Impacts of Leakage, Whistleblowing, and the Rise of Propaganda

Perry L. Lyle
Columbia College of Missouri, USA

Ashraf M. Esmail
Dillard University, USA

IGI Global
Scientific Publishing
Publishing Tomorrow's Research Today

Vice President of Editorial Melissa Wagner
Managing Editor of Acquisitions Mikaela Felty
Managing Editor of Book Development Jocelynn Hessler
Production Manager Mike Brehm
Cover Design Phillip Shickler

Published in the United States of America by
IGI Global Scientific Publishing
701 East Chocolate Avenue
Hershey, PA, 17033, USA
Tel: 717-533-8845
Fax: 717-533-8661
Website: https://www.igi-global.com E-mail: cust@igi-global.com

Library of Congress Cataloging-in-Publication Data

Names: Lyle, Perry, 1950- editor. | Esmail, Ashraf, editor.
Title: Impacts of leakage, whistleblowing, and the rise of propaganda / edited by Perry Lyle, Ashraf Esmail.
Description: Hershey, PA : IGI Global Scientific Publishing, 2025. | Includes bibliographical references and index. | Summary: "Leakage and disseminating fake news have become increasingly detrimental issues in modern society, as political operatives and whistleblowers use leaks to shape public opinion, decision-making, and power distribution. The truth-finder must dig deeper and work harder to validate the legitimacy of their sources and the quality of the information provided"-- Provided by publisher.
Identifiers: LCCN 2024055957 (print) | LCCN 2024055958 (ebook) | ISBN 9798369374689 (hardcover) | ISBN 9798369374696 (paperback) | ISBN 9798369374702 (ebook)
Subjects: LCSH: Leaks (Disclosure of information). | Fake news. | Propaganda. | Whistle blowing.
Classification: LCC JF1525.S4 I67 2025 (print) | LCC JF1525.S4 (ebook) | DDC 320.01/4--dc23/eng/20250210
LC record available at https://lccn.loc.gov/2024055957
LC ebook record available at https://lccn.loc.gov/2024055958

British Cataloguing in Publication Data
A Cataloguing in Publication record for this book is available from the British Library.

I am with gratitude and with a multitude of blessings to have a wonderful Son, Perry Lyle, 2, and a great daughter, Michele Lyle Bishop, along with my extended family which provides me will loving support and inspiration for my life's work and joy of living.

Perry Lyle

We would like to dedicate the book to diligent citizens and officials who have confronted and worked to address propaganda. We also dedicate the book to the authors who have contributed to it. They not only advance the field but also ensure that field alone maintains and follow the highest quality, integrity, and ethical standards.

Ashraf Esmail & Perry Lyle

Table of Contents

Detailed Table of Contents

Foreword

Ever since Johannes Gutenberg, the inventor of the printing press, blanketed continental Europe with the practical reality of reproducible information, the power of information, influencing the individual and the nation, has been indispensable to society, to what it is, as well as to what it does. Now, in the digital age, the reach and resources of information flows and distribution have increased in new and unprecedented ways, posing new challenges of trust and authenticity and control. Leakage and whistleblowing, once the reserve of the hardcore within societies intent on change and reform, whether subversive or heroic, or both, have developed into sub rosa essentials of greater or lesser levels of institutional transparency within both the public and private sectors. Meanwhile propaganda, in the various forms, new and old, of the persuaders of public opinion, tends to intrude upon the authentic with more visible and less invisible forms of deviancy.

In this timely edited volume by Perry Lyle, PhD and Ashraf Esmail, PhD scholars from the fields of criminology, sociology, communication studies, law and media studies come together to address leakage, whistleblowing and propaganda and their impact on the political, social and economic fabric of our world. Together with the editors, the prestigious professors and authors examine the global landscape forced to navigate on multiple fronts: by new modes of regulation and contestation, state and non-state actors, information and pseudo-information, science and pseudo-science, journalism and propaganda, honesty and mayhem and, by emerge and re-emerging diseases. They offer an abundance of theoretical and methodological research, combined with illustrative case studies, on subjects of primary importance for the present but with crucial implications in years to come.

What were once more or less shadowy forms of punctuation in the larger story of capitalist modernity – at once transgressions and triumphs, at once violations and testaments – have come to dominate modern discourses on governance, and on ethics and accountability in business. From the leak of classified government files to the release of company secrets, whistleblowing is no longer just dark art. It has become a prominent and powerful tool of reform, of transparency, and of justice. Edward Snowden and Chelsea Manning are only the two most prominent whistleblowers – both US government contractors – who have brought issues to the public's attention that tend to transcend the immediate cases and events that surfaced with their leaks. These range from the role (and limits) of privacy in contemporary life, and the size and scope of state surveillance and judicial intrusion, to the behavior of large corporations, and what liberty means – or ought to mean – in the digital age.

Although ostensibly aimed at fighting 'fake news', propaganda is also morphing from overt government-led efforts such as PSYOPS into more subtle, more nuanced forms of persuasion – often but not exclusively via the world wide web and social media. Fake news and deepfakes are becoming commodities, as well as forms of targeted political advertising, aiding political campaigns and altering the fabric of democratic life. The boundaries between propaganda and PSYOPS are still clear enough: propaganda is not necessarily state-driven, though it may be, and typically aims to influence civil discourse while PSYOPS is government action targeting a vulnerable enemy populace as battlefield support, concentrating on inflaming existing tensions. It's not even clear why we still make a distinction. Countries that are not totalitarian use propaganda and PSYOPS all the time, whether to influence the outcome of elections, divide a populace and foster anti-government sentiment, or control and incite violence for a military campaign.

With the dynamic that most information is now globally dispersed, this book attends to an uglier, pressing reality: modern societies must grapple with new kinds of problems at the global level as leaks proliferate across world economies – and political systems and networks – much like PSYOPS propaganda lurks to shape political processes and sensibilities, globally. In a world in which leaks and information can create just as many opportunities for empowerment as destabilization, any serious discussion about governance, politics and the well-being of any society needs to come to terms with leakage, whistleblowing and PSYOPS.

Its overall structure in some part mirrors this multidimensionality, with separate parts devoted to entangled areas of this multidimensional mass. Media, Communication and Fake News lodges itself in the quagmire of fake news diffusion and function: how media – both mainstream and social – act as disseminators and fire lines in the struggles for truth. Separate chapters in the Political Propaganda and Influence part examine how propaganda is operative in electoral communications and politics, as well as driving extremist movements and the operation of fringe groups. The Government, Policy and Whistleblowing section addresses leaks and whistleblowing operations, especially in the political sphere and at the corporate level, with chapters sharing light on the legal and ethical issues they bring about. Social and Cultural Narratives investigates the propensity for and operation of fake news in sustaining false consciousness about both minority groups and major political issues, including history itself – and perhaps religion too.

In this they bring an astounding array of voices together that offer sustained reflection on some of the most consequential realities confronting the world today. Both scholars bring a range of experience to bear on the remarkable testament of thoughtful statements manifest in this book. Dr Perry Lyle brings more than three decades of experience as public safety leadership in law enforcement, the intelligence realm as well as higher education. Dr Lyle's academic record spans criminal justice, leadership studies and social justice that makes him the ideal person destined to spearhead a project of this order. Dr Ashraf Esmail has earned a stature as a thought leader in the realm of racial justice and social equity and is the director of the Center for Racial Justice. His editorial leadership through multiple scholarly journals on education and political science also assures that the book about furies confronts its topic matter with the requisite pragmatics and rectitude.

While his book is a scholarly contribution, it is also a rallying cry, a provocation calling on everyone, from policymakers and academic scholars to journalists and activists, to take stock of themselves and the systems around them when it comes to leaks, whistleblowing and propaganda. When will they open their eyes?

As you explore the chapters, bringing their lessons to bear on our everyday information landscapes, my desire is for you to see authority and power in new ways, and to question our assumptions and unexamined judgments about them. I hope that you come away with a richer understanding of how power works in mediated spaces, and that you grasp the potential for positive change if those of us who process, use and create information learn to do so in ways that truly expand our ability to reason collaboratively – rather than putting us on the illusory path to near-total (and ever-shifting) compliance with the views of powerful individuals and institutions that would otherwise do so with little resistance. May students, disinformation analysts, journalists, think tankers, human-rights workers, community organizers and all citizens be enriched by its lessons. May its lessons help us see what can be salvaged from the wreckage of the information battlefield, and also help us envision a far superior construction of ‘truth,’ ‘truthiness,’ and all that lies in between, and afford us all the opportunity to dwell on it.

Given that the dichotomy between truth and falsehood has been fractured by forces it could not contain, the work proposed here leads one through labyrinthine obstacles in the information age. Leakage, whistleblowing and propaganda are not mere abstractions. If we wish to enable those in power – especially ourselves – to make informed decisions, we need to become adept at harnessing leakage, whistleblowing and propaganda: we need to rethink their components and decode their impact.

As educators, we should all thank Dr Perry Lyle and Dr Ashraf Esmail, the co-editors of this volume, for having been the first to reach out to such a range of scholars, and for putting it together. More important, I hope that this book will spur on further research, commentary and action.

Arthur Wayne Turner
US Army (Retired), USA

Preface

In a world where the line between truth and falsehood grows increasingly indistinct, understanding the mechanisms of information dissemination and manipulation has never been more critical. The rapid evolution of digital media has transformed how we access, share, and perceive information, often with profound implications for society, politics, and culture. This book, *The Historical Impacts of Leaking, Whistleblowing, and the Rise of Propaganda*, explores the intricate interplay of media, communication, fake news, and propaganda. Through a collection of scholarly chapters, it traces their historical origins, examines their contemporary forms, and analyzes their impacts on public opinion, policy, and global relations. Spanning historical perspectives, technological advancements, political strategies, and socio-cultural narratives, this volume offers a comprehensive lens on how information—whether accurate or deceptive—shapes our reality.

The subject matter of this book lies at the intersection of media studies, political communication, and social dynamics. It addresses the multifaceted nature of information as both a tool for enlightenment and a weapon for manipulation. From the historical use of fake news to sway public sentiment to the modern challenges posed by social media and artificial intelligence, the chapters collectively illuminate the enduring power of information and the urgent need to understand its effects. This book does not merely document these phenomena; it seeks to equip readers with the knowledge to critically engage with the information ecosystem that surrounds them.

RELEVANCE IN TODAY'S WORLD

The topic of this book is acutely relevant in the context of today's digital age. The advent of the internet, social media platforms, and 24-hour news cycles has democratized information dissemination, allowing anyone with a device to become a publisher. Yet, this accessibility has a darker side: the unchecked spread of fake news, propaganda, and misinformation. These forces have tangible consequences—undermining democratic elections, fueling extremist ideologies, eroding public trust in institutions, and even jeopardizing public health, as seen during global crises like the COVID-19 pandemic. Governments, corporations, and individuals alike grapple with the challenge of discerning truth from falsehood in an environment where information travels faster than verification. This book arrives at a pivotal moment, offering insights into how we arrived at this juncture and proposing pathways to mitigate the risks while harnessing the benefits of our interconnected world.

TARGET AUDIENCE

This book is designed for a diverse yet discerning audience. It primarily targets academics, researchers, and students in fields such as media studies, communication, political science, sociology, and journalism, providing them with rigorous analyses and interdisciplinary perspectives. Beyond academia, it appeals to professionals—journalists seeking to navigate the ethics of reporting, policymakers crafting regulations to address misinformation, and technologists developing tools to detect and counter fake news. Additionally, the book speaks to a broader readership: anyone intrigued by the complex dynamics of information in modern society. Whether a concerned citizen or an expert in the field, readers will find value in its blend of historical context, contemporary case studies, and forward-looking solutions.

IMPORTANCE OF EACH CHAPTER

The book is organized into four sections, each containing chapters that contribute uniquely to the overarching theme. Below is a description of each chapter's significance.

Section 1: The Historical Impacts of Media, Communication, Fake News, and Propaganda in Contemporary Society

Chapter 1: The Historical Impact of Fake News by Perry L. Lyle and Ashraf Esmail

This chapter lays a foundational understanding by exploring how fake news has shaped public opinion and policy throughout history. By examining notable historical examples—such as wartime disinformation campaigns, it draws connections to today's digital misinformation, emphasizing that the manipulation of truth is not a new phenomenon but one with evolved tactics.

Chapter 2: Contagion: The Disease of Spreading Fake News in the Digital World by Rouby Mavyan, Ashraf Esmail, and Hovsep Mavyan

Offering an innovative perspective, this chapter likens the spread of fake news online to a contagious disease. It employs epidemiological models to analyze how misinformation propagates through digital networks, providing a scientific framework that enhances our grasp of its rapid, pervasive reach in the internet era.

Chapter 3: Social Media and the Internet: Fake News and Clickbait by Ghosh Thinnakkakath

This chapter zeroes in on the role of social media platforms in amplifying fake news, focusing on the use of clickbait to capture attention. It critiques how algorithms prioritize engagement over accuracy, underscoring the need for media literacy to counteract these pervasive digital influences.

Chapter 4: A Comprehensive Review on Advancements and Challenges in Fake News Detection by Anuradha Thota, Chanakya .C.N, Bhumika Sharma, Aarthy. S.T, Ketki P. Kshirsagar, and Monica Bhutani

A technical cornerstone, this chapter surveys cutting-edge methods—such as machine learning and natural language processing—used to detect fake news. It balances optimism about technological progress with a candid discussion of challenges, like the adaptability of misinformation creators, making it essential for those tackling this issue practically.

Chapter 5: Mapping the Misinformation Ecosystem in India: Insights into Key Areas and Pathways of Dissemination by Apoorva Mahiwal, Saad Ullah Khan, Sadaf Khan, and Mani Sachdev

This chapter provides regional case studies, dissecting the misinformation landscape in India. By identifying key sources and dissemination channels, it offers a model for understanding how cultural and political contexts shape misinformation, with lessons applicable globally.

Section 2: The Power of Political Communication Lies in its Propagation and Influence Permeating Society on a Global Scale

Chapter 6: Propaganda: The Lifeblood of Terrorism and Extremism by Perry L. Lyle and Retired Lt. Colonel Arthur Wayne Turner

This chapter examines how terrorist and extremist groups leverage propaganda to recruit and radicalize individuals. Its focus on media as a strategic tool highlights the high stakes of information control, urging countermeasures to disrupt these dangerous narratives.

Chapter 7: Fake News, Propaganda, and Other Influences on Elections by Ghosh Thinnakkakath

Investigating the manipulation of electoral processes, this chapter uses recent election case studies to reveal how fake news and propaganda sway voters. It underscores the threat to democracy, making it vital for understanding political integrity in the digital age.

Chapter 8: Artificial Intelligence, Online Algorithms, and the Influence of Propaganda by Kadir Uludag

This chapter explores how AI and algorithms enhance propaganda's reach, targeting audiences with precision. It raises ethical questions about technology's role in amplifying manipulation, offering a forward-looking perspective on a rapidly evolving challenge.

Chapter 9: Conflict Caught in Propaganda Nationalism: An Analysis of the India-Pakistan Newspaper Coverage of Mumbai, Uri, and Pulwama Attacks by Keerthana Thankachan, Thomas P E, and Vishnu Achutha Menon

This chapter dissects how Indian and Pakistani newspapers framed major conflicts, highlighting propaganda's role in fostering nationalism. Its focus on media bias during crises offers a compelling lens on information's power in geopolitics.

Section 3: The Global Ramifications of Government Policy and Whistleblowing

Chapter 10: The Impacts of Leaking in Government and Business Enterprises by Perry L. Lyle

Exploring the fallout from leaks in governmental and corporate spheres, this chapter uses cases like WikiLeaks to assess their effects on trust and stability. It bridges public and private domains, emphasizing the broader implications of transparency.

Chapter 11: Scope of Judicial Review and Oversight of Administrative Actions Affecting India and Other Jurisdictions by Saurabh Chandra and Boddu Harshith Sai

Focusing on legal oversight, this chapter compares judicial review frameworks across jurisdictions, particularly India. It connects governance to information control, showing how legal systems respond to policy and disclosure challenges.

Chapter 12: Corporate Data Mining and Manipulation in Marketing by Henrietta Okoro

This chapter critiques how corporations exploit data mining to influence consumers, raising ethical concerns about privacy and manipulation. It ties corporate practices to broader misinformation trends, broadening the book's scope.

Section 4: Social and Cultural Narratives Shaping Misinformation

Chapter 13: From Victims to Voices: The Power of Words in Breaking and Healing Through Whistleblowing by Jyoti Kukreja

Highlighting whistleblowing's transformative potential, this chapter shows how it empowers victims and fosters healing. Its humanistic approach complements the book's technical and political analyses.

Chapter 14: The "Other Columbine": Myths and Misinformation About the Columbine School Shooting by Selina E. M. Kerr.

By debunking myths about Columbine, this chapter illustrates how misinformation distorts collective memory. It stresses the importance of accurate narratives in understanding pivotal events.

Chapter 15: Conspiracy Theories Eroding Institutional Confidence: Past and Present by Komanduri S. Murty and Johnny R. Green

This chapter traces how conspiracy theories undermine trust, blending historical and modern examples. Its focus on institutional erosion ties misinformation to societal stability.

Chapter 16: Did God Say That? The Role of Religion in the Dissemination of Information by Toiya Marie McGruder

Examining religion's dual role in spreading truth and falsehood, this chapter enriches the cultural narrative discussion. It highlights belief systems as amplifiers of information dynamics.

Chapter 17: Fake News Defamation and Sabotage of Prominent Civil Rights Leaders, and President Obama by Tara D. Miller

This chapter reveals how fake news has historically targeted civil rights figures, offering a poignant historical perspective. It connects misinformation to social justice struggles.

Chapter 18: Dual Narratives on Social Media and the Future of Trust and Reliability in Indian Politics by Kesavan Dhanapal, Sivaprakkash S., Naveenraj Xavier, and Marianand N.

Analyzing social media's impact on Indian political trust, this chapter explores competing narratives' effects on reliability. It projects future challenges in digital political discourse.

CONCLUSION: IMPACT AND CONTRIBUTION

Impacts of Leakage, Whistleblowing, and the Rise of Propaganda stands as a vital contribution to the study of information's role in shaping our world. By weaving together historical insights, technological analyses, political critiques, and sociocultural explorations, it offers a holistic view of a pressing global issue. Its interdisciplinary approach bridges academia and practice, providing scholars with theoretical depth, practitioners with actionable strategies, and the public with tools for critical engagement. The book impacts the field by synthesizing diverse perspectives into a cohesive narrative, advancing our collective understanding of misinformation and propaganda. It contributes by not only diagnosing the problem but also inspiring solutions—be it through improved detection technologies, informed policies, or enhanced media literacy. In an era defined by information overload, this volume is both a beacon and a call to action, urging us to reclaim truth in a landscape of deception.

Acknowledgment

We extend our heartfelt thanks to the distinguished authors who have contributed to this volume. Their vast knowledge, education, and experience have been instrumental in the success of this undertaking. Their exceptional abilities in crafting and writing their book chapters are evident throughout this work. This book is poised to make a significant impact on academic circles worldwide. Moreover, it will provide invaluable insights to policymakers, NGOs, government officials, and politicians, aiding in the promotion of truth-telling and the mitigation of fake news, misinformation, election manipulation, and other threats to our vital institutions.

Section 1
The Historical Impacts of Media, Communication, Fake News, and Propaganda in Contemporary Society

Chapter 1
The Historical Impact of Fake News

Perry L. Lyle
https://orcid.org/0009-0009-2363-6005
Columbia College of Missouri, USA

Ashraf Esmail
Dillard University, USA

ABSTRACT

Fake news, also known as Yellow Journalism, emerged in the late 19th century in the United States when Joseph Pulitzer purchased the New York World for $346,000. The term was coined in the mid-1890s to describe sensational journalism in the circulation war between Pulitzer and Willam Randolf Hurst's New York Journal. Fake news has become mainstream with the advent of the Internet, social media, and other mass media technologies. The problem with fake news is that it presents content as factual new stories or events, deceiving the reader. Manipulation methods make them appear factual and enticing to share them. Fake news is deeply intertwined with human cognition, social dynamics, and technological infrastructures. The chapter presents a literature review of the history, key terms, different types of fake news, public opinion, prevention, broader consequences for society and democracy, technological and educational approaches, theoretical framework, and lessons learned.

PROBLEM STATEMENT

By the late 19th century, in the US, the journalistic landscape that would produce fake news (then called Yellow Journalism) took shape. In 1883, Joseph Pulitzer purchased New York World for $346,000. In his first editorial, he ordered the staff to use 'sensationalism, slick words, exaggeration, and crusades against all sorts of corruption and politics,' all to improve circulation. The term 'Yellow Journalism' first entered the lexicon in the mid-1890s, during a circulation war between Pulitzer's New York World and William Randolph Hearst's New York Journal according to Arndt, G. (2024, October 2).

Fake news is not new – it has existed since the advent of modern mass media and, specifically, since the 19th century. But it has grown exponentially with the advent of the Internet, social media and other mass media technologies. This fake news can be best defined by the fact that is presented as a fact-based

DOI: 10.4018/979-8-3693-7468-9.ch001

news story or event, often by the use of 'dark patterns' that make this story look 'real', and sometimes trigger the reader's reflex to share it immediately. The other characteristic of the phenomenon is the fact that, in practice, the term fake news has been used to delegitimize the work of legitimate media, thus causing confusion regarding the difference between fake news and real news, and ultimately promoting the delegitimization of the media in general as note in *Research Guides: "Fake News," Lies and Propaganda: How to Sort Fact from Fiction: What is "Fake News"?* (n.d.).

Given the fact that fake news is not just about misinformation but is deeply rooted in human cognition, sociality and infrastructural media technologies, the aim of this chapter is to map the literature on the historical development of fake news, outlining key terms and types, discussing the effects of fake news on public opinion and behavior as well as strategies to prevent or mitigate fake news. It will also review possible consequences for society and democracy at large, before moving on to discuss technological and pedagogic approaches. It will also provide a general theoretical framework for understanding fake news.

INTRODUCTION

"A lie gets halfway around the world before the truth has a chance to get its pants on" Khurana, S. (2023, April 5). A famous quote given credited to Sir Winston Churchill, which has been popular for years. Notably, there is dispute that others before him utter similar words used in the quote. Nonetheless, the point is presented for an introductory of just how powerful lies and all forms of deception and how fast fake news can spread. Fake news is not a new phenomenon and has been around for centuries but is an issue that has become increasing problematic for all people globally. In the run up to the 2016 election in the U. S., people from around the globe had a front row seat of just how fake new, disinformation, and propaganda are to tilt an American presidential election.

Fake news has become a significant digital epidemic, with fake news stories posing a threat to the media, government, and democracy. In the past, fake news stories, such as the Comet Ping Pong incident, [The 'Podesta e-mails' revealed the existence of a secret society of pedophiles operating through a pizza place loosely connected to Hilary Clinton associate David Brock.] LaCapria, K. (2016, November 21). A fake narrative led Reddit user u/DumbScribblyUnctious to publish a thread titled:

> "Comet Ping Pong - Pizzagate Summary" "to subreddit r Donald Trump (a community of Donald Trump supporters), which appears to have touched off a complex and detailed conspiracy theory involving WikiLeaks 'release of e-mails from former Hillary Clinton presidential campaign chair John Podesta, child exploitation, and a Washington, D.C., pizzeria called Comet Ping Pong." (LaCapria, 2016)

Other campaigns have allegedly been plagued by fabricated stories, such as suggesting Ted Cruz's father engaged in the Kennedy assassination plot and claiming violent crime was at an all-time high. However, this trend is about to change as text-based stories become more prevalent (LaCapria, 2016).

Audio and video technology advancements are becoming so sophisticated that they will replicate real news in unprecedented and indecipherable ways. Researchers at Stanford University and the University of Erlangen-Nuremberg showed how technologists could record videos of someone talking and then change their facial expressions in real time. This technology could take a news clip of Vladimir Putin and alter his facial expressions in real-time in hard-to-detect ways according to Stacey (2021, September 16).

Future Developments

This is only one part of the future fake news menace. Other similar technologies have been in the works in universities and research labs for years, but they have never really pulled off what computers can do today. For example, "The Digital Emily Project" [photorealistic digital facial performances.], created digital actors that could substitute in lieu of real people, The Wikihuman Project (n.d.). However, technologies now used by Hollywood and the video game industry have made digital avatars almost indecipherable from real people. The popular phrase, get ready for a 'brave new world' appears to be right for fake modern technologies on the horizon.

Audio advancements may be just as harrowing. Adobe showed off a new product called "Photoshop for audio," which allows users to feed about ten to 20 minutes of someone's voice into the application and then type words that are expressed in that exact voice. This technology could ease the ability to feed one of Trump's interviews or stump speeches into the application and then type sentences or paragraphs in his spoken voice.

The scariest reality is that this sort of technology will transcend academies and institutions to the point where you or I can create fake digital clips as easily as regular people created fake news stories during this cycle. According to Dr. Perry Lyle, foreign adversaries can highjack our real time screaming of news to provide false narratives thus even further undermining our news sources.

OVERVIEW OF THE CHAPTER'S STRUCTURE AND RELEVANCE

The Relevance of contemporary societies cannot be underestimated. Globally, societies and their cultures are intertwined as never before, more dependent on each other for a myriad of reasons, not to mention security and sustainability. The use of fake news and false narratives by evil doers are designed to minder mind confidence and trust in governmental institutions and the free press. During and after the 2016 U. S. presidential election fake news articles proliferated at an unpresented rate seen in any time of history DiLascio-Martinuk, T. (2024). The bases of power and control are the main goals of undermining any legitimate authority. Whether it be in a corporate board room or a governmental organization, coups and takeover attempts are always at the heart of the design. Chapter One is organized to provide a solid foundation and perspectives on the subject matter.

Chapter one is organized to present a through literature review of the history of fake news, key terms and definitions, different types of fake news, how public opinion and behaviors can be influenced, how fake news can be prevented or at least mitigated, the broader consequence for society and democracy, the technological and educational approaches, the theorical framework of fake news, and lessons learned. Finally, the authors look at how the landscape of fake news expected to evolve.

UNDERPINNING THEORETICAL FOUNDATIONS

The cost and other barriers to entering the media industry has decreased significantly with the expansion of the World Wide Web. Publishing and spreading "news" articles with dubious or non-existent credibility has become easier than ever. Since these articles can be created and published by individuals in other countries, especially those hostiles to the United States as they are beyond the reach of U.S. authorities, and content prohibited in the US might not be in another country. There are numerous criticisms of news sources. The ethical holdings once taught in journalism universities has been overshadowed by more pernicious bias reporting and personalized addenda advancement DiLascio-Martinuk, T. (2024).

Bias refers to news outlets presenting information about events or facts in a way intended to further their own agenda. Citizens in America are becoming increasingly aware of political narratives aimed to sway voters toward a particular agenda, even without considering the repercussions or harm they may do to their own nation. When a news source is said to have a liberal or conservative slant, this is usually what is meant. However, a news source may also be skewed for a host of other reasons, such as financial gain over ideology.

Conspiracy Theories

The American landscape abounds with numerous conspiracy theories. It is difficult today for the average citizen or guest to have a meaningful conversation about politics, a war, a significant incident such as 911, COVID-19 pandemic, or any other high-profile news story without the injection of a conspiracy. Those sensationalized stories are replete with explanations or suggestions of a secretly manipulated behind the scenes forces or politicians. These theories are taken and spread in our culture through a combination of psychological, social, and technological means. Many conspiracy theories are often promoted on a global scale unprecedented in early history.

"New World Order" (NWO) is a term used to refer to longstanding right-wing conspiracy theories about a socialist or communist one world government. These conspiracies have been popular for decades, but this term became particularly popular among anti-government extremists from the 1990s onwards. It has replaced older theories about a global communist conspiracy. "New World Order" conspiracists believe that a tyrannical, socialist "one-world" conspiracy has already taken over most of the planet and schemes to eliminate the bastion of freedom, the United States, with the help of collaborators within the government ADL.org (2024).

The American NWO Conspiracy Theory

Conspiracy theories with anti-Semitic overtones that have proliferated worldwide have not spared America. During the past few decades, the United States has seen a comparable rise of conspiratorial fringe characters. As anti-Semitic conspiracy theories proliferated throughout the world, the United States saw a boom of fringe conspiratorial groups in the middle of the 20th century, which greatly aided in the NWO's mainstream acceptance Flores, M. (2022, May 22).Popular organization such as the John Birch Society (JBS) became powerful and very influential in the U. S. and around the globe. Initially, their calling was making claims of global plots by the communist elites.

These claims laid the foundation for future conspiracy theories of elites striving for global domination. Organizations such as the Illuminati and Free Masons were part and partial of all these abounding conspiracy organizations look to promote the NOW. "As a result, the combination of the countercultural interest in secret societies alongside the anti-elite conspiracism of the JBS created the infrastructure for broad belief in the existence that secret global organizations seek control over the United States" Flores, M. (2022, May 22). Debunking offers insights into the modern dissemination of false narrative and those conspiracy minds hard at work to convince their most ardent supporters to spread the gospel. During the 60s and 70s, the Illuminati were trying the world's affairs while secretly establishing the NOW primarily through financial manipulation of global markets Flores, M. (2022, May 22). The 911 terror attacks would set off a new wave of conspiracies in America.

9/11 A BRAVE NEW WORLD

It did not take long for conspiratorial theorists to grab hold of the headlines and videos of that tragic terrorist attack that occurred on the fateful day of 9/11. Over 3,000 people died when al-Qaeda launch a massive attack on U. S. soil using fueled up commercial airlines to crash into the Pentagon, the World Trade Center (Twin-towers) in NYC, along with the orchestration of the downing of flight 93 crashing in Shanksville, PA. It would be almost ten years before the United States would be able to hunt down and put an end to Osma bin Laden, who was the mastermind behind the terrorist plot while operating in Afghanistan's. His hatred for the United States and the West began from earlier history.

It was the secret agreement known as the Sykes-Picot Agreement by the British and French governments following post WW1 which divided Arab lands (Ottoman Empire) up and keep them under British and French spheres that had had steeped into Osama bin Landen's sole that so angered him. His radicalized ideology and hatred for the West would later provide the pivotal influence in plotting his revenge against the United States History.com Editors (2019, July 29).

Flight 93 Conspiracy Theory

The passengers and crew of Flight 93 gallantly fought back against the terrorists to no avail. The plane crashed into an empty field in Shanksville. The attackers took part in a larger terrorist plot and would likely be used to carry out further attacks on U.S. soil. The hijacked plane carried 38 passengers, 7 crew members put the four Islamic hijackers that had boarded the plane with boxcutters. One of the most common conspiracy theories about this awful event was that the United States military jets in lieu of allowing the flight to continue shot down flight 93 History.com Editors (2023, July 18).

Inside Job Conspiracy Theory

One of the most prevalent fake news theories that appeared months after the 9/11 attack, Twin-towers specifically were orchestrated by the military elite, in concert with aims of (NOW extremists), to allow later military actions in the Middle East and the implementation of new security measures, i.e. The Patriot Act. Unknown agents were allowed to plant the explosives, allowing for the blasts and destruction of the Towers.

The CIA's Counterterrorism Center in December 1998, the CIA's provided a reported to then President Bill Clinton that al-Qaeda was preparing for attacks in the U.S. that might include hijacking plane Schmidt, S. (2004, July 18). Nuggets of truth such as these are woven into the fabric of fake news stories and particularly conspiracy theories to give the audience plausibility.

Hence undermining citizens' personal freedoms and gain added controls by the government. "Few legislative acts in American history have caused polarization, as die the United and Strengthening America by Providing Appropriate Tools Required to Intercept and Obstruct Terrorism" (Smith, C. and Hung, Li-ching (2010). Finally, another plot was propagated that suggested that the U. S. Intelligence Agencies had foreknowledge and permitted the attacks by keeping hands-off.

THE IMPACTS OF FAKE NEWS

No matter where the fake news originates from and why, the are impacts and cultural consequences for fake news and propaganda. From a commonsense perspective, fake news stories often undermine the societal established norms, and the trust people have in their government leaders. United States adversaries, namely China and Russia most assuredly used AI and other forms of public opinion stories to play a role in the 2016 presidential elections. According to Dr. Perry Lyle, one of the top aims involving manipulation of political agenda and ideology is to plant and sow seeds of distrust against politicians and legitimate institutions. There are many psychological factors that contribute to the way and means creators of fake news use to make them effective.

Confirmation biases allow for people to have a natural tendency to see and use common patterns and connections for their preconceived notions and opinions. In other words, the mind wants to make sense of any new phenomenon and simply seeks out that which supports existing views. For example, in times of crisis, conspiracy theories can offer a simple explanation for complex events such as 911. Naturally, if I have a perceived notation and mistrust of the government, the natural tendency will be to consider those narratives that justify my preconceived opinions, even against contrary information, most often dismissed.

Unfortunately, everyone suffers from having confirmation bias. Even if you believe you are open-minded, you are probably not aware just how adapted your mind is to search, sorting, and only observing the information that supports what you already know or believe in. It is very likely that some bias will shape your opinion in the end. This natural tendency is very difficult to combat. To be open-minded you must train yourself to search for oppositional information and data if you are truly interested in objectivity. "We don't [sic] see things as they are, we see things as we are" (Wocado.com).

When psychologists Amos Tversky and Daniel Kahneman presented their research in the 1970s scientists were able to show that humans have limited abilities to make rational decisions. Their research demonstrated that most people rely on specific ways to simplify the decision-making process. It forces us to rely on mental shortcuts to make sense of our world. It follows that heuristics are educated guesses or rules of thumb that are used to solve our everyday problems Cherry, K. (2020, January 10).

ARTIFICIAL INTELLIGENCE (AI) FAKE NEWS AS AN EMERGENT THREAT

The rise of omnipresent and highly capable generative artificial intelligence (AI) presents a plausible concern for national security due to the potential for exploitation by adversaries of the United States, particularly in the realm of social media manipulation. It is imperative that the U.S. government, together with the wider technological and policy community, take proactive measures to address this issue promptly. The authors primarily center their attention on China and its *People's Liberation Army* as a representative instance of the potential menace. However, it is important to note that a range of entities, including technically advanced non-state players (both domestic and foreign), might employ generative artificial intelligence for the purpose of manipulating social media. The capabilities and concerns addressed in this Perspective are likely to have relevance for other players, including Russia and Iran, who have already been involved in the manipulation of social media Marcellino, W., et al. (2023). For a chart highlighting several select social media manipulation and potential implications of Generative AI see Figure 1.

Figure 1.

Select Social Media Manipulation Tactics and Potential Implications of Generative AI

Tactic	Definition	Potential Implication
Algorithm gaming	Driving specific content via algorithmic understanding (e.g., search engine optimization or hashtag manipulation)	Likely to be broadly relevant and further exploited by large-scale synthetic (bot) accounts, though gaming may still require some human expertise
Bots for astroturfing	Using large numbers of inauthentic (fake) accounts (bots) to create the appearance of a broad consensus on a topic	Likely to increase dramatically, since it will become orders of magnitude cheaper to produce convincing, unique content, and thus will be harder to detect
Advertising	Paid promotional content to support a cause or actor	May diminish, because generative AI makes other methods (e.g., astroturfing) so much cheaper
Cheapfakes and recontextualized media	Supporting a campaign either with simple edits or by repurposing media (usually, images)	May diminish, because generative AI is likely to be cheaper, faster, and more effective at generating high-quality, customized media
Memes and meme wars	Use of easily shared "units of culture" (often, a slogan incorporated into an image) to promote a cause or actor	Unclear, because generative AI may help speed up production, but effective memes may still need human insight
Misinfographics	Infographics that appear professional and authoritative but are inaccurate or misinforming	Unclear, because generative AI may help speed up production, but effective infographics likely still need human insight

SOURCE: Adapted from Harvard Kennedy School Shorenstein Center for Media, Politics, and Public Policy, 2022.

Source: *Havard University Kennedy School, available through public forum and use.*

Microtargeting and Voter Suppression

According to Ashrif Esmail, Ph.D., AI can analyze vast datasets to *micro-target voters* with tailored messages, potentially spreading divisive content or suppressing voter turnout. Malicious actors could influence election outcomes by identifying vulnerable populations and exploiting their fears or beliefs. It raises the question; can American democracy continue to survive with the divisiveness and mistrust of government institutions? The global stage of political ramifications will be equally challenged. Finally, most scholars agree that believing in conspiracy theories can strengthen in-group identities giving members a sense of belonging.

How Can Fake News be Detected and Mitigated?

Most scholars of journalism and communication experts agree that in todays age of AI, digital manipulation of headlines and stories, the only practical way to deal with fake news is personal accountability. Since the beginning of the Internet, there are hardly any restrictions on the information people may access. Therefore, being a consumer of the media means having to be much more alert and informed on the sources for accuracy. Making poor decisions in social, personal, and professional contexts may result from discovering and using misleading information from the internet. People must take more control over their own cognitive and affective mind processing than ever before because of the way our memories function and the biases we have when choosing and interpreting information. As illustrations: Most people are more likely to accept information that is congruent with their preconceived ideas, and simply repeating something can boost confidence in its apparent veracity, to others. Additionally, even after finding that the original wrong information is no longer available, it can still have an impact.

When evaluating information, readers according to Britt, A., Rout, J-F., Blaum, D., and Millis, K. (2019, March 8), encouraged to take into account the following: "(a) establish and track their objectives for completeness, correctness, and coherence; and (b) to employ strategies to achieve these goals; and (c) to value this time- and effort-consuming systematic evaluation." These recommendations support a reasoned approach to fake news and manipulation. Is there a practicality to these approaches? Reader decides. Suggested recommendation:

IMPLICATIONS FOR PRACTICE STUDIES

To counter and mitigate the unending amount of false information, fake news, and propaganda that making its way through our daily lives, Congress and our national leadership must form a bi-partisan commission that seeks to improved public and private information that is distributed. Most assuredly, artificial intelligence has good and bad usage.

AI influences people's daily lives due to significant advancements in language processing, computer vision, and pattern recognition. These developments range from assisting with movie selection to supporting medical diagnosis. However, with that achievement comes a new urgency to comprehend and address the drawbacks and hazards associated with AI-driven systems, such as algorithmic discrimination or the intentional use of AI to mislead. To ensure that AI's drawbacks are as few as possible, computer scientists must collaborate with social sciences and law specialists Stacey, K. (2021, September 16). A juxtaposition of fake news, misinformation, and propaganda, challenges – detection, curtailment, mitigation, and long-term strategies by Dr. Lyle.

Table 1. Juxtaposition for Solutions

Methods	Recommendations	Responsibility
Detection		
Technology	Develop and deploy advanced AI and machine learning algorithms to detect fake news	Government and Private Industry support by scientific community and universities.
Collaborate with Tech Companies	Work closely with social media platforms to be transparent. Develop tools to remove real-time fake news	Corporations and other NGOs. Global cooperation.
Fact-Checking-Partnerships	Create centralized data bases and partner with independent organizations.	Corporations and non-profit NGOS. Global cooperation.
Curtailment		
Legislation and Regulation	Enforcement of regulations and holding individuals and organizations accountable for spread of fake news.	Government, public, and media.
Transparency Requirements	Require social media platforms to be transparent about their content and policies and algorithms. Mandated disclosures.	Government, corporations, and all other NGOs including universities and the scientific community.

continued on following page

Table 1. Continued

Methods	Recommendations	Responsibility
Media Literacy	Invest in public education campaigns to improve media literacy among citizens	Government and NGOs.
Mitigation		
Influence Quality Journalism	Provide financial and institutional support for quality journalism and local news outlets. Not censorship.	Investigative reporting and in-depth analysis to counteract false information and hidden agendas.
Crisis Communications	Develop strategies for the development and implement of crisis communication strategies to address fake news during emergencies.	Timely and accurate information. Media outlets, government, and public.
International Cooperation	Collaborate with other countries and international organizations to tackle fake new globally.	Best practices shared with governments, private organizations, academia, NGOs.
Long-term Sustainability		
Research and Development	Fund research into the psychology or misinformation and the effectiveness of various interventions.	Government, public, private enterprise, NGOs, and academia.
Public Awareness Campaigns	The continuous running of public awareness campaigns highlighting the dangers of fake news and the importance of accurate information.	Media, Hollywood, and the scientific community.

These steps are aimed at creating a more informed and resilient society that is better equipped to handle the challenges posed by fake news.

Notable Case Studies Examined

Most realize that fake news spreads rapidly without censorship. The Internet is a pipeline filled to the brim with stories ripe for conspiracy theories such as Pizzagate. Pizzagate fed into another conspiracy theory known as QAnon. QAnon in 2016 was the "Big tent conspiracy theory" that falsely claims that former President Trump is facing down a shadowy cabal of Democratic pedophiles" December 2016, a man in Washington DC entered the Ping Pong Pizzeria with a semiautomatic assault rifle and a handgun and began blasting shots several times. Fortunately, no one was injured or killed and his reasoning that he offers police authorities was that he had been motivated by online reports that Democrats such as Hillary Clinton was harboring child sex slaves, and there was ample evidence to prove those allegations. Investigations into the story uncovered some reputable media outlets that uncovered several fake news sources originating from several countries such as Russia and Macedonia; others form the U. S. (LaCapria, K., 2016, November 21).

The Case in Veles, Macedonia (2016)

In 2016, 18-year-old Paul (changed for identity) from Veles, Macedonia, discovered a lucrative opportunity in the digital world by creating fake news websites. His articles, primarily shared on Facebook, generated significant traffic, leading to Paul earning $16,000 over a few months. This led to over a hundred political websites in Veles, many of which produced similar content. Paul and his fellow fake news publishers were motivated by profit, with the most popular stories being pro-Trump. Companies like

Google AdSense and AppNexus placed ads as intermediaries between advertisers and small publishers like Paul, reported by: Wired (2017, February 14).

The proliferation of fake news became a major scandal during the 2016 US election, with debates about whether sites like those run by Paul contributed to Trump's victory. Tech giants like Google and Facebook took measures to combat fake news, but continuous innovation and vigilance are necessary to combat the ever-evolving landscape of fake news Cimili, Z. and Satter, R. (2016, December 2).

Pizzagate (2016)

Previously discussed, a conspiracy theory was launched that falsely claimed a child trafficking ring involving high-profile politicians was being run out of a Washington D.C, pizzeria known as Comet Ping Pong. Former Secretary of State Hillary Clinton, and opposition candidate to Donald Trump was allegedly in charge of the Kolb.

The impact of this fake news led to an armed man entering the pizzeria to "self-investigate," which resulted in gunfire but fortunately no injuries. The incident underscored the real-world dangers of conspiracy theories propagated online" Reese, K. (2021, September 3).

The Pope Endorsement of Presidential Candidate Donald Trump (2016)

During the 2016 U. S. presidential election cycle, a fake news story circulated claiming that Pope Francis had endorsed Donald Trump. While not true, even more significant is that Pope's do not make political endorsements. Naturally, there was an impact that this fake story, which was widely shared on social media platforms globally, could have influence public opinion during this critical election. This is an example of how easily misinformation can be spread and unfortunately believed. According to one study, 8 percent of registered voters believe the enforcement was true Blake, A. (2018, April 3).

Brexit Misinformation (2016)

There were long-term consequences from the impact of the misinformation campaign leading up to and after the Brexit referendum, including the exaggerated figures about the financial benefits of for citizens of the U.K. for leaving the EU. The financial benefits claims would be later debunked, however, not before shaping the public's opinion and interest Blake, A. (2018, April 3). "Ever since David Cameron announced the UK's EU referendum in February 2016, discussions about Fake News during the Brexit campaign have been thriving and sparking debates on the role of social media in the run-up to Brexit" Höller, M. (2021).

2016 Impact on U. S. Presidential Election

Ohio State University academics' study suggests that false news significantly impacted Hillary Clinton's election-day support decline, with around 4% of Obama supporters deterred from voting in 2016 due to their trust in false information as report in 2018 by Blake, A. (2018, April 3).

This alone does not prove that fake news made a difference, of course. A Princeton-led study of fake news consumption during the 2016 campaign found that false articles made up 2.6 percent of all hard-news articles late in the 2016 campaign, with the stories most often reaching intense partisans who probably were not persuadable. And it wouldn't be surprising if Obama voters who weren't reliable Democratic supporters were more apt to believe fake news stories that affirmed their decision not to vote for Clinton, sourced from - Blake, A. (2018, April 3).

Ultimately, according to Dr. Perry Lyle, Ph.D., everyone has an individual responsibility to fact-check information they believe is important. You cannot abandon individual responsibility.

WHAT IS THE FUTURE OF FAKE NEWS?

On whether false and misleading narratives on the internet will decline in the next ten years, experts are evenly divided. 50/50. Those who predict progress put their faith in societal and technological answers. Some believe that technology serves to enhance rather than repress the darker aspects of human nature. As we know from Karl Marx's Conflict Theory, elitists and those in control will continue to dominate the landscape and keep the masses divided. Fake news, misinformation, and propaganda have always been an essential element in division. The Internet is credited with the ability to spread more diverse viewpoints and of course, lies. It is hard not to take a page from the past with the infamous and popular tabloids like the *National Enquirer* or *News of the World*, which for decades were impugned for spreading gossip of the stars' substance use, pregnancy rumors, affairs of the rich and famous, and even alien visitors DiLascio-Martinuk, T. (2024). A more pessimistic view centers on the behavioral nature of man:

> Most respondents who expect the environment to worsen said human nature is at fault. For instance, Christian H. Huitema, former president of the Internet Architecture Board, commented, "The quality of information will not improve in the coming years, because technology can't improve human nature all that much."

Let us not forget that we have Donald Trump squaring off again against each other in the 2024 run-up-to-the-election in the U. S. According to Lyle, bad information has always been around. The challenge remains for individuals to take responsibility and to stay skeptical, consider fact-checking and consider your own biases.

On the Horizon

Social media is expected to play a significant role in the spread of disinformation during Donald Trump's second term as President of the United States, which began on January 20, 2025. Several key factors are contributing to this trend: Relaxed Content Moderation and major social media platforms have rolled back their content moderation policies such as:

Meta (Facebook and Instagram) has eliminated U.S.-based fact-checkers, aiming to "dramatically reduce the amount of censorship" on its platforms.

X (formerly Twitter), under Elon Musk's ownership, has seen a significant increase in misinformation, with an EU official describing it as the biggest source of fake news and disinformation among social media platforms Atmos. (2025, January 24).

The Amplification of False Information is likely to be spurred on by influential figures, including Elon Musk, that has gained massive reach. For example, Musk's posts about the U.S. election were viewed 2 billion times, with a single false tweet about illegal voters receiving over 47 million views Steffen, S. (2024, November 14). X's algorithm changes have favored political messages supporting Trump, serving as a gateway between fringe and mainstream content (2024, November 14).

The proliferation of misleading content will continue to be a global issue influencing not only the U. S. 2024 election campaign which saw a surge in false and misleading claims on social media, targeting both presidential candidates according to Steffen, S. (2024, November 14) utilizing AI-generated content, including deepfakes, has emerged as a new tool for spreading disinformation, though its impact was not as widespread as initially feared. Loss of trust is an inevitable outcome.

Erosion of trust in traditional media Trump's continued use of terms like "fake news" is likely to further erode public trust in traditional news sources. This erosion of trust could lead to increased skepticism towards verified information and greater fragmentation of the information landscape Lever, R. (2024, November 12). Challenges for Fact-Checkers and Journalists

The dismantling of fact-checking programs and the rise of AI-generated content present significant challenges for maintaining information integrity, (2024, November 12) journalists and fact-checkers will need to navigate an era of intensified information warfare that has just been propelled to new height on inauguration day, January 20, 2025.

Muzzling the Media

Trump's attacks on the media have also raised alarm bells about coverage of his administration. Journalist and author Kyle Paoletta acknowledged that he fears "Trump's assault on the press will become a fusillade of discrete attempts to quash whatever reporting he views as antagonistic" and questions whether reporters will maintain access or face harassment. In a similar way, social media has retreated in content moderation as misinformation researchers face threats and attacks from conservative lawmakers.

Since taking over Twitter, now known as X, Elon Musk -- who may join Trump's cabinet has amplified rather than curbed misinformation. Matt Gertz of the left-leaning watchdog Media Matters recently said in a blog post that Trump won over supporters thanks in part to "a right-wing media complex that bombards them with falsehoods and grievances while dissuading them from consulting any alternative sources of information, be they legacy news outlets or government officials or medical experts." Daniel Kreiss a professor and researcher at the University of North Carolina Center for Information, Technology and Public Life), said the failure of fact-checking and traditional reporting to stem the spread of misinformation could be "devastating."

"What we're going to see are concerted campaigns to undermine democratic institutions and democratic norms," Kreiss said Lever, R. (2024, November 12).

Global Implications- The spread of disinformation through social media is expected to have impacts beyond U.S. borders, potentially influencing elections and public discourse in other countries Quadri, F. (2025, January 21). In conclusion, social media platforms are poised to become even more significant vectors for the spread of disinformation during Trump's second term. The combination of relaxed content moderation, algorithmic amplification of controversial content, and the erosion of trust in traditional media sources creates a fertile environment for the proliferation of false and misleading information Quadri, F. (2025, January 21) and Lever, R. (2024, November 12).

CONCLUSION

Fake news, also known as yellow journalism, emerged in the late 19th century in the United States, with Joseph Pulitzer purchasing the New York World in 1883 for $346,000. The term was coined in the mid-1890s to describe sensational journalism in the circulation war between Pulitzer and Willam Randolf Hurst's New York Journal. Fake news has become mainstream with the advent of the Internet, social media, and other mass media technologies.

The real problem with fake news is that the content is presented as factual news stories or events, deceiving the reader. Manipulation methods are deployed to make them appear factual and arranged through psychological means, enticing the reader to share them. The term has also been used to undermine established media outlets by questioning the validity of actual, factual news and decrying its legitimacy. Fake news is deeply intertwined with human cognition, social dynamics, and technological infrastructures.

Fake news has become a significant digital epidemic, posing a threat to the media, government, and democracy. In the past, fake news stories, such as the Comet Ping Pong incident, have been prevalent, can spawn violence, even mass shootings. However, this trend will change as text-based stories become more prevalent. Audio and video technology advancements are becoming so sophisticated that they will replicate real news in unprecedented and indecipherable ways. The scariest reality is that this sort of technology will transcend academies and institutions to the point where people can create fake digital clips as easily as regular people create fake news stories during this cycle Anderson, J. and Rainie, L. (2017, October 19).

Anderson, J. and Rainie, L. (2017, October 19), make this observation - “the conflict is too big for tech. The general population needs to support and fund the creation of impartial, truthful information. Additionally, it needs to make information literacy the main objective of schooling;” and from Elon Musk, [sic], “we can't have, like, willy-nilly proliferation of fake news. That's crazy. You can't have more types of fake news than real news. That's allowing public deception to go unchecked. That's crazy “. Elon Musk Quotes. (n.d.). Finally, this chapter underscores the difficulty that the world with have with putting the Jennie back in the bottle, as society continues to deal with fake news.

REFERENCES

ADL.org. (2024). New World Order. Glossary of Hate and Extremism. *Adl.org*. Accessed May 20, 2024, from https://extremismterms.adl.org/glossary/new-world-order

Anderson, J., & Rainie, L. (2017, October 19). The Future of Truth and Misinformation Online. https://www.pewresearch.org/internet/2017/10/19/theme-5-tech-cant-win-the-battle-the-public-must-fund-and-support-the-production-of-objective-accurate-information-it-must-also-elevate-information-literacy-to-be-a-primary-goal-of-educat/

Arndt, G. (2024, October 2). *The Newspaper Wars: Pulitzer vs Hearst*. Everything Everywhere. https://everything-everywhere.com/the-newspaper-wars-pulitzer-vs-hearst/

Bilton, N. (2017, January 26). Fake News is About to Get Scarier than you Ever Dreamed. Vanityfair.com. Retrieved May 19, 2024, from https://www.vanityfair.com/news/2017/01/fake-news-technology

Blake, A. (2018, April 3). A new study suggests fake news might have won Donald Trump the 2016 election. https://www.washingtonpost.com/news/the-fix/wp/2018/04/03/a-new-study-suggests-fake-news-might-have-won-donald-trump-the-2016-election/

Britannica, T. Editors of Encyclopedia (2024, May 2). *Yellow journalism. Encyclopedia Britannica.* https://www.britannica.com/topic/yellow-journalismcirculation

Britt, A., Rout, J.-F., Blaum, D., & Millis, K. (2019, March 8). A Reasoned approach to Dealing with Fake News, Sage Journals. https://journals.sagepub.com/doi/full/10.1177/2372732218814855

Cherry, K. (2020, December 11, 2020). How Confirmation Bias Works. Accessed from https://www.verywellmind.com/what-is-a-confirmation-bias-2795024

Cimili, Z., & Satter, R. (2016, December 2) Macedonia's Fake News Hub, Ten Show AP how it's Done. https://www.nbcconnecticut.com/news/national-international/in-macedonias-fake-news-hub-teen-shows-ap-how-its-done/1989346/

CITS.ucsb.edu. (n.d.) What is fake news? *Center for Information Technology & Society. University of California Santa Barbara.*https://cits.ucsb.edu/fake-news/what-is-fake-news

DiLascio-Martinuk, T. (2024). Fake News: Overview. *APA Points of ViewFake News: Overview: Cougar Search.* ccis.edu

Elon Musk Quotes. (n.d.). BrainyQuote.com. Retrieved May 23, 2024, from *BrainyQuote.com Web site:*https://www.brainyquote.com/quotes/elon_musk_949273

Flores, M. (2022, May 22). The New World Order: The Historical Origins of a Dangerous Modern Conspiracy Theory. https://www.middlebury.edu/institute/academics/centers-initiatives/ctec/ctec-publications/new-world-order-historical-origins-dangerous

Höller, M. (2021). The human component in social media and fake news: The performance of UK opinion leaders on Twitter during the Brexit campaign. *European Journal of English Studies*, *25*(1), 80–95. DOI: 10.1080/13825577.2021.1918842

http://www.youtube.com/watch?v=frjTitjisY

LaCapria, K. (2016, November 21). Is Comet Ping Pong Pizzeria Home to a Child Abuse Ring Leg by Hillary Clinton? *Snopes.com*. Accessed May 29, 2024, from https://www.snopes.com/fact-check/pizzagate-conspiracy/

Lever, R. (2024, November 12). Donald Trump's second term presents fresh disinformation challenges. *AFP.com*. Accessed January 25, 2025. https://factcheck.afp.com/doc.afp.com.36M84UR

Merriam-Webster. (n.d.-a). Filter bubble. Noun. *Merriam-webster.com*. https://www.merriam-webster.com/dictionary/filter%20bubble

Merriam-Webster. (n.d.-b). Echo chamber. Noun. *Merriam-webster.com*.https://www.merriam-webster.com/dictionary/echo%20chamber

Merriam-Webster. (n.d.). *Algorithm Definition & Meaning*. Merriam-Webster.

Quadri, F. (2025, January 21). What Trump's second term means for information resilience, media credibility. *FactCheckHub.com*. Accessed January 25, 2025. https://factcheckhub.com/what-trumps-second-term-means-for-information-resilience-media-credibility/

Reese, K. (2021, September 3). What is QAnon? the Viral Pro-Trump Conspiracy Theory. https://www.nytimes.com/article/what-is-qanon.html

Research Guides: "Fake News," Lies and Propaganda: How to Sort Fact from Fiction: What is "Fake News"? (n.d.). https://guides.lib.umich.edu/fakenews

Schmidt, S. (2004, July 18). 1998 Memo Cited Suspected Hijack Plot by Bin Laden. http://www.washingtonpost.com/wp-dyn/articles/A58615-2004Jul17.html

Simran, K. (2019, March 12). Winston Churchill Quotations. Retrieved from https://www.thoughtco.com/winston-churchill-quotations-2831679

Smith, C. & Hung, L-C. (2010). *The Patriot Act: Issues and Controversies*. Thomas Publishing Co.

Stacey, K. (2021, September 16). New Report Assesses Progress and Risks of Artificial Intelligence. Academic Press.

Stanford University. (2024). New report assesses progress and risks of artificial intelligence. Stanford HAI. https://hai.stanford.edu/news/new-report-assesses-progress-and-risks-artificial-intelligence

Steffen, S. (2024, November 14). Fact check: Disinformation's impact on the US election. *dw.com*. https://www.dw.com/en/fact-check-what-role-did-disinformation-play-in-the-us-election/a-70729575

The Wikihuman Project (n.d.). The Digital Emily Project: Achieving a Photoreal Digital Actor. usc.edu

Wired. (2017, February 14). Here's How Fake News Works (and How the Internet Can Stop it). *Wired*.

KEY TERMS AND DEFINITIONS

Algorithms: A set of rules or calculations used by computers to perform tasks. Social media algorithms often figure out what content users see, which can influence the spread of fake news. Merriam-Webster. (n.d.).

Bot: Automated accounts on social media platforms that can spread information, including fake news. Bots can amplify the reach of disinformation campaigns. Merriam-Webster. (n.d.).

Click Bait: A term used to describe articles, either real or fake, that have attention-grabbing headlines and intentionally inflammatory content, designed to entice readers to click on the article and share the content DiLascio-Martinuk, T. (2024).

Echo Chamber: An environment where a person only meets information or opinions that reflect and reinforce their own beliefs. Social media can create echo chambers by showing users content like what they already engage with Merriam-Webster. (n.d.).

Fake News: Fake news means "news articles that are intentionally and verifiably false" designed to manipulate people's feelings of facts, events, and statements. It is about information presented as news known by its promoter to be false based on demonstrably incorrect facts, statements, or events that verifiably did not happen CITS.ucsb.edu (n.d.).

Filter Bubble: A situation wherein the internet user meets only information and opinions that conform to the reinforcement of their preconceived beliefs, created by algorithms that personalize the content. Confirmation biases Merriam-Webster. (n.d.).

Yellow Journalism: the use of lurid features and sensationalized news in newspaper publication to attract readers and increase circulation Britannica, T. Editors of Encyclopedia (2024, May 2).

Chapter 2
Contagion:
The Disease of Spreading Fake News in the Digital World

Rouby Mavyan
https://orcid.org/0009-0001-3515-5921
Fresno Pacific University, USA

Ashraf Esmail
Dillard University, USA

Hovsep Mavyan
Fresno Pacific University, USA

ABSTRACT

Fake news on the internet refers to intentionally concocted or falsely presented licit information. The purpose is to negatively influence public opinion for several reasons, which include political agendas, monetary profit, and propaganda. Disinformation on the internet is circulated through websites and social media. It can take various forms, including but not limited to erroneous headlines, falsified stories, distorted images, and fabricated content mirroring truthful news reports. Fake news flourishes in areas where trust in credible media sources is low and political division is high. The propagation of false data across the internet is rooted in technology, psychology, and society. This concept likens fake news to infectious disease. Fake news on the web can be transmitted from person to person. By referring to fake news as a contagious disease, it is easier to understand the variables affected, the rapid spread, the detrimental effects, and the vigorous steps necessary to combat the problem.

PROBLEM STATEMENT

The modern digital era has shifted society's dependence toward online platforms for information which stands in direct contrast to historical reliance on journalists and reputable media as truth sources. The spread of fake news presents a pressing difficulty since users need to distinguish between facts and false information—a challenge that dates back to ancient Rome's use of propaganda and World War I's misinformation tactics by superpowers to shape public views. Yellow journalism in the early 1900s

DOI: 10.4018/979-8-3693-7468-9.ch002

intensified this problem through characters like Joseph Pulitzer who created fake stories to increase newspaper sales and established a foundation for modern online misinformation. Historical analysis of fake news development remains essential since it dictates current political discussions and public confidence in digital communication. This literature review research seeks to explore the historical roots of misinformation from ancient propaganda through yellow journalism to uncover patterns and strategies that affect modern fake news spread while developing strategies for improved digital literacy and response.

INTRODUCTION

In the past, fundamental sources of information came from journalists and reputable media channels. Today, society uses the digital world to access information. Whether the content is accurate, or fake is left up to the user to investigate—fake news dates to ancient civilizations. Kreis (2017) described that, in ancient Rome, politicians used propaganda to manipulate public opinion and damage opponents' reputations. This tactic shaped the current practice of disseminating false news to alter politics and public opinions. During World War I, both superpowers used detailed propaganda to spread misinformation, shift public perception, and advance a positive outlook. In the early 20th century, yellow journalism surfaced. As Schudson (2003) stated, yellow journalism intended to publish fabricated stories to boost profits from newspaper sales. Notable authors such as Joseph Pulitzer used yellow journalism to post misleading headlines to increase the circulation of their published work (Schudson, 2003). This era established the framework for the *modern-day contagion* of spreading false information in the digital realm.

THE EVOLUTION OF THE INTERNET

In the early days of the Internet, email frauds and false stories spread through online forums. The speed and minimal effort needed to share information extended the influence of fake news, compared to traditional media sources. Fake news in the digital world refers to intentionally concocted or falsely presented licit information. Allcott and Gentzkow (2017) reported that the drive of false news is to negatively influence public opinion for several reasons, such as political agendas, monetary profit, and advertising purposes. Studies have exhibited that two-thirds of American adults attain news from social media outlets regardless of concern about its validity (Pew Research Center, 2018).

Faux news on the Internet is circulated through websites and social media (Lazer et al., 2018). It can take various forms, including, but not limited to, erroneous headlines, falsified stories, conspiracy theories, fake political statements from presidential candidates, distorted images, and fabricated content mirroring truthful news reports. As Quandt et al. (2019) presented, seven types of misinformation exist:

Satire content, which intends to trick viewers, rather than cause harm.

Misleading content, which aims to condemn a person or an issue.
Imposter content, which mimics genuine content.
Fabricated content, which is newly created fake content intended to cause harm.
False connections, which include a disconnect between headlines and content.
False context, which includes instances where factual content is shared with false context.

Manipulated content, that is, real images and videos are purposely manipulated to deceive viewers.

The propagation of false data across the Internet is rooted in technology, psychology, and society. This concept likens fake news to infectious disease. Fake news on the Web can be transmitted from person to person. This happens through social media platforms, websites, and blogs. By referring to fake news as a contagious disease, it is easier to understand the rapid spread, the detrimental effects, and the vigorous steps necessary to combat the problem.

The Internet is an easily accessible and free digital world where anyone can effortlessly publish information without verification. Fake news is intentionally published to push a specific agenda or for monetary gain. The easy creation and distribution of content allows falsified information to be produced and spread without restriction. Headlines that attract attention are more likely to be shared through social media. Websites such as ABCnews.com.co and wtoe5news.com resemble legitimate websites to disinform viewers (Allcott & Gentzkow, 2017).

REASONS FOR THE SPREAD OF FAKE NEWS

The following crucial elements influence the spread of fake news quickly: Monetary incentives, virality, confirmation bias, algorithms, and easy access to content distribution and echo chambers. Monetary compensation significantly increases the reproduction of fake news. Fake websites operate based on the volume of traffic brought to their sites, and the more users visit their sites, the more revenue the site owners generate. Financial motivation pushes the production of fake news to attract user attention and buy-in continuously. Furthermore, the algorithms used on these platforms promote content to generate website traffic and thus lead to the advancement of the contagious spreading of fake news. Subsequently, the rapid spread of unverified information becomes viral (Tufekci, 2018).

Virality refers to the hasty sharing of content through social networks, which quickly magnifies the effects of fake news. Virality comprises emotionally motivated content that attracts user attention, pushing them to share the information within their social links. This often leads to the standardization and belief that false information is accurate.

Fake news tends to thrive in environments where trust in credible media resources is low and political polarization is high. Research shows that individuals are more likely to spread fake news if it aligns with their political opinions (Guess et al., 2019). This underscores the concerning influence of fake news on public opinion and the need for increased digital literacy and critical thinking.

One of the main factors impacting the widespread of fake news is confirmation bias. Confirmation bias is a type of rational bias. It occurs because it is convenient, connects people to the same beliefs, and feeds their emotions. It causes people to accept true or false information that backs their existing views (Vosoughi et al., 2018). When fake news is dispersed online and resonates with one's presumed beliefs, it can make it easier to trust and pass on that information. The ease of creating and spreading content offers little hindrance to false information spreading. The risk of confirmation bias arises when people choose to believe and understand information as they interpret it. Misinformation becomes credible to users when it confirms their existing beliefs.

Confirmation bias increases with the presence of filter bubbles. Often, users are unaware that the content presented is executed purposefully to support their beliefs and interests. Filter bubbles, also known as personalized bubbles, are created when users accept website cookies through personalized searches in which the websites promote content based on previous searches and click history. These personalized bubbles keep users away from content that does not align with their ideologies.

Like other major media platforms, Google uses filter bubbles through its search engine. Because of confirmation bias, filter bubbles cannot be avoided. People will be unable to think critically, and misinformation will continue to spread like an infectious disease without a cure.

LIMITATIONS OF THE STUDY

The research provides beneficial historical understanding about misinformation progression yet faces multiple limitations that restrict how its results can be applied. The study operates exclusively through a literature review by using secondary sources instead of primary interviews or archival materials and experimental data. The study's conclusions are interpretive because they rely on existing scholarly work that could have its own biases and historical coverage gaps.

The research faces another major limitation because it encompasses both ancient Roman propaganda tactics and contemporary digital disinformation campaigns. The broad scope provides a valuable comparative framework but could lead to simplifications of the distinct socio-political complexities present in each historical period. Technological capacities and cultural practices combined with media frameworks from different historical periods create boundaries for directly comparing misinformation tactics.

The examination of Western media history that emphasizes Joseph Pulitzer's influence and yellow journalism's emergence threatens to sideline non-Western viewpoints on propaganda and fake news creation. This focused perspective fails to adequately represent the development and response to misinformation across different geopolitical settings such as the Global South, authoritarian systems, and oral community networks.

The historical and theoretical nature of this study excludes empirical data and real-time case studies needed for evaluating current misinformation countermeasures. Digital literacy and public response recommendations remain provisional without current data and intervention research which necessitates more empirical validation.

This study represents an essential starting point to connect past media practices with current digital obstacles despite their limitations. Subsequent studies could build on this base through cross-cultural evaluations, empirical evaluations of media literacy initiatives or by applying computational methods to study disinformation trends across digital platforms.

PROS AND CONS OF FAKE NEWS

While spreading fake news can pose a lot of risks, it does entail some advantages. One of the benefits includes the heightened awareness it offers of information flow and the importance of media literacy. As fake news on the Web becomes more popular, society becomes more aware and diligent in detecting and combating false content. As a positive effect, this leads to continued public awareness and the ability to critically analyze and recognize inauthentic content. Likewise, falsified content has allowed for the advancement of AI and machine learning to help tackle the spread of misinformation. Tech companies have strategized and developed tools and algorithms to detect and remove non-credible information from social media websites. Lastly, although not always authentic information, the vast spread of news online proves the power of social media platforms in promoting heightened engagement. Content that produces heightened emotions is more likely to be shared and spread (Pennycook & Rand, 2018).

On the opposite end, the consequences of spreading fake news on social media include distrust in media platforms, worsening of societal divides, and the negative impact on health and safety. When most of society widely propagates and believes misinformation is accurate, it challenges the trust in credible media sources. This mistrust has significant consequences for democracy and social unity (Lazer et el., 2018). In addition, this amplifies misinformation and creates a division in public opinion. Vosoghi et al. (2018) noted that misinformation can easily and rapidly become peoples' reality, mainly when it corresponds with their existing beliefs. The division in public opinion has unfavorable impacts on public health and safety.

Health Misinformation and COVID-19

Recent examples of significant societal and political impacts due to the spread of misinformation include conspiracy theories regarding the COVID-19 pandemic, its origin and treatment, and vaccine efficacy. The term "pandemic" characteristically refers to the universal spread of a disease. In the case of fake news and misinformation, it can be seen as a single widespread disease.

People search for health information to learn about various diseases, illnesses, and preventative measures. Information can be obtained through multiple sources such as primary care physicians, friends, family, newspapers, magazines, television, and the radio (Warner, 2004). Today, most of society no longer seeks out those sources, and many defer to the Internet for validation.

There is infinite Web content and platforms that Internet users utilize to look up health information and share updates on health information. Many websites contain accurate information; however, several misleading sites promote inaccurate health evidence. Reputable websites such as WebMD and other credible health education outlets allow users to post user-generated content (i.e., comments) on their websites. The challenge arises when the accuracy of the user-posted content is not validated, and people start to believe false information because it was posted on a reputable site such as WebMD. When Internet users read reviews, they find it hard to differentiate between facts and opinions, authentic vs. fake information.

When the world dealt with pandemics and epidemics in the past, information was limited, and the spread was contained. During the H1N1 outbreak, false information was spread only during social outings and between families and friends (Nguyen & Nguyen, 2020). Technology today allows millions of online users to create rumors and spread fake information. Given that most digital information and news are free to access, the opportunity for misrepresentation is immeasurable. A substantial cause of misinformation is the lack of accuracy in proving the information as false. Popular social media platforms such as Facebook and Twitter are common culprits of fake news propagation, especially regarding health education (pandemics, epidemics, vaccine effects, medical treatments, and non-transmittable diseases).

When COVID-19 surfaced in February 2020, the digital world failed to offer educational and valuable information regarding the pandemic. The recommendations from educational sites and medically governed agencies were limited, and all other COVID-19-relevant content was based on propaganda to promote a specific agenda.

The dissemination of fake news on the Web during the COVID-19 pandemic had a monumental impact on public health directives, vaccine efforts, compliance with safety protocols, the public trust in government, healthcare workers, and credible media sources (Pennycook & Rand, 2020). Subsequently, society was confused about the preventable measures such as social distancing, mask mandates, and the vaccine's benefits. The vaccine hesitancy arose from the false claims on the safety and efficacy (Mheidly & Fares, 2020). Internet hearsay kept buzzing about the vaccine affecting women's fertility and genetic alteration for those who received the injection (Cinelli et al., 2020). Furthermore, as former president Donald Trump suggested, fraudulent claims about the effectiveness of specific treatments, such as drinking bleach or using hydroxychloroquine, circulated like wildfire on social media and Internet websites (Constine, 2020).

Platforms such as Twitter use bots to impersonate human users to post content. Moreover, Internet trolls and users who are trying to promote a deceitful agenda hop onto these sites to promote health-related disinformation to cause chaos and confusion within society. The most recent COVID-19 pandemic is the latest public health crisis affected by false information on the Web. The pandemic became an infodemic because misinformation became contagious and spread infinitely on the Internet (Govindankutty & Gopalan, 2023). One example is the impact of vaccines created solely for political and financial gain.

During the prime of COVID-19, people took advantage of the unfortunate circumstances to gain monetary compensation. Srivastava (2021) reported that social media influencers and pharmacies took advantage of the pandemic to promote ineffective homeopathic medicine, prescription, and nonprescription medications, as well as counterfeit vaccines as a cure for COVID-19. Due to the uncertainty and fear of the unknown, Internet users fell victim to purchasing the falsely advertised COVID-19 cures.

In the summer of 2020, 34% of people in the United States believed in the effectiveness of the COVID-19 vaccine, with a significant political divide between the Democrats and the Republicans (Tyson et al., 2020). By spring 2021, the vaccine acceptance slightly increased, yet the Republicans remained skeptical. The reason was that the Republicans were more susceptible to believing misinformation regarding vaccine efficacy as it aligned with their beliefs. They followed right-wing mainstream ideas, dividing society from dishonest leaders (Motta, 2021).

Bode and Vraga (2018) conducted a study on the harmful effects of presenting false information on the COVID-19 pandemic, resulting in a more significant societal divide, the instillation of fear, the stigmatization of certain groups, and the promotion of discrimination. The opposition weakened the attempts to battle the pandemic jointly.

SOCIETAL DIVISIONS

In addition to the societal divide and increase in stigmatization due to misinformation on COVID-19, the Asian community became the main target of racism. Coined on the Twitter platform as the "Chinese Virus" by Trump, the virus became racialized, rather than a biological threat. This caused a significant increase in detrimental fake news about the COVID-19 spread and anti-Asian racism (McGuire, 2020). Those who believed in the misinformation used the Asian population as victims to accuse and discriminate against. Consequently, the Asian population became stigmatized and targeted with physical, verbal, and emotional violence.

Mcguire (2020) reported that, from 2020 to 2021, there were 3800 incidents of racism against Asian Americans.

Forms of racism towards Asian Americans included the spreading of hate comments on social media tied to misinformation about the origination of the virus, evictions from businesses, discrimination at the workplace, and property destruction. Twenty-nine percent of Americans believed the Coronavirus was leaked from a lab in Wuhan, China, and twenty-three percent believed it was purposefully done. Moreover, by March 2020, twenty-nine percent of Americans believed China created the virus as a tactic for biological warfare (Romer & Jamieson, 2020).

Mental health challenges and trauma resulting from the pandemic affected much of society. The online hoaxes that continued circulating regarding COVID-19 posed a significant challenge for health workers working around the clock to fight the virus. It added to their already high-stress lifestyles and led some to depression and severe mental disorders (Alhouri et al., 2023). The negative influence of COVID-19 played a tremendous role in society. However, the Asian Americans experienced a domino effect. They suffered mental and emotional challenges along with trauma, stress, fear, depression, and anxiety because of the racism and criticism they continued to experience (McGuire, 2020).

To limit the amount of misinformation on public health issues circulating on the Web, medical governing agencies must ensure that evidence-based information overpowers public health to limit false information to society. Universities, hospitals, and credible healthcare agencies should collaborate with governments to create policies and continuously share health education information supported by evidence (Mheidly, 2020). The more accessible and credible information is, the higher the chances of spreading it for the common good.

Fact-checking content published on the Internet is essential to ensure reliability and trust with consistent verification. Fact-checking digital media sources during the pandemic was critical and necessary to validate credibility and recommendations from the World Health Organization and Centers for Disease Control and Prevention. Public health actions and safety policies were significantly impacted, and educating society on safety measures was a vital factor in preventing the spread of the virus.

Pandemic Conspiracy Theories Thrive

During the pandemic, when conspiracy theories, such as the virus being created in a lab in China, were circulating on the Web regarding the virus's origin, fact-checking conceded for evidence-based information to combat false theories (Flemming, 2020).

Social media platforms, although guilty of spreading fake news about COVID-19, China, and Asian American hate, have also helped with combating the discrimination against Asians. Mcguire (2020) reported that platforms such as Facebook, Twitter, and Instagram supported the targeted minorities from exploitation by pushing campaigns such as #IAmNotAVirus on their websites.

The National Institutes of Health recommended that Internet users be mindful of Web content by checking its accuracy. To do so, the following factors had to be considered. The website's sponsorship, the author's credibility, whether the author was a health official or not, the purpose of the Web content, and the date of publication, all signified the validity of the content (Pennycook & Rand, 2018). Accurate sources promote health education and health decisions. Vulnerable populations such as the elderly, minorities, and communities who do not have easy access to health care are at most risk of believing false health information because they lack education on evidence-based health information. This increases the likeliness of them falling victim to conspiracy theories.

Politics and Elections

Fake campaigns can shape public opinion by spreading false information on viewpoints, leading to a societal divide. When society cannot differentiate between credible sources and fake news, they lose faith in the reliability of information and sway away from politics (Alcott & Gentzkow, 2017). During elections, false information about the voting process, candidate speeches, and election dates undermine democratic elections.

Political Falsehoods

The spread of falsehood in politics has been studied as a "top to bottom" phenomenon (Lasser et al., 2020), with political figures being at the top, flowing down to noncredible websites and social media platforms. The distribution of misinformation in politics is also used as a weapon to attack candidates, creating more opposition than expected in a democracy. This decreases the chances of a well-functioning system, risking citizen distrust in the government. In May 2022, a national survey was conducted to understand the motivations of social media users and their intent of sharing misinformation. The respondents were asked if they participated in generating or sharing false information through online platforms; 14% admitted that they did (Littrell et al., 2023). They also reported that the purposeful sharing was due to their support for political carnage, their political views being aligned with extremist groups such as QAnon and White supremacists, and, lastly, their desire to participate in running for office. According to the same survey, users who purposely shared false content admitted to using social media sites such as Telegram and Truth Social to promote misinformation and conspiracy theories (Littrell et al., 2023)

It is equally important to note that there are Internet users who are not extremists or political figure advocates who also intentionally share false political information to mislead others due to their agendas (Buchanan & Benson, 2019). They aim to ensure their posted content quickly spreads and goes viral to attract the most attention. Lastly, users can post false information to discredit political groups or create chaos online.

The problem with fake political news also extends to worldwide concerns. Fake campaign news becomes a tool for foreign entities, allowing them to distort the democratic process intentionally. The most recent attempts include the 2016 Russian influence during the U.S. presidential elections and the 2016 Brexit vote in the United Kingdom. During the 2016 presidential election campaign, thousands of fake Russian accounts posted propaganda against Hillary Clinton, branding her a criminal to sway voters' opinions (Allcott & Gentzkow, 2017). As part of this propaganda, it was reported that the Russian government led a campaign that included hacking and bots to disseminate false news across the Internet in efforts to sway the public trust in the U.S. election process and to tarnish candidate reputations. The campaign included more than one million posts on Twitter, hundreds of thousands of Facebook and Instagram feeds, and thousands of YouTube videos, generating and attracting almost three hundred million views (Polyakova & Boyer, 2017).

THE CHINA CONNECTION

China's government (PRC), on the other hand, is strict with access to foreign social media platforms (i.e., Google, Facebook, and YouTube) within the country, banning the use of these platforms through strong firewalls. Social media allowed in China includes Chinese-created platforms strictly monitored by the government to push progovernment propaganda to avoid antigovernment agendas. On the contrary, however, China uses foreign social media sites to spread advertisements (authentic or fake) to other countries, such as the United States. Consumers in China spent five billion dollars on Facebook advertisements in 2018, making them the largest buyers of advertisements in Asia (King et al., 2017).

China has also interfered with foreign government campaigns such as Russia's election propaganda influence forces. According to Horton (2018), during the 2018 Taiwan presidential elections, the Chinese government led months long of vast propaganda to discredit Taiwan's president and the democratic party to have them removed from office and replaced with the opposing party. Furthermore, China has used platforms like LinkedIn to connect with business leaders in America, using misleading suggestions to establish relationships and offer money in exchange for intelligence information (King et al., 2017).

Bogus Iranian propaganda has also tried to influence the U.S. with its policy interests aligned with the Iranian government, such as anti-Israel and pro-Palestine propaganda and anti-Trump agendas, due to Trump's decision to pull America out of the nuclear agreement with Iran (Guess et al., 2019). Iran has created close to one hundred fake websites to spread disinformation to fifteen countries, including the United States. One of their fabricated websites posted a fake story alleging that Israel threatened a nuclear attack on Pakistan if they aided with sending their troops to Syria. Without validating whether these claims were valid or not, Pakistan responded with an actual attack via a social platform viewed globally (Guess et al., 2019). Tensions decreased once it was determined that the content was indeed fabricated.

Iran has similarly successfully gathered followers and views by creating slogans that are most often about topics that divide society. Their tactics include creating and posting fake images of celebrities to promote political or racial divides, generating hundreds of thousands of shares.

Fact-checked information is correlated to positive outcomes through the confirmation of correct information. The impact, however, decreases during elections. On January 6, 2021, rioters ambushed Capitol Hill because of fake election conspiracy theories, which until today are widely accessible on the Internet. The 2024 election will prove far worse when spreading false campaigns due to more robust and enhanced propagation tools. The surge and advancement in AI have simplified the spreading of misinformation to sway voters and manipulate elections. Fake images, videos or audio clips named deepfakes have already been implemented into campaign ads, impersonating candidates' plans that will negatively impact society. Although fact-checking websites have debunked these advertisements, credible digital sources that once invested in fact-checking practices have shifted their interests (Kim et al., 2019).

ADVERTISING

Advertising has revolutionized due to the rise of social media, which has allowed endless opportunities to market to a broader audience. In advertising, especially in the digital world (e.g., TikTok, Twitter, Instagram, and Facebook), fake narratives influence consumer behavior, brand character, and market dynamics (Lewandosky et al., 2012). Vosoghi et al. (2018) claimed that buyers are deceived by false commercials that change market competition, ignoring moral advertising models. Ahmed (2017) predicted that eighty-eight percent of online purchasers follow customer reviews before purchasing, and seventy-two percent of consumers believe a web-page's trustworthiness is due to positive reviews.

Not all online advertisements are authentic. Falsified ads, which include misleading information, negatively impact society. Those who fall for false advertising fraud can suffer financial losses. For example, rapidly spreading false advertisements on weight loss medications that encourage quick and easy results can lead people to spend copious amounts on products that have no results and can pose a health risk. This financial plummet can cause consumers to lose trust in online products. As the skepticism about online products increases, motivation to shop online decreases, impacting business owners and e-commerce (Kumar, 2021).

Market dynamics suffer equally due to false advertisements. When false advertisements promote quality products, the competition becomes biased. Authentic businesses with credible advertisements fall into the shadows of rapidly spread misleading promotions, resulting in a loss of profit. Beyond consumers and legitimate business owners suffering financial losses, there are regulatory costs. Government agencies such as the Federal Trade Commission spend copious amounts of money investigating and prosecuting falsified ads (Federal Trade Commission, 2021).

Lastly, spreading false advertisements poses a greater risk to algorithmic exploitation and cybersecurity. Algorithm recommendations can be manipulated by user interaction rather than credibility. The spread of fake data quickly increases due to those algorithms. Consequently, the spread of this information negatively impacts the credibility of online information. Moreover, false advertisements online cause cybersecurity threats such as phishing or virus distribution. These misleading ads can also manipulate consumers to provide credit cards or personal information, compromising identity theft (Felt et al., 2014).

NATURE OF GENERATIVE CONTENT

The driving force in generating and distributing fake content on the Web is achieving maximum webpage traffic in exchange for revenues (Chahal, 2017). The financial gains triumph over the consequences when the disease of fake news spreads on platforms such as Facebook. The conception of fake news through advertising is seen as an effective digital marketing tool, targeting interest groups who share common beliefs to widen the spread of misinformation.

The spread of deceptive information affects advertising, which, in turn, impacts branding. In order to be transparent, credible companies prioritize where their advertisements appear. When brands are associated with false advertisements, their reputations are at risk, causing buyers to lose their trust in the company. Reports from the Pew Research Center (2021) confirm that fake advertisements led to decreased interest in online advertisements, impacting the overall digital marketplace.

A substantial portion contributing to the growth of online advertising is attributed to giant media distributors such as Facebook and Google, though large dependable companies, such as Walmart and Starbucks, have been shying away from digital advertising in fear of falling victim to fake propaganda (Solon, 2017). Reputable brands continue to be seen as reliable sources when placing online advertisements. They, too, hesitate to advertise through other media channels due to the lack of control between the advertiser and the outlet source (Lemon et al., 2016). It is apparent that Facebook and other platforms significantly promote false advertisements and fake news. However, the issue also lies with the spread of misinformation by Internet users themselves

The negative impact of spreading false advertisements on social media could be challenged by redirecting the spread to accurate advertising. To decrease the spread of fake news in advertising, purchasers must critically analyze online information, verify reputable sources, and avoid ads that seem too perfect. There are various strategies for overcoming the consequences of false advertising in the digital realm. Controlling credible websites restricts illegitimate advertisement pop-ups explicitly created to distribute falsified content (Ghosh, 2020).

THE ROLE OF AI, RACE, AND SOCIAL CONFLICT BY FAKE NEWS

AI is the imitation of human aptitude supported by machines. AI is based on data and algorithms to predict human behavior, allowing for the same capability of understanding, logic, and problem-solving (Bontridder & Poullet, 2021). AI has the power to make people believe false information is accurate. Generative AI, being more advanced, can produce updated content. It can create modified visual and audio content, making verifying real or fake content difficult. Generative AI can serve two purposes: Creating and disseminating fake content as well as detecting it. Generative AI's capability to produce fake news has become a challenge in social media, where misinformation is easily accessible, and credibility is not popular.

Media content created by AI, also known as deepfakes, is specifically meant to generate and distribute deceptive content. Deepfakes pose threats to society because of their capability to combine algorithms and facial mapping to illicitly generate data into digital content (Bontridder & Poullet, 2021). The growth of deepfakes has negatively impacted society through politics, advertising, and the spread of misinformation. Deepfakes are to blame for politicians saying things they never said by promoting fake audio or video content generated by AI. For example, most recently, robocalls utilizing AI were used to impersonate President Joe Biden's voice, urging citizens not to vote to sway the election outcomes in November (Lu et al., 2022). The realistic audio of Biden's voice created new channels for manipulating and spreading fake news to society. In other instances, videos and images allegedly taken in Israel, Gaza, and Ukraine to sway the American opinion of the wars proved to be fake. This is detrimental to American society as the misinformation causes a deeper political divide.

Advertisements correlated to digital marketing allow companies to use images, videos, and content to promote their brands. Identifying online advertisements' credibility is essential to avoid falling victim to monetary loss. Deepfakes played a large part during the peak of the COVID-19 pandemic. Their intent was to publish misleading information regarding social distancing, mask mandates, and the effectiveness of vaccines. A fraudulent video of Dr. Anthony Fauci, an immunologist and infectious disease expert who was the chief medical advisor to the U.S. president at that time, was circulating across social media platforms urging people to abstain from COVID-19 vaccination. This created uncertainty in society and caused a gap in trust between top health officials and the government.

On the other hand, there are benefits to the emergence of AI, one being its ability to detect fake content. Firstly, AI can identify and measure data and trends that suggest falsified information. It can also cross-reference facts with credible sources and raise the alarm about fake information. Through social media channels, it can identify and compare user behavior with false information generation to intervene with early efforts in stopping the spread. Second, AI can also be used to educate online consumers and readers, providing them with strategies to identify fake information by verifying information and Web sources. Lastly, AI can track the spread of information on social media platforms, identifying suspicious patterns and user behavior associated with disinformation campaigns. This allows for the early detection of emerging trends and targeted intervention strategies.

IMPLICATIONS FROM THE DATE RESEARCH

Past research has proved that the propagation of fake news on the Internet can spread racism, especially towards African Americans. Social media plays a prominent role in broadcasting racist views. In the past, when the public was presented with a video of a particular incident, it was trusted that the incident happened as portrayed in the video. Deepfake videos modify real videos by using technology to alter faces and voices. This is becoming especially dangerous for ostracized communities who have no voice, such as the existing incidents of police brutality, especially towards African Americans. Witnesses and police body cameras have captured the factual encounters of police misconduct; however, with access to deepfakes, false videos and audio have been altered to protect law enforcement instead. This has challenged the efforts of seeking justice for police brutality.

Wu et al. (2023) highlighted that, following the death of George Floyd in 2020, the Black Lives Matter (BLM) movement took an uprising when members began to protest around the country to fight for justice against police brutality. During these protests, Internet users took advantage and began posting fake news articles about the intent of BLM. Additionally, deepfake images began circulating the Web about the BLM movement and the false intent of their fundraising efforts. To support the BLM movement, an NBA team advertised BLM on their team buses. A distorted image of the buses was shared on social media, and an article claimed that the fundraising money was spent on luxury charter buses, rather than for the cause (Georgacopoulos & Poche, 2024). The fake content that spread on the Web involving the BLM movement resulted in negative attention and increased racism towards African Americans.

Proving that fake images or videos are not authentic is more challenging than proving that real videos are not fake. Verification technology (specifically through smartphones) now offers tools to validate the time and place the footage was recorded. It also discloses if the image or data attached has been manipulated (Lu et al., 2022). The goal of these tools is to safeguard the credibility of the images with facts. There is, however, a downside to this benefit. In modern society, where abundant video evidence is still not enough to convict a police officer for violence, enhancing technology may not be the answer, as it can create more significant inequalities. The cost of adding such functionality to smartphones will increase the selling price, which some people may not be able to afford. One study found that Whites and high-earning income people had higher rates of smartphone ownership than Black people (Pew Research Center, 2024). Unless the verification technology tool is equally attainable for all, the existing disparities to digital access increase. These consequences take a step further, causing inferences for police liability and for Black lives. Technological verifications will not be practical if they are only available to upper-class White people who are more favored in society than minorities. The threat of deepfakes might lessened with such technology, but systemic racism will continue to augment.

According to the Pew Research Center (2024), four out of five Black people feel the Internet and the news falsely depict their race. Significantly, with its potential to generate fake news, AI can also affect racial bias and racism. The developers and researchers of AI technology can lack diversity, which contributes to the dissemination of racial bias. Algorithms unfamiliar with large data sets and lacking diversity inhibit fundamental biases. For example, software that detects facial recognition has higher error rates for African Americans, due to the lack of training data (Bontinder & Poullet, 2021).

AI in decision-making is especially detrimental to people of color. According to Bontinder and Poullet (2021), the spread of falsified views regarding specific races further increases when automated decisions are made in employment pronouncements and/or in the criminal justice system, and AI does not include testing for racial bias. To overcome the racial basis in AI, the algorithms and data collection must be diverse to ensure fairness and accuracy in automated decision-making processes (Lu et al., 2022).

POPULATION AT RISK

It is essential to understand that fake news does not entertain everyone. Understanding the target audience of those who are responsive to fake news is necessary to create approaches to stop the impact of the spread. The increased vulnerability of those falling for fake online propaganda differs by demographics, age, socioeconomic status, and low educational achievement (Pennycook & Rand, 2018). Senior citizens are most at risk of believing falsified information due to their age and competence in navigating the World Wide Web. They are less versed, have less familiarity with social and digital media, and cannot analyze content as real or fake. Furthermore, individuals with low levels of education are not as knowledgeable in discerning between credible and non-credible sources. Also, they do not possess the same analytical thinking skills as those with degrees. Knoll et al. (2011) found that college students are also susceptible to misinformation due to the lack of knowledge of political and world views vs. an older person with more experience. Lastly, people with low socioeconomic status are more prone to relying on false information and contributing to the spread due to economic pressures and uncertainty.

Psychological and emotional vulnerabilities are just as significant to note. Emotional triggers play a fundamental role in the transmission of fake news. Emotions spark irrational thoughts and can limit critical thinking and overbearing logical reasons to analyze the reliability of online sources (Pew Research Center, 2017). Emotions that spark fear, anger or joy are more likely to be shared. Emotions also tie in with the level of trust people have towards information.

Confirmation and cognitive biases impact individuals prone to believing and spreading fake news. As mentioned previously, people with solid confirmation bias are the ones who hold firm political stances and are more likely to spread false news that they hold strong opinions about. Lewandowsky et al. (2017) reported that confirmation bias impacts how people process information and share and spread false information with people of like minds. Thus, fake news resulting from confirmation bias is more likely to spread through echo chambers.

Like confirmation bias, the bandwagon effect is a social influence where people behave or believe in information because others do. This type of influence vastly contributes to the spread of false news. When Internet surfers see widely spread content, they are more inclined to share it themselves regardless of its reliability. Vosoghi et al. (2018) confirmed that the bandwagon effect plays a prominent role in disseminating false news online.

Another vulnerable group includes teenagers who grow up in the world of social media and influencers. Teenagers only follow news that corresponds with their beliefs and interests. Furthermore, teenagers often avoid watching news altogether. Avoidance stems from a lack of current news knowledge, leading to their gullibility in believing false news (Cohen et al., 2021). Teenagers also consume news with the least attention as they navigate multiple sites simultaneously. Subsequently, the distraction disables them from recognizing the difference between real and fake news. Disregarding the importance of distinguishing and disseminating real news, teenagers share and spread news on social media platforms if it interests them. Fake news supporting racism is another common type of news that teenagers are exposed to. Deceptions of race are used as a broad strategy to unload negative comments and stereotypes on social media periodically (Cohen et al., 2021).

Extreme social media users are equally at risk because they may encounter more misinformation due to the contagious spread of content and the algorithmic echo chambers that support existing beliefs. Finally, individuals who are less familiar with how news is produced, verified, and distributed may struggle to recognize the difference between credible and deceptive content (Pennycook & Rand, 2018).

Strategies to Combat Fake News

Fake news continues to govern the digital world, and the trust crisis continues. The challenge lies in the ever-changing nature of social media and online communication, the lack of media literacy, and collaborative efforts with all stakeholders, including the government. A real-time system is needed to detect and identify fake news. Google has recently created an online fact-checker system called Google News Initiative to combat Web-based propaganda (Williams, 2017). This system will allow users to subscribe and access quality and truthful information while helping viewers recognize distorted content.

Cinelli et al. (2020) suggested strategies to combat the spread of misinformation on the Internet. Firstly, it is imperative to promote digital media literacy and critical thinking skills, so that individuals can easily distinguish fake news from credible content. Because all Internet users are educated on recognizing misinformation online, educating the public on media literacy is imperative. Integrating this into university curriculums will make the younger generation aware and equip them with the tools to differentiate between credible and noncredible news and its detrimental impacts on society. Secondly, utilizing the enhancement of technology, algorithms, content limitation, and fact-checking mechanisms can assist in controlling the spread of fake news (Guess et al., 2020).

Thirdly, policy frameworks play a vital role in placing accountability on fake news sources, further advancing the creation of a trustworthy and safe online atmosphere.

Kim et al. (2019) proposed three levels of source rating that can be applied to published articles. Expert ratings include expert reviewers' fact-checking of information, user article ratings consisting of users rating the published information, and user source ratings, in which users rate the website's credibility. Results found that users who trusted the Web source automatically trusted the posted content. This reiterates that confirmation bias plays a significant role in disseminating false information due to alignment with one's beliefs.

Social Media Platforms

Social media platforms, specifically Facebook, are vulnerable to disseminating fake content. They also hold great significance in stopping the propagation of fake news online. Measures such as adjusting website algorithms and reputable platforms such as Twitter and Facebook have tried to remove fake or suspicious content from their sites (Vosoghi et al., 2018).

Fake online accounts created by humans and bots spread fake news, distorted images, videos, and false advertisements.

When the 2016 presidential campaign revealed the disinformation dissemination crisis, Facebook began working on approaches to combat the digital plague of false content distribution. Their tactic consisted of flagging fake news to garner the attention of Facebook administrators by allowing viewers to report false content through a set reporting option. A second strategy encompassed the use of fact-checkers to rate the validity of the posted content by requesting ratings on validity and ranking inaccurate content at the bottom of user news feeds. In 2018, the fact-checking operation spread to twenty-three countries. In addition, Facebook created tools to detect false information and assist fact-checkers in their efforts (Kim et al., 2019). Fake news can go viral quickly, and fact-checkers may miss the verification period between when the content is created and spread. Therefore, these tools will help speed up the fact-checker process.

Lastly, collaborative efforts are needed to tackle the spread of disinformation online. Strategies between the government, tech establishments, and civil organizations are essential to mitigate the spread. Government policies and regulations can aid by mandating that platforms be more accountable for the content they allow to be posted to their websites.

CONCLUSION

The disease of spreading fake news in the digital world is complex, influencing public health, democratic processes, brand reputation, racism, and AI. These factors impair the propagation of misinformation and make it challenging to address. Political actors may use fake news to distort opinions, false advertisements unintentionally disseminate disrupting content, and racist content promotes biases to influence perceptions. Although AI has benefits, it can heighten the spread of fake information through virality, disregarding credibility. The COVID-19 pandemic proved to society how detrimental false information can jeopardize public health and safety.

Fundamental steps to lessen the harmful impact of false news are essential. The goal is to safeguard credible information and reinforce liability. Promoting transparency on digital platforms, enhancing critical thinking and media literacy skills, supporting fact-checking, and holding all participants, such as society, policymakers, and digital platforms, accountable are critical moves to avoid the harmful bearings of fake news. Addressing this challenge is not just about curtailing misinformation but also about emphasizing the reliability of information and ensuring a restored more educated democratic society.

REFERENCES

Alhouri, A., Abu Shokor, M., Marwa, K., Sharabi, A., Mohammad Nazir Arrouk, D., Al Houri, F. N., & Al Houri, H. (2023). COVID-19 and Its Impact on Healthcare Workers: Understanding Stigma, Stress, and Quality of Life. *Cureus, 15*(4), e37846. DOI: 10.7759/cureus.37846 PMID: 37214008

Allcott, H., & Gentzkow, M. (2017). Social media and fake news in the 2016 election. *The Journal of Economic Perspectives, 31*(2), 211–236. DOI: 10.1257/jep.31.2.211

Bode, L., Vraga, E. K., & Borah, P. (2018). See something, say something: Correction of global health misinformation on social media. *Health Communication, 33*(9), 1131–1140. DOI: 10.1080/10410236.2017.1331312 PMID: 28622038

Bontridder, N., & Poullet, Y. (2021). The role of artificial intelligence in disinformation. *Data & Policy, 3*, e32. DOI: 10.1017/dap.2021.20

Bradshaw, S., & Howard, P. N. (2018). Challenging truth and trust: A global inventory of organized social media manipulation. Oxford Internet Institute's Computational Propaganda Research Project. https://comprop.oii.ox.ac.uk/wp-content/uploads/sites/93/2018/07/ct2018.pdf

Buchanan, T., & Benson, V. (2019). Spreading disinformation on Facebook: Do trust in message source, risk propensity, or personality affect the organic reach of "fake news"? *Social Media + Society, 5*(4). DOI: 10.1177/2056305119888654

Chahal, M. (2017). The fake news effect and what it means for advertisers. *Marketing Week*.https://www.marketingweek.com/2017/03/27/the-fake-news-effect/

Cinelli, M., Quattrociocchi, W., Galeazzi, A., Valensise, C. M., Brugnoli, E., Schmidt, A. L., Zola, P., Zollo, F., & Scala, A. (2020). The COVID-19 social media infodemic. *Scientific Reports, 10*(1), 1. Advance online publication. DOI: 10.1038/s41598-020-73510-5 PMID: 33024152

Cohen, A., Ekwueme, P. O., Sacotte, K. A., Bajwa, L., Gilpin, S., & Heard-Garris, N. (2021). "Melanincholy": A Qualitative Exploration of Youth Media Use, Vicarious Racism, and Perceptions of Health. *The Journal of adolescent health: official publication of the Society for Adolescent Medicine, 69*(2), 288–293._DOI: 10.1016/j.jadohealth.2020.12.128

Cuan-Baltazar, J. Y., Muñoz-Perez, M. J., Robledo-Vega, C., Pérez-Zepeda, M. F., & Soto-Vega, E. (2020). Misinformation of COVID-19 on the Internet: Infodemiology study. *JMIR Public Health and Surveillance, 6*(2), e18444. DOI: 10.2196/18444 PMID: 32250960

Felt, A. P., Ha, E., & Han, S. (2014). Measuring the effectiveness of security and privacy mechanisms in mobile applications. *Proceedings of the 2014 ACM Conference on Computer and Communications Security,* 1006-1018._DOI: 10.1145/2661433.2661445

Fleming, N. (2020). Infodemic management: A key component of COVID-19 pandemic response strategy. *Health Education & Behavior, 47*(2), 283–286. DOI: 10.1177/1090198120922984

FTC. (2021). The Federal Trade Commission: Protecting consumers and competition. https://www.ftc.gov

Georgacopoulos, C., & Poche, T. (2024). Fake news, disinformation, and the George Floyd protests. *Fight Fake News.* https://faculty.lsu.edu/fakenews/about/protestfakenews.php

Ghosh, D. (2020). Brand safety and the digital advertising ecosystem: The case of fake news. *Journal of Advertising Research, 60*(4), 395–408. DOI: 10.2501/JAR-2020-038

Govindankutty, S., & Gopalan, S. P. (2023). From fake reviews to fake news: A novel pandemic model of misinformation in digital networks. *Journal of Theoretical and Applied Electronic Commerce Research, 18*(2), 1069–1085. DOI: 10.3390/jtaer18020054

Guess, A., Nagler, J., & Tucker, J. (2020). Less than you think: Prevalence and predictors of fake news dissemination on Facebook. *Science Advances, 6*(14). Advance online publication. DOI: 10.1126/sciadv.aay3539 PMID: 30662946

Guess, A., Nyhan, B., & Reifler, J. (2019). Selective exposure to misinformation: Evidence from the consumption of fake news during the 2016 U.S. presidential campaign. European Research Council (ERC). *Grant, 2018*, 1–40.

Horton, C. (2018, November 22). Specter of meddling by Beijing looms over Taiwan's elections. *New York Times.* https://www.nytimes.com/2018/11/22/world/asia/taiwan-elections-meddling.html

Kim, A., Moravec, P. L., & Dennis, A. R. (2019). Combating fake news on social media with source ratings: The effects of user and expert reputation ratings. *Journal of Management Information Systems, 36*(3), 931–968. DOI: 10.1080/07421222.2019.1628921

King, G., Pan, J., & Roberts, M. E. (2017). How the Chinese government fabricates social media posts for strategic distraction, not engaged argument. *The American Political Science Review, 111*(3), 484–501. https://gking.harvard.edu/50C. DOI: 10.1017/S0003055417000144

Knoll, S., Eisend, M., & Steinhagen, J. (2011). Gender roles in advertising: Measuring and comparing gender stereotyping on public and private TV channels in Germany. *International Journal of Advertising, 30*(5), 867–888. DOI: 10.2501/IJA-30-5-867-888

Kumar, A. (2021). Consumer behavior and online advertising: An overview. *JMR, Journal of Marketing Research, 58*(3), 451–463. DOI: 10.1177/0022243721996970

Lasser, J., Aroyehun, S. T., Simchon, A., Carrella, F., Garcia, D., & Lewandowsky, S. (2022). Social media sharing of low-quality news sources by political elites. *PNAS Nexus, 1*(4). Advance online publication. DOI: 10.1093/pnasnexus/pgac186 PMID: 36380855

Lazer, D. M., Baum, M. A., Benkler, Y., Berinsky, A. J., Greenhill, K. M., Menczer, F., Metzger, M. J., Nyhan, B., Pennycook, G., Rothschild, D., Schudson, M., Sloman, S. A., Sunstein, C. R., Thorson, E. A., Watts, D. J., & Zittrain, J. L. (2018). The science of fake news. *Science, 359*(6380), 1094–1096. DOI: 10.1126/science.aao2998 PMID: 29590025

Lemon, K., & Verhoef, P. (2016). Understanding customer experience throughout the customer journey. *Journal of Marketing, 80*(6), 69–96. DOI: 10.1509/jm.15.0420

Lewandowsky, S., Ecker, U. K., & Cook, J. (2017). Beyond misinformation: Understanding and coping with the "post-truth" era. *Journal of Applied Research in Memory and Cognition*, *6*(4), 353–369. DOI: 10.1016/j.jarmac.2017.07.008

Littrell, S., Klofstad, C., Diekman, A., Funchion, J., Murthi, M., Premaratne, K., Seelig, M., Verdear, D., Wuchty, S., & Uscinski, J. E. (2023). *Who knowingly shares false political information online? Harvard Kennedy School (HKS).* Misinformation Review. DOI: 10.37016/mr-2020-121

Lu, Z., Li, P., Wang, W., & Yin, M. (2022). The effects of AI-based credibility indicators on the detection and spread of misinformation under social influence. *Proceedings of the ACM Human-Computer Interaction, 6*(CSCW2), Article 461. DOI: 10.1145/3555562

McGuire, E. (2020, April 5). Anti-Asian hate continues to spread online amid COVID-19 pandemic. *Al Jazeera.*https://www.aljazeera.com/news/2020/04/anti-asian-hate-continues-spread-online-covid-19-pandemic-200405063015286.html

Mheidly, N., & Fares, J. (2020). Leveraging media and health communication strategies to overcome the COVID-19 infodemic. *Journal of Public Health Policy, 41*(4), 410–420. DOI: 10.1057/s41271-020-00247-w PMID: 32826935

Motta, M. (2021). Can a COVID-19 vaccine live up to Americans' expectations? A conjoint analysis of how vaccine characteristics influence vaccination intentions. *Social Science & Medicine*, *272*, 113642. DOI: 10.1016/j.socscimed.2020.113642 PMID: 33414031

Nguyen, H., & Nguyen, A. (2020). COVID-19 misinformation and the social (media) amplification of risk: A Vietnamese perspective. *Media and Communication*, *8*(2), 444–447. DOI: 10.17645/mac.v8i2.3227

Pennycook, G., & Rand, D. G. (2018). The implied truth effect: Attaching warnings to a subset of fake news stories increases perceived accuracy of stories without warnings. *Management Science*, *67*(11), 6525–6543. DOI: 10.1287/mnsc.2020.3797

Pennycook, G., & Rand, D. G. (2020). Fighting misinformation on social media using crowdsourced judgments of news source quality. *Proceedings of the National Academy of Sciences of the United States of America*, *117*(0), 6882–6884. DOI: 10.1073/pnas.1912444117 PMID: 30692252

Pew Research Center. (2018). News use across social media platforms 2018. https://www.journalism.org/2018/09/10/news-use-across-social-media-platforms-2018/

Pew Research Center. (2020). Americans who mainly get their news on social media are less engaged, less knowledgeable. https://www.pewresearch.org/fact-tank/2020/12/02/americans-who-mainly-get-their-news-on-social-media-are-less-engaged-less-knowledgeable/

Pew Research Center. (2021). Digital news fact sheet https://www.pewresearch.org

Pew Research Center. (2024). https://www.pewresearch.org/wp-content/uploads/sites/20/2024/01/PI_2024.01.31_Home-Broadband-Mobile-Use_FINAL.pdf

Polyakova, A., & Boyer, S. P. (2018). The future of political warfare: Russia, the West, and the coming age of global digital competition. Brookings Institution. https://www.brookings.edu/wp-content/uploads/2018/03/the-future-of-political-warfare.pdf

Quandt, T., Frischlich, L., Boberg, S., & Schatto-Eckrodt, T. (2024). Fake news. In Vos, T. P., Hanusch, F., Dimitrakopoulou, D., Geertsema-Sligh, M., & Sehl, A. (Eds.), *The International Encyclopedia of Journalism Studies*. DOI: 10.1002/9781118841570.iejs0128

Romer, D., & Jamieson, K. H. (2020). Conspiracy theories as barriers to controlling the spread of COVID-19 in the U.S. *Social Science & Medicine, 263*, 113356. Advance online publication. DOI: 10.1016/j.socscimed.2020.113356 PMID: 32967786

Shahi, G. K., Dirkson, A., & Majchrzak, T. A. (2021). An exploratory study of COVID-19 misinformation on Twitter. *Online Social Networks and Media, 22*, 100104. DOI: 10.1016/j.osnem.2020.100104 PMID: 33623836

Solon, O. (2017). Facebook's failure: Did fake news and polarized politics get Trump elected? *The Guardian*. https://www.theguardian.com/technology/2016/nov/10/facebook-fake-news-election-conspiracy-theories

Srivastava, K. (2021). Fake COVID vaccines boost the black market for counterfeit medicines. *BMJ (Clinical Research Ed.), 375*(2754), n2754. Advance online publication. DOI: 10.1136/bmj.n2754 PMID: 34789457

Tufekci, Z. (2018). YouTube, the great radicalizer. *The New York Times,10*(3).

Tyson, A., Johnson, C., & Funk, C. (2020). *U.S. public now divided over whether to get COVID-19 vaccine*. Pew Research Center. https://www.pewresearch.org/science/2020/09/17/u-s-public-now-divided-over-whether-to-get-covid-19-vaccine/

Vosoughi, S., Roy, D., & Aral, S. (2018). The spread of true and false news online. *Science, 359*(6380), 1146–1151. DOI: 10.1126/science.aap9559 PMID: 29590045

Williams, W. (2017, April 7). *Google rolls out new 'Fact Check' tool worldwide to combat fake news*. Christian Science Monitor. https://www.csmonitor.com/Technology/2017/0407/Google-rolls-out-new-Fact-Check-tool-worldwide-to-combat-fake-news

Wong, J. I. (2016). Almost all the traffic to fake news sites is from Facebook: New data show. *Quartz*. https://qz.com/848917/facebook-fb-fake-news-data-from-jumpshot-its-the-biggest-traffic-referrer-to-fake-and-hyperpartisan-news-sites/

KEY TERMS AND DEFINITIONS

Confirmation Bias: Believing in information because it aligns with your beliefs and opinions (Vosoughi et al., 2018).

Digital Literacy: Knowing how to effectively analyze digital content and differentiate between credible vs. noncredible data (Cinelli et al., 2020).

Fake News: Deliberately misleading false content to support a specific agenda (Alcott & Gentzkow, 2017).

Filter Bubbles: These are created by algorithms to promote content that aligns with users' beliefs (Vosoughi et al., 2018).

Internet: A network of information sharing connecting people across the world (Alcott & Gentzkow, 2017).

Misinformation: Fake information created to deceive people (Quandt et al., 2019).

Propaganda: Distorted information to promote political agendas (Solon, 2017)

Virality: Motivated by emotion, is the rapid sharing of information on the Internet (Tufekci, 2018).

Chapter 3
Social Media and the Internet:
Fake News and Clickbait

Ghosh Thinnakkakath
https://orcid.org/0009-0002-1684-7217
University of the Cumberlands, USA

ABSTRACT

This chapter examines fake news and clickbait as two of the most significant challenges digital communication poses to information dissemination. It explores how the internet and social media have democratized access to information, facilitated global connectivity, and revolutionized communication in the digital age. Fake news refers to false or misleading information presented to the public as if it were credible. While this chapter focuses on mechanisms for distributing fake news, it begins by discussing the role of social media algorithms and sensational content in the diffusion of all news. It also demonstrates how clickbait—the use of sensational or misleading headlines to provoke clicks—undermines public trust. To foster a more informed and resilient digital society, the chapter emphasizes the need for media literacy, greater accountability from social media platforms, and collaborative regulatory efforts.

SOCIAL MEDIA AND THE INTERNET: FAKE NEWS AND CLICKBAIT

The digital age has fundamentally changed our modes of communication, how we access information, and how we relate to the world. Key drivers of global connectivity include the internet and social media, where people share ideas, news, and personal updates instantly across the globe. This democratization of information has empowered individuals, facilitated global community formation, and fueled social movements. However, along with the many benefits of the digital age, there are considerable challenges. Chief among these is the proliferation of fake news and the widespread use of clickbait strategies. In fact, the prevalence of fake news has become a serious issue, as many people now rely on online news without verifying its accuracy (Al Ghamdi et al., 2024).

One of the most pervasive problems is fake news, which involves spreading false or misleading information disguised as legitimate news. This tactic exploits the trust users place in online sources of information. Furthermore, on social media, misinformation often goes viral, further spreading confusion. Galli et al. (2022) highlight that fake news is posted on a large scale through social media, posing serious threats to democracy, justice, and public trust. Conversely, clickbait uses sensational or mislead-

DOI: 10.4018/979-8-3693-7468-9.ch003

ing headlines to generate clicks and attract visitors, often at the expense of content quality and truth. These practices undermine the credibility of legitimate news, contribute to increasing polarization in society, and erode public trust. Consumers are often drawn to clickbait, which drives traffic (Chatterjee & Panmand, 2022), making it difficult to manage and reduce this content for a better user experience on social media platforms.

This chapter investigates two significant problems of social media and the internet: fake news and clickbait. It examines their origins and consequences, highlighting their significance in today's digital world. The chapter analyzes possible solutions and strategies to mitigate the harm caused by these phenomena. In other words, the goal is to contribute toward a more informed and resilient digital society.

The Rise of Digital Communication

The advent of digital communication transformed how individuals and organizations communicate, creating broad social, economic, and political implications. New digital platforms enable instant communication from any part of the globe, effectively eliminating geographical borders in the realm of information dissemination. This has democratized access to knowledge, opened up opportunities for sharing opinions, and become an essential tool for activism, marketing, and personal connections. A study by Omar and Ondimu (2024), which analyzed 32 peer-reviewed articles and case studies published between 2016 and 2024, reveals that social media platforms facilitate global connectivity and foster community building. However, they also pose significant challenges, including superficial connections, social isolation, and the spread of misinformation. The pervasive nature of digital communication requires ongoing adaptation and regulation to mitigate its adverse effects while maximizing its benefits (Anderson & Rainie, 2018).

Fake News and Clickbait

Fake news involves presenting false or misleading information as legitimate news with the intent to deceive or mislead people. Recently, it has gained significant momentum with the shift to digital media, where information spreads at lightning speed, often outpacing efforts to verify its accuracy. Stories are fabricated, facts distorted, and images manipulated—all made to appear like credible news sources. The principal goals of fake news include influencing public opinion, sowing confusion, or even triggering political or social instability. It exploits the trust audiences place in traditional news formats, making it difficult for individuals to distinguish factual reporting from falsehoods. Algorithms on social media platforms often promote sensational and emotionally charged content, further amplifying the reach and impact of fake news. The European Union has responded with regulations to contain internet companies, particularly those spreading misinformation, in an effort to protect democratic processes and ensure the credibility of digital content. The European Union enacted the Digital Services Act, which requires tech firms to take additional steps to prevent the spread of misinformation. In Germany, a strict law fines social media companies that fail to remove xenophobic, fake, or terrorist content. France is introducing legislation that will grant magistrates the power to remove false news during election campaigns, while a European Union-wide survey found that 83% of citizens consider fake news a threat to democracy (Khan, 2018).

Clickbait is closely related to the concept of fake news. It involves using sensationalized or misleading headlines to attract clicks and drive web traffic. Often, the content behind these headlines falls short of what was promised, leading to user disappointment and sometimes eroding trust in the source of information. Clickbait thrives due to financial incentives in the digital advertising model, which generates revenue with every click or view. This practice can degrade the quality of online journalism and information by prioritizing engagement over accuracy and substance. It also contributes to the spread of fake news, as both clickbait and fake news rely on qualities that provoke curiosity and emotional responses. Given how widespread clickbait has become, the most effective way for consumers to navigate the complex and sometimes misleading landscape of digital information is through media literacy and critical thinking. As a result, detecting and predicting clickbait virality is a crucial challenge for social media platforms, essential to ensuring a clickbait-free environment and improving user experience (Chatterjee & Panmand, 2022).

THE EVOLUTION OF SOCIAL MEDIA

Early Days of Social Media

Social media began in the late 1990s with the launch of sites like Six Degrees in 1997, which allowed users to build social networks and profiles. In 2002, Friendster took the initiative to introduce social networking focused on connections between friends of friends. Myspace followed in 2003, achieving great success by offering customized user profiles. These early platforms were the forerunners of today's social media (Boyd & Ellison, 2007). They laid the foundation for internet-based social networking, where users could create personal profiles, connect with others for friendship, and share content within online communities. SixDegrees.com, often credited as the first true social networking site, allowed users to create profiles, list their friends, and browse the friend lists of other users.

At this time, social media focused on person-to-person connections and social interaction in a virtual environment. The user experience was relatively simple, featuring basic elements such as friend lists, message boards, and primitive photo-sharing. Although these early platforms may seem rudimentary by today's standards, they were highly innovative at the time and laid the groundwork for the more advanced social media that would emerge in the following years. These early platforms shaped how people engaged with this new environment, introducing concepts that would eventually become core social networking principles. They also demonstrated the internet's potential as a powerful tool for social connection, paving the way for the global, multifaceted platforms we see in today's digital landscape. While simpler than current platforms like Facebook, Twitter (now X), TikTok, and Instagram, the innovations of Six Degrees, Friendster, and Myspace are considered landmark moments in the history of online communication and community.

Expansion and Popularity

Advancements in information technology and internet access have led to the development of high-speed social media platforms, which are now widespread and in high demand. In the mid-2000s, the launch of major social media platforms like Facebook, X, and LinkedIn drastically changed how people connect. Facebook, in particular, revolutionized social media with its user-friendly interface, enabling users to interact with friends and family and share updates within various online communities. The introduction of the news feed transformed information consumption, allowing users to receive real-time updates and engage with content continuously. This era also saw significant changes due to advancements in mobile technology.

As smartphones became more affordable and widespread, social media platforms optimized their interfaces for mobile use. This allowed users to stay connected regardless of their location. The ability to access social media accounts on the go further facilitated this trend, enabling users to engage with content, post updates, and communicate with others directly from their mobile devices. This integration of social media into daily routines significantly impacted traditional models of news and information consumption. The rise of diverse channels and sources of information, coupled with enhanced opportunities for user interaction and content co-creation, have transformed how news is consumed (Pentina & Tarafdar, 2014)

The introduction of multimedia features—such as pictures, videos, and live streaming—has increasingly engaged users and provided new ways for them to interact and generate content. This has made the social networking space more dynamic and comprehensive in terms of how people communicate and share experiences. Instagram, for instance, has excelled in this area, focusing on visual content and contributing significantly to the visual domain. Meanwhile, Facebook and X have incorporated these features to enhance user experience. The ability to spread multimedia content instantly has amplified the virality of information and trends, making social media a powerful tool for communication and influence.

With the evolution of social media, it has become central to individuals' lives, influencing their social relationships and media consumption and even shaping public opinion. This expansion has contributed to the complex digital landscape we navigate today, where sources of connection and entertainment also play significant roles in the dissemination of information—sometimes including misinformation through fake news and clickbait.

Social Media Platforms: An Overview

Today, social media sites have evolved into complex systems of diverse networks that cater to various topics, demographics, and user needs. As these platforms become integral to our daily lives, they shape how we interact, consume information, and perceive the world. Among the leading sites, Facebook stands out as the largest social network in the world, with billions of users. It focuses on personal networking and community building, allowing users to stay connected with friends and family, join groups of shared interests, and engage with content that reflects their social circles.

With its focus on visuals, Instagram has become the favorite among influencers, brands, and younger audiences who prioritize aesthetics. The app is designed primarily for sharing images and short-form videos, appealing to users interested in curating their digital personas. X continues to be a crucial platform for real-time updates, news, and public discourse. Its concise format and hashtag system enable users to follow trending topics and engage in global conversations, making it a powerful tool for journalists, politicians, and other thought leaders.

LinkedIn is the leading professional networking site on the web, focusing on business and industry content. It enables users to share professional achievements, explore job opportunities, and engage in discussions within their fields of expertise. TikTok, on the other hand, is immensely popular among Generation Z, driving creative trends with short video content and viral challenges. Its algorithmic approach to content distribution allows users to achieve significant visibility and reach, even with a relatively small number of followers.

Truth Social aims to cater to users seeking alternative spaces for political and social discussion, focusing on free speech and views not typically represented on larger platforms. This positioning distinguishes it from established social media networks. Meanwhile, Snapchat continues to attract a younger audience with its unique features, such as ephemeral messaging (multimedia messages that disappear after being viewed), Stories, and augmented reality lenses, fostering a creative and spontaneous environment. Truth Social and other right-leaning networks, including Parler and Rumble, offer alternatives by drawing audiences interested in politically charged debates and perspectives that often counter mainstream narratives.

From personal interactions to complex virtual information consumption, each type of social media platform has pursued different objectives within the social media landscape. They cater to a range of needs and preferences among diverse users, shaping the formation and maintenance of digital communities. Their influence spans from personal relationships to global movements, illustrating the dynamic nature of social media. These platforms contribute to the multifaceted nature of social media, as highlighted by Boyd and Ellison (2007), influencing global interrelationships and interactions.

FAKE NEWS: DEFINITION AND IMPACT

What Constitutes Fake News?

Fake news refers to the deliberate spread of disinformation or misleading information disguised as legitimate news. This includes fabricated stories, distorted facts, and manipulated images that appear to be credible news sources. The motivations behind creating fake news often involve misleading public opinion, inciting political or social unrest, or driving web traffic for economic gain through advertisement revenue. By exploiting the audience's trust in the new format, fake news deceived people into mistaking false information for genuine reporting.

Historical Context of Fake News

Fake news is not a recent phenomenon; its origins can be traced back to propaganda and sensational reporting, such as yellow journalism, practiced in the 19th and early 20th centuries. According to Carlos (2019), the first instance of what we now call "fake news" occurred in 1835, when the Sun, a New York newspaper, published a story claiming that the moon was inhabited. The story caused a significant stir in the United States. Historically, fake news has been used by various entities—governments, political organizations, or media outlets—as a strategic tool to manipulate public perception for political, social, or economic objectives. For example, during wars or political crises, misinformation and propaganda have been employed to sway public opinion and justify military actions or undermine opponents. The manipulation of information has often played a crucial role in shaping historical events by selectively presenting facts or fabricating them outright.

The invention of the printing press was a significant milestone in the spread of fake news, as printed materials—whether pamphlets, newspapers, or books—could now reach larger audiences. Another turning point occurred in the 20th century with the advent of radio and television, which introduced new ways of transmitting information. These forms of media made it easier for misinformation and sensationalism to spread at unprecedented rates, marking a new era for both true and false information. Often, they promoted exaggerated or false narratives, sometimes with significant effects on public opinion and policy.

However, with the rise of the internet and social media in the digital age, the reach, speed, and impact of fake news have grown enormously. Unlike the centralized dissemination of the past, the internet is decentralized and widely accessible, allowing anyone with access to a digital platform to create and share content, regardless of its accuracy. With algorithms that prioritize high engagement, social media has become fertile ground for fake news, particularly on sensational or emotional topics. This has escalated the issue to a much larger and harder-to-handle scale, as false information now spreads globally within minutes, often reaching millions before corrections can be made. The historical evolution of fake news highlights this persistent challenge and underscores the need for vigilance and innovation in addressing its spread in our increasingly digital world.

The Impact of Fake News on Society

The impact of fake news on society is wide-ranging and profound, influencing public opinion, intensifying social polarization, and eroding trust in credible information sources (Lazer et al., 2018). As digital platforms become central to how people access and share information, these adverse effects of fake news are becoming increasingly apparent. This disrupts informed decision-making, shapes political landscapes, and distorts public understanding of critical issues, leading to severe repercussions across many areas of society.

Political Manipulation

One of the most concerning and dangerous aspects of fake news is its transformation into a political tool of manipulation. Political actors, both domestic and foreign, have increasingly recognized how fake news can be used to sway public opinion against opponents or even influence election outcomes. A notable example is the 2016 U.S. presidential election, where fake news was strategically deployed to create confusion and mistrust among voters (Allcott & Gentzkow, 2017). Social media was flooded with fabricated stories aimed at misleading specific voter demographics about candidates, policies, and the electoral process. Similarly, during the Brexit referendum in the United Kingdom, fake news proliferated, particularly around false claims about immigration and its economic impact, shaping public sentiment and influencing the course of history.

These examples illustrate the strategic use of fake news to manipulate democratic processes. It creates an environment where truth becomes elusive, leaving voters to navigate a maze of conflicting information. This kind of manipulation not only undermines the democratic process but poses significant risks to the legitimacy of election results, as decisions are made based on falsehoods rather than facts.

Social Division

Fake news has played a significant role in deepening social divisions beyond the political sphere. While digital technology allows information to spread rapidly, it also fosters echo chambers where individuals are exposed only to content that reinforces their pre-existing beliefs. This is particularly dangerous in the case of fake news, as it creates counter-narratives filled with falsehoods that deepen biases and misconceptions within certain communities.

Sensitive social issues, such as race, religion, and immigration, are often exploited by fake news to exacerbate existing divisions. For example, stories that distort or fabricate details of crimes committed by specific ethnic or religious groups can fuel fear and hatred, leading to increased tension and hostility between social groups. These divisive narratives promote an "us versus them" mentality, making people more polarized and less likely to engage in meaningful dialogue with those who hold differing views.

One of the most harmful effects of fake news is its erosion of social cohesion. By dividing communities through misinformation, it weakens the bonds that hold societies together, making it harder to address collective challenges or build a society based on mutual respect.

Public Misinformation

Another serious consequence of the spread of fake news is public misinformation, particularly in the areas of health and science. Vaccine hesitancy offers some of the most alarming examples of the impacts of fake news. Over the years, social media has circulated vast amounts of false information about the safety and efficacy of vaccines, causing many people to avoid vaccinations for themselves and their children. This has contributed to the re-emergence of preventable diseases, posing a significant public health risk.

In addition, fake news distorts public perception of other critical issues, such as climate change and medical treatments. For example, stories about miracle cures or the denial of scientific consensus on climate change can encourage harmful behaviors and lead to misguided policy choices. Such misinformation undermines the public's ability to make informed decisions. As Kuczabski (2022) demonstrated, social media users remain vulnerable to fake news despite being aware of it. This highlights the need for targeted media education, training programs, and awareness campaigns to help users critically evaluate information and reduce their susceptibility to misinformation.

Public misinformation has far-reaching consequences, affecting not only individual behaviors but also the well-being of society. The spread of misinformation affected areas like the environment, public health, and security. In addition, the erosion of trust in reliable information sources exacerbates the issue as individuals become more susceptible to sensational and misleading content.

The theoretic spheres in which fake news affects society are numerous and multi-sectoral, ranging from political outcomes to deepening social divisions and contributing to widespread public misinformation. As we continue to confront the challenges of the modern age, it is essential to develop strategies to combat these issues and ensure a more informed and resilient society. Addressing these challenges requires a collective effort from governments, technology companies, educators, and individuals, guided by the principles of truth and accuracy in information to shape norms in our highly interconnected world.

THE MECHANICS OF CLICKBAIT

Understanding Clickbait

Clickbait refers to digital content that is deliberately sensationalized or misleadingly titled to entice users into clicking its links. The primary goal of clickbait is to generate traffic to a website, often prioritizing clicks over creating engaging or accurate content. It relies on provocative, exaggerated, or curiosity-driven headlines that promise more than they deliver, drawing users to pages that frequently fail to meet the initial claims. The rise of clickbait is closely tied to the advertising model of digital media, where revenue is often generated based on clicks or views, incentivizing publishers to adopt these tactics.

Psychological Triggers in Clickbait

The use of clickbait is a strategic approach that leverages psychological triggers to attract users to click on content. Curiosity is one of the most potent triggers. Most clickbait headlines are designed to provoke curiosity by posing intriguing questions or implying that crucial information is just one click away. This tactic exploits the brain's natural tendency to seek out missing information and resolve uncertainty, making it difficult for users to resist clicking the link. Clickbait provides just enough detail to spark interest but not enough to satisfy curiosity, compelling users to click to learn more (Chua et al., 2021).

Emotional responses also play a prominent role in making clickbait effective. Content that triggers shock, fear, excitement, or anger tends to be shared and clicked more frequently. For example, headlines designed to evoke fear or anger tap into fundamental human emotions, prompting action with minimal critical evaluation. Emotionally charged material speaks directly to the reader, bypassing rational thought processes and driving impulsive behavior.

Another psychological mechanism exploited by clickbait is social validation. Users are more likely to click on content that is highly shared or has substantial engagement due to a tendency to follow popular trends or actions, known as social proof. The notion of "everyone else is doing it" can strongly influence the decision to engage with content, even if its quality is questionable.

Curiosity, emotional arousal, and social validation are key psychological drivers used by clickbait. These tactics appeal to basic human instincts, making clickbait headlines effective at grabbing attention and driving website traffic. While such strategies may yield short-term engagement, they also contribute to the spread of misinformation and erode trust in online content, raising ethical concerns about their use in digital media.

The Role of Algorithms in Promoting Clickbait

Algorithms play a crucial role in spreading clickbait across social media and other digital platforms. These algorithms are designed to maximize user engagement by promoting content that generates high levels of interaction, such as likes, shares, comments, and views. With its emotionally charged and curiosity-inducing headlines, clickbait is particularly effective at driving this kind of engagement. The effectiveness is not coincidental but rather a direct result of how these algorithms are designed to operate.

State-of-the-art algorithms power the feeds on platforms like Facebook, X, and YouTube. These algorithms analyze vast amounts of data on users' past behaviors, preferences, and reactions to predict what content is likely to engage them. Clickbait, with its sensational and often misleading headlines, frequently meets the criteria for high engagement and, therefore, is prioritized and amplified by these algorithms. As a result, users are more likely to encounter clickbait in their feeds, whether they want to or not.

This algorithmic promotion of clickbait creates a self-reinforcing cycle. Each time users engage with clickbait, the algorithms interpret this as a preference for such content and push even more clickbait to the forefront. This incentivizes publishers and content developers to produce more clickbait, driven by the potential increase in traffic and revenue. Over time, this trend can negatively affect the quality of information users receive, as sensationalistic content designed to provoke emotions often overshadows substantive and accurate reporting.

The consequences of this dynamic are far-reaching. If clickbait becomes prevalent in digital media, it can distort public discourse, facilitate the spread of misinformation, and undermine trustworthy news sources. This erosion of trust can make it increasingly difficult for users to distinguish fact from fiction in a crowded digital environment. Addressing this issue will require both a reevaluation of how algorithms prioritize content and a collective effort to enhance media literacy and critical thinking among users.

CASE STUDIES OF FAKE NEWS AND CLICKBAIT

Fake news and clickbait are powerful tools for misinformation and manipulation in the digital age. Digital extremism strategically exploits online platforms to spread extremist ideologies, recruit members, and incite violence, often coordinating illicit activities. Clickbait articles with exaggerated or misleading headlines frequently distort the truth, contributing to widespread misinformation. Extremists have used the internet's vast reach and anonymity to amplify their messages, making radicalization easier. These tactics underscore the need for enhanced digital literacy and effective content moderation to combat hate speech, disinformation, and propaganda.

Case studies on fake news and clickbait illustrate how sensationalist or provocative content is crafted to attract attention and provoke an emotional response, often with the intent to deceive. These real-world examples of extremist strategies highlight the importance of developing approaches to debunk misinformation and promote digital literacy.

High-Profile Fake News Incidents

High-profile incidents of fake news have repeatedly altered political landscapes and influenced public opinion, demonstrating the extensive reach and impact of misinformation in the digital age. Fake news spreads rapidly across social media due to its broad reach and speed, making it challenging for accurate information to keep pace. This misinformation affects individual beliefs, election outcomes, and public health responses. Examining specific cases reveals just how profound and widespread the impact of fake news can be.

U.S. Presidential Elections

In the U.S. presidential elections of 2016 and 2020, various high-profile fake news incidents affected both Republicans and Democrats. The 2016 election was notably influenced by increased partisan reporting by news organizations, polarizing rhetoric from cable media outlets, and the vitriolic opinions expressed by citizens online (Mihailidis & Viotty, 2017).

Pizzagate

One notable case is the "Pizzagate" conspiracy theory, which falsely claimed that a child trafficking ring was being operated from a pizzeria in Washington, D.C. Despite having no basis in fact, the story spread widely on the internet. The situation escalated when a man carrying a firearm entered the pizzeria to "investigate" the claims (Mihailidis & Viotty, 2017). The case highlights not only the dangers of fake news in the real world but also how easily misinformation can be weaponized in politically charged environments.

COVID-19 Misinformation

During the pandemic, there was a surge in fake news, particularly regarding false remedies and conspiracy theories. Misinformation about the virus, its origin, and potential cures spread rapidly across digital platforms during this global health crisis. One notable example involved a social media claim that combining sodium chlorite solution with citric acid to produce chlorine dioxide—a powerful bleaching agent—could provide antimicrobial, antiviral, and antibacterial benefits when consumed (Mian & Khan, 2020). Promoted falsely as a cure for the virus, this dangerous misinformation not only endangered lives but also eroded trust in legitimate health advisories and responses.

Brexit Campaign

Another recent case is the Brexit referendum in the United Kingdom, where fake news significantly influenced public opinion. A notable example was the claim that the United Kingdom would save £350 million every week by leaving the European Union. This figure was prominently displayed on campaign buses and became a central talking point for the Leave campaign. However, it was later revealed that this figure had grossly misinterpreted the financial implications (Howard & Kollanyi, 2016). Despite this correction, significant damage had already been done, as many of the voters had based their decisions on this misinformation, illustrating how fake news can have lasting effects even after it has been debunked.

Russian Interference and the Steele Dossier

The 2016 U.S. presidential election was further complicated by allegations of Russian interference, detailed in the Steele Dossier. This dossier included claims of collusion between the Trump campaign and the Russian government, which were widely reported by the media and significantly influenced public discourse. Although many of these claims were later debunked as unsubstantiated (Johnson, 2019), they deepened partisan divisions and altered political opinions, highlighting the powerful impact of media coverage on public opinion and political processes, even when based on dubious sources.

Donald Trump's Tax Returns

The controversy surrounding Donald Trump's tax returns exemplifies the impact of fake news and clickbait. Reports claimed that Trump paid very low taxes, but many of these reports misrepresented the complexities of the U.S. tax system. Sensational headings often highlighted simplified aspects, such as the $750 tax payment, without providing proper context. While Trump did pay relatively low taxes in some years, many headlines lacked crucial details about legal deductions and strategies used by the wealthy. This oversimplification led to widespread misinformation through sensationalized clickbait headlines. The case highlights how engagement can sometimes come at the expense of accuracy in a polarized political environment, where nuanced topics can easily be distorted.

These high-profile incidents of fake news and clickbait underscore the urgent need for enhanced media literacy and more robust regulatory frameworks to curb the spread of misinformation. The real-world consequences—ranging from jeopardizing public health to influencing national elections—demonstrate the profound impact of false information on society. As digital platforms continue to evolve, there is a critical need to innovate strategies for combating fake news and safeguarding the integrity of information in the public domain.

Analysis of Clickbait Strategies

Clickbait strategies in digital media use sensationalized and often misleading headlines to attract clicks and boost a website's traffic. These methods are specifically engineered to exploit human curiosity and emotions through psychological triggers that entice users into clicking on links. Traditional clickbait headlines create curiosity by presenting information gaps and employing exaggerated or sensationalist language to prompt clicks (Scott, 2023). However, these links often fail to meet user expectations, resulting in weakened trust in online content.

One common clickbait tactic involves exaggeration, where headlines amplify the content's significance beyond what is presented. Examples include "You'll Be Astonished by What Happens Next," "The Surprising Truth About [Topic]," "10 Foods That Could Endanger Your Health," or "Reverse Your Diabetes in 30 Days." These vague headlines create a sense of urgency or intrigue, leaving users with questions they feel compelled to answer by clicking through. Shock value is another common tactic in which headlines hint at something alarming or sensational, tapping into users' emotional responses to encourage engagement.

These strategies are designed to exploit social media algorithms, which are likely to prioritize content with high levels of clicks, shares, and comments. As a result, poor or misleading material can circulate widely, often rivaling more credible and informative sources. This diminishes the overall quality of information online and perpetuates the cycle where sensationalism is favored over substance. Analyzing these tactics reveals how easily users can fall prey to engaging with misleading content, underscoring the need for greater awareness and critical thinking when using digital media.

Lessons Learned from Case Studies

Analyzing case studies of fake news and clickbait offers valuable lessons for individuals, media organizations, and policymakers. First, there is an urgent need for media literacy education to help people distinguish credible information from falsehoods. Educating the public on source verification, recognition, and critical evaluation can reduce the spread of misinformation. Social media platforms must enhance their efforts in algorithm development and moderation practices to detect and limit the circulation of fake news and clickbait. This can be achieved through more stringent and efficient fact-checking mechanisms and clearer guidelines for content creators. Additionally, strong collaboration among governments, tech companies, and civil society is essential for developing comprehensive strategies to curb misinformation while preserving freedom of expression. These lessons highlight the necessity of a multi-faceted approach to effectively address the challenges of fake news and clickbait in the digital age.

THE ROLE OF SOCIAL MEDIA PLATFORMS

Responsibility and Accountability

In the modern information age, social media platforms hold significant responsibility due to their influential roles in shaping public opinion and information flow. As major sources of news, these platforms must ensure the integrity of the information they disseminate. The power wielded by likes, shares, and comments on platforms such as Facebook, X, and YouTube comes with the responsibility to contain the spread of misinformation and harmful content. Balancing freedom of expression with the need to limit misinformation is delicate, requiring these companies to develop and implement effective policies. Tafesse and Korneliussen (2021) found that pre-use experience, brief training, and internet support are strong predictors of organizational social performance, contributing to the collective efficacy of social media teams. As fake news and clickbait become increasingly prevalent, the debate about the extent of these platforms' responsibility continues.

Measures Taken to Combat Fake News

Social media platforms need to implement strategies to slow the spread of disinformation. A common approach involves deploying advanced algorithms and AI to automatically detect and flag potentially false or misleading content. These technologies are designed to identify patterns and behaviors indicative of disinformation, such as sensational headlines or a high volume of shares from dubious sources. Nasery et al. (2023) emphasize that the issue of fake news on social media is complex and multidisciplinary, requiring more than just detection. Strategies for preventing the creation and circulation of fake news, as well as mitigating its effects after detection, are also necessary. The authors advocate for greater proactivity from the information systems community and propose a holistic framework that incorporates comprehensive strategies for addressing the fake news problem.

In addition to technical measures, the defense has become more comprehensive; social media companies have increasingly collaborated with independent fact-checking organizations. These partnerships facilitate content verification by experts, assessing the truthfulness of information spread across networks like Facebook or X. Misinformation can be flagged or accompanied by hyperlinks to more accurate sources, providing users with context for a more informed evaluation. Social media platforms have also introduced tools for reporting suspicious or false information, fostering collaboration between the platform and the community. Moreover, deliberate efforts have been made to enhance media literacy among users, enabling them to critically appraise and distinguish between credible and unreliable sources.

Effectiveness of Current Strategies

The effectiveness of current fake news strategies on social media platforms is a subject of ongoing debate. While progress has been made in identifying and reducing the spread of misinformation, challenges remain. Algorithms and AI systems are not flawless; they can sometimes miss content or incorrectly flag it. Fact-checking partnerships and user reporting mechanisms are essential but are often slow and resource-intensive. Additionally, the sheer volume of content produced daily makes detailed monitoring difficult. Galli et al. (2022) describe the issue as one of early detection, given the limited information available on the propagation of news. The study benchmarks various machine learning and deep learning techniques for detecting fake news, highlighting their advantages and limitations in real datasets. Despite these challenges, ongoing technological advancements and greater integration between platforms, governments, and civil society are necessary. Strategies must continually evolve and adapt to address the ever-changing tactics of fake news spreaders and clickbait creators.

COMBATING FAKE NEWS AND CLICKBAIT

Media Literacy and Education

Media literacy and education are critical elements in overcoming fake news and clickbait. Users must be educated about how disinformation and false news are propagated and their societal ramifications, such as creating distrust in official sources and deepening political, religious, racial, and social divides (Wardle & Derakhshan, 2017). Media literacy initiatives could significantly reduce the spread of disinformation, enabling the public to critically analyze information sources, identify reliable resources, and distinguish between true and false information. Educational efforts, starting from early childhood and continuing through all levels, should include courses in critical thinking, digital literacy, and fact-checking. Moreover, public awareness campaigns and adult workshops can further enhance the general population's ability to navigate the complex media landscape. Media literacy and education equip individuals with the knowledge to become informed, savvy citizens, fostering a resilient society less susceptible to the more harmful aspects of fake news and clickbait.

Technological Solutions

Technological solutions are considered the most effective way to combat fake news and clickbait. Pop (2020) discusses how new technologies have advanced manipulation processes, contributing to the rise of fake news. The widespread adverse effects across various domains have urged specialists to find timely solutions to counter the rapid spread of misleading information. Advanced algorithms and AI can be used to identify and flag deceptive content on social media platforms. Machine learning helps analyze patterns and detect fake news by considering factors such as language, source credibility, content, and dissemination patterns. Other common tools include browser extensions and built-in fact-checkers that allow users to verify the accuracy of information. Collaboration between tech firms and independent fact-checking organizations can lead to the development of more effective tools and systems for curbing misinformation. In this way, the practice of spreading fake news and clickbait can be significantly reduced, making the digital world more reliable and trustworthy.

Policy and Regulation

National Policies

National policies are pivotal in addressing the challenges of fake news and clickbait. Governments can implement policies that hold social media companies accountable for the content available on their platforms. Current deterrents against fake news on social media are generally weak, highlighting the need for stronger legislation, regulation, and policy frameworks to reduce the practice and its proliferation.

However, research by Nasery et al. (2023) found that people often view such regulations as limiting freedom of speech, especially in cases where governments are mistrusted, or laws are seen as avenues for corruption. Effective policies could include obligatory transparency reports and firm measures against the spread of misinformation, with heavy fines for non-compliance.

Wardle and Derakhshan (2017) propose that, in today's connected digital world, the solution to information pollution should involve the engagement of policymakers, legislators, researchers, technologists, and practitioners. This could include mandating media literacy programs in educational institutions to ensure that future citizens are more effective at distinguishing credible information. National policies should also foster collaboration between the public and private sectors to build robust strategies against misinformation while preserving freedom of expression and maintaining the open nature of the internet.

International Cooperation

Global collaboration is critical to taking deliberate and concrete actions to address the spread of fake news and clickbait, which contribute to an increasingly polluted information space through misleading headlines, misuse of statistics, and unattributed quotes (Wardle & Derakhshan, 2017). Misinformation often crosses borders, requiring a coordinated response. International organizations, such as the United Nations, the European Union, and other alliances, can support the sharing of best practices, technological breakthroughs, and regulatory frameworks among countries. Joint actions might include cross-border fact-checking networks, collaborative research on misinformation, and harmonized regulations to ensure a unified approach. This global cooperation can strengthen the resilience of the information ecosystem and improve the ability to counter fake news and clickbait worldwide.

THE FUTURE OF SOCIAL MEDIA AND NEWS CONSUMPTION

Trends in Digital Media

With the progress of digital media, a variety of emerging trends shape the future landscape of social media and news consumption. Key trends include the increasing adoption of multimedia content, from videos to podcasts and interactive graphics, which are more engaging than text. Another trend is the growing emphasis on personalization, where platforms use algorithms to customize content based on individual preferences and behaviors. Additionally, integrating social media with other digital services, such as e-commerce and entertainment, creates seamless user experiences across different aspects of online life. The increased use of decentralized platforms and blockchain technology may further change how information is shared and authenticated, potentially reducing fake news. For instance, Petratos and Faccia (2023) concluded that fake news, misinformation, and disinformation can significantly impact the supply chain, especially when caused by external or intentional events. Their study found that blockchain technology offers a promising way to manage these risks through enhanced cooperation and information sharing, improving the resilience of supply chains in the face of such challenges.

The Role of AI

AI is set to take center stage in the future of social media and news consumption. AI algorithms are applied in content curation, fake news detection, and enhancing the user experience by predicting and responding to preferences. Machine learning models analyze large datasets to identify patterns and trends, allowing for more accurate content recommendations and effective targeted advertising. Akhtar et al. (2023) address this challenge by proposing the fake news and disinformation model, which uses AI and machine learning to verify authenticity and filter out false information by cross-referencing multiple online sources. The authors suggest future research in areas such as case studies, operational performance measures, new algorithm implementation, and longitudinal studies to refine the model's effectiveness. Furthermore, AI-driven tools are being developed to improve news authenticity by detecting inconsistencies and flagging problematic content. As AI technology advances, the scope of information flow management and optimization on social media will expand significantly.

Predicting Future Challenges

While digital media and AI offer many potential benefits, emerging challenges cannot be overlooked. A significant issue lies in the ethical considerations surrounding AI, particularly in areas such as privacy, data protection, and algorithmic bias. Ensuring that AI systems are transparent and accountable is crucial for maintaining user trust. Daunt et al. (2023) emphasize that one way to defend against belief in political fake news is by increasing awareness of disinformation. Their research shows that raising public awareness can serve as a protective mechanism, and they suggest future efforts focus on practical ways to enhance disinformation awareness and develop strategies to safeguard the public from its negative effects. Another challenge is the potential for increased polarization and the formation of echo chambers, as personalized content reinforces existing biases and limits exposure to diverse perspectives. Furthermore, the fast-paced evolution of social media and technology requires constant adaptation from users, regulators, and media organizations. The rapid dissemination of misinformation remains a persistent challenge that must be addressed through enhanced digital literacy and effective countermeasures.

CONCLUSION

Summarizing Key Points

The chapter examines in greater detail how social media and the internet have influenced the dissemination of fake news and clickbait. It begins with a definition, explores the roots, and describes how digital communication platforms have accelerated this growth. The discussion then turns to the tactics used in creating fake news and clickbait, as well as the psychological mechanisms that make these strategies so effective. The chapter also addressed the erosion of trust in traditional media and the rise of polarization in public opinion, situating these trends within their broader societal implications. It discusses the roles of algorithms and economic incentives in driving this phenomenon, along with the regulatory and ethical challenges involved in tackling sensationalist content. The chapter makes a strong case for critical thinking and media literacy as tools to combat such issues. Overall, it provides a broad overview of the challenges posed by fake news and clickbait in the digital age, along with potential solutions.

The Path Forward

The challenges posed by fake news and clickbait require holistic solutions and call for a collaborative approach. The following points may guide us toward creating a more trustworthy and enriching digital environment.

Higher Media Literacy

A critical step in this direction involves increasing the public's media literacy. As digital platforms grow, users need to develop a critical eye for the content they encounter online. Educational programs should equip users with techniques for source identification, recognizing deceitful tactics behind fake news and clickbait, and distinguishing between credible and questionable information. Public awareness campaigns can play a crucial role in heightening consciousness about the risks of misinformation and helping users become vigilant and informed consumers of digital content.

Buschman (2019) concludes that combating fake news requires a multifaceted approach rooted in a nuanced understanding of democracy and the role of libraries. While libraries are essential in fostering critical thinking and informational discernment, their broader educational mission is crucial in supporting a democratic society. Library and information science efforts to counteract fake news are promising, but they must be seen as the beginning of a long-term commitment to empowering citizens through education and engagement with the complexities of democratic life.

Accountability for Social Media Platforms

In this regard, Karine et al. (2021) revealed that intensity of usage, trust in social media, social credibility, and digital literacy are significant factors influencing users' ability to identify fake news. The research demonstrated that while higher usage intensity and social credibility increase trust in social media, they decrease verification behavior. Meanwhile, digital skills enhance verification behavior and fake news detection. The study highlighted the complex relationship between trust, verification behavior, and the identification of fake news, necessitating further investigation across various demographics and regions.

This underscores the need for increased accountability from social media platforms. Fine-tuning algorithms to better prioritize accurate and high-quality information and developing fact-checking mechanisms to detect and flag false content are essential. Clear policies on content moderation—outlining how and why content is promoted or removed—can further build user confidence. Such measures by platforms can reduce misinformation, creating a more secure and safe environment for all users.

Joint Regulatory Efforts

To develop regulations for containing misinformation without compromising freedom of speech, collaboration between governments, technology companies, and civic societies is essential. This collaboration would bring together stakeholders to formulate effective policies for addressing the complexities of digital communication. Nasery et al. (2023) highlight the importance of joint regulatory efforts in the fight against fake news. They argue that both legislative and non-legislative avenues, such as educational programs, are crucial for preventing the production and circulation of misinformation. They emphasize the need for complex, multi-stakeholder strategies involving governments, social media platforms, and educational initiatives to counter fake news. Further studies on the psychological and social dynamics of fake news and clickbait will be instrumental in regulatory efforts, providing a deeper understanding of the drivers of misinformation. This approach aims to create a digital space where information is not only accessible but also trustworthy and conducive to societal development.

REFERENCES

Akhtar, P., Ghouri, A. M., Khan, H. U. R., Amin ul Haq, M., Awan, U., Zahoor, N., Khan, Z., & Ashraf, A. (2023). Detecting fake news and disinformation using artificial intelligence and machine learning to avoid supply chain disruptions. *Annals of Operations Research, 327*(2), 633–657. DOI: 10.1007/s10479-022-05015-5 PMID: 36338350

Al Ghamdi, M. A., Bhatti, M. S., Saeed, A., Gillani, Z., & Almotiri, S. H. (2024). A fusion of BERT, machine learning and manual approach for fake news detection. *Multimedia Tools and Applications, 83*(10), 30095–30112. DOI: 10.1007/s11042-023-16669-z

Allcott, H., & Gentzkow, M. (2017). Social media and fake news in the 2016 election. *The Journal of Economic Perspectives, 31*(2), 211–236. DOI: 10.1257/jep.31.2.211

Anderson, J., & Rainie, L. (2018). *The future of well-being in a tech-saturated world.* Pew Research Center. https://www.pewresearch.org/internet/2018/04/17/the-future-of-well-being-in-a-tech-saturated-world/

Boyd, D. M., & Ellison, N. B. (2007). Social network sites: Definition, history, and scholarship. *Journal of Computer-Mediated Communication, 13*(1), 210–230. DOI: 10.1111/j.1083-6101.2007.00393.x

Buschman, J. (2019). Good news, bad news, and fake news: Going beyond political literacy to democracy and libraries. *The Journal of Documentation, 75*(1), 213–228. DOI: 10.1108/JD-05-2018-0074

Carlos, S. A. (2019). La primera "fake news" de la historia [The first "fake news" in history]. *Historia y Comunicación Social, 24*(2), 411–431. DOI: 10.5209/hics.66268

Chatterjee, S., & Panmand, M. (2022). Explaining and predicting click-baitiness and click-bait virality. *Industrial Management & Data Systems, 122*(11), 2485–2507. DOI: 10.1108/IMDS-01-2022-0003

Chua, A. Y. K., Pal, A., & Banerjee, S. (2021). "This will blow your mind": Examining the urge to click clickbaits. *Aslib Journal of Information Management, 73*(2), 288–303. DOI: 10.1108/AJIM-07-2020-0214

Daunt, K. L., Greer, D. A., Jin, H. S., & Orpen, I. (2023). Who believes political fake news? The role of conspiracy mentality, patriotism, perceived threat to freedom, media literacy, and concern for disinformation. *Internet Research, 33*(5), 1849–1870. DOI: 10.1108/INTR-07-2022-0565

Galli, A., Masciari, E., Moscato, V., & Sperlí, G. (2022). A comprehensive benchmark for fake news detection. *Journal of Intelligent Information Systems, 59*(1), 237–261. DOI: 10.1007/s10844-021-00646-9 PMID: 35342227

Howard, P. N., & Kollanyi, B. (2016). *Bots, #StrongerIn, and #Brexit: Computational propaganda during the UK–EU referendum. SSRN.* DOI: 10.2139/ssrn.2798311

Johnson, D. E. (2019). Russian election interference and race-baiting. *Columbia Journal of Race and Law, 9*(2), 191–264. DOI: 10.7916/cjrl.v9i2.3409

Karine, A. B., Dabbous, A., & Tarhini, A. (2021). An empirical approach to understanding users' fake news identification on social media. *Online Information Review, 45*(6), 1080–1096. DOI: 10.1108/OIR-08-2020-0333

Khan, M. (2018, March 12). EU urged to take a tougher line with tech groups over "fake news." *FT.com*. https://www.proquest.com/trade-journals/eu-urged-take-tougher-line-with-tech-groups-over/docview/2122401079/se-2

Kuczabski, M. J. (2022). Fake news as a threat to social resilience. *European Research Studies*, *25*(1), 765–782. https://www.proquest.com/scholarly-journals/fake-news-as-threat-social-resilience/docview/2639719067/se-2

Lazer, D. M. J., Baum, M. A., Benkler, Y., Berinsky, A. J., Greenhill, K. M., Menczer, F., Metzger, M. J., Nyhan, B., Pennycook, G., Rothschild, D., Schudson, M., Sloman, S. A., Sunstein, C. R., Thorson, E. A., Watts, D. J., & Zittrain, J. L. (2018). The science of fake news. *Science*, *359*(6380), 1094–1096. DOI: 10.1126/science.aao2998 PMID: 29590025

Mian, A., & Khan, S. (2020). Coronavirus: The spread of misinformation. *BMC Medicine*, *18*(1), 89. DOI: 10.1186/s12916-020-01556-3 PMID: 32188445

Mihailidis, P., & Viotty, S. (2017). Spreadable spectacle in digital culture: Civic expression, fake news, and the role of media literacies in "post-fact" society. *The American Behavioral Scientist*, *61*(4), 441–454. DOI: 10.1177/0002764217701217

Nasery, M., Turel, O., & Yuan, Y. (2023). Combating fake news on social media: A framework, review, and future opportunities. *Communications of the Association for Information Systems*, *53*(1), 833–876. DOI: 10.17705/1CAIS.05335

Omar, A., & Ondimu, K. (2024). The impact of social media on society: A systematic literature review. *The International Journal of Engineering and Science*, *13*(6), 96–106. https://www.researchgate.net/publication/381800701_The_Impact_of_Social_Media_on_Society_A_Systematic_Literature_Review

Pentina, I., & Tarafdar, M. (2014). From "information" to "knowing": Exploring the role of social media in contemporary news consumption. *Computers in Human Behavior*, *35*, 211–223. DOI: 10.1016/j.chb.2014.02.045

Petratos, P. N., & Faccia, A. (2023). Fake news, misinformation, disinformation and supply chain risks and disruptions: Risk management and resilience using blockchain. *Annals of Operations Research*, *327*(2), 735–762. DOI: 10.1007/s10479-023-05242-4 PMID: 37361081

Pop, M.-I. (2020). Scoring model for the detection of fake news. *Studia Universitatis "Vasile Goldis" Arad—Economic Series, 30*(1), 91–102. DOI: 10.2478/sues-2020-0006

Scott, K. (2023). "Deceptive" clickbait headlines: Releusers' intentions, and lies. *Journal of Pragmatics*, *218*, 71–82. DOI: 10.1016/j.pragma.2023.10.004

Tafesse, W., & Korneliussen, T. (2021). On the collective efficacy of social media teams. *Marketing Intelligence & Planning*, *39*(3), 438–453. DOI: 10.1108/MIP-03-2020-0118

Wardle, C., & Derakhshan, H. (2017). *Information disorder: Toward an interdisciplinary framework for research and policy making*. Council of Europe. https://rm.coe.int/information-disorder-toward-an-interdisciplinary-framework-for-researc/168076277c

KEY TERMS AND DEFINITIONS

Algorithmic Prioritization: The process by which algorithms determine the order and visibility of content in digital platforms, often influencing what users see first.

Clickbait: The practice of using sensational or misleading headlines to attract clicks and drive traffic to online content, often at the expense of accuracy or relevance.

Content Moderation: The practice of monitoring, reviewing, and managing user-generated content to enforce platform policies and community standards.

Digital Communication: Using digital tools such as email, social media, instant messaging, and other online tools to exchange information.

Echo Chambers: Situations in which information, beliefs, or opinions are amplified within a closed system, limiting exposure to differing perspectives.

Fact-Checking: The process of verifying the accuracy of information, often conducted by independent organizations to combat misinformation.

Fake News: Information presented as news that is deliberately false or misleading to deceive or mislead.

Information Dissemination: The process of distributing information widely across various media channels to reach a broad audience.

Media Literacy: Making informed decisions and resisting misinformation by critically evaluating, understanding, and creating media content.

Political Manipulation: The strategic use of information, propaganda, or other tactics to influence public perception and achieve political goals.

Sensationalism: The use of exaggerated or shocking content to provoke strong emotional responses and attract attention.

Social Media: A digital platform or application that allows users to create, share, and interact with content and each other in a virtual community.

Chapter 4
A Comprehensive Review on Advancements and Challenges in Fake News Detection

Anuradha Thota
G. Narayanamma Institute of Technology and Science, India

Chanakya C. N.
Bangalore University, India

Bhumika Sharma
https://orcid.org/0000-0002-3963-6036
Sharda School of Law, Sharda University, Greater Noida, India

Aarthy S. T.
https://orcid.org/0000-0002-1537-6575
SRM Institute of Science and Technology, India

Ketki P. Kshirsagar
https://orcid.org/0000-0002-5851-1749
Vishwakarma Institute of Technology, Pune, India

Monica Bhutani
https://orcid.org/0000-0003-1924-3056
Bharati Vidyapeeth College of Engineering, New Delhi, India

ABSTRACT

Fake news, a product of the digital age, poses significant threats to social stability, democracy, and political processes. This review critically examines the state-of-the-art in fake news detection, highlighting progress, challenges, and key insights. Detection methods often utilize machine learning, NLP, and deep learning models to analyze linguistic patterns, source credibility, and propagation networks. Fact-checking, both automated and human-assisted, complements traditional content-based and social-contextual approaches. The review underscores the evolving nature of fake news, the need for localized detection solutions, and the lack of large-scale benchmark datasets as major challenges. Future research should focus on cross-platform data integration, explainable AI, and real-time tracking to preempt fake news spread. The interdisciplinary nature of the problem and ethical concerns around detection system misuse are also discussed, emphasizing the need for collaborative, ethically sound solutions.

DOI: 10.4018/979-8-3693-7468-9.ch004

1. INTRODUCTION

Fake news refers to the dissemination of intentionally false or misleading information presented as credible news. It is characterized by its intent to deceive and manipulate audiences for various purposes, including political, economic, or ideological gains. Unlike satire or parody, which aim to entertain or critique societal issues, fake news seeks to misinform and create confusion. Its scope extends across multiple domains, including politics, health, finance, and entertainment, and it can take various forms, such as fabricated stories, manipulated multimedia, and out-of-context reporting.

The digital revolution has exacerbated the reach and impact of fake news. Platforms like social media, where information spreads rapidly and without rigorous verification, have become breeding grounds for misinformation. Fake news is no longer limited to text-based articles; it now includes images, videos, and even sophisticated deepfakes, complicating detection efforts. The scope of fake news is further broadened by its ability to exploit human cognitive biases, such as confirmation bias and the tendency to trust familiar or emotionally charged content.

1.1 Historical Context and Evolution of Fake News

Fake news is not a new phenomenon. Its roots can be traced back to the ancient world, where misinformation was used as a tool for propaganda and manipulation. For example, political leaders spread false narratives during Roman times to discredit their opponents. Similarly, fabricated stories were employed in medieval Europe to influence religious and political outcomes (Ahmed, H. F., & Yassin, A. S. 2021).

The invention of the printing press in the 15th century marked a significant shift in the dissemination of information, including fake news. Pamphlets and books became tools for spreading rumors and misinformation, often leading to social unrest. In the 19th and early 20th centuries, the rise of mass media, particularly newspapers, further amplified the potential for fake news. Sensationalism and "yellow journalism" became prevalent, driven by the pursuit of profit and readership.

The internet and social media have transformed the fake news landscape, making it more pervasive and impactful. Unlike traditional media, where editorial oversight acted as a gatekeeper, online platforms enable anyone to create and share content. This democratization of information has led to the proliferation of fake news unprecedentedly. Algorithms designed to maximize engagement often prioritize sensational or polarizing content, inadvertently amplifying fake news. The rise of bots and coordinated disinformation campaigns has further complicated the fight against fake news, as they can generate and disseminate false information with remarkable efficiency (Al-Rubaian, M. 2023).

1.2 Importance of Addressing Fake News in the Digital Age

In the digital age, fake news poses significant risks to societies worldwide. It undermines trust in institutions, erodes democratic processes, and fuels social polarization. For instance, fake news can influence voter perceptions and decisions during elections, potentially altering outcomes (Anwar, S., & Kumar, V. 2022). The spread of misinformation during the COVID-19 pandemic highlighted its dire consequences in public health, as false claims about treatments and vaccines jeopardized lives.

The economic impact of fake news is also considerable. Businesses can suffer reputational damage and financial losses due to false reports, while misinformation about markets can lead to economic instability (Bharti, A., & Prakash, A. 2021). Furthermore, fake news can exacerbate societal tensions, incite violence, and disrupt social cohesion. High-profile cases, such as the role of fake news in the 2016 U.S. presidential election and the spread of false narratives during the Brexit campaign, underscore its ability to shape public opinion and policy decisions (Guntuku, S. C., & Preoţiuc-Pietro, D. 2022).

From a technological perspective, the rapid evolution of fake news necessitates equally advanced detection and mitigation strategies. Traditional fact-checking methods are insufficient to combat the volume and speed of fake news dissemination. AI and machine learning have emerged as critical tools in this fight, offering scalable solutions for detecting and debunking fake news. However, the same technologies can be exploited to create more convincing and difficult-to-detect fake content, such as deepfakes, highlighting the need for continuous innovation and vigilance (Gupta, A., & Roy, P. 2022).

Addressing fake news is not only a technological challenge but also a societal one. It requires collaboration among governments, tech companies, researchers, and the public. Media literacy programs are essential to equip individuals with the skills to critically evaluate information and identify misinformation. Additionally, policies and regulations must strike a balance between curbing fake news and preserving freedom of speech.

1.3 Objectives and Structure of the Chapter

This chapter aims to provide a comprehensive review of the progress and challenges in detecting fake news. It seeks to answer critical questions, such as:

1. What are the key characteristics and drivers of fake news?
2. How have detection techniques evolved over time?
3. What are the limitations and ethical considerations of current approaches?
4. What emerging technologies and methodologies show promise in combating fake news?

The chapter is structured as follows:

- **Understanding Fake News**: This section categorizes fake news types, explores its motivations, and examines the psychological and sociological factors that contribute to its spread.
- **Detection Techniques: An Overview**: This section reviews traditional and automated methods for identifying fake news, emphasizing AI and machine learning advancements.
- **Challenges in Fake News Detection**: This section highlights the limitations of existing approaches, including dataset availability, evolving tactics, and cross-cultural challenges.
- **Evaluation Metrics and Benchmark Datasets**: This section discusses the tools used to assess the performance of fake news detection systems.
- **The Role of Social Media and Platforms**: This section examines how social media algorithms contribute to fake news dissemination and the measures taken by platforms to mitigate its spread.
- **Emerging Trends and Technologies**: This section explores cutting-edge solutions, such as blockchain and multi-modal detection models, and their potential to enhance fake news detection.
- **Future Directions**: This section outlines strategies for integrating detection technologies with societal efforts, such as media literacy and interdisciplinary collaboration.

By systematically addressing these topics, the chapter aims to provide readers with a nuanced understanding of the fake news phenomenon, its detection methods, and the ongoing efforts to combat its impact. It also underscores the importance of a multi-faceted approach that combines technological, educational, and policy interventions to address this complex issue effectively.

2. UNDERSTANDING FAKE NEWS

Fake news is a multifaceted phenomenon that has significant implications for individuals, societies, and institutions worldwide. This section explores the various dimensions of fake news, including its types, the motivations behind its creation and dissemination, and the psychological and sociological factors that contribute to its widespread impact. Understanding these aspects is essential for developing effective strategies to combat fake news and its consequences (Hassan, A. S., & Shakil, K. 2021).

2.1 Types of Fake News

Fake news can be classified into three broad categories: misinformation, disinformation, and misinformation. Each type has distinct characteristics and consequences, although they often overlap in practice. Recognizing these types is critical to developing targeted detection and mitigation strategies (Jain, A., & Srivastava, P. 2023).

2.1.1 Misinformation

Misinformation refers to false or inaccurate information that is shared without malicious intent. It typically arises from misunderstandings, misinterpretations, or incomplete knowledge. For instance, during a natural disaster, incorrect information about rescue operations or safety measures might circulate due to a lack of reliable updates. While the intent behind misinformation is not harmful, its effects can still be significant, leading to confusion, panic, or inappropriate responses (Kaur, N., & Chahal, P. 2023).

2.1.2 Disinformation

Disinformation is deliberately created and spread to deceive and manipulate audiences. This type of fake news is often associated with propaganda, where the intent is to influence opinions or behaviors for political, economic, or ideological purposes. A notable example is the use of fake news during election campaigns to sway voter perceptions or undermine opponents. Disinformation is particularly dangerous because it is crafted to exploit biases and vulnerabilities, making it more persuasive and harder to detect.

2.1.3 Malinformation

Malinformation involves the use of genuine information in a misleading or harmful context. Unlike misinformation and disinformation, which rely on falsehoods, misinformation distorts real facts to achieve a specific agenda. For example, leaking private information about an individual to damage their reputation is a form of malinformation. This type of fake news is especially insidious because it undermines trust in authentic sources and blurs the line between truth and manipulation (Lee, J., & Lee, K. 2021).

2.2 Motivations Behind Creating and Spreading Fake News

The creation and dissemination of fake news are driven by various motivations, ranging from individual interests to broader societal objectives. Understanding these motivations can help in designing interventions that address the root causes of fake news proliferation.

2.2.1 Political Motivations

Political agendas are one of the most common drivers of fake news. Governments, political parties, and interest groups often use fake news as a tool for propaganda, influencing public opinion, or destabilizing adversaries. For example, during geopolitical conflicts, fake news campaigns may be used to spread false narratives about opponents, weaken alliances, or gain international sympathy. Social media platforms amplify the reach of politically motivated fake news, creating echo chambers where misleading information thrives.

2.2.2 Economic Motivations

Economic incentives also play a significant role in the proliferation of fake news. Many fake news creators generate revenue through clickbait articles that attract high web traffic and advertising income (Li, Q., & Sun, M. 2022). The sensational nature of fake news often ensures higher engagement compared to factual reporting. Additionally, companies might spread fake news about competitors to damage their reputation or gain a market advantage. In some cases, the fake news industry operates as a business model, with organized networks producing and distributing content for profit.

2.2.3 Social and Psychological Motivations

Fake news can also be driven by social and psychological factors, such as the desire for attention, validation, or influence. Individuals may share fake news to appear knowledgeable or to gain social status within their communities. In some cases, fake news serves as a means of reinforcing group identity or advancing ideological beliefs. This type of motivation is particularly evident in conspiracy theories, where fake news supports narratives that align with the group's worldview (Liu, X., & Chen, W. 2020).

2.3 Psychological and Sociological Factors Influencing Fake News Dissemination

The widespread dissemination of fake news is not solely a result of technological advancements or malicious intent. Psychological and sociological factors play a crucial role in determining how and why individuals interact with fake news.

2.3.1 Cognitive Biases

Cognitive biases are mental shortcuts that influence how people process information, often leading to errors in judgment. Several biases contribute to the spread of fake news:

- **Confirmation Bias**: People are more likely to believe and share information that aligns with their pre-existing beliefs, even if it is false.
- **Availability Heuristic**: The tendency to judge the likelihood of an event based on how easily examples come to mind can make sensational fake news seem more plausible.
- **Illusory Truth Effect**: Repeated exposure to false information increases its perceived accuracy, making fake news more convincing over time.

These biases are exploited by fake news creators, who design content that resonates with the target audience's beliefs and emotions.

2.3.2 Emotional Appeal

Emotion plays a significant role in the spread of fake news. Content that evokes strong emotions, such as anger, fear, or excitement, is more likely to be shared. For instance, fake news stories about public health crises or political scandals often go viral because they trigger immediate emotional responses. Social media algorithms, which prioritize engagement, further amplify emotionally charged content, increasing its visibility and reach (Martínez-Ruiz, M. J., & González, J. 2021).

2.3.3 Social Dynamics

Social dynamics, such as peer influence and groupthink, also contribute to the dissemination of fake news. In online communities, individuals often share information to maintain social bonds or gain approval from their peers. Groupthink can lead to the uncritical acceptance of fake news, especially in environments where dissenting opinions are discouraged. Additionally, the anonymity of online platforms reduces accountability, making it easier for individuals to share fake news without fear of consequences.

2.3.4 Trust and Credibility

Trust in sources plays a crucial role in determining whether people believe and share information. Fake news often masquerades as credible journalism by mimicking the appearance and tone of legitimate news outlets. This tactic exploits the general public's limited ability to discern credible sources, particularly in the digital age, where the sheer volume of information can be overwhelming. Moreover, declining trust in traditional media and institutions creates a fertile ground for fake news to flourish (Patel, M., & Singh, D. 2022).

2.3.5 Technological Amplification

Technological advancements, particularly in social media and artificial intelligence, have amplified the impact of psychological and sociological factors. Algorithms designed to maximize user engagement prioritize sensational and controversial content, inadvertently promoting fake news. Bots and automated accounts further accelerate the spread of fake news by generating and sharing content at a scale that far exceeds human capabilities. This technological amplification exacerbates the challenges posed by fake news, making it a persistent and evolving threat (Biswas, S., & Sood, M. 2024).

In conclusion, understanding the types, motivations, and underlying factors influencing fake news is essential for developing effective countermeasures. By addressing the psychological and sociological drivers of fake news dissemination, alongside its technical aspects, researchers and policymakers can work toward a more informed and resilient society.

3. DETECTION TECHNIQUES: AN OVERVIEW

The detection of fake news requires a multi-faceted approach combining manual and automated methods. While manual methods rely on human expertise and critical analysis, automated approaches leverage technological advancements to detect fake news on a larger scale. This section explores these two broad categories, their evolution, and their unique contributions to addressing the fake news challenge (Cai, W., & Xu, P. 2023).

3.1 Manual Approaches to Fake News Detection

Manual detection techniques involve human-led efforts to verify the authenticity of news and information. These methods emphasize critical thinking, expertise, and thorough analysis, often executed by professional fact-checkers, journalists, and independent organizations.

3.1.1 Fact-Checking Organizations

Fact-checking organizations play a vital role in combating fake news. Entities like PolitiFact, Snopes, and FactCheck.org evaluate the accuracy of claims made by public figures, media outlets, and viral social media content. Their methodologies typically involve:

- **Identifying Claims**: Selecting statements or stories that warrant verification, often based on their public impact or virality.
- **Cross-Referencing Sources**: Comparing claims against credible databases, primary sources, and subject-matter experts.
- **Publishing Results**: Sharing detailed analyses with the public, often accompanied by transparency regarding the fact-checking process.

Fact-checking organizations operate as the first line of defense against misinformation, but their reach is limited by the time and labor-intensive nature of the work. They often struggle to keep up with the sheer volume of fake news circulating on digital platforms (Chan, H., & Zhang, X. 2023).

3.1.2 Crowdsourcing and Collaborative Efforts

Collaborative efforts, such as community-driven fact-checking, are another manual method. Social media platforms like Facebook and Twitter have introduced initiatives where users can flag or annotate potentially false information. While these efforts democratize the detection process, they are susceptible to biases and inconsistent reliability(Chen, Y., & Zhao, L. 2024).

3.1.3 Challenges of Manual Detection

Manual detection faces several limitations:

- **Scalability**: Human fact-checkers cannot verify the massive volume of fake news generated daily.
- **Speed**: The time required for thorough verification can delay responses to rapidly spreading misinformation.
- **Subjectivity**: Human biases may influence the fact-checking process, leading to inconsistent results.

3.2 Automated Approaches: Evolution of Technology in Fake News Detection

To address the limitations of manual methods, automated approaches leverage computational technologies to detect fake news more efficiently and at scale. These methods have evolved significantly, ranging from basic keyword matching to advanced artificial intelligence (AI) and machine learning (ML) techniques (Das, R., & Prasad, N. 2023).

3.2.1 Early Approaches: Rule-Based Systems

Initial efforts in automated fake news detection relied on rule-based systems. These systems used predefined criteria, such as:

- Identifying sensational language or specific keywords associated with fake news.
- Flagging discrepancies in publication dates, author credibility, or website authenticity.

While effective in detecting straightforward cases, rule-based systems struggled to adapt to the evolving tactics of fake news creators and lacked contextual understanding.

3.2.2 Machine Learning-Based Techniques

The integration of machine learning marked a significant advancement in automated fake news detection. ML models are trained on labeled datasets to identify patterns and features indicative of fake news. Techniques include:

- **Text Classification**: Using natural language processing (NLP) to analyze linguistic features such as sentiment, readability, and syntax.
- **Content Analysis**: Comparing claims within an article to verified facts or external databases.

- **User Behavior Analysis**: Studying patterns of sharing, commenting, and liking to detect coordinated disinformation campaigns.

Supervised learning algorithms, such as support vector machines (SVM) and decision trees, are widely used in these systems. They require extensive datasets, annotated with examples of fake and real news, to achieve high accuracy.

3.2.3 Advanced Techniques: Deep Learning and Neural Networks

Deep learning models, particularly neural networks, have revolutionized fake news detection by enabling more nuanced analysis. These models excel in handling unstructured data, such as text, images, and videos, making them ideal for detecting complex forms of fake news like deepfakes. Techniques include:

- **Recurrent Neural Networks (RNNs)**: Used for sequential data analysis, such as tracking changes in narratives over time.
- **Convolutional Neural Networks (CNNs)**: Applied to multimedia content, such as detecting manipulated images or videos.
- **Transformer Models**: State-of-the-art NLP models like BERT and GPT analyze contextual relationships between words, improving text-based fake news detection.

Deep learning techniques require large computational resources and high-quality datasets but offer superior performance in complex scenarios.

3.2.4 Emerging Technologies and Trends

The continuous evolution of technology has introduced innovative approaches to fake news detection:

- **Blockchain Technology**: Ensures content authenticity by providing immutable records of its origin and history.
- **Multimodal Detection Models**: Combine textual, visual, and behavioral data for comprehensive analysis.
- **Real-Time Detection**: AI-powered tools capable of identifying and flagging fake news within seconds of its publication.

3.2.5 Challenges of Automated Detection

Despite their advancements, automated approaches face several challenges:

- **Adversarial Adaptation**: Fake news creators constantly evolve their tactics to bypass detection algorithms.
- **Dataset Limitations**: High-quality, annotated datasets are scarce, limiting model performance.
- **Ethical Concerns**: Automated systems risk overreach, such as censoring legitimate content or infringing on free speech.

Manual and automated approaches each play a crucial role in fake news detection. While manual methods provide depth and reliability, automated systems offer scalability and speed. The integration of these approaches, supported by continuous technological innovation and interdisciplinary collaboration, is essential for addressing the dynamic and persistent challenge of fake news (Dhiman, G., & Kumar, M. 2023).

4. MACHINE LEARNING AND AI IN FAKE NEWS DETECTION

The application of machine learning (ML) and artificial intelligence (AI) has significantly advanced the detection of fake news, enabling scalable and effective solutions. This section examines the role of supervised learning techniques, unsupervised and semi-supervised approaches, and deep learning advancements in combating fake news.

4.1 Supervised Learning Techniques

Supervised learning techniques rely on labeled datasets to train models to classify news as fake or real. These methods have been foundational in the development of AI-driven fake news detection systems(Fu, X., & Wang, Q. 2024).

4.1.1 Classification Models

Classification models form the backbone of supervised learning in fake news detection. Common algorithms include:

- **Support Vector Machines (SVM)**: SVMs create hyperplanes to separate classes, making them effective in binary classification tasks. They perform well in detecting fake news when combined with well-engineered features.
- **Naive Bayes**: This probabilistic model assumes independence between features, making it computationally efficient. It is particularly useful in text classification tasks due to its simplicity and speed.
- **Decision Trees**: These models use a tree-like structure to classify data based on feature thresholds. Decision trees are easy to interpret and serve as the basis for ensemble methods like Random Forest and Gradient Boosting.

4.1.2 Feature Engineering

Feature engineering plays a critical role in enhancing the performance of supervised models. Key features include:

- **Linguistic Features**: Analysis of textual characteristics such as sentiment, readability, and grammar helps identify discrepancies typical of fake news.
- **Content-Based Features**: Metrics like the frequency of certain keywords, named entities, and the presence of hyperlinks can differentiate authentic news from fake content.

- **User Behavior Features**: Patterns in user interactions, such as sharing frequency and comment sentiment, provide additional context for classification models.

4.2 Unsupervised and Semi-Supervised Approaches

Unsupervised and semi-supervised methods address the challenge of limited labeled data, which is a common limitation in fake news detection(Ghosh, A., & Singh, A. 2023).

4.2.1 Clustering Algorithms

Clustering techniques group similar data points without predefined labels, making them useful for identifying patterns in unlabeled datasets:

- **K-Means Clustering**: Groups news articles into clusters based on feature similarity, enabling the identification of outliers that may indicate fake news.
- **Hierarchical Clustering**: Builds a hierarchy of clusters, providing insights into the relationships between data points and facilitating anomaly detection.

4.2.2 Anomaly Detection Techniques

Anomaly detection identifies data points that deviate significantly from the norm, which can indicate fake news. Common methods include:

- **Isolation Forests**: These models isolate anomalies by partitioning data points based on random feature splits.
- **Autoencoders**: Neural network-based models that learn to reconstruct input data. Significant reconstruction errors can flag fake news articles as anomalies.

4.3 Deep Learning Advancements

Deep learning has revolutionized fake news detection by enabling sophisticated analysis of complex data. These models excel in handling unstructured data, such as text, images, and videos.

4.3.1 Neural Networks

Deep neural networks, such as CNNs and RNNs, have proven effective in detecting fake news:

- **Convolutional Neural Networks (CNNs)**: Typically used for image and text analysis, CNNs extract hierarchical features from input data, making them suitable for detecting fake multimedia content.
- **Recurrent Neural Networks (RNNs)**: Designed for sequential data, RNNs analyze temporal dependencies in text. Variants like Long Short-Term Memory (LSTM) networks are particularly effective for understanding contextual nuances in news articles.

4.3.2 Pre-Trained Language Models

Pre-trained language models leverage vast amounts of textual data to achieve state-of-the-art performance in fake news detection:

- **BERT (Bidirectional Encoder Representations from Transformers)**: BERT's ability to analyze context in both directions makes it highly effective in understanding nuanced language.
- **GPT (Generative Pre-trained Transformer)**: GPT models excel in generating coherent text and identifying inconsistencies in news articles.

These models can be fine-tuned on domain-specific datasets to improve their accuracy and relevance in detecting fake news.

Machine learning and AI have transformed fake news detection through a combination of supervised, unsupervised, and deep learning techniques. By leveraging the strengths of various algorithms and models, these approaches offer scalable and efficient solutions to an ever-evolving problem. Future advancements in AI promise to enhance the accuracy, robustness, and adaptability of fake news detection systems (Gupta, S., & Verma, S. 2024).

5. CHALLENGES IN FAKE NEWS DETECTION

The detection of fake news, while advanced in many aspects, faces numerous challenges that hinder its effectiveness. These challenges stem from technical, cultural, and ethical dimensions, each requiring unique solutions and collaborative efforts.

5.1 Lack of Labeled Datasets for Training

One of the most significant barriers in fake news detection is the scarcity of high-quality, labeled datasets. Supervised machine learning algorithms, which form the backbone of many detection systems, require vast amounts of labeled data to achieve high accuracy. However, labeling fake news is a labor-intensive and subjective task, often requiring domain expertise to discern factual accuracy, context, and intent (Han, J., & Liu, T. 2024).

Additionally, fake news evolves rapidly, and outdated datasets may not represent current trends. For instance, a dataset focusing on misinformation during the COVID-19 pandemic might not be applicable to political disinformation in elections. The lack of datasets representing diverse languages, regions, and media formats further exacerbates the problem, limiting the ability of detection systems to generalize across different scenarios.

5.2 Multimodal Fake News (Text, Images, Videos)

Modern fake news is not confined to textual content. It increasingly incorporates images, videos, and audio, creating multimodal content designed to enhance believability and emotional appeal. For example, altered images or misleading captions can spread misinformation faster than text alone. Videos, especially those manipulated through deepfake technologies, present even greater challenges due to their complexity and realism (He, X., & Wang, C. 2023).

Detecting multimodal fake news requires sophisticated algorithms capable of analyzing and correlating multiple data types simultaneously. However, integrating textual, visual, and audio analysis in a cohesive framework is computationally expensive and technically challenging. Furthermore, the sheer volume of multimodal content generated daily on platforms like YouTube, TikTok, and Instagram makes real-time detection nearly impossible with current capabilities.

5.3 Cross-Lingual and Cross-Cultural Detection Challenges

Fake news is a global problem, but most detection systems are designed for dominant languages like English, leaving non-English content largely unaddressed. This linguistic limitation allows misinformation to proliferate in regions where such tools are unavailable or ineffective. For instance, during elections or crises, fake news in local languages can have devastating consequences, yet it often goes unnoticed by mainstream detection efforts (Huang, L., & Zhao, L. 2024).

Cultural nuances further complicate detection efforts. What is considered fake or misleading in one cultural context might not be perceived the same way in another. For example, satire or hyperbolic expressions are common in some cultures but may be misunderstood as genuine content elsewhere. Developing culturally and linguistically adaptive models is essential but requires significant resources and collaboration between local experts and global technology providers.

5.4 Evolution of Fake News Tactics (e.g., Deepfakes)

As detection technologies improve, so do the tactics used by fake news creators. Sophisticated methods like deepfakes—AI-generated content that convincingly mimics real people's voices and appearances—pose a significant challenge. Deepfakes have been used to impersonate public figures, spread political propaganda, and even commit financial fraud, making them a potent tool for disinformation (Jain, R., & Nair, R. 2023).

The dynamic nature of fake news ensures that detection systems are often reactive rather than proactive. For instance, a method effective against current text-based misinformation might struggle to identify future deepfakes or AI-generated articles. The arms race between creators and detectors requires continuous innovation, rapid updates to detection algorithms, and anticipatory research into emerging threats.

5.5 Ethical and Legal Concerns (e.g., Censorship, Privacy)

The fight against fake news is fraught with ethical and legal dilemmas. Efforts to curb misinformation, such as content moderation and algorithmic filtering, risk infringing on freedom of speech. Determining what constitutes fake news often involves subjective judgment, raising concerns about censorship and bias. For example, political or ideological biases in detection algorithms could lead to the disproportionate flagging of certain viewpoints, undermining public trust (Kaur, P., & Yadav, S. 2023).

Privacy is another critical issue. Many detection systems require access to vast amounts of user-generated data to analyze and identify fake news patterns. This data collection raises questions about user consent, data security, and the potential misuse of personal information. Striking a balance between effective detection and ethical practices is a persistent challenge that requires transparent governance, accountability, and adherence to privacy standards.

Addressing the challenges in fake news detection requires a multi-pronged approach. Collaboration among technologists, policymakers, and societal stakeholders is essential to develop robust, ethical, and inclusive solutions. Future efforts must focus on building diverse datasets, advancing multimodal detection technologies, and addressing cross-lingual and cultural limitations while maintaining ethical integrity. Only through a coordinated effort can the battle against fake news be effectively sustained (Khan, M., & Iqbal, J. 2024).

6. EVALUATION METRICS AND BENCHMARK DATASETS

The evaluation of fake news detection systems is a critical component in assessing their effectiveness and performance. This section discusses commonly used datasets for fake news detection, key evaluation metrics, and the challenges faced in standardizing evaluation methods.

6.1 Commonly Used Datasets for Fake News Detection

Datasets play a fundamental role in training, validating, and testing fake news detection models. Several benchmark datasets have been created to support research in this area. These datasets offer a range of features, including textual content, metadata, and context-specific information, which are essential for developing accurate detection systems.

- **LIAR Dataset:** One of the most widely used datasets in the field of fake news detection, the LIAR dataset consists of around 12,800 labeled short statements collected from the fact-checking website PolitiFact. These statements are classified into six categories: true, mostly true, half true, mostly false, false, and pants on fire (indicating extreme falsity). Each statement is annotated with metadata such as the speaker's identity, speaker's political affiliation, and the context in which the statement was made. LIAR is valuable for training models to understand subtle linguistic patterns and factual discrepancies in political discourse.
- **FakeNewsNet:** This dataset is designed specifically for the detection of fake news on social media platforms. It contains both news content (text) and the associated social context (such as user comments, shares, and the credibility of the news sources). FakeNewsNet is unique because it integrates news data from the political domain, providing both news articles and metadata on the dissemination of news across social networks. It is often used for training models to identify fake news in real-time scenarios, where the content's virality plays a crucial role in the detection process.
- **Kaggle Fake News Dataset:** Hosted on Kaggle, this dataset contains labeled articles from news websites categorized as real or fake. The dataset includes features such as title, text, and the publisher's details, which are useful for both traditional machine learning models and deep learning models. Researchers often use this dataset to test the efficiency of their models in distinguishing between real and fake news based solely on the content.
- **CrisisMMD:** CrisisMMD focuses on detecting misinformation in the context of crisis events, such as natural disasters or emergencies. It is a specialized dataset containing news articles and

social media posts about specific crisis events. The data includes content from reliable and unreliable sources, providing a unique challenge for detection systems that must handle the high volume of rapidly disseminated information in such situations.

- **CREDBANK:** This dataset contains over 60,000 tweets with labels indicating whether the tweets are credible or not. The data is collected from multiple domains, including politics and natural disasters, making it versatile for general-purpose fake news detection as well as domain-specific tasks. CREDBANK is especially useful for studying the dynamics of news credibility in real-time online environments.

These datasets offer a variety of challenges and opportunities for researchers working on fake news detection, enabling them to train and benchmark models under different conditions and types of misinformation (Lee, S., & Kim, H. 2024).

6.2 Evaluation Metrics for Fake News Detection Systems

The evaluation of fake news detection systems is crucial for determining their accuracy and real-world applicability. Several evaluation metrics are commonly used in research to assess the performance of these systems.

- **Area Under the Curve (AUC):** AUC refers to the area under the Receiver Operating Characteristic (ROC) curve, which plots the true positive rate (recall) against the false positive rate. AUC is a robust metric for evaluating the performance of a detection system, as it assesses how well the model distinguishes between fake and real news, irrespective of the threshold used for classification. A higher AUC value indicates a better model performance across various classification thresholds.
- **Accuracy:** Accuracy is the simplest and most commonly used metric, representing the proportion of correct predictions (both fake and real news) out of the total number of predictions. However, accuracy may not always be a reliable measure, especially in the case of imbalanced datasets, where one class significantly outnumbers the other.

6.3 Challenges in Standardizing Evaluation Methods

While the evaluation of fake news detection systems is essential, it is hindered by several challenges in standardizing evaluation methods. These challenges stem from the complexity and variety of fake news, as well as the evolving nature of misinformation across different domains.

- **Lack of Standardized Datasets:** Despite the availability of several benchmark datasets, there is no universally accepted dataset for fake news detection. Each dataset comes with its unique characteristics, such as the domain of news (e.g., politics, health, entertainment) or the type of content (e.g., articles, tweets). This diversity makes it difficult to compare models consistently, as each dataset may emphasize different features of fake news, such as linguistic cues, social network metadata, or the propagation patterns of misinformation.
- **Imbalanced Data Distribution:** In many datasets, there is a significant class imbalance between real and fake news articles, with real news being more prevalent. This imbalance can skew the evaluation metrics, especially accuracy, which may show high values even for models that fail to

detect fake news effectively. Precision and recall become more relevant in these cases, but they too can be influenced by the class imbalance, requiring techniques such as resampling or cost-sensitive learning.

- **Subjectivity in Labeling:** The process of labeling fake news is inherently subjective, and human annotators may disagree on what constitutes fake news. This subjectivity can introduce inconsistencies in the dataset and make it challenging to evaluate detection systems reliably. For example, a news story that may be deemed fake by one fact-checking organization might be considered legitimate by another. This issue is further complicated by the rapid evolution of misinformation and the dynamic nature of public opinion.
- **Dynamic Nature of Fake News:** Fake news is not a static concept; it evolves over time. New methods for generating and disseminating fake news emerge frequently, which means that detection systems must adapt to changing patterns in misinformation. This makes it difficult to evaluate models effectively, as a model trained on one set of data may not perform well on a different set of data or under new conditions. As a result, evaluation metrics must account for these evolving challenges.
- **Contextual Complexity:** Fake news detection is not just about identifying misleading text but also understanding the context in which it is presented. Factors such as the credibility of the source, the platform on which the news is shared, and the demographic and social contexts in which the news is consumed play significant roles in determining whether news is perceived as fake. Existing evaluation methods often fail to capture these complexities, making it difficult to assess models holistically.

In conclusion, while various datasets and evaluation metrics exist for fake news detection, challenges such as dataset diversity, class imbalance, subjectivity in labeling, and the dynamic nature of fake news hinder the standardization of evaluation methods. To overcome these challenges, future research needs to develop more standardized, adaptable, and context-aware evaluation frameworks that can better capture the complexities of detecting fake news across different platforms and domains.

7. THE ROLE OF SOCIAL MEDIA AND PLATFORMS

Social media has revolutionized the way information is disseminated, making it easier for news to reach a global audience. However, this vast reach also creates opportunities for the rapid spread of fake news. This section explores the role of social media platforms in the dissemination of fake news, the algorithms that fuel this spread, the countermeasures implemented by these platforms, and the importance of collaboration among platforms, governments, and researchers to combat misinformation.

7.1 Algorithms Driving Fake News Dissemination

The role of algorithms in driving the spread of fake news on social media platforms is one of the most critical factors in understanding why misinformation can go viral. Social media platforms, such as Facebook, Twitter, and YouTube, rely on sophisticated algorithms to determine what content users see. These algorithms are designed to maximize user engagement by promoting content that is likely to capture attention and spark reactions, such as likes, shares, and comments. However, this design has unintended consequences when it comes to fake news.

- **Echo Chambers and Filter Bubbles:** One of the most significant phenomena contributing to the spread of fake news is the creation of echo chambers and filter bubbles. An echo chamber is a situation where individuals are exposed to information that reinforces their preexisting beliefs, leading to a closed loop of ideologically similar content. Filter bubbles, on the other hand, occur when algorithms prioritize content based on users' past behavior, limiting exposure to diverse viewpoints and creating an environment where false or misleading information can thrive unchecked. These environments foster the rapid spread of fake news, as sensational or emotionally charged stories are more likely to be shared and circulated within these bubbles.
- **Algorithmic Amplification:** The algorithms used by social media platforms are designed to prioritize content that generates high levels of engagement. Fake news articles, especially those with sensational or polarizing headlines, tend to attract more attention and engagement compared to factual or neutral news. This engagement triggers the algorithm to further amplify the content, increasing its visibility and potential for virality. This amplification effect is particularly concerning in the context of fake news, as misinformation can spread rapidly before being debunked, potentially causing significant harm to public discourse and decision-making.
- **Polarization and Misinformation:** The algorithms also contribute to the polarization of public opinion by exposing users to extreme or divisive content. As individuals engage with content that aligns with their beliefs, the algorithm learns to recommend even more extreme content, further entrenching users' views and making them more susceptible to fake news. This process creates a feedback loop where misinformation feeds into users' existing biases, reinforcing false narratives and distorting their perception of reality.

7.2 Social Media Platforms' Countermeasures

In response to the growing concerns about the spread of fake news, social media platforms have implemented a variety of countermeasures aimed at detecting, mitigating, and preventing the dissemination of misinformation. These efforts are critical in reducing the impact of fake news on public opinion, elections, and social stability.

- **Content Moderation:** One of the primary countermeasures employed by social media platforms is content moderation, which involves monitoring and filtering content based on established guidelines. Content moderation can take several forms, including automated detection using algorithms, manual review by human moderators, or a combination of both. Platforms like Facebook and Twitter have developed machine learning models that can flag posts containing misinformation, hate speech, or harmful content. While automated moderation can be effective at scale, it is not foolproof and can sometimes lead to false positives or negatives. As a result, platforms also rely on human moderators to review flagged content and make final decisions about its removal.
- **Flagging and Labeling Misinformation:** Another key countermeasure is the use of flagging and labeling systems, where platforms attach warnings or labels to content that is deemed potentially false or misleading. For example, Twitter has implemented a system of labeling tweets that may contain misinformation, directing users to credible sources or fact-checking organizations.

Similarly, Facebook has partnered with third-party fact-checkers to assess the accuracy of news articles and label those that are deemed false or misleading. These labels serve to inform users about the reliability of the content they are consuming, encouraging them to think critically before sharing or believing the information.

- **User Education and Media Literacy Campaigns:** In addition to moderating content, social media platforms have begun to invest in educating users about the dangers of misinformation. Initiatives aimed at improving media literacy can help users identify false or misleading content on their own. For example, platforms may offer prompts or educational materials that teach users how to spot fake news or fact-check articles before sharing them. These efforts are especially important in combating the spread of misinformation during times of crisis, such as during elections or public health emergencies, when the spread of fake news can have serious consequences.
- **Promoting Credible Sources:** Some social media platforms are also working to promote content from credible sources. For example, Google's News initiative prioritizes articles from well-established news organizations, while Facebook has developed algorithms that aim to elevate authoritative sources in users' news feeds. By promoting reputable outlets and suppressing content from unreliable sources, these platforms aim to reduce the visibility of fake news and ensure that users are exposed to accurate information.

7.3 Collaboration Between Platforms, Governments, and Researchers

Given the complex and pervasive nature of fake news, effective solutions require collaboration across multiple sectors, including social media platforms, governments, and academic researchers. Each of these stakeholders plays a vital role in developing and implementing strategies to combat misinformation.

- **Platform-Government Partnerships:** Governments around the world have recognized the importance of addressing the spread of fake news, particularly in the context of elections and national security. In response, governments have initiated collaborations with social media platforms to develop regulations and guidelines for managing misinformation. For example, the European Union has introduced the Digital Services Act (DSA), which mandates that large platforms take responsibility for preventing the spread of illegal content, including fake news. In the United States, lawmakers have proposed similar legislation to hold platforms accountable for their role in spreading misinformation. However, these collaborations often face challenges, such as balancing the need for regulation with the protection of free speech and privacy.
- **Researcher-Platform Collaborations:** Academic researchers play a crucial role in studying the spread of fake news and developing new methods for detecting and preventing misinformation. Collaborations between researchers and social media platforms can help improve the effectiveness of countermeasures by providing valuable insights into the algorithms and behaviors that drive the spread of fake news. For example, researchers may develop new machine learning models that can detect fake news more accurately or propose new approaches to content moderation. Platforms, in turn, can provide researchers with access to data and tools to test their hypotheses and solutions at scale.
- **International Cooperation:** Fake news is a global issue, and combating its spread requires international cooperation. Misinformation can easily cross borders, making it difficult for individual governments or platforms to address the problem on their own. International bodies, such as the

United Nations and the G7, have recognized the need for global solutions to tackle the spread of fake news, and discussions are underway to create common frameworks for regulating misinformation. These collaborations can help standardize the approach to fake news detection, ensuring that platforms around the world adhere to similar guidelines and practices.

- **Public-Private Partnerships:** In addition to collaborations between platforms, governments, and researchers, public-private partnerships are also essential for addressing fake news. Many non-profit organizations, fact-checking agencies, and civil society groups are working to combat misinformation, and their efforts can be strengthened through partnerships with private companies and tech platforms. These collaborations can help to create a more transparent and accountable ecosystem for information sharing, making it more difficult for fake news to flourish.

In conclusion, social media platforms play a central role in the dissemination of fake news, driven by algorithms that prioritize engagement and amplify misinformation. However, platforms have begun implementing countermeasures such as content moderation, flagging systems, and media literacy campaigns to combat the spread of fake news. The fight against misinformation also requires collaboration among platforms, governments, and researchers, with each stakeholder contributing valuable resources and expertise to address this complex issue. Through these collective efforts, it is possible to mitigate the impact of fake news and promote a more informed and responsible online environment.

8. EMERGING TRENDS AND TECHNOLOGIES

The fight against fake news is evolving as new technologies and methods emerge to improve the detection, verification, and prevention of misinformation. In this section, we explore some of the most promising emerging trends and technologies in the field of fake news detection, including the use of blockchain for verifying authenticity, network-based approaches for source tracing, multi-modal and multi-lingual detection models, and real-time detection systems.

8.1 Use of Blockchain for Verifying Authenticity

Blockchain technology, best known for its use in cryptocurrencies like Bitcoin, has garnered attention in recent years for its potential to address issues related to the verification of information. Blockchain's key feature is its decentralized and immutable nature, meaning that once data is recorded on the blockchain, it cannot be altered or deleted without consensus from the network participants. This characteristic makes blockchain a promising tool for ensuring the authenticity and traceability of news content.

- **Verifying Content Origins:** One of the primary ways blockchain can be used in fake news detection is by providing a secure and transparent method for tracking the origin of news content. By embedding metadata such as timestamps, authorship information, and source verification into the blockchain, it is possible to create an immutable record of the content's creation and subsequent changes. This record can help verify whether a news article has been manipulated or distorted as it circulates across the internet.
- **Decentralized Fact-Checking:** Blockchain can also support decentralized fact-checking systems, where multiple independent verifiers (fact-checkers, journalists, or even automated systems) can

validate the authenticity of news content before it is widely disseminated. These fact-checking results can be recorded on the blockchain, ensuring that the verification process is transparent and tamper-proof.

- **Combating Deepfakes:** In addition to combating traditional fake news, blockchain can help authenticate multimedia content, including videos and images, which are increasingly used to spread misinformation. By associating media files with blockchain records that track their origin and editing history, blockchain can make it easier to detect manipulated or fabricated media, such as deepfakes, ensuring that the public has access to accurate information.

8.2 Network-Based Approaches for Source Tracing

Another emerging trend in fake news detection is the use of network-based approaches for tracing the source and propagation of misinformation. Social media platforms are dynamic networks where content is shared and reshared, making it challenging to identify the original source of fake news. Network-based approaches aim to track the dissemination of information and uncover the origins of false or misleading stories.

- **Tracking Content Spread:** By analyzing how content spreads across social media networks, researchers can trace the origins of fake news and identify key actors involved in its dissemination. For example, network analysis tools can help identify the first account or group that shared a piece of misinformation and how it subsequently spreads through various connections, such as followers, retweets, or shares. This information can be used to trace misinformation back to its source and identify patterns of malicious or coordinated activity, such as bot networks or coordinated disinformation campaigns.
- **Identifying Trusted Sources:** Network-based approaches can also help identify credible sources of information by analyzing the network of content sharers and fact-checkers. For instance, if multiple credible accounts, such as reputable news outlets or verified experts, consistently share a particular story, it can be classified as more trustworthy. Conversely, if a piece of content is repeatedly shared by untrustworthy or suspicious sources, it may raise red flags for potential misinformation.
- **Graph-Based Approaches:** Graph theory and machine learning techniques are increasingly being used to model the relationships between users, content, and topics. By building graph structures that represent the connections between different social media entities (e.g., users, pages, and posts), it is possible to identify clusters of fake news and detect influential accounts or coordinated efforts to spread misinformation. These approaches provide a powerful way to uncover hidden patterns in the dissemination of fake news.

8.3 Multi-Modal and Multi-Lingual Detection Models

As fake news continues to spread across the globe, it is becoming increasingly important to develop models that can detect misinformation across multiple formats and languages. Multi-modal and multilingual detection models are emerging as crucial tools for tackling misinformation in a diverse and multilingual online environment.

- **Multi-Modal Detection:** Multi-modal detection involves combining various types of data, such as text, images, and videos, to improve the accuracy of fake news detection systems. Since fake news often comes in the form of multimedia content (e.g., misleading headlines paired with manipulated images or videos), single-modal detection methods (which focus solely on text) may not be sufficient. Multi-modal models analyze both the content of the text and the visual elements, allowing them to better understand the context and authenticity of the news. For example, a model might analyze a news story along with the associated images or videos to determine if the visuals match the textual content or if they have been doctored.
- **Multi-Lingual Detection:** As misinformation is a global issue, detecting fake news in multiple languages is crucial. Multi-lingual models aim to improve detection by incorporating text in different languages, making them more adaptable and capable of addressing the challenges posed by cross-lingual fake news. Traditional fake news detection models often struggle with languages beyond English, but advancements in natural language processing (NLP) have led to the development of multi-lingual models capable of processing content in a wide range of languages. These models use shared representations of text across languages, enabling them to detect fake news in diverse linguistic contexts.
- **Cross-Domain Applications:** Multi-modal and multi-lingual models can be further enhanced by integrating data from various domains, such as social media platforms, news websites, and forums. This approach helps create more robust detection systems that can recognize fake news regardless of the platform or language in which it appears. For example, a model trained on data from Twitter might struggle to detect misinformation on a video-sharing platform like YouTube, but a multi-modal, multi-lingual model can bridge this gap by analyzing content from both platforms simultaneously.

8.4 Real-Time Detection Systems

Real-time detection of fake news is an emerging priority for both researchers and social media platforms, as misinformation often spreads rapidly and has immediate consequences. Real-time detection systems aim to identify and flag fake news as it is being disseminated, allowing for quicker responses and interventions.

- **Speed of Detection:** In contrast to traditional fake news detection systems, which often require manual analysis or post hoc fact-checking, real-time detection systems can automatically analyze content as it is being shared, allowing for the rapid identification of fake news. These systems rely on real-time data from social media platforms and news websites to analyze the content and assess its credibility. Machine learning algorithms, such as natural language processing (NLP) and image recognition, are used to quickly process text, images, and videos to determine their authenticity.
- **Early Warning Systems:** Real-time detection systems can be integrated with early warning systems that alert users, platforms, and fact-checkers about the potential spread of fake news. For example, if a news story begins to gain traction quickly and is flagged by an automatic detection system, the platform can issue a warning or prompt users to review the information before sharing it. Similarly, real-time systems can automatically alert journalists and fact-checking organizations to investigate suspicious content, allowing them to act swiftly and minimize the impact of misinformation.

- **Integration with Social Media Algorithms:** Real-time detection systems can also be integrated with the algorithms used by social media platforms. By incorporating real-time fake news detection into the content recommendation process, platforms can suppress the spread of misinformation before it reaches a large audience. This integration could involve automatic flagging of suspicious content or downgrading its visibility in users' feeds until it is verified by a trusted source.

9. CONCLUSION

The proliferation of fake news has emerged as one of the most pressing challenges in the digital age. It has the potential to destabilize societies, influence elections, exacerbate public health crises, and distort public discourse. In this review, we have examined the progress made in understanding the nature of fake news, the technologies and strategies developed to detect it, and the challenges that remain in combating it effectively.

At the heart of the issue is the complexity of identifying misinformation, which often masquerades as legitimate news. Fake news can take many forms, from fabricated stories to manipulated media, and it can be spread by a variety of actors, including individuals, groups, and even state-sponsored entities. This diversity in form and origin makes it difficult to develop a one-size-fits-all solution to fake news detection.

Current approaches to detecting fake news rely heavily on machine learning and artificial intelligence, which offer powerful tools for analyzing large volumes of data quickly. Models trained on text, images, and other multimedia content have made significant strides in identifying misleading information. Additionally, fact-checking organizations, social media platforms, and governments have implemented various countermeasures, such as content moderation systems, flagging protocols, and transparency efforts, to reduce the spread of misinformation. However, these efforts are not without their limitations. Automated systems can struggle with nuanced content, and human moderation can be prone to biases. The lack of standardization in evaluation metrics and benchmarks further complicates the effectiveness of detection systems, as it makes it difficult to compare results across different studies and platforms.

The role of social media platforms is central to the dissemination of fake news, as algorithms designed to maximize engagement often prioritize sensational and polarizing content. Social media platforms have started to implement countermeasures, such as flagging systems, content moderation, and partnerships with fact-checking organizations. However, these efforts alone are insufficient, as they fail to address the underlying issues related to algorithmic bias, user behavior, and the sheer volume of content. A more holistic approach is needed, involving collaboration between platforms, governments, researchers, and civil society organizations.

Emerging technologies, such as blockchain for content verification, network-based approaches for source tracing, and real-time detection systems, offer promising avenues for improving the detection and verification of fake news. These technologies aim to create more transparent, accountable, and effective methods for combating misinformation. However, their widespread implementation will require overcoming significant technical, ethical, and regulatory challenges. For instance, blockchain's scalability and integration with existing infrastructure remain hurdles, while real-time detection systems must balance speed with accuracy to avoid false positives.

In conclusion, while considerable progress has been made in understanding and addressing the issue of fake news, much work remains. The spread of misinformation is a complex, multifaceted problem that requires coordinated efforts across various sectors. As the digital landscape continues to evolve, so too must our strategies for combating fake news, ensuring that the information we consume and share is accurate, reliable, and trustworthy.

10. FUTURE DIRECTIONS

As we move forward in the battle against fake news, several key areas warrant attention and further research. While the detection of fake news has seen significant advancements, emerging technologies, and innovative approaches hold the promise of more effective solutions. The future of fake news detection will likely be shaped by the ongoing development of new methodologies, technologies, and collaborative efforts aimed at creating a more robust, scalable, and equitable framework for addressing misinformation.

One of the most exciting areas for future research lies in the development of more advanced artificial intelligence and machine learning techniques for detecting fake news. While current models primarily rely on text-based features, the integration of multi-modal approaches (such as images, audio, and video) holds the potential to significantly improve detection systems. Future AI systems will likely focus on a deeper understanding of context, sentiment, and source credibility, enhancing their ability to discern subtle manipulations or hidden biases in content. Additionally, there is a growing interest in explainable AI (XAI), which seeks to make AI decision-making processes more transparent and understandable. The ability to interpret why a certain piece of content was flagged as fake news could improve trust in detection systems and provide clearer insights into the underlying data and reasoning.

The use of blockchain for content verification represents a promising future direction for tackling misinformation. Blockchain's decentralized and immutable characteristics make it an ideal tool for verifying the authenticity of news content. As blockchain technology matures, we can expect to see more widespread adoption of decentralized content verification systems that can trace the origin and modifications of digital media, ensuring transparency and trustworthiness. In the coming years, integration with AI and machine learning could further strengthen blockchain's ability to detect and verify fake news in real-time. However, challenges related to blockchain's scalability, energy consumption, and integration with existing media infrastructure will need to be addressed before these systems can be deployed at scale.

The fight against fake news cannot be won by any single entity working in isolation. In the future, collaboration between social media platforms, governments, academic researchers, and civil society organizations will be crucial to developing more comprehensive and effective solutions. Governments will need to strike a balance between regulating content and protecting freedom of expression, ensuring that policies are transparent, proportionate, and designed to foster trust in digital platforms. One promising avenue for policy development is the creation of international frameworks for combating misinformation that encourage cross-border cooperation. Furthermore, as the regulatory landscape evolves, platforms will likely be required to be more transparent about their content moderation practices, ensuring accountability in how they handle misinformation.

An essential aspect of addressing fake news lies in improving public awareness and media literacy. As misinformation becomes increasingly sophisticated, empowering individuals to critically evaluate the information they encounter will be crucial. Future efforts should focus on integrating media literacy education into formal and informal education systems, helping people of all ages become more discerning consumers of news. Social media platforms can also play a role in this by promoting media literacy campaigns that encourage users to verify information before sharing it. Research into the psychological and behavioral factors that contribute to the spread of fake news will also be important, as it could reveal new ways to influence user behavior and reduce the impact of misinformation.

REFERENCES

Ahmed, H. F., & Yassin, A. S. (2021). Fake news detection: A survey of machine learning approaches. *International Journal of Computer Applications*, *175*(2), 19–27.

Al-Rubaian, M. (2023). Blockchain-based solutions for fake news detection. *Journal of Information Security Research*, *9*(3), 144–158.

Anwar, S., & Kumar, V. (2022). Fake news detection in the age of AI: A deep learning perspective. *Journal of Artificial Intelligence*, *41*(1), 56–72.

Ayed, R. B., & Boudriga, N. (2021). The role of social media in spreading fake news and the challenges of mitigating its effects. *Journal of Digital Information Management*, *19*(4), 312–324.

Bharti, A., & Prakash, A. (2021). Detection of fake news using machine learning: A review. *International Journal of Computer Science and Network Security*, *21*(7), 93–100.

Biswas, S., & Sood, M. (2024). Detecting fake news using neural networks and ensemble learning techniques. *Neural Computing & Applications*, *36*(2), 547–561.

Cai, W., & Xu, P. (2023). Network-based approaches for identifying sources of fake news. *Journal of Computational Social Networks*, *10*(2), 185–200.

Chan, H., & Zhang, X. (2023). Fake news detection with multi-modal fusion: A new approach. *Journal of Information Science and Engineering*, *42*(1), 44–58.

Chen, Y., & Zhao, L. (2024). Fact-checking algorithms: Advancing accuracy in fake news detection. *Journal of Computational Intelligence*, *15*(1), 112–125.

Das, R., & Prasad, N. (2023). Challenges in multi-lingual fake news detection: A case study of Asian languages. *Journal of Natural Language Processing*, *31*(5), 1009–1022.

Dhiman, G., & Kumar, M. (2023). Social media sentiment analysis for fake news detection: A survey. *Journal of Digital Media and Communication*, *9*(3), 245–260.

Fu, X., & Wang, Q. (2024). Hybrid deep learning models for fake news detection on Twitter. *Journal of Social Media and Digital Technologies*, *14*(1), 33–47.

Ghosh, A., & Singh, A. (2023). Detecting misinformation with hybrid AI-based models: A deep learning perspective. *Computers in Human Behavior*, *88*(4), 91–106.

Guntuku, S. C., & Preoţiuc-Pietro, D. (2022). A survey of machine learning and deep learning models for fake news detection. *Journal of Data Science : JDS*, *20*(4), 398–414.

Gupta, A., & Roy, P. (2022). Advancements in multi-modal fake news detection. *IEEE Transactions on Knowledge and Data Engineering*, *34*(6), 1489–1503.

Gupta, S., & Verma, S. (2024). Multi-source data fusion for fake news detection on social media. *IEEE Transactions on Information Technology*, *21*(1), 67–82.

Han, J., & Liu, T. (2024). Using blockchain to trace the origin of fake news: A novel approach. *Journal of Digital Information Security*, *19*(2), 202–216.

Hassan, A. S., & Shakil, K. (2021). Fake news detection using natural language processing techniques. *Journal of Data Mining and Knowledge Discovery*, *45*(3), 274–289.

He, X., & Wang, C. (2023). A survey on AI-based fake news detection systems: Challenges and future directions. *AI & Security*, *6*(1), 12–27.

Huang, L., & Zhao, L. (2024). Real-time fake news detection using convolutional neural networks. *Journal of Machine Learning in Media*, *17*(2), 125–138.

Jain, A., & Srivastava, P. (2023). The impact of social media on the spread of fake news: A review. *International Journal of Media and Communication Studies*, *13*(1), 22–39.

Jain, R., & Nair, R. (2023). Leveraging deep reinforcement learning for social media content moderation. *Journal of Artificial Intelligence Research*, *49*(6), 1675–1690.

Kaur, N., & Chahal, P. (2023). Social media platforms' role in fake news detection and mitigation: A critical review. *International Journal of Social Media and Online Communities*, *7*(2), 91–103.

Kaur, P., & Yadav, S. (2023). Fake news detection using text mining and deep neural networks: A review. *Journal of Big Data*, *12*(3), 87–104.

Khan, M., & Iqbal, J. (2024). Fake news detection and prevention: Challenges and perspectives. *Journal of Information Management and Technology*, *25*(2), 44–58.

Lee, J., & Lee, K. (2021). Multi-lingual detection of fake news on social media: A comparative study. *Journal of Computational Linguistics*, *48*(2), 213–230.

Lee, S., & Kim, H. (2024). Real-time misinformation detection on social media platforms: A study of deep learning models. *Journal of Social Computing*, *17*(1), 76–92.

Li, Q., & Sun, M. (2022). Fake news detection using deep learning: Recent advances and future challenges. *Journal of Artificial Intelligence Research*, *58*(4), 442–459.

Liu, X., & Chen, W. (2020). Leveraging blockchain for content verification in news dissemination. *Journal of Information and Media Ethics*, *28*(3), 244–261.

Martínez-Ruiz, M. J., & González, J. (2021). Fake news detection: Insights from machine learning algorithms. *Journal of Data Science and Technology*, *9*(4), 158–174.

Patel, M., & Singh, D. (2022). Network analysis for identifying the spread of fake news. *Journal of Computational Social Science*, *17*(1), 51–67.

Chapter 5
Mapping the Misinformation Ecosystem in India:
Insights Into Key Areas and Pathways of Dissemination

Apoorva Mahiwal
https://orcid.org/0009-0002-8087-5298
Amity School of Communication, Amity University, Jaipur, India

Saad Ullah Khan
https://orcid.org/0000-0002-3392-7844
Centre for Media and Mass Communication Studies, Jamia Hamdard, New Delhi, India

Sadaf Khan
https://orcid.org/0009-0005-1348-0386
IEC College of Engineering and Technology, Greater Noida, India

Mani Sachdev
https://orcid.org/0009-0000-8284-9718
Amity Institute of Behavioural and Applied Sciences, Amity University, Jaipur, India

ABSTRACT

India, known for its remarkable unity in diversity with numerous languages, religions, and traditions, faces significant challenges in information dissemination. Its linguistic variety, along with widespread digital platforms and varying levels of digital literacy, has created an environment where fake news can thrive. Despite the emergence of fact-checking initiatives, nearly 45% of people in a 2018 survey were unaware of these efforts. Recent surveys also highlight false information as India's highest risk, surpassing other critical issues. This research analyses the characteristics of fake news in India by examining debunked stories from 10 fact-checking outlets. The goal is to understand the nature and distribution of fake news, offering insights to improve strategies against misinformation and enhance efforts to protect Indian society from its adverse effects.

DOI: 10.4018/979-8-3693-7468-9.ch005

1. INTRODUCTION

The phenomenon of fake news has become a ubiquitous and consequential issue in the contemporary media landscape, impacting societies globally and posing significant challenges to democratic discourse, public trust, and social cohesion. In India, a country with a diverse media ecosystem and expanding digital population, the spread of fake news has acquired alarming dimensions. This phenomenon not only undermines the credibility of mainstream media sources but also challenges the foundations of public trust in information (Ognyanova et al., 2020). From fabricated stories to manipulated visuals and misleading narratives, fake news poses significant challenges. As technologies evolve and digital platforms continue to proliferate, understanding and addressing the impacts of fake news have become imperative tasks for societies globally.

This global trend is exacerbated by rapid advancements in artificial intelligence (AI), which have ushered in a new era of technological disruption (Singh Bawa, 2024). In the context of India's diverse media landscape and expanding digital footprint, the proliferation of deepfakes adds a layer of complexity to the fight against misinformation.

1.1 Fake News Scenario in India

In India, the proliferation of fake news has become a pressing concern with diverse landscape of media consumption. Internet penetration increased by 3% in 2023, reaching deeper into rural areas. With 950 million smartphone data subscriptions in the same year, India showcases a vast active online audience of 525 million, reflecting the extensive reach and influence of digital media. Notably, Indians led global statistics in the amount of time spent on their phones in 2023, highlighting the pervasive nature of digital engagement across the country (FICCI & EY, 2024). The country's diverse media landscape, coupled with rapid digital expansion, has created fertile ground for the spread of fake news across various platforms. Owing to such a vast and diverse media landscape in the country, India has become particularly susceptible to the spread of fake news. According to a digital news consumption survey conducted in March 2023 (Basuroy, 2024), over 60 percent of respondents acknowledged encountering potentially fake news online. Conversely, a small minority, three percent, claimed they had never encountered such content, underscoring the widespread reach of fake news across various online platforms. In recent years, incidents related to fake news have escalated in India, posing significant challenges. Studying the phenomenon of fake news is crucial not only for understanding its prevalence and impact but also for developing effective strategies to combat its spread.

1.2 Significance of the Study

According to the World Economic Forum's 2024 Global Risk Report, India is the country where the risk of disinformation and misinformation is ranked the highest. Experts have identified fake news as the foremost risk faced by the nation, placing it ahead of critical issues such as infectious diseases, illicit economic activities, wealth and income inequality, and labour shortages (Fleck, 2024). This recognition underscores the urgent need for research, awareness, and proactive measures to combat the spread of fake news. It further sets the stage for a comprehensive exploration of the fake news landscape in India.

This study aims to provide a nuanced understanding of the prevalence, themes, dissemination channels, and evolving nature of fake news in the Indian context. By analysing debunked stories from reputable fact-checking outlets and examining trends over the past decade, the research seeks to uncover patterns, identify vulnerable areas, and inform evidence-based interventions. Moreover, this study contributes to the academic literature on media studies and communication by offering insights into the mechanisms underlying the spread of fake news. This insight is vital for stakeholders, including policymakers, educators, and media organizations, to develop targeted strategies to combat the spread of fake news and enhance media literacy among the public. Understanding the trends in fake news will enable stakeholders to anticipate nature of fake news and proactively address emerging challenges.

1.3 Objectives of the Study

(1) Identify key platforms and distribution channels including social media, TV news, print media, and other digital platforms, that are predominantly used to spread fake news.
(2) Examine annual trends in themes in the prevalence of different themes and sources of fake news, identifying which themes and platforms have become more prominent or diminished over the past decade.
(3) Explore the characteristics of fake news, including its categorization into types like misinformation and disinformation, as well as the different formats it takes, such as text, images, videos, audio, and the language used.
(4) Investigate the prevalence of fake news stories reported by fact-checking outlets and identify various themes of fake news such as political, health, religious, and other categories to understand the dominant narratives.

1.4 Theoretical Frameworks

The theoretical framework for studying fake news often includes the agenda-setting theory, which explores how media influences the public agenda by highlighting certain issues (McCombs & Shaw, 1972). This theory posits that media doesn't tell people what to think but rather what to think about. In the context of fake news, there is an intricate relationship with online partisan media, both responding to and setting the issue agenda, thereby shaping public perception and discourse (Vargo et al., 2017). Additionally, the framing theory is pertinent, examining how media shapes perception by presenting information in particular ways (Goffman, 1974). This theory suggests that the way information is presented (framed) in the media significantly influences how audiences interpret and understand the information. In the case of fake news, different framing techniques can manipulate public opinion and reinforce existing biases, making it a powerful tool for misinformation and disinformation campaigns.

1.5 Review of Literature

Fake news, defined as false stories presented as news to influence views of the people (Cambridge Dictionary, 2023), has emerged as a significant issue globally, particularly with the advent of digital media. In India, a nation known for its diversity in languages, religions, and cultures, the spread of fake news poses unique challenges. Fake news frequently exploits the vulnerabilities of subaltern communities by leveraging their marginalization and restricted access to reliable information, thereby amplifying misinformation that perpetuates stereotypes and biases (Woolley, 2022). Ironically, OTT platforms are pivotal in delivering more authentic representations of these communities, challenging existing misrepresentations and offering a platform for diverse perspectives (Khan, Khan & Mukherjee, 2024). By presenting accurate and empathetic narratives, OTT series contribute to counteracting misinformation and fostering a more informed and equitable public discourse.

2. PREVALENCE OF FAKE NEWS: AN INDIAN SCENARIO

The prevalence of fake news in India is alarming, with numerous studies and reports highlighting its widespread nature. A 2019 survey by Microsoft ranked India as the country most affected by fake news, with 64% of respondents encountering false information regularly (Press Trust of India, 2019). Indians were notably more likely to encounter fake news and internet hoaxes, scoring seven points higher than the global average (Microsoft, 2019). The issue remains persistent in 2024, with a survey finding that misinformation and disinformation were identified by experts as the number one risk for India, surpassing infectious diseases, illicit economic activity, inequality, and labour shortages (Fleck, 2024). These findings demonstrate the profound impact of fake news, which affects public opinion, incites violence, and undermines trust in media and institutions.

2.1 Themes of Fake News

The themes of fake news in India are diverse, reflecting the country's complex social and political landscape. Among these, disaster, health, and politics are particularly significant, as misinformation in these areas can lead to severe consequences, including casualties and irreversible effects (Muhammed & Mathew, 2022). Political themes dominate, with fake news often targeting elections, political figures, and policies. For instance, a study finds that during the 2014 Indian general elections, social media played a crucial role in spreading political content, much of which was fake news and rumours. (Sen et al., 2019) Health themes also represent a major category, particularly evident during the COVID-19 pandemic. The spread of false information and conspiracy theories related to the coronavirus outbreak significantly increased public confusion (Rocha et al., 2021). Religious themes are prevalent as well, with fake news frequently inciting communal tensions. One study concluded that in India, fabricated and misleading information—especially on social media—has played a significant role in instigating communal violence (Panigrahi & Singh, 2017).

2.2 Distribution Channels of Fake News

Mapping the misinformation ecosystem in India elucidates how globalization and advancements in new media technology significantly influence and amplify the propagation of false information. The swift evolution of digital platforms and the increasing interconnectedness of global communication networks have markedly transformed traditional media landscapes, underscoring the extensive impact of contemporary technological and global forces on information dynamics (Tamandehrou & Khan, 2015). A thorough understanding of these factors is imperative for devising effective strategies to combat misinformation and bolster media literacy in the 21st century. Notably, the distribution channels for fake news in India are multifaceted, with digital platforms emerging as pivotal vectors in the spread of disinformation. Meel & Vishwakarma in 2019 indicated that information pollution, including fake news, rumours, misinformation, and disinformation, has become a prevalent by-product of the digital communication ecosystem, posing significant dangers. Fake news proliferates widely across various platforms such as social media, websites, and messaging apps, which leverage their extensive reach and high user engagement to disseminate misinformation rapidly (Geeng et al., 2020). Notably, platforms like WhatsApp have significantly amplified this issue by facilitating the swift and extensive spread of false information, enabling users to generate, share, and coordinate collective actions based on misleading content (Farooq, 2018). This trend reflects the critical role digital technology plays in the propagation of fake news.

2.3 Characteristics of Fake News

Fake news in India exhibits various characteristics that complicate its detection and mitigation. It derives its power from its appeal to partisanship and perceived novelty, often amplified through repeated exposure by both automated bots and human users sharing it online (Tandoc, 2019). This type of misinformation is intentionally crafted to mislead and manipulate the public, employing sensationalist headlines and false information to provoke strong emotional responses (Watson, 2018). Studies have shown that fake news with such features, particularly those with sensationalist headlines, doctored images and the absence of credible sources, tends to spread more widely (Gunawan & Suwandi, 2020). The rapid dissemination of fake news is facilitated by digital platforms and social media, which lack the credibility of established news sources, thereby enhancing its reach and impact. Addressing this challenge requires a multifaceted approach that includes improving media literacy, enhancing fact-checking mechanisms, and fostering greater accountability among digital platforms to curtail the spread and influence of fake news.

2.4 Challenges in Combatting Fake News

The challenge of combating fake news is intensified by the need to balance democratic values like freedom of speech with the use of advanced technology to detect and address misinformation, while navigating competitive battles over AI frameworks, data, and infrastructure (Figueira & Oliveira, 2017). As average data consumption per user rises—from 16 GB in 2020 to an anticipated 74 GB in 2029—the volume of information, including fake news, grows significantly. The rise of generative AI and deep-fake technologies further complicates this issue, making it increasingly difficult to distinguish between genuine and misleading content. Despite technological advancements, 61% of survey respondents have reported encountering fake or misleading news recently, with one in three unable to verify its authenticity (FICCI & EY, 2024). This highlights the urgent need for effective self-regulation and clear boundaries to manage the evolving landscape of digital misinformation. The challenge of combating fake news lies in balancing the protection of democratic values like freedom of speech with the use of advanced technology and resources to objectively identify and address misinformation, while navigating competitive battles over AI frameworks, data, and infrastructure.

2.5 Strategies to Combat Fake News

To combat the proliferation of fake news effectively, a multifaceted strategy involving various stakeholders is essential. Social media platform providers must deepen their understanding of the risks associated with the cascading effects of fake news and its societal impact (Olan et al., 2022). The false information ecosystem in India is influenced by a complex interplay of factors and actors, exacerbated by the rapid adoption of internet platforms like WhatsApp and Facebook. To combat this, increased funding for independent fact-checking organizations, enhanced public awareness of fact-checking services, and collaborative efforts in hosting digital literacy workshops are recommended. Legislative measures should protect human rights and avoid overbroad censorship. Technology companies should integrate educational features on misinformation into their platforms and ensure transparency and accountability in their content moderation efforts. Traditional news outlets must invest in training journalists to navigate the false information environment effectively (Singh, 2019). Furthermore, it is crucial for social media users to be vigilant about verifying the authenticity of the information they encounter and share (Destiny Apuke & Omar, 2021). The limited ability of users to distinguish between facts and opinions highlights the need for improved media literacy. Initiatives to enhance media literacy should be supported by a comprehensive understanding of news ownership patterns to assess information based on source credibility (Balili, A., & Desai, P., 2019). Broader effort involving collective action from government bodies, political parties, fact-checking organizations, technology companies, and users should be encouraged (Singh, 2019). By leveraging the reach and immediacy of social media responsibly and fostering collective efforts, we can address and mitigate the challenges posed by fake news. This review highlights the complexity of the fake news landscape, driven by diverse themes, extensive digital distribution channels, and distinct characteristics that complicate detection and response. Despite advancements in technology, the challenge of balancing democratic values with effective misinformation management remains significant, particularly with the rise of generative AI and deepfake technologies. To address this, a multifaceted strategy involving increased funding for fact-checking, enhanced media literacy, legislative safeguards, and greater transparency from technology companies is crucial. Hence, understanding the nature of the fake news landscape is essential to frame effective combating strategies. By fostering collective action from all stakeholders—including government bodies, political parties, media outlets, and users—we can better navigate the evolving fake news landscape and work towards a more informed and resilient society.

2.6 Research Methodology

Research methodology is a set of systematic techniques used to guide and conduct research. It involves describing and analysing methods, highlighting their limitations and resources, and clarifying their assumptions and consequences (Igwenagu, 2016). A well-defined research methodology provides a detailed plan that ensures the legitimacy and scientific soundness of the research, making the process smooth, effective, and manageable (Indeed Editorial Team, 2021).

3. RESEARCH DESIGN

The research adopted for this study is quantitative, aiming to provide a comprehensive analysis of the fake news landscape in India. This design employs a set of strategies, techniques, and assumptions to study the psychological, social, and economic processes involved in the spread of fake news through the exploration of numeric patterns (University of Texas Arlington, 2023). By focusing on debunked fake news stories from selected fact-checking outlets, the approach involves collecting numerical data on the themes, distribution channels, language, source and formats of fake news, followed by analysis to identify trends over the past decade. Content analysis is utilized as research method. Content analysis is a research tool for assessing the specific words, themes, or concepts within qualitative data. This method enables researchers to quantify and examine the occurrence, meanings, and relationships of these elements, providing a systematic approach to analysing qualitative data within a quantitative framework (Columbia University, 2019).

3.1 Data Source

To provide a comprehensive analysis of the fake news landscape in India, this study utilizes data from ten carefully selected fact-checking outlets. These outlets include signatory fact check portals of India mentioned in the International Fact-Checking Network (IFCN). The International Fact-Checking Network (IFCN) at Poynter, established in 2015, is a global leader in promoting fact-checking excellence through resources, grants, training, and networking opportunities for over 100 operations worldwide (Poynter, 2024).

3.2 Selection Criteria

The study considers the list of 18 fact-checking outlets in India that are signatories to the International Fact-Checking Network (IFCN) (IFCN, 2024). However, outlets focused on specific themes, such as Digital Forensics, Research and Analytics Centre (D-FRAC), FactChecker.in, First Check, and THIP Healthtech Pvt Ltd, are excluded from the study. Additionally, only fact-checking outlets that publish debunked stories in English are included, leading to the exclusion of Telugupost.com, TV Today Network Limited - The Lallantop, and Youturn. Soft Media Hub LLP is also excluded due to its lack of showcased debunked stories. The remaining outlets considered for this study include:

Table 1. List of Selected Fact Check Outlet

Sr. No.	Fact Check Outlet
1.	Vishvas News
2.	BOOM
3.	Factly Media & Research
4.	Fact Crescendo
5.	News Mobile
6.	Newschecker

continued on following page

Table 1. Continued

Sr. No.	Fact Check Outlet
7.	Newsmeter (Fifth Estate Digital Private Limited)
8.	Press Trust of India
9.	T. V. Today Network Ltd. - India Today Fact Check
10.	The Quint

3.3 Time Frame

The study covers debunked fake news stories from the selected fact-checking outlets from their inception till June 2024. This time frame allows for a comprehensive analysis of trends and patterns in the fake news landscape over a significant period.

3.4 Content Analysis Method

Content analysis is a research method employed to identify the presence of various concepts, words, and themes within texts (Damyanov, 2023). Conventional content analysis approach is particularly useful in scenarios where there is limited or no prior knowledge about a phenomenon, when investigating and describing new phenomena, or when seeking to understand the nuances of a social setting without relying on preexisting theories and categories (Akhter, 2023).

Content analysis is chosen for this study because, given the novelty of fake news exposure in India and the lack of comprehensive research on its impact, it offers a holistic approach to understanding the various forms of debunked fake news through a detailed examination of different fact-checking outlets.

3.5 Selection of Content from Fact-Check Outlets Year-Wise Selection

The study selects content from fact-checking outlets on both year-wise and month-wise basis to provide a comprehensive view of their debunked stories. It includes content from the establishment of each outlet up to June 2024, using systematic sampling to collect data on the 1st and 15th of each month. If content is not available on these specific dates, the nearest prior or subsequent dates are used, and any months with no debunked stories are noted in the analysis.

3.6 Total Number of Debunked Stories Analysed in the Study

This study has analysed debunked stories from ten fact-checking outlets from their inception up to June 2024. The total number of debunked stories from each outlet is as follows:

Table 2. Total Number of Debunked Stories Analysed

Sr. No.	Fact-Check Outlet	No. of Debunked Stories
1.	Vishvas News	129
2.	BOOM	163
3.	Factly Media & Research	12
4.	FactCrescendo	122
5.	NewsMobile	124
6.	Newschecker	113
7.	Newsmeter (Fifth Estate Digital Private Limited)	114
8.	Press Trust of India	56
9.	T. V. Today Network Ltd. - India Today Fact Check	109
10.	The Quint	123
Total No. of Debunked Stories Studied		1065

Additionally, it is important to note that the content from Factly Media & Research was only accessible for the year 2024, thus the data collected for this outlet pertains solely to the current year.

3.7 Categorical Variables

Categorical variables represent the original verbal information, which can then be analysed using standard statistical methods. (*Content Analysis: A Methodology for Structuring and Analyzing Written Material*, 1996) In this study, these categorical variables have been converted into numeric data based on their frequency of appearance in fact-checking outlets each month. The converted data is tabulated for statistical comparison and analysis. The variables considered are as follows:

- Theme (Health, Communal, Sports, Social, National, International, Politics, Bollywood, Finance, Technology)
- Keywords (COVID-19, Farmer's Protest, BJP, International Conflict, etc)
- Source of Fake News (AI Generated, Edited, Old content, Unrelated content, Scripted content, False Claim)
- Format (Audio, Video, Image or Text)
- Language (English, Hindi or other)
- Fake News Platform (News portals, Print media, TV Channels, social media)

3.8 Limitations of the Study

This study's reliance on data from debunked fake news stories, while providing valuable insights, may not capture the full spectrum of fake news, including emerging or lesser-known narratives that have not yet been widely addressed. Additionally, the analysis may be constrained by the scope of digital platforms and social media channels covered.

Furthermore, while the research focuses on the Indian context, the results may have limited generalizability to other regions with different social, political, and technological environments. Technical constraints related to the use of fact-check outlets' web portals for data collection could introduce limitations regarding the accuracy and completeness of the data, along with potential biases inherent in these tools.

To address these limitations, future research could benefit from incorporating qualitative methods to explore the emotional and psychological effects of fake news on audiences. Expanding research to include diverse data sources and incorporating interdisciplinary approaches can further enrich the analysis of fake news and its societal implications.

4. DATA ANALYSIS AND INTERPRETATION

The data analysis and interpretation provide a comprehensive examination of the debunked fake news stories collected from the selected ten fact-checking outlets. This section begins with the preparation and cleaning of data, converting categorical variables into numeric values to facilitate analysis. The findings are then interpreted to draw insights into the fake news landscape, considering limitations and contextual factors.

4.1 Themes of Fake News

Based on the frequency data for themes of fake news, political themes are the most common, with a total of 289 instances. This indicates that political fake news is the most prevalent in India, reflecting the high level of interest and engagement with political content among the Indian population. Politics, often being a contentious and highly debated topic, has significant potential to influence public opinion and behaviour, making it a prime target for fake news.

The second most common theme is social issues, with 197 instances. Social themes, which encompass a wide range of societal concerns, also have a broad appeal and impact on the Indian masses. Both political and social fake news are likely to resonate strongly with the public, as they tap into prevalent concerns and discussions within the country. This analysis highlights the critical areas where misinformation is most rampant and underscores the need for robust fact-checking and public awareness efforts in these domains.

Figure 1. Frequency of Themes

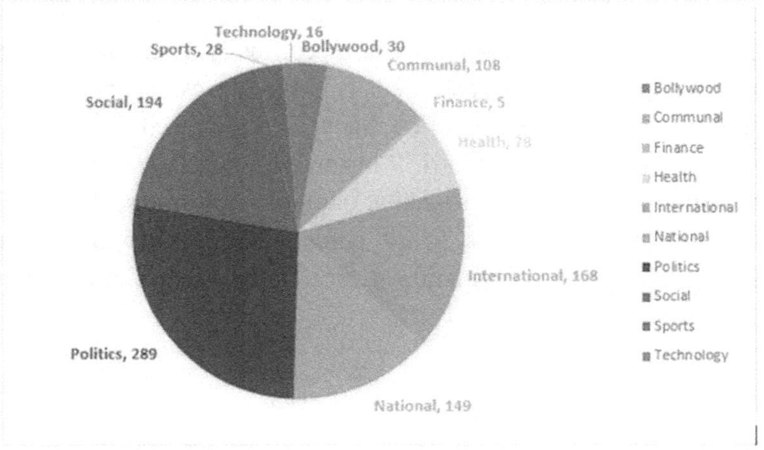

Additionally, the analysis of the keyword frequency data provides insights into the prevalent topics of fake news in India. Among the themes identified, COVID-19 emerges as the most common keyword under the health theme, reflecting the widespread dissemination of fake news related to the pandemic; and is also the most frequently occurring keyword across all themes.

In terms of communal themes, 'Muslim' stands out as the most common keyword, and 'BJP' is the most commonly used word for fake news under Politics theme. Under the national theme, 'protest' is the dominant keyword with the frequency of mention 38, which includes 25 mentions of Farmer's Protest.

Moreover, specific international conflicts such as those involving keywords like Syria (6), Palestine (8), Ukraine (11), Russia (14), and Israel (14) are mentioned under International Armed Conflict in below graph, suggesting that these geopolitical events are also subject to misinformation and manipulation in the Indian fake news landscape. The frequency of other dominant keywords are listed as follows:

Figure 2. Frequency of Keywords

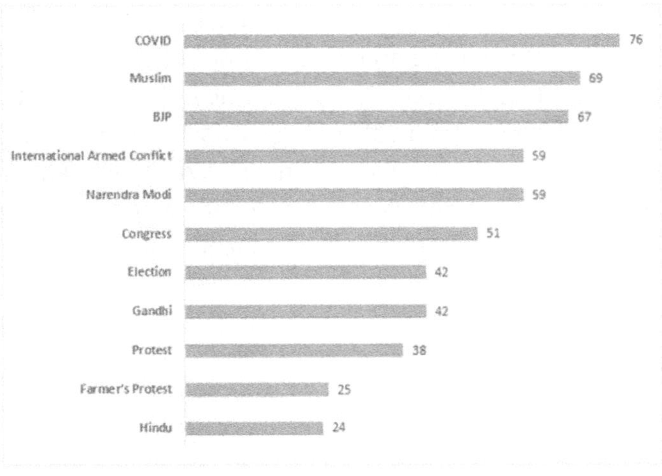

4.2 Distribution Platforms for Fake News

Based on the frequency data provided, it is evident that social media platforms are the predominant channels for the dissemination of fake news in India. Specifically, Facebook emerges as the most frequently cited platform, with 294 instances recorded. This showcases Facebook's significant role in the propagation of misinformation and disinformation due to its wide reach and user engagement features. Additionally, X (formerly Twitter) showcases 159 instances, indicating a substantial presence of fake news on unspecified online platforms. Additionally, outdoor platforms such as rallies, hoardings, and offices collectively account for 7 mentions. While comparatively fewer in frequency, these physical platforms also contribute to the spread of misinformation in the public domain. News Agency include News Portals and TV News Channels collectively.

Figure 3. Frequency of Use of Media Platform for Fake News

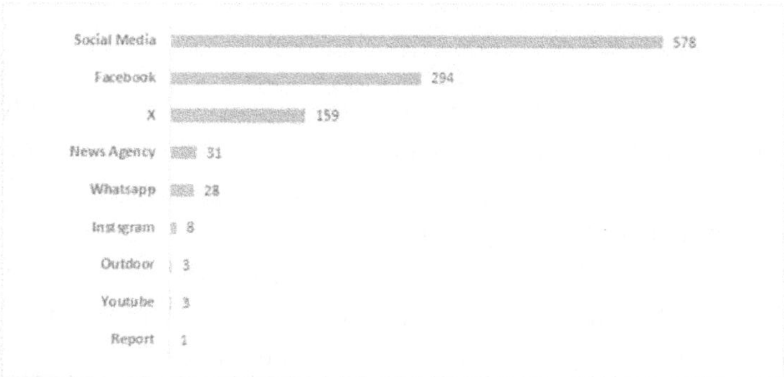

4.3 Sources of Fake News

The analysis of the different formats of fake news reveals that the most common type is false claims, with a frequency of 341. This category involves spreading narratives based on incorrect information. The second most prevalent format is unrelated content, with a frequency of 287. This includes videos, images, or audio that are completely unrelated but are used to falsely describe certain events. Old content, which involves presenting years-old content as recent, has a frequency of 231. Edited content, which includes any manipulated, altered, or morphed content shared, appears 156 times. Scripted content and satire, with frequencies of 18 and 4 respectively, involve content created intentionally false or satirical but then shared as real. AI-generated content and impersonated accounts, with frequencies of 15 and 13, involve content created by artificial intelligence and fake accounts pretending to be celebrities, respectively.

Figure 4. Source of Content of Fake News

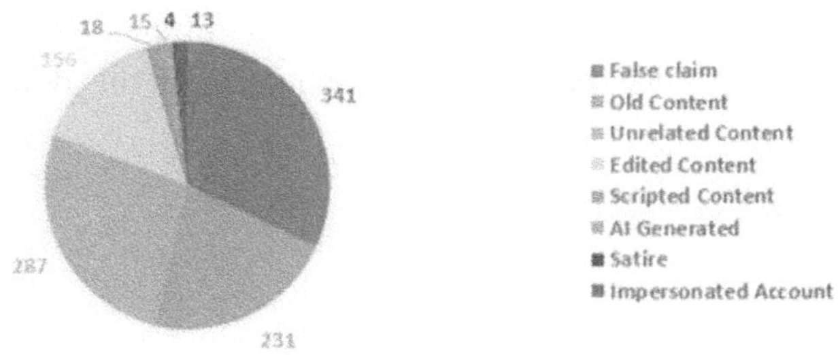

The analysis of old content repurposed as recent reveals that videos are the most frequently shared format among the categories of videos, images, and articles. Within these outdated videos, the dominant themes are politics and international affairs.

Figure 5. Frequency of Old Content Formats

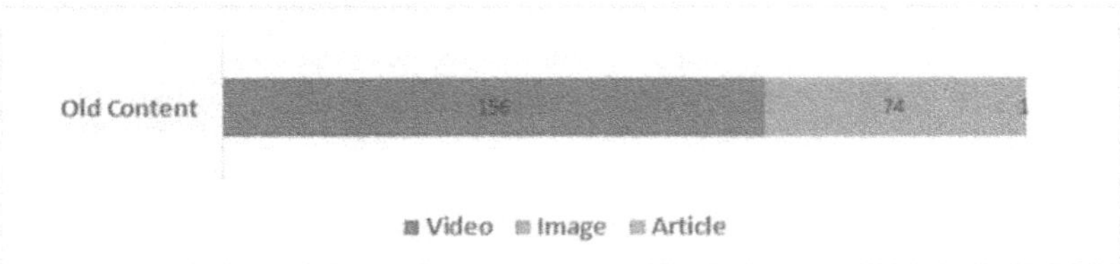

The graph of unrelated content illustrates how videos, images, and audio have been shared with different narratives and contexts. The insights reveal that images are the most frequently shared format of unrelated content. Among these images, political themes dominate, indicating a significant use of unrelated images to spread political misinformation. For unrelated videos shared as fake news, international and social themes have the highest occurrences, highlighting how videos are manipulated to misinform the public about global and societal issues.

Figure 6. Frequency of Unrelated Content

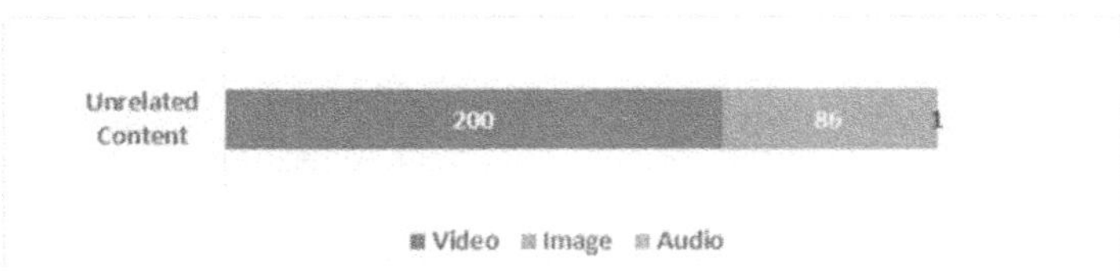

The analysis of edited content in fake news reveals various forms of manipulated media used to deceive the public. This includes doctored/altered/edited videos, clipped videos, and edited/morphed/photoshopped images, AI-generated content (comprising 6 images, 1 video, and 1 audio) and Deepfake videos. Among these, images are the most frequently shared format, with a frequency of 102. Further, political themes dominate the edited content category, with 77 out of 177 edited stories, accounting for approximately 43% of the total. This indicates a significant use of manipulated media in political fake news, highlighting the need for greater scrutiny and fact-checking in this domain.

Figure 7. Frequency of Edited Content

The prevalence of manipulated media, particularly in the form of edited images and videos, within political fake news underscores the critical need for heightened scrutiny and rigorous fact-checking measures. Further, the sophistication of techniques such as video clipping, image morphing, and AI-generated content poses significant challenges for traditional verification methods.

4.4 Formats of Fake News Content

The analysis of content formats used in fake news reveals that videos are the most widely shared format, with a total frequency of 504. This indicates that videos are particularly effective in spreading misinformation, likely due to their engaging and attention retaining nature. Images are the second most common format, with a frequency of 361, followed by text-based content, which has a frequency of 197. Audio content is the least shared format, with only 3 instances.

Figure 8. Formats of Fake News Content

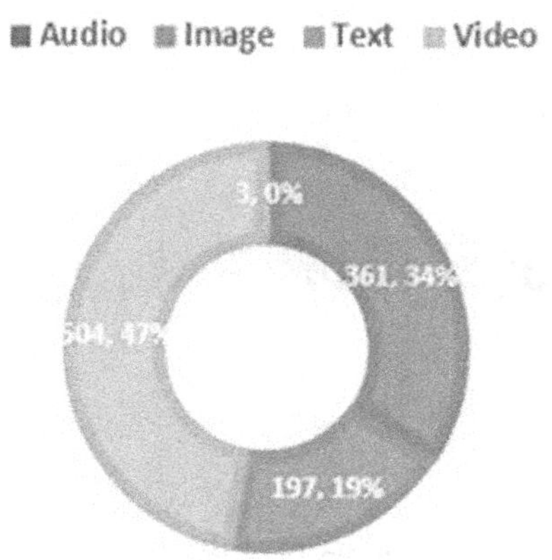

The dominance of videos in fake news highlights the need for enhanced video verification processes to combat the spread of misinformation effectively. While image reverse search tools have become standard for fact-checking outlets in debunking fake news stories based on images, the complexity of verifying video content demands more advanced tools. Some fact-checking organizations have employed similar techniques, utilizing frame-by-frame analysis and reverse image search across multiple frames to trace the origins of misleading/fake videos. This underscores the necessity for continuous technological advancements and robust methodologies in tackling the evolving challenges posed by video-based misinformation, ensuring accuracy and reliability in combating the spread of fake news effectively.

4.5 Language of Fake News Content

Language plays a pivotal role in the spread of fake news, shaping how information resonates with different audiences and communities. Hindi and English, being the official languages of India, are prominently used for wider reach and impact. Further, other regional languages such as Bengali, Gujarati, Telugu, and Malayalam also feature, albeit to a lesser extent, highlighting the nuanced approach taken to manipulate public discourse and influence perceptions in specific region or state. Below mentioned chart showcases the frequency of use of different languages in fake news content.

Figure 9. Frequency of Different Languages used in Fake News Content

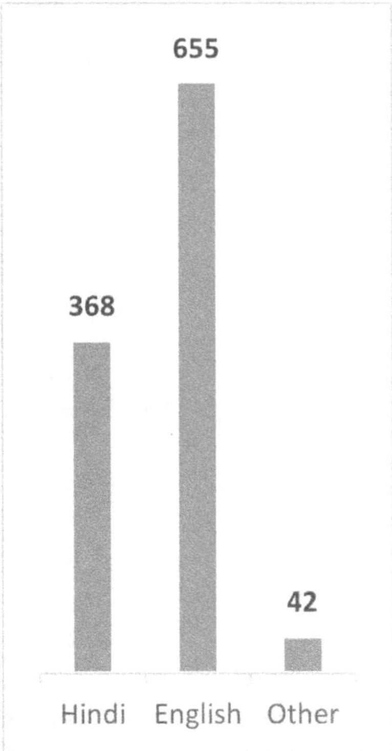

Figure 10. Frequency of Different Languages used in Fake News Content

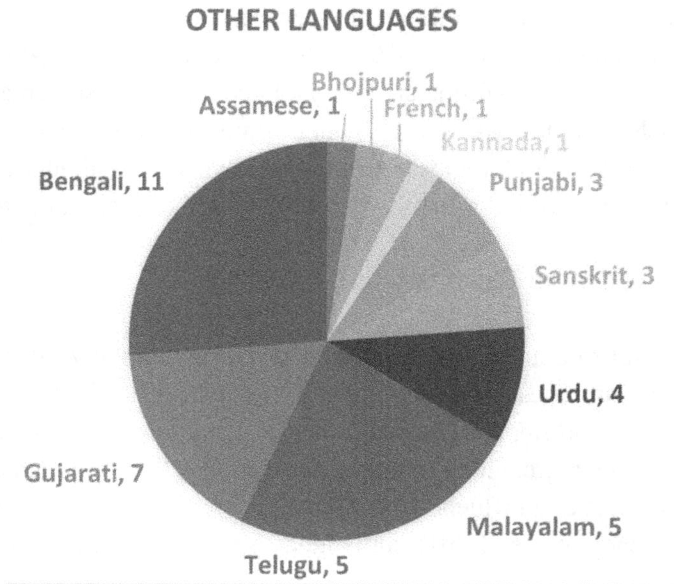

Figure 11. Frequency of Hindi and English Language vis-à-vis Fake News Themes

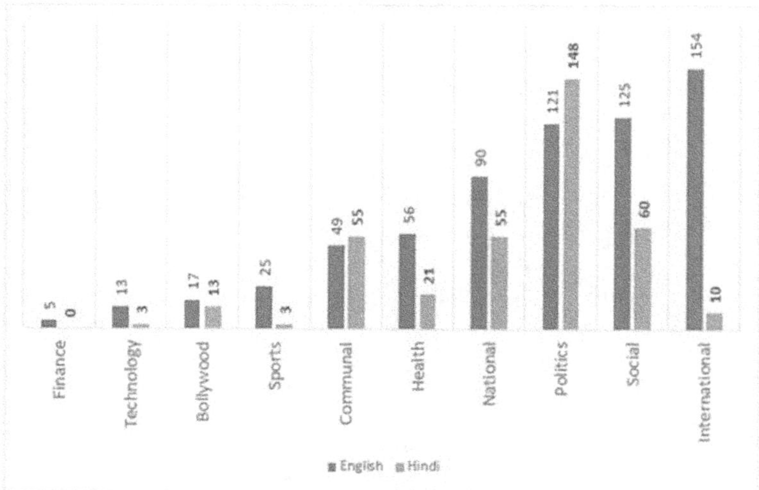

The chart illustrates the frequency of Hindi and English languages used in debunked stories across various themes of fake news content. It is noteworthy that Hindi is predominantly used in themes related to politics and communal issues, surpassing English in these two categories. This language preference showcases the targeted dissemination of fake news to cater to regional and linguistic demographics within India. The prominence of Hindi in political and communal narratives suggests an intentional effort to resonate with Hindi-speaking audiences, potentially amplifying the impact of Fake News.

4.6 Trends in Fake News Over the Past Five Years

The trends in fake news over the past five years have been systematically studied to understand the changing landscape of Fake News in India. Although data collection spans the inception of the fact-check outlets, with the earliest data from 2017, consistent data is available from the year 2020 onward. This consistency across all selected fact-check outlets allows for a comprehensive analysis of trends from 2020 to June 2024. The data collection extends up to June 2024, making the 2024 data representative of only half of the year.

Figure 12. Trends in Themes of Fake News Over Last 5 Years

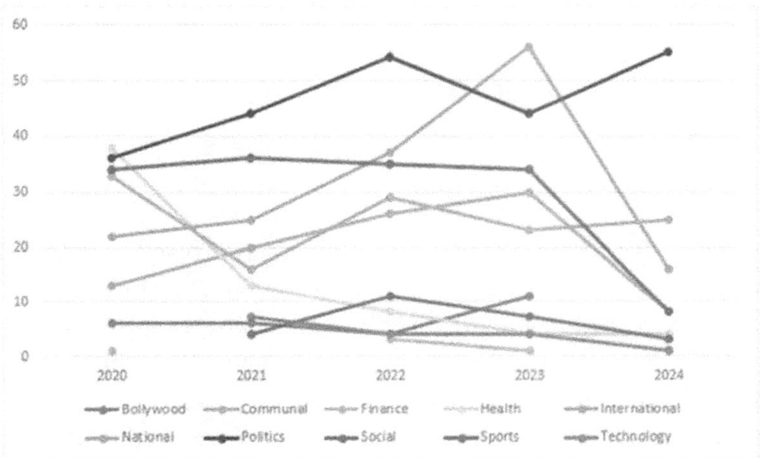

In 2020, health emerged as the most trending theme of fake news, closely followed by politics. This spike in health-related fake news can be attributed to the COVID-19 pandemic, which dominated global discourse. However, the prevalence of health-related fake news saw a significant decline in subsequent years. Conversely, political fake news consistently remained prominent in India, with the highest number of stories in 2021, 2022, and 2024. Notably, even with data from only the first half of year 2024, there is a significant number of political fake news, due to the General Elections in India in 2024. In 2023, there was a surge in fake news related to international themes, predominantly covering the Russia-Ukraine conflict and the Israel-Hamas conflict.

This analysis underscores how specific events and periods exert a profound influence on the thematic focus of fake news in India. The rise of health-related misinformation during the COVID-19 pandemic illustrates how crises can amplify false information, exploiting public anxieties and uncertainties. As the pandemic stabilized, the narrative shifted to political fake news, particularly during election years, where misinformation can sway voter opinions and electoral outcomes. Additionally, the surge in fake news surrounding international conflicts like the Russia-Ukraine and Israel-Hamas disputes in 2023 reflects how global events can shape local misinformation narratives, influencing public perceptions on international affairs. These shifts highlight the dynamic nature of fake news, where themes ebb and flow with the prominence of current events and societal concerns, underscoring the need for adaptable strategies in media literacy, fact-checking, and regulatory frameworks to safeguard the integrity of public discourse in India.

Figure 13. Trends in the Format of Content of Fake News Over Last 5 Years

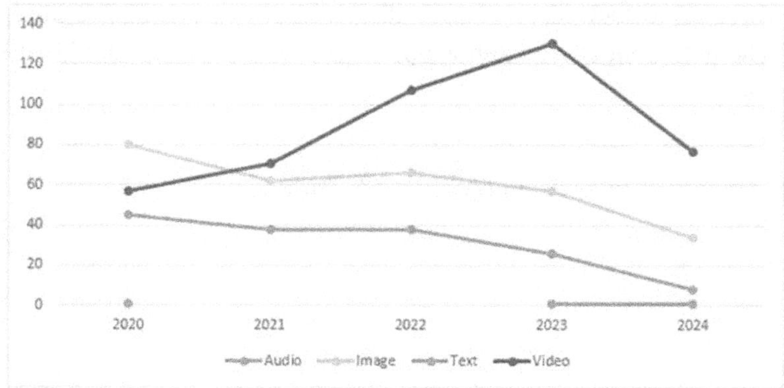

Over the past five years, the format of fake news content has evolved significantly. In 2020, images were the most common format for spreading fake news. This could be attributed to the rapid sharing of images on social media platforms, making them an effective tool for misinformation. However, since 2021, videos have become the most prevalent format for fake news. This shift can be justified by the increasing consumption of video content online and the persuasive power of videos in conveying narratives. Videos combine visual and auditory elements, making them more engaging and believable to viewers.

The shift from images to videos as the predominant format for spreading fake news over the past five years underscores a significant evolution in how misinformation is disseminated and consumed. This trend highlights the adaptability of those seeking to manipulate public opinion, leveraging technological advancements and changing media consumption habits to disseminate misinformation in increasingly impactful and convincing ways.

Figure 14. Trends of Source of Fake News Over Last 5 Years

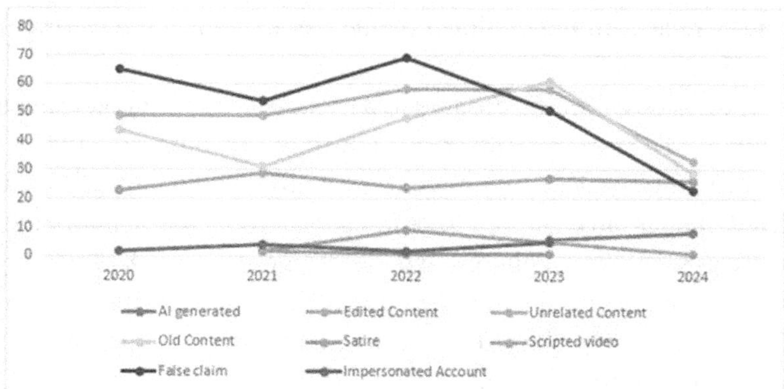

The trends in the source of fake news over the last five years signify a notable shift in the strategies employed to disseminate misinformation in India. As seen from the chart, setting a false narrative with incorrect information has been the most common source of spreading fake news content. During the COVID-19 pandemic, a significant portion of debunked fake news stories originated from this type, where random incorrect claims were widely shared among the masses. Up until 2022, spreading fake news with the foundation of false claims was the most common strategy. However, in 2023 and 2024, this trend saw a decline, and fake news content was more frequently shared using old or unrelated content to describe recent events. For instance, videos or images of past protests, floods, or rallies were shared as if they related to current events. This shift in strategy, where previously unrelated or outdated content is repurposed to fit a new narrative, has overtaken the 'false claim' approach in the past two years.

This shift indicates that fake news creators are becoming more sophisticated and resourceful. By recycling older content and recontextualizing it to fit current events, they can create a false sense of continuity and credibility, making it more challenging for the public to discern truth from falsehood. This approach leverages the familiarity of old content and the immediacy of new events to amplify misinformation's impact.

5. CONCLUSION

The phenomenon of fake news has become a pressing issue in India's contemporary media landscape. Over the years, the dissemination strategies, themes, formats, and sources of fake news have evolved, reflecting broader societal and technological changes. The comprehensive analysis sheds light on the shifting nature of fake news, highlighting the dominance of themes, the growing use of certain format of content, the strategic deployment of language, and the methods employed by fake news creators.

Based on the findings of this study, it is evident that political themes dominate the landscape of fake news in India, indicating a widespread influence on public discourse. Nearly 80 percent of India's first-time voters find themselves bombarded with fake news on popular social media platforms, according to a survey by the digital rights organization Social & Media Matters. (TOI News Desk, 2024) Social issues follow closely behind, reflecting broad societal concerns that are similarly susceptible to misinformation. Further, keyword analysis reveals significant focus on COVID-19 in health-related fake news, while political narratives often centre around specific identities and international armed conflict related content also trended. The prevalence of these themes and keywords underscores the critical need for enhanced media literacy, robust fact-checking mechanisms, and targeted educational initiatives to mitigate the harmful effects of fake news on public trust and societal stability in India.

Based on the frequency data of distribution platforms of fake news, it is clear that social media platforms, particularly Facebook, play a pivotal role in the dissemination of fake news across India, leveraging its extensive user base and interactive features to amplify false narratives. Similarly, X (formerly Twitter) highlights significant role in the propagation of fake news. Although outdoor platforms such as rallies, hoardings, and offices collectively contribute somewhat lesser, their physical presence underscores another avenue through which misinformation can influence public perception. Social Media platforms appear to be most susceptible for spread of fake news. These findings showcase the urgent need for platform accountability and enhanced digital literacy efforts.

The analysis on sources of fake news reveals that false claims are the most common type of fake news, indicating that spreading narratives based on incorrect information is a prevalent tactic. It is followed by unrelated content, repurposing videos, images, or audio to falsely describe events and old content, presenting years-old material as recent. The dominant themes in unrelated content are political and international affairs, particularly highlighting the significant use of unrelated images and edited political content to spread fake news. Edited content, including manipulated media, scripted content and satire, AI-generated content, and impersonated accounts have lower frequencies.

The analysis of content formats used in fake news reveals that videos are the most widely shared format, indicating their effectiveness in spreading fake news due to their engaging nature. It is followed by images, text-based content and audio content respectively. This dominance of videos highlights the need for enhanced video verification processes, as traditional image reverse search tools are insufficient for the complexity of video content. Advanced tools such as frame-by-frame analysis and reverse image search across multiple frames are necessary to trace the origins of misleading/fake videos, underscoring the need for continuous technological advancements and robust methodologies to combat video-based misinformation effectively.

Language plays a pivotal role in the spread of fake news in India, with English and Hindi being prominently used due to being official language of India. Further, regional languages like Bengali, Gujarati, Telugu, and Malayalam are also featured, reflecting a strategic approach to influencing public perception in specific regions. Analysis reveals that Hindi is predominantly used in fake news themes related to politics and communal issues, surpassing English in only these two categories. This targeted dissemination indicates an intentional effort to resonate with Hindi-speaking audiences, potentially amplifying the impact of fake news.

Additionally, the trends in fake news over the past five years in India reveal a dynamic landscape influenced by specific events and societal concerns. In 2020, health-related fake news surged due to the COVID-19 pandemic, but this theme significantly declined in subsequent years. Conversely, political fake news remained consistently prominent, peaking during election years such as 2021, 2022, and 2024, where misinformation can impact voter opinions and electoral outcomes. In 2023, international themes like the Russia-Ukraine and Israel-Hamas conflicts drove a surge in fake news, demonstrating how global events can shape local misinformation narratives. These shifts highlight the need for adaptable strategies in media literacy, fact-checking, and regulatory frameworks to maintain the integrity of public discourse in India.

Over the past five years, there has been a significant evolution in the format of fake news content in India. In 2020, images were the most common format for spreading misinformation, likely due to their rapid shareability. However, since 2021, videos have become the predominant format, reflecting the growing consumption of video content online and their persuasive power in conveying narratives. This shift from images to videos highlights how those disseminating fake news adapt to technological advancements and changing media consumption habits, using increasingly impactful and convincing methods to manipulate public opinion. This is further supported by the data from the M&E Report 2024 by FICCI, which states that the popularity of short videos is twice as high in tier 2 cities. Additionally, the average minutes per user per day spent on short videos increased in 2023. With this trend continuing, it demands the need for greater preparedness in addressing the spread of fake news through video content. (FICCI & EY, 2024)

The trends in the sources of fake news over the past five years in India reveal a significant shift in fake news content strategies. Initially, setting false narratives with incorrect information was the most common approach, especially during the COVID-19 pandemic when random incorrect claims were widely shared. However, 2023 onwards, there has been a notable increase in the use of old or unrelated content to describe recent events, surpassing the 'false claims' method. This involves recycling videos or images of past incidents, such as protests, armed conflicts or floods, and presenting them as current, creating a false sense of continuity and credibility. This shift shows that fake news creators are becoming more sophisticated and resourceful, using familiar old content and the immediacy of new events to enhance fake news content's impact and make it harder for the public to distinguish truth from falsehood.

In conclusion, the evolving landscape of fake news in India underscores the urgent need for comprehensive strategies to combat fake news. The shifting themes, formats, and sources of fake news, coupled with the growing influence of social media and regional languages, highlight the necessity for enhanced media literacy, technological advancements in verification, and proactive platform accountability. Addressing these challenges effectively is crucial for safeguarding public trust and ensuring the integrity of democratic discourse in an increasingly complex media environment.

REFERENCES

Akhter, N. (2023). Fake News in India a study of online and TV News since 2014. https://shodhganga.inflibnet.ac.in/handle/10603/549446

Balili, A., & Desai, P. (2019). Fake News and Social Media: Indian Perspective. *Media Watch, 10*(3). Advance online publication. DOI: 10.15655/mw/2019/v10i3/49687

Basuroy, T. (2024, June 26). *India: frequency of seeing fake news online 2023.* Statista. https://www.statista.com/statistics/1406289/india-frequency-of-seeing-fake-news-online/

Cambridge Dictionary. (2023, October 11). *Fake news.* https://dictionary.cambridge.org/dictionary/english/fake-news#google_vignette

Columbia University. (2019). *Content Analysis.* www.publichealth.columbia.edu. https://www.publichealth.columbia.edu/research/population-health-methods/content-analysis#:~:text=Content%20analysis%20is%20a%20research

Content Analysis: A Methodology for Structuring and Analyzing Written Material. (1996). United States General Accounting Office. http://archive.gao.gov/f0102/157490.pdf

Damyanov, M. (2023, March 21). *What is Content Analysis? Uses, Types & Advantages.* Dovetail.com. https://dovetail.com/research/content-analysis /

Destiny Apuke, O., & Omar, B. (2021). Fake News and COVID-19: Modelling the Predictors of Fake News Sharing among Social Media Users. *Telematics and Informatics, 56*, 101475. DOI: 10.1016/j.tele.2020.101475

Farooq, G. (2018). Politics of Fake News: How WhatsApp Became a Potent Propaganda Tool in India. *Media Watch, 9*(1). Advance online publication. DOI: 10.15655/mw/2018/v9i1/49279

FICCI & EY. (2024). *Reinvent india's media & entertainment sector is innovating for the future.* FICCI & EY.

Figueira, Á., & Oliveira, L. (2017). The current state of fake news: Challenges and opportunities. *ScienceDirect, 121*, 817–825.

Fleck, A. (2024, January 24). *Survey Finds False Information Risk Highest in India.* The Wire. https://thewire.in/media/survey-finds-false-information-risk-highest-in-india

Geeng, C., Yee, S., & Roesner, F. (2020, April 21). Fake News on Facebook and Twitter: Investigating How People (Don't) Investigate. *Proceedings of the 2020 CHI Conference on Human Factors in Computing Systems.* DOI: 10.1145/3313831.3376784

Goffman, E. (1974). Frame analysis: An essay on the organization of experience. Northeastern University Press.

Gunawan, F., & Suwandi, V. (2020). Identifying the most influencing characteristics of fake news. *ICIC International, 11*(1), 93–101. DOI: 10.24507/icicelb.11.01.93

IFCN. (2024). *IFCN Code of Principles.* https://ifcncodeofprinciples.poynter.org/signatories

Igwenagu, C. (2016). Fundamentals of research methodology and data collection. *ResearchGate*. https://www.researchgate.net/publication/303381524_Fundamentals_of_research_methodology_and_data_collection

Indeed Editorial Team. (2021, December 15). *What Is Research Methodology and Why Is It Important?* Indeed Career Guide. https://www.indeed.com/career-advice/career-development/research-methodology#:~:text=Why%20is%20a%20research%20methodology

Khan, S. U., Khan, S., & Mukherjee, T. (2024). The 'Subaltern' Will Speak: Investigating Portrayals in the Acclaimed OTT Series of India and Pakistan. In Kalorth, N. (Ed.), *Exploring the Impact of OTT Media on Global Societies* (pp. 1–24). IGI Global. DOI: 10.4018/979-8-3693-3526-0.ch001

McCombs, M., & Shaw, D. (1972). The agenda-setting function of mass media . *Public Opinion Quarterly*, *36*(2), 176. DOI: 10.1086/267990

Meel, P., & Vishwakarma, D. K. (2019). Fake news, rumor, Information Pollution in Social Media and web: A Contemporary Survey of state-of-the-arts, Challenges and Opportunities. *Expert Systems with Applications*, *153*(1), 112986. DOI: 10.1016/j.eswa.2019.112986

Microsoft. (2019, February 5). *Microsoft releases digital civility index on Safer Internet Day*. Microsoft Stories India. https://news.microsoft.com/en-in/microsoft-digital-civility-index-safer-internet-day-2019/

Muhammed, S. T., & Mathew, S. K. (2022). The Disaster of misinformation: A Review of Research in Social Media. *International Journal of Data Science and Analytics*, *13*(4), 271–285. DOI: 10.1007/s41060-022-00311-6 PMID: 35194559

Ognyanova, K., Lazer, D., Robertson, R. E., & Wilson, C. (2020). Misinformation in action: Fake news exposure is linked to lower trust in media, higher trust in government when your side is in power. *Harvard Kennedy School Misinformation Review*, *1*(4), 1–19. DOI: 10.37016/mr-2020-024

Olan, F., Jayawickrama, U., Arakpogun, E. O., Suklan, J., & Liu, S. (2022). Fake news on Social Media: The Impact on Society. *Information Systems Frontiers*, *1*(1), 1–16. DOI: 10.1007/s10796-022-10242-z PMID: 35068999

Panigrahi, S., & Singh, J. (2017). *RGICS BRIEF Deadly Combination of Fake News and Social Media*. https://www.rgics.org/wp-content/uploads/policy-issue-briefs/Policy-Brief-Deadly-Combination-of-Fake-News-and-Social-Media-September-2017.pdf

Poynter. (2024). *About IFCN*. Poynter. https://www.poynter.org/ifcn/about-ifcn/

Press Trust of India. (2019, February 5). *Microsoft survey: Indians are more likely to encounter online fake news*. https://www.business-standard.com/article/pti-stories/microsoft-survey-india-topping-fake-news-menace-globally-119020501427_1.html

Rocha, Y. M., de Moura, G. A., Desidério, G. A., de Oliveira, C. H., Lourenço, F. D., & de Figueiredo Nicolete, L. D. (2021). The impact of fake news on social media and its influence on health during the COVID-19 pandemic: A systematic review. *Journal of Public Health*, *1*(10). Advance online publication. DOI: 10.1007/s10389-021-01658-z PMID: 34660175

Sen, R., Naumann, K., & Murali, V. S. (2019, December 18). *The Impact of Digital Media on the 2019 Indian General Election*. Regional Programme Political Dialogue Asia. https://www.kas.de/en/web/politikdialog-asien/single-title/-/content/the-impact-of-digital-media-on-the-2019-indian-general-election

Singh, S. (2019). *The False Information Ecosystem in India*. https://toda.org/assets/files/resources/policy-briefs/t-pb-55_spandana-singh_the-false-information-ecosystem-in-india.pdf

Singh Bawa, J. (2024, July 17). *Opinion: Opinion | From Misinformation To Fraud, The Alarming Rise Of Deepfakes In India*. https://www.ndtv.com/opinion/from-misinformation-to-fraud-the-alarming-rise-of-deepfakes-in-india-6124014

Tamandehrou, A., & Khan, S. U. (2015). Assessing the importance of globalisation and new media technology in 21st century: An analytical overview. *International Journal of Multifaceted & Multilingual Studies*, *1*(4).

Tandoc, E. C.Jr. (2019). The facts of fake news: A research review. *Sociology Compass*, *13*(9), e12724. Advance online publication. DOI: 10.1111/soc4.12724

TOI News Desk. (2024, January 16). Around 80% first-time voters have encountered fake news on social media: Survey. *The Times of India*. https://timesofindia.indiatimes.com/india/fake-news-on-social-media-survey/articleshow/106899024.cms

University of Texas Arlington. (2023). *Subject and course guides: Quantitative and qualitative research: Understand what quantitative research is*. https://libguides.uta.edu/quantitative_and_qualitative_research/quant

Vargo, C. J., Guo, L., & Amazeen, M. A. (2017). The agenda-setting power of fake news: A big data analysis of the online media landscape from 2014 to 2016. *New Media & Society*, *20*(5), 2028–2049. DOI: 10.1177/1461444817712086

Watson, C. A. (2018). Information Literacy in a Fake/False News World: An Overview of the Characteristics of Fake News and its Historical Development. *International Journal of Legal Information*, *46*(2), 93–96. DOI: 10.1017/jli.2018.25

Woolley, S. (2022, July 18). *In Many Democracies, Disinformation Targets the Most Vulnerable*. Centre for International Governance Innovation. https://www.cigionline.org/articles/in-many-democracies-disinformation-targets-the-most-vulnerable/

ADDITIONAL READING

Barclay, D. A. (2020). *Fake News, Propaganda, and Plain Old Lies: How to Find Trustworthy Information in the Digital Age*. Rowman & Littlefield Pub Inc.

Baud, J. (2023). *Governing by Fake News: 30 Years of Fake News in the West*. Max Milo Editions.

Brotherton, R. (2020). *Bad News: Why We Fall for Fake News*. Bloomsbury Sigma. DOI: 10.5040/9781472962867

Giusti, S., & Piras, E. (2020). *Democracy and Fake News: Information Manipulation and Post-Truth Politics*. Routledge. DOI: 10.4324/9781003037385

Greifeneder, . (2020). *The Psychology of Fake News: Accepting, Sharing, and Correcting Misinformation*. Routledge. DOI: 10.4324/9780429295379

Rusbridger, A. (2021). *News and How to Use It: What to Believe in a Fake News World.* Canongate Books.

Sharma, A., & Kumar, S. (2022). *Fake News and Challenges in the Digital Era.* Evincepub Publishing.

Sood, G. (2023). *Fake News: Spot It, Stop It.* Penguin Business.

KEY TERMS AND DEFINITIONS

Artificial Intelligence: An interdisciplinary field within computer science focused on developing systems and algorithms capable of performing tasks that require human-like cognitive functions, such as learning, reasoning, and problem-solving. AI encompasses technologies like machine learning and neural networks, which enable automated systems to process and analyze vast amounts of data.

Censorship: The practice of suppressing or restricting access to information, ideas, or expressions by governmental or institutional authorities. Censorship is often implemented to control or limit content deemed objectionable, sensitive, or threatening to specific interests, thereby influencing public access to and perception of information.

Content Analysis: A research method employed to systematically analyze and interpret textual, visual, or audio materials. This technique identifies recurring patterns, themes, and underlying meanings within content, facilitating a deeper understanding of media narratives and their potential impact on audiences, commonly used in fields like media studies and communications.

COVID-19 Pandemic: A global health crisis triggered by the SARS-CoV-2 virus, which emerged in late 2019 and precipitated widespread illness, mortality, and socioeconomic disruption. The pandemic has led to significant changes in global health policies, emergency responses, and public health practices aimed at curbing the virus's spread.

Debunked Stories: Information or reports that have been conclusively disproven through detailed fact-checking and empirical evidence. These stories, once accepted as credible, are revealed as inaccurate or intentionally misleading, highlighting the effectiveness of verification processes in maintaining informational accuracy and integrity.

Digital Literacy: The skill set needed to proficiently navigate and utilize digital technologies and online platforms. This includes the ability to locate, evaluate, and create digital content, as well as understanding issues related to online privacy, security, and digital ethics.

Fact-Check Outlets: Specialized entities or platforms dedicated to the systematic verification of factual claims, statements, and news narratives. These organizations employ rigorous methodologies to assess the accuracy and truthfulness of information, thereby serving as a critical mechanism for maintaining the reliability of public information and countering misinformation.

Fake News: Intentionally fabricated or distorted information presented as factual news with the aim of misleading or manipulating public opinion. This phenomenon often leverages emotional, sensational, or provocative content to advance particular political, ideological, or commercial agendas, thus undermining the integrity of public discourse.

Fake News Trends: Analytical observations of the evolving patterns, dissemination methods, and impact of misinformation across various media platforms. These trends reveal how false information adapts and spreads, influencing public perception and behavior over time, and are crucial for understanding the dynamics of misinformation in contemporary media environments.

Media Literacy: The proficiency required to effectively access, analyze, evaluate, and produce media content across various platforms. Media literacy empowers individuals to critically assess the credibility and validity of information, fostering informed decision-making and enhanced engagement with the media landscape.

Section 2

The Power of Political Communication Lies in Its Propagation and Influence Permeating Society on a Global Scale

Chapter 6
Propaganda:
The Lifeblood of Terrorism and Extremism

Perry L. Lyle
https://orcid.org/0009-0009-2363-6005
Columbia College of Missouri, USA

Arthur Wayne Turner
Boone County S. O., USA

ABSTRACT

Propaganda is any strategic, rational, systematic force, and means of spreading information to pursue set goals and objectives having levels of prejudice, falsehoods, and distortions. This thinking frames broader psychological assumptions about the spread of information, reflecting core thinking about propaganda. Extremist propaganda is a highly effective dispersal medium in which terrorists and other actors who operate in the jihadist framework of disinformation use. High-impact graphic images serve as the emotional trigger to increase the potency of the message; vibrancy is. Extremists disseminate propaganda by virtual messaging, da'wah, journals, audio, and video files to recruit and enthuse sympathizers, political personalities, mujahideen, and soldiers of the cause. Messaging would all be of marginal consequence if extremists failed in adjudicating the instrumentality and ambitions of propaganda, achieving extensive dissemination and influence over people's hearts and minds. Propagandized information has constituted a force multiplier in reshaping worldviews and motivations.

PROBLEM STATEMENT

Propaganda is the lifeblood of communications across the globe for terrorist and extremist groups and governments of all kinds. It is what makes things 'go' and what powers the heart. Propaganda manipulates perceptions, pushes agendas, and persuades people at all levels of society, but it is essential for more than that. It creates narratives people believe in and can rally around, pulling at the heartstrings for emotional persuasion and ideological support. Terrorists and extremists use propaganda to recruit people, radicalize minds, legitimize operations, and justify violence. Governments use propaganda to control and legitimize policies and national causes. Moreover, it is easy to see how the line between

DOI: 10.4018/979-8-3693-7468-9.ch006

information and certain kinds of propaganda can get blurred, with all kinds of power centers carefully exerting control over 'the narrative.' Propaganda is weaponized communication.

With the advent of digital media, propaganda has become more sophisticated, reaching global audiences with unprecedented speed and efficiency. The relevancy of understanding propaganda cannot be overstated, as it plays a pivotal role in contemporary conflicts, political campaigns, and social movements. This chapter aims to examine the historical impacts, science, and politics of propaganda. At the same time, it may be self-evident: to place this all-purpose tool of persuasion center-stage so that we can better recognize it and resist it, thereby ensuring that globally, people can better identify the susceptible fodder for unscrupulous manipulators bent on fabricating a highly malleable and fully mobilizable public.

INTRODUCTION

To amplify their actions, terrorists and extremists rely heavily on media sources. While terrorist incidents may not always have a high number of casualties compared to other mass causes of death and injury or a major natural disaster or a pandemic, the media coverage these crimes receive creates a disproportionately substantial impact and is often referred to as a *theatrical* crime. The net propaganda benefit to the organizers is huge. To illustrate, a single mass shooting with casualties at a grade school in the United States goes viral and stays in the public's eye for days and weeks as media coverage dissects the cause and effect of the tragedy. Globally, the extensive coverage reaches a wide audience, exposing people to terrorist intentions and threats that they might not otherwise be aware of or a target of. Without this media attention, the public awareness and impact of extremists' acts would likely be significantly diminished Combs, C. (2022-07-29, p. 233). The media is only one subject of the terrorist or extremist target audience for being manipulated. The adage is, "If it bleeds, it leads.

Media's Amplification of Terrorist Propaganda

The media unintentionally boosts terrorist propaganda by offering extensive coverage which becomes a powerful force in present-day information environments. Research indicates that terrorists receive the mass media attention they desire through a well-documented symbiotic relationship White, J. (2020).

Studies show that Muslim-perpetrated terror attacks receive approximately 357% more media attention compared to attacks committed by other groups. Media outlets provide unequal attention to attacks which may lead to false impressions about their frequency and generate discriminatory beliefs according to Varela, A. (2019, May 23). Digital advances which speed up the news cycle intensify the media's function as a distributor of terrorist propaganda White, J. (2020).

The issue exists not with the media's decision to report on terrorism but with their reporting methods OCP Policy Center & Elshimi, M. (2018). When media outlets share violent extremist propaganda without proper analysis, they help promote extremist messages which extends their reach according to H. J. Ingram from the Australian National University (2017). The digital age demonstrates a significant amplification effect through social media platforms which enable quick dissemination of extremist content to worldwide audiences Shah, M. (2024, July 4).

Media outlets must employ responsible reporting practices that critically examine extremist propaganda while steering clear of sensationalist coverage White, J. (2020). Media organizations that follow these practices can break down terrorist propaganda's strategic framework instead of unintentionally boosting its message Ingram, H. J. & Australian National University. (2017).

Unregulated and unrestricted, the Internet provides a place whereby organizations such as terrorist groups can craft and disseminate their messaging forms of propaganda with ease. Terrorist groups tailor their pitch toward their agenda with seamless websites and other social media platforms. With the advent of AI, groups now provide a barrage of content 24 x 7 at their target interest. Their style of content is sophisticated digit words most often laced with Hollywood style videos complete with tricks, effects, and glamor that even top production artist must tip their hats to. ISIS is one of the most sophisticated groups harnessing some of the most successful recruitment propaganda Liberman, A. V., (2017-2018). By operating poly-sites, terrorism can promote propaganda in many forms from multiple sites having the capacity to "go-dark" at any given time and they pop up again from another country location. Intelligence agencies have extreme difficulty in the identification and monitoring of these ghost sites. Sites may be turned on and off like a light switch.

As an example, the ability for pro-western governments to suspend pro-ISIS media sites goes away when the organizations shut down operation only to quickly spring up again with a replacement. It represents a cat and mouse game that drains resources of legitimate governments. "The Islamic State of Iraq and Syria—also known as ISIS or ISIL—is a jihadist militant group and terrorist organization that formed in 1999" History.com Editors (2019, June 7). While the group has been weakened over the past few years, the organization is still very capable of launching horrific acts of terrorism against its enemies and particularly the West.

The Islamic State, (aka ISIS) has been skillful at grabbing worldwide media attention with shocking videos of beheadings of their intended victims. Along with the beheadings, the militant group infuses pro-jihadi songs called "nasheeds" in the content to help spread their messaging. "It's a catchy song [sic], admits Phillip Smyth, a researcher at the University of Maryland. "Lyrics aside – and the knowledge that the song is representing something very bad for the Middle East – it's a catchy tune".

RATIONAL AND LIMITATIONS

This chapter explores the complex relationship between technology, culture, and human behavior, focusing on the impact of terrorism and extremism promoted by propaganda. It provides a comprehensive analysis of how technology reshapes cultural norms, values, and practices, affecting communication patterns and identity formation. The chapter is of utmost importance to readers in the fields of technology, sociology, anthropology, and cultural studies. Balancing breadth with depth is a delicate task, and this chapter may lean more towards a broad overview rather than an in-depth analysis of each subject involved. Interested readers and researchers are encouraged to explore the vast amount of publicly available literature available on diverse subject matter.

The chapter has limitations. The rapidly evolving nature of technology may cause some discussions and examples to become outdated quickly, potentially affecting the relevance and applicability of the findings. The scope of the cultural contexts examined may not fully address all variations and nuances. The interdisciplinary approach may also pose challenges, as integrating insights from various fields may lead to a need for more depth in specific areas.

Lastly, the chapter relies on existing literature and case studies, which may introduce biases based on the availability and selection of sources. Future research with empirical data and longitudinal studies would provide a more robust understanding of the long-term effects of propaganda and the future use of technology on culture.

In conclusion, while this chapter offers valuable insights into the relationship between technology and culture, readers should be mindful of its limitations. Acknowledging these constraints allows for a more critical engagement with the content, paving the way for further research and discussion in this vital study area.

HISTORICAL CONTEXT

While the term propaganda may not be easily defined, most would agree that the word has negative connotations in the modern age. That does not necessarily have to be the case. In the ancient City of Athens great Greek scholars had incredibly wise ideas about City/State affairs and most scholars agree that *Ethos* was shaped through ideas here to last throughout the ages. These great men of Philosophy intentionally propagated their ideas for others to follow, especially their protégés. Propaganda today does not always have to be controversial or a matter that offends the mind, accessed from Historians.org. (n.d.) Ideologies and beliefs that are utilitarian in nature and considered good can be shaped to support broad interest and appeal. Of course, propaganda today is most often used in controversial matters, to spread disinformation and lies for hidden agendas. The search for truth appears to be ignored in our modern-day world.

Long before "Fake News," the Greeks had a lively set of ideas about truth. The philosopher Socrates argued that absolute Truth (*Sophia*) is knowable and that we communicate best when we communicate only that Truth. His student, Plato, went further, saying that one can arrive at the Truth through the method of dialectic—which meant a process of questioning and testing. Taken together, Socrates and Plato proposed that wisdom isn't [sic] based purely on possessing the "truth," but—rather ironically—on being aware of one's own ignorance of it Rangappa, A., and Mercieca, J. (2020, June 7).

Early History

Tyrannicides in Athens: The most notable instance is the assassination of Hipparchus by Harmodius and Aristogeiton in 514 BCE during the Panathenaic festival as seen by Teegarden, D. A. (2022, January 13). They aimed to kill the tyrant Hippias but ended up killing his brother. This act was later celebrated in Athens as a symbol of resistance against tyranny. This historical event reflects the complex political dynamics of the time and the use of violence for political ends, which can be seen as an early form of what we might today call terrorism. The use of propaganda evolved significantly throughout the ages, shaped by the prevailing political and religious climates, and the culture context of the different eras.

Early Religious Era

After the Roman Empire fell, three major religions—Christianity, Judaism, and Islam—flourished and vied for influence and control. Although not seen as a formal religion, Paganism was practiced during these times. Despite widespread belief, pagan practice in the Middle Ages was much more subtle and complicated than that. A cultural fabric as varied as Europe maintained a rich undercurrent of pagan ideas and rituals alongside the new faith, even though Christianity was widely adopted throughout the continent Dupres, L. (2024, January 14). The Crusades, starting in 1096 and lasting 200 years, saw Christian kings, nobles, soldiers, and knights attacking Muslim cities in Palestine to gain dominance. Christianity was the predominant religion across Europe's royal families, nobility, and most of the general population. Islam, established in 622 A.D., dominated the Middle East, and boasted a rich culture in religion, art, science, and urbanization Britannica, T. Information Architects of Encyclopaedia (2024, June 16).

Judaism, while a minority religion, consisted of tradespeople, merchants, and farmers. Paganism, common before the medieval era, involved the belief in gods residing in natural objects. Monasteries, founded in Egypt in the third century, dedicated their lives to serving God and supported themselves by offering goods and services to the public and the crown. These monasteries also produced some of the oldest books in Europe.

During the Middle Ages, Christian churches significantly influenced art and architecture by constructing grand cathedrals. These large buildings featured intricate woodwork, paintings, murals, tapestries, and sculptures. The Crusades occurred in waves as power shifted between Christians and Muslims, who often fought back to reclaim their territories. By 1291, the Crusades ended, and the crusading soldiers had returned home Britannica, T. Information Architects of Encyclopaedia (2024, June 16).

History also records that Europe fell into darkness due to a plague that ostensively changed medieval Europe. The Black Death, which occurred between 1347 and 1352 wiped out one-half of the population. It changed society and affected every aspect of those that survived, including the arts, government, religion, commerce, and culture. Religion became even more important to daily lives and for Europe's revival Mark, J. (2020, April 16).

Throughout the ages, propaganda has been artfully utilized by many in numerous created ways. Mans' abilities to sew ways of deceit and manipulation consisted of words, art, images, monuments to the kings, and other historical relics. Used to promote and conduct battles and war strategies, men of power such as Egyptian pharaohs learned how to operationalize technologies of their day. Ancient civilization in Egypt often took form in monumental architectures and sculptures to deify and glorify rulers as seen in the pyramids. In medieval times, propaganda was utilized to reinforce and ignite wars and to manipulate opponents. No historical scholars have understated the power of religious propaganda controls used during this era. The continent of Africa was making great strides in forging significant civilization of unique cultures.

The Medieval Period

During the medieval period, from the fifth to the late 15th century, the region now known as Nigeria was home to several prominent kingdoms and societies, each with a unique culture, governance, and contribution to the region's history. Some of the most notable kingdoms and societies include the Kanem-Bornu Empire, a powerful Islamic state that played a crucial role in trans-Saharan trade. "Kanem-Bornu empire also traded slaves to people in North Africa in exchange for war horses" Britannica, T. Editors of Encyclopedia (n.d.). Chieftains developed propaganda messaging to control and manipulate their populations. It was known for its military prowess, strategic trade routes, and diplomatic relations with other states in North Africa and the Middle East.

With the advent of the print revolution in the 15th century by Johannes Gutenberg, the dissemination of propaganda became revolutionized. Pamphlets, books, and posters became powerful tools for those with agendas to promote. Ideological, religious, and extremist messages could be widely disseminated. The Protestant Reformation illustrates just how powerful print propaganda had become in the mobilization of the masses. Martin Luther a German monk and professor [1483 – 1546] advocated the removal of the impurities and corruption from church institutions and more reliance on the teaching from the Holy Bible. This included printing the Bible in the language of the reader vs. Latin. Luther was excommunicate from the Catholic Church in 1521 Harvey, R. (2024, March 15). State propaganda and nation-states began to use propaganda to consolidate power exemplified by the new Spanish and French monarchies. Military leaders like Napoleon Bonaparte wielded propaganda extensively to legitimize his rule and to promote a nationalist fervor.

Modern Era

The Industrial Revolution would bring modern technologies and close the communication gaps between nations. The printing press gave capabilities for mass distribution of print communication like no other invention of the time. Through newspapers a whole new wave of mass communication became available. Newspapers could be used to harness propaganda in very deceitful ways for politicians, businesspeople, religious leaders, and others. Their agendas could now be promoted by endless attacks against opponents. Newspapers in competition began a practice of "yellow journalism" to sensualize news to achieve growth. This practice was the forerunner on what today is coined as "fake news."

In the United States, the young country saw even more dynamic changes in the rapidly growing population. America had been through a great civil war and was on the verge of completing its *Manifest Destiny*, Heidler, J. T. and Heidler, David S. (2024, May 28). With a massive influx on new immigrants, the country transformed from an agricultural economy to embrace the industrial revolution and shift from rural population centers to metropolitan centers. With many of its men folks off to Europe to fight in World War One, American social changes would now incorporate women voters and the alcohol probation era for the next 13 years, [1920 -1933]. Newspapers and radio stations would now take center stage not only at providing news but also including fake news and propaganda in messaging, primarily for the politicians of the day. WW1 and WW 2 raised the bar and used propaganda in unprecedented ways.

WW1 and WW2 marked the height of propaganda used by world governments. All governments can be seen from historical literature, music, print materials, films, posters, and the alike to promote and operationalize propaganda in their war efforts to demonize their enemies and garner support for their political positions, battles fought, and to mobilize their populations for recruitment of soldiers. These were desperate times and called for extreme measures to gain support.

Although President Wilson and Congress saw the need for the United States' entry into the global conflict, it was necessary to convince the American people of their need to support the war effort. This was not an easy task as the president had won re-election based on his promise to keep the United States out of the fighting. President Wilson and his administration developed a series of propaganda campaigns that focused on the patriotic duty of all Americans to back the war effort to defeat the enemy, thus enabling the preservation of democracy at home and abroad. On April 14, 1917, President Wilson established a propaganda organization called the Committee on Public Information (CPI) and appointed

George Creel, an investigative reporter and writer, as chair. The committee remained active until June 30, 1919, Delaware.gov. (n.d.)

Joseph Gobbles, [1987 - 1945] of Germany, took center stage at the onset of Hitler's regime building efforts. Gobbles crafted one of the most effective propaganda machines in history HistoryStaff.com (2019, June 7). A trusted and loyal confident of Adolf Hitler, the Nazi politician and philologist was at one time the district leader of Berlin. Later, the Chief propagandist of the Nazi party. Gobbles studied at the University of Heidelberg earning a doctorate in 1921. He was highly adaptive of crafting and using his position as head of the Third Riech's propaganda ministry for propagandizing through radio and film for motiving German people to believe in the great lie, that German woes laid at the hands of the Jews and Christian churches. All roads that led to the Jewish holocaust can be traced back to the propaganda machine created by Gobbles and Hitler's inner circle of henchmen. A new type of warfare would follow the close of WW2 and the new prosperity of the ages.

The end of World War 2 consolidated a huge power grab by the Soviet Union. Eastern Bloc nations fell to the commonest party's efforts to use the victory over Germany to build and consolidated a new empire. A new age of *Cold War* strategies would entail the use of propaganda to again mobilize the masses under the new regime and dictatorship Duda, A. (17 September 2022). The "Soviet empire" can be seen as *imperialist* through the lens of the soviet foreign policies and dissemination of propaganda world-wide. Their intent was to use political, economic, and military interventions for regime change of neighboring Eastern states such as: Eastern German, (fall of Berlin), Hungary (1956) Czechoslovakia in 1968, and Poland from 1980 to 1983. These states were referred to as Satellite States of the USSR. Additional Soviet adventurism included Cuba in the 1960s and Afghanistan form 19709 – 1989 Duda, A. (17 September 2022). The Ukrainian people remember a former Soviet leader, by the name of Joseph Stalin.

"The Ukrainian famine—known as the Holodomor, a combination of the Ukrainian words for "starvation" and "to inflict death"—by one estimate claimed the lives of 3.9 million people, approximately13 per cent of the population" according to Kiger, P. (2019, April 16). Stories tell of the brutality imposed by Stalin as he sought to punish the Ukrainians for their desire for independence and the ability to feed their own through family-owned farms, Stalin's *policy* known as collectivism. History today is recording more of the truths about two of the world's most sinister and evil dictators, Adolf Hitler, and Joseph Stalin. In summary, the combined death toll from the policies and actions of Hitler and Stalin is estimated to be between twenty-three million and thirty-seven million people.

The Cold War between the U. S. and the Soviet Union lasted many decades before a thaw in relations took place. The best period of "detente" was when Premier Gorbachev (USSR) and President Reagan, [1980s] were both leaders of their respective counties. The old Soviet Union collapsed costing them to lose grip on several former Satellite countries under their dominance, to include East Berlin, Germany. As Vladimir Putin came to power in Russia, as former KGB officer, Putin's ambition was to again rebuild Russia back to its former prestige and world stage actor with all its former military might.

Technological Era

During the 1980s, computer technology became available globally, primarily for government and military usage. Computer usages expanded rapidly along with the means to mass communicate digitally. Old analog telephones went by the wayside and the new era was dubbed the "information age" and later the "digital age." Propaganda usage took on a whole fresh look. Hybrid warfare has "gained significant currency and relevance in recent years as states employ non-state actors and information technology to subdue their adversaries during or—more importantly—in the absence of a direct armed conflict" Bilal, A. (2021, November 21).

Today, approximately 70 percent of the population on earth has access to some form of computer technology and the means to communicate via the Internet; many from the palm of their hands by 'smart phones', laptop computers, and other digital recording equipment. Asymmetrical warfare, (unconventional tactics, such as terrorism), is the modern way to attack your enemies and adversaries. The world-wide web created a seismic change in the way people conduct their daily activities. Cyber-attacks happen routinely by nation states, proxy states, terrorist organizations, and a multitude of extremist groups bend on disrupting opponents. Hybrid Warfare involves a combination of traditional military tactics and propaganda, often blurring the lines between truth and misinformation. The use of "deep fakes," [the art and science of deceptive video editing] has now become the most sophisticate psychological means to render chaos to your adversary, say a local politician. Artificial intelligence as the modern-day game changer.

AI is revolutionizing our lives on a daily basis. This new technology is being self-promoting technology that will supersede human thought capabilities in the next five years. "The pernicious advantage of computational propaganda is in enabling the rapid distribution of large amounts of content, sometime personalized in order to foll users into thinking that messages originate in their extended network of family and friends" Woodley, S., and Howard, P. (2019).The use of automated social actors (AI) robots can be used to bolter particular politicians and policy positions supporting candidates in chatrooms and on other platforms used the politicians to communicate with the public.

THEORETICAL FOUNDATIONS AND KEY CONCEPTS

PsyOps

The Weaponization of propaganda in modern times is a powerful tool used by ideologs, extremists, terrorists, government, politicians, individuals, and groups of sorts, underpins the theoretical concepts of this chapter. Propaganda, as a strategic tool in [Psyops], uses many means to disseminate information to shape specific goals, influence behaviors, and mobilize individuals towards specific goals. The power of Psychological Operations, commonly referred to as (PsyOps) has been of keen interest to both legitimate and non-state government organizations for years. Intelligence agencies have developed sophisticated and multifaceted tools designed to manipulate perception and behaviors of a wide variety channels, continuously adapting to feedback, and studying results to become more influential of target manipulation. According to Dr. Perry Lyle, Ph.D., one primary objective of a terrorist organizations' goals is to instill fear, psychological anxiety, and cast doubts of their target to provide safety and security for inhabitants. The government is seen as impotent and loses authority and creditability in governance of their people FP Team (2023, September 5). A special disinformation and propaganda campaign by the U.S.S.R. directed toward the U. S. in the 1980s was successful.

The U.S.S.R. and the international security operations of the East German government (Stasi) along with the Soviet's KGB launch an Anti-American campaign against the United States in the 1980s suggesting that the U. S. government's bio-chemical warfare center at Ft. Derick, (Maryland) had been responsible for the creation of HIV/AIDs and was responsible for its distribution of the disease to various countries, in particular, African nations.

The Soviet Union used the campaign to undermine the United States' credibility, foster Anti-Americanism, to isolate America abroad, and create tensions between host countries and the U.S. over the presence of American military bases (which were often portrayed as the cause of AIDS outbreaks in local populations) Globalsecurity.org (1987, August 1).

Governments will make use of forged documents and special reports, and other disinformation materials to make it plausible that such activities or events had occurred. The campaign was referred to as Operation Denver and also known as Operation "INFECKTION." The Soviet Union's Communist party operationalized all forms of mass media to include state run radio, television, newspapers, and other mass media outlets to disseminate the propaganda. In the aftermath of this disinformation campaign, a poll taken in the U. S. in 1992 showed that an alarming 15 percent of Americans believe that the U. S. had created the virus *Boghardt*, T. (December 2009). In 2005 a Rand and Oregon State University study revealed that 50 percent of African Americans believed that AIDs was human-caused, 12 percent believed that is had been spread by the CIA, and that 15 percent felt that the virus targeted Black people for genocide. PsyOps may also be viewed as political warfare.

Table 1. Juxtaposition Illustration for Propaganda: Tactics, Styles, Materials, and Content

Tactics	Influencer	Objective
Emotional Appeals	Fear, anger, and pride	Emotional Responses
Misinformation and Disinformation	Information	Confuse and or manipulate public perceptions
Echo Chamber	Closed Communication Networks	Reinforce Organization Messaging
Victim Narratives	Disguised Victimization	Gain Sympathy and Support
Glorification of Violence	Celebrate Acts of Violence and Martyrdom	Claim heroic Status
Dehumanization of Opponents	Depicting enemies as less than human	Justify Violence Including Children
Call to Action	Urging Supporters to Engage in Specific Tasks	Raising Money, Recruitment, Engagement of Violence
Manipulation or Religious Beliefs	Ideological Beliefs	Twisting Religious texts or Ideological Principles for Justifications
Local Grievances	Exploiting Local Issues	Gain Support and Legitimacy
Styles	**Influencer**	**Objective**
Narrative	Story telling	Compelling stories that Resonate with Target
Visual Imagery	Powerful Images	Videos, and symbols to convey messages quickly/ effectively
Music and Poetry	Incorporates Culture elements	Songs, Poems, and others makes messages relatable
Humor and Satire	Using humor to Ridicule Opponents	Extremist Ideas Become More Palatable
Profession Production	High Quality Videos, Magazines, and Online Content	More Credible and Sophisticated
Grassroots Aesthetics	Low Budget and Amateur cooking	Creates a Sense of Authenticity for Grassroot Support
Materials	**Influencer**	**Objective**

continued on following page

Table 1. Continued

Videos	Documentaries, Clips of Speeches, and Footage of Attacks	Training, Again Sympathy, Support, and Stream Live
Social Media Posts	Tweets, Facebook posts, Instagram Images, You Tube, and Tik Tok	Messaging, Spreading News Globally in Nanoseconds
Pamphlets and Flyers	Printed materials Distribution in Communities	Messaging of Content, Low-budget Resources
Online Magazines	Digital Publications with Articles, Interviews, and other Propaganda Pieces	Example: Inspire Magazine; Training, and Call to Action Support, Recruitment
Books and Essays	Long-form, Deeper Content for Ideological Justifications	Gain Support for Agenda, Political Manifestos
Podcasts	Recorded Messages from Leaders and Ideologues	Digital Messaging aided by AI Responses
Website and Blogs	Dedicated Online Platforms for Disseminating Content	Reach Audiences 24 x 7
Graffiti and Street Art	Public Displays of Slogans, Symbols, and Messages	Slogans, Inspire Hate and Anger for Victimization, and Martyrdom
Content	**Influencer**	**Objective**
Justification of Ideology	Explaining and Rationalization	Convenience other of Beliefs
Success Stories	Highlighting Successful Operations	Perceived Growth of Movement and Advocacy
Enemy Atrocities	Showcasing Real or Fabricate Crimes and Deaths	Inspire Movement, Justification for Retaliations
Historical Narratives	Reinterpreting History to Distort and Support	Claims of Legitimacy and Promote Victimization
Religious or Ideological Teachings	Tests and Sermons	Religious Ideological Validation
Personal Stories	Testimonies from Group Members	Recruitment, Validation of Causes and Claims
Threats and Warnings	Issuing Threats to Enemies	Alert Members to Consequences – Promote Fear and Doom to Opposition
Strategic Goals	Outline Short-term and Long-term Goals	Provide Sense of Direction to Members. Help in Recruitment Campaigns
Calls for Unity	United We Stand – Divide We Fall	Building Solidarity Among Followers. Unity Against Oppressors
Declarations and Manifestos	Formal Statements and Religious Edicts as in Fatwas	Contains Objective, Directions, and Calls to Action

The Cultivation Theory/PSY/OPS

The strategies of the cultivation theory integrated with uses of mass media, particularly television, explores the lasting effects of media consumption and hypothesizes that individuals who spend more time watching television tend to perceive the real world through a lens aligned with prevalent depictions and messaging. While the original hypothesis originated out of the immense amount of time viewers relied on T. V. for their daily content of news, sports, and other forms of entertainment, scholars believe that much of the psychological manipulation may be transferred to social media platforms today.

America finds itself in a strategic age where numerous actors are conducting operations combining across levels and domains of political, informational, military, and economic measures to sway, compel, intimidate, or otherwise dually compromise or undercut US or friends' and allies' interests; much of this is routinely identified by the term 'political warfare.' A "death by a thousand cuts," originating in ancient Chinese history, metaphorically refers to a gradual, relentless decline or deterioration caused by a series of minor setbacks or challenges. An Asymmetrical warfare/PSYOPs tactic deployed by Osama bin Laden against the West.

The previous illustration examined political warfare as it is conducted today, by state and non-state actors, and offered recommendations on the most effective means by which the US government and its allies and partners can pursue or counter this kind of competitive hostility for US ends and US interests Robinson, L, et al. (2018). Despite the problem above, which is still with us today, PSYOPs are an essential non-lethal force multiplier in both war and peace.

ASYMMETRICAL WARFARE, TERRORISM, EXTREMISM, AND PROPAGANDA

If some is coming to kill you, rise up and kill him first – "Sanhedrin 72a". According to Lt. Colonel Arthur W. Wayne Turner, M. S., US Army [Retired], asymmetrical warfare, unconventional strategies, cyber-attacks, and emerging technologies will continue to be impactful in shaping terrorists and extremist actions for the 21st century and beyond. Efforts to reap the propaganda benefits using intimidation, and other forms of hostilities will be on centerstage. Some of the significant strategies will include:

1. Asymmetrical/ Hybrid Warfare:
    - Asymmetrical warfare refers to conflicts with a significant disparity in military power and capabilities between opposing forces. Terrorist groups often engage in asymmetrical warfare because they lack the conventional military strength to confront state actors directly. According to Lyle, Iran, and other rouge nations such as Norh Korea will use proxies to carry-out terrorists' activities against the West. Iran has been utilizing Hamas, (Palestinian nationalist and Islamist movement), and the Lebanese militant group Hezbollah, (Party of God), its proxy war against Israel since the attack on March 7, 2023, from Britannica, T. Editors of Encyclopedia (2024, June 14).
    - Terrorist organizations will continue to exploit the advantages of asymmetrical warfare, such as blending into civilian populations, using hit-and-run tactics, and targeting soft targets to maximize their impact while minimizing their vulnerabilities. Remember, "lone wolves' are the hardest for western democracies to detect.
    - To deal with these uneven and often blurred strategies, governments and anti-terrorism groups must change their plans and focus on gathering information, stopping people from becoming radicalized, and making their country safer. Legitimate government leaders need to apply ample resources by developing effective counterintelligence strategies and a hybrid form of solutions that include unconventional methodologies.
2. Unconventional Strategies:
    - Terrorist groups may employ unconventional strategies to achieve their objectives, such as psychological warfare, cyberattacks, and economic disruption. Disruption of advisory's digital communication systems is a prime weaponized tactic. These methods can create widespread fear and instability without resorting to traditional violence. Propaganda techniques aided by AI will continue to evolve into strategies used by terrorist actors such as Hezbollah, al Quada, and Hamas.

- To stop unconventional strategies like cyberattacks, and hacking, counterterrorism efforts need to use a broader range of methods, such as sharing intelligence and working with other countries to deal with the root causes of terrorism.

3. Emerging Technologies:
    - Emerging technologies, such as drones, artificial intelligence, and biotechnology, can provide terrorist groups with new tools and capabilities. Drones, for example, can be used for surveillance, reconnaissance, and even conducting attacks, such as those being used by Hamas in the on-going conflict in the Mid East. "Hezbollah has stepped up its use of drones to attack Israeli military positions, while Israel has hit back with targeted strikes against the militants" according to AFP (2024, June 12). This follows the terrorist organization raining down rockets on Israel aimed at causing mass destruction and casualties. Most experts agree that these actions were orchestrated by Iran's military leadership.
4. State Actors:
    - Governments and other adversaries such as China have found it convenient to attack other countries directly, but in most cases like Iran against Israel, by using proxies, such as Hamas. In the case of China, PRC has found that by providing the drug fentanyl and the precursor ingredients to manufacture fentanyl to Mexico, the PRC can wage an under-the-table campaign against the U. S.
    - Congress members are accusing China of asymmetric war against the United States due to the influx of Chinese fentanyl. The drug enforcement agency estimates that 90% of fentanyl comes from Chinese companies, which are subsidized and paid for by the Chinese Communist Party. China sends precursor chemicals to Mexico, which are processed and manufactured into synthetic opioids by Mexican drug cartels. The fentanyl crisis is not an area of dispute, but China claims it is an American domestic issue. In 2022, over 100,000 Americans died from overdoses in the United States, and fentanyl poisoning became the leading cause of death for Americans aged 18 to 45. Prescription opioids accounted for 44% of the decline in labor force participation among men in asymmetric warfare. China is accused of exploiting America's appetite for illicit drugs and weaponizing fentanyl. The Opium Wars, which began in the mid-19th century, led to China's "Cyber Century of humiliation a day" and stifled international efforts. The influx of fentanyl has become deeply ingrained in foreign diplomacy today, with some Americans believing China is the primary source of fentanyl in the United States Task & Purpose. (2023, November 5).
5. Propaganda and Recruitment:
    - The Internet and social media platforms have provided terrorist organizations with powerful engines for propaganda, recruitment, and radicalization. Online content can quickly reach a global audience, making it easier for groups to spread their ideologies and attract new members. Terrorists make use of their abilities to pop-up websites only to go-dark at a moment's decision frustrating intelligence agencies in their monitoring activities.
    - Counterterrorism efforts must focus on countering online radicalization and propaganda through initiatives that promote counter-narratives, monitor online activity, and cooperate with technology companies to remove extremist content.
    - Governments and law enforcement agencies will need to develop strategies and technologies to detect and mitigate the potential threats posed by emerging technologies. This may in-

clude developing counter-drone systems, monitoring online communications, and regulating the sale and use of specific technologies.

6. International Cooperation:
    - Asymmetrical warfare, unconventional strategies, and emerging technologies transcend national borders. Therefore, international cooperation among governments and organizations will be crucial in addressing these challenges effectively.
    - Multinational efforts to share intelligence, coordinate responses, and implement joint strategies will play a vital role in combating terrorism in the 21st century.
7. U. S. Domestic Terrorism and Extremism
    - Extremism in the United States is a complex and multifaceted phenomenon that encompasses a range of ideologies and actions that fall outside the mainstream political and social norms. It is important to note that extremism can manifest in various forms and is not limited to any group or belief system. Here is a summary of extremism in the United States:

    A. Political Extremism:

    - Right-Wing Extremism: This includes groups and individuals who hold far-right ideologies, such as white supremacy, anti-government sentiments, and extremist nationalism. Some notable examples include the Proud Boys, Oath Keepers, and various white supremacist organizations. Extremist often incorporate racism and ethnic hate as part of their justification to strike out against other individuals and or groups.
    - Far-right extremism has spread extensively across online platforms. Flourishing within echo chambers, these groups propagate different types of online and offline actions and advance their hateful ideologies to a wide-ranging audience. This chapter highlights the issues surrounding far-right extremism, which distinguishes it from terrorism and examining its contemporary digital manifestations. Importantly, it sheds light on how far-right groups utilize online platforms for communication, radicalization, and on-ground actions, relying on alternative truths, misinformation, conspiracy theories, fashion, and memes to connect with like-minded individuals. The chapter also addresses content moderation challenges and the impact of rising populism in today's political climate, which fuels societal divisions and uncertainty.
    - Left-Wing Extremism: On the opposite end of the spectrum, there are left-wing extremist groups that advocate for radical social and political change. Antifa, for instance, is a loosely organized movement that opposes fascism and racism through direct action, sometimes involving violent confrontations.
    - Left wielding extremist with their patented contentious ideologies in many cases would rather bring about change with scorched earth policies that destroy the freedoms and liberties of others for their own benefit.

    B. Religious extremism

    - Religious extremism can be found among various religious groups in the U.S. Some individuals or minor factions within religious communities may hold extremist beliefs and engage in acts of violence or terrorism in the name of their faith. Examples include extremist interpretations of Islam or fringe Christian groups.

In summary, the evolving nature of terrorism in the 21st century will require adaptive and multi-dimensional counterterrorism strategies. To effectively counter the threats that asymmetrical warfare, unconventional methods, and innovative technologies pose, governments, law enforcement agencies, and international organizations must remain alert, constantly change their strategies, and invest in technology and intelligence Combs, C. (2023 pgs. 460-493).

LONEWOLF ATTACKS IN THE UNITED STATES

"The joint report from the Federal Bureau of Investigation and the Department of Homeland Security shows 2019 was "the most lethal year" for *domestic violent extremist* attacks since 1995 – with 32 people killed, 24 of them by White supremacists. The report focuses on data from 2017-2019" Wild, W. and Sands, G. (2021, May 15). DHS and the FBI conduct thousands of domestic terrorism investigations against terrorist organizations and domestic extremism organizations on America soil each year. Motivations are often brewed from radicalized individuals with a seething hatred against the government institutions. Propagandized conspiratorial theories help fuel the radicalized cause.

Political disagreements within the United States could present opportunities for **DVEs** to engage in violence against individuals perceived to have opposing ideologies, prominent political or public figures, or members of the media covering these events," the agencies wrote, referring to domestic violent extremists (2021, May 15).

Government officials note that the lone-wolf attack is the most difficult form of a terrorist attacks to detect and prevent. Usually well planned, with no warning or social footprint to detect, the perpetrators can with little cost and with an abundance of online information, organize their attack.

Unfortunately, President Joe Biden's feckless immigration policies have allowed millions of illegal immigrants to cross the U. S. borders, particularly, the U. S. southern border, unfetter, and unscreened. Illustrating the need for stricter immigration policies and to curtail the massive number of illegals crossing our borders was the arrest and detention of eight men form Tajikistan that Immigration and Customs Enforcement (ICE) claims to have potential ties to ISIS out of central Asia. The men were pickup in New York, Philadelphia, and Los Angeles demonstrating how quickly and easily these "clean skins" individuals were able to freely move about the U. S. once in according to Ainsley, J., Winter, T., Blankstein, A., and Planas, A. (2024, June 11). Using the CBP One app, created by the Biden administration to easy efforts for those seeking asylum, one of the men crossed the border in the 2023 booking an appointment for asylum inside the U. S. These adventurous actions use an inordinate amount of law enforcement resources in protecting America's citizens and interest.

The FBI's Joint Terrorism Task Force monitors potential terrorist threats and have had a focus on threats originating out of central Europe. A number or recent of innocent American citizens by undocumented immigrants crossing the southern borders has forced the Biden administration to take increased enforcement actions against those that are deemed to be potential threats. Biden is running against in arch enemy, former Donald Trump, in the 2024 presidential election with showing the Biden lack confidence by the American majority for border control.

Significant Case Reviews

Preceding the 9/11 tragedy in America, The United States was shaken by a horrific terrorist attack by two of its own citizens and one who had served his country in the armed forces. Home-grown terrorism was the new dawn from the massive carnage left in the wake of the Oklahoma City bombing occurring on April 19, 1995 (History.com staff, 2009). Using a rental truck, Timothy McVeigh parked rental in front of the Alfred P. Murrah Federal Building, setting off the truck bomb causing 168 deaths and injured victims scores. A right-wing radical extremist, McVeigh had been sentenced to death and was executed in 2001 by lethal injections administered while in a federal prison in Terre Haute, Indiana. A co-conspirator, Terry Nichols, was convicted and is serving life without the possibility of parole. McVeigh's motivations and propaganda against the U. S. government.

McVeigh has espoused extreme hatred for the U. S. government and particularly against the ATF for their actions against private citizens at Ruby Ridge and for the siege and illegal killings against the religious cult membership at Waco. His anti-government sentiments included protested foreign policies that he advocated has caused numerous innocents to be killed in foreign lands by the military. For these causes, he propagandized that his actions were justified at Oklahoma City in 1995. McVeigh was radicalized while serving in the military himself. While in the Army, McVeigh met Nichols and Michael Fortier. Each shared a common interest in survivalist techniques and training. The men bonded on their penchant for survivalist interest and later joined a survivalist group based in Michigan. Michael Fortier, who had known of McVeigh's bombing plan, was convicted, and received a reduced sentence testifying on the government's behalf. Nineteen young children located in a daycare center for employees died that day.

The event was the worst terrorist attack on U. S. soil before 9/11 (History.com staff, 2009). Following the tragedy, undertook a massive review of all government buildings to place restrictions on parking near facilities, including erecting barriers and adding layers of protection against future bombing attempts.

Figure 1. Other Lone Wolf Attacks on U. S. Soil

Perpetrators	Location in U. S.	Summary	Date
Eastern			
Dzhokar & Temerin Tsarnaev, (brothers) Mid-Eastern	Boston, MA	Bombing - Brothers were self-raticalized terrorist that used Inspire online al-Qaeda magazine to construct pressure cooker bombs that killed 5, injured 281 Boston Marathon event including 17 that lost limbs from the Islamic motivated attack	4/15/2013
Dillen Roof, white male	Charleston, SC	Shooting - killed 9 Africian American worshipers while attending Emanuel Episcopel Church Bible Study. Lone wolf style attack. White xxtremist motivation	6/17/2015
Syed Rizman Farook /Tasheen Malik, Mid-Eastern, (married couple)	San Bernardino, CA	Shooting- Attacked occurred during a holiday lunch. 16 killed, including the two perpetrators. Islamic terrorism motivation.	12/2/2015
Omar Mateen, Mid-Eastern	Orlando, FL	Shooting - 49 killed and 50 injuried at the Pulse Nightclub bar, known to cater to LGBTQ customers. Islamic terrorism motivation.	6/12/2016

Worth, K. (2016, July 14).

In recent times, our societal landscape has included the portrayal of uniformed police and military as key villains to be targeted and high-velocity firearms as the attacker's weapon of choice. The research shows that the typical lone-wolf terrorist is an unemployed, single white male who is older, less educated, and more prone to mental illness. Radicalization by propaganda.

The radicalization model explains the process by which lone wolf terror begins with personal and political grievances that build into the identification of an enabler, the broadcasting of terrorist intent, and, finally, a triggering event. For the law enforcement and intelligence communities, detecting and preventing lone-wolf terror requires a comprehensive understanding of these processes. Broadcasting intent is essential since the lone wolf seeks to lift his cause into the public's consciousness through spoken statements, threats, screeds and broadsides, e-mails, texting, and videotaped proclamations Worth, K. (2016, July 14). ISSI has recently been calling for more lone wolf attacks against the West and has been funneling operative into U. S. homeland across the Mexican border.

In June 2024, the Al-Azaim Foundation, an unofficial pro-Islamic State (ISIS) media group linked to the Islamic State Khorasan Province (ISKP), published posters in English on the pro-ISIS Rocket Chat server, rallying lone wolves to continue to adhere to ISIS's agenda of violence and encouraging attacks in the West against Christians and Jews.

On June 22, 2024, the Al-Azaim Foundation published a poster titled “O Muwahhid [Monotheist] Who Follows the Sunnah of The Prophet!” The image depicts a hooded operative watching U.S. and Israeli flags go up in flames. The text on the poster read:

“Set fire to the towns of the Crusaders and the Jews and make them one of the fiery towns.”

It continued: “Do not underestimate a match you light. Beware of things that put yourself in danger. Take the necessary security. Put your trust in Allah. Turn them into towns that will destroy the disbelievers and strike fear into their hearts” See Figure [02. a] Appendices; sourced from Rocket.Chat, June 22, 2024.

We will become more aware of the terror threat that lone wolf terrorists pose as a result of their pathological intensity and desire to kill both themselves and others in large numbers. Focusing on the threat that lone wolf terrorism poses may prove to be a unique advantage.

ETHICAL CONSIDERATIONS

Propaganda can raise questions about ethics. While using propaganda does not in itself involve anything wrong, spreading falsehoods, skewing valuable information and dissent are potentially ethically wrong, and propaganda has been argued to be incompatible with a free and democratic process by undermining individual autonomy Bjola, C. (2018). Recall that the Nazis propagandizing in the Second World War and Americans propagandizing in the Cold War, to name a few examples, have faced scrutiny for their ethics Black, J. (2001). Do remember, though, that context is important: propagandizing might be acceptable in wartime or in a political campaign for the sake of boosting morale or getting people valuable information about a special situation, although effectiveness should not disrupt ethics badly. Collective thoughts by the author:

Therefore, the message of media ethics is threefold:

1. Propaganda is ubiquitous and dangerous.
2. The media needs to adequately police propaganda in modern political campaigns and inform the electorate about substantive policy issues, such as Trump-era politics versus the Deep State. Think about your own confirmation biases.
3. It becomes incumbent upon individuals to educate themselves so they may vote in an informed way.

Citizens must demand more of their candidates, the media, and themselves.

Ethical Considerations in Terrorism and Extremism Research

The study of terrorism and extremism raises significant ethical challenges that researchers and policymakers must navigate carefully. A key consideration is striking the appropriate balance between security measures and individual privacy rights Conway, M. (2021). While governments have a duty to protect their citizens from terrorist threats, it's crucial that counter-terrorism powers do not infringe on fundamental freedoms and civil liberties. The role of whistleblowers associated with propaganda and extremism should not be dismissed.

Whistleblowers have played a pivotal role in exposing possible government overreach and sparking public debate on the ethics of surveillance and national security practices. In recent U. S. history, two prominent examples illustrate this impact:

Edward Snowden

In 2013, Edward Snowden, a former NSA contractor, leaked classified documents revealing the existence of mass surveillance programs conducted by U.S. intelligence agencies *Edward Snowden: A 'Nation' interview | The Nation*. (2015, June 29). His disclosures exposed:

The scale of data collection on American citizens
Cooperation between tech companies and intelligence agencies
International surveillance activities

Snowden's actions ignited a global conversation about privacy rights in the digital age and led to reforms in surveillance laws *Edward Snowden: A 'Nation' interview | The Nation*. (2015, June 29). While some view him as a traitor, others consider him a hero who sacrificed his freedom to defend civil liberties The National Whistleblower Center. (2021, February 23).

Chelsea Manning

Chelsea Manning, a former U.S. Army intelligence analyst, leaked hundreds of thousands of classified documents to WikiLeaks in 2010 Wikipedia contributors. (2025, January 7). Her disclosures included:

Diplomatic cables revealing sensitive communications
Military logs from the Iraq and Afghanistan wars
Videos showing potential war crimes

Manning's leaks shed light on military operations and foreign policy decisions, prompting debates about government transparency and accountability in wartime Allyn, B. (2017, November 30). Her actions resulted in court-martial and imprisonment but also raised questions about the ethics of classifying information that could be in the public interest of Wikipedia contributors. (2025, January 7).

As we have seen, the impact on policy and public perception can be broad considering the revelations by Snowden and Manning and their far-reaching consequences. In fact, Snowden's disclosures led to the UDA Freedom Act, which has placed some limits of bulk data collection by intelligence agencies *Edward Snowden: A 'Nation' interview | The Nation*. (2015, June 29).

The above examples and discussions provide a more nuanced exploration of the ethical dimensions of terrorism and extremism research, as well as the complex interplay between mechanisms propaganda and how government collects data for prevention of terrorism, improvements in security, privacy, and government accountability in the digital age. The treatment of whistleblowers has become a battleground for competing narratives as the government strives to balance national security with civil liberties.

IMPLICATIONS FOR PRACTICE KNOWLEDGE

When thinking about practicing knowledge in the context of propaganda, extremism, or terrorism, it is helpful to consider the ethical obligations and the strategic options available. The following has some implications:

Knowing the tools of propaganda: successful counterterrorism (CT), that counters the manipulative pull of terrorist narratives must be built on knowledge about the techniques employed in radicalization and recruitment, including emotional appeals, misinformation, and simplification. Practice understanding in this regard would support the design and use of counter-narratives and educational programs to expose the deception of terrorist narratives and provide alternative information that dismantles myths Helmus, T., & Bodine-Baron, E. (2020, September 11).

Ethical Issues: The empirical work and practice on the study of terrorism and extremism involve important ethical considerations. The balance between security and privacy and avoiding any counter-terrorism powers that infringe on individual rights and freedoms must be considered. The prevention of censorship in the free world has always been a cornerstone of a free society absent of government involvement.

Prevention and intervention: Understanding practice knowledge is essential for creating prevention and intervention programs and curricula that properly assess risk factors associated with radicalization—and, ultimately, with violence—and support structures and measures that help people resist the influence of extremist ideologies. These include community engagement programs, online monitoring, and mental health support.

Policy and regulation: Practice knowledge can inform policymaking and promote the formation of laws and rules that respond to the underlying causes and symptoms of extremism and terrorism, from policy on internet governance to counter-terrorism efforts through international cooperation accessed from Countering and Exposing Terrorist Propaganda and Disinformation. (n.d.).

Training and Education: Frontline professionals, such as policemen, social workers, teachers, and community leaders, need to be trained using emerging practice-based knowledge on radicalization, especially how extremist groups recruit and root their cause and the importance of responding early at the lowest possible level.

Promoting practice knowledge: Research on persuasion and propaganda has implications for building societal resilience toward extremism and propaganda. Strategies that encourage critical thinking skills, media literacy, and community cohesion can help societies become more resistant to and resilient against terrorist ideologies, strategies, and messaging.

In short, the application of practice knowledge to propaganda, extremism, and terror should not be defensive (we'll pursue the terrorists, we'll crush the jihadists, we'll show them who's tough) but forward-looking, preventative, educational, and ethically committed.

CONCLUSION

Propaganda as seen from ancient societies on through to modern times has been used to message and persuade people toward varying perceptions, to influence behaviors, and mobilize individuals, politicians, governments, non-state actors, groups, and others towards specific goals. Early on in history, technology did not exist for the rapid and universal dissemination of propaganda. Nonetheless, propaganda was used to influence and manipulate people (targets) and the use was effective. Intertwined with 'yellow journalism' or fake news in America during the early twentieth century, propaganda became more powerful as a tool for those with political agendas. A seismic shift occurred in World War 1 and 2 that saw countries using propaganda effectively to recruit and motivate their populations toward war and to demonize their enemies.

This chapter has explored various strategies and ethical considerations when addressing the complex challenge of counterterrorism and extremism, particularly propaganda and radicalization. Joseph Gobbles, [1987 - 1945] of Germany, took center stage at the onset of Hitler's regime building efforts. [See appendices, illustration – figure 01 a.] Gobbles crafted one of the most effective propaganda machines in history HistoryStaff.com (2019, June 7). Gobbles as a trusted confident of Adolf Hitler, along with Hitler's henchmen, oversaw the propaganda machine that would be utilized in persuading German leaders and their countrymen toward the extermination of Jews as one of the prime villains behind Germany's economic woes and suffering. Today's terrorist organizations use lessons learned from the Nazi's propaganda successes to promote their agendas.

Terrorist organizations effectively use social media and disinformation to amplify their influence and recruit members. Groups like ISIS have historically utilized high-quality content to project power and attract followers. However, their capabilities have diminished over time due to more stringent controls by social media platforms. To counter these narratives, initiatives like the Global Engagement Center (GEC) work globally to analyze and disrupt extremist propaganda by collaborating with local and state-level partners to provide alternative narratives, including those from former extremists and community leaders – Global Engagement Center - Dept. of State (2023, March 22). How propaganda is used over the Internet, on social media platforms, and other means for recruitment and radicalization is always of research interest.

Dr. Paul Gill, a researcher at the University College of London who has collected a database of more than 100 'lone wolf' attacks in Europe and the US since 1990, has said it is as pointless to try to draw a single profile of a lone wolf attacker as it is to draw a profile of a generic criminal. 'What arsonists are interested in and what influences them is very different for sexual offenders and burglars,' he said in an online lecture in 2015. He also suggested that there might be variations in the psychological profiles of far-right extremists, ISIS supporters, and "single-issue" radicals who support a single political cause, such as the environment or abortion. Like the Patriot Act following 9/11, (2001), new laws and methods have to be continuously updated and implemented to counter threats stemming from U. S. adversaries.

Executive Order 13721 (n.d.) On March 14, 2016, U. S. President, Berack Obama signed Executive Order 13721, which established the Global Engagement Center (GEC) whose mission is to coordinate, integrate, and synchronize Government wide communication activities directed at foreign audiences abroad. Its goal is to counter the messaging and diminish the influence of international terrorist organizations, including the Islamic State of Iraq and the Levant ISIL (ISIS) and al Qaeda.

Finally, Insights from practice knowledge and empirical research should guide policymaking and the development of laws to tackle the root causes and manifestations of extremism and terrorism Worth, K. (2016, July 14) This involves understanding extremists' platforms and methods and developing targeted interventions that can be more directly applied within specific cultural and operational contexts.

"Only the dead have seen the end of war." Plato

REFERENCES

AFP (2024, June 12). Hezbollah rains rockets down on Israel after strike kills commander. msn.com

Ainsley, J., Winter, T., Blankstein, A., and Planas, A. (2024, June 11). 8 suspected terrorists with possible ISIS ties arrested in New York, L. A., and Philadelphia, sources say. NBCnews.com.

Allyn, B. (2017, November 30). No regrets, Chelsea Manning tells Penn audience. https://whyy.org/articles/no-regrets-chelsea-manning-tells-penn-audience/

Bilal, A. (2021, November 21). Hybrid Warfare – New Threats, Complexity, and 'Trust' as the Antidote. www.nato/int

Black, J. (2001). Semantics and Ethics of Propaganda. *Journal of Mass Media Ethics, 16*(2&3), 121–137. http://www.communicationcache.com/uploads/1/0/8/8/10887248/semantics_and_ethics_of_propaganda.pdf

Boghardt, T. (2009, December). Soviet Bloc Intelligence and Its AIDS Disinformation Campaign (Operation INFEKTION). *Studies in Intelligence.*

Britannica, T. Editors of Encyclopedia (2024, June 14). Hamas. Encyclopedia Britannica. https://www.britannica.com/topic/Hamas

Britannica, T. Information Architects of Encyclopaedia (2024, June 16). Crusades. Encyclopedia Britannica. https://www.britannica.com/facts/Crusades

Britannica, T. Editors of Encyclopedia (n.d.). Kanem-Bornu Empire https://kids.britannica.com/kids/article/Kanem-Bornu-Empire/353330

Combs, C. C. (2022-07-29). Terrorism in the Twenty-First Century, 9th Edition [VitalSource Bookshelf version]. Retrieved from vbk://9781000609844

Conway, M. (2021). Online Extremism and Terrorism Research ethics: Researcher safety, informed consent, and the need for tailored guidelines. *Terrorism and Political Violence, 33*(2), 367–380. DOI: 10.1080/09546553.2021.1880235

Countering and Exposing Terrorist Propaganda and Disinformation. (n.d.). The Washington Institute. https://www.washingtoninstitute.org/policy-analysis/countering-and-exposing-terrorist-propaganda-and-disinformation

Davis, M. (2002). The Concise Dictionary of Crime and Justice. Thousand Oaks, CA. Sage Publications.

Duda, A. (2022). Remembering Soviet imperialism. https://www.taipeitimes.com/News/editorials/archives/2022/09/17/200378545

Edward Snowden: A 'Nation' interview. (2015, June 29). The Nation. https://www.thenation.com/article/archive/snowden-exile-exclusive-interview/

Executive Order 13721—Developing an Integrated Global Engagement Center To Support Government-wide Counterterrorism Communications Activities Directed Abroad and Revoking Executive Order 13584. (n.d.). https://www.presidency.ucsb.edu/documents/executive-order-13721-developing-integrated-global-engagement-center-support-government

FBI. (n.d.). Terrorism. Retrieved on March 9, 2016, from https://www.fbi.gov/about-us/investigate/terrorism/terrorism-definition for-strategic-impact/

Forrest, J. (2015). Center for Terrorism and Security Studies. *UMASS Lowell.*https://www.uml.edu/research/ctss/about/

Global Engagement Center - United States Department of State. (2023, March 22). United States Department of State. https://www.state.gov/about-us-global-engagement-center-2/

Globalsecurity.org (1987, August 1). *U. S. Department of State. A Report on Active Measures and Propaganda, 1986-1987).* globalsecurity.org

Harvey, R. (2024, March 15). Protestant Reformation. *Free speech center @jMiddle Tennessee State University.*https://firstamendment.mtsu.edu/article/protestant-reformation/

Heidler, J. T. & Heidler, D. S. (2024, May 28). Manifest Destiny. Encyclopedia Britannica. https://www.britannica.com/event/Manifest-Destiny

Helmus, T., & Bodine-Baron, E. (2020, September 11). *Are Counter Violent Extremism Interventions Effective?* RAND. https://www.rand.org/pubs/commentary/2020/09/are-counter-violent-extremism-interventions-effective.html

Historians.org. (n.d.). American Historical Association. Propaganda. https://www.historians.org/about-aha-and-membership/aha-history-and-archives/gi-roundtable-series/pamphlets/em-2-what-is-propaganda-(1944)/some-limitations-of-propaganda

History.com Editors. (2019, June 7). ISIS. History.com.

HistoryStaff.com. (2009). Oklahoma City bombing. Retrieved from https://www.history.com/topics/oklahoma-city-bombing

HistoryStaff.com. (2019, June 7). Joseph Goebbels. https://www.history.com/topics/world-war-ii/joseph-goebbels

Incorporating Human Rights Principles Into National Security Measures. (n.d.). Rights Commission. https://humanrights.gov.au/about/news/speeches/incorporating-human-rights-principles-national-security-measures

Ingram, H. J. & Australian National University. (2017). “That is what the terrorists want”: Media as amplifier or disrupter of violent extremist propaganda. *Australian National University.* https://icct.nl/sites/default/files/import/publication/INGRAM-paris-speech.pdf

Jaafari, S. (2014, December 14). How ISIS uses catchy, violent tunes for propaganda. Theworld.org/stories

Kiger, P. (2019, April 16). How Joseph Stalin Starved Millions in the Ukrainian Famine. History.com.

Lewis, S. (2020, April 27). *Tyrannicide*. https://www.britannica.com/topic/tyrannicide

Liberman, A. V. (2017-2018). *Terrorism, the Internet, and Propaganda: A Deadly Combination*. heinonline.org/HOL/LandingPage?handle=hein.journals/jnatselp9&div=9&id=&page=

Mark, J. (2020, April 16). The Effects of the Black Death on Europe. Accessed from. Effects of the Black Death on Europe. World History Encyclopedia.

OCP Policy Center & Elshimi, M. (2018). *Thinking about the symbiotic relationship between the Media andPolicy Center* [Policy Brief]. https://www.policycenter.ma/sites/default/files/2021-01/OCPPC-PB1812.pdf

Rangappa, A., & Mercieca, J. (2020, June 7). The Ancient Greeks' Guide to Rejecting Propaganda and Disinformation. www.zocalopublicsquare.org

Robinson, L. (2018). Modern Political Warfare: Current Practices and Possible Responses. Santa Monica, CA: RAND Corporation, https://www.rand.org/pubs/research_reports/RR1772.html

Rocket.Chat, June 22, 2024. Media Group Linked to Islamic State Khorasan Province (ISKP) Publishes Posters Instructing Lone. . . . *MEMRI*. https://www.memri.org/jttm/media-group-linked-islamic-state-khorasan-province-iskp-publishes-posters-instructing-lone

Saul, B. (2006). Defining Terrorism in International Law. Oxford: Oxford University Press on Demand. https://scirp.org/reference/referencespapers?referenceid=3010902

Shah, M. (2024, July 4). *The digital weaponry of radicalization: AI and the recruitment nexus*. GNET. https://gnet-research.org/2024/07/04/the-digital-weaponry-of-radicalisation-ai-and-the-recruitment-nexus/

Task & Purpose. (2023, November 5). *The Fentanyl War is Worse Than You Think* [Video]. YouTube. https://www.youtube.com/watch?v=BjsSuWKz2s0

Team, F. (2023, September 5). *Psychological Operations (PsyOps): Influencing Minds for Strategic Impact*. Fact Protocol.

Teegarden, D. A. (2022, January 13). Tyrannicide in Ancient Greek Political Culture. In *The Oxford Handbook of the History of Terrorism*. DOI: 10.1093/oxfordhb/9780199858569.013.001

The National Whistleblower Center. (2021, February 23). *The case of Edward Snowden*. National Whistleblower Center. https://www.whistleblowers.org/news/the-case-of-edward-snowden/

Varela, A. (2019, May 23). Terror attacks by Muslims get 357 percent more media coverage than other terror attacks, study shows. *Georgia State News Hub*. https://news.gsu.edu/2019/02/19/terror-attacks-by-muslims-get-disproportionate-news-coverage/

Vinney, C. (2023, December 26). What Is Cultivation Theory in Media Psychology? https://www.verywellmind.com/slug-placeholder-5214376

What Is a Chatbot? (n.d.). https://www.ibm.com/topics/chatbots

White, J. (2020). Royal United Services Institute for Defense and Security Studies, & Private Office of the Assistant Commissioner of Specialist Operations for the London Metropolitan Police Service. Terrorism and the mass media. *RUSI Occasional Paper* [Report]. https://ocd.lcwu.edu.pk/cfiles/International%20 Relations/EC/IR-404/terrorism_and_the_mass_media_final_web_version.pdf

Whitehead, J., & Whitehead, N. (2022, June 8). Everything Is a Weapon: The U.S. Government Is Waging Psychological Warfare on the Nation. https://www.rutherford.org/publications_resources/john_whiteheads_commentary/everything_is_a_weapon_the_u.s_government_is_waging_psychological_warfare_on_the_nation

Wikipedia contributors. (2025, January 7). *Chelsea Manning*. Wikipedia. https://en.wikipedia.org/wiki/BradleyManning

Wild, W. & Sands, G. (2021, May 15). FBI and DHS report finds deaths at hands of racially motivated violent extremists on the rise in US. *cnn.com*

Woodley, S., & Howard, P. (2019). *Computational Propaganda*. Oxford University Press.

Worth, K. (2016, July 14). Lone Wolf Attacks Are Becoming More Common — And More Deadly. *Pbs.org.*

KEY TERMS AND DEFINITIONS

Asymmetric War: Warfare that is between opposing forces which differ greatly in military power and that typically involves the use of unconventional weapons and tactics (such as those associated with guerrilla warfare and terrorist attacks) Merriam-Webster. (n.d.).

Bot: Automated accounts on social media platforms that can spread information, including fake news. Bots can amplify the reach of disinformation campaigns. Merriam-Webster. (n.d.).

Chatbots: A chatbot is a computer program that simulates human conversation with an end user. While conversational AI chatbots can digest a users' questions or comments and generate a human-like response, generative AI chatbots can take this a step further by generating updated content as the output. This updated content can include high-quality text, images and sound based on the LLMs they are trained on What Is a Chatbot? | IBM. (n.d.).

Clean-Skins: Have no criminal record and typically would not be identified as radicalized with connections to a terrorist organization such as al-Qaeda. Martin Chulov's contention that "clean skins" or home-grown terrorists acting on their own participated in the London bombings in 2005 They are hidden and almost impossible to stop before they wreck their havoc (Forrest, J. (2015, p. 73).

Cultivation Theory: Proposes that repeated exposure to mass media over time influences viewers' perceptions of social reality. Vinney, C. (2023, December 26).

Cybercrime: "Crime committed with, or facilitated by, computers, the Internet, the World Wide Web, and other online services." (Davis, M., 2002, p. 79). Today's technologies now permit enemies of the state to engage in acts of asymmetrical warfare to damage and exploit weaknesses in their opponent's defenses." So, cyberterrorism must involve destructive acts against innocent persons or against the systems vital to their survival and must be motivated by political goals.

Deep Fake: An image or recording that has been convincingly altered and manipulated to misrepresent someone as doing or saying something that was not actually done or said Merriam-Webster. (n.d.).

Domestic Terrorism: USA "Domestic terrorism" means activities with the following three characteristics: Involve acts dangerous to human life that violate federal or state law. Appear intended to intimidate or coerce a civilian population; (ii) to influence the policy of a government by intimidation or coercion; or (iii) to affect the conduct of a government by mass destruction, assassination, or kidnapping; and Occur primarily within the territorial jurisdiction of the U.S. 18 U.S.C. § 2332b defines the term "federal crime of terrorism" as an offense that: Is calculated to influence or affect the conduct of government by intimidation or coercion, or to retaliate against government conduct; and Is a violation of one of several listed statutes, including § 930(c) (relating to killing or attempted killing during an attack on a federal facility with a dangerous weapon); and § 1114 (relating to killing or attempted killing of officers and employees of the U.S. (FBI, n/d).

Eco Chamber: A room with sound-reflecting walls used for producing hollow or echoing sound effects —often used figuratively. Living in a kind of echo chamber of their own opinions, they pay attention to information that fits their conclusions and ignore information that does not Merriam-Webster. (n.d.).

Lone Wolves: A person who prefers to work, act, or live alone. In the case of a terrorist who may act independently without the benefit of a controller Merriam-Webster (n.d.).

Propaganda: The propaganda may include virtual messages, presentations, magazines, treatises, audio and video files, and video games developed by terrorist organizations or sympathizers Combs, C. (2022, p. 149).

APPENDIX

Figure 2. Joseph Gobbles

Joseph Goebbels was Nazi propaganda minister under Adolf Hitler. *AP File Photo*

The photo free use World Wide Web / https://www.usatoday.com/story/news/world/2015/04/22/secretary-pomsel-recalls-nazi-joseph-goebbels/26066809/

Figure 3. ISIS Lone Wolf Propaganda Poster

The photo free use World Wide Web / Rocket.Chat, June 22, 2024.

Chapter 7
Fake News, Propaganda, and Other Influences on Elections

Ghosh Thinnakkakath
https://orcid.org/0009-0002-1684-7217
University of the Cumberlands, USA

ABSTRACT

This chapter demonstrates how misinformation and propaganda greatly influence modern elections. Election integrity is central to ensuring democratic processes are free and fair. New threats have emerged with the rise of social media and digital platforms, including fake news, disinformation, and algorithmic echo chambers. These issues distort public perception, affect voting behavior, and increase polarization. Throughout history, from the Nazi election of 1932 to the Brazilian election in 2018, propaganda and misinformation have paved the way for outcome manipulation. Key methods of influencing voters include psychological manipulation, cognitive biases, and emotive fake news. Media literacy, fact-checking, technological interventions, and policy regulations are proposed as potential solutions to these risks. In light of the digital revolution, election integrity has become a collective responsibility of governments, technology firms, media, and the people.

FAKE NEWS, PROPAGANDA, AND OTHER INFLUENCES ON ELECTIONS

Overview of Election Integrity

Election integrity is at the heart of any democracy. It ensures that the electoral process is free, fair, and representative of the citizens' will, supported by valid voter identification. Election integrity is built on transparency, accountability, and inclusiveness, aiming to create an open, level playing field for election activities and prevent manipulation, fraud, or undue influence from affecting outcomes. With these principles in place, voters can trust that their votes are accurately counted and that election results truly reflect the collective will of the voting population.

In the modern age, ensuring the integrity of the electoral process has become increasingly challenging. With the rise of technology and the rapid flow of information, new opportunities for interference and manipulation have emerged. Long-standing concerns in the electoral process include voter suppression, gerrymandering, and dark money in campaigns. Partisan gerrymandering undermines the connection

DOI: 10.4018/979-8-3693-7468-9.ch007

between voting and representation, leading to unresponsive electoral outcomes and limiting voters' ability to align with their preferred party (Wang, 2016). Social media and digital platforms have added to these complex challenges, introducing issues such as fake news, propaganda, and strategic leaks that threaten the integrity of elections. These factors can shape public opinion and voter behavior, potentially altering election outcomes in ways that do not reflect the true democratic will of the people.

The Role of Information in the Democratic Processes

In any democracy, information is the lifeblood of the electoral process. It informs citizens, enables decision-making, and ensures accountability among candidates and voters. Democracies thrive when their electorates are well-informed and can make informed decisions based on an understanding of critical issues, government policies, and candidates. The free flow of information is essential to ensuring that elections are fair, and outcomes are legitimate. When democracy emerged as an ideal, political actors argued that informed citizens were crucial for its success (Hochschild, 2010).

Disinformation spreads rapidly online, making it difficult to distinguish truth from falsehood. This creates a dilemma between safeguarding free speech and protecting democracy from harmful propaganda. In recent times, the role of information in democratic processes has become increasingly muddled. Social media and the internet have transformed the way information is shared and consumed. While these platforms provide quick access to vast amounts of information, they also serve as conduits for misinformation, disinformation, and propaganda. Fake news, often spread via social media, can mislead voters, distort public perception, and influence election outcomes. This manipulation of information poses a significant threat to election integrity. In the digital age, harmful content such as hate speech, extremism, propaganda, and political agendas can be easily disseminated online. Combating the spread of fake news has become a major challenge in today's digital landscape (Al Ghamdi et al., 2024).

Modern propaganda differs from traditional political campaigning, becoming more subtle and pervasive. When driven by partisanship, individuals are more likely to support information that favors their party and dismiss evidence that contradicts it, even when facts suggest otherwise. This can lead to selective perception and skewed judgment about political realities (Vail et al., 2023). Strategic leaks of both true and false information are used to discredit candidates or divert attention from crucial election issues. These tactics undermine the democratic process by distorting the informational landscape, preventing voters from making free choices.

HISTORICAL CONTEXT

Early Instances of Election Manipulation

The manipulation of elections is as old as democracy itself. Throughout history, political actors have sought to influence electoral outcomes at the expense of free and fair voting processes. Ancient Rome provides one of the earliest documented examples where wealthy candidates used their resources to bribe voters, finance extravagant public spectacles, and sway public opinion. According to Lintott (1990), while electoral bribery distorted democratic processes by shifting power to affluent candidates, it was often accepted as part of Roman politics and did not significantly alter the broader political landscape or control of key offices. Election manipulation has persisted in many forms throughout history, often by those in power.

Election manipulation became more sophisticated in Europe and the United States during the 18th and 19th centuries. For instance, the infamous "rotten boroughs" in the United Kingdom were small constituencies with very few voters that could still elect members to Parliament (Aidt & Franck, 2013), giving disproportionate influence to large landowners and the wealthy elite. Meanwhile, in the United States, the "Tammany Hall" political machine exemplified how organized groups could manipulate elections through bribery, intimidation, and falsifying lists of qualified voters. Tammany Hall, rooted in Martin Van Buren's political theory, initially helped integrate immigrants into American society through patronage and social activities but eventually shifted toward self-serving behavior (Frankel, 2024). These early examples highlight an important point: Democratic systems have historically been vulnerable to manipulation by individuals or groups seeking to advance their personal or political agendas.

Evolution of Propaganda Techniques

Modern propaganda began in the early 20th century, when governments systematically used it to shape public opinion in support of the war effort during World War I. This conflict marked a milestone as the first global war accompanied by a concurrent disinformation campaign of hoaxes and incomplete news (Barceló Sánchez et al., 2023). Propaganda is the structured dissemination of information—whether true or false—that aims to influence public opinion. During this era, state-sponsored propaganda campaigns employed posters, newspapers, and radio broadcasts to shape mass perception and stir nationalistic fervor. Emotionally charged imagery and slogans became hallmarks of these early efforts, invoking fear, pride, and anger in equal measure.

As technology developed, so did the vehicles for disseminating propaganda. Television added a new dimension to propaganda in the mid-20th century, allowing governments to broadcast messages directly into citizens' homes. Propaganda during this period became a fine art for governments and political actors, using sophisticated visual and audio tools with manipulated stories to shape public opinion. During the Cold War, there was an intense, immediate propaganda clash between the United States and the Soviet Union, with each side using media to distort the other's image and promote its own ideology. The book *Russia and the Media* examines how Western media shapes a negative image of Russia through propaganda, focusing on mutual paranoia in geopolitical conflicts, though it lacks coverage of how Russian media portrays the West (Khafizullina, 2021). Both the Soviet Union and the United States extensively used propaganda during the Cold War as part of their broader strategy to influence global public opinion and advance their geopolitical goals. In this context, propaganda was more than just the art of selling policies; it became the very perception of reality as both sides launched disinformation campaigns that blurred the line between truth and falsehood.

The digital era has made propaganda even more pervasive and challenging to detect. Social media has become the new battleground where state and non-state actors spread information with little oversight or accountability. Engagement-based algorithms have unintentionally become propaganda tools, as sensational or emotionally charged content tends to go viral faster than factual information. Modern propaganda is focused on narrative control, flooding the information space with conflicting data and leaving people to determine what is true and false. The nature of influence has shifted: The goal is no longer to convince but to confuse and overwhelm.

Case Studies of Past Elections Influenced by Propaganda

The use of propaganda in elections has become a consistent feature of modern history, with several notable examples demonstrating how media manipulation can affect election outcomes.

Nazi Germany (1932 Elections)

One of the most frequently cited examples is the 1932 German election, in which Adolf Hitler and his Nazi Party effectively used propaganda to win power. The strategic use of propaganda heavily influenced Hitler's rise during this election. Joseph Goebbels, Nazi Minister of Propaganda, employed posters, films, and mass rallies to portray Hitler as a decisive leader. This campaign manipulated economic desperation and fear of communism to appeal to nationalist sentiments (Lindenfeld & Kershaw, 1988). The 1932 election is often considered a classic example of how public opinion can be manipulated through propaganda to enable extremist parties to take power.

Soviet Union (Post-1917 Bolshevik Seizure of Power)

Following the October Revolution of 1917, the Lenin regime relied heavily on propaganda to justify its rule and demonstrate the correctness of its policies. The slogan "Peace, Land, Bread" stirred patriotic fervor among war-weary, impoverished citizens. Through elaborate public speeches, posters, and pamphlets, the regime crafted a narrative of itself as the savior of the working class (Brandenberger, 2012). Propaganda helped the Bolsheviks gain popular support during the elections to the Constituent Assembly, though they dissolved the Assembly when it failed to produce their desired outcome.

Iran (1979 Islamic Revolution)

During the 1979 Islamic Revolution, Ayatollah Khomeini used cassette tapes, leaflets, and underground media networks to spread propaganda against the Shah of Iran. Khomeini's messages depicted the Shah as corrupt and aligned his own image with the people's aspirations for religious and economic reform (Abrahamian, 1982). In this way, propaganda played a crucial role in generating the support necessary for the revolution and ensuring the success of the new regime during a national referendum vote.

Brazil (2018 Election)

The 2018 Brazilian presidential election was marked by the widespread use of digital propaganda and misinformation, particularly on platforms like WhatsApp. Jair Bolsonaro's campaign exploited disinformation and fueled public fears of crime, corruption, and communism to discredit his opponent, Fernando Haddad. The election underscores the growing role of digital propaganda in shaping modern elections. The role of WhatsApp in spreading disinformation through the "Office of Hatred," a government-backed operation that emerged after Bolsonaro's 2018 election, is particularly notable (Ozawa et al., 2023). Expert interviews trace the Office of Hatred's tactics, focusing on disinformation campaigns against the Brazilian Workers' Party and its evolution within WhatsApp groups, with broader implications for populist and authoritarian regimes worldwide.

These case studies demonstrate how propaganda can turn the tide of an election. It remains a powerful tool for any individual or group seeking to manipulate public opinion and democratic processes through traditional and digital media. Recognizing and countering these tactics is a growing challenge in an increasingly interconnected world, where the boundaries between fact and falsehood are often deliberately blurred. While the struggle against propaganda is not new, it has never been more critical than in the digital era.

FAKE NEWS AND ITS IMPACT

Definition and Characteristics of Fake News

Fake news plays a significant role in politics and elections today, particularly in contemporary discourse. It refers to fabricated information presented as factual, often sourced to appear credible. Fake news is a longstanding issue that dates back to the 15th century, resurfacing with the advent of new technologies, such as the printing press, postal systems, mass media, film, radio, television, and, more recently, digital software and the internet (Buschman, 2019).

Unlike simple misinformation, which can occur accidentally, fake news is intentionally created to deceive, misinform, or manipulate its audience. Typically, it is presented in a way that mimics credible reporting, using the style, tone, and structure of traditional journalism to cloak it in an air of legitimacy. Richardson and Stähler (2021) analyzed the competition between a news provider offering truthful but uncertain information and two fake news providers who exploit cognitive dissonance by confirming prior beliefs. Their findings suggest that although real news is valued more as information variability increases, fake news providers can still thrive financially.

Key characteristics of fake news include sensationalism, emotional appeal, and the frequent use of attention-grabbing images or headlines. While the intent behind fake news is often to tell compelling stories, it usually contains distorted truths or is entirely fabricated. Fake news serves a variety of purposes, including political manipulation, financial gain, social engineering, and cultural disruption. In this context, the term "fake news" is closely tied to influencing voter opinions—misleading voters or emphasizing societal divisions.

Mechanisms of Spread in the Digital Age

The rise of digital technology has significantly amplified the spread of fake news, primarily through social media platforms like Facebook, X (formerly Twitter), and Instagram. Unlike traditional news, which undergoes editorial scrutiny, digital platforms allow anyone to share content without verification. This lack of regulation has enabled fake news to spread more rapidly than fact-checkers can keep up with. Social media algorithms, designed to optimize user engagement, favor content that evokes strong emotions such as fear and anger, making sensationalist fake news more likely to go viral. Once it gains traction, it can reach thousands in a matter of hours.

The echo chamber effect on social media exacerbates this problem. Users are often grouped into communities with similar beliefs, where information that aligns with their views circulates freely while opposing perspectives are excluded. This selective exposure reinforces misinformation, making it harder to correct. Richardson and Stähler (2021) argue that, especially in uncertain news environments, echo chambers become more powerful, particularly among those with extreme views. They suggest that public media, media education, and competition policies are more effective in mitigating fake news than simple fact-checking efforts.

Beyond social media, the spread of fake news extends to other forms of digital communication, such as email chains, messaging applications, and online forums. These platforms offer users greater anonymity and privacy, allowing misinformation to flow more freely with less public scrutiny than on social media. Together, these channels create an environment conducive to the rapid spread of fake news, especially during sensitive periods like election cycles.

Psychological Impact on Voters

The psychological influence of fake news on electorates is deep and multi-dimensional, gradually eroding confidence in traditional media and democratic institutions. Daunt et al. (2023) state that exposure to misinformation causes individuals to generalize distrust, making it difficult to distinguish between credible news and baseless accusations, which further fuels voter apathy, cynicism, and disengagement from the political process. These effects are compounded by cognitive biases, including confirmation bias and the availability heuristic. Confirmation bias predisposes individuals to favor information that aligns with their beliefs, while the availability heuristic overvalues information because it is more easily accessible.

The problem with fake news stories, especially those designed to elicit outrage or fear, is that their emotional appeal becomes a significant determinant in voting behavior. Voters often make decisions based on immediate feelings rather than thoroughly considering the issues. Misinformation reinforces false beliefs due to the illusory truth effect; it appears more valid after repeated exposures, particularly within the social media echo chamber. This leads to the rigid polarization of the electorate, with repeated misinformation keeping individuals further away from considering alternative viewpoints or even the truth.

Notable Examples of Fake News in Recent Elections

Several high-profile examples in recent years have vividly shown the influence of fake news on elections. One such example was the sensational "Pizzagate" conspiracy during the 2016 U.S. presidential election, in which rumors claimed that a children-trafficking ring involving leading Democrats was being run from a Washington, D.C. pizzeria. Despite the lack of evidence, the story spread like wildfire on social media and led to real-world consequences: A gunman entered the pizzeria, intending to "investigate." This is another example of how fake news can have dangerous, real-life repercussions.

Another notable example is the widespread dissemination of misinformation during the Brexit referendum in the United Kingdom. The most famous claim was that the United Kingdom would save £350 million a week by leaving the European Union, a figure prominently displayed on campaign buses and circulated widely on social media. As it turned out, this claim was false, but it played a significant role in shaping public perception. The Brexit campaign thus demonstrated how political manipulation using fake news can unfold on a large scale, with lasting political and economic consequences for years to come.

As noted by Rea (2022), media outlets often emphasized the most sensational aspects of memos from former British Intelligence Officer Christopher Steele to suggest that Donald Trump was compromised and blackmailed by Russian actors. However, the U.S. Senate Select Committee on Intelligence later concluded that many of the allegations in the "Steele dossier" were unverified and potentially influenced by Russian security services. Additionally, there was a significant surge in fake news during the 2020 U.S. presidential election, both from and about the candidates. Amplified by social media algorithms and extensive user sharing, this spread of misinformation polarized the election landscape and created an intense atmosphere. The proliferation of fake news further undermined public trust in the electoral process and highlighted the ongoing battle against online misinformation.

Examples like these demonstrate how fake news influences perception and behavior, potentially affecting the outcomes of democratic processes or even swaying elections. As digital platforms continue to play a significant role in shaping public discourse, the challenge of fake news will likely persist, necessitating ongoing efforts to address it. In essence, fake news seriously undermines the integrity of elections and democratic processes. By manipulating cognitive biases, stirring emotions, and disseminating information at high speeds, it becomes a powerful tool for any actor intent on influencing the course of voting. Tackling fake news will require enhancing media literacy, holding social media platforms accountable, and implementing appropriate regulatory mechanisms.

PROPAGANDA IN MODERN ELECTIONS

Definition and Techniques of Propaganda

Election propaganda is information disseminated to voters, often unilateral or distorted, with the goal of influencing their opinions in favor of a specific candidate, party, or ideology. While propaganda can be based on the truth, it is typically presented in a way that manipulates emotions, distorts facts, or omits relevant context to achieve the desired effect. Propaganda in modern elections goes beyond merely informing voters; it aims to persuade, indoctrinate, or manipulate the electorate.

The realm of electoral propaganda typically employs several techniques. Seven propaganda devices, well-known in communication theory, are bandwagoning, card stacking, glittering generalities, name-calling, testimonial propaganda, transfer, and plain folks (Sproule, 2001). *Bandwagoning* urges people to vote for a candidate because others are doing so, creating an impression of inevitable success or universal acceptance. *Card stacking* presents only one side of an issue while omitting contradictory information to serve a specific agenda. *Glittering generalities* use sweeping, emotive, and vague words or phrases that apply universally, offering little substance. *Name-calling* involves labeling opponents with negative terms to discredit their character or policies without addressing the substance of their ideas. *Testimonial propaganda* utilizes celebrities, public figures, or influential leaders to lend credibility to a candidate or cause. *Transfer* associates the authority, prestige, or appeal of something respected—such as a symbol, institution, or person—with a particular idea, group, or product. Finally, the *plain folks* appeal aims to present a candidate as just like the average voter, regardless of background or intentions, creating an emotional appeal based on relatability.

These are often combined in practice to create a multi-dimensional approach aimed at influencing voter perception and behavior. Whether propaganda succeeds in elections depends on its ability to appeal to the emotions of the electorate, confirm and justify their prejudices, and simplify complex issues into easily understandable narratives.

Media's Role in Propaganda Dissemination

The media plays a central role in disseminating propaganda, particularly during elections. While traditional media such as television, radio, and print have historically been used for this purpose, the rise of digital and social media has exponentially accelerated its spread. The internet enables the rapid transmission of information, often bypassing editorial checks, which makes it easier to tailor messages to specific audiences. Platforms such as Facebook, X, and YouTube are especially effective at spreading propaganda because their algorithms prioritize emotionally engaging content.

Whether intentionally or not, news organizations may amplify propaganda by framing stories to fit certain narratives. As a result, individuals are exposed only to information that reinforces their preexisting beliefs, creating echo chambers. Additionally, "alternative" media outlets, which often have fewer journalistic standards, contribute to the proliferation of propaganda by promoting falsehoods and ideologically biased content that mainstream outlets typically avoid. The combined influence of traditional, social, and alternative media plays a significant role in shaping public opinion through propaganda.

Government and Non-Government Propaganda Sources

Propaganda can originate from governments and non-governmental sources, each employing various motives and methods. Governments often use propaganda to maintain power, control public opinion, or justify policies. This is typically achieved through state-sponsored media, public relations campaigns, and subtle messaging that promotes the ruling party while discrediting opposition voices. In extreme cases, governments may suppress dissent, spread disinformation, and manipulate media to fit a favorable narrative.

Non-governmental propaganda sources include political parties, interest groups, private companies, and foreign governments. Political parties and interest groups use campaign ads, speeches, and social media to promote their causes and discredit opponents. Private companies may influence elections by funding ads, sponsoring research, or manipulating platforms to subtly shape public opinion. In recent years, foreign governments have increasingly played a role in election-based propaganda, using social media to sow discord, hack sensitive information, or support particular candidates to influence election outcomes in other nations. These organized efforts aimed at gaining political advantage can significantly impact democracy.

This multi-faceted approach to propaganda reveals its pervasive role in shaping political landscapes and influencing public perception domestically and internationally. Lewis et al. (2021) provide insights into how non-governmental organizations shape political and social narratives, often through propaganda techniques, focusing on their diffuse nature compared to centralized governmental propaganda. They cover the broad impact of these organizations on policy, influence, and ideological advancement. While governmental propaganda tends to be more centralized, non-governmental propaganda can be more diffuse and more challenging to track, making it a potent force in modern elections.

SOCIAL MEDIA AND DIGITAL PLATFORMS

Influence of Social Media on Election Campaigns

Social media has rewritten the definition of election campaigns in the digital era. These platforms have become essential tools for political candidates to connect with voters, shape public discourse, and inform campaign strategies. The ability to engage directly with millions offers unique opportunities to influence voter opinions and mobilize support.

Social media's impact on election campaigns is immense, as it allows candidates to reach the public without interference from traditional media gatekeepers. This direct communication channel enables candidates to construct their narratives, respond promptly to controversies, and tailor messages to specific demographics. For instance, Twitter (now X) played a pivotal role in the 2016 U.S. presidential election, particularly in how Donald Trump engaged directly with voters, bypassing traditional media filters (Galdieri et al., 2017). His tweets not only energized his base but were also widely covered by media outlets, extending his message beyond his immediate followers.

Modern political campaigns use social media to target specific groups based on data such as online behaviors, interests, and demographics. This allows for highly personalized ads that can effectively sway key voter segments, increasing the efficiency of campaign spending and influence. However, the rise of social media in elections also raises concerns about misinformation and the formation of echo chambers, which threaten the integrity of the electoral process. These challenges underscore the need to address the risks of disinformation in political campaigns.

Algorithms and Echo Chambers

At the heart of how social media influences electoral results lies the role of algorithms. As previously discussed, the primary function of these algorithms is to amplify user engagement by personalizing content based on the data the user generates through their behavior and interests. While personalization helps retain user engagement, it also nurtures the now-infamous echo chamber—a cocoon where individuals are continuously exposed to information and perspectives that reinforce their existing worldviews.

What is particularly alarming, however, is how these algorithms contribute to the creation of echo chambers by amplifying misinformation and disinformation. The more a piece of misinformation resonates with a user's experiences and beliefs, the more the algorithm recommends that content, leading to its widespread dissemination within like-minded communities. This creates a toxic cycle, where misinformation circulates unchecked and erodes trust in credible news sources as users become increasingly insulated within their echo chambers. Milhazes-Cunha and Oliveira (2023) explore the role of echo chambers in amplifying COVID-19 disinformation and hate speech on social media, particularly within the Portuguese Facebook community. Their study shows how groups like "Doctors for the Truth" used their influence to spread false COVID-19 narratives, fostering toxic discourses and reinforcing misinformation.

The ongoing challenge for social media platforms is to balance user engagement with the promotion of diversity and the pursuit of accurate information. While a few recent experiments have attempted to adjust algorithms to reduce the impact of echo chambers—such as recommending content from more diverse sources, fact-checking, and flagging misinformation—these efforts are still in the early stages, and their effectiveness remains to be proven.

Misinformation and Disinformation on Social Media

Social media has become a breeding ground for false information, posing significant threats to electoral integrity. Misinformation refers to false information that is spread innocently, without the intent to deceive, while disinformation involves deliberately fabricated information designed to mislead. Both types of false information seriously affect the electoral process, confusing the electorate, distorting public debates, and eroding trust in democratic institutions.

A significant factor contributing to the spread of misinformation and disinformation on social media is the viral nature of false content. Such information is often crafted to be sensational or emotionally charged, increasing its likelihood of going viral and spreading quickly across platforms. The situation is exacerbated by social media algorithms, which prioritize content based solely on high engagement, regardless of its veracity. Unlike traditional media, platforms like Facebook operate with a fundamentally different structure, enabling users to share content with minimal third-party filtering, fact-checking, or editorial oversight. This allows individuals—even those without established reputations—to occasionally reach as many readers as prominent news outlets like Fox News, CNN, or the New York Times (Allcott & Gentzkow, 2017).

Misinformation and disinformation can take many forms, from fake news and manipulated photos to false statistics and fabricated endorsements. These tactics target the psyche of specific voter groups, aiming to create chaos and influence their mindset. Misinformation and disinformation are multi-faceted problems on social media that require a multi-pronged approach. Most platforms respond by taking action against the spread of fake news, flagging or removing misleading content with the help of fact-checking organizations, and promoting media literacy. However, the sheer volume and speed at which this content spreads often make it difficult to provide proper contextual coverage.

Those behind disinformation campaigns are often sophisticated and adaptive, constantly evolving their methods to evade detection. These campaigns could be conducted by state actors, political operatives, or individuals with malevolent intentions seeking to influence the outcome of an election. The stakes are high: these campaigns shape mass perceptions, sway undecided voters, and sometimes even incite violence.

Role of Influencers and Fake Accounts

Influencers and fake accounts have become increasingly impactful in elections, alongside algorithms and fake news. With their large social media followings, influencers can sway public opinion by endorsing candidates and spreading political messages. Their reach makes them valuable assets for political campaigns, but this influence is a double-edged sword. While they can mobilize voters, raise awareness, and encourage civic engagement, the lack of regulation in the influencer space allows for the unchecked dissemination of partisan or misleading information.

Additionally, fake accounts, often controlled by bots or malicious actors, amplify misinformation and distort civic discourse. These accounts can create the illusion of grassroots support and manipulate public opinion by flooding social media with political content or attacks on opponents. Proven instances of coordinated fake accounts have exposed efforts to manipulate voting behavior.

An integrated approach is needed to address these challenges. Regulation, platform accountability, and public education are essential to combat misinformation and ensure transparency. Influencers must be held to standards of transparency, while platforms should take steps to eliminate fake accounts. Public awareness campaigns can help citizens recognize and resist manipulation. Ultimately, while social media democratizes information and political participation, it also creates risks that must be mitigated to ensure fair elections based on reliable information.

PSYCHOLOGICAL MANIPULATION TACTICS

Modern political manipulation remains an underestimated factor in shaping public opinion and influencing election results. While campaigns and political messages continue to exploit the capabilities offered by social media and digital platforms, it has become increasingly urgent to understand the psychological tactics at play. This section will address three key topics: the use of fear and emotion in campaigns, cognitive biases, fake news and propaganda, and strategies to counter deceptive maneuvers effectively.

Use of Fear and Emotion in Campaigns

The emotion of fear ranks among the highest in shaping human behavior and has been used extensively in political campaigns to sway voters' opinions. Political campaigns can be overwhelming emotionally, causing groups to share fear-driven concerns about safety, economic stability, or cultural identity, often drowning out rational considerations. This common method is used to create urgency or a sense of danger, mobilizing people to support a candidate or cause out of a desire for preservation.

Campaigns often highlight issues, such as immigration, linked to national security threats or economic instability. By playing on these fears, such campaigns can quickly turn anxiety into support for policies or candidates who promise protection or security—even when those policies may not be in voters' best interests. Fear-based messages often focus on threats such as crime, terrorism, or economic collapse, exaggerating or distorting facts to reinforce the perceived danger.

Emotionally charged messaging goes beyond fear—it taps into a range of powerful emotions, including anger, pride, and hope. Westen (2007) argues that emotions play a dominant role in political decision-making, particularly during elections when values, images, and emotional appeals outweigh logical arguments. He explains that voters tend to prioritize their emotional responses to political parties, candidates, and policies when casting their ballots. One campaign may use national flags or images of soldiers to stir patriotic feelings, while another may focus on ordinary people facing hardship to invoke empathy and solidarity. By emotionally connecting with voters, campaigns can make their messages so personal that voters are reluctant to reject them, making the messages more persuasive.

Cognitive Biases Exploited by Fake News and Propaganda

Fake news and propaganda exploit cognitive biases that influence how individuals process information, often leading to irrational decision-making. One key bias is *confirmation bias*, in which people favor information that supports their preexisting beliefs while disregarding contradictory evidence. Fake news takes advantage of this bias by presenting false or distorted information that aligns with the reader's worldview, reinforcing their stance and reducing the likelihood of seeking alternative perspectives.

Karine et al. (2021) examine the *illusory truth effect*, noting that humans are more likely to believe something the more they hear it. This effect explains how repeated exposure to false information can make it appear more credible. In the digital age, the rapid spread of fake news across social media and news platforms amplifies this effect, making it increasingly difficult for individuals to distinguish fact from fiction. These cognitive distortions can significantly alter public perceptions, influencing behaviors such as voting in ways that contradict factual evidence.

Strategies to Counter Psychological Manipulation

Given the depths to which psychological manipulation during elections can reach, there is a clear need for a strategy that acts as an antidote and encourages better decision-making. Improving people's media literacy can empower them to critically assess information that captures their attention. In politics, social media has transformed campaign strategies and public discourse, contributing to both polarization and the spread of misinformation. Additionally, its impact on mental health is multi-faceted—providing support networks and resources but also contributing to anxiety, depression, and cyberbullying (Omar et al., 2024).

The purpose of media literacy programs is to help individuals recognize emotional manipulations and biases, as well as to seek out credible and balanced information. Education on fact-checking, distinguishing news from opinion, and identifying reliable sources makes learning more engaging. Digital platforms now offer fact-checking tools to combat misinformation. Transparency in political advertising—through clear labeling and disclosure of funding—helps voters identify the source of information. Media consumption can be diversified to counteract echo chambers and open up broader perspectives, while critical thinking enables individuals to question information and weigh the evidence, ensuring decisions are based on facts rather than manipulation or misinformation.

REGULATORY AND ETHICAL CONSIDERATIONS

Current Laws and Regulations

In the digital age, information management has become increasingly complex, especially during elections, as governments around the world struggle with fake news and propaganda. Various laws and regulations have been implemented to safeguard electoral integrity, emphasizing transparency, accountability, and the prevention of undue influence. In the United States, the Honest Ads Act requires online political ads to disclose their funding sources, similar to traditional advertising. This legislation and other controls were introduced after the 2016 U.S. presidential election when foreign interference and the spread of misinformation on digital platforms raised significant concerns. The Federal Election Commission also proposed rules to ensure political advertisers reveal their identities and include disclaimers on digital content.

The General Data Protection Regulation is a foundational European regulation that protects personal data but struggles to address modern AI systems capable of inferring sensitive information, such as user habits and emotional states. Newer laws, such as the Digital Services Act and the Artificial Intelligence Act, enhance protections but still contain critical gaps that require further attention (Sposini, 2024). Other countries, including those with laws like the Internal Security Act and Online Harms Bill, are similarly adapting their regulatory frameworks to address the rapid and often uncontrollable flow of information, which poses serious risks to democratic processes.

Challenges in Regulating Digital Campaigns

Regulating digital campaigns remains challenging despite numerous laws and regulations. First, the global nature of the internet allows information to cross borders easily, making the application of national laws difficult. Misleading information may originate in one country and quickly influence elections in another, bypassing legal oversight. The rapid evolution of digital platforms and technologies outpaces regulatory frameworks, creating loopholes for manipulation through techniques like bots, deep fakes, and micro-targeting. These technologies develop faster than lawmakers can keep up, leaving significant gaps in regulation.

Moreover, the sheer volume of content generated online during election cycles makes it nearly impossible for regulators to monitor effectively. Unlike traditional media, which has a limited number of broadcasters, the internet democratizes content creation, overwhelming regulators. Although automated systems like AI-based content moderation tools exist, they are imperfect and may inadvertently suppress legitimate speech or allow harmful content to slip through. Additionally, digital platforms lack transparency in how they surface and prioritize content through algorithms, further complicating regulation. Laws like the Honest Ads Act and General Data Protection Regulation require some level of disclosure, but the opaque nature of algorithms makes it difficult for regulators to understand how or why specific content is targeted, undermining trust in the electoral process.

Ethical Considerations for Media and Political Entities

In the digital age, media organizations and political entities face significant ethical challenges, particularly in the context of digital campaigns. Due to the prevalence of fake news and propaganda, reporting accurately, fairly, and in a balanced manner has become increasingly important. Media organizations are ethically obligated to ensure the accuracy of their content, but the pressure for speed often leads to the spread of misinformation when fact-checking is inadequate. This not only distorts public discourse but also erodes trust when false information is repeatedly propagated. Ethical journalism demands that errors be corrected transparently and promptly.

Political entities, on the other hand, must also uphold democratic values and respect for the electorate. When political campaigns resort to dishonest tactics, such as fake news or clickbait, the integrity of the electoral process is compromised, potentially leading to a long-term loss of public trust in government institutions. Additionally, both media and political actors have an ethical responsibility to handle personal data carefully, particularly in the realms of micro-targeting and digital manipulation. The ethical use of personal information in campaigns must prioritize transparency and consent. Ultimately, both media outlets and political organizations must advocate for truth, transparency, and respect to uphold the integrity of democratic processes.

STRATEGIES FOR COMBATTING FAKE NEWS AND PROPAGANDA

A growing proportion of fake news and propaganda is structurally changing the information space, especially in the context of elections. These phenomena distort public opinion and further undermine the integrity of democratic procedures. Daunt et al. (2023) highlight that belief in political fake news is heavily influenced by social identity and patriotism, with susceptibility to fake news acting as a catalyst for further engagement with disinformation. Their research underscores the need for strategies that enhance media literacy and critical thinking while also addressing the vulnerabilities of those with strong conspiracy-driven mentalities. The study suggests that platforms should use AI to identify and counteract disinformation that exploits patriotic tensions or conspiracy theories. A multi-faceted response is required to combat such threats; therefore, media literacy, fact-checking organizations, technology, and policy recommendations are the four main areas of countermeasures.

Media Literacy and Public Awareness Campaigns

Media literacy is the foundation of any strategy to combat fake news and propaganda. As misinformation runs rampant on social media platforms, teaching the public how to critically analyze the information they encounter has become crucial. Media literacy involves teaching people how to identify reliable sources, recognize hidden biases, and question what is presented to them as reality. Nowhere is the importance of such skills more acutely critical than during election periods, when even small amounts of disinformation can easily sway voter sentiment.

Raising awareness among the general public can greatly facilitate media literacy. This can be done through schools, community-based initiatives, or online campaigns. For example, media literacy could be integrated into school curricula so that young students are equipped with the tools necessary to navigate an increasingly complex media landscape. In addition, public awareness campaigns can target specific groups that are particularly vulnerable to misinformation, such as older adults or those without easy access to trustworthy news sources.

By fostering media literacy and conducting public awareness campaigns, we can begin to address the root causes of fake news and propaganda. This can help nurture a culture of critical thinking and skepticism, making people less susceptible to false information. Ultimately, this approach would contribute to securing the integrity of democratic processes.

Role of Fact-Checking Organizations

Fact-checking organizations play a vital role in the fight against fake news and propaganda. Their work is essential for authenticating the information that the public receives, especially during election periods. This process is conducted efficiently to ensure that the public is informed by facts rather than fabrication. Fact-checking organizations come in various forms; some are designed to verify information in real time, swiftly debunking false stories as they spread across social media. Others conduct more extensive investigations into the origins and motivations behind deceptive reports. Regardless of the methodology, one thing is clear: The singular purpose is to defend truth and enhance public understanding. Political fact-checking has evolved into a global movement, originating in the United States and expanding internationally, with the aim of establishing unbiased journalism through standardized practices and reliable funding (Graves, 2016).

Collaboration between fact-checking organizations and media outlets is crucial. Integrating fact-checking into the editorial processes of news organizations can help them avoid disseminating misinformation. Social media platforms can also work with fact-checkers to flag and hide false content from immediate visibility, limiting its potential harm. However, fact-checking organizations face significant challenges, including the overwhelming tide of misinformation, the rapid pace at which it spreads, and skepticism from some audiences regarding fact-checkers' credibility. This underscores the need for continuous support in the form of funding, collaboration, and public endorsement. By strengthening their infrastructure, we can enhance their ability to combat fake news and propaganda effectively.

Technological Solutions to Detect and Mitigate Fake News

As technology advances at an unprecedented rate, technological solutions have become increasingly important in combating propaganda and fake news. Disinformation, particularly on social media, has become a global issue, and while progress has been made in detection, significant challenges remain due to its complexity (Shu et al., 2020). Machine learning and AI tools are increasingly being adopted to detect and flag misinformation automatically. These technologies analyze language, sources, and patterns of dissemination to assess content credibility. Key technological approaches include algorithmic detection on social media platforms, which can flag posts exhibiting signs of misinformation, such as sensational headlines or a lack of credible references. AI tools are also used to study misinformation networks, identifying key influencers who spread false information and enabling targeted interventions to disrupt its flow.

In addition to social media algorithms, browser extensions and apps are being developed to provide real-time fact-checking capabilities. These tools cross-check content against established fact-check databases, warning users about potential misinformation. However, while these technological solutions are powerful, they are not infallible. Misinformation evolves quickly, necessitating regular updates to the tools. Furthermore, transparency in algorithmic function is crucial to avoid the unintended suppression of legitimate content. Ultimately, these technological solutions are just one component of a larger strategy, which must also include media literacy and robust fact-checking initiatives to effectively combat fake news and propaganda.

Policy Recommendations

To effectively combat fake news and propaganda during elections, governments must collaborate with tech companies, civil society organizations, and international bodies. The goal is to strike a balance between preserving free expression and protecting the public from misinformation. Key recommendations include creating clear guidelines for social media platforms on content regulation, defining misinformation, clarifying platforms' roles in managing it, and increasing transparency in moderation processes. Additionally, periodic reports from platforms should be mandated to assess their efforts in controlling fake news, the effectiveness of algorithms, and the outcomes of moderation practices.

Those who intentionally spread disinformation should face strict sanctions, including fines and prosecutions. However, regulatory actions must be carefully crafted to avoid infringing on free speech rights. Since misinformation knows no borders, international cooperation is essential. Governments and the private sector should work together to establish global standards for countering fake news, potentially involving joint fact-checking operations and coordinated responses to cross-border disinformation campaigns.

Furthermore, policies should promote research into psychological and social factors that influence people's susceptibility to false information. Lewandowsky et al. (2017) explore psychological factors contributing to the acceptance of misinformation and discuss strategies such as media literacy and fact-checking to mitigate its effects. They suggest that responses to this issue should incorporate technological solutions grounded in psychological principles, an interdisciplinary approach called "technocognition."

By understanding these factors, policymakers can design targeted interventions—such as media literacy programs and fact-checking initiatives—that ultimately strengthen society's resilience to misinformation.

CONCLUSION

Summary of Key Points

This chapter aimed to describe the growing influence of misinformation, propaganda, and similar tactics on the credibility of contemporary elections. Digital communication, especially social media, has radically transformed how information is spread, providing a platform for falsehoods and propaganda. These fraudulent actions are typically designed to manipulate public opinion, alter voting habits, and disrupt democratic processes. The chapter reviewed key events in which propaganda and fake news have shaped electoral outcomes, highlighting the dangers posed by unregulated information. Additionally, it discussed how algorithms and economic incentives prioritize sensationalism over factuality, increasing the spread of deceptive narratives. This underscores the challenge of distinguishing between real news and fabricated stories in a media landscape where truth and falsehood often blur.

The Future of Election Integrity

In the future, the integrity of elections will depend on how well societies manage to address and mitigate the effects of fake news and propaganda. As digitalization progresses, it will continue to present both opportunities and challenges for securing elections. Emerging threats such as deepfakes, targeted disinformation campaigns, and other sophisticated forms of content manipulation pose growing risks to democratic processes. However, further advancements in science and technology will make these threats easier to detect and counter, helping to safeguard election integrity. In this context, an informed and discerning electorate, fostered by media literacy, will play a critical role in defending against manipulation. This effort will be further supported by the development of transparent and responsible social media platforms equipped with effective control mechanisms to ensure that elections remain free and fair. Ultimately, the future of election integrity will hinge on the ability of governments, technology companies, and civil societies to adapt to these evolving challenges.

Call to Action for Stakeholders

Ensuring election integrity in the face of fake news and propaganda requires coordinated efforts from all stakeholders. Governments must lead by enacting regulations that hold platforms accountable for the content they host while safeguarding freedom of speech. Tech companies should innovate, developing and deploying tools to trace and prevent the spread of unverified information. Educators and civil society groups play a crucial role in promoting media literacy, equipping people with the critical thinking skills needed to assess online information. Journalists and media organizations bear the primary responsibility for upholding high standards and countering misinformation through rigorous fact-checking. Finally, it is up to citizens to stay vigilant, seek credible sources of information, and actively challenge falsehoods. Together, these efforts can foster an information environment where trust prevails, elections are secure, and democracy thrives.

REFERENCES

Abrahamian, E. (1982). *Iran between two revolutions*. Princeton University Press.

Aidt, T. S., & Franck, R. (2013). How to get the snowball rolling and extend the franchise: Voting on the Great Reform Act of 1832. *Public Choice, 155*(3–4), 229–250. DOI: 10.1007/s11127-011-9911-y

Al Ghamdi, M. A., Bhatti, M. S., Saeed, A., Gillani, Z., & Almotiri, S. H. (2024). A fusion of BERT, machine learning and manual approach for fake news detection. *Multimedia Tools and Applications, 83*(10), 30095–30112. DOI: 10.1007/s11042-023-16669-z

Allcott, H., & Gentzkow, M. (2017). Social media and fake news in the 2016 Election. *The Journal of Economic Perspectives, 31*(2), 211–236. DOI: 10.1257/jep.31.2.211

Barceló Sánchez, J. M., Mateos Abarca, J. P., & Álvarez Rivas, D. (2023). Propaganda gubernamental, censura informativa Y fake news durante la Primera Guerra Mundial. *Historia y Comunicación Social, 28*(2), 407–418. DOI: 10.5209/hics.92243

Brandenberger, D. (2012). *Propaganda state in crisis: Soviet ideology, indoctrination, and terror under Stalin, 1927–1941*. Yale University Press.

Buschman, J. (2019). Good news, bad news, and fake news: Going beyond political literacy to democracy and libraries. *The Journal of Documentation, 75*(1), 213–228. DOI: 10.1108/JD-05-2018-0074

Daunt, K. L., Greer, D. A., Jin, H. S., & Orpen, I. (2023). Who believes political fake news? The role of conspiracy mentality, patriotism, perceived threat to freedom, media literacy and concern for disinformation. *Internet Research, 33*(5), 1849–1870. DOI: 10.1108/INTR-07-2022-0565

Frankel, G. (2024). Old Kinderhook and civic integration in America. *The Independent Review, 29*(1), 5–30. https://www.proquest.com/scholarly-journals/old-kinderhook-civic-integration-america/docview/3063799102/se-2

Galdieri, C. J., Lucas, J. C., & Sisco, T. S. (Eds.). (2017). *The role of Twitter in the 2016 US election*. Palgrave Pivot., DOI: 10.1007/978-3-319-68981-4

Graves, L. (2016). Boundaries not drawn: Mapping the institutional roots of the global fact-checking movement. *Journalism Studies, 19*(5), 613–631. DOI: 10.1080/1461670X.2016.1196602

Hochschild, J. L. (2010). If democracies need informed voters, how can they thrive while expanding enfranchisement? *Election Law Journal, 9*(2), 111–123. DOI: 10.1089/elj.2009.0055

Karine, A. B., Dabbous, A., & Tarhini, A. (2021). An empirical approach to understanding users' fake news identification on social media. *Online Information Review, 45*(6), 1080–1096. DOI: 10.1108/OIR-08-2020-0333

Khafizullina, E. (2021). Russia and the media: The makings of a New Cold War. *Insight Turkey, 23*(3), 276–278. https://www.proquest.com/scholarly-journals/russia-media-makings-new-cold-war/docview/2575925280/se-2

Lewandowsky, S., Ecker, U. K. H., & Cook, J. (2017). Beyond misinformation: Understanding and coping with the "post-truth" era. *Journal of Applied Research in Memory and Cognition*, *6*(4), 353–369. DOI: 10.1016/j.jarmac.2017.07.008

Lewis, D., Kanji, N., & Themudo, N. S. (2021). *Non-governmental organizations and development* (2nd ed.). Routledge.

Lindenfeld, D. F., & Kershaw, I. (1988). The "Hitler myth": Image and reality in the Third Reich. *German Studies Review*, *11*(2), 329. DOI: 10.2307/1430004

Lintott, A. (1990). Electoral bribery in the Roman Republic. *Journal of Roman Studies*, *80*, 1–16. DOI: 10.2307/300277

Milhazes-Cunha, J., & Oliveira, S. (2023). The impact of echo chambers on COVID-19 disinformation and hate speech in the Portuguese Facebook community. *Journal of Social Media Studies*, *15*(2), 254–278.

Omar, A. S., & Ondimu, K. O. (2024). The impact of social media on society: A systematic literature review. *The International Journal of Engineering and Science*, *13*(6), 96–106. DOI: 10.9790/1813-130696106

Ozawa, J. V. S., Woolley, S. C., Straubhaar, J., Riedl, M. J., Joseff, K., & Gursky, J. (2023). How disinformation on WhatsApp went from campaign weapon to governmental propaganda in Brazil. *Social Media + Society*, *9*(1). Advance online publication. DOI: 10.1177/20563051231160632

Rea, S. C. (2022). Teaching and confronting digital extremism: Contexts, challenges and opportunities. *Information and Learning Science*, *123*(1), 7–25. DOI: 10.1108/ILS-08-2021-0065

Richardson, M., & Stähler, F. (2021). Some economics of echo chambers. *Journal of Institutional and Theoretical Economics*, *177*(2), 205–219. DOI: 10.1628/jite-2021-0004

Shu, K., Wang, S., Lee, D., & Liu, H. (2020). Mining disinformation and fake news: Concepts, methods, and recent advancements. In Shu, K., Wang, S., Lee, D., & Liu, H. (Eds.), *Lecture Notes in Social Networks* (pp. 1–19). DOI: 10.1007/978-3-030-42699-6_1

Sposini, L. (2024). Neuromarketing and eye-tracking technologies under the European framework: Towards the GDPR and beyond. *Journal of Consumer Policy*, *47*(3), 321–344. DOI: 10.1007/s10603-023-09559-2

Sproule, J. M. (2001). Authorship and origins of the seven propaganda devices: A research note. *Rhetoric & Public Affairs*, *4*(1), 135–143. https://www.jstor.org/stable/41939653. DOI: 10.1353/rap.2001.0014

Vail, K. E.III, Harvell-Bowman, L., Lockett, M., Pyszczynski, T., & Gilmore, G. (2023). Motivated reasoning: Election integrity beliefs, outcome acceptance, and polarization before, during, and after the 2020 U.S. Presidential Election. *Motivation and Emotion*, *47*(2), 177–192. DOI: 10.1007/s11031-022-09983-w PMID: 36188156

Wang, S. S. (2016). Three tests for practical evaluation of partisan gerrymandering. *Stanford Law Review*, *68*(6), 1263–1321. https://www.proquest.com/scholarly-journals/three-tests-practical-evaluation-partisan/docview/1807470903/se-2

Westen, D. (2007). *The political brain: The role of emotion in deciding the fate of the nation*. Public Affairs Books.

KEY TERMS AND DEFINITIONS

Algorithms: Computational processes used by digital platforms to prioritize and recommend content based on user behavior.

Cognitive Biases: Psychological tendencies that cause individuals to process information in ways that deviate from rationality.

Confirmation Bias: The tendency to favor information that confirms one's preexisting beliefs while ignoring contradictory evidence.

Deepfakes: AI-generated synthetic media that manipulates video or audio to create highly realistic yet fake content.

Disinformation: Deliberately false information spread with the intent to mislead, often for political purposes.

Election Integrity: The assurance that electoral processes are transparent, fair, and free from manipulation.

Media Literacy: The ability to critically assess, analyze, and evaluate the credibility of media content.

Misinformation: Incorrect or misleading information spread without the intent to deceive.

Propaganda: Information, often biased or misleading, used to promote a specific political cause or viewpoint.

Technocognition: An interdisciplinary approach that combines technology and psychological principles to combat misinformation and its effects on public opinion.

Voter Manipulation: Efforts to influence voter behavior through deceptive or unethical tactics, including misinformation and propaganda.

Chapter 8
Artificial Intelligence, Online Algorithms, and the Influence of Propaganda

Kadir Uludag
https://orcid.org/0000-0003-3713-4670
Shanghai Jiao Tong University, China

ABSTRACT

In the digital age, the intersection of artificial intelligence, online algorithms, and the pervasive influence of propaganda has become a focal point of concern and study. This chapter delves into the intricate relationship between these elements, exploring how AI technologies, particularly online algorithms such as total likes, are leveraged to amplify the dissemination of propaganda across various digital platforms. Propaganda, with its ability to mold opinions and shape narratives, finds a potent ally in AI-driven algorithms that tailor content to individual preferences, beliefs, and biases. This synergy raises critical questions regarding the ethics, transparency, and societal implications of utilizing AI in the propagation of propaganda. By analyzing the mechanisms through which AI and online algorithms facilitate the spread of propaganda, this chapter aims to shed light on the evolving landscape of information dissemination, the challenges posed by algorithmic manipulation, and the imperative for ethical considerations and regulatory frameworks.

1. INTRODUCTION

The intersection of Artificial Intelligence (AI), Online Algorithms, and the influence of propaganda presents a complex landscape that shapes information dissemination in the digital age. Digital organizational propaganda refers to the deliberate and persuasive communication efforts by organizations using digital platforms, characterized by unethical motives such as dishonesty (Lock & Ludolph, 2020). In the early 1800s, propaganda had a harmless, limited definition. However, its connotation turned negative

DOI: 10.4018/979-8-3693-7468-9.ch008

in World War I, and even publicity was not unaffected by the war's impact (McCluskey, Hamilton, & Reynolds, 2023).

Previously, war propaganda is considered incitement not just for trying to encourage highly violent ideologies but also for directly provoking widespread violence. By defining war propaganda in this manner, tribunals have transformed the offense of incitement from a concept of mere initiation to one centered on causation (Kiper, 2015). Furthermore, information warfare involves exploiting media systems to erode trust (Hashemi & Hall, 2019). In addition, previous bibliometric analysis reveals that propaganda on social media has been more extensively researched within the social sciences, while the field of computer science is gaining ground (Chaudhari & Pawar, 2021). The utilization of digital propaganda in times of crises and elections to sway public perception, stifle opposition, and suppress the voices of activists (Neyazi, 2020).

Overall, the intersection of AI, online algorithms, and digital propaganda, characterized by unethical motives and the manipulation of public opinion, has transformed information dissemination, influencing crises, elections, and eroding institutional trust in the digital age.

Our objective in the manuscript was to explore the connection among AI, Online Algorithms, and the Impact of Propaganda. Understanding how AI and algorithms interact with and potentially amplify the effects of propaganda is essential in comprehending the dynamics of online communication, the spread of misinformation, and the potential manipulation of public opinions. By examining these connections, we can gain insights into the mechanisms behind the dissemination of information in the digital age and develop strategies to mitigate the negative impacts of propaganda on society.

2. METHODS

The literature was summarized on AI and propaganda. It is important to know that it is not a systematic review. SANRA narrative review guidelines was used (Baethge, Goldbeck-Wood, & Mertens, 2019). We have summarized recent studies related to online algorithms and propaganda.

3.RESULTS

According to main results, based on the primary outcomes, recent studies have surfaced regarding AI and propaganda. Upon researching the terms "artificial intelligence" and "propaganda," we identified 44 studies, with the majority of them conducted between 2020 and 2024. Nevertheless, a few of the outcomes were related to the subject matter.

4. DISCUSSION

In the era of digital advancements, the convergence of AI, Online Algorithms, and the widespread impact of propaganda has emerged as a significant area of interest and investigation. This manuscript examines the complex interplay among these components, investigating how AI tools, especially online algorithms, are utilized to magnify the spread of propaganda on diverse digital channels.

4.1. Trends in Social Media

Social media trends have the potential to educate individuals about significant subjects and may be associated with propaganda. The topics trending on social media platforms can serve as a source of information and knowledge for individuals, helping them stay informed about important issues. However, it also implies a cautionary note by mentioning the association with propaganda, indicating that some trending content on social media may be biased, misleading, or designed to manipulate opinions rather than provide objective information. This highlights the dual nature of social media trends, which can both enlighten and potentially deceive users depending on the credibility and intentions behind the content.

4.2. Monopoly of Social Media and Propaganda

The monopoly of social media platforms has significantly impacted the dissemination of information and the spread of propaganda in contemporary society.

With a handful of major social media companies (e.g., Twitter, Facebook) holding substantial control over online communication channels, the potential for spreading propaganda and manipulating public opinion has increased. These platforms have become powerful tools for shaping narratives, influencing ideologies, and even swaying political outcomes.

The algorithms employed by these platforms often prioritize content that garners the most engagement, leading to the amplification of sensational or divisive messages, including propaganda. This can create echo chambers where individuals are exposed to information that aligns with their existing beliefs, further reinforcing polarized viewpoints.

Moreover, the lack of transparency in content moderation and the proliferation of fake news and misinformation on social media have made it easier for propaganda to masquerade as legitimate information. This blurring of lines between truth and falsehood poses a significant threat to public discourse and democracy.

To combat the negative effects of social media monopolies on propaganda, there is a growing call for increased regulation. Additionally, media literacy and critical thinking skills have become essential tools for individuals to navigate the complex landscape of information online and discern fact from fiction.

Ultimately, addressing the monopoly of social media and its role in propagating misinformation requires a multifaceted approach that involves collaboration between policymakers, tech companies, and society.

4.3. Education against propaganda

Education serves as a powerful antidote to propaganda by nurturing critical thinking, media literacy, civic engagement, cultural understanding, ethical considerations, and information literacy. By investing in a well-rounded education that equips individuals with the skills and knowledge to discern truth from falsehood, societies can build a more resilient defense against the insidious influence of propaganda.

Education has the dual potential to serve as a tool for spreading propaganda, while also possessing the capacity to nurture essential abilities like critical thinking, which are crucial for recognizing and resisting propaganda (Silitră, 2020). Digital literacy encompasses a broad range of intricate cognitive, physical, social, and emotional skills beyond basic software usage and device operation, essential for effective functioning in digital spaces (Eshet, 2004).

In conclusion, education stands as a potent remedy against propaganda, fostering critical thinking, media literacy, civic engagement, cultural awareness, ethical discernment, and information fluency. By investing in a comprehensive education that empowers individuals to distinguish truth from deception, societies can fortify themselves against the pervasive impact of propaganda, thus highlighting the dual role of education in combating misinformation while also cultivating essential skills for navigating digital landscapes.

4.4. Influence of Online Bots

Amplification of Messages: Online bots can rapidly amplify messages by creating the illusion of widespread support or opposition. They can flood social media platforms with content, making certain narratives appear more popular or credible than they actually are. Manipulation of Trends: Bots can artificially inflate hashtags or topics, influencing what trends on social media platforms. This manipulation can distort public discourse and steer conversations in particular directions. Disinformation Campaigns: Bots are often used to spread false information or propaganda, contributing to the dissemination of misinformation, fake news, and conspiracy theories. This can lead to confusion, distrust, and division within society.

The results of prior analysis confirm that bots achieved measurable levels of influence in the 2016 US election. Hence, it is clear that bots did influence the spread of information during this particular event (Woolley & Guilbeault, 2017). Furthermore, in a different study, following accusations of Russian involvement in the 2016 US presidential elections, there was a spotlight on advanced trolls—automated accounts(Pavlíková, Šenkýřová, & Drmola, 2021).

4.5. Online Propaganda and Extremism

Online propaganda and extremism have become increasingly prevalent in the digital age, leveraging the vast reach and anonymity provided by the internet to disseminate radical ideologies and recruit followers.

There exist terrorist organizations that, with minimal upfront costs, are producing videos of such high quality that they rival BBC or CNN broadcasts to the extent that the distinction becomes insignificant and, these groups have immediate access to a worldwide audience through the internet (Dauber & Winkler, 2014). Following the emergence of the Islamic State, a general agreement has formed regarding the correlation between extremism and social media. Specifically, it is widely acknowledged that ISIS' effectiveness as a terrorist group is, in part, attributable to its adept utilization of social media platforms (Ferrara, 2017).

4.6. Personalized Advertisement and Politics

There is a scarcity of literature on personalized advertising and its intersection with politics.

Personalized advertising and propaganda can be closely intertwined, especially in the realm of political campaigns where targeted messaging can have a significant influence on public opinion. Politicians can use personalized advertising to propagate their message and potentially influence people on a large scale:

Personalization results in higher click-through rates for companies that employ explicit data gathering methods (Aguirre, Mahr, Grewal, de Ruyter, & Wetzels, 2015).

Example Scenario

Imagine a political candidate running for office who wants to target specific voter demographics with tailored messages to sway their opinions in their favor. By leveraging personalized advertising on social media platforms, the candidate's campaign team can create custom ads that resonate with different segments of the population based on their interests, behaviors, and demographics.

Microtargeting: Using data analytics and algorithms, the campaign team can identify key issues that are important to different groups of voters. For instance, they may create ads addressing healthcare for older voters, economic policies for young professionals, and education reform for parents.

Psychographic Profiling: By analyzing social media behavior and interactions, the campaign can create psychological profiles of voters to understand their beliefs, values, and preferences.

A/B Testing: The campaign can run multiple versions of ads with slight variations in messaging, imagery, or calls to action to determine which ones are most effective in eliciting the desired response from different segments of the population.

Echo Chambers: Through targeted advertising, the campaign can reinforce existing beliefs and opinions within specific groups, creating echo chambers where individuals are exposed to content that aligns with their viewpoints. This can deepen polarization and make it challenging for alternative perspectives to penetrate these bubbles.

Disinformation and Manipulation: In extreme cases, personalized advertising can be used to spread misinformation, manipulate facts, or distort reality to serve the interests of the campaign. This can lead to the propagation of propaganda that aims to deceive or mislead voters for political gain.

Number of Likes and Dislikes

Users express preferences for entertainment by liking or disliking content; they engage in socializing through commenting and uploading videos (Khan, 2017). Predicting the popularity of User Generated Content is a subject of interest to the Internet service providers, content makers, social media researchers, and online advertisers (Halim, Hussain, & Hashim Ali, 2022).

In the context of social media platforms, the number of likes and dislikes on a post can be seen as an algorithm that influences the visibility and engagement of that content. This could also evolve over time as the website updates its algorithms.

1. Likes and Dislikes Count:
    - The number of likes and dislikes a post receives is a significant metric for social media platforms.
2. Engagement Measurement:
    - Likes and dislikes are used as indicators of user engagement with a post. Higher engagement often leads to increased visibility of the post.
3. Algorithmic Impact:
    - The number of likes can influence the algorithm that determines which posts are shown to users. Posts with more likes are often prioritized and shown to a larger audience.

Networking Rules

Networking rules in social media (e.g., Facebook, Linkedin, and Instagram) are essential for maintaining a professional image and fostering meaningful connections.

Be Authentic: Authenticity is crucial in networking on social media. Be genuine, transparent, and true to yourself in your interactions.

Professional Profile: Ensure your profile is professional and up-to-date. Use a clear profile picture and bio that accurately represent you and your professional interests.

Engage Thoughtfully**: When engaging with others, be thoughtful and respectful in your comments and messages. Avoid controversial topics that may harm your professional reputation.

Quality Over Quantity: Focus on building quality connections rather than amassing a large number of followers. It's better to have a few meaningful connections than many superficial ones.

Personalized Communication**: When reaching out to new connections, personalize your messages. Mention common interests or connections to make your approach more genuine.

Share Valuable Content**: Share content that is relevant and valuable to your network. This could include industry insights, articles, or personal achievements.

Maintain Professionalism**: Maintain a professional tone in all your interactions. Avoid using slang or language that may be perceived as unprofessional.

Privacy: Respect the privacy of others on social media. Avoid sharing personal information without permission and be mindful of tagging others in posts.

Networking Groups: Join networking groups related to your industry or interests. Engage in discussions, provide value, and build relationships with other members.

Algorithmic Detection of Propaganda:

Natural Language Processing (NLP): NLP techniques are often employed to process and analyze text data to detect patterns indicative of propaganda. Sentiment analysis, topic modeling, and text classification are common NLP methods used for this purpose.

Machine Learning Algorithms: Supervised and unsupervised machine learning algorithms can be utilized to train models to recognize propaganda based on labeled datasets. These algorithms can learn to distinguish between normal content and propaganda through features such as language use, source credibility, and emotional appeal.

Other document introduces a technique utilizing topic modeling to detect texts containing propaganda. The method outlined consists of four main steps: creating corpus partitions, generating a topic model for a combined corpus, estimating imbalances in each topic within the corpora (Kirill et al., 2020). Also,a linguistic/game-theoretic approach was suggested to detect propaganda (Barfar, 2022).

5. CONCLUSION

In conclusion, the intricate interplay between Artificial Intelligence, Online Algorithms, and propaganda in the digital sphere underscores pressing concerns that necessitate thorough examination and proactive measures. As AI technologies, particularly online algorithms, are increasingly harnessed to amplify the reach of propaganda, the ethical implications and societal consequences of this alliance come into sharp focus.

Limitations

This is not a systematic review. Researchers may exhibit bias towards particular disciplinary perspectives in certain fields, leading them to prioritize extreme cases in order to achieve more notable outcomes.

Suggestions for Further Studies

Additional studies could educate participants on how to recognize propaganda.

Acknowledgment

None.

Funding

There is no funding associated with this study.

Author Statement

K.U. wrote the manuscript.

Conflict of Interest Statement

There is no conflict of interest to state.

REFERENCES

Aguirre, E., Mahr, D., Grewal, D., de Ruyter, K., & Wetzels, M. (2015). Unraveling the Personalization Paradox: The Effect of Information Collection and Trust-Building Strategies on Online Advertisement Effectiveness. *Journal of Retailing*, *91*(1), 34–49. DOI: 10.1016/j.jretai.2014.09.005

Baethge, C., Goldbeck-Wood, S., & Mertens, S. (2019). SANRA—A scale for the quality assessment of narrative review articles. *Research Integrity and Peer Review*, *4*(1), 1–7. DOI: 10.1186/s41073-019-0064-8 PMID: 30962953

Barfar, A. (2022). A linguistic/game-theoretic approach to detection/explanation of propaganda. *Expert Systems with Applications*, *189*, 116069. DOI: 10.1016/j.eswa.2021.116069

Chaudhari, D. D., & Pawar, A. V. (2021). Propaganda analysis in social media: A bibliometric review. *Information Discovery and Delivery*, *49*(1), 57–70. DOI: 10.1108/IDD-06-2020-0065

Dauber, C. E., & Winkler, C. K. (2014). *Visual propaganda and extremism in the online environment*. USAWC Press.

Eshet, Y. (2004). Digital literacy: A conceptual framework for survival skills in the digital era. *Journal of Educational Multimedia and Hypermedia*, *13*(1), 93–106.

Ferrara, E. (2017). Contagion dynamics of extremist propaganda in social networks. *Information Sciences*, *418-419*, 1–12. DOI: 10.1016/j.ins.2017.07.030

Halim, Z., Hussain, S., & Hashim Ali, R. (2022). Identifying content unaware features influencing popularity of videos on YouTube: A study based on seven regions. *Expert Systems with Applications*, *206*, 117836. DOI: 10.1016/j.eswa.2022.117836

Hashemi, M., & Hall, M. (2019). Detecting and classifying online dark visual propaganda. *Image and Vision Computing*, *89*, 95–105. DOI: 10.1016/j.imavis.2019.06.001

Khan, M. L. (2017). Social media engagement: What motivates user participation and consumption on YouTube? *Computers in Human Behavior*, *66*, 236–247. DOI: 10.1016/j.chb.2016.09.024

Kiper, J. (2015). Toward an Anthropology of War Propaganda. *Political and Legal Anthropology Review*, *38*(1), 129–146. DOI: 10.1111/plar.12090

Kirill, Y., Mihail, I. G., Sanzhar, M., Rustam, M., Olga, F., & Ravil, M. (2020). Propaganda Identification Using Topic Modelling. *Procedia Computer Science*, *178*, 205–212. DOI: 10.1016/j.procs.2020.11.022

Lock, I., & Ludolph, R. (2020). Organizational propaganda on the Internet: A systematic review. *Public Relations Inquiry*, *9*(1), 103–127. DOI: 10.1177/2046147X19870844

McCluskey, L. M., Hamilton, J. M., & Reynolds, A. (2023). When Propaganda Became a Dirty Word. *Journalism History*, *49*(2), 140–157. DOI: 10.1080/00947679.2023.2203026

Neyazi, T. A. (2020). Digital propaganda, political bots and polarized politics in India. *Asian Journal of Communication*, *30*(1), 39–57. DOI: 10.1080/01292986.2019.1699938

Pavlíková, M., Šenkýřová, B., & Drmola, J. (2021). Propaganda and disinformation go online. *Challenging online propaganda and disinformation in the 21st century*, 43-74.

Silitră, N. C. (2020). 21st Century Propaganda and Education–Friends or Foes? *Bulletin of the Transilvania University of Braşov, Series VII: Social Sciences and Law, 13*(1-Suppl), 143-154.

Woolley, S., & Guilbeault, D. (2017). Computational propaganda in the United States of America: Manufacturing consensus online. Academic Press.

Chapter 9
Conflict Caught in Propaganda Nationalism:
An Analysis of the India–Pakistan Newspaper Coverage of Mumbai, Uri, and Pulwama Attacks

Keerthana Thankachan
Apollo University, Chittoor, India

Thomas P. E.
Bharathiar University, India

Vishnu Achutha Menon
https://orcid.org/0000-0003-4028-3685
Institute for Educational and Developmental Studies, India

ABSTRACT

This chapter delves into the emerging themes and trends of propaganda journalism in the print media of India and Pakistan, focusing on their coverage of the Kashmir conflicts. Through a thematic comparative analysis of case studies, including the Mumbai, Uri, and Pulwama attacks, the research uncovers the biases and reliance on stereotypical reporting in national newspapers. It critically examines how Indian and Pakistani newspapers, specifically The Hindu and Dawn, act as agents of peace and conflict, shaping propaganda narratives of war and reconciliation. By analyzing the framing of nationalist ideologies within the context of these conflicts, the chapter provides insights into the intricate relationship between media, nationalism, and propaganda. The findings reveal that the print media in both countries perpetuate nationalist propaganda, influencing public opinion and fueling ongoing tensions. The study also highlights the need for a paradigm shift in media framing to foster positive propaganda that promotes peace and reconciliation between India and Pakistan.

DOI: 10.4018/979-8-3693-7468-9.ch009

INTRODUCTION

It's a hard reality to accept that studies on media intervention in India-Pakistan conflicts are often biased and fragmented. The editor of 'Friday Times,' a Pakistani English-language independent news-weekly, analyzed how media coverage remains entrenched in narrow nationalism. He critically examines the media's tendency to exacerbate conflicts rather than work towards proposing solutions. Reports on India-Pakistan conflicts often reflect national agendas, consisting of arguments and counter-arguments that pit the two nations against each other. For instance, Indian dailies report that Pakistan engages in hostile propaganda against India (The Hindu, 2023), while Pakistani newspapers accuse India of propagating terror in what they call Indian-occupied Kashmir.

From the Shimla, Agra, and Lahore Summits to ceasefires and the Delhi–Lahore Bus service, peace initiatives have consistently failed to find a sustainable solution to the ongoing tensions between India and Pakistan. The 2008 Mumbai attack disrupted the ongoing peace process, with the media playing a significant role in perpetuating the conflict. Numerous political and historical researchers have studied the potential threat these conflicts pose, recognizing that a major war or nuclear strike would be catastrophic for world peace and humanity as a whole (Siraj, 2008).

Journalists attending a gathering in New Delhi acknowledged the bitter truth that exaggerated reports from newspapers in both countries have fueled Hindu-Muslim riots since partition (Jabbar, 2012). Various organizations, such as SAFMA (South Asian Free Media Association), have been formed, and others have joined hands to promote peace initiatives between the nations. However, the solutions proposed often fail to achieve lasting peace, as these initiatives and recurring conflicts are entangled in propaganda-driven nationalism. This propaganda nationalism is further amplified through emerging social and digital media platforms, where news coverage portrays the two countries as fierce enemies rather than potential allies (Siraj, 2008; Paul & Paul, 2005).

Approaches to India-Pakistan Conflict Coverage

The absence of a centralized code of ethics for media in the coverage of conflict stories allows news organizations to create their own moral frameworks, which are often closely aligned with organizational policies and interests rather than national interests. The modern newsroom has become a hub focused on maximizing viewership through "anchor-driven" content, "competitive news," and selective coverage of events (Seth, 2016; Kaur et al., 2018). Propaganda nationalism in India-Pakistan news coverage often operates by manipulating emotions. However, modern scholars argue that the impact of propaganda on nationalism can be minimal, and it may even backfire, undermining national pride (Cantoni et al., 2017; Huang, 2018). The limitations of propaganda in influencing minds and emotions, as opposed to its perceived persuasive power in media, have also been explored by contemporary media scholars (Wedeen, 1999; Carter and Carter, 2019).

In this context, the present chapter becomes crucial in dissecting conventional wisdom to determine whether traditional media coverage manipulates nationalism for the purposes of propaganda.

Direction of the Study and Goals

The mission and the focus of the chapter are to understand the emerging themes and trends of propaganda journalism in the print media between India and Pakistan.The research explores how the national newspapers of India and Pakistan become agents of peace and conflict in framing the propaganda of war and reconciliation. When the reports of the Ministry of External Affairs (MEA) in 2022 argued the engagements of "hostile and fabricated propaganda", the study became vital to analyse the framing of propaganda nationalism in The Dawn and The Hindu which are the prominent newspapers of India and Pakistan. The chapter will be an eye-opener to understand the intense correlation between newspaper propaganda and framing of nationalism in Indian and Pakistani Newspapers. From the background of the contents and contexts of 3 case studies, namely, Mumbai, Uri, and Pulwama attacks a comparative examination is done to distinguish the narrative construction of propaganda framed in the consensus of nationalism. Therefore, the study is structured for a thematic comparative analysis of the coverage of India-Pakistan Conflicts to deconstruct the extent of propaganda nationalism.

Intent and Targets

From the first War of Independence in India to the modern war of words, the role and contribution of newspapers in advancing the cause of freedom and propagating ideas (Barns, 1940; Bhargava, 1987) cannot be overlooked. From pamphlets to modern digital newspapers, print media has continuously evolved, finding new ways to manipulate emotions and shape nationalism through the power of persuasion. This chapter analyzes the capacity of print media in India and Pakistan to frame nationalist sentiments, serving either the propaganda of peace or the rhetoric of war. The study offers a crucial perspective on the modern framing strategies employed by media in the enduring conflicts between India and Pakistan.

By examining key events such as the Mumbai attack on 26th November 2008 and the Pulwama attack on 14th February 2019, this content analysis provides a comprehensive framework for understanding the changing patterns of propaganda and the portrayal of nationalism in both countries.

The study serves as a window for dialogue between the neighboring nations, offering insights into how each country handles media messages during conflicts. These messages often become the primary source of information for readers, with significant consequences such as internet shutdowns and digital warfare. The underlying frames of nationalist propaganda can manipulate emotions and intensify identity-based disputes, thereby fueling the venom of war. Conversely, these same frames have the potential to elevate peace journalism, providing interactive cues for conflict resolution and fostering friendly coexistence.

The main objectives of this chapter are to explore and underline the researchers' understandings (Hussain, 2018; Joshi, 2016) of whether media coverage in such contexts is propagandistic or highly escalatory.

Objectives

1. To understand how propaganda is represented in the newspaper articles of the case studies.
2. To explore the framing of national ideology in newspapers and its role in promoting either peace or conflict.
3. To identify whether the news media has become a tool for propagating nationalist content during India-Pakistan conflict coverage.

4. To analyze the portrayals of propaganda and identity in order to define the frameworks used to shape nationalism.

FLASHES OF PREVIOUS RESEARCH INSIGHTS

From the concepts of traditional media theories, authoritarianism has gradually evolved to use nationalist propaganda as a tool to strengthen mass support. Propaganda nationalism in media operates by manipulating emotions (Carter and Carter, 2019; Nugent, 2017), often by invoking perceived violations of national sovereignty and integrity under the guise of patriotism. This approach leverages media's capacity to increase regime support or incite hatred for mass influence (Wedeen, 1999). A notable historical example is Soviet propaganda, which effectively mobilized the Russian people against German forces using traditional communication strategies. Similarly, during the Second World War, posters were a major medium for disseminating French propaganda that incited hatred against their Allies (Çakı and Gülada, 2018). These examples demonstrate how propaganda can be deeply rooted in nationalism and strategically spread through media for calculated outcomes.

Today, coordinating propaganda campaigns has become easier with the widespread availability of media outlets across countries (Fahmy, 2019; Hoskins & O'Loughlin, 2015; Grondin, 2012). It's a well-known fact that military operations around the globe, including those in the United States, India, and Pakistan, optimally utilize media platforms, particularly social media, for propaganda purposes and to portray nationalism (Tumber & Webster, 2006; Tanchak, 2017; Till, 2020). On the other hand, researchers have studied online propaganda by terrorist groups (Klausen, 2015; Fahmy, 2019) and confirmed that organizations like Al-Qaeda and ISIS rely on various media outlets to promote their ideologies and recruit members. This becomes particularly alarming when considering the ongoing conflicts between India and Pakistan.

The shift from civic nationalism to ethnic nationalism (Paul, 2006) occurs when religion is intertwined with the emotions of patriotism. Indian and Pakistani newspapers have long been part of national identity propaganda (Carter and Carter, 2021). The article "Pakistan: Between Radicalisation and Democratisation in an Unfolding Conflict" (2009) clearly analyzes how The Dawn newspaper was founded with the mission to propagate Jinnah's politics and his goal of creating an independent Pakistan (Bose, 2011). Similarly, Indian newspapers, predating Independence, were ignited by nationalist movements, turning them into powerful tools with sharp propaganda and ideological orientation (Bose, 2011).

In the context of modern media business, even a free media outlet in India during wartime, as Hastings aptly put it, "becomes an extension of war" (Tonite, 2024). This perspective aligns with the views of researchers like Sandra Borden (2010) and Galtung and Ruge (1965), who emphasize the media's responsibility to go beyond nationalist ideologies and embrace constructive and peace journalism, aiming for harmony. The Kargil War, which exploded in the electronic media, became a tool for the Indian government to promote nationalism (Bose, 2011). The Mumbai attacks, with their intense insurgencies and inhuman events, followed suit, further fueling war hysteria and societal vulnerability. From print to social media, emotional narratives propagated through the media have exacerbated hatred and intensified the situation, particularly regarding Kashmir, which remains a constant theme in both Indian and Pakistani national media.

From the extensive reviews gathered (Cohen, 1967; Ankit, 2016; Gerbner, 1991), it is evident that the India-Pakistan conflict serves as adrenaline for the media, offering significant news value for extensive coverage. However, there is also criticism of Indian media's coverage of India-Pakistan issues, with claims that a free press often behaves similarly to the Pakistani press, lacking true independence and freedom of choice. Researchers have expressed concern over the jingoistic journalism that prevails even 75 years after Independence. Therefore, a comprehensive analysis of media content in portraying nationalistic propaganda during India-Pakistan conflicts is urgently needed to identify the modern print media propaganda caught in the waves of nationalism.

THEORETICAL BACKGROUND AND CONCEPTUALIZATION

The study is grounded in the media theories of framing and propaganda. The theory of framing, as explained by theorists like Goffman (1974) in Frame Analysis and further expanded by Fairhurst and Sarr (1996), highlights how media focuses attention on particular events to shape the meanings that audiences derive. This strategic placement of information influences how readers process structured messages, guiding them on how to think about specific issues. The media's ability to frame events offers a framework with two key distinctions: natural and social. Through these frameworks, along with personal experiences, media framing plays a critical role in shaping societal interpretations of issues. The functional role of media framing acts as a social force, directing public attention to specific topics within the backdrop of an agenda. Framing represents a conscious choice in modern gatekeeping, designed to present ideas in a way that yields intended and relatable results.

Propaganda and framing are two sides of the same coin, both integral to the process of agenda-setting. The theory of propaganda, particularly in media and political contexts, is concerned with persuading audiences to adopt an agenda through the strategic use of framing. Like framing, propaganda is selective and represents a deliberate choice. The concept of propaganda in the media was notably introduced by Edward S. Herman and Noam Chomsky (1988) in their seminal work Manufacturing Consent: The Political Economy of the Mass Media, where they discuss its use for ulterior motives. This book illustrates how news and contexts can be structured to reflect inherent conflicts of interest. "Power elites" leverage media to manufacture biased communication, a concept that gained prominence during the Cold War and remains relevant today in highlighting elite interests. C. Wright Mills (1956) also addresses this issue in his book The Power Elite, explaining how control groups interweave their interests into media messages, thereby shaping the judgments of less powerful readers.

This study integrates these theoretical foundations to analyze how nationalism is portrayed through media content via framing and propaganda. Nationalistic propaganda, often emerging from elite consensus, is disseminated through media frames that focus on conflict, peace, motivation, manipulation, and intention. This study examines how these frames are applied in select cases, such as the Mumbai, Uri, and Pulwama attacks, through news stories, articles, features, and other media formats. It investigates how propaganda and framing are strategically employed in newsrooms to project organizational goals, with a focus on dissecting the processes of content formation and the elements of nationalism embedded within them. The research adopts a rational approach, grounding the study in these two influential theories of mass media, which directly intersect with politics, nationalism, and public perception. The conceptualization aims to observe how media frames and propagates nationalist ideas in reporting stories related to India and Pakistan, particularly during periods of insurgency or major civilian attacks that disrupt the stability and economy of both nations.

METHODOLOGY

Using a non-experimental ex-post facto research design, as described by Kothari (2004), this study conceptualizes its approach by identifying three major crisis cases in India and Pakistan through a pilot study based on audience preferences. Out of seven potential cases, the Mumbai, Uri, and Pulwama attacks were selected by respondents, who identified significant nationalistic elements in the content presented for analysis. A qualitative content analysis was then undertaken using variables associated with framing, nationalism, and propaganda, based on the coders' identification.

The content analysis technique involved counting manifest or observable content. This analysis was conducted by counting the frequency of themes (sentences, propositions) and tabulating the occurrences of various categories of "events data" (news accounts of actual happenings) as they appeared in the leading news headlines. The frames of identity, peace, dispute, manipulation, and emotional motivation were taken into account, based on a pre-determined coding sheet that included actors, emotions, images, mood, verbology, and tone of the content. The unit of analysis was words, categorized by their positive, negative, or neutral valence, which helped in developing the coding scheme.

Method and Sampling

For content analysis, one prominent newspaper from each country—The Hindu from India and Dawn from Pakistan—was selected. The analysis covered a one-month period following each of the three attacks, considering all forms of published stories, including news articles, feature stories, editorials, opinions, and cartoons. Specifically, there were 1,099 news stories in The Hindu and 436 in Dawn following the Mumbai attack; 523 stories in The Hindu and 425 in Dawn following the Uri attack, including coverage of the Surgical Strike; and 638 stories in The Hindu and 526 in Dawn following the Pulwama attack and the subsequent Balakot strike. The content was coded based on characteristics related to the significant presence of themes, using typical case sampling, a type of purposive sampling. Each occurrence of a unit was assigned a code in the pre-designed coding scheme, which was developed based on the themes and frames of conflict coverage. The analysis proceeded from conceptual analysis to relational analysis, aiming to determine the relationships among concepts in the texts for comparison between the two newspapers.

Reliability and Validation of Codes

The analysis also considered the frequency of repetition, the extent of themes, and the selection of words within the conflict contexts. Word segments were categorized logically and transparently based on predefined or interactively developed categories related to nationalism, identity, and framing. Inter-rater reliability and inter-coder reliability, as described by Tinsley and Weiss (2000), were employed to minimize errors and ensure consistent judgments. Reproducibility and accuracy were key criteria for ensuring reliability, while the closeness of categories, conclusiveness, and generalizability of results were the main criteria for validating the content analysis. Although there were predetermined variables for analysis and code creation, an inductive approach was employed to explore underlying recommendations for further research. The findings are based on the interconnection of variables related to frames, nationalism, and propaganda, analyzed in the context of the stories' portrayals.

RQ1: Is the mainstream public print media in India and Pakistan independent, or is it controlled in propagating frames of nationalism during conflict coverage?
RQ2: Do Indian and Pakistani newspapers use emotional frames to influence public opinion in favour of propaganda nationalism in select cases?
RQ3: Do newspaper contents related to India-Pakistan conflicts promote peace, or do they instigate conflict by framing content around disputes?
RQ4: Is there a nationalistic propaganda approach in newspapers during times of conflict to promote specific themes or stakeholders?
RQ5: Are the contents and contexts of India-Pakistan conflicts framed within the bounds of propaganda nationalism?

MEDIA AND CONFLICT COVERAGE SYMBIOSIS: THE CASE OF MUMBAI

The civilian attack on Mumbai, India's financial capital, which lasted three days and resulted in over 700 fatalities, brought the nation to a standstill. The nature of the attack, characterized by multiple direct assaults on civilians, set it apart from other India-Pakistan conflicts. The Indian government, still grappling with the terrifying effects of the event, underscores the relevance of studying the role of traditional media as watchdogs. Newspapers played a crucial role in disseminating information, shaping public opinion, and creating propaganda that allowed the international community to grasp the extent of terror and foreign hostility during the attack.

The framing of the 'Mumbai attack' differed significantly from other cases, as civilians were the primary victims, leading to the use of critical frame combinations centered on soft targets. The tone, language, and reporting style in Indian and Pakistani newspapers were framed from either an antagonistic or a protagonist perspective, depending on the national viewpoint. In the Indian daily The Hindu, the propaganda of nationalism leaned on themes of 'ancient hatred' and 'contention for power,' often employing stereotypical blame games. Unlike typical nationalism-focused propaganda seen in India-Pakistan news stories, such as cricket matches or bilateral relations, the Mumbai attack's framing combined sentiments that intensified political tensions.

Frames and Propaganda of Conflict Mitigation: Extracts From Mumbai Reports

According to The Hindu's reports, the crisis underscored the need for international diplomacy and political cooperation. In contrast, Pakistani news daily Dawn focused on the vulnerability of being targeted by accusations without proper evidence. Both Indian and Pakistani newspapers used nationalistic frames to either assert dominance or promote diplomacy. In comparison, international dailies influenced and shaped the framing adopted by national newspapers. For instance, The Hindu included columns and content discussing the propaganda and perceptions that emerged from international meetings, summits, and other engagements, often referencing the Mumbai attack during these discussions. The anticipation of international discourse on the Mumbai attack and the propaganda supporting conflict resolution became key points of discussion due to the attack's nature. Dawn, meanwhile, dedicated ample space to projecting Pakistan's national voice, defending its identity and innocence in the face of international scrutiny through political talks, interviews, articles, and historical analyses.

The first three days of coverage were marked by a flood of information and misinformation, with Indian reports often reflecting confusion, possibly due to the dominance of social and electronic media coverage in the initial stages, despite safety concerns. Themes of justice, family and national emotions, and animosity toward Pakistan-based terror outfits dominated the initial reports in The Hindu. In contrast, Pakistani newspapers focused on themes of national identity, prestige, retaliation, and false accusations aimed at Pakistan. Analysis of The Hindu's coverage reveals that public responses and aggressive political rhetoric served the terrorists' agenda by instilling panic and fear within the nation.

Dawn's reports clearly conveyed the magnitude of the attack by the next day, reflecting a 24-hour analysis of the situation. The restraint from an anticipated war was evident in the context of national security and international pressure. As international attention focused on the Mumbai attack, Pakistan faced increasing pressure to defend its national identity and frame its stance on the attack. Indian media outlets, including The Hindu, referenced the perpetrators' Pakistani connections, creating a vulnerable situation for Pakistan as it sought to maintain its reputation on the global stage.

The Political Context of the Framing of Nationalism in 26/11

The Hindu dedicated significant coverage to the political repercussions of the 26/11 Mumbai attacks, including resignations and political shifts. Messages from Indian Muslim organizations condemning the attack, alongside opinions from prominent figures, were prominently featured on the front and editorial pages. Over the weeks, opinions from business leaders, international dignitaries, and organizations, along with condolences to the victims, filled the pages of The Hindu. The newspaper effectively utilized strategic framing to push for prioritizing Pakistan in international forums, creating a sense of national unity aimed at isolating Pakistan for its alleged support of terrorism. Social networking tools, especially Twitter and Flickr, played a supportive role in sustaining the widespread anger of the Indian public, amplifying traditional media's coverage.

India cancelled major events with Pakistan, including a cricket tour, as part of its accusation that Islamabad was not curbing terrorist outfits based in Pakistan. Dawn's reports clearly reflected the freeze in relations. In-depth features and articles in Dawn called for a healthier relationship between the neighbours, invoking discussions on peace and security. The Pakistani daily consistently framed its content around the theme of maintaining peace, contrasting with the more animosity-driven and anger-filled reports in The Hindu. Dawn also focused on countering the accusations with demands for more evidence, questioning the linkage of Pakistan to the Mumbai attacks. The theme of false allegations was a recurring propaganda tool, with Dawn pointing to incidents like airspace violations to counter Indian accusations.

Media Narratives of Uri Attack: Framing and Propaganda

Compared to 26/11, the Indian newspaper The Hindu adopted a more balanced reporting style during the Uri attack, despite the war of words on social media. The Uri attack on an army camp in Jammu & Kashmir, followed by a counter-attack termed as a surgical strike, was framed within the context of Indian nationalism. Operatives linked to Jaish-e-Mohammad were quickly connected to Pakistan, leading to sensational headlines in The Hindu that called for retaliatory action. Phrases like "It's time for payback," "Lessons for Pakistan," and "War or peace?" dominated the narrative. Politicians fuelled this rhetoric, with the call for a "jaw for a tooth" becoming a dominant national sentiment, pushing the government towards action.

The Indian press, driven by public pressure, framed the attack as a call to war, while Dawn countered with defensive frames, portraying India's aggressive political agenda as a threat to Pakistan's national identity. The ongoing insurgencies in Kashmir were used by Dawn to postpone any potential reconciliation, framing India as the epicentre of terrorism. Jingoistic headlines in both newspapers, such as "Befitting response," "Hit back," and "Isolate," heightened the tension. The Hindu's extensive coverage, including columns like "India sticks to diplomatic offensive," emphasized the need to globally isolate Pakistan, reflecting national sentiment. The Uri crisis coverage, with its heavy reliance on pro-government frames, eventually led to India's surgical strike, a response widely supported by the media and public alike.

The Propaganda of General Elections Associated With the Uri Attack

The content analysis of The Hindu and the outcomes of the review clearly link the propaganda surrounding the upcoming general elections to the messaging around the Uri attack. As the nationalist Bharatiya Janata Party (BJP) sought to secure power for the next term, the media's framing of responses—including comments, judgments, and arguments—was both swift and substantial. The frequent references to the BJP and its leaders in The Hindu serve as a prime example of this connection. Retribution calls were immediate and were supported by election stakeholders, who sought to exploit the public's emotional response, which was shaped by nationalist frames of identity.

The surgical strike that followed the Uri attack was not just a military response but also a media-fueled event, where stakeholders—including the media, the public, and political leaders—pushed for immediate action rather than measured deliberation. The media played a significant role in this, helping to justify the urgency of the response under the pretext of saving face before the international community. This explains the extensive international references and interventions discussed and framed in both The Hindu and Dawn. Dawn, alongside Pakistani national leaders, became responsible for addressing international and national queries, as they anticipated a looming cold war-like scenario.

Uri and Pulwama Attack: Two Sides of the Same Coin

The media coverage of the Uri and Pulwama attacks in the context of India-Pakistan relations is more than mere reportage; it is a performance shaped by national identity and political agendas. The difference in how these attacks were framed compared to the Mumbai attack lies in the exploitation of emotions and sentiments. Terms like "war on terror" and emotionally charged language such as "remorse," "anger," and "pride" became central to the narrative, leading to a media-driven, ongoing war on terror in both the Uri and Pulwama incidents.

The symbiotic relationship between media and national identity is clear and transparent, with mediatisation shaped by the demands of national narratives. In today's context, mediatisation is unavoidable, but the responsibility lies with the dailies to critically frame content for an audience concerned about peace settlements. When discussing India-Pakistan conflict reporting, particularly in the Indian and Pakistani news dailies, nationalism and political propaganda are inextricably linked. The Pulwama attack coverage, for instance, redirected readers' focus to the deteriorating situation in Kashmir, with the media glorifying and justifying the actions of suicide bombers as "freedom fighters."

Kashmir remains a persistent nationalistic frame in both Indian and Pakistani media, even as Indian media celebrated the airstrike response as a victory. Meanwhile, the Pakistani daily countered with claims of "false propaganda," asserting that terrorist activities did not exist on their soil. Pakistan's initiatives for diplomatic settlement were clearly framed in terms of national identity, with the return of the Indian pilot portrayed as an act of innocence and goodwill.

The content analysis of these cases reveals that the media narratives of both nations are not directed toward fostering freedom or peace. Instead, the media's role in these engagements tends to amplify terror rather than promote peace. The politics of nationalism and the propaganda surrounding Kashmir are two central pillars in how Indian and Pakistani media frame the Kashmir issue. These projections differ according to national agendas, with the frames shaped by principles of national identity. As such, the second objective of this study—understanding the symbiotic relationship between nationalism and framing—is closely linked to the third objective, which examines how these frames perpetuate conflict rather than promote peace. The analysis clearly shows that the framing of the Uri and Pulwama attacks was never aimed at peace but was instead part of a broader narrative of national consciousness and political propaganda.

The War of Words: Extracts From Pulwama Attack

The Indian and Pakistani dailies were direct counterparts in their reporting on the Pulwama attack and the subsequent Balakot strike. The Hindu projected the airstrike as a symbol of victory, while the Pakistani daily countered with frames of denial, dismissing Indian claims of casualties as false. Despite this, the war of words between the two continued, with both sides framing the attacked area as free from terrorist operations, even as Indian media celebrated a victory aimed at undermining terror outfits. Nationalistic propaganda reached new heights, with Dawn repeatedly emphasizing their government's official stance, responding with a declaration that Pakistan would choose the appropriate time to respond.

The intensity of the verbal exchange between the two nations escalated further, with the Indian media adopting an unrestrained tone that called for revenge. The release of the Indian pilot was celebrated as a significant victory in The Hindu, with national authorities framing it as a demand met. Soon after, the aggressive rhetoric shifted towards calls for peace, with both media outlets projecting a desire for stability in the region. The Indian government's assurance of a withdrawal from armed actions until provoked was framed as a sign of strength and a commitment to peace.

On the other side, Dawn continued to argue for Pakistan's innocence, taking a critical stance against what it described as India's conventional deterrence and nuclear bluff. The Pakistani daily portrayed Indian aggression as futile in the context of the Pulwama attack, positioning Pakistan as a nation led by mature statesmen. The return of the Indian pilot was framed as an act of peace and reconciliation, reinforcing Pakistan's innocence and its independence from terror activities.

In summary, both dailies were deeply entrenched in mainstream politics, heavily influenced by the agendas of their respective governments, rather than providing independent analysis. The voice of nationalistic propaganda was unmistakable in the coverage of the India-Pakistan conflict. Media intervention aligned closely with government narratives, with nationalism serving as the key driving force in the framing of content.

MEDIA INDEPENDENCE VS. NATIONALISTIC NARRATIVES: PROPAGANDA THROUGH EMOTION

Evidence From Mumbai

The reporting pattern of the Mumbai attack differed markedly from that of the Uri and Pulwama attacks. While the latter incidents were framed with elements of nationalism and identity, the Indian press adopted a tone of radical fury, akin to a soldier in battle. The Mumbai attack reports exerted pressure on Pakistan, forcing it to redefine its strategic priorities. The Indian press produced a vast amount of content across various contexts—national, international, articles, opinions, and editorials—over an entire month after the conflict, intensifying public sentiment against Pakistan, which found itself caught in a blame game.

References to 9/11 alongside the 26/11 attack in Indian news reports reflected a deliberate effort to highlight the dangerous animosity and the need for international attention. The reports frequently linked the attackers to militants affiliated with Lashkar-e-Taiba, an organization with a history of initiating terror assaults and ties to Pakistan's military and intelligence services. Pakistani media, on the other hand, framed content to protect national identity and address fears of a full-scale war between the neighbors. The competing propaganda from both nations aimed to influence international narratives and garner support, evident in the tone and language used.

The situation escalated as Dawn projected Pakistan's rigid stance, counter-accusing India of shortcomings in Kashmir and along the Line of Control. Cricket, once a tool for promoting bilateral engagement, became a symbol of deteriorating trust between the nations. The stubbornness of both countries, coupled with the wounds to their national identities, was clearly reflected in the content of both newspapers, highlighting differences in how they framed nationalism, often influenced by religious backgrounds. Pakistan's disappointment with being placed in a vulnerable position was evident, with Dawn projecting a nationalism tinged with ambiguity. Consequently, the media coverage of 26/11 in both Indian and Pakistani newspapers was marked by opportunistic framing.

Uri and Pulwama Attack: The Dimensions of Propaganda, Emotions, and Nationalism

The framing in both dailies was dense with themes of revenge, following the usual pattern of victimization on one side and victory on the other. The perceived duplicity and hypocrisy of the neighboring country fueled an escalation of the war of words, with both media outlets employing charged language like "extreme benevolence," "humiliation," and "won." However, the reality is that such extreme rhetoric seldom leads to a win-win solution; rather, it diminishes the possibility of a 'benevolent gesture of peace.' Media institutions, driven by national agendas, often set themes based on these agendas—whether related to general elections, cricket matches, or international summits—when forming and framing conflict coverage. Whether it was Pakistan's celebratory tone or India's blame game, as projected by the media, the perception of victory was successfully created. This perception then became a criterion for the media to craft a national theme of extreme caution and skepticism. It is evident that media narratives serve as spokespersons for national constituencies, appealing to political establishments rooted in their independence. The politics of representation and the degree of alignment between government intent and media propaganda remain open for debate in the context of India-Pakistan conflict coverage and media intervention.

Media Frames: Promoting Harmony or Deepening Indo-Pak Divisions?

An Analysis of the framing of the Mumbai (2008), Uri (2016), and Pulwama (2019) attacks by Indian and Pakistani print media predominantly framed these events often using emotionally charged language and imagery to induce public outrage and solidarity against a perceived external threat by Indian daily. Headlines like "Pakistan the Terror Hub" and "Revenge Must Follow" emphasized emotional justice, further polarizing the discourse and reducing the chances of promoting reconciliation. On the other hand, Pakistani newspapers framed these attacks as either "false flag operations" or baseless accusations projected to harm Pakistan's international image. Articles often highlighted India's assumed "hegemonic intentions" while portraying Pakistan as a victim of propaganda, deflecting attention from terrorism concerns. Such narratives entrenched the "us vs. them" dichotomy, reinforcing nationalistic ideologies and deepening societal divides eliminating the chances of diplomacy during crisis.

Such selective framing patterns adopted by the newspapers on both sides take the limelight discussions on cross-border dialogue and the socio-political complexities fuelling anger and frustrations to point the other side as enemy and deepening the existing wound. By prioritizing sensationalism over balanced reporting, it is a sour truth to accept that the media has created an environment of mistrust, where peace-building initiatives were marginalized, and public opinion was steered toward hostility rather than reconciliation. The consistent focus on blame and counter-blame in print media coverage has significantly contributed to conclude that media was a fuel to intense the heighten tensions rather than an advocate of peace.

DISCUSSION AND EXTRACTS OF THE ANALYSIS

Accusations exchanged between India and Pakistan during times of conflict are a major source of media reports, highlighting the pervasive presence of nationalism in recurring content. The tone of revenge and themes of vengeance are compounding factors that intensify the manipulative content found in motivational frames. Indian newspapers, particularly following civilian attacks like Mumbai, are marked by intense emotions of hate, with follow-up stories providing opportunities for the administration and stakeholders to leverage these sentiments for their intended benefits. Similarly, nationalistic frames of propaganda are evident in Pakistani newspapers, where content is often defensive, aimed at evading Indian allegations. A cross-sectional analysis of the content from Mumbai to Kashmir reveals how the unfinished agenda of Kashmir continues to prompt moral, ideological, and regulatory conflicts between India and Pakistan.

The structure of language—through words and sentences that evoke strong emotions—often embeds nationalism within the broader propaganda of war, overshadowing messages of reconciliation. The content reveals the influence of manipulative elites who control the media, stoking the flames of ancient hatred and advancing the commercial agendas of opinion leaders, particularly in counterattacks like the Uri and Pulwama incidents. The key findings of this chapter support McQuail's (1994) argument that mass media constructs social reality "by framing the images of reality," whether through nationalism or propaganda. Print media often establishes emerging propaganda, which later spreads through digital platforms. The opinion and article sections of newspapers reveal the presence of political and religious contexts that form the basis of the content, with India-Pakistan conflict frames in print media emitting emotions of hate and anger in the current scenario.

From the Mumbai attack to the Pulwama incident over the past decade, there has been no significant paradigm shift in media themes—from addressing the problems to understanding the underlying reasons. Hegemony, a dominant theme in Indian newspapers, frames the propaganda of partition's failures and the identity crisis that ensued. Conversely, Dawn participates in national propaganda, with any potential paradigm shift contingent on changes in the national agenda. This study underscores the necessity of changing the principles within administrative systems when addressing India-Pakistan conflicts from both sides of the border.

The conflict-media intervention theory, developed from the study's outcomes, reveals that media frames are inherently subjective, shaped by the nature of the attack being reported. Consequently, nationalistic propaganda in India-Pakistan conflicts is deeply intertwined with the nature and impact of these attacks.

CONCLUSION

Addressing the gaps in identity and religious instabilities is crucial for resolving the core issues between India and Pakistan and promoting a positive propaganda of peace. Media plays a vital role as a powerful tool to stir up contexts that encourage progressive settlement. A significant shift in the framing of India-Pakistan issues in the print media could lead to the emergence of peace-oriented narratives. Currently, the framing of opinions in both Indian and Pakistani dailies is dichotomous, with carefully crafted language that creates vivid, often nationalistic representations of events. The intimate presentation style, which adopts a structure of dynamic dissimulation, directly fuels nationalistic propaganda through psychological processes.

The repeated frames and recurring thematic combinations in these dailies illustrate the different types of relationships that readers can associate with the portrayal of India-Pakistan conflicts. Developing a model through which media can be used as a tool for peace promotion presents an important opportunity for future progress in both countries. By rethinking how conflicts are framed in the media, there is potential to move from a narrative of division and hostility to one that fosters reconciliation and mutual understanding.

REFERENCES

AnkitRakesh. (2016). *The Kashmir Conflict: From Empire to the Cold War, 1945–66*. Routledge.

Barns, Margarita, 1904-. (1940). The Indian press; a history of the growth of public opinion in India, by Margarita Barns. [London]: G. Allen &Unwin ltd

Bhargava, MotiLal, 1917-. (1987). Role of press in the freedom movement / MotiLalBhargava. New Delhi: Reliance Pub. House

Borden, S. (2010). The moral justification for journalism. In Meyers, C. (Ed.), *Journalism ethics: a philosophical approach*. Oxford University Press. DOI: 10.1093/acprof:oso/9780195370805.003.0004

Çakı, C., & Gülada, M. O. (2018). Vichy Fransası'ndaİşgalPropagandası. *TrakyaÜniversitesiİktisadiveİdariBilimlerFakültesiDergisi*, *7*(1), 53–80.

Cantoni, D., Chen, Y., Yang, D. Y., Yuchtman, N., & Zhang, Y. J. (2017). Curriculum and ideology. *Journal of Political Economy*, *125*(2), 338–392. DOI: 10.1086/690951

Carter, E. B., & Carter, B. L. (2021). Propaganda and Protest in Autocracies. *The Journal of Conflict Resolution*, *65*(5), 919–949. DOI: 10.1177/0022002720975090

Carter & Carter. (2019). When Autocrats Threaten Citizens WithViolence: Evidence from China. Working Paper, University of Southern California. Available at: http://www.erinbcarter.org/documents/chinaThreats.pdf

Cohen Bernard, C. (1967). Mass Communication and Foreign Policy. In Rosenau, J. N. (Ed.), *Domestic Sources of Foreign Policy* (pp. 195–212). Free Press.

Dwaipayan, B. (2011). Journalism caught in narrow nationalism: The India-Pakistan media. Available at: https://reutersinstitute.politics.ox.ac.uk/sites/default/files/2017-10/Journalism_Caught_in_Narrow_Nationalism_The_India-Pakistan_Media_War.pdf

Fahmy, S. (2019). Personal Choice or Political Provocation: Examining the Visual Framing and Stereotyping of the Burkini Debate. *Journalism & Mass Communication Quarterly*, *96*(4), 1076–1098. DOI: 10.1177/1077699019826093

Fairhurst, G. T., & Sarr, R. A. (1996). *The Art of Framing: Managing the Language of Leadership*. JosseyBass.

Galtung, J., & Ruge, M. H. (1965). The Structure of Foreign News: The Presentation of the Congo, Cuba and Cyprus Crises in Four Norwegian Newspapers. *Journal of Peace Research*, *2*(1), 64–90. DOI: 10.1177/002234336500200104

George, G. (1991). The Image of Russians in American Media and the "New Epoch". In Dennis, E. E., Gerbner, G., & Zassoursky, Y. N. (Eds.), *Beyond the Cold War: Soviet and American Media Images* (pp. 31–35). SAGE.

Goffman, E. (1974). Frame Analysis: An Essay on the Organization of Experience. Harper & Row.

Grondin, S. (2012). Violation of the scalar property for time perception between 1 and 2 seconds: Evidence from interval discrimination, reproduction, and categorization. *Journal of Experimental Psychology. Human Perception and Performance*, *38*(4), 880–890. DOI: 10.1037/a0027188 PMID: 22390291

Herman, E. S., & Chomsky, N. (1988). *Manufacturing consent: the political economy of the mass media*. Pantheon Books.

Hoskins, A., & O'Loughlin, B. (2015). Arrested War: The Third Phase of Mediatization. *Information Communication and Society*, *18*(11), 1320–1338. Advance online publication. DOI: 10.1080/1369118X.2015.1068350

Huang, H. (2018a). The pathology of hard propaganda. *The Journal of Politics*, *80*(3), 1034–1038. DOI: 10.1086/696863

Hussain, A. (2018b). Muhammad Iqbal's constitutionalism. *Indiana Law Review*, *2*(2), 135–158. DOI: 10.1080/24730580.2018.1544023

Jabbar, J. (2012). *Prospects of improving Pakistan-India relations through media*. Pildat PakistanIsntitute of Development and Transparency.

Joshi, S. (2016). Raiders in Kashmir: India's Pakistan problem. *Survival*, *58*(6), 195–208. DOI: 10.1080/00396338.2016.1257204

Kaur, K., Nair, S., Kwok, Y., Kajimoto, M., Chua, Y. T., Labiste, M. D., ... Lin, L. (2018). Information Disorder in Asia: Overview of Misinformation Ecosystem in India, Indonesia, Japan, the Philippines, Singapore, South Korea, and Taiwan. Academic Press.

Klausen, J. (2015). Tweeting the Jihad: Social media networks ofwestern foreign fighters in Syria and Iraq. *Studies in Conflict and Terrorism*, *38*(1), 11–22. DOI: 10.1080/1057610X.2014.974948

Kothari, C. R. (2004). *Research Methodology: Methods and Techniques* (2nd ed.). New Age International Publishers.

Mills, C. W. (1956). *The power elite*. Oxford University Press.

Nugent, N. (2017). *The government and politics of the European Union (8.)*. Palgrave, Macmillan Education.

Pakistan: Between radicalisation and democratisation in an unfolding conflict. (2019, January 31). IMS. https://www.mediasupport.org/publication/pakistan-between-radicalisation-and-democratisation-in-an-unfolding-conflict/

Paul, T. V. (2006). Why has the India-Pakistan Rivalry Been so Enduring? Power Asymmetry and an Intractable Conflict. *Security Studies*, *15*(4), 600–630. DOI: 10.1080/09636410601184595

Paul, T. V., & Paul, T. V. (Eds.). (2005). *The India-Pakistan conflict: an enduringrivalry*. Cambridge University Press. DOI: 10.1017/CBO9780511616112

Seth, V. (2016). India-Pakistan legislators and public officials dialogue on sharing of experiences on governance and democracy [Report]. https://www.pildat.org/Publications/publication/FP/IndiaPakistanLegislatorsandPublicOfficialsDialogue_Mar10_2016.pdf

Siraj, S. A. (2008). War or Peace Journalism in Elite US Newspapers: Exploring News Framing in Pakistan-India Conflict. In Annual Meeting of the International Communication Association, Montreal, Canada.

Tanchak, P. N. (2017). The invisible front: Russia, trolls, and the information war against Ukraine. In O. Bertelsen (Ed.), Revolution and war in contemporary Ukraine: The challenge of change (pp. 253–281). Columbia University Press.

Till, C. (2020). Propaganda through "reflexive control" and the mediated construction of reality. *New Media & Society*, *23*(6), 1362–1378. DOI: 10.1177/1461444820902446

Tinsley, H. E. A., & Weiss, D. J. (2000). Interrater reliability and agreement. In Tinsley, H. E. A., & Brown, S. D. (Eds.), *Handbook of applied multivariate statistics and mathematical modeling* (pp. 95–124). Academic Press. DOI: 10.1016/B978-012691360-6/50005-7

Tonite, H. (2024, July 6). Media at War: Issues & Limitations with References to Kargil, Vietnam, and Gulf War. Himachal Tonite. https://himachaltonite.com/himachal/media-at-war-issues-limitations-with-references-to-kargil-vietnam-and-gulf-war/

Tumber, H., & Webster, F. (2006). Journalists Under Fire: Information War and Journalistic Practice. London: Sage. 192 pp. ISBN 1412924073. *Journal of Peace Research*, *44*(5), 641–641. DOI: 10.1177/00223433070440050717

Wedeen, L. (1999). *Ambiguities of domination: Politics, rhetoric, and symbols in contemporary Syria.* University of Chicago Press.

Section 3
The Global Ramifications of Government Policy and Whistleblowing

Chapter 10
The Impacts of Leaking in Government and Business Enterprises

Perry L. Lyle
https://orcid.org/0009-0009-2363-6005
Columbia College of Missouri, USA

ABSTRACT

From the perpetuation of war to the downfall of corporate giants, leakages affect national defense and business operations; digitalization and interdependence exacerbate these risks. Security threats hamper government activities; service outages and loss of public trust jeopardize government credibility; financial losses, reputation damage, and legal liabilities can gravely impact the business. The remarkably high dependency on the information economy has created exposure that must be understood for governments and companies to control. These pages aim to understand leakage dynamics of effects, prevention best practices, and incident handling to guide policymakers and business leaders in developing security frameworks and governance policies. The comprehensive analysis of high-profile leakages and emerging trends frames the need to safeguard the public interest, national security, competitive advantage, and customer trust for governments and businesses.

PROBLEM STATEMENT

Leakage is a threat to governments, businesses or organizations of any size, as it could cost large amounts of money, lead to the destruction of an organization's brand name, result in a number of legal liabilities, and give advantage to competitors. Adding to these risks, the digitalization of operations and the interdependency of systems adds more serious risks to an organization's operations. Governments might be caught in the crossfire of risk exposures, including national security and legal liabilities, while government officials battle conspiracy theories and the erosion of the public's confidence in government

DOI: 10.4018/979-8-3693-7468-9.ch010

particularly government leadership. Americans already disillusioned by the Vietnam War, become even more distrustful of their homeland's government.

Then, in June 1971, The New York Times began publishing excerpts from a classified Department of Defense history of US involvement in Vietnam from 1945 to 1967, part of a study ordered by the secretary of defense Robert McNamara that came to be known as the 'Pentagon Papers'. The papers showed that four successive presidential administrations had deceived Congress and the US public about the nature, purpose and course of the war in Vietnam cited by Pruitt, S., & Pruitt, S. (2024, June 11). During his period, it was one of the most impactful black eyes on a nation that had boosted itself on a land of opportunity and freedom.

Leakage affects governments, businesses, and organizations in multiple ways. It is costly to suffer financial losses and brand-name destruction, reducing revenue, the value of the organization, and the trustworthiness that customers have in the organization. In addition, a cost could arise from legal liabilities. Competitors, internal whistleblowers, and compelled disclosure by law enforcement could seize upon a weakened brand name to expose an organization, which could result in financial loss, though not exclusively. The chapter will help us understand how leakages result, their direct and indirect effects, the best practices to avoid or a strategy to handle a leakage incident, and what can be corrected. Leakage remains one of the most vexing problems that organizations must address particularly online carriers of vast amounts of digital information

INTRODUCTION

Leaking, whistleblowing, fake news, and propaganda is nothing new. Planting and disseminating fake news dates as far back as ancient Egypt. Every President in modern times has anguished over the volume of holes and types of unauthorized information sharing from the bowls of their inter-circles, primarily engaged in policymaking, or implementing policies. Former President Richard Nixon had Carl Bernstein of the Washington Post to contend with. Years later, 'Deep Throat' was revealed, and Carl Bernstein anguished over his source's information. It would be the primer for bringing down the Presidency of the United States of America.

What is evolving today is that leakers are willing to damage the very fabric of their county or company in a *scorched-earth* ideology with the full intent of potential damage to their country/organization or themselves. Many journalists from around the globe are willing contributors of biased dogma, replete with likeminded soldiers of their partisan ideological camps ready for their benefactors' bidding. The truth finder must dig deeper and work harder to validate the legitimacy of their sources and the quality of provided information.

HISTORICAL SIGNIFICANCE OF LEAKING

While there are unwavering differences, leakers may try to sabotage the administration's new policies by leaking the Leaking and the dissemination of fake news to distort facts and influence others with bold out-right-lying appears to have been trivialized in our modern society. The gamut of recent data releases and new methods deployed by political operatives to influence public opinion transform the process. State and non-state actors controlling the flow of information (from politicians and governments to those seeking to destabilize them, such as whistleblowers) have long used leaks strategically to shape public opinion, decision-making and the distribution of power itself. Increasingly leaks are used within a networked propaganda strategy to offer pressures and opportunities unique to our globalized digital age. Usually, hold-over bureaucrats who maintain their civil servant careers, leakers have various levels of access to government or otherwise, privileged information. If they differ along ideological lines and have information to the press. Scholars examining the Nixon Presidency are still analyzing all the key elements of Nixon's presidency as an integrated interrelated whole, tracing Nixon's rise and fall and the how and why of the Watergate scandal.

Many years later, 'Deep Throat was revealed, and Carl Bernstein said about his source of leaks:

> To this day, I don't know all of Mark Felt's motives. There's [sic] no way to know the motives of another person totally, even a person that you know very well. Our responsibility is to the principle, and that principle is that if we want to know the facts an come up with a truthful picture of something, it will often require that we can tell people with the information that we will not identify them under any circumstances, Carl Bernstein-(PBS Frontline, 2007).

Today's media operates from an **a-moral** standard of ethical behavior from their colleges of decades past. Members of the media have made no secret that they have paid informants strategically placed at all levels of the U. S. government and corporate America. There are laws, and criminal sanctions available to hold those accountable who violate the government's trust and non-disclosure agreements. But, according to Dr. Perry Lyle, Ph.D., those unethical media soldiers are all but impossible to find, especially when protected by the administration they serve.

Edward Snowden was sued by the U. S. Government in 2019 for the publication of the "Permanent Record" a book, which revealed and disclosed many classified secrets held by the government. The disclosures as claimed by the Department of Justice were in violation of non-disclosure agreements Snowden had signed while employed by both the NSA and the CIA. On September 29th, 2020, the U.S. District Court for the Eastern District of Virginia ruled that the government is entitle to more than $ 5.2 million in royalties from book sales and has established a trust for future earnings of Snowden residing in Russia according to Reuters staff (2020 October 1). According to Perry Lyle, PhD., there are those that regard Snowden as a patriot for the disclosures showing that the United States Int'l agencies were spying on private U. S. citizens, [privacy issues] and those that see his actions as self-greed enemy of the state.

Courts have regularly enforced government non-disclosure agreements (government or private enterprises) designed to protect sensitive information. The government has been given considerable latitude to declare what is confidential and what may not be disclosed. Courts have enforced government nondisclosure agreements aimed at protecting sensitive information. In Snepp v. the United States, the Supreme Court found these arrangements to create enforceable fiduciary duties. The Snepp case offers further clarification.

In Snepp, a former CIA employee, the Court found that whether the information was classified was not the determinative threshold relating to the actual data. Snepp was writing for publication and failed to submit his manuscripts for agency review and ran flow of the law. During a campaign "intelligence work" by opposition operative is nothing new. Those engaged on President Richard Nixon staff were the impetus to bring down his presidency over the famous Watergate scandal. At the time, the forces of Nixon team were unprecedented in the nature and intensity of their clandestine activities.

As proven, charges included: assembling real and fake dossiers of opposition lives, leaking false and manufactured information to the press, burglarizing, and stealing confidential campaign files and the active investigation of the lives of dozens of Democratic candidates and their families mining for dirt.

The new paradigm of the digital age allows for the spread of information in alternative forms of the Internet, social media, and blogs. What people say and share via emails is vulnerable to being hacked and exposed. The old saying, "don't write or say anything in an email you are not willing to share with the world," seems to be excellent advice. To underpin this research, Affective Events Theory (AET), developed by organizational psychologists Howard M. Weiss (Georgia Institute of Technology) and Russell Cropanzano (University of Colorado), Fripp, G. (2023, November 24), to explain how emotions and moods can influence job performance and job satisfaction. Also utilized will be the Equity vs. Expectancy Theory - analyzing the relationship between employee and employer as cited in Equity Theory vs. Expectancy Theory - *What's the Difference? | This vs. That.* (n.d.). Both theories were developed in the 60s by J. Stacey Adams and Victor Vroom, respectively.

Workplace deviance resulting from the leaking of information, most often sensitive and or secret, is a common occurrence in today's digital society. While it is nothing new, the avalanche of public disclosures is costing vast sums of money and negative energy for government and private enterprises from around the globe to protect their secrets. It is a pervasive problem that affects all types of organizations; big and small, government and NGOs. According to (Haper, 1990), during recent times, it has been estimated that between 33% and 75% of are engaged in deviant behaviors that range from thefts of assets to included intellectual properties to vandalism, theft, fraud, and deliberate absenteeism.

WikiLeaks' Australian founder, Julian Assange, faced allegations that led to his seeking asylum in Ecuador's London embassy as he fled from the United States seeking protection. Established as an online source, WikiLeaks noted for posting secret documents from anonymous leakers. They provided a massive disclosure of U.S. government and military information in 2010. In April 2019, President Lenín Moreno of Educator accused WikiLeaks of spying and intercepting his private phone calls and hacking photos of his bedroom, his meals, and his wife and daughters dancing; Moreno has provided no evidence yet. WikiLeaks calls the charges "bogus." The U. S government, released and unsealed indictments against the founder in 2018, alleging on charges that he 'conspired to commit computer intrusions' Welna, D. (2019, April 11). He has been arrested by Ecuadorian authorities and face deportation to the United States to face charges. Assange appears to have outstayed his welcome in Educator.

On February 5, 2020, the United States Senate voted largely along party lines Wednesday to acquit President Donald Trump on articles of impeachment for abuse of power and obstruction of Congress. This historical vote closed the book on the months-long impeachment inquiry that has dominated both chambers of Congress, the press, and in a large part, the country already split along partisan lines. The probe began before the President's inauguration, based upon leaked information. Many believe, especially those that supported Trump, the whole matter was contrived by the leftist political Democratic party Thomsen, J. (2020, February 5).

While leaking is not new, the progression of recent data releases and new methods deployed by political actors to influence public opinion transform voting processes. State and non-state actors controlling the flow of information (from politicians and governments to those seeking to undermine them, such as whistleblowers) have long used leaks strategically to shape public opinion, decision-making and the distribution of power itself. Propaganda has been used heavily by the Russians ever since the cold war initiated in 1945. Increasingly leaks are used within a networked propaganda strategy to offer pressures and opportunities unique to our globalized digital age.

Powerful, competing elites, and those seeking to disrupt or question their power, both combine leaking with emerging advanced methodologies in hacking, (counter-) surveillance and propaganda, meaning these cannot be understood in isolation in today's information environment. It is the intent of this writing to introduce readers to scholarly and popular debates regarding strategic leaking, propaganda, and journalistic reporting. Yes, there are honest hardworking members of the journalist profession trying to inform you. Legitimate media seeks to inform you – fake news seeks to deceive you.

Globally, as humankind heads deeper into the 21st century, the mind shapes out to be the new frontier – and not just from a military standpoint of view. The new battleground – as governmental-military-corporate organizations become enmeshed with each other to push the same AI (Artificial Intelligence) driven agenda of an NWO (New World Order). Research is feverishly underway with the aim of completely understanding and decoding the brain, with the idea that such an understanding will lead to many 'useful' benefits for the rich and powerful. Leaking and political hacking is just a part of the whole process to undermine, discredit and destabilize your opponent. *Winston Churchill once famously said,* "A lie gets halfway around the world before the truth has a chance to get its pants on." *That quote originated many years before the advent of social media.*

One of the first social media sites was the advent of SixDegrees.com in 1997. At its highpoint, the company boasted of a million subscribers allowing members to set up a profile page and share network information across its platform. It was sold for $125 million and shuttered in 2000. The social media outlets of the present day rely less on object facts and more on personal emotions and beliefs. One of the problems is that subscribers are easily influenced by a gamut of distorted and often unreliable information. Many individuals rely on their social networks to obtain information thanks to social media's ability to promote and share information rapidly over a much larger landscape. Yes, most subscribers enjoy their own protection of bubble that allows them to filter their information based on personal ideologies.

So much information is readily available through social media platforms. If ever there was a better vehicle for sharing of fake news and disinformation, this is it according to Dr. Perry Lyle, most often, the consumer of this information, i.e., the everyday user, gravitates toward the unbalanced load of information that is most palatable with their existing views and values. They seek out "facts" and data (most often mere opinions) that specifically supports their preconceived conclusions and proports information contradictory to their beliefs as fake news.

According to the World Economic Forum (2013), a significant concern arises from the proliferation of incorrect information, commonly referred to as "digital wildfires," which rapidly spreads online and poses a substantial threat to governments and societies. The discourse pertaining to the phenomenon of "fake news" has existed for several decades, albeit under several terminologies, and it is only in recent times that the word has gained widespread recognition and usage Lee, T. (2019). According to the Miriam-Webster Dictionary (n.d.), the term "fake news" has been in circulation for more than 125 years, although it has acquired a distinct connotation in recent times. The term "fake news" is commonly employed to refer to a type of news that is often associated with political narratives that are perceived as detrimental to a certain organization, entity, or individual. When leakers disseminate private or classified documents, the culprits may join the documents with fake news information other forms of propaganda to bring about the intended impact of conspiratorial scandalous behaviors against their intended target.

According to Allcott and Gentzkow (2017), the subjects in question have been widely addressed in the academic literature of various disciplines, including economics, psychology, political science, and computer science. Over the course of the last decade, researchers in the field of academia have undertaken an examination of the potential influence that entertainment might exert on political dynamics. The impact of entertainment-driven journalism on the political landscape has been brought into question, specifically in relation to the satirical tone of talk shows like The Daily Show with Jon Stewart or The Colbert Report. In his scholarly investigation about the intersection of entertainment television and politics, Holbert (2005) provided a definition of The Daily Show as "a program that exemplifies the subgenre of fake news."

The author provided a more precise characterization of the genre as one that encompasses programming where either the primary emphasis of the program or a distinct and clearly delineated segment is dedicated to political satire. This observation underscores the significance of the prevalence of fabricated narratives, with a particular focus on political themes, and cautions against underestimating the consequential effects these falsehoods have exerted on nations.

RATIONAL AND LIMITATIONS

This chapter explores the complex relationship between technology, culture, human behavior and organizational behavior, focusing on the impact of leaking on government and business enterprises. It provides a comprehensive analysis of how psychological theories, altruism and public interest integrated with technology reshape cultural norms, values, and practices, affecting communication patterns and identity formation. The chapter is of utmost importance to readers in the fields of political science, ethics, technology, sociology, anthropology, and related cultural studies. Balancing breadth with depth is a delicate task, and this chapter may lean more towards a broad overview rather than an in-depth analysis of each subject involved. Interested readers and researchers are encouraged to explore the vast amount of publicly available literature available on diverse subject matter.

The chapter has limitations. The rapidly evolving nature of technology may cause some discussions and examples to become outdated quickly, potentially affecting the relevance and applicability of the findings. The scope of the cultural contexts examined may not fully address all variations and nuances. The interdisciplinary approach may also pose challenges, as integrating insights from various fields may lead to a need for more depth in specific areas. While motivations may vary, political and or ideological motivations are usually top identifiers on why people risk leaking information, secrets, and classified documents.

Lastly, the chapter relies on existing literature and case studies, which may introduce biases based on the availability and selection of sources. Future research with empirical data and longitudinal studies would provide a more robust understanding of the long-term effects of the phenomena of leaking in society.

In summation, while this chapter offers valuable insights into the relationship between psychology, technology, and culture, readers should be mindful of its limitations. Acknowledging these constraints allows for a more critical engagement with the content, paving the way for further research and discussion in this vital study area.

SIGNIFICANT HISTORICAL CASES OF POLITICAL LEAKING

The leaking of sensitive and classified information has had profound impacts on government, business, and the political spectrum throughout the past century. Some of the most significant cases and their effects include the Pentagon Papers, Watergate, and the Iran Contra Affair to illustrate just a few. The table below illustrates ten from around the world. Today, according to Dr. Lyle, leaks are now part of a frenzied daily news cycle, as opposed to where they were once the first step in the meticulous investigative process of journalism. A war started with the terrorist group, Hamas, when the terrorist organization launch a strike into Israel from the Gaza strip on October 7, 2023, just months following another major leak as tensions were already high.

Hudson, J., & Loveluck, L. (2023, April 14) in a recent report by US media suggested that senior Mossad officials encouraged protests against the Israeli government's judicial overhaul plans. This claim was based on leaked US intelligence documents. However, the Mossad and the Prime Minister's Office have strongly denied these allegations, calling them "completely false and absurd."

The reports, cited by The New York Times and The Washington Post, claimed that Mossad leadership advocated for both agency members and citizens to protest the judicial reforms. These reports were based on a Pentagon document dated March 1, which indicated that the information was obtained through signals intelligence, implying US espionage. It is easy to see the damage created by the leak in an area that is already a powder-keg of explosive tensions.

Despite these claims, a statement from the Prime Minister's Office asserted that Mossad officials did not promote any protests or political activities. Experts have also questioned the accuracy of the leaked intelligence, suggesting it may have confused former spy chiefs involved in the protests with current agency officials.

ETHICS – THE FUTURE OF AI IN VETTING INFORMATION DUMPS

Nieman Reports. (2019, February 25), that anonymous sources and leaks are becoming an increasingly important part of reporting. AI can help journalists vet the huge files and document dumps that are being provided by anonymous sources. Here are a few ways AI resources can be leveraged:

Data Parsing and Extraction - AI tools can quickly parse documents and extract key information, search for datapoints and pull out a summary of the document, including the most crucial parts (through natural language processing, or NLP).

Pattern Recognition - Algorithms have the ability to detect patterns, inconsistencies or anomalies, all of which can be an indicator of experiment fabrication, forgery or data corruption.

Source Verification - Machine learning algorithms can determine the reliability of a source by cross-referencing with known databases, known historical accuracy of sources, and other relevant metrics. AI can flag suspicious sources or those known to provide dubious information.

Fact-Checking - Automated fact-checking tools, which can cross-reference utterances and data against curated databases and past data, can rapidly ferret out factually false and misleading information.

Using some of these valuable tools, it is hoped that journalists and others can better vet and source the information and apply ethical standards in the release. Not to do so it going to feed into less transparency and promote the use of fake news and propaganda. AI can also help to trace the origins of anonymous leaks by analyzing writing styles, metadata, and other digital footprints.

Table 1. Cases of Political Leaking

Date	Country	Political Event	Outcome
December, 1772	USA	**The Hutchinson Letters**- Governor of Massachusetts, Hutchinson had urged the British government to send more troops to put down rebellions in the colony. Franklin disclosed the letter to Samual Adams who published the letters in Boston that increased the tensions among rebellious colonists.	Benjamin Franklin dismissed as Postmaster General by British Parliament and the event help fuel the Revolutionary War with England.
1848	USA	**The Treaty of Guadalupe Hidalgo –** A reported for the New York Herald, published an **unsigned** Treaty of Guadalupe Hidalgo which had concluded a 2-year war between the U. S. and Mexico.	An outranged U. S. Senate demanded that reporter John Nugent reveal his sources. He did not and stood steadfast claiming that he was not a member of the Senate, and it was free speech. He was held in House arrest for over a month before being released, never revealing his source. Ten years later, Nugent was commission for a special assignment by President James Buchanan. It became evident that Buchanan, then Secretary of State was the most probable source for the leaked treaty.
June, 1971	USA	**The Pentagon Papers** – The New York Times published excerpts from a top-secret study that had been commissioned by then Secretary of Defense, Robert McNamara. The study was America's involvement in the Vietnam War from 1945-1967. 4 successive presidents had deliberately misled Congress and the American public about the scope, objectives and progress of early on and subsequent direct involvement in Vietnam.	Daniel Ellsberg, a military analyst who opposed the war and had surreptitiously photocopied and leaked [photostats] the documents to the newspaper. He was prosecuted under the 1917 Espionage Act. A judge would later dismiss the charges and it took 40 years later for the documents to be declassified.
1972	USA	**Watergate** – The scandal was touched off by innocuous five men (cut-outs) caught by DC police in the break-in of the Offices of the National Democratic Party's H.Q. for surreptitious and illegal bugging of the offices. "Deep Throat" code name for an anonymous source for reporters of the Washington Post, Carl Bernstein and Bob Woodard provided information over a period of time after a Special Prosecutor was commission for the Watergate affair and Congressional investigation.	The Watergate scandal would ultimately lead to President Richard Nixon's resignation from office resulting from leaked information. He was the 37 President of the United States, (1/20/1969 – 8/9/1974) succeed by V.P. Gerald R. Ford. The anonymous source for Bernstein and Woodward remained secret for 33 years until 2005 when former retired FBI agent, Mark Felt, revealed himself as "Deep Throat" the anonymous source. down a setting U. S. President.
July 2003	USA	**The Plame Affair** -Joseph Wison, a former CIA envoy to Niger in 2002, had published an op-ed article in the NY Times that President Geore R. Bush's claim that Iraq's attempt to purchase uranium from the country were not substantiated. Valerie Plame was a CIA operative working at the Agency's H. Q. was compromise when columnist Robert Novak, a conservative, outed her CIA employment as Wilson claimed was retribution.	The Bush administration came under fire and a special prosecutor, Patrick Fitzgerald, was appointed to investigate the leak and the affair. The investigation drew in the President's V.P. Chaney, and several reporters including Chaney's chief of staff. Libby was convicted of perjury as a result of lying to the prosecutor during hearings and received 30 months, which was later commute by Busch. In the aftermath of the War with Iraq, no weapons of mass destruction wherever found.

continued on following page

Table 1. Continued

Date	Country	Political Event	Outcome
May, 2005	England	**The Downing Street Memo -** Only the head of the British Secret Intelligence Services (MI6), meeting with Tony Blair's national security team in 2002 and briefed on secret US meetings, said that 'military action was now seen as inevitable'. Attacked at home for failing to stop 9/11, the former chief of US Central Command was eager to show he could 'smoke out' Saddam Hussein.	Critics celebrated the Downing Street Memo as the 'smoking gun' proving that George W. Bush and P. M. Tony Blair had made a secret decision to invade Iraq and then spin the intelligence to fit it. The leaked memo showed that the meeting between the two leaders had been held 9 months before the invasion.
October, 2010	USA	**Iraq War Logs-WikiLeaks founder Julian Assange at a November 2010 press conference.** In 2010, WikiLeaks published 400,000 Iraq War-related classified military documents that showed that the US military intentionally ignored detainee abuse and that there had been an additional 15,000 civilian casualties than previously reported.	Assange personally passed the documents on to the press. This resulted in Chelsea Manning's conviction under the Espionage Act, receiving 35 years imprisonment. She was pardoned in 2017 by President Obama. "The emails sparked criticism of the committee and Hillary Clinton's campaign. On April 11, 2019, Assange was arrested by British authorities inside the embassy of Ecuador in London."
2013	USA	**Edward Snowden-** Edward Snowden a contractor working for the National Security Agency revealed classified documents of NSA's PRISM program's Internet data collecting. The NSA and FBI said the surveillance program prevented the terrorist strikes in justification PRISM.	For some, Snowden was a legitimate whistleblower by some, and others called Snowden a traitor. Despite criticism He received asylum in Russia after Espionage Act charges were filed against him by federal prosecutors. The Washington Post and Guardian printed the leaks provided by Snowden.
April, 2016	Panama	**The leak of the "Panama Papers." -** Mossack Fonseca's Panama-based database leaked 11.5 million files in 2016 revealing rich and public leaders' personal finances.	After receiving the data from an unidentified source, the German newspaper Sueddeutsche Zeitung shared them with the worldwide Consortium of Investigative Journalists (ICIJ), which then shared them with a network of worldwide news sites, including BBC and the Guardian. "People who used offshore tax havens to shelter their fortunes were the presidents of Argentina, Ecuador and Ukraine; the king of Saudi Arabia; the prime ministers of Australia and Iceland; members of the Spanish royal family; and a number of prominent athletes, actors and businesspeople around the world."
November, 2017	Panama and England	**The Paradise Papers-** According to the 13.4 million "Paradise Papers," Queen Elizabeth II and U. S. Secretary of Commerce, Wilbur Ross Facebook, Nike, as corporations utilized offshore investments to hide wealth, profit, and tax avoidance.	The "Paradise Papers." Stolen from the offshore law firm Appleby, [one of the world's most prestigious] documents leaked to the German newspaper *Sueddeutsche Zeitung* (who also received the Panama Papers in 2016). It was estimated that around $ 10 trillion worth of investments was made in the scheme to conceal the profits and avoid taxes. A considerable amount of embarrassment against the Queen played out in the press resulting from the leaks.

Sourced from: Pruitt, S., & Pruitt, S. (2024, June 11).

In theory, AI could be used to augment journalists' due diligence, making it easier to sort and check massive data dumps. But for as much good as AI might offer, its deployment also needs to be carefully managed in order to set ethical boundaries and maintain public trust in journalism. The cases above illustrate that most of the leaks were propagated by people of statute and authority.

These above cases show how leaks of sensitive, personal, and secret information that often is accompanied by classified documents can affect government policies, political debate, and commercial activities. Most often, in the arena of politics, the motives are advocacy and activism, political gain, and ideological beliefs. Leakers are most adaptive at their efforts to conceal their identities or position themselves for deniability or plausibility in secretly disseminating the information.

THEORETICAL FOUNDATIONS

The decision to leak government documents is complex and multifaceted, often driven by a combination of emotional responses, perceived injustices, and rational considerations. Affective Events Theory, (AET), highlights the role of emotional triggers, Equity and Equality Theory (EET), underscores the importance of fairness and justice, and Rational Choice Theory (RCT), provides a framework for understanding the calculated decisions individuals make. Together, these theories offer a robust explanation for why individuals might choose to leak sensitive information, shedding light on the interplay between emotional, ethical, and rational motivations.

Affective Events Theory (AET)

To underpin this research, Affective Events Theory (AET), developed by organizational psychologists Howard M. Weiss (Georgia Institute of Technology) and Russell Cropanzano (University of Colorado), Fripp, G. (2023, November 24), is used to explain how emotions and moods can influence job performance and job satisfaction.

Affective Events Theory (AET), proposed by Weiss and Cropanzano in 1996, posits that workplace events trigger affective reactions which influence attitudes and behaviors. In the context of government document leaks, AET suggests that emotional responses to specific workplace events can lead individuals to leak documents. For instance, an employee might feel frustration, anger, or moral outrage due to perceived unethical practices, lack of transparency, or systemic injustices within the government. These strong emotional reactions can motivate an individual to leak documents as a form of protest or to bring about change, driven by a sense of moral duty or the desire to correct perceived wrongs. Net responses and reprisals may flow from other organizational misbehaviors or injustices with organizations.

Equity and Equality Theories (EET)

Placed side by side, the Equity and Equality Theories, (EET) gives a unique understanding about organization structure and how people respond to injustices, real or perceived and plausible responses to injustice in the workplace when they occur. Equity and Equality Theory developed by J. Stacey Adams in the 60s and the Equality Theory, developed by Victor Vroom, (Equality Theory), also in the 60s may be compared and contrasted regarding the injustices or imbalances experienced by employees Fripp, G. (2023, November 24).

When people perceive an imbalance—believing their efforts are undervalued or their rewards insufficient compared to others—they may experience feelings of inequity and injustice. In the context of government leaks, employees who perceive unfair treatment or observe inequitable practices within the organization might feel compelled to leak documents. This could be seen as an attempt to restore equity by exposing these practices and seeking corrective measures. Additionally, Equality Theory emphasizes the importance of fairness and equal treatment. Leakers may be motivated by a desire to ensure equal access to information and to rectify situations where they perceive certain groups or individuals are being unfairly advantaged or disadvantaged.

Rational Choice Theory as an Over Arching Theory

Rational Choice Theory (RCT), rooted in economics and associated with scholars like Gary Becker, Becker, G. S. (1976) and Coleman, J. (1990), both who posits that individuals make decisions by weighing the costs and benefits to maximize their personal advantage prior to leaking sensitive or classified documents. To do so, actors must consider the ethical, legal, and possible civil and or criminal sanctions involved prior to doing so. When applied to the act of leaking government documents, RCT suggests that leakers generally analyze the cost-benefit analysis before deciding to leak.

Factors in this analysis might include the potential personal risks (e.g., legal consequences, loss of employment) versus the perceived benefits (e.g., personal satisfaction, public recognition, or the impact of the leaked information on public policy or government accountability). Individuals may also consider the potential positive outcomes for society, such as increased transparency and justice, when making their decision to leak documents. According to Dr. Lyle, it is very similar to the Rational Choice Theory of Criminology. (2024, February 13). RCT as a criminological theory, criminals' way the benefits of committing a crime and getting caught and punished over the benefits of the reward or loot they will receive. In other words, is the "pain worth the gain." The 18th century saw Beccaria and Bentham arguing that a conscious endeavor to minimize pain and maximize pleasure governs human behavior (Beccaria, 1764, 1789) cited in Rational Choice Theory of Criminology (2024, February 13).

IMPLICATIONS FOR PRACTICE KNOWLEDGE – LEAKING IN THE 21ST CENTURY

The Panama Papers – described, accurately, as 'the biggest leak in the history of data journalism' – represented about 11.5 million documents sent to the German newspaper Sueddeutsche Zeitung by an anonymous source. The symbolism of the moment is this: even more important than the I-got-scoop-you-didn't scene in Allen and Carell's drama is the fact that what happened in 2015 with the Panama Papers is yet another link in an evolutionary shift that started in 2010, with WikiLeaks' cooperation according to with news organizations for the leak of the Afghan war logs Kenton, W. (2024, June 28).

"Julian Assange, an Australian computer programmer, was also noted computer hacker and activist who pleaded guilty to a host of cybercrimes charges in 1991, but, because of his youth, he received only minimal punishment. He was inspired to create WikiLeaks by Daniel Ellsberg's 1971 release of the Pentagon Papers." Assange founded Wikileaks in 2006 as a media website for clearing classified information according to Ray (2024). In June 2024, Julian Assange, now 54, brokered a deal between the U. K. authorities and a U. S. Judge to leave a British prison and return home to Australia Said-Moorhouse, L. and Manglona, T. (2024, June 26).

These noted events had inspired moments in history that were real and lasting: it represents the realization when journalists learned and, in doing so, normalized a behavior that is now integral to the way news is reported today. Learning has now become the normalized and it has regenerated, dovetailed and evolved into a new trend Kenton, W. (2024, June 28)

The Afghan war logs were just 92,000 rows of military data, much smaller even than the Panama Papers, and truly represent the first in a new series, in which concrete cross-national newsroom collaborations and advanced data-journalism techniques were very much involved from the start. In addition to wikileaks.org as the interposed filter, the totality of leaks examined here shows the characteristic elements of anonymous sources using encrypted channels, along with interposed organizations that mediate access and collaboration, cross-national newsroom collaborations, and advanced data-journalism techniques. A new breed of leaks that has seismic consequences Weise, N. K. (2020, April 11).

This debate reached its height when WikiLeaks was at the zenith of its media prominence with the release of the war logs and 'Cablegate' in 2010, with the question then being: was WikiLeaks a journalistic institution in its own right, or was it a source for traditional journalists? The Panama Papers illustrated that it was ultimately a debate about the evolution of journalism itself, and that far from cloning WikiLeaks, journalism adapted to it by imbibing new, sophisticated practices while making the best of established journalistic values.

According to Von Hein, M. (2024, June 25), November 28, 2010, was the day the bomb dropped — with five leading Western publications initiating the simultaneous publication of secrets from the engine room of American diplomacy. Their raw material: 251,287 documents from the State Department, most of them top secret and confidential, gathered by American embassies around the world. Together, they gave a less than pretty picture of US foreign policy.

After 274 consulates, embassies, and diplomatic missions worldwide transmitted classified cables to the U.S. State Department, WikiLeaks began releasing them on November 28, 2010.

News media organizations are adopting similar technologies to WikiLeaks's, including the encrypted whistleblower submission system SecureDrop, (used by 60 news outlets for submitting whistleblowing activities) which is being used by dozens of news organizations around the world and was authored by the Freedom of the Press Foundation. Journalists now routinely use basic encryption. For the 2016 Panama Papers investigations, journalists used 'a variety of technical means to protect the whistleblower, the leak and the reporting of the story, the ICIJ noted with some excitement. A generation ago, such tools did not exist - Working with Whistleblowers. (n.d.).

Further, non-profit organizations such as the International Consortium of Investigative Journalists (ICIJ) have stepped in to play a mediating role by granting access to leaks and developing tools to facilitate cross-border collaboration. Unlike WikiLeaks, which espouses a philosophy of radical transparency, these organizations embrace the norms of responsible journalism, respect privacy for those outside the public eye, and release only what's in the public interest. The future of data journalism and collaboration. Icij. (2023, May 3). Below is the organization's Mission Statement as quote:

Mission: To show people how the world really works through stories that rock the world; forcing positive change.

Vision: We expose wrongdoing so the world can make it right [Icij. [2023, May 3].

In this sense, the Panama Papers have shown how leaking has helped to accelerate the development of data journalism and a sharing and collaboration culture. Data journalism procedures – and related methodologies required for the management of big leaks – have become a lot more sophisticated, making it possible for journalists to filter and process enormous amounts of unstructured data. This has led to the creation of dedicated data teams in newsrooms and has further highlighted the emphasis on collaboration.

Cooperation via leaks, moreover, points to a break in the long tradition of investigative journalism based on ego and fierce competition for scoops. Revealing the stories suggests the influence of open-source culture displayed in sharing and cooperation, although journalists retain their role as producers of information and gatekeepers of the press. Automated journalism and the future of the press is being increasingly criticized for the loss of public confidence in reporting fake news. AI-operated blogs, internet sites and news stories are confronting journalism with new and profound challenges. Finally, this synthesis begs questions about the agency of news. Journalists of automation, preserving values of impartiality and objectivity, so that the essence of journalism endures.

For this reason, too, automation is essential to handling large-scale leakage. The Panama Papers investigation demonstrated that computation works in newspapers, too. This is as far as the dream of automated journalism has gone so far. The targets look more like a hybrid species, half-man, half-machine algorithm. Data still needs to be interpreted by someone. At the heart of the media complex money and finances and survival will top motivators for staying competitive.

Big data leaks are obviously changing both how journalism is done and how that work is financed: news organizations are by necessity moving closer together as they work on complex, collaborative data analysis and deployment, and they are confronting a new age for the management and handling of information.

UNDERSTANDING THE LAWS ON LEAKING CLASSIFIED DOCUMENTS

The legal framework governing the unauthorized disclosure of classified information in the United States is complex, with several key statutes and regulations. While whistleblower protections exist, they do not shield individuals who leak classified information to unauthorized entities. It is important for whistleblowers to follow proper channels that will ensure both the protection of classified information and their own legal wellbeing. Listed below is a breakdown of the primary laws and protections involved:

U. S. Federal Laws

1. Espionage Act *(18 U.S.C. §§ 793-798):*
    - The above act criminalizes the unauthorized possession and transmission of national defense information.
    - Specific sections, such as *18 U.S.C. § 793*, address the unlawful retention and communication of classified information.
    - Penalties include fines and imprisonment, with sentences up to 10 years for each count of unauthorized disclosure.
2. Intelligence Identities Protection Act *(50 U.S.C. § 3121 et seq.:*
    - The act makes it a federal crime to intentionally disclose information identifying a covert agent, knowing that such disclosure could harm U.S. intelligence efforts.
3. National Security Act of 1947 *(50 U.S.C. § 3024(i)):*
    - This act includes provisions for the protection of intelligence sources and methods.
    - The act also prohibits unauthorized disclosure of such information.

4. Classified Information Procedures Act *(CIPA) (18 U.S.C. App. III):*
    - CIPA provides procedures for handling classified information in criminal cases to prevent unauthorized disclosure during litigation.
5. Executive Orders:
    - *Executive Order 13526:* The Presidential Executive order outlines the classification system for national security information, including levels of classification and procedures for handling, protecting, and declassifying such information.

Penalties for Leaking Classified Information

Penalties vary based on the specific laws violated but may include:

- Imprisonment: Violators can face significant prison sentences. For example, under the Espionage Act, individuals can be sentenced to up to 10 years in prison for each count of unauthorized disclosure.
- Fines: Monetary fines can be substantial.
- Loss of Security Clearance: This can effectively end careers in government or related fields.
- Employment Consequences: Administrative actions, including termination of employment, can occur in addition to legal penalties.

Protections for Whistleblowers

There are laws designed to protect whistleblowers who report wrongdoing through proper channels:

- Whistleblower Protection Act *(5 U.S.C. § 2302(b)(8)):*
- Protects federal employees who disclose information they reasonably believe evidence a violation of law, rule, or regulation; gross mismanagement; gross waste of funds; abuse of authority; or substantial and specific danger to public health or safety.
- Intelligence Community Whistleblower Protection Act *(50 U.S.C. § 3234):*
- Provides procedures for intelligence community employees to report urgent concerns, including classified information, to Congress through proper channels while protecting their identities.

Additional Considerations

Imagine you are a government employee who stumbles upon evidence of serious misconduct that could harm the public or national security. You want to do the right thing and report this misconduct, but you know the information is classified. It is crucial to navigate the legal landscape carefully. Leaking this information to unauthorized persons, even with good intentions, could lead to severe consequences, including imprisonment and the end of your career. However, by following the proper legal channels provided by whistleblower protection laws, you can report the wrongdoing while safeguarding both the classified information and your own legal standing. Understanding these laws and protections helps ensure that the truth can come to light without compromising national security or personal safety.

CONCLUSION

Online poll YouGov.com poll revealed that 68 per cent of Americans believe the person who leaked classified US military documents is a criminal. A YouGov survey, based on 1,072 interviews, further reveals that 57 per cent of the Americans say the person behind the leak is a criminal, while 16 per cent call the person a hero.

The diplomatic cables of US intelligence operations in Russia, Ukraine and South Korea were leaked this past year and exposed details that ranged from resettlement of refugees in Moscow and uprooting of nuclear-armed submarine base near Vladivostok in Russia, to the assassination of rebels by government forces in Kiev and repression of Oligarchs by Russians in Baku, and the influence of South Koreans on Japan.

A lopsided majority of Americans agreed with US espionage on the Russians and Ukrainians, while a lean majority opposed CIA infiltration in South Korea. Concern about the leak is bipartisan – Democrats and Republicans expressed serious concern. American concern on the leak came from people of all ages, educational degrees, races, religions and gender as reported by Sanders, L. and Frankovic, K. (2023, April 20). The U. S. government and governments globally are working to keep their vital secrets protected, not just from hackers and cybercrime, but from their own people.

An **Unauthorized Disclosures Program Implementation Team** (UDPIT) instituted in 2012 by the Office of the Under Secretary of Defense for Intelligence was dubbed 'to help prevent and deter conscious illegal disclosures of classified information'. But it is an effort that's 'partial, fragile, and perhaps temporary' because of 'strategic and operational impediments. RAND issued 22 recommendations ranging from 'how to keep the snowball rolling' (to use their graphic) to continued emphasis on top-down support, coupled with metrics, accountability, and a timelier focus on triage response Bruce, J., & Jameson, G. (2013).

THE DEPARTMENT OF DEFENSE FACES STRATEGIC OBSTACLES IN STEMMING DISCLOSURES

Media leaks have many causes but few feasible and effective solutions.

There is a longstanding organizational culture in DoD that treats leaking classified information to the media as nearly risk-free, which suggests to some that the behavior is acceptable.

To be fully effective, remedies must address the full range of security, classification, and particularly UD-related behavior, and establish an end-to-end accountability process from initial UD identification through the imposition of effective penalties for violations sourced from Bruce, J., & Jameson, G. (2013).

This paradoxical idea, e.g., free speech has to be limited in order to preserve freedoms of speech, and artists' caricatures of those in power, aptly capture the inevitable tension in American democracy between the security demands of the nation-state on one hand and the first amendment rights of the citizenry on the other. For any nation to survive as an entity and to stay reasonably secure in the face of enemies, it will need to be able to protect the secrecy of its national security plans and operations.

The US Constitution, of course, guarantees free speech and these free speech demands directly pinch against the demands for secrecy. All governments that practice a certain level of democracy from around the world will need to maintain the security of some of their secrets and to provide enough levels of openness and transparency in their governance to meet the public's demands for secrecy and trust in order to maintain a certain degree of power. The nation-state and liberty will continue to be quite contentious bedfellows.

REFERENCES

A Handyman's Guide to Fixing National Security Leaks: An Analytical Framework For Evaluating Proposals To Curb Unauthorized Publication Of Classified Information (1989) 5 J. L. & Pol. 759. - GMSR Appellate Lawyers - Los Angeles | San Francisco. (2016, December 9). GMSR Appellate Lawyers - Los Angeles | San Francisco. https://www.gmsr.com/publication/a-handymans-guide-to-fixing-national-security-leaks-an-analytical-framework-for-evaluating-proposals-to-curb-unauthorized-publication-of-classified-information/

Allcott, H., & Gentzkow, M. (2017). Social Media and Fake News in the 2016 Election. *The Journal of Economic Perspectives*, *31*(2), 211–236. DOI: 10.1257/jep.31.2.211

A.P. (n.d.). Fake News definition. *AP News.com*. Retrieved from https://apnews.com/article/11853adb8811487ca5805a0451156c19

Becker, G. S. (1976). *The Economic Approach to Human Behavior*. University of Chicago Press.

Britannica (n.d.) Yellow Journalism. *Britannica.com*. Retrieved from https://www.britannica.com/topic/yellow-journalism

Bruce, J., & Jameson, G. (2013). Assessing the Department of Defense's Approach to Preventing and Deterring Unauthorized Disclosures. RAND Corporation. Accessed July 30, 2024, from https://www.rand.org/pubs/research_reports/RR409.html

Coleman, J. S. (1990). *Foundations of Social Theory*. Harvard University Press.

Dictionary, C. (n.d.). Troll definition. *Cambridgedictionary.org*. Retrieved from https://dictionary.cambridge.org/us/dictionary/english/troll

Equity Theory vs. Expectancy Theory - *What's the Difference?* (n.d.). *This Vs. That*. https://thisvsthat.io/equity-theory-vs-expectancy-theory#:~:text=While%20Equity%20Theory%20emphasizes%20the%20importance%20of%20fairness,organizations%20seeking%20to%20enhance%20employee%20motivation%20and%20performance

Fripp, G. (2023, November 24). *What is the Affective Events Theory? - Organizational Behavior*. My Organizational Behaviour Notes. https://www.myorganisationalbehaviour.com/what-is-the-affective-events-theory/

Harper, D. (1990). Spotlight abuse-save profits. *Industrial Distribution*, *79*, 47–51.

Holbert, R. L. (2005). A typology for the study of entertainment television and politics. *The American Behavioral Scientist*, *49*(3), 436–453. DOI: 10.1177/0002764205279419

Hudson, J., & Loveluck, L. (2023, April 14). Israeli spy chiefs led secret revolt against Netanyahu overhaul plans, leaked documents say. *Washington Post*. https://www.washingtonpost.com/national-security/2023/04/08/leaked-documents-israel-mossad-judicial-reform/

ICIJ. (2023, May 3). *About*. ICIJ. https://www.icij.org/about/

Kenton, W. (2024, June 28). *The Panama Papers Scandal: Who Was Exposed & Consequences.* Investopedia. https://www.investopedia.com/terms/p/panama-papers.asp

Laufman, D. (2012, August 12). *Prosecuting Leaks of Classified Information.* HuffPost. https://www.huffpost.com/entry/prosecuting-leaks_b_1585193

Lee, T. (2019). The global rise of "fake news" and the threat to democratic elections in the USA. *Public Administration and Policy, 22*(1), 15–24. DOI: 10.1108/PAP-04-2019-0008

Lee, W. (2017, February 24). "Whistleblowing" and "Leaking" Explained. *Voice of America.* https://www.voanews.com/a/whistleblowing-and-leaking-explained/3736863.html

Pruitt, S., & Pruitt, S. (2024, June 11). 10 Consequential Political Leaks Through History. History. https://www.history.com/news/9-leaks-that-changed-the-world

Rational Choice Theory of Criminology. (2024, February 13). Simply Psychology. https://www.simplypsychology.org/rational-choice-theory-of-criminology.html

Ray. (2024, July 27). WikiLeaks. Encyclopedia Britannica. https://www.britannica.com/topic/WikiLeaks

Reports, N. (2019, February 25). Nieman Reports. The Ethics of Leaks. Accessed July 28, 2024, from https://niemanreports.org/articles/the-ethics-of-leaks/

Reuters Staff. (2020 October 1). Whistleblower Edward Snowden book earning should go to the U. S. government, court rules. Ruetersnews.com. https://www.reuters.com/article/us-usa-security-snowden-lawsuit/whistleblower-edward-snowdens-book-earnings-should-go-to-us-government-court-rules-idUSKBN26M76P

Said-Moorhouse, L. & Manglona, T. (2024, June 26). Julian Assange returns home a free man to Australia after a plea deal with U. S. CNN.

Sanders, L., & Frankovic, K. (2023, April 20). *Most Americans view the person behind the leak of classified military documents as a criminal.* YouGov. https://today.yougov.com/politics/articles/45600-most-americans-view-person-behind-leak-classified-

Snyder, W. E. (2015). Leaks and Their Consequences: A Guide to the Controversy Over Secrecy vs. Open Government. *American Intelligence Journal, 32*(2), 13–16. https://www.jstor.org/stable/26202131

Strömbäck, J., Tsfati, Y., Boomgaarden, H., Damstra, A., Lindgren, E., Vliegenthart, R., & Lindholm, T. (2020). News media trust and its impact on media use: Toward a framework for future research. *Annals of the International Communication Association, 44*(2), 139–156. DOI: 10.1080/23808985.2020.1755338

Thompson, E., & Phua, F. T. T. (2012). A Brief Index of Affective Job Satisfaction. *Group & Organization Management, 37*(3), 275–307. DOI: 10.1177/1059601111434201

Thomsen, J. (2020, February5). Senate Republicans Just Acquitted Trump in the Impeachment Trial. This Is How We Got Here. The National Law Journal. Retrieved from https://www.law.com/nationallawjournal/2020/02/05/senate-republicans-just-acquitted-trump-in-the-impeachment-trial-this-is-how-we-got-here/?slreturn=20200124142442

Thomson Reuters Legal. (2024, May 16). 4 things you should know about non-disclosure agreements. https://legal.thomsonreuters.com/en/insights/articles/4-things-to-know-about-non-disclosure-agreements

Von Hein, M. (2024, June 25). WikiLeaks "Cablegate" 10 years on. *dw.com*. https://www.dw.com/en/wikileaks-cablegate-10-years-on-unvarnished-look-at-us-foreign-policy/a-55755239

Weise, N. K. (2020, April 11). A Reading List to Put the WikiLeaks "War Logs" in Context. *ProPublica*. https://www.propublica.org/article/A-Reading-List-to-Put-the-WikiLeaks-War-Logs-in-Context

Welna, D. (2019, April11). 12 Years of Disruption: A WikiLeaks' Timeline. NPR online. Retrieved from www.npr.org/2019/04/11/712306713/12-years-of-disruption-a-wikileaks-timeline

Working with Whistleblowers. (n.d.). https://gijn.org/resource/working-with-whistleblowers/

KEY TERMS AND DEFINITIONS

Bot: A computer program that performs automatic repetitive tasks Merriam-Webster (n.d.).

Fake News: Consists of deliberately false stories that appear to come from credible, journalistic sources. They were designed originally to be spread around the Internet. A.P. (n.d.).

'Leaking': a: To become known despite efforts at concealment confidential information leaked out. b: [leaker], to be the source of an information leak. The nuances between whistleblowing and leaking have more to do with the intent. Example: A whistleblower may have protection against retribution against criminal or civil liability to report illegal or unethical conduct against an employer. A leaker may be releasing classified documents or secrets of an organization, or sensitive information to cause public harm due to friction or reprisals against the organization with intent to do harm Lee, W. (2017, February 24).

Non-Disclosure Agreement: Non-disclosure agreements (NDAs) are legally binding agreements to keep information confidential. They go by other names in certain contexts, including confidentiality agreements (CAs), confidential disclosure agreements (CDAs), and proprietary information agreements (PIAs) Thomson Reuters Legal (2024, May 16).

Plausibility: Superficially fair, reasonable, or valuable but often deceptively so a plausible pretext. The suspected leaker of classified documents offered a plausible method on how the information was leaked to the press. Merriam-Webster. (n.d.).

Propaganda: The spreading of ideas, information, or rumor for the purpose of helping or injuring an institution, a cause, or a person Merriam-Webster (n.d.).

Yellow Journalism: The use of lurid features and sensationalized news in newspaper publishing to attract readers and increase circulation. The phrase was coined in the 1890s to describe the tactics employed in the furious competition between two New York City newspapers, the World and the Journal (Britannica, n.d.).

Chapter 11
Scope of Judicial Review and Oversight of Administrative Actions Affecting India and Other Jurisdictions

Saurabh Chandra
https://orcid.org/0000-0003-4172-9968
Bennett University, India

Boddu Harshith Sai
https://orcid.org/0009-0009-4884-4126
Bennett University, India

ABSTRACT

The state policy has shifted away from the laissez-faire ideology that advocated minimal interference of government in the financial affairs of the state and individualism, in favor of the welfare state theory, which emphasizes collective action, socio economic rights, and state-directed policy. The discretionary, regulatory, and managerial powers of the administrative authorities are enormous. Since there is no codified body of administrative law, the administration's discretion in exercising its powers is subject to its own interpretation, rather than being constrained by any objective standards. Judicial review aids in maintaining checks and balances to prevent the abuse of power by other government organs. In India, the laws in relation to the judicial review of administrative actions have been derived from the common law. The author asserts that judicial control of administrative actions refers to courts oversight on actions of the government based on the norms established by the court.

LITERATURE REVIEW

Judicial review of administrative actions is a crucial aspect of administrative law, serving as a check on executive power (Oster, 2008; NandishC, 2020). The scope of judicial review varies across jurisdictions and is often determined on a case-by-case basis, influenced by constitutional, statutory, and regulatory provisions (Daly, 2021). Courts exercise control over administrative actions through writs such as ha-

DOI: 10.4018/979-8-3693-7468-9.ch011

beas corpus, mandamus, certiorari, prohibition, and quo warranto (NandishC, 2020). The doctrine of ultra vires is a key principle in this process (NandishC, 2020). While separation of powers traditionally divides state functions, some overlap is now considered inevitable and desirable, with judicial review being an example of this convergence (Mehta, 2018). Administrative law values, including individual self-realization, good administration, electoral legitimacy, and decisional autonomy, provide guidance in understanding and navigating the jurisprudence surrounding judicial review of administrative actions (Daly, 2021).

Judicial review, a crucial aspect of administrative law, allows courts to assess the legality and propriety of decisions made by public authorities (Aas Muhammad et al., 2023). Its scope has expanded beyond its traditional role of controlling statutory powers exercised by the government (M. Elliott, 2011). In India, the constitution provides for judicial review through various articles, making it more firmly established than in the USA (Shyam Pandey, 2020). The scope of judicial review differs between countries; for instance, in the US, courts defer to administrative interpretations when Congress has not addressed an issue, while in Germany, administrative courts primarily control rather than decide (Jan Oster, 2008). Recent developments, such as Brexit and the COVID-19 pandemic, have raised questions about the judiciary's role in relation to government and parliament actions in the UK (Aas Muhammad et al., 2023). Determining the appropriate scope of judicial review requires consideration of its normative foundations, including respect for the rule of law and the need for good governance (M. Elliott, 2011).

Judicial review, a crucial mechanism for controlling government actions and ensuring good governance, has evolved significantly across jurisdictions. In the UK, its scope has expanded beyond statutory powers, raising questions about its application in atypical settings (Elliott, 2011). The practice is rooted in respect for legality, government control, and public interest (Elliott, 2011). In India, judicial review is constitutionally enshrined through various articles, making it more firmly established than in the USA (Pandey, 2020). Recent developments, such as Brexit and the COVID-19 pandemic, have challenged the judiciary's role in relation to government actions in the UK (Muhammad et al., 2023). Despite variations across jurisdictions, administrative law values like individual self-realization, good administration, and electoral legitimacy provide guidance in understanding and navigating judicial review cases (Daly, 2021). The scope of judicial review continues to adapt to evolving governance techniques and constitutional changes.

Judicial review, the practice of courts examining the constitutionality of laws, has evolved differently across nations. While originating in the United States, it has spread globally with varying implementations (Kommers, 1976). Some countries, like Indonesia and Germany, have established specialized constitutional courts, while others, such as the US, rely on existing judicial institutions (Wijaya & Nasran, 2021). France initially rejected judicial review but has shown growing interest in adopting it (Haines, 1930). The effectiveness of judicial review varies, working well in advanced democracies like Japan and Germany, but struggling in many emerging nations (Kommers, 1976). The growth of judicial review has been influenced by factors such as the need to protect individual rights and limit government power (Calabresi, 2021). Overall, judicial review has become a significant feature of constitutional governance worldwide, adapting to each country's unique legal and political context (Wijaya & Nasran, 2021; Calabresi, 2021).

Judicial review of legislation, once considered a uniquely American practice, has become widespread globally (Haines, 1930). Various models have emerged, including review by existing courts, specialized constitutional courts, and non-judicial institutions (Wijaya & Nasran, 2021). The United States, Germany, and France exemplify these approaches, respectively. While judicial review has been adopted in many countries, its effectiveness varies, working best in advanced, middle-class societies committed to limited government (Kommers, 1976). The extent of judicial activism in reviewing secondary legislation differs across nations, influenced by factors such as legislative efficiency, judicial recruitment, and career patterns. For instance, the United States exhibits high judicial activism, while the UK has traditionally shown lower levels, though this may be changing. France's Council of State appears to intervene less formally but may influence regulation drafting more extensively (Shapiro, 2002). These variations reflect each country's unique legal and political contexts.

Judicial review in America, often associated with Marbury v. Madison (1803), allows courts to evaluate government actions against constitutional principles (Wrzoszczyk, 2020). However, this power is not explicitly stated in the Constitution (Wrzoszczyk, 2020). Before and after Marbury, courts also developed a form of judicial review based on common law principles (Edlin, 2006). The concept evolved from the King-in-Council's role in reining in errant colonies and the political space created by bicameralism, separation of powers, and federalism (Calabresi, 2021). The doctrine's scope has expanded to include executive and legislative realms, transforming the judiciary from a reticent to an interventionist institution (Yasin et al., 2022). Post-Civil War amendments and statutory expansions of federal court jurisdiction further strengthened judicial review, leading to a situation where the Supreme Court now checks state legislatures similarly to how the King-in-Council once controlled colonial legislatures (Calabresi, 2021).

Judicial review, a practice originating in the United States, has been adopted in various forms by numerous countries worldwide (Haines, 1930; Kommers, 1976). Three main approaches to judicial review have emerged: review by existing judicial institutions (e.g., the U.S. Supreme Court), review by specialized constitutional courts (e.g., in Indonesia, Germany, and South Korea), and review by non-judicial institutions (e.g., in France) (Wijaya & Nasran, 2021). The influence of judicial review has been particularly notable in Latin America, while European nations initially rejected it as incompatible with their separation of powers doctrine (Kommers, 1976). Post-World War II, many countries, including emerging nations in Asia and Africa, have adopted judicial review in their constitutions (Kommers, 1976). However, its effectiveness varies, with greater success observed in advanced, middle-class societies committed to limited government, such as Japan, West Germany, and Italy (Kommers, 1976). The implementation of judicial review continues to evolve, with ongoing discussions in countries like Switzerland (Haines, 1930).

Judicial review in the United Kingdom is a crucial mechanism for assessing the legality and propriety of public authorities' actions (Aas Muhammad et al., 2023). Its scope and application have evolved significantly, influenced by recent political and constitutional changes such as Brexit and the COVID-19 pandemic (Aas Muhammad et al., 2023). The UK's uncodified constitution and devolution have led to variations in administrative law across the country, with the UK Supreme Court acting as a harmonizing force (S. Nason, 2021). The adoption of the Human Rights Act 1998 has expanded judicial review, drawing inspiration from international models and addressing human rights concerns (S. Calabresi, 2021). However, tensions between the executive, legislature, and judiciary persist, with ongoing debates about the proper limits of judicial power (P. Birkinshaw, 2021). Despite these challenges, judicial review remains a fundamental aspect of the UK's constitutional framework, ensuring government accountability and upholding the rule of law (P. Birkinshaw, 2021).

Judicial review, a crucial aspect of democratic governance, differs significantly between the United Kingdom and the United States. The UK's system, rooted in an oral legal culture, emphasizes flexibility and context-specific interpretation (Pratt, 2022). In contrast, the US relies on a written constitution, promoting a unified national understanding (Pratt, 2022). This distinction extends to administrative law, where UK courts maintain supremacy in statutory interpretation but defer to administrative factual findings, while US courts respect agency interpretations but scrutinize factual determinations (Ip, 2015). The UK's approach to judicial review has evolved, influenced by recent events like Brexit and the COVID-19 pandemic, raising questions about the judiciary's role in relation to government actions (Muhammad et al., 2023). Both systems, despite their differences, aim to ensure constitutional supremacy and check arbitrary powers of the legislature and executive (Jain, 2024).

Judicial review practices differ significantly between the United Kingdom, European Union, and United States. The UK's approach is rooted in an oral legal culture with a flexible, unwritten constitution (Pratt, 2022). In contrast, the US relies heavily on its written constitution for judicial review, emphasizing procedural democracy (Bignami, 2016). The EU's judicial review model focuses on protecting fundamental economic and social rights (Bignami, 2016). The European Court of Justice has been particularly active in reviewing member states' policies to ensure alignment with the single market (Koch, 2001). The EU's landmark case Costa v. ENEL established the supremacy of EU law, drawing comparisons to the US case Marbury v. Madison in its significance for judicial review (Puder, 2004). As global trade regimes evolve, judicial review principles from both EU and US legal systems are likely to influence the development of global law (Koch, 2001).

Judicial review practices differ significantly between the United Kingdom, European Union, and United States. The UK's approach is rooted in an oral legal culture with a flexible, unwritten constitution (Pratt, 2022). In contrast, the US relies heavily on its written constitution for judicial review, emphasizing procedural democracy (Bignami, 2016). The EU's judicial review model focuses on protecting fundamental economic and social rights (Bignami, 2016). The European Court of Justice has been particularly active in reviewing member states' policies to ensure alignment with the single market (Koch, 2001). The EU's landmark case Costa v. ENEL established the supremacy of EU law, drawing comparisons to the US case Marbury v. Madison in its significance for judicial review (Puder, 2004). As global trade regimes evolve, judicial review principles from both EU and US legal systems are likely to influence the development of global law (Koch, 2001).

Judicial review in European countries has evolved differently from the United States, with many nations adopting specialized Constitutional Courts rather than a diffuse system (De Andrade & G. Fernandes, 2001). This development was influenced by factors such as legal education, the role of judges in policy issues, and the need to protect individual liberties (De Andrade & G. Fernandes, 2001). While most Western countries have embraced judicial review, some, like the UK and Netherlands, have been more reluctant (De Andrade & G. Fernandes, 2001; Visser, 2013). The rise of constitutional adjudication in Europe has led to diverse institutional designs and purposes (Visser, 2013). Despite variations in philosophical backgrounds and organizational models, there is a growing trend towards a common model of judicial control over administrative authorities across Europe (Woehrling, 2006). The character of judiciaries within Europe is shaped by various factors, resulting in distinct systems in countries such as France, Germany, Spain, Sweden, and England (Bell, 2006).

Judicial review in European countries has undergone significant changes, with many nations adopting constitutional courts modeled after Western European systems (Wright Sheive, 1995). These courts have expanded their roles beyond classical judicial review to include functions such as reviewing political party activities and resolving constitutional disputes (Kustra-Rogatka, 2019). Unlike the U.S. system, European constitutional courts can practice abstract review, examining legislation's constitutionality without specific case contexts (Wright Sheive, 1995). At the supranational level, the European Court of Human Rights has emerged as a potential 'Supreme Court of Europe' for judicial review (Daiber, 2024). The adoption of constitutional courts in Europe was influenced by factors such as legal education, the role of judges in policy issues, the concentration of executive and legislative powers, and the need to protect individual liberties (De Andrade & Fernandes, 2001). These developments reflect Europe's evolving approach to constitutional oversight and rights protection.

The development of judicial review in France has been a gradual process, marked by significant shifts from traditional resistance to constitutional control. Until 1958, France rejected judicial review of legislation, viewing judicial power as oligarchic and opposed to progress (Calabresi, 2021). The Constitution of the Fifth Republic in 1958 introduced a system of checks and balances and established the Conseil constitutionnel, empowered to determine the limits of parliamentary authority (Beardsley, 1975). Judicial review expanded significantly in 1971, 1974, and 2008 for various reasons (Calabresi, 2021). However, no constitutional provision explicitly provides for judicial review of administrative measures; this is only envisaged by laws and regulations (De Costa, 2021). The Conseil Constitutionnel's evolving role represents an attempt to integrate constitutional control into a tradition of parliamentary supremacy, inviting comparisons with developments in other countries like Canada and the United States (Morton, 1988).

Judicial review in France has evolved significantly since the French Revolution. Initially rejecting judicial oversight of legislation, France gradually introduced constitutional review through the Conseil Constitutionnel (S. Calabresi, 2021). The administrative courts now exercise extensive control over public administration acts, though some remain beyond review (De Costa, 2021). The Conseil Constitutionnel's role expanded in 1971, 1974, and 2008, paralleling developments in other countries like Canada (F. Morton, 1988; S. Calabresi, 2021). Recent reforms have enhanced the roles of both the Conseil Constitutionnel and Conseil d'Etat in reviewing legislative impact assessments, aiming to improve evidence-based lawmaking and institutional balance (J. Duprat, 2012). While no constitutional provision explicitly provides for judicial review of administrative measures, the Administrative Justice Code and the Code of Relations between the Public and the Administration govern this process (De Costa, 2021). These developments represent a significant shift from France's traditional view of judicial power as potentially oligarchic and opposed to progressive causes (S. Calabresi, 2021).

Judicial review in Germany is characterized by a specialized Constitutional Court with extensive powers, surpassing even those of the U.S. Supreme Court (Kommers, 2006). This system, developed after World War II, was designed to protect rights and serve as a federalism umpire (Calabresi, 2021). Unlike the U.S., where constitutional questions are incidental to cases, Germany allows for special proceedings focused solely on constitutional issues (Rupp, 1960). The German model has been widely adopted by civil law countries due to its compatibility with their legal systems (Calabresi, 2021). While judges are typically appointed by the government, these decisions are subject to strict judicial review, ensuring a fair assessment of candidates based on constitutional requirements (Riedel, 2020). The Federal Constitutional Court's authority extends to abstract questions of constitutional law and lacks a political question doctrine, making it a powerful institution in German governance (Kommers, 2006).

Judicial review of administrative actions is a crucial form of external oversight, ensuring legality and protecting citizens' rights (Batalli, 2015). Administrative and judicial oversight are both important, with judicial oversight being considered more effective due to its independence and objectivity (Jassim, 2022). Congressional oversight of the executive branch is another significant means of influencing agency decision-making, with oversight hearings being particularly effective in altering agency behavior (Feinstein, 2018). The effectiveness of oversight hearings is linked to the credibility of potential legislative sanctions, and they are most likely to occur when there is alignment between Congress, relevant committees, and agencies (Feinstein, 2018). Congressional procedures play a crucial role in shaping oversight and administrative law, with committees, appropriations processes, and differences between

Senate and House procedures influencing various aspects of governance, including military action, environmental efforts, and Medicare budgets (Tiefer, 1998).

ORIGIN AND HISTORICAL BACKGROUND OF THE CONCEPT OF JUDICIAL REVIEW

The concept of judicial review, a cornerstone of constitutional governance, empowers courts to assess the constitutionality of state actions, including legislation (Bhattarai, 2023). Originating in English law and significantly developed in the United States, judicial review has become a crucial feature of legal systems worldwide (Pandey, 2020). In the U.S., despite no explicit constitutional mention, it evolved through landmark cases and judicial interpretation (Yasin et al., 2022). The Supreme Court established a two-step framework for reviewing agency interpretations of statutes in Chevron, providing much-needed guidance for lower courts (Lynch, 1985). While judicial review serves to protect civil liberties and maintain the rule of law, it faces criticism for potentially undermining democratic legitimacy (Bhattarai, 2023). The scope of judicial review encompasses legislation, executive actions, and judicial decisions, with grounds for review including illegality, irrationality, and procedural impropriety (Bhattarai, 2023; Yasin et al., 2022).

Judicial review is a crucial mechanism for ensuring constitutional supremacy, protecting civil liberties, and controlling government arbitrariness (Bhattarai, 2023). It serves as a form of transnational legal control over domestic public decision-making, particularly benefiting foreign investors in the context of investment treaties (Ortino, 2012). The establishment of strong-form judicial review influences and is influenced by prevailing conceptions of legal and political authority, which can form stable judicial review regimes (Roux, 2018). Judicial review, along with political oversight, acts as a mechanism of mediated legitimacy in administrative governance, helping to reconcile tensions between democracy, technocracy, and juristocracy (Lindseth, 2019). However, the concept is not without criticism, facing challenges related to democratic legitimacy and the potential for arbitrary judicial interference (Bhattarai, 2023). Comparative analysis of judicial review systems can provide insights into their varying implementations and purposes across different polities (Lindseth, 2019).

The doctrine of judicial review has been originated from U.S in the late 18th century. It was first witnessed in the U.S Supreme Court case of *Marbury v. Madison, 1803*, which has entrenched the concept of judicial review by stating that Supreme Court has the authority to declare the acts and legislations made by the U.S. congress unconstitutional. One of the major exponents of judicial review can be traced back to the English philosopher John Locke, who has proclaimed that government actions should be limited to certain extent and the individuals should have the right to liberty and remedies against unjust laws. This doctrine further came to light by the some of the legal philosophers who believed in thought of separation of powers and rule of law.

It was for the first time in the year 1803 that the U.S Supreme Court in Marbury v. Madison (1803) declared that the legislative actions are also under the purview of the judicial review. The Constitution of the U.S.A. does not provide any provision for the exercise of the power of the review by the judiciary. It is argued that through the case of Marbury the Court assumed the power of judicial review in itself.

In England, there has always been the supremacy of the Parliament. The judiciary was not supposed to review the acts of the Parliament, as the Parliament is supreme to all. Judicial review remained restricted to the executive actions(B.S,Chauhan,2018).

The genesis of the doctrine of judicial review in India can be traced back to the Constitution of India, which was ratified in 1950. The Constitution instituted the Supreme Court as the preeminent court within the nation and bestowed upon it the authority of judicial review in relation to legislation and executive measures. Following India's independence in 1947, the Indian Constitution was formulated and ratified, thereby instituting a tripartite system of governance comprising the legislature, executive, and judiciary. The Constitution instituted the Supreme Court as the ultimate authority on legal matters and vested it with the authority to conduct judicial review. Subsequently, the Indian Supreme Court and judicial entities has exercised its authority of judicial review to invalidate statutes and executive measures that are considered to be in violation of the constitution. The landmark decision of the Supreme Court, *Kesavananda Bharati v. State of Kerala, 1973* was acclaimed as the annals of judicial review in India. In this case, the Supreme Court opined that any amendment to the Constitution that would substantially modify its fundamental structure or essential features would be deemed unconstitutional. The notion of judicial review has significantly influenced Indian democracy and the legal system, serving as a crucial mechanism for ensuring governmental responsibility and safeguarding the liberties and entitlements of Indian inhabitants. Its continued relevance underscores its significance as a means of upholding the rule of law.

INTRODUCTION

The term "judicial review" is commonly understood to refer to the ability of courts to scrutinize the actions of other branches of government, in order to maintain a system of checks and balances and prevent abuse of power by these organs. The author is of the opinion that a key component of ensuring that the government abides with the Constitution and the law is judicial review and monitoring of administrative acts. The idea of judicial review and monitoring of administrative acts impacting India and other countries will be examined in this research paper. It will also look at pertinent legal precedents, case law, and other important statutes. The ability of the judiciary to assess and closely examine the activities of the executive branch of government is referred to as "judicial review and oversight of administrative actions." When citizens and the government disagree, the court serves as a neutral, impartial and independent arbitrator. The idea of judicial inspection and review of administrative decisions is based on the separation of powers doctrine. The process of judicial review involves the declaration of invalidity of any law that is deemed unconstitutional by a court. This feature was incorporated into our system from the United States Constitution. The process of rectifying this particular aspect of our constitution spanned several years. The judiciary assumes a significant role in this matter. The process of judicial review encompasses the evaluation of constitutional amendments, legislative actions, and laws that have been enacted by the legislature.

The legislative, executive, and judicial departments of government are divided into equal parts under this theory. In order to make sure that the executive arm of government is acting in accordance with the Constitution and the law, the judiciary acts as a check on it and prevents abuse of power. When a person or group files a specific legal challenge because they feel that a government action has infringed their rights, judicial review is sometimes used as a defense. The court will assess the parties' evidence and arguments to decide whether or not the government's conduct is legal. Judicial review is valued as a crucial component of constitutional systems in many nations, including the US, and the constitution explicitly grants courts the authority to examine government acts. However, judicial review's breadth and depth may differ based on the nation and legal system under consideration.

The term administrative action can be understood as any action other than judicial and legislative action, through this paper I have manifest those administrative actions has no legal responsibilities in terms of assembling facts or comparing arguments. In the landmark decision of the Supreme Court in the case of *A.K. Kraipak v. Union of India, 1970,* based on the factual matrix the apex court has held that a person or an individual who serves on a committee for a job should not be a candidate appearing for that job himself. The court further stated that to determine whether the actions of administrative authority actions are in nature of quasi-judicial or administrative, one has to examine the nature of power that is conferred, who have granted the authority, what ate consequences of giving such authority and what is the mechanism that has been practiced to confer such power. India's governmental structure comprises three distinct agencies, namely the legislative, executive, and judicial branches. The legislative branch is responsible for the creation and making of laws, while the executive branch is tasked with their execution and enforcement of the laws and legislations made by the legislative wing. The judiciary branch conducts oversight of both the legislative and executive branches and also has the potentials to interpret the laws made by the legislative wing, ensuring that the laws created and enforced are in accordance with the Indian Constitution and do not exceed its prescribed limits. The separation of powers is a constitutional feature that enables agencies to operate within their respective mandates.

The Indian constitution's Article 50 pertains to the division of powers. In contrast to the United States, where this concept was embraced, it is not adhered to as rigorously in this context. The notion of judicial review is derived from the United States Constitution. The judiciary possesses the authority to nullify any legislation enacted by the parliament in the event that it contravenes the provisions of the Indian Constitution. In the event that a law enacted by the legislative branch is found to be in conflict with the provisions of the constitution, it is within the purview of the judiciary to declare said law null and void. In accordance with Article 13(2) of the Constitution of India, any legislation enacted by the Parliament that curtails the fundamental rights of individuals as outlined in Article 3 of the Constitution is deemed null and void ab initio. The judiciary holds the authority to comprehensively interpret the Indian Constitution. The Indian Constitution is safeguarded by this entity. According to the Indian Constitution there are several articles, including 13(1), 32(2), 131-136, 143, 226, 145, 246, 251, 254, and 372, confer judicial review powers. The matter addressed in Article 372(1) pertains to the judicial review of pre-constitutional laws that were operative prior to the adoption of the Indian Constitution.

According to Article 13(2), the courts have the authority to declare any legislation passed by Parliament subsequent to the constitution's implementation as null and void. The Supreme Court and high court are commonly regarded as the upholders of the fundamental principles that are enshrined in the constitution. In the event that an individual's fundamental rights are infringed upon, they have the option to initiate legal proceedings in a court of law pursuant to the provisions outlined in Article 32 and Article 226 of the Constitution. As per the provisions of Articles 251 and 254, in the event of a conflict between union law and state law, the former shall take precedence and the latter shall be rendered invalid.

RELEVANCE OF JUDICIAL REVIEW IN INDIA

The Constitution of India, which was ratified on January 26, 1950, is where the idea of judicial review first appeared in India. The Constitution created a government structured on the idea of separation of powers, with the judiciary serving as an independent and impartial mediator of conflicts between the executive and legislative departments. Articles 13, 32, 226, and 227 of the Constitution all provide the right to a judicial review. If any provisions of legislation are found to be in violation of the rights protected by part III of the Constitution, then that law is null and invalid. The Supreme Court can be petitioned under Article 32, which states about right to constitutional remedies and article 32 (1) confers the rights to individuals have the right to move the supreme court through appropriate proceedings and high courts can issue writs to ensure that basic rights be respected under Articles 226 and 227.

Throughout the years, the Indian judiciary has exercised its authority of judicial review to invalidate statutes that are considered to be in violation of the constitution. The *Keshavananda Bharati case (1973)* is considered a seminal and consequential case, as it led to the establishment of the basic structure doctrine by the Supreme Court. As per this doctrine, the Constitution is believed to possess an inherent framework that is impervious to modifications by the legislative body via constitutional amendments. The Supreme Court ruling in the *Maneka Gandhi case* of 1978 established that the privilege to travel overseas is a fundamental right that is protected by Articles 14, 19 and 21 of the Indian Constitution. The Supreme Court, in the *Olga Tellis* case of 1985, established that the fundamental right to livelihood was recognized under Article 21 of the Indian Constitution. In India, the exercise of judicial review is regulated by specific rules and principles. The principle of separation of powers is a fundamental tenet that mandates the judiciary to function as an autonomous and unbiased mediator in conflicts that arise between the remaining two branches of governance.

Furthermore, it is noteworthy that the Indian judiciary adheres to the doctrine of stare decisis, which means that to stand by the already decide matters by the courts or the judicial bodies, whereby it is obligated to abide by its own prior rulings as well as those of superior courts. The aforementioned principle serves to establish uniformity and foreseeability within the legal system.

NATURE AND SCOPE OF JUDICIAL REVIEW

The Constitutional principle of Judicial Review constitutes a fundamental characteristic of the Indian Constitution. The Constitution is distinguished by this characteristic. This evolution holds significant importance in the realm of public law. The Supreme Court and High Courts bear the responsibility of serving as the ultimate interpreters of the rule of law as guaranteed under Article 32 and 226 of the Indian Constitution respectively. Their primary function is to ascertain the scope and boundaries of the power wielded by the executive and legislative branches, which are of equal standing, and ensure that they do not exceed their prescribed limits. Its absenteeism would result in a lack of governance by laws, thereby rendering the rule of law as a mere illusion and an unfulfilled promise. In contemporary times, the scope of judicial review pertaining to administrative action has notably broadened and intensified. According to the previous doctrine, judicial authorities were limited to intervening solely in instances of power overstepping, inadequacy, or misuse. With the proliferation of State activities and the emergence of massive public corporations, it is justifiable to increase public and judicial oversight to safeguard the interests of the public exchequer.

The individual have the right to challenge the legislative enactments which were found to be held unconstitutional by approaching the Supreme Court and the High Court under the Indian Constitution. The author through this paper would like to specify the grounds for challenges of such laws/legislations in the following:

- Violation of fundamental rights guaranteed under Part III of the Indian Constitution
- If the legislations are found to be contrary to constitutional provisions
- If the provisions are outside the competence of the authorities which has enacted it

JUDICIAL REVIEW AND CONTROL OF ADMINISTRATIVE ACTIONS

Judicial review of administrative actions is a crucial aspect of administrative law, serving as a primary mechanism for controlling government power and protecting citizens' rights (D. NandishC, 2020; H. Rawlings, 1986). Courts exercise this control through writs such as habeas corpus, mandamus, and certiorari (D. NandishC, 2020). However, the effectiveness of judicial review in controlling central government has been questioned due to factors like executive power to reverse judicial decisions and civil service characteristics (H. Rawlings, 1986). Recent developments show an increasing inclination of courts to review public authorities' actions, reflecting the expanding public sphere (Hugh Corder, 1998). Constitutional reforms have provided a basis for judicial review of administrative actions, though additional legislation may be necessary for clarification (Hugh Corder, 1998). The primary purpose of judicial review is to safeguard citizens' interests from administrative authorities' abuse of power or unlawful acts (M. Aronson et al., 1996).

Judicial review plays a crucial role in controlling administrative actions in India. The Constitution empowers the Supreme Court and High Courts to review administrative decisions through writs like quo-warranto, habeas corpus, mandamus, certiorari, and prohibition (Bhagyashree A. Deshpande, 2024; D. NandishC, 2020). This mechanism helps maintain the rule of law and keeps administrative authorities within legal limits. The judiciary's role extends to interpreting the constitution, safeguarding its supremacy, and deciding disputes between citizens and the state (D. NandishC, 2020). Police actions, being administrative in nature, are also subject to judicial review based on factors like compliance with the doctrine of ultra vires and principles of natural justice (Kriti Sharma, 2023). However, some argue that judicial review fails to significantly control central government due to the executive's ability to reverse judicial decisions through legislation and the civil service's lack of legal training (H. Rawlings, 1986).

The Indian legal system places significant emphasis on the judicial review and control of administrative actions within the country. Judicial review enables the courts to scrutinize the conduct of administrative bodies and ascertain that they are operating within their prescribed jurisdiction and in compliance with the legal framework. This serves to guarantee the safeguarding of citizens' rights and the imposition of accountability on the government for its conduct. Article 226 and Article 32 of the Indian Constitution establish the provision for judicial review of administrative actions. The provision of Article 226 confers authority upon the High Courts to grant writs to any individual or entity, including the government, for the purpose of upholding fundamental rights and other objectives. Article 32 confers authority upon the Supreme Court to grant writs for the purpose of upholding fundamental rights.

In addition, to the afore-mentioned fundamental rights the author strongly affirms that there exist various statutes that allow for the judicial examination of administrative decisions, such as:

1. **The Administrative Tribunals Act of 1985** serves to institute administrative tribunals that are tasked with the responsibility of resolving disputes that may arise between the government and its employees.
2. **The Right to Information Act of 2005** is a legislative provision that guarantees access to information held by public authorities and outlines the procedures for acquiring such information.
3. **The Prevention of Corruption Act of 1988** is a legislative measure aimed at preventing and combating corruption in India. The aforementioned legislation entails provisions aimed at the deterrence of corrupt practices perpetrated by individuals in the employ of the government, as well as the imposition of penalties for such transgressions.

There are also several pertinent judicial precedents concerning the judicial review and regulation of administrative actions in India includes:

1. The case of ***Maneka Gandhi v. Union of India (1978)*** established that the fundamental right to travel abroad is subject to reasonable restrictions in accordance with the law. The Supreme Court ruled that any limitations on this right must be justifiable and lawful.
2. The landmark case of ***Kesavananda Bharati v. State of Kerala (1973)*** established the principle that the Constitution holds the highest authority and any legislation or conduct that contradicts it can be invalidated by the judiciary.
3. The case of ***A.K. Kraipak v. Union of India (1970)*** established the principle that the exercise of appointment power must be conducted in a fair and objective manner. The Supreme Court ruled that subjective satisfaction alone is insufficient to justify an appointment.
4. The case of ***Union of India v. Association for Democratic Reforms (2002)*** established that the electorate's fundamental right to be informed of a candidate's background is legally recognized by the Supreme Court.
5. In the landmark case of ***State of U.P. v. Raj Narain (1975)*** established that the judicial review of government actions is permissible if such actions are deemed arbitrary, capricious, or influenced by extraneous factors. The Supreme Court of India rendered this decision.

GROUNDS UPON WHICH JUDICIAL REVIEW OF ADMINISTRATIVE DISCRETION MAY BE EXERCISED

Judicial review is a crucial mechanism for challenging administrative decisions, ensuring they align with the rule of law (Dennett, 2021; Dennett, 2019). The grounds for judicial review, as established in landmark cases like Wednesbury and CCSU, primarily include illegality, irrationality, and procedural impropriety (Parpworth, 2018; Dennett, 2021). Additional grounds encompass relevant/irrelevant considerations, improper purpose, bad faith, proportionality, and legitimate expectations (Parpworth, 2018). Boynton (1986) notes that courts will not substitute their judgment for that of the decision-maker. Judicial review remedies include unique prerogative orders such as mandatory, prohibiting, and quashing orders (Dennett, 2021; Dennett, 2019). While judicial review protects against arbitrary or unlawful use of power, challenges exist, including the need to seek leave within three months and establishing sufficient interest to sue (Boynton, 1986). Recent decisions have expanded the concept of public law in this context (Boynton, 1986).

In the Indian legal system, the judiciary holds the power to conduct a judicial review of administrative discretion based on multiple criteria. Judicial review of administrative discretion may be exercised on various grounds, including:

- Illegality pertains to situations where decision-making procedures do not conform to legal requirements. In such cases, the judiciary may intervene and nullify the decision. In instances where an individual without proper authorization makes a decision or when a decision is made in contravention of a compulsory procedure, it is possible for the decision to be deemed unlawful.
- In cases of procedural irregularity, the judiciary has the authority to intervene and nullify a decision if it is deemed to be flawed or unjust. In instances where the decision-making process was conducted without affording the affected parties an opportunity to express their views, or where the decision-maker exhibited bias or had a conflict of interest, the decision may be invalidated.
- In cases where a decision is deemed to be highly unreasonable to the extent that it falls outside the bounds of rationality, the judicial system may intercede and render the decision null and void. In instances where a decision is founded upon extraneous factors or lacks coherence with the fundamental tenets of fairness, it may be deemed irrational.
- In the context of legal proceedings, it is within the purview of the courts to invalidate a decision if it is deemed disproportionate to the objective it aims to accomplish. In instances where a decision places an undue burden on an individual that outweighs the benefit it confers upon society; it may be invalidated.

Case Laws Concerning the Judicial Review of Administrative Discretion in India Include

- The case of *LIC of India v. Consumer Education and Research Centre (1995)* established that administrative discretion must be guided by reason and relevant considerations, rather than extraneous factors. The Supreme Court ruled accordingly.
- The landmark case of *E.P. Royappa v. State of Tamil Nadu (1974)* established the principle that administrative discretion must be exercised in a manner that is fair, non-arbitrary, non-discriminatory, and non-capricious, as per the ruling of the Supreme Court.
- The case of *Maneka Gandhi v. Union of India (1978)* established that the administrative decision-making process must adhere to the principles of natural justice and be deemed reasonable.

Judicial review over administrative discretion can be exercised by courts in other jurisdictions, such as the United States, based on similar grounds including illegality, procedural irregularity, and irrationality. The principle of proportionality is acknowledged in several other legal systems, including the European Union and Canada.

THE ADVANTAGES OF JUDICIAL REVIEW IN THE EXERCISE OF ADMINISTRATIVE DISCRETION

The judicial review mechanism serves as a protective measure against the capricious use of authority by the government and guarantees the preservation of the basic rights of individuals. The judiciary possesses the authority to invalidate statutes or conduct that contravene the Constitution or encroach upon the essential liberties of individuals. The concept of accountability in government is upheld through the mechanism of judicial review, which serves to ensure that the government is held responsible to the citizenry and operates within the confines of its legally prescribed powers. The principle of preventing the government from acting in an arbitrary or capricious manner and ensuring that its actions are subject to scrutiny and oversight is upheld. The promotion of good governance is facilitated by judicial review, which fosters transparency, accountability, and equity in the process of decision-making. The aforementioned statement highlights the significance of ensuring that governmental actions are grounded on logical reasoning and substantiated by empirical evidence, while also being carried out in the best interest of the general public. The evolution of legal principles is facilitated by judicial review, which furnishes direction and lucidity on matters of law. The establishment of legal precedents serves as a guiding force for future decisions and promotes uniformity and predictability in the legal system.

Case Laws Pertaining Against Administrative Action

- The case of *Kesavananda Bharati v State of Kerala (1973)* resulted in the affirmation by the Supreme Court of India of the doctrine of the basic structure of the Constitution. This doctrine serves to restrict the authority of the government in amending the Constitution. The aforementioned ruling safeguarded essential liberties and set a significant standard for the scrutiny of constitutional amendments by the judiciary.
- The case of *Maneka Gandhi v Union of India (1978)* resulted in a ruling by the Supreme Court of India that recognized the fundamental right to travel abroad under the Constitution. The court further held that any limitations imposed on this right must be just and equitable. The aforementioned ruling broadened the range of essential entitlements and set a significant standard for the assessment of governmental measures by the judiciary.
- The case of *Indian Medical Association v V.P. Shantha (1995)* pertains to a legal matter that was brought before the court. The Supreme Court of India invalidated a governmental directive that curtailed physicians' entitlement to conduct medical practice in private clinics. The aforementioned determination safeguarded the entitlements of medical practitioners and set a significant standard for the assessment of administrative measures that encroach upon personal liberties.

In India, the practice of judicial review of administrative discretion holds considerable advantages that are pivotal in maintaining the supremacy of law and safeguarding the fundamental rights of individuals.

THE DRAWBACKS OF JUDICIAL REVIEW IN THE EXERCISE OF ADMINISTRATIVE DISCRETION

Although judicial review of administrative discretion is widely acknowledged as advantageous, it is not without potential drawbacks in the context of India. Several drawbacks are associated with this phenomenon. The process of judicial review has the potential to consume a significant amount of time, resulting in a delay in the decision-making process. The urgency of certain situations, such as those pertaining to national security or public health, can pose significant challenges. The concept of judicial review has been criticized for potentially impeding the executive branch's policy-making process, as it may be perceived as an unwarranted intrusion. The aforementioned circumstance has the potential to generate strain between the judiciary and the remaining branches of government, resulting in allegations of judicial overreach. Judicial review has the potential to impose a burden on the judicial system, resulting in a backlog of cases and hindering the timely resolution of other legal disputes.

The concept of unintended consequences is applicable to judicial review, as it may result in public officials being hesitant to take prompt action due to the possibility of facing legal challenges.

Case Laws Against the Administrative Discretion

- The case of *Maneka Gandhi versus Union of India in 1978* is a notable legal matter. The present instance witnessed an expansion of the ambit of the right to life and personal liberty enshrined in the Constitution by the Supreme Court of India. Although the ruling was hailed as a significant legal precedent for safeguarding personal liberties, it was also met with allegations of judicial overstepping and encroachment on the domain of policymaking.
- The case of *Union of India v. Raghubir Singh (1989)* saw the Supreme Court of India invalidate a government directive that permitted detention without trial under specific circumstances. Although the ruling was perceived as a triumph for personal liberties, it also resulted in setbacks in the execution of governmental measures pertaining to national security.
- The legal case of *R. S. Nayak v. A. R. Antulay,* which took place in 1984, is of academic interest. The apex court of India ruled that the authority of scrutinizing legislative actions, commonly known as judicial review, is applicable to the legislative arm of the government. The ruling was perceived as a triumph for the principles of responsibility and openness, yet it also elicited apprehensions regarding the division of authority and the likelihood of judicial intervention in the lawmaking procedure.

In general, the process of judicial review pertaining to administrative discretion serves as a crucial tool in upholding accountability and safeguarding the rights of individuals. However, it may inadvertently result in unforeseen outcomes and generate conflict between the judiciary and other governmental branches.

WHAT IS DOCTRINE OF PROPORTIONALITY AND ITS RELEVANCE TO JUDICIAL REVIEW?

The doctrine of proportionality has emerged as a significant principle in judicial review of administrative actions, gradually replacing the Wednesbury reasonableness test in common law countries (Ajoy Pb, 2024). While the Indian Supreme Court accepted this doctrine in 2000, its practical application remains limited (A. Chandrachud, 2013). Proportionality is argued to be a more objective and preferred standard for reviewing administrative actions (Ajoy Pb, 2024). Some scholars advocate for proportionality as a general principle of judicial review, applicable to both rights-based and non-rights cases (P. Craig, 2010). The institutionalization of proportionality-based judicial review is seen as a practice of Socratic contestation, potentially improving outcomes by addressing political decision-making pathologies and complementing the basic institutional commitments of liberal democratic constitutionalism (M. Kumm, 2009). However, challenges remain in fully integrating the doctrine into legal systems, particularly in India (Ajoy Pb, 2024; A. Chandrachud, 2013).

The principle of proportionality, which is a component of the judicial review framework, would guarantee that in cases where the decision of the Court-Martial pertains to an area that falls exclusively within its jurisdiction, if the sentence handed down by the Court is a flagrant violation of reason, then the sentence would not be exempt from rectification. Judicial Review acknowledges irrationality and perversity as valid grounds. All governmental authorities are subject to legal constraints. In the prominent case of *Coimbatore Distt. Central Co-operative Bank v. Employees Association, (2007)* is noteworthy precedent on the very concept of the judicial review. A group of employees engaged in an unlawful work stoppage. They impeded the performance of duties by others. It was determined that the actions constituted a severe breach of conduct. The penalty of withholding increments from employees cannot be deemed excessive in relation to the accusations that have been alleged and substantiated against said employees.

The Hon'ble Supreme Court of India upheld the Test of Proportionality in the case of *K. S. Puttaswamy v. Union of India, 2017,* often regarded as Aadhar Judgment. It has been established that in cases involving proportionality, the assessment of a measure must take into account the limitations imposed by the State on the fundamental rights of individuals. In addition to examining the legal and physical limitations, it is imperative to consider the psychological impact of such restrictions on the general public, while also evaluating the appropriateness of the measures taken. In the case of *Anuradha Bhasin v. Union of India, 2019,* the constitutional validity of the imposition of internet shutdown and movement restrictions in Jammu and Kashmir was contested before the esteemed Supreme Court. The text outlines the need to adhere to the doctrine of proportionality by authorities prior to imposing any order that may limit the fundamental rights of individuals. The primary objective of a measure aimed at imposing restrictions must be identified in the initial stage. It is important to acknowledge that any objective must be deemed lawful. Prior to adopting the aforementioned measure, it is imperative for the governing bodies to evaluate the presence of any alternative mechanism that can facilitate the attainment of the aforementioned objective.

The suitability of the aforementioned measure is contingent upon its impact on fundamental rights and its essentiality. The aforementioned ruling indicates that the State must only employ the most minimal measures, while taking into account the relevant facts and circumstances. Finally, given that the order carries significant consequences for the fundamental rights of those impacted, it is imperative that it is backed by substantial evidence and is subject to judicial scrutiny.

WEDNESBURY'S PRINCIPLE AND ITS RELEVANCE TO THE CONCEPT OF JUDICIAL REVIEW

The Wednesbury Principle can be traced back to the United Kingdom's famous case of *Associate Provincial Picture Houses Ltd v. Wednesbury Corporation, 1948* in which Lord Greene defined an irrational decision as one that is so preposterous that no reasonable person would make it, and any person could have ever imagined making it. Lord Diplock beautifully "summarizes wednesbury unreasonableness as a principle that applies to a decision that is so outrageous in its defiance of logic or accepted moral standards that no reasonable person who applied his or her mind to the issue at hand could have reached it." The Wednesbury principle of judicial review is founded on the tenet that executive actions must not be excessively unreasonable or drastic in order to achieve a desired outcome. The reasoning behind the observation made in the seminal case of Wednesbury Corporation is that the courts can intervene when it appears that an executive's administrative action is so arbitrary and offensive that no reasonable administration could have taken it. This was necessary to keep the executive's actions and powers in check. In the preceding case, the court also considered the extent to which it is appropriate for the courts to exercise their intervention authority.

Any authority with discretion must act responsibly and only consider relevant and mandatory matters. He is acting unreasonably if he breaks the law. In *Dy. Director of Consolidation v. Deen Bandhu Rai*, the official refused an exchange application because it would overburden them. The Honorable Supreme Court found the rejection reason irrelevant and inappropriate. In another instance, *Barium Chemicals Ltd. v. corporate Law Board*, the Company Law Board Secretary ordered inspectors to investigate corporate affairs under Section 237(b) of the Companies Act, 1956. In this instance, the Supreme Court decided that the discretion under section 237 of the Act can only be employed in limited cases when the authority feels proper according to the Act's principles. In a similar case, *Shalini Soni vs Union of India*, the Supreme Court stated, "It is an unwritten rule of the law, constitutional and administrative, that whenever a decision-making function is entrusted to the subjective satisfaction of a statutory functionary, there is an implicit obligation to apply his mind to pertinent and proximate matters only, eschewing the irrelevant and the remote."

DOCTRINE OF LEGITIMATE EXPECTATION AND ITS RELEVANCE TO THE JUDICIAL REVIEW

The doctrine of legitimate expectations has been recognized by both the English and Indian legal systems in recent times. This concept is the most recent addition to the extensive array of criteria that courts have established to assess administrative actions. The Doctrine of Legitimate Expectations, fundamentally, establishes a duty to operate with equity. Due to the substantial and expeditious escalation in governmental operations, it is unfeasible to furnish a comprehensive inventory. The rapid and volatile nature of these fluctuations renders it such that prior to reaching the midpoint of our enumeration, the initiation would have already reached its ultimate conclusion. However, it is evident. According to the court's perspective, it is deemed inappropriate for a court to utilize its jurisdiction in order to evaluate an administrative action or decision.

In administrative law, India adheres to the notion of legitimate expectation. The concept posits that individuals who hold a justifiable anticipation of being treated in a particular manner by a governmental entity possess a valid anticipation that the entity will behave in conformity with that expectation. The doctrine of legitimate expectation is intricately associated with the notion of judicial review in India. The judiciary has the potential possesses the authority to scrutinize the conduct of public entities to guarantee that they are operating within their lawful jurisdiction and adhering to the tenets of fairness and impartiality. This entails an assessment of whether the governmental entity has fulfilled the reasonable anticipations of the persons impacted by its conduct. The Supreme Court ruling *in Union of India v. Hindustan Development Corporation (1993)* established that the doctrine of legitimate expectation is a legally recognized principle that can be invoked to contest the actions of public authorities. The Supreme Court ruling in *LIC of India v. Consumer Education and Research Centre (1995)* established the legitimacy of the doctrine of legitimate expectation as a basis for judicial review. It was further established that public authorities are obligated to act in accordance with the legitimate expectations of individuals.

JUDICIAL PRECEDENTS THAT ESTABLISHED THE CONCEPT OF JUDICIAL REVIEW IN INDIA

The following jurisdictions have contributed to the advancement and expansion of judicial review in India:

1. The landmark case of *Kesavananda Bharti v. the State of Kerala, 1973*. This case commonly referred to as the Fundamental Rights Case is notable for having introduced the Fundamental Structure Doctrine into legal discourse. The Indian Constitution is governed by a legal principle that asserts the existence of fundamental features that are immutable and impervious to any modifications or annulments by the Parliament.
2. The case of *Minerva Mills v. Union of India, 1980*. The case in question represents a significant milestone in the jurisprudence of the Supreme Court of India. It serves to expound upon the interpretation of the basic structure doctrine, as previously established in the Kesavananda Bharti v State of Kerala case. As per the Court's verdict, the ability of Parliament to make amendments is not a deleterious power and, as a result, it is impermissible for Parliament to obstruct the essential rights of individuals, such as the right to freedom and impartiality, which are guaranteed under the Indian Constitution.
3. The case of *Golak Nath v. the State of Punjab, 1967*. Before the aforementioned ruling, the Supreme Court maintained that the laws pertaining to amendments were not of an ordinary nature and therefore could not be invalidated through the implementation of Article 13, which states about the laws that are inconsistent with or in derogation of the fundamental rights established by the Constitution. The Supreme Court rendered a groundbreaking decision in a case that contested the legitimacy of the 1st, 4th, and 17th amendments. The Court reversed its previous ruling that had upheld the Article 368 provision, which enabled Parliament to restrict fundamental rights under Chapter III of the constitution.

4. In the case of *P.A. Inamdar v State of Maharashtra, 2005*, the Supreme Court rendered a decision to eliminate state quotas in privately owned and unsupported vocational institutions. The ruling specifically addressed the state's role in such institutions. It was not possible to implement reservations in institutions that did not have the necessary support. The aforementioned event resulted in the enactment of the Constitution (Ninety-third Amendment) Act 2005 by the legislative body in December of the same year.
5. The case of *Champakam Dorairajan v. the State of Madras, 1951*. The Champakam Dorairajan case pertains to the reservation of seats in state medical and technical colleges by the Madras government for various communities based on their religion, race, and caste. This practice has been contested on the grounds of being unconstitutional. The government has justified its directive by citing Article 46 of the Constitution, which authorizes the state to advance the educational and economic welfare of the less privileged segments of society, particularly the scheduled castes and scheduled tribes, while taking special measures to guarantee social equity. The Supreme Court invalidated the aforementioned order on the grounds of violating the equality safeguarded under Article 15(1). The Court further observed that the directive principles cannot supersede the fundamental rights that are guaranteed. The Constitution (First Amendment) Act of 1951 saw the introduction of Clause (4) to Article 15 by Parliament.

CONSTRAINTS ON THE POWER OF THE JUDICIARY

There are limits to what a court may do by definition. Its strength is in the resolution of administrative disputes rather than the execution of administrative tasks. The executive is responsible for managing the rule of law and the judicial system are responsible for ensuring that the government abides with its constitutional obligations. An abuse of discretion occurs when a decision-making body acts outside its jurisdiction, makes a mistake of law, disregards the principles of natural justice, or reaches a conclusion that no reasonable person would have reached. The administrative authority's decision may be deemed reasonable, rational, and not arbitrary, or in violation of Article 14 of the Indian Constitution, by the court. The power of judicial review cannot be used unless the order issued by an administrative authority is illegal or unconstitutional. As long as the Administrator's experiments are conducted in good faith and stay within the scope of their power, no outside intervention should be required.

The author through this paper would like to state few of the limitations on the application of the concept of judicial review because the principle of Judicial Review has been acknowledged by courts as a fundamental aspect of the legal system, although there remain specific domains in which it is not applicable. It has been widely acknowledged that the contemporary State has assumed the role of a provider of social welfare services from changing its role as police state, where there is an excessive state control on the citizens. In order to ensure comprehensive care for its citizens throughout their entire lives, it is necessary for the State to have authoritative control in certain domains. The exclusion of judicial review is evident in instances where the state's actions, political affairs, policy determinations, and similar matters are concerned. The exclusion of judicial review may take on various forms, including partial or total exclusion, unconditional and unqualified exclusion, or conditional and qualified exclusion. The authority of Judicial Review, which is bestowed upon the High Courts and the Supreme Court by Articles 32, 136, 227, and 266 of the Constitution of India, is considered an integral component of the fundamental framework of the Constitution. It is noteworthy that this power cannot be revoked, even though amendments made to the Constitution.

THE FACTORS THAT TAKE PRECEDENCE OVER OTHERS

The author is of opinion that there are two primary factors serve to limit the extent of Judicial Review they are as follows:

- The expectation is that judges will not assume the role of a superior board or a pedantic schoolmaster in lieu of administrative expertise when providing due defense.
- The primary reason for the perfunctory affirmation of the majority of agency decisions is the time constraints imposed by the judicial calendar.

THE CONCEPT OF JUDICIAL REVIEW IN U.S.

Judicial review is a legal authority vested in the courts of the United States to examine and invalidate legislation and governmental conduct that contravenes the provisions of the Constitution. The Constitution does not make a direct reference to this authority; however, it was instituted through the significant legal decision of Marbury v. Madison (1803). In this case, the Supreme Court proclaimed its ability to nullify laws that were deemed unconstitutional. The fundamental purpose of judicial review in the United States is to verify that the government operates within the boundaries of its constitutional jurisdiction and upholds the liberties of individuals. The principle of separation of powers forms the basis of the doctrine of judicial review. This principle mandates that the legislative, executive, and judicial branches of government function autonomously and are subject to checks and balances.

The concept of judicial review, a cornerstone of constitutional governance, empowers courts to assess the constitutionality of state actions, including legislation (Bhattarai, 2023). Originating in English law and significantly developed in the United States, judicial review has become a crucial feature of legal systems worldwide (Pandey, 2020). In the U.S., despite no explicit constitutional mention, it evolved through landmark cases and judicial interpretation (Yasin et al., 2022). The Supreme Court established a two-step framework for reviewing agency interpretations of statutes in Chevron, providing much-needed guidance for lower courts (Lynch, 1985). While judicial review serves to protect civil liberties and maintain the rule of law, it faces criticism for potentially undermining democratic legitimacy (Bhattarai, 2023). The scope of judicial review encompasses legislation, executive actions, and judicial decisions, with grounds for review including illegality, irrationality, and procedural impropriety (Bhattarai, 2023; Yasin et al., 2022).

In this writing piece the author has mentioned several pertinent legal precedents regarding the doctrine of judicial review in the United States exist. The landmark case of *Marbury v. Madison in 1803* established the principle that the Constitution is the ultimate authority in the United States and that it is incumbent upon the judiciary to construe the Constitution and invalidate any legislation that violates its provisions. Chief Justice John Marshall delivered the opinion of the Court, which articulated this fundamental doctrine. The landmark case of McCulloch v. Maryland (1819) affirmed the constitutionality of the Bank of the United States and established the legal doctrine of implied powers. This principle maintains that the federal government possesses the authority to undertake actions that are deemed necessary and appropriate to fulfil its constitutional obligations. The landmark case of *Brown v. Board of Education (1954)* resulted in the Supreme Court's ruling that the practice of segregation in public schools was in contravention of the Equal Protection Clause of the Fourteenth Amendment, thereby invalidating the "separate but equal" doctrine. The landmark case of *Roe v. Wade (1973)* established that the Due Process Clause of the Fourteenth Amendment guarantees a woman's constitutional right to obtain an abortion. In the case of *Citizens United v. Federal Election Commission in 2010* is a landmark decision in the field of election law. The Supreme Court ruled that corporations possess the privilege of free speech as protected by the First Amendment, and that any limitations imposed on political expenditures by corporations would be deemed as a violation of the First Amendment.

Judicial review is a pivotal component of the United States legal system, serving as a means for the courts to safeguard individual rights and verify that the government operates within the boundaries of its constitutional jurisdiction.

THE CONCEPT OF JUDICIAL REVIEW IN U.K.

Judicial review is a legal mechanism in the United Kingdom that enables the courts to scrutinize the actions of public entities, such as government agencies, local councils, and other public bodies. The principle of judicial review is rooted in the notion of the rule of law, which posits that no entity, including the government, is exempt from legal accountability. The fundamental purpose of judicial review in the United Kingdom is to verify that governmental entities operate within the boundaries of their legal jurisdiction and adhere to the principles of natural justice, equity, and rationality. The judiciary is primarily focused on evaluating the procedural aspects of a decision-making process and its compliance with legal requirements, rather than the substantive merits or underlying policy considerations.

Judicial review in the United Kingdom empowers courts to assess the legality and procedural correctness of public authorities' actions, maintaining checks and balances (Aas Muhammad et al., 2023). Its scope has evolved significantly, influenced by recent political and constitutional changes like Brexit and the COVID-19 pandemic (Aas Muhammad et al., 2023). The UK's uncodified constitution makes the constitutional provisions for judicial review somewhat controversial, though it is considered essential for the rule of law (Nason, 2021). The Criminal Justice and Courts Act 2015 limits remedies in cases where outcomes would likely remain unchanged (Nason, 2021). Judicial review expanded significantly in the late 20th century, with the incorporation of the European Convention on Human Rights in 2000 marking a notable shift (Schwarze, 2002). The principle provides crucial protection for individuals against abuse of power by public authorities (Schwarze, 2002; Sule, 2022).

Judicial review in the United Kingdom has evolved significantly, empowering courts to assess the legality and propriety of public authorities' actions (Aas Muhammad et al., 2023). This practice ensures checks and balances, particularly in light of recent political changes (Aas Muhammad et al., 2023). The conceptual framework for judicial review includes grounds such as systemic unfairness and access to justice (Adams-Prassl & Adams-Prassl, 2020). It serves to control government arbitrariness, protect civil liberties, and maintain the rule of law (Bhattarai, 2023). The scope of judicial review encompasses legislation, executive actions, and judicial decisions (Bhattarai, 2023). The adoption of the Human Rights Act 1998 expanded judicial review in the UK, borrowing from international models and coinciding with power devolution to Scotland, Wales, and Northern Ireland (Calabresi, 2021). Despite criticisms regarding democratic legitimacy, judicial review remains crucial for establishing constitutional supremacy and the rule of law (Bhattarai, 2023).

There are pertinent judicial precedents and case laws regarding the notion of judicial review in the United Kingdom include:

1. The legal case of *Associated Provincial Picture Houses Ltd v Wednesbury Corporation (1948)* established the principle that an administrative decision may be subject to challenge if it is deemed to be so unreasonable that it would not have been made by a reasonable person. The aforementioned principle, commonly referred to as the "Wednesbury principle," continues to be utilized in contemporary judicial review.
2. The case of *Council of Civil Service Unions v Minister for the Civil Service*, which was decided in 1985, is of academic significance. The court in this instance determined that the government's utilization of prerogative powers was susceptible to judicial scrutiny, and that the courts possessed the authority to scrutinize the government's decision-making procedures.
3. The case of *R v Secretary of State for the Home Department, ex parte Simms (1999)* is a notable legal precedent. The court's ruling in this instance stipulated that adherence to the principle of legality necessitates the use of unambiguous and unequivocal language in the abrogation of fundamental rights. Additionally, the court cautioned against presuming that Parliament intended to supersede fundamental rights.
4. The legal precedent of *R (Miller) v. The Prime Minister in the year 2019*. The court in this instance determined that the Prime Minister's counsel to the Queen to suspend Parliament was capable of being adjudicated and open to legal scrutiny. It was found that the counsel was illegal as it impeded or obstructed Parliament's capacity to execute its constitutional duties.

In the United Kingdom's legal system, judicial review is an essential mechanism that guarantees public bodies operate within the boundaries of their legal jurisdiction and that their actions are subject to examination and responsibility. The judiciary system holds a crucial function in maintaining the supremacy of the law and safeguarding the fundamental rights and freedoms of individuals.

Judicial review in the United Kingdom has evolved significantly over the past decades, expanding its scope and influence (Schwarze, 2002). It serves as a crucial mechanism for assessing the legality and propriety of public authorities' actions, maintaining checks and balances (Muhammad et al., 2023). The UK Supreme Court acts as a final harmonizing authority for case-law principles, although administrative law differs across the UK due to devolution (Nason, 2021). Recent developments, including Brexit and the COVID-19 pandemic, have raised questions about the judiciary's role in relation to government and parliament actions (Muhammad et al., 2023). The Supreme Court has shown renewed interest in developing a rights-jurisprudence at common law, attempting to synthesize it with the Human Rights Act. However, this effort has created tensions between responding to external pressures and maintaining the internal coherence of common law review (Varuhas, 2018). Despite these challenges, judicial review remains essential for protecting individuals and preventing abuse of power by public authorities (Schwarze, 2002).

CONCLUSION

The aforementioned piece of writing pertains to the topic of Judicial Review of Administrative Discretion and the diverse provisions that enable the exercise of Judicial Review of Administrative Discretion. The utilization of any form of authority must adhere to the limitations and regulations established by the law, as per a fundamental principle of jurisprudence. The fundamental principle in question is not exempt from the utilization of administrative authority. The fundamental principles of administrative law pertain to the identification and preservation of such constraints. According to Article 13(2) of the Indian Constitution, it is impermissible for the state to enact any legislation that infringes upon or curtails the fundamental rights that are enshrined in the Constitution. Any law that contravenes this provision will be deemed null and void to the extent of the inconsistency.

In a system that upholds the rule of law, unbridled discretion is precluded. The potential for abuse exists within any form of power, and the efficacy of judicial review is ultimately determined by its ability to prevent such misuse. The administration is obligated to implement unclear and indistinct statutory provisions. As the need to tailor requirements to particular cases has increased, the significance of exercising discretion has escalated on a daily basis. Further, the author with this article has believes that comprehending current issues within a wide framework can be a daunting task. The administrator encounters a multitude of novel and intricate challenges that pose a difficulty in resolution due to their complexity and the administrator's limited knowledge. In certain situations, there may be a lack of established legal or regulatory frameworks. In such circumstances, it is imperative that the administrator manages these situations in a rational manner, akin to how an individual would typically exercise their authority in comparable scenarios.

REFERENCES

Bhattarai, S. K. (2023). Conceptual Framework of Judicial Review with Reference to Nepal. *Advances in Sciences and Humanities*, *9*(2), 52–57.

Carelli, D., & Pierre, J. (2024). When the cat is away: How institutional autonomy, low salience, and issue complexity shape administrative action. *Public Administration*, *102*(1), 207–221. DOI: 10.1111/padm.12912

Castillo-Ortiz, P. (2020). Constitutional Review in the Member States of the EU-28: A Political Analysis of Institutional Choices. *Journal of Law and Society*, *47*(1), 87–120. DOI: 10.1111/jols.12210

Daly, P. (2021). *Understanding administrative law in the common law world*. Oxford University Press. DOI: 10.1093/oso/9780192896919.001.0001

Drolc, C. A., & Keiser, L. R. (2021). The importance of oversight and agency capacity in enhancing performance in public service delivery. *Journal of Public Administration: Research and Theory*, *31*(4), 773–789.

Hillebrandt, M., & Leino-Sandberg, P. (2021). Administrative and judicial oversight of trilogues. *Journal of European Public Policy*, *28*(1), 53–71. DOI: 10.1080/13501763.2020.1859598

Hillebrandt, M., & Leino-Sandberg, P. (2021). Administrative and judicial oversight of trilogues. *Journal of European Public Policy*, *28*(1), 53–71. DOI: 10.1080/13501763.2020.1859598

Ionita, G. B. (n.d.). Particularities of the Administrative Oversight in the Context of the Commissioner Exercise of the Action for Annulment Based on the Provisions of the Law no. 554/2004 of the Administrative Contentious and the Administrative Code. In Administrative Law and Public Administration in the Global Social System (pp. 83-91). Societatea de Stiinte Juridice si Administrative.

Jain, A. G. (2016). Indian practice relating to international law. *Indian Journal of International Law*, *56*(3), 503–536. DOI: 10.1007/s40901-017-0062-7

Jassim, A. L. E. M. (2022). Administrative and Judicial Oversight of Administrative Decisions. *Journal of Juridical and Political Science*, *11*(2).

Lindseth, P. (2020). 'Always Embedded' Administration: The Historical Evolution of Administrative Justice as an Aspect of Modern Governance. In The Economy as a Polity: The Political Constitution of Contemporary Capitalism (pp. 117-135). Routledge.

Lindseth, P. L. (2023). Administration and Democracy. In Public Administration and Expertise in Democratic Governments (pp. 242-255). Routledge.

Mayeda, G. (2024). Reasonableness as Responsiveness in Administrative Law in the United States, United Kingdom, and Canada: Kant and Arendt on the Role of the Community in Deferential Judicial Review. *The American Journal of Comparative Law*, avae006.

Mejía, L. E. (2021). Judicial review of regulatory decisions: Decoding the contents of appeals against agencies in Spain and the United Kingdom. *Regulation & Governance*, *15*(3), 760–784. DOI: 10.1111/rego.12302

Morton, F. L. (1988). Judicial Review in France: A Comparative Analysis. *The American Journal of Comparative Law*, *36*(1), 89–110. DOI: 10.2307/840185

Nandish, C. D. (2020). Administrative law and judicial review of administrative action through writs: Ground of review. *Journal of Emerging Technologies and Innovative Research.*

Nggilu, N., Moha, M. R., Sinaga, M. R., & Rachmaniar, A. (2024). Judicial Review of Constitutional Amendments: Comparison Between India, Germany, Colombia, and the Relevancy with Indonesia. *Lex Scientia Law Review*, *8*(1), 261–298.

Onyango, G. (2020). Legislative oversight and policy-reforms in "unsettled" political contexts of public administration. *International Journal of Public Administration*, *43*(3), 213–228. DOI: 10.1080/01900692.2019.1627556

Onyango, G. (2020). Legislative oversight and policy-reforms in "unsettled" political contexts of public administration. *International Journal of Public Administration*, *43*(3), 213–228. DOI: 10.1080/01900692.2019.1627556

Oster, J. S. (2008). The Scope of Judicial Review in the German and US Administrative Legal System. *German Law Journal*, *9*(10), 1267–1297.

Pandey, S. P. (2020). Constitutional provision of judicial review in India: An evaluation. Asian Journal of Advances in Research, 291-301.

Pavone, T., & Stiansen, Ø. (2022). The shadow effect of courts: Judicial review and the politics of preemptive reform. *The American Political Science Review*, *116*(1), 322–336. DOI: 10.1017/S0003055421000873

Raffler, P. J. (2022). Does political oversight of the bureaucracy increase accountability? Field experimental evidence from a dominant party regime. *The American Political Science Review*, *116*(4), 1443–1459. DOI: 10.1017/S0003055422000181

Sadurski, W. (2011). Constitutional Review in Europe and in the United States: Influences, paradoxes, and convergence. Forthcoming, Sydney Law School Research Paper, (11/15).

Vázquez, C. M. (2004). Judicial Review in the United States and in the WTO. *Some Similarities and Differences. Geo. Wash. Int'l L. Rev.*, *36*, 587.

Wijaya, A., & Nasran, N. (2021). Comparison Of Judicial Review: A Critical Approach To The Model In Several Countries. *Jurnal Legalitas*, *14*(2), 85–106. DOI: 10.33756/jelta.v14i2.11809

Wrzoszczyk, M. (2019). The idea of judicial review in the United States of America: the context of creating and early judgments of the Supreme Court. Academic Press.

Chapter 12
Corporate Data Mining and Manipulation in Marketing

Henrietta Okoro
https://orcid.org/0009-0005-9124-1954
Colorado Technical University, USA

ABSTRACT

In today's viable business setting, examining and manipulating huge datasets is critical for effective promotional approaches. The digital revolution of readiness has become imperative as it shakes various aspects of the business as the latent for embracing innovative technologies raises, including the rise of propaganda, impacts of leakage, mobile technologies, cloud technologies, and the internet of things. This chapter highlights an inclusive plan for implementing data mining and manipulation techniques to enhance marketing efforts within corporations. It explores the critical role of data mining and manipulation in modern corporate marketing strategies and provides an ample analysis of how corporations can leverage data to drive marketing decisions, enhance big data management, customer engagement, and increase profitability. The chapter covers theoretical foundations, practical applications, case studies, future trends, and recommendations in data-driven marketing.

PROBLEM STATEMENT

The essential skill of analyzing and manipulating extensive data sets must be master's in modern competitive business settings to develop successful marketing strategies. Innovative technologies like Big Data analytics and social media have driven enterprise digital transformation which now alters multiple business operation aspects. This transformation offers both prospects and obstacles because companies need to manage technological complexity to maintain their competitive edge. Numerous organizations face difficulties when trying to use data mining and manipulation techniques to boost their marketing strategies. The challenges of creating targeted marketing campaigns and accurately segmenting customers together with managing big data sets and making strategic marketing choices along with increasing customer interaction limit companies' revenue potential and competitive advantage.

Modern business success depends heavily on data-driven insights which makes addressing these issues essential. The strategic application of data becomes essential to drive business profitability and maintain customer relationships while securing long-term competitive advantages in today's digital

DOI: 10.4018/979-8-3693-7468-9.ch012

age with advanced analytical tools. This chapter explores cutting-edge data mining and manipulation methods that target existing challenges to improve marketing results. This analysis aims to demonstrate how companies can utilize these methods to optimize big data management and use them to guide marketing strategies while growing profitability and enhancing customer engagement. The chapter prepares businesses to maximize their data assets for marketing success by examining theoretical foundations and real-world case studies alongside emerging trends and practical applications and recommendations.

INTRODUCTION

In today's competitive business environment, the ability to analyze and manipulate large datasets is critical for effective marketing strategies. The digital transformation of the enterprise has become very important as it affects various facets of the business as the potential for adopting innovative technologies grows, including impacts of leakage, rise of propaganda, Big Data analytics, social media, mobile technologies, the Internet of Things, and cloud technologies (Morakanyane, 2017; Mydyti and Kadriu, 2021c; Pejić Bach, Pivar, & Krstić, 2019). Artificial intelligence and advanced analytics are robust digital technologies that drive business and information analytics, prediction, and business process monitoring (West and Allen, 2018).

Data mining, the practice of separating valuable insights from enormous datasets, plays a critical role in decision-making across various domains. However, along its advantages, data mining also bestows security and ethical challenges, mainly in the areas of whistleblowing, information leakage, and propaganda (Bloch-Wehba, 2024; Zurini, 2012). Leakage of sensitive data could be intentional or accidental and can expose privacy and lead to reputational damage. Equally, whistleblowing, frequently induced by data analysis, could uncover unethical practices, raising inquiries about the reliable use of extracted information. Moreover, data driven propaganda forces directed algorithms to influence public awareness, swaying opinions and actions on a enormous scale. As data mining methods grow, it is essential to equalize their possible innovation with precautions against misapplication, ensuring moral and clear applications (Domnik & Holland, 2024).

This chapter focuses on exploring data mining and manipulation methods to improve marketing efforts within companies. By leveraging innovative data mining and data analytics, it aids to develop optimized marketing campaigns, customer targeting, and increase overall revenue. It investigates the critical role of manipulation and data mining in modern corporate marketing policies and offers a generous analysis of how companies can leverage data to enhance big data management, drive marketing decisions, increase profitability, and customer engagement. The chapter covers theoretical foundations, case studies, future trends, practical applications, and recommendations in data-driven marketing.

BACKGROUND

Data Mining Overview

Data mining involves finding patterns, variances, and correlations, in big datasets to forecast outcomes. Data mining relates to numerous techniques such as: clustering, regression, classification, variance detection, and association rules. Data mining aids in customer Segmentation and marketing by classifying distinct customer clusters based on purchasing behavior. This allows personalized marketing strategies and basket analysis. Using data mining helps to reveals products frequently bought together, supports cross-selling, and upselling efforts (Vleugel, Spruit, & Anton, 2010, Saarenvirta, 1998).

The process helps to predict customer churn. For example, analyzing patterns to predict which customers are likely to stay or leave and thereby helps in creating retention strategies. The data analytics systems and smart applications allow companies to demonstrate the importance of delivering results to improve decision making, productivity, and effectiveness (Bughin et al., 2017). Companies use technology to perform analytics, such as simple reports and a dashboard that present past performance reviews and investigation reports. (Bumblauskas et al., 2017). Most companies share a common goal of using digital technology to improve their decision-making capabilities as they continue their digital journey (Schwertner, 2017). Data mining, interconnect with machine learning, and help companies to reduce costs and improve the customer experience (Sima et al., 2020; Chen et al., 2015; Palmer et al., 2011), especially in the era of Big Data (Pejic-Bach et al., 2019; Pivar, & Krstić, 2019).

Scope of Data Manipulation

Data manipulation and cleaning involves detecting and adjusting errors and discrepancies in data to recover data quality. Financial fraud has been increasing since the twenty-first century due to several succeeding scandals, including WorldCom, Lehman Brothers (US), Enron, Parmalat Spa (Italy), Vivendi and BPN (Portugal). According to PricewaterhouseCoopers (PwC) 2018 Global Economic Crime and Fraud Survey, 49% of organizations exposed as fraud and the global effect of fraud is close to $US 3 trillion dollars. The process of correcting data manipulation assists with handling misplaced values, correcting errors, removing duplicates, and ensuring data dependability. It also leads to data transformation, which is the process of converting data into a suitable format or structure for analysis (Harb, Nasrallah, Khoury, & Hussainey, 2023). However, adequate data manipulation involves normalization, aggregation, discretization, and creating new attributes. This leads to data integration, by combining data from different sources to provide a unified view. Hence, the resultant data merging, data consolidation, and resolving data heterogeneity.

Importance of Data Mining

Data mining has numerous advantages in advertising that comprise of targeted marketing operations, customer segmentation, market basket analysis, trend analysis, customer churn prediction, and customer lifetime value (CLV) prediction.

1. *Targeted Marketing Operations*

The usage of targeted marketing operations helps in analyzing customer data, companies can create promotions that fit specific customer sections. This method helps to increase the effectiveness and efficiency of marketing strengths, leading to better returns on investment (ROI) and greater conversion rates.

2. *Customer Segmentation*

Data mining supports companies to categorize their stakeholders into diverse groups based on purchasing preferences, behaviors, and demographics. Consequently, it permits personalized marketing, targeted promotions, and improved customer relationship management (CRM).

3. *Market Basket Analysis*

The practice of market basket analysis aids in classifying items that often coincide in transactions. Subsequently, it supports upselling strategies and cross-selling by recommending products that are regularly purchased together, thus increasing sales (Zurini, 2012).

4. *Trend Analysis*

Data mining supports recognizing and analyzing patterns and trends over time. This procedure allows companies to stay ahead of market variations, seize new opportunities, and adapt strategies accordingly.

5. *Customer Churn Prediction*

Data mining practices assists to forecast which customers are likely to leave based on their behavior patterns. Therefore, it aids in creating retention strategies, maintaining a stable customer base, and reducing churn rates.

LIMITATIONS OF STUDY

The discussion in this chapter about corporate data mining evaluates both its mechanisms and ethical concerns yet faces multiple scope limitations. The research work predominantly examines academic publications and publicly accessible content that may fail to represent the real-time corporate techniques alongside their proprietary methods. Confidentiality rules and non-disclosure contracts prevent researchers from directly examining corporate data mining algorithms and decision-making structures as well as the actual datasets used. The analysis remains primarily focused on legal and ethical perspectives within jurisdictions known for their established data protection regulations including the European Union and the United States. Due to these constraints the research does not provide a complete analysis of data mining practices across regions that possess different legal standards or weaker enforcement systems.

The fast-paced advancements in corporate data mining technologies represent a crucial limitation. The ongoing progress in artificial intelligence research combined with machine learning developments and big data analytics evolution could render some insights in this chapter obsolete due to emerging techniques and new regulation standards. This study examines socio-political and economic effects from corporate data mining but avoids an in-depth analysis of algorithms development techniques and cybersecurity risks that emerge from data breaches. Primary empirical research like insider interviews and experimental data mining studies is not included in this chapter because time and access restrictions prevented such activities. The existing restrictions demonstrate the necessity for continued research efforts and collaborative work across multiple disciplines to grasp the complex nature and developing challenges of corporate data mining.

THEORETICAL FOUNDATIONS

Main Notions in Data Mining

Data mining involves finding correlations, patterns, and variabilities in big datasets to forecast outcomes and obtain valuable insights. Digital transformation is observed as the function of new technologies (Mydyti, Kadriu, & Mirjana, 2023). Digital technologies enable significant operational improvements, such as improving customer experience, mitigating processes, or creating new models. The key drivers of digital transformation are digital capabilities and technologies. Digital technologies are essential to all efforts and provide business opportunities (Morakanyane, 2017; Orfanidis, 2018; Mydyti and Kadriu, 2021c). According to Mydyti, Kadriu, & Mirjana (2023) study, the positive impact of the primary attribute of service quality, time taken to resolve complaints, is critical as the study proves that data mining improves decision making and increases efficiency by analyzing business forecasts. The data mining approach empowers managers to make strategic decisions, and the use of data mining technologies is key to improving business performance. By helping companies, managers and researchers to become the main beneficiaries, this paper highlights the positive aspects of data mining, which serves as a contemporary approach to facilitate the digital transformation of companies (Mydyti, Kadriu, & Mirjana, 2023). The three key concepts are data processing, patterns and models, and overfitting and underfitting.

(a) Data Preprocessing: Data mining involves preparing raw data for analysis by cleaning, transforming, and organizing it. This process does through data cleaning by handling missing values, removing duplicates, correcting errors. This results to data integration by combining data from different sources as well as data transformation, normalizing and aggregating data, and data reduction by reducing data volume while maintaining integrity.
(b) Patterns and Models: Data mining patterns and models refer to regularities and structures in data, while models are mathematical representations used to describe and predict data behavior. For example, using an Association rule, classification models, clustering patterns to define structures.
(c) Overfitting and Underfitting: The process of data mining overfitting is a model that is too complex and captures noise along with the underlying pattern. The underfitting model relates to failing to capture the underlying pattern. The importance of overfitting and underfitting models helps to ensure a balance to achieve a model that generalizes well to new data (Schoormann, Schweihoff, Jussen, & Möller, 2023).

Big Data Function in Marketing

Big data contributes vigorously to a role in marketing by allowing companies to gain richer insights into marketing strategies, customer behavior, and striving better decision-making. The nine perceptions of big data in marketing include: targeted marketing, customer perceptions, optimizing marketing promotions, customer retention, product development, pricing strategies, social media promotions, improving customer experience, and measuring return on investment (Cordeiro, Deschamps, & de Lima, 2017; Pivar & Krstić, 2019).

1. *Customer Perceptions*: The notion of customer perceptions includes understanding customer behavior. So, big data lets companies analyze huge amounts of data from numerous sources, such as website interactions, social media, and purchase history, to comprehend customer behaviors, preferences, and trends. In addition, incorporating personalization by leveraging big data into industries supports to create product recommendations tailored to individual customer preferences and vastly personalized marketing messages (Hu, Sun, & Li, 2024).
2. *Targeted Marketing:* Targeted marketing relays to using big data breakdown to support in segmenting customers into discrete groups based on geographic, psychographic, demographic, and behavioral data. This dissection allows for more levelled and effective marketing campaigns. Subsequently, this aids predictive analytics on marketers to expect future customer preferences and behaviors, permitting for proactive marketing approaches and improved customer engagement (Pivar & Krstić, 2019).
3. *Optimizing Marketing Promotions:* Optimizing marketing promotions includes performance analysis of the big data to deliver real-time insights into the performance of marketing campaigns, enabling marketers to make data-driven adjustments and optimize campaign effectiveness. Hence marketers can use big data to conduct various tests on marketing elements such as ad creatives, email subject lines, and landing pages to define what works best for their targeted audience.
4. *Customer Retention:* Customer retention relays to managing blend analysis by examining customer data to tolerate corporations identify patterns that specify potential customer blend. This improves the development of retention approaches to keep customers involved and loyal. Accordingly, it results to using loyalty plans on the big data in designing and managing customer preferences and purchase history to offer relevant incentives and rewards (Pivar & Krstić, 2019).
5. *Product Development:* Product development in big data promotion includes using customer feedback to help companies gather and analyze customer feedback from numerous sources, such as surveys, reviews, and social media, to identify areas for innovation and improvement. This scores to market trends analysis and customer preferences, to help businesses develop new services and products that meet evolving needs and stay ahead of the competition.
6. *Pricing Strategies:* Vibrant Pricing in big data marketing allows dynamic pricing strategies by analyzing features such as competitor pricing, demand, and customer behavior in real-time, letting companies adjust prices for extreme profitability. This leads to price optimization by helping marketers to establish the optimal price points for services and products, balancing customers' readiness to pay with business goals.
7. *Social Media Promotions:* Social media marketing allows us to use big data tools to apply, listen, and monitor social media conversations and sentiment, providing insights into customer opinions and brand perception. This results to marketing influencer by analyzing social media data, businesses can identify and collaborate with influencers who have a significant impact on their target audience.
8. *Improving Customer Knowledge:* Big data marketing aids in planning and personalizing customer drives, safeguarding that customers receive appropriate and timely interactions at each stage. By incorporating data from numerous channels, companies can deliver a seamless and consistent customer capability across all stages, from online to in-store.
9. *Defining Return on Investment (ROI):* Big data lets companies determine sales and adaptations to definite marketing events, providing a robust ROI and the effectiveness of different marketing networks. The use of performance metrics lets marketers to track key performance indicators (KPIs) such as customer lifetime value (CLV), customer acquisition cost (CAC), and return on marketing investment (ROMI) to gauge success and make informed decisions.

DATA COLLECTION AND PREPARATION

Classifying applicable data sources is a vital step in the data mining practice. It contains shaping where to get the data that will offer the most valuable perceptions for a particular business goal or analysis. Some examples of relevant data sources include the following:

Examples of Relevant Data Sources

(a) Transactional Data are Point of Sale (POS) Systems that capture sales transactions and inventory data.
(b) E-commerce Platforms track online sales, customer interactions, and product views.
(c) Customer Data such as CRM Systems stores customer contact details, interaction history, and purchase behavior.
(d) Surveys and Feedback Forms are used to collect customer opinions, satisfaction ratings, and preferences.
(e) Web and Social Media Data using website analytics tools like Google Analytics to provide data on website traffic, user behavior, and conversion rates. Also, social media platforms integrating APIs from platforms like Twitter, Facebook, and Instagram provide data on user interactions, posts, and sentiment.

Market and Competitive Data

The idea of market research reporting helps to provide insights into industry trends, market size, and competitive landscape. Industry trends is one of the core components of a market research report that helps with market identification and industry analysis. These trends could range from consumer behavior shifts to regulatory changes, technological innovations, and economic variations. By market research reports and prediction emerging patterns help companies anticipate variations, adapt proactively, and remain competitive.

Market Size and Growth Potential

Understanding the size of a market is essential for evaluating opportunities and risks. Hence, market size typically showing the revenue potential, market volume, and historical and projected growth rates. Market research reports break down the data to allow companies assess whether entering a market or launching a product is worth the investment. Subsequently, reports help to provide market segmentation insights, enabling businesses to target specific niches. For instance, breaking a market into segments like geography, demographics, and purchasing behavior helps firms tailor their offerings and marketing efforts to the most lucrative segments.

Data Collection and Sources

Data Collection and Sources refers to gathering information from various channels, like social media, surveys, government reports, and market studies. This data helps companies understand consumer preferences, market demand, and regulatory landscapes, forming a foundation for data-driven marketing strategies. The market and growth potential has several data collection and sources that includes the following:

- Consumer Preferences and Social Media Analysis: Energy companies use social media and survey data to understand public opinion on green energy initiatives, identifying key demographics interested in renewable solutions. For example, higher interest in sustainable options, which can guide targeted advertising.
- Government Policy and Incentives: Most companies analyze government data on renewable energy subsidies, grants, and incentives to position themselves strategically in markets where support for green energy is robust.
- Market Demand Forecasting: The data from environmental organizations, economic reports, and utility companies is mined to predict demand for renewable sources, allowing companies to tailor marketing campaigns to anticipated market shifts.

Data Manipulation Targeting and Segmentation

Data manipulation and segmentation is the practice where companies use gathered data to distribute customers into discrete groups based on interests, behaviors, or demographics. It involves data analysis methods to predict which groups are best likely to respond to specific marketing efforts, allowing for vastly targeted, personalized promotions that increase conversion and engagement rates.

- Behavioral Segmentation: By tracking customer behaviors, for example, (home energy use, interest in eco-friendly products, location), companies can segment audiences based on likelihood to adopt renewable energy.
- Predictive Analytics for Customer Targeting: Using predictive models, firms assess which customers are most likely to invest in renewable energy solutions, adjusting marketing efforts accordingly. Data from IoT devices in smart homes, for instance, can help identify energy-saving behaviors, promoting energy-efficient options to specific customer groups.

Data Insights Marketing Strategies

Data insights marketing strategies include using data analysis to shape personalized marketing approaches. This involves customizing content for specific audiences, targeting through influencer partnerships, tailoring campaigns to regional preferences and enhancing engagement and effectiveness.

- Content Personalization: Renewable energy companies tailor their messaging and ad content to resonate with segmented audiences. For instance, consumers identified as environmentally conscious might receive messaging highlighting the ecological benefits of green energy, while cost-sensitive customers might see ads focused on potential savings.
- Influencer Marketing and Partnerships: Companies use data on social media trends to collaborate with influencers who advocate for sustainability, reaching target demographics with high engagement rates through relatable figures.

- Localized Marketing Efforts: By analyzing geographic data, companies can launch campaigns targeting regions where renewable resources like solar or wind power are most feasible, making the marketing relevant to each area's specific energy potential.

Data-Insights Corporate Social Responsibility (CSR) Edges

Data-driven corporate social responsibility (CSR) edges use data to design and promote CSR efforts that align with consumer values, such as sustainability. This aids companies build trust by clearly sharing their environmental effect and adapting CSR promotions to meet audience anticipations.

- Transparency and Trust Building: By mining data on public opinion regarding environmental responsibility, companies create CSR campaigns that highlight their contributions to sustainability, appealing to socially conscious consumers.
- Sustainability Reporting and Accountability: Data analysis enables companies to measure their environmental impact, which they can publicize to reinforce brand integrity and customer loyalty.

Ethical Considerations and Data Challenges

Ethical considerations and data challenges convey issues like consumer trust, data privacy, and regulatory compliance. Businesses must balance data-driven advertising with respect for user privacy, follow data protection laws, and avoid manipulative tactics, to maintain ethical standards.

- Privacy Concerns: As companies collect more consumer data, particularly related to personal energy use, ethical issues around privacy emerge. The renewable energy sector must address transparency in data usage and provide clear data privacy policies.
- Manipulation vs. Influence: The line between persuasive marketing and manipulation becomes blurred as companies use data to influence decisions. The renewable energy sector must consider how marketing practices impact consumer autonomy and trust.
- Regulatory Compliance: With increasing regulations around privacy, data usage, and renewable energy corporations must safeguard their data mining practices to align with local laws, such as GDPR and international laws to avoid reputational loss and legal repercussions.

In summary, the global renewable energy market influences data mining and manipulation to shape marketing strategies, navigate ethical, attract environmentally conscious consumers, and regulatory landscapes. Incorporating specific examples and potential data sources could provide a comprehensive overview of the powerful role that data plays in modern renewable energy marketing.

Competitive Panorama

Competitive Panorama is the analysis of an industry's key players, market trends, and strategies. Understanding this helps companies identify opportunities, assess threats, and position themselves effectively within the market. Another critical component of market research reports is an analysis of the competitive landscape. It provides a comprehensive overview of the main players within the industry, their market shares, strengths, weaknesses, and competitive strategies.

By comparing and benchmarking competitors, companies can adjust their market approach, address potential gaps, and identify areas for differentiation. For example, using a Smartphone Industry. The Smartphone Industry is a segment focused on planning, manufacturing, and selling smartphones. It comprises businesses competing on features like brand, technology, design, and price, frequently innovating to meet consumer demands and stay ahead in a very competitive market (Han, 2014). The ability to report and analyze the global smartphone industry provides the competitive landscape section for major players like Apple and Samsung. There is a growing opportunity for mid-tier manufacturers in emerging markets. This insight could encourage new entrants or smaller companies to invest in these markets where competition is less saturated.

Market Drivers and Limitations

Market drivers are factors that influence the growth of an industry. Drivers propel market growth, like technological advancements or high demand, while restraints hinder it, such as regulatory challenges or economic downturns. The market research reports and analyze key factors driving or hindering market growth. Understanding the limitations and drivers is vital for making sound tactical decisions. Market drivers may include technological innovations, changing consumer preferences or favorable economic conditions. Conversely, limitations, comprise regulatory issues, high operational costs, and supply chain challenges. For instance, using Electric Vehicles (EV). Electric Vehicles are automobiles propelled by using energy accumulated in batteries, rather than conventional internal incineration engines.

DATA CLEANING AND INTEGRATION METHODS

Data Cleaning involve excluding duplicates and errors from data while integration methods helps to combine data from diverse sources into a joined format to ensure consistency and accuracy for analysis. Data Cleaning are vital in data preparation, to ensure data accuracy and ready for analysis. These strategies help improve the quality of data, making it more consistent for decision-making and modeling.

Data Cleaning Methods

Data Cleaning Methods involve eliminating errors and variations in data to progress its quality. Common practices include handling missing values and removing duplicates, standardizing formats, detecting outliers, fixing errors, and converting data categories to ensure reliability and accuracy. Data cleaning includes classifying and rectifying issues in the dataset to increase its quality. Common techniques include:

(a) Removing Duplicates: Duplicates can distort analysis and lead to incorrect conclusions. Data cleaning tools detect and remove duplicate records.
(b) Handling Missing Data: Missing values can result from incomplete data entry, or errors during collection. Various methods to handle missing data include imputation and deletion. The imputation relates to replacing missing values with mean, median, mode, or predicted values while the deletion relates to removing rows or columns with missing values if they significantly impact analysis.

(c) Standardization and Normalization: Ensures consistency in data format, such as converting all date formats to a standard. For instance, ensuring arithmetic values are within a reliable range such as MM-DD- YYYY.
(d) Outlier Discovery and Usage: Categorizing outliers and data themes vary from different sources. Determining the option of whether to eliminate, retain, or adjust a data follows the significance to the analysis.
(e) Error Adjustment: Spotting and fixing data entry errors, such as incorrect values, misspellings, or discrepancies. For instance, USA vs United States.
(f) Data Type Conversion: Ensuring that data is in the correct type. For example, converting text values to numerical values, or vice versa.

Data Integration Methods

Data integration comprises data from diverse sources, creating a unified view of information. Integration can be intricate, as data might be in numerous formats or have different structures.

Key techniques include:

(a) Schema Incorporation: Different data sources might use diverse data types, schemas, and tables. Schema incorporation ensures that data from diverse sources can be combined into a consistent format. This can involve mapping fields from different systems to a unified schema.
(b) Object Determination: Identifying and unifying records from diverse sources that refer to similar real-world objects, such as toning customer records from two diverse databases that signify to the same person. This is vital to avoid data repetition when integrating datasets.
(c) Data Charting: Charting data from one structure to another. For instance, charting customer data from a CRM technique to an ERP system's customer profile. This ensures that fields from diverse systems align correctly.
(d) Data Transformation: Transforming data into a format appropriate for integration. This can include processes such as converting units, aggregating data, miles to kilometers or switching time zones.
(e) Data Consolidation: Joining data from numerous sources, such as flat files, databases, and application programming interface (API) into a unified or single dataset. This often includes merging, duplication, or joining tables from diverse sources.
(f) ETL Process (Extract, Transform, Load): A widely used technique in data integration. It involves extracting by pulling data from different sources. Transforming by cleaning, normalizing, and converting the data to a suitable format. Loading by inserting the transformed data into a target system, such as a data warehouse.

Data Cleaning Integration and Challenges

(a) Challenges in data cleaning integration comprise data variations across sources, incomplete data, missing mismatches, managing big volumes of data efficiently, and systematizing the cleaning and integration process, especially with frequently changing or unstructured data.

(b) Data Variation: Different data sources might have opposed information, that would require decision-making on which to entrust the data.
(c) Data Format Disparity: Joining data from numerous sources with different formats. For example, dates, text, numbers that requires extensive transformation.
(d) Scalability: Classifying big volumes of data efficiently while ensuring correctness and speed during cleaning and incorporation (Kohavi, Mason, Parekh, Zheng, 2004).
(e) Automation: Automating the cleaning and integration process can be complex, especially when dealing with unstructured data or sources with frequent changes.

Data Cleaning Tools

The process of data mining requires data cleaning tools to ensure data mining efficieny. These tools automate various practices to enhance transformation, data cleaning, and integration for reliable, accurate, and joined datasets analysis. Numerous tools help to automate and streamline data cleaning and integration processes, such as:

(a) Data Cleaning Tools: Trifacta, OpenRefine, Talend, Alteryx.
(b) ETL Tools: Informatica, Apache NiFi, Microsoft SSIS (SQL Server Integration Services), and Talend.
(c) Data Integration Platforms: Dell Boomi, Informatica PowerCenter, and MuleSoft

Data Best Practices

Best Practices in data cleaning include regularly validating and updating data, standardizing formats, handling missing values appropriately, detecting and correcting errors, maintaining clear documentation, and using automated tools for consistency and efficiency. Ensuring data quality through regular monitoring is key to accurate analysis.

(a) Data Quality Assurance: Continuously monitor and validate the quality of integrated data to ensure it remains accurate and useful.
(b) Documentation: Document data sources, integration steps, and assumptions to maintain clarity in complex projects.
(c) Scalability Considerations: Implement solutions that can scale as data volume increases, ensuring long-term efficiency.

Therefore, data cleaning and integration techniques are fundamental to ensuring that data is accurate, consistent, and ready for meaningful analysis. These techniques enhance the reliability of business insights and decision-making by addressing challenges related to data quality and unification.

Data Consistency and Quality

Data consistency and quality comprises validating data accuracy, reliability, and completeness across diverse sources. It contains standardizing formats, handling missing data, removing errors, and implementing checks to preserve uniformity, ensuring data is dependable for analysis and decision-making. Ensuring data consistency and quality is vital for preserving reliable and accurate data across systems, ensuring it is appropriate for analysis, decision-making, and reporting. This process involves several key practices and techniques:

(a) Data Accuracy: Ensuring that the data is precise and free from mistakes. This involves implementing validation rules at the data entry stage. For example, field type checks, range checks. This includes using automated data justification tools to identify discrepancies and cross-check data against dependable sources or benchmarks.
(b) Data Completeness: Ensuring that all essential data is present and there is no missing information. This involves establishing clear guidelines on mandatory fields and data entry requirements and implementing processes for handling missing or incomplete data. For example, imputation and data collection follow-ups. Hence, it requires regular auditing of data sources for gaps or missing records.
(c) Data Consistency: Ensuring that the same data values are consistent across different systems, datasets, and processes. This involves standardized formats such as dates, currency, addresses, across data sources and using data integration tools to ensure that data merged from different systems aligns correctly. Applying rules to avert conflicting information in multiple records for instance, a customer's address should be reliable across all systems.
(d) Data Integrity: Maintaining the reliability and trustworthiness of the data over time. This involves using checksums and data validation during transfers to avoid corruption and emplcying version control to track and verify changes to the data. This helps to implement auditing mechanisms to detect and prevent unauthorized or accidental changes.
(e) Data Standardization: Ensuring that data is formatted and structured consistently across sources. This involved developing data standards and naming conventions to ensure uniformity and using automated tools to enforce data transformations. For example, converting all phone numbers to a specific format.
(f) Data Validation: Verifying that the data entered meets specific criteria and is within acceptable parameters. This involves implementing real-time validation checks during data entry and using automated systems to identify data anomalies. For example, values outside predefined ranges.

Error Detection and Data Correction: Identifying and fixing mistakes in the data. This involves using error detection algorithms to flag outliers or inconsistencies. It also helps to perform regular data quality checks, such as manual review or machine learning-based anomaly detection. Using data cleaning techniques helps to correct erroneous values such as misspellings and duplicate records.

Data Consistency and Quality Benefits

The process of data consistency and quality is essential for companies to maintain trust, make informed decisions, and simplify operations. Consequently, data consistency and quality is a standardization method for multi-step process validation, error discovery, and governance for retaining the reliability and integrity of data. The application of these practices, companies could maintain data is both consistent and accurate format for driving better decisions and insights. Some key advantages include:

(a) Enhanced Decision-Making: Accurate and consistent data leads to better-informed decisions.
(b) Improved Efficiency: Reduces time spent on fixing errors, allowing for smoother processes.

(c) The Regulatory Compliance: relates to data-related guidelines and rules for applying compliance to data mining processes. For instance, the enforcement of Health Insurance Portability and Accountability Act (HIPAA) and General Data Protection Regulation (GDPR). Both regulations share the unilateral goals of retaining obligations upon administrations to properly store, manage, and protect users' personal data.
(d) Improved Customer Trust: Dependable data leads to improved customer experiences and satisfaction.

DATA MINING METHODS IN MARKETING

Data mining methods in marketing include analyzing big sets of customer data to discover patterns and perceptions that can notify marketing tactics. Common techniques include:

(a) Clustering: Grouping similar customers for targeted campaigns.
(b) Classification: Predicting customer behavior or segment membership.
(c) Association Rule Mining: Identifying relationships between products or services.
(d) Regression Analysis: Forecasting sales or customer behavior.
(e) Emotion Analysis: the process of analyzing customer reactions to measure brand perception.

These practices aid marketers to improve customer engagement, optimize targeting, and enhance decision-making (Song & Hua, 2022).

Analysis of Marketing Data Manipulation

The analysis of marketing data manipulation comprises of the transformation of market data and raw customers into actionable perceptions. This embraces structuring, cleaning, and organizing data, shadowed by using numerical and analytical techniques to classify patterns, trends, and relationships.

The objective is to enhance marketing approaches, improve customer segmentation, forecast trends, and progress decision-making for more applicable promotions and product offerings. Handling and analysis of marketing data is a vital process in marketing that converts raw data into valuable insights for better decision-making. It involves several key stages such as data preparation, manipulation, analysis, reporting, and optimization.

Data Collection and Preparation is the practice of collecting raw information from numerous sources for exploration, decision-making, or application in certain tasks. Data collection ensures that accurate, relevant and sufficient data is acquired for the intended purpose. The three processes are data collection, cleaning, and transformation. The collection involves gathering data from various sources like customer interactions, online behavior, sales transactions, social media, surveys, etc. The cleaning removes inaccuracies, duplicates, and irrelevant data, and handling missing or inconsistent information while the transformation, structures data into a usable format by standardizing units, categories, and time frames, ensuring consistency. The importance of Data Collection and Preparation include:

(a) Data Quality: Reliable data leads to accurate insights and decisions.
(b) Moderates Errors: Cleaning and organizing data minimize inaccuracies.
(c) Facilitates Analysis: Properly prepared data is easier to analyze and visualize.

(d) Saves Time: Structured and clean data reduces the effort needed during analysis.

Data Manipulation denotes to the practice of altering, organizing, or analyzing data to make it more valuable, clear, and suitable for purposes. This can comprise various operations such as cleaning, filtering, sorting, converting, gathering, or removing data, often to prepare it for further analysis or to create meaningful perceptions. The three steps of data manipulation are aggregation, filtering, and normalization. The aggregation summarizes data by grouping it such as sales by product category to identify trends and patterns. The filtering helps to select specific subsets of data to focus on relevant information, such as filtering out data for a particular region or period. Normalization conveys regulating data to a common format or scale, making it easier to link such as converting currencies to a single value.

Data manipulation is a vital step in the data lifecycle, ensuring that raw data is converted into a format that adds value to systems and users. The benefits of data manipulation comprise:

(a) Enhances data usability and accuracy.
(b) Simplifies complex datasets for analysis and visualization.
(c) Provides actionable insights for informed decision-making.
(d) Prepares data for automation or advanced applications, such as Artificial Intelligence (AI).

Data Mining Analysis

Data mining analysis is the practice of analytically inspecting, organizing, and inferring data to discover relationships, patterns, trends, and perceptions that can solve specific problems or inform decisions. It includes using mathematical, statistical, and computational techniques to transform raw data into meaningful information. For instance, data analysis includes predictive, descriptive, segmentation, prescriptive, and association analysis.

(a) Predictive Analysis: involves the use of numerical models and machine learning to predict future sales patterns or customer behaviors such as predicting customer demand or churn.
(b) Descriptive Analysis: focuses on visualizing and summarizing data through trends, averages, and charts to comprehend current states and past behaviors.
(c) Segmentation: requires the grouping of customers into sections based on shared characteristics, such as demographics, and purchasing behavior to construct targeted marketing approaches.
(d) Prescriptive Analysis: relates to recommending activities based on data insights, such as product promotions or signifying optimal pricing strategies.
(e) Association Analysis: involves classifying relationships between variables, such as repeatedly bought-together products, to expand cross-selling and upselling strategies.

Data Reporting and Visualization

The data reporting and visualization shows the graphical illustration of data using visual rudiments such as graphs, charts, and maps. It supports users hastily and intuitively to understand multipart data designs, insights, and trends. The visualization tools uses graphs, dashboards, and charts to present multifaceted data perceptions in an easily logical format for decision-makers, while the reporting connects main findings, actionable insights, and trends to stakeholders through presentations. Consequently, visualization aids to make data simpler to interpret and actionable by converting raw numbers into meaningful visuals.

The common types of data visualization include:

- Bar Charts: Compare categories or track changes over time.
- Line Graphs: Show trends or changes over continuous periods.
- Pie Charts: Represent proportions or percentages of a whole.
- Scatter Plots: Display relationships between two variables.
- Heat Maps: Highlight intensity or concentration in specific areas.
- Dashboards: Combine multiple visualizations for a holistic view of metrics.

The benefits of data visualization include:

- Simplifies complex data.
- Enhances understanding and retention of insights.
- Classifies outliers, trends, and relationships at a glance.
- Eases communication between technical and non-technical audiences.

Data Optimization

Data optimization indicates the practice of cultivating and improving how data is gathered, analyzed, and used to exploit the success of marketing promotions. It ensures that promotions are data-driven and distribute the best possible outcomes by allowing more accurate decision-making. The main elements involve exact data collection, segmentation, and performance metrics evaluation.

(a) Data Collection: the process of gathering data from reliable sources, such as demographics, user behavior, and campaign performance metrics for instance, clickable rates, adaptation rates, using tracking tools such as tags, cookies, and analytics platforms to ensure consistency.
(b) Data Segmentation: is the process of dividing audiences into meaningful sections based on characteristics such as location, age, or behavior. This consents to targeting specific groups and refining engagement and relevancy.
(c) Performance Metrics Evaluation: involves classifying and focusing on main performance indicators (KPIs) that support the campaign goals, such as engagement, ROI, or lead generation. This allows the adjusting of metrics that do not contribute to actionable insights.

Data Manipulation Analysis Benefits

The process of data manipulation analysis attracts many benefits that involve transforming raw data into actionable perceptions that improve decision-making, optimize marketing strategies, advance customer targeting, heighten customer satisfaction, and surge return on investment (ROI). In essence, handling and analyzing marketing data allows companies to convert huge amounts of data into actionable insights that drive efficient marketing decisions, improve customer engagement, and eventually, expand profitability. This leads to more effective promotions, better resource allocation, and competitive advantage.

(a) Improved Targeting: is the process of classifying the most profitable customer sections and modifying marketing efforts to their needs. It allows personalized marketing by recognizing crucial customer segments.
(b) Informed Decision-Making: is the process of data-driven insights providing strong direction for marketing approaches, leading to better apportionment of resources. It provides data-driven perceptions to guide marketing tactics.
(c) Enhanced Customer Experience: By evaluating customer behavior, companies can offer personalized experience and improve satisfaction. It helps to tailor offerings to meet customer needs and boost satisfaction.
(d) Competitive Advantage: process access to customer preferences and market trends that helps businesses stay ahead of competitors. It identifies market trends and customer preferences to stay ahead of competitors.
(e) Optimized ROI: helps to ensure effective data manipulation analysis for marketing budgets on the most successful tactics and maximizing return on investment. It ensures marketing budgets are spent on the most effective plans to maximizing greater returns.

CASE STUDIES AND IMPLICATIONS FOR PRACTICE STUDIES

Data Mining Implementation in a Large Retail Corporation

The implementation by a big retail corporation, functioning on e-commerce platforms and physical stores, to enhance its marketing efforts, improve customer experience, and optimize inventory management. The business faced challenges in predicting demand for products, understanding customer preferences, and personalizing marketing messages (Dorador, 2022). Big retail corporation and E-commerce is a vital sphere for data mining (Kohavi & Provost, 2001), with massive amounts of clickstream and transactional data that dwarf in size data warehouses from a few years ago (Kimball & Merz, 2000).

Objectives

The corporation aimed to: (a) Increase Customer Segmentation: to strongly comprehend customer preferences and behaviors. (b) Improve Sales and Marketing Approaches: to prsonalize promotions and provide different customer sections. (c) Optimize Inventory Management: to predict demand patterns to decrease understocking and overstocking issues. (d) Increase Customer Retention: to identify issues influencing customer loyalty and decrease churn.

Data Mining Practice Implementation

(a) Customer Segmentation: the corporation used clustering algorithms called K-means to slice customers based on demographic data, purchasing behavior, and browsing patterns. This allowed the merchant to classify seasonal shoppers, high-value customers, and discount-sensitive segments.

(b) Market Bucket Analysis: the corporation applied association rule mining, such as Apriori algorithm to analyze customer purchase data and identify product combinations often bought together. This view helped the company to target product promotions, shoved offers, and product assignments, increasing up-selling and cross-selling opportunities.
(c) Predictive Analytics: embodies regression analysis and trend series for calculating the request for specific activities based on historical data, seasonality, and external factors like promotions and holidays. This helped the company to optimize inventory levels, ensuring that the right products are in stock at the right time.
(d) Personalized Promotion: the use of data mining techniques such as logistic regression and decision trees, the company classified patterns in shopping behaviors and customer preferences. This information was used to create personalized product recommendations, email campaigns, and promotions, leading to advanced engagement and conversion rates.
(e) Customer Mix Analysis: allows the company to classify the models such as decision trees, support vector machines to classify customers at risk of churning based on past behavior and purchase history. The company applied targeted retention strategies, such as special offers, loyalty programs to re-engage these customers (Dorador, 2022; Kimball & Merz, 2000).

Results

- Enlarged Sales: By identifying promotions and product endorsements, the company saw a substantial increase in sales, especially from up-sell and cross-sell initiatives.
- Enriched Customer Retention: The churn forecast model allowed the company to proactively engross with reducing churn, at-risk customers, and growing customer lifetime value.
- Improved Inventory: allowed thriving demand forecasting, the company condensed excess inventory and evaded stockouts, leading to improved operational efficiency and cost savings.
- Heightened Marketing Return on Investment (ROI): this targeted marketing promotions that led to advanced response rates and improved resource allocation, resulting in an enriched return on investment for marketing efforts.

Outcome

The successful application of data mining in the large retail company allowed the business to influence sales and customer data efficiently, leading to better customer segmentation, enhanced inventory, and more personalized marketing approaches. By using data-driven perceptions, the retailer was able to boost sales, operational efficiency, and improve customer satisfaction.

Case Study 2: E-Commerce Industry Trends

Market research reports are vital tools that guide businesses in making informed decisions about new markets, product launches, and strategic growth. These reports deliver comprehensive analyses that reveal industry trends, evaluate market size, and assess competitive landscapes. By offering actionable insights, market research reports become instrumental in shaping organizational strategy and fostering competitive advantage (Bonsu, 2019). A good business model gives answers to the following questions: Who is the customer? What does the customer value? How do we make money? What is the underlying economic logic that explains how to deliver value? (Magretta, 2002, p. 4). The business model concept is widely understood as a (management) tool to facilitate different activities (Pateli & Giaglis, 2004). The use of industry trends delves into the key components of market research reports, displaying the role of industry dynamics, market potential, and the factors that influence competitive positioning. For example, industry trends relates to the e-commerce and market research reports that showcase the significant shift from desktop to mobile shopping over the last decade. As mobile devices became more predominant, businesses with early access to such visions were able to capitalize in mobile-optimized platforms and mobile marketing plans, gaining a competitive edge (Paun, Ivascu, Olteteanu, & Dantis, 2024; MarketLine, 2023).

Background

The e-commerce business has faced rapid development over the past decade, propelled by expansions in changes in consumer behavior, technology, and the explosion of online platforms. Amazon: adoption of the leveraged AI-driven program engines, resulting in 35% of its revenue from personalized recommendation plan, such as the TikTok influencers boosting brand engagement and awareness, with over 100 million app downloads in 2023 (MarketLine, 2023). By 2023, the global e-commerce market was projected to exceed $6 trillion, with significant contributions from mobile commerce, personalization, and artificial intelligence (AI) applications. Key trends include the rise of social commerce, sustainability initiatives, omnichannel experiences, and increased reliance on data analytics (Magretta, 2002).

Objective

The case study purposes explore how a leading e-commerce company, ShopEase, adapted to evolving trends to optimize operations, boost customer engagement, and sustain competitive advantage in a rapidly advancing market.

Implementation

According to Desouza (2024), ShopEase focused on three key trends:

1. Adoption of AI for Personalization:
    - o Integrated AI algorithms to analyze customer behavior and preferences.
    - o Used predictive analytics to recommend products tailored to individual customers.
2. Expansion into Social Commerce:
    - o Partnered with major social media platforms like Instagram and TikTok.
    - o Leveraged influencer marketing and direct shopping features to drive sales.
3. Adoption to Sustainability:
    - o Initiated eco-friendly packaging.
    - o Offered a "green shopping" filter to highlight sustainable products.

To implement these strategies:

- ShopEase invested in cutting-edge technology and data science teams.

- Integrate the content creators and influencers and to boost its presence on social media.
- Partner with suppliers to ensure viable sourcing and packaging materials.

Results

The implementation yielded measurable success:

- AI Personalization: Conversion rates improved by 20%, and average order value increased by 15% (MarketLine, 2023)
- Social Commerce Expansion: Sales through social platforms grew by 35% year-over-year (Desouza, 2024).
- Sustainability Efforts: Customer retention rates increased by 10%, as 68% of customers reported a preference for brands with sustainable practices (Fischer & Goad, 2024; Harvard Business Review, 2022)

Outcome

The plans enabled ShopEase to reinforce its market position, attaining a 25% revenue growth in a highly competitive ecosystem. The company's emphasis on sustainability and innovation which resonated with Gen Z customers, millennials, and aligning with their values and purchasing preferences (Harvard Business Review, 2022; Magretta, 2002).

RISKS AND ETHICAL FAILURES

While data mining provides weighty advantages, it also aids vital threats and ethical challenges. One main worry is data leakage, where complex information is unprotected inadvertently, leading to financial loss and confidentiality gaps. A remarkable example is the Facebook Cambridge Analytica outrage, where private data of masses of users was reaped without consent, impelling sparking global arguments and political campaigns on data privacy. Likewise, whistleblowing incidents, such as Edward Snowden's disclosures about mass surveillance, focus how data mining can be leveraged for government supervision while nurturing interests about civil independences and ethical limitations (Cormier & Magnan, 2017).

Another persistent concern is the use of data mining for publicity and misinformation. Advanced algorithms can influence social media feeds, magnifying wrong storylines to influence public opinion. For example, in the 2016 U.S. presidential election, data-driven hype was used to target voters with misrepresenting content, stimulating polarization. Such incidents highlight the need for sterner transparency and regulations in data-driven decision-making.

To address these issues, companies need to embrace vigorous ethical strategies, ensure accountability in data-driven processes, and rank data security. While technical features like data cleaning remain vital for accuracy, they can be reorganized to preserve focus on ethical considerations in real-world applications.

THE FUTURE TRENDS IN DATA-DRIVEN MARKETING

As the panorama of marketing is speedily changing and data technology is advancing. The future of data-driven marketing will continue to advance in data collection, mining, analysis, and personalization. Some of the main trends that are recommended drive the future of data-driven marketing:

(a) Machine Learning (ML) and Artificial Intelligence (AI) contributes to improved personalization, predictive analysis, and systematized promotions. The AI and ML help to forecast future trends and customer behavior. In the future, these technologies will allow more precise predictions, helping marketers adjust campaigns in real time and expand customer retention strategies. The improved personalization sanctions for hyper-personalized marketing at scale by analyzing massive amounts of customer data, including preferences, purchasing behavior, and engagement. This results in more tailored content, offers, and experiences. The automated movements relate to the machine learning algorithms that progressively automate decision-making in marketing promotions, adjusting in real-time to customer behaviors, responses, and preferences.

(b) Visual and Voice Search Optimization relays to voice search and visual search. With the increasing popularity of voice-activated devices such as Google Assistant and Amazon Alexa, the voice search will develop into a critical part of the customer voyage. Businesses will boost content for voice queries, ensuring that their products or services appear in voice-based search results. Visual search tools like Google Lens and Pinterest are prominent in the visual search. In the future, customers will be able to search for products using graphics, virtual, images, and marketers will influence visual search data to target customers based on the images they engage with.

(c) Advanced Analytics and Big Data: conveys to data integration, real-time data processing, predictive and prescriptive analytics. Real-time data processing examines big amounts of data in real-time and will regenerate to improve, allowing marketers to adjust instantly to customer behavior and market changes. This enables more immediate and impactful decision-making. The data integration handles more data sources and companies increasingly integrate various data streams, such as social media, CRM systems, website behavior, and IoT data to build more comprehensive customer profiles. This will enable more nuanced and effective targeting. The projecting and prescriptive analytics support the future outcomes and prescribing the best actions to take. This helps in optimizing marketing strategies before problems arise.

(d) Privacy-First Promotion: recounts to data privacy rules and zero-party data. The data privacy policies help to develop consumer responsiveness such as the California Consumer Privacy Act (CCPA) and General Data Protection Regulation (GDPR) that necessitates businesses to embrace privacy-first strategies. This comprises offering clients extra power over their data, greater transparency in data collection practices, and ensuring compliance with privacy laws. The zero-party data help Companies to rely on zero-party data, which is data openly offered by customers, as opposed to third-party data that may be firmer to obtain due to privacy limitations. This data can include preferences, interests directly shared by customers, and feedback allowing for more visible and customer-centric promotion.

(e) Amplified Reality (AR) and Virtual Reality (VR): involves to immersive client drives and data-driven personalization. Both (AR and VR) generates more attractive customer experiences. For example, AR permit clients to visualize products in their own setting before buying. For instance, clothing and furniture, while VR deals with immersive brand practices or virtual store tours. The (AR and

VR) are data from user connections for further personalization practices, helping marketers design extra engaging and targeted content that vibrates with individual preferences.

(f) Conversational Business and Chatbots includes conversational business and AI-Powered Chatbots. The AI-Powered Chatbots driven by natural language and AI processing play an important role in customer interfaces. They support responding to customer questions to endorsing products based on client data. The Conversational Business functions through messaging platforms like Facebook Messenger, WhatsApp, or SMS, and promote businesses to engage clients in real-time exchanges. These communications will be driven by data intuitions that predict client needs and offer personalized product promotions and recommendations.

(g) Blockchain Trust: involves Ad Fraud Prevention and Data Security. Data Security uses Blockchain technology to pull and safeguard data transparency and security in data-driven promotion. It helps to validate and secure customer data, unauthorized access, preventing fraud, and safeguarding that customers' data is used fairly and in compliance with privacy rules. Ad Fraud Prevention uses blockchain to resolve problems related to ad scams by offering traceable and transparent advertising data. Marketers could footprint their advertising cost and ensure that their promotions reach the intended audience without being averted by deceitful actors (PricewaterhouseCoopers, 2022; 2020; 2018).

(h) Engaging Content Formats: includes interactive content, video, and user-generated content (UGC). Interactive Content and Video aids to build more engaging video promotions and shoppable content will make it simpler for customers to act immediately after watching and enhancing conversion rates. User-Generated Content play a vital role in future marketing promotions. Companies will leverage data to classify and promote user-generated content that echoes with the audience, trust, and building authenticity.

(i) Content Creation by AI-Driven: narrates the automated content personalization and content creation. Automated Content Creation uses natural language and AI in handling data and allow varieties to automate the formation of personalized content on a scale. AI-powered tools can create everything from social media posts to emails, blog articles, and product descriptions, ensuring they support with customer behaviors and preferences. Consequently, Content Personalization uses AI to generate content that adjusts to learning from their browsing behavior, individual user preferences, past purchases, and demographic data to create messages that reverberate on a personal level. Hence, the future of data-driven promotion is branded by more refined technologies, improved personalization, and a greater focus on ethical practices and privacy. Successively, marketers will need to stay ahead of evolving trends and persistently adapt their approaches to leverage new insights and tools, all while safeguarding and maintaining customer trust and delivering significant practices. As data becomes more dominant, the brands that successfully combine invention, ethical considerations, and customer-centricity will lead the way.

RECOMMENDATIONS OF DATA MINING MARKETING STRATEGIES

The recommendations plan to improve service quality and communication between customer service companies and subcontractors, retailers, wholesalers, and manufacturers. According to (Mydyti, Kadriu, & Mirjana, 2023), users interact with the recommendation system without having to log in to process the information generated by the classification algorithm - the decision tree. Users have the advantage of receiving probability predictions - data and charts. This chapter provides the following five recommendations for applying data mining in data-driven promotions:

1. *Exploit Customer Segmentation for Targeted Operations:* The power in using data mining methods like classification and clustering to fragment customers based on demographics, purchasing patterns and behavior. Tailoring promotion messages to these fragments for more effective campaigns and personalization. For instance: A apparel retailer can produce separate advertising campaigns for different purchaser segments, such as first-time visitors, frequent shoppers, or clients with excessive spending potential.
2. *Classify Upselling Chances and Cross-Selling:* The capacity to use association rule mining to discover hidden designs in customer buying behavior. This can assist classify chances for upselling, cross-selling, increasing revenue from current customers. For instance: An e-commerce platform might determine that consumers who purchase a camera are also likely to buying accessories like tripods or lenses, stimulating targeted upselling promotions.
3. *Optimize Pricing Approaches:* helps to engage data mining to explore competitor pricing, patterns, and customer thoughtfulness to price variations. This perception will enhance pricing tactics for different consumer fragments or product classes. For instance: A travel agency can use data mining to change flight and hotel prices vigorously based on customer preferences, seasonality, and competitive pricing.
4. *Enhance Customer Preservation:* involves operating predictive analytics to categorize consumers at risk of implementing preservation approaches and churn. For instance, use cataloging algorithms to identify consumers who have shown signs of detachment. For instance: A telecommunication firm can offer incentives to consumers predicted to churn and personalized discounts thus cultivating retention rates.
5. *Personalize Email Promotion Campaigns:* The ability to implement recommendation systems based on data mining algorithms to send personalized product recommendations and offers in email campaigns. Use customer purchase history, browsing behavior, and preferences for customization. For example: An online bookstore can recommend books to customers based on past purchases or browsing history, increasing open rates and conversion.
    (a) *Improve Social Media Targeting:* The ability to use data mining to analyze social media data and identify trends, influences, and audience behaviors. This supports in improving ad levelling and content tactics on platforms such as Instagram, Facebook, and LinkedIn. For instance: A brand may use data mining to recognize which social media posts resound best with demographics, permitting for more targeted promotion.
    (b) *Enrich Marketing Attribution Prototypes:* this helps in data mining to cultivate advanced attribution prototypes that evaluate the effectiveness of diverse marketing campaigns and channels. These succors dealers to apportion their budgets more proficiently by understanding which channels push the greatest value. For example: A company can use data mining to determine the exact contribution of paid search ads, email marketing, and social media campaigns to conversions, leading to more strategic budget allocation (Zahara, Ikhsan, Santi, & Farid, 2023).

By leveraging data mining methods, companies can discover perceptions that push more efficient, personalized, and effective marketing approaches. These recommendations offer actionable ways to harness the power of data to optimize marketing efforts, improve customer experience, and ultimately increase revenue.

CONCLUSION

As data mining revives to contour businesses and people, it is vital to recognize both its merits and demerits. Outside boosting innovation and decision-making, data mining could lead to unplanned effects, such as data leakage, which looms security and privacy. While whistleblowing enabled by data mining can aid as a form of misconduct and corruption. whistleblowing also advances ethical dilemmas about liable disclosure and data ownership. Besides, the misappropriation of mined data for hype underlines the need for awareness against algorithmic misinformation and handling. To connect the influence of data mining reliably, it is vital to apply ethical strategies, transparency to alleviate the risks, robust security measures, and safeguard data-driven perceptions to positively enhance the society. Big data is transforming promotion by providing companies with tools to comprehend their consumers better, generate more personalized and effective marketing tactics, and eventually drive business development. By leveraging big data, dealers can optimize their campaigns, make data-driven decisions, and deliver remarkable customer experiences. Applying data mining and manipulation methods in marketing will deliver corporations' weighty competitive advantage. Leveraging data will drive marketing approaches, as they can improve campaigns, increase customer targeting, and ultimately increase income. It offers the opportunity to convert marketing efforts through higher data analytics. Therefore, classifying relevant data sources is essential to the success of data mining projects. By steadily evaluating external and internal data sources, considering integration potential, measuring data quality, and businesses can gather the greatest relevant data to push insightful evaluation and informed decision-making. This process safeguards the data used, maintain high-quality, and actionable tasks to align with the business goals. Equally, market inquiry reports help as a valuable resource for companies looking to benefit an exhaustive understanding of the business they control or wish to penetrate. By proposing insights into business trends, competitive dynamics, market size, and market drivers, these reports endow administration to make data-driven decisions. Whether it's classifying new growth chances, benchmarking against competitors, or understanding customer preferences, market research reports are crucial tools for business victory. Manipulation in promotion involves approaches designed to impact customer behavior, often through deceptive or persuasive tactics. Though it could be an efficient way to drive brand and sales awareness, it long-term risks and increases ethical concerns. Advertising and promotions should target to foster authentic relationships with consumers and build trust by offering value and transparency. When manipulation marks ethical boundaries such as exploiting vulnerabilities, misleading advertising, or withholding critical information it can harm a brand's reputation and erode customer trust. To balance efficiency with integrity, dealers should emphasize ethical practices such as fair representation and transparency of products or services and recognizing consumer independence. By ranking ethical considerations, advertising can not only attain short-term success but also shape sustainable, long-term connections with its audience. In the end, ethical advertising helps not just customers but also corporations, creating a basis of loyalty and trust that pushes lasting success. Hence, this chapter delivers valuable perceptions into the strategic use of data mining and manipulation in business promotions to evade bias from whistleblowing, data leakage, and propaganda. By linking theoretical foundations with case studies, and practical applications, it aims to be an indispensable resource for practitioners and academics in the field.

REFERENCES

Bloch-Wehba, H. (2024). The promise and perils of tech whistleblowing. *Northwestern University Law Review, 118*(6), 1503–1562. https://coloradotech.idm.oclc.org/login?url=https://www.proquest.com/scholarly-journals/promise-perils-tech-whistleblowing/docview/3049832414/se-2

Bonsu, S. (2019). Corporate Social Responsibility: Assessing the Alignment of Theory and Practice Utilizing Case Studies. *Journal of Marketing Management, 10*(1), 1–18. https://coloradotech.idm.oclc.org/login?url=https://www.proquest.com/scholarly-journals/corporate-social-responsibility-assessing/docview/2234961050/se-2

Bughin, J., Hazan, E., Ramaswamy, S., Chui, M., Allas, T., Dahlstrom, P., Henke, N., & Trench, M. (2017). *Artificial intelligence: the next digital frontier?* McKinsey Global Institute.

Bumblauskas, D., Nold, H., Bumblauskas, P., & Igou, A. (2017). Big data analytics: Transforming data to action. *Business Process Management Journal, 23*(3), 703–720. DOI: 10.1108/BPMJ-03-2016-0056

Cordeiro, G. O., Deschamps, F., & de Lima, E. P. (2017). Developing a Big Data/Analytics project: a case study in the auto industry. *IISE Annual Conference Proceedings,* 1753-1758. https://coloradotech.idm.oclc.org/login?url=https://www.proquest.com/scholarly-journals/developing-big-data-analytics-project-case-study/docview/1951123574/se-2

Cormier, D., & Magnan, M. (2017). Does a firm's exposure to ethical failures matter to financial markets? A governance perspective. *The Journal of Management and Governance, 21*(2), 267–289. DOI: 10.1007/s10997-016-9341-9

Desouza, E. (2024). *AfroTech - Blavity: Ready For Your Startup? Here Are Unique Business Name Ideas To Drive Success.* Newstex.

Domnik, J., & Holland, A. (2024). On Data Leakage Prevention Maturity: Adapting the C2M2 Framework. *Journal of Cybersecurity and Privacy, 4*(2), 167–195. DOI: 10.3390/jcp4020009

Dorador, B. (2022). *Nonprofit Business to Business Social Media Interventions: A Qualitative Case Study* (Order No. 28969306). Available from ABI/INFORM Collection. (2641884338). https://coloradotech.idm.oclc.org/login?url=https://www.proquest.com/dissertations-theses/nonprofit-business-social-media-interventions/docview/2641884338/se-2

Fischer, M., & Goad, S. (2024). Greenhouse Gas Emission – A Perspective. *Journal of Strategic Innovation and Sustainability, 19*(2), 1–13. DOI: 10.33423/jsis.v19i2.6991

Han, E. (2014). *The Future of Smartphone Industry: New Opportunities and Breakthroughs.* (). Taipei: Institute For Information Industry. Retrieved from ABI/INFORM Collection https://coloradotech.idm.oclc.org/login?url=https://www.proquest.com/reports/future-smartphone-industry-new-opportunities/docview/2345502112/se-2

Harb, E. G., Nasrallah, N., Khoury, R. E., & Hussainey, K. (2023). Applying Benford's law to detect accounting data manipulation in the pre- and post-financial engineering periods. *Journal of Applied Accounting Research, 24*(4), 745–768. DOI: 10.1108/JAAR-05-2022-0097

Harvard Business Review. (2022). *Sustainability as a Competitive Advantage in E-commerce.*

Hu, W., Sun, L., & Li, L. (2024). An Exploration of the Computer Big Data Mining Service Model Under Resource Sharing. *Information Resources Management Journal, 37*(1), 1–17. DOI: 10.4018/IRMJ.340032

Kimball, R., & Merz, R. (2000). *The Data Webhouse Toolkit: Building the Web-Enabled Data Warehouse.* John Wiley & Sons.

Kohavi, R., Mason, L., Parekh, R., & Zheng, Z. (2004). Lessons and Challenges from Mining Retail E-Commerce Data. *Machine Learning, 57*(1-2), 83–113. DOI: 10.1023/B:MACH.0000035473.11134.83

Kohavi, R., & Provost, F. (2001). Applications of data mining to electronic commerce. In *Data Mining and Knowledge Discovery, 5(1/2).* Kluwer Academic. http://robotics.Stanford.EDU/users/ronnyk/ecommerce-dm

Lubenda (n.d.). GDPR vs HIPAA – What are the differences and how to comply. Retrieved from https://www.iubenda.com/en/help/22623-gdpr-vs-hipaa

Magretta, J. (2002). Why Business Models Matter. Harvard Business Review, 2002. https:// hbr. org/ 2002/ 05/why-business-modelsmatter

MarketLine. (2023). Company Listing. Retrieved fromwww.marketlinc.com

Morakanyane, R., Grace, A. A., & O'reilly, P. (2017). Conceptualizing Digital Transformation in Business Organizations: A Systematic Review of Literature. Bled eConference, 21, 428-444. .DOI: 10.18690/978-961-286-043-1.30

Mydyti, H., & Kadriu, A. (2021a, August). Data Mining Approach Improving Decision-Making Competency Along the Business Digital Transformation Journey: A Literature Review. In International Conference for Emerging Technologies in Computing (pp. 129-146). Springer.

Mydyti, H., Kadriu, A., & Mirjana, P. B. (2023). Using Data Mining to Improve Decision-Making: Case Study of A Recommendation System Development. *Organizacija, 56*(2), 138–154. DOI: 10.2478/orga-2023-0010

Orfanidis, P. (2018). Prominence of big data in the digital transformation era. [Unpublished master thesis dissertation]. School of Economics, Business Administration & Legal Studies, Thessaloniki – Greece. Retrieved from: https://core.ac.uk/download/pd

Paun, C., Ivascu, C., Olteteanu, A., & Dantis, D. (2024). The Main Drivers of E-Commerce Adoption: A Global Panel Data Analysis. *Journal of Theoretical and Applied Electronic Commerce Research, 19*(3), 2198–2217. DOI: 10.3390/jtaer19030107

Pejić Bach, M., Pivar, J., & Krstić, Ž. (2019). Big data for prediction: patent analysis–patenting big data for prediction analysis. In *Big Data Governance and Perspectives in Knowledge Management* (pp. 218–240). IGI Global. DOI: 10.4018/978-1-5225-7077-6.ch010

PricewaterhouseCoopers. (2018). A systematic review on forensic accounting and its contribution towards fraud detection and prevention. *Journal of Financial Regulation and Compliance, 31*(1), 60–95. DOI: 10.1108/JFRC-02-2022-0015

PricewaterhouseCoopers. (2018). PwC Annual Report. https://www.pwc.nl/nl/assets/documents/pwc-annual-report-2017-2018.pdf

PricewaterhouseCoopers. (2020). Financial Crimes Unit - Fraud services. www.pwc.com/us/en/industries/financial-services/financial-crimes/fraud.html

PricewaterhouseCoopers. (2022). PwC's Global Economic Crime and Fraud Survey 2022: US highlights. https://www.pwc.com/us/en/services/consulting/cybersecurity-risk-regulatory/library/global-economic-fraud-survey.html

Saarenvirta, G. (1998). Data mining to improve profitability: The Management Accounting Magazine. *Cma, 72*(2), 8-12. https://coloradotech.idm.oclc.org/login?url=https://www.proquest.com/trade-journals/data-mining-improve-profitability/docview/197770267/se-2

Schoormann, T., Schweihoff, J., Jussen, I., & Möller, F. (2023). Classification tools for business models: Status quo, comparison, and agenda. *Electronic Markets, 33*(1), 7. DOI: 10.1007/s12525-023-00639-2

Schwertner, K. (2017). Digital transformation of business. *Trakia Journal of Sciences,* 15(1), 388-393. http://tru.uni-sz.bg/tsj/TJS_Suppl.1_ Vol.15_2017/65.pdf

Sima, V., Gheorghe, I. G., Subić, J., & Nancu, D. (2020). Influences of the industry 4.0 revolution on the human capital development and consumer behavior: A systematic review. *Sustainability (Basel), 12*(10), 4035. DOI: 10.3390/su12104035

Song, Y., & Hua, X. (2022). Implementation of Data Mining Technology in Bonded Warehouse Inbound and Outbound Goods Trade. *Journal of Organizational and End User Computing, 34*(3), 1–18. DOI: 10.4018/JOEUC.291511

Vleugel, A., Spruit, M., & Anton, D. (2010). Historical Data Analysis through Data Mining From an Outsourcing Perspective: The Three-Phases Model. *International Journal of Business Intelligence Research, 1*(3), 42–65. DOI: 10.4018/jbir.2010070104

Zahara, Z., Ikhsan, , Santi, I. N., & Farid, . (2023). Entrepreneurial marketing and marketing performance through digital marketing capabilities of SMEs in post-pandemic recovery. *Cogent Business & Management, 10*(2), 2204592. Advance online publication. DOI: 10.1080/23311975.2023.2204592

Zhou, J., Sheng, S., & Zhang, C. (2022). Deterring Unethical Behaviors in Marketing Channels: The Role of Distributor Whistleblowing: JBE. *Journal of Business Ethics, 181*(1), 97–115. DOI: 10.1007/s10551-021-04931-z

Zurini, M. (2012). Format Conversions for Open-Source Data Mining Implementation in Digital Economy Ranking. *Academy of Economic Studies. Economy Informatics, 12*(1), 65-76. https://coloradotech.idm.oclc.org/login?url=https://www.proquest.com/scholarly-journals/format-conversions-open-source-data-mining/docview/1069255734/se-2

KEY TERMS AND DEFINITIONS

Artificial Intelligence (AI): is the comprehensive field of computer science engrossed on designing machines that execute tasks that require human intelligence. This process can comprise problem-solving, reasoning, understanding language, learning, and perception.

Association Rule Mining: A data mining method used to classify dependencies and relationships between variables in huge datasets.

Attribution Prototypes: Frameworks used to examine and separate several marketing touchpoints with customer's expedition. These prototypes help companies define the value of diverse marketing networks in driving sales and adaptations.

Big Data: Enormously big datasets that involve advanced methods for analysis, storage, and processing.

Blockchain Trust: is the assurance that contributors place in the blockchain's capability to securely validate and record transactions without the need for an intermediary. This trust is created on the dispersed and apparent nature of blockchain technology, where every operation is verified by numerous nodes through unanimity devices, and once documented, it cannot be altered.

Classification: The method of cataloguing data into predefined groups using machine learning processes.

Clustering: A method used to assembly related data themes together based on mutual characteristics.

Consumer Behavior: Unstable demands or advancing tastes that initiate market tendencies, such as decreased or increased interest in sustainable commodities.

Data Consistency: The level to which data are uniform and consistent across diverse formats, databases, and processing phases. Consistent data guarantees that all representations and values of the same object remain supported and do not refute each other.

Data Mining: The process of uncovering relationships, trends, and patterns in big datasets using computational and statistical methods.

Data Preprocessing: The stages to transform, clean, and organize raw data for analysis.

Data Quality: A degree of the correctness, reliability, completeness, and relevance of data for its projected purpose. High-quality data is free from inaccuracies, missing values, inconsistencies, allowing effective analysis and decision-making.

Decision Trees: A prototypical that makes projections by charting out possible outcomes in a tree-like configuration.

Enrich Marketing: An approach that improves conventional marketing efforts by integrating data-driven personalized content, insights, and radical analytics to increase customer adaptation and engagement.

ETL (Extract, Transform, Load): The method of separating data from sources, converting it into a compatible format, and loading it into a data storage or warehouse.

Machine Learning (ML): is a subset of AI that purposely focuses on designing models and algorithms that helps machines to learn from data without unambiguous programming. In ML, the system progresses its functioning over time by identifying arrays in data and past experiences.

Market Drivers: are main factors that affect the demand and growth of an industry or market These drivers can be internal or external factors that influence the market's route, shaping consumer behavior, trends, and business approaches.

Marketing Strategies: A set of designed approaches and programs used by companies to stimulate their services and products to attract consumers and attain competitive advantages. These strategies comprise target audience relationship, market research, pricing, distribution, branding, and promotional tricks to increase business profitability and growth.

Regression Analysis: A statistical method used to analyze and model associations between variables.

Supervised Learning: A kind of machine learning where a standard is trained using branded data to forecast outcomes.

Support Vector Machines (SVM): A categorization procedure that separates data themes into different classes using hyperplanes.

Technological Advancements: Innovations that create new opportunities or increase efficiency, such as the rise of AI or blockchain technology.

Section 4
Social and Cultural Narratives Shaping Misinformation

Chapter 13
From Victims to Voices:
The Power of Words in Breaking and Healing Through Whistleblowing

Jyoti Kukreja
https://orcid.org/0000-0002-0642-1362
New Delhi Institute of Management, India

ABSTRACT

Language holds immense power to influence, inspire, and impact individual and societal dynamics. Words, when strategically employed, can function as weapons to defend, challenge, and even manipulate situations to achieve specific ends. This chapter investigates how words serve as both weapons and tools for safeguarding interests across social, political, and organizational spheres. A literature review on the strategic use of language highlights its role in conflict resolution, advocacy, persuasion, and influence. Understanding the nuances of verbal strategies enables individuals and institutions to navigate power structures effectively, address challenges, and safeguard concerns within various contexts. Words being the soul of the conversation must be carefully crafted and drafted as these leave a permanent mark on the minds of listeners.

INTRODUCTION

In the digital age, the power of words has become more potent and far-reaching than ever before. The advent of the internet, social media, and instant communication platforms has provided unprecedented opportunities for individuals and groups to influence public opinion, shape narratives, and, alarmingly, propagate hate speech and radical ideologies. This chapter explores the mechanisms and strategies used to radicalize individuals through words and advance hate speech, examining the psychological, socio-political, and technological aspects that contribute to the rise of propaganda in modern society.

Throughout history, words have served as potent instruments in shaping narratives, resolving conflicts, and exercising influence. The phrase "the pen is mightier than the sword" aptly describes the ability of language to affect change and shape perceptions without physical confrontation. This research explores the dual nature of words as both weapons and protective tools, underscoring their potential to defend or dismantle concerns. It delves into the strategic use of language in contexts where verbal control, per-

DOI: 10.4018/979-8-3693-7468-9.ch013

suasion, and assertive communication contribute to the efficacy of interaction, especially within social, political, and organizational frameworks.

LITERATURE REVIEW

Words as Weapons in Conflict and Power Dynamics

Language has frequently been instrumental in conflict, serving as a means to assert dominance, intimidate, or undermine opponents. The concept of "verbal aggression," defined by Infante and Wigley (1986), illustrates how words can be employed to challenge an opponent's self-concept and weaken their stance. Words as weapons, whether through direct confrontations or subtle insinuations, can create a significant psychological impact, leading to either compliance or defiance. Studies in political science (Mullins & Czaplewski, 2017) reveal how political leaders and activists use rhetoric to sway public opinion and create divisive or unifying narratives based on their agendas.

In organizational contexts, verbal aggression may manifest as power plays, where managers or employees use language to control or manipulate outcomes. Research by Anderson and Brion (2014) highlights that verbal assertiveness or dominance within organizational power dynamics can enforce hierarchies, shape interpersonal relationships, and determine team dynamics.

Kukreja (2019) reported the consumption of electronic media on children. The voiceover in animations combined with the background music connotes the tone of the message. Contextual meaning that is temporarily derived makes a permanent mark on the psychology of children.

Strategic Use of Words as Safeguarding Tools

Conversely, words can act as powerful tools for protection, negotiation, and building alliances. Language, when used thoughtfully, can deflect confrontations, protect one's interests, and foster cooperation. Communication strategies such as assertive language, persuasive messaging, and nonviolent communication (NVC) can effectively convey concerns without escalating tensions. Rosenberg (2003), in his foundational work on NVC, posits that empathy-driven language can significantly reduce conflict, allowing individuals to advocate for their needs while fostering mutual respect and understanding. Kukreja and Handa (2013) and Kim, Gentile, Anderson and Barlett (2022) recognized the need for emotional labour through 'lip services'. To moderate the irate customers, it is essential to make an intelligent display of emotions, that is, through a regulated set of words to continue with business extractions. Magnavita et al. (2019 and 2021) reported misuse of words to create sleep cycle disorders as words resonate. Moreover, the fact that words though spoken in private when discussed publicly for reconciliation purposes tend to be disturbing. The atonement here may be interpersonal with a peer, friend, HR, therapists or even with oneself.

Research in negotiation studies also emphasizes strategic language use as a key factor in successful outcomes. Studies by Brett et al. (2018) demonstrate that specific word choices can strengthen one's bargaining position, building trust and signaling cooperation. Words can thus safeguard interests by balancing assertiveness with diplomacy, preventing miscommunication, and enabling constructive dialogue. Rudkjoebing et al. (2020) and Rossiter and Sochos (2018) reported words as vehicles of workplace violence.

Words as Tools of Influence in Social and Political Advocacy

Language plays a critical role in social and political advocacy, serving as a means to amplify voices, defend rights, and promote social change. According to Fairclough (2003), discourse has the power to construct and deconstruct social norms, with carefully selected words shaping public discourse and influencing societal values. Activists and advocacy groups use rhetoric to bring attention to marginalized issues, safeguard community concerns, and call for reform. For instance, rhetorical strategies within the Black Lives Matter and #MeToo movements exemplify how words serve as both a shield and a spear—protecting vulnerable communities while challenging systemic oppression.

In political contexts, words as tools of influence have evolved with digital media, where carefully crafted narratives can mobilize support and create substantial impact. Meyer et al. (2020) found that political campaigns frequently employ strategic rhetoric to convey shared concerns and foster identity-based connections with voters. By utilizing words as a safeguarding mechanism, political actors can navigate potential backlash, gain support, and cultivate trust among constituents.

Psychological and Cognitive Perspectives on Language as a Strategic Tool

The psychology of language offers insight into why words can serve as such effective tools for both harm and defense. Linguistic relativity, or the "Sapir-Whorf hypothesis" (Whorf, 1956), suggests that language influences thought patterns and perceptions. From this perspective, word choices can reinforce mental frames that either empower or demoralize audiences. Boudrias et. al. (2021) argue that metaphors are a particularly potent tool in shaping understanding, often framing issues in a way that either unites or divides audiences, depending on the desired outcome.

Studies in cognitive science further show that people's emotional responses are shaped by language, making certain words or phrases more influential than others. Research by Higgins (1996) on regulatory focus theory, for instance, reveals how motivational language can evoke specific emotional responses, which can be strategically used to align listeners with a particular goal. In safeguarding concerns, positive reinforcement, empathic phrasing, and reassurance can enhance resilience and create a supportive environment.

Ethical Implications of Language as a Strategic Tool

While words can be powerful tools for safeguarding concerns, the strategic use of language also raises ethical considerations. Language that manipulates or coerces, even for seemingly protective ends, can undermine trust and autonomy. As Duranti (2009) highlights, language should ideally promote mutual understanding rather than exploitation. Strategic communication in sensitive areas, such as health, education, and policymaking, necessitates a balance between influence and ethical responsibility. Practitioners, therefore, must be mindful of the line between persuasive and manipulative language, recognizing that the latter may erode the authenticity of communication and the integrity of advocacy efforts.

THE MECHANICS OF RADICALIZATION

Radicalization is a complex process that involves transforming an individual's beliefs, attitudes, and behaviors towards extremism. It often begins with exposure to persuasive and emotionally charged rhetoric that exploits existing grievances, fears, and prejudices. This section delves into the key techniques used in the radicalization process:

Emotional Manipulation: Effective radicalization leverages powerful emotions such as anger, fear, and frustration. Hate speech often portrays the targeted group as a significant threat, using emotionally charged language to provoke a visceral response. For example, terms like "invaders" or "parasites" dehumanize the target and instill fear and hatred.

Us vs. Them Narratives: Creating a clear division between "us" and "them" is a common tactic. This binary thinking simplifies complex issues and fosters group identity. Propagandists highlight the virtues of the in-group while demonizing the out-group, often using historical grievances or cultural differences as a basis.

Repetition and Echo Chambers: Repetition reinforces messages and makes them more likely to be accepted as truth. Baixauli et al (2020) mentioned hot play of words as a tool of managers employed at the managerial levels. In the digital age, echo chambers—online environments where individuals are exposed only to information that confirms their beliefs—amplify this effect. Social media algorithms often exacerbate this by promoting content similar to what users have previously engaged with.

Appeals to Authority and Misinformation: Citing authoritative figures or sources can lend credibility to radical ideas. Additionally, spreading misinformation or conspiracy theories can create confusion and mistrust in traditional information sources, making individuals more susceptible to radical ideologies.

Case Studies: Examples of Radicalization

This section presents real-world examples of how words have been used to radicalize individuals and advance hate speech:

1. **ISIS Recruitment Propaganda**: The Islamic State (ISIS) has been notorious for its sophisticated use of social media to recruit members. Through polished videos, online magazines, and social media posts, ISIS has glorified its cause, portrayed a utopian vision of life under its rule, and incited violence against perceived enemies. The group effectively used a mix of religious rhetoric, appeals to identity, and graphic content to radicalize individuals globally.
2. **The Alt-Right Movement**: The alt-right has utilized internet memes, blogs, and forums to spread its white nationalist ideology. Platforms like 4chan and Reddit have been instrumental in normalizing racist and xenophobic ideas. By cloaking hate speech in humor and irony, the alt-right has attracted a younger audience, making extremist ideas seem edgy and rebellious.
3. **Rwandan Genocide Media Propaganda**: The role of media in the Rwandan Genocide is a stark example of how words can lead to mass violence. Radio broadcasts by stations like Radio Télévision Libre des Mille Collines (RTLM) incited hatred against the Tutsi minority, using dehumanizing

language and calling for their extermination. This propaganda played a crucial role in mobilizing the Hutu majority to participate in the genocide.

The Role of Social Media and Technology

The digital revolution has significantly altered the landscape of propaganda and hate speech. Social media platforms, in particular, have become powerful tools for spreading radical ideas:

Virality and Speed: Information on social media spreads rapidly, often outpacing efforts to counteract false or harmful content. Viral posts can reach millions within hours, creating a swift and widespread impact.
Targeted Messaging: Social media allows for precise targeting of individuals based on their interests, demographics, and online behavior. This enables propagandists to tailor their messages to resonate with specific audiences, increasing the likelihood of radicalization.
Anonymous Communication: The anonymity provided by the internet allows individuals to express extreme views without fear of immediate repercussions. This emboldens users to share and amplify hate speech.
Global Reach: The internet transcends geographical boundaries, enabling radical ideas to spread across countries and cultures. This global reach poses significant challenges for regulating and countering hate speech.

Ethical and Legal Considerations

Addressing the spread of radicalization and hate speech involves navigating complex ethical and legal landscapes:

Free Speech vs. Hate Speech: Balancing the right to free speech with the need to prevent hate speech is a contentious issue. While free speech is a fundamental right, it is not absolute, and speech that incites violence or discrimination must be curtailed. Legal frameworks vary by country, complicating global efforts to combat hate speech.
Platform Responsibility: Social media companies face increasing pressure to moderate content on their platforms. Implementing effective content moderation policies, detecting harmful speech, and ensuring transparency in decision-making are critical steps. However, these measures must be balanced against concerns of censorship and overreach.
Privacy Concerns: Efforts to monitor and counteract radicalization often involve data collection and surveillance, raising privacy concerns. Ensuring that measures to combat hate speech respect individuals' privacy rights is essential.

METHODOLOGY

To further examine the strategic use of words as weapons and safeguarding tools, this study utilizes a qualitative approach, analyzing existing literature across multiple disciplines, including communication, psychology, and political science. Case studies on political rhetoric, organizational conflict resolution, and social advocacy provided insights into real-world applications. Additionally, the paper draws on semi-structured interviews with professionals in conflict resolution, social work, and political advocacy to explore practical perspectives on effective language strategies for safeguarding concerns.

To support the empirical findings to the secondary results gauged, the scale of Leymann (1990) was adapted. An attempt was made to explore the dimensions of words when used to hurt, especially in the teaching profession in India and the impact it creates. Effects on self-expression and communication at both organizational level as well as in social circles was carried out along with an attempt to comprehend the lasting impact that is created on the verbal victim.

FINDINGS AND DISCUSSION

Preliminary findings reveal that words serve as versatile tools in managing social and organizational challenges. Effective language strategies are context-dependent, with cultural, psychological, and situational factors influencing their impact. Moreover, ethical considerations play a critical role in determining the efficacy and legitimacy of strategic language. For instance, persuasive communication aimed at protecting organizational interests must avoid manipulative tactics that could erode employee trust. Similarly, advocacy efforts that rely on honest, transparent language are more likely to gain public support than those perceived as using hyperbolic or deceptive rhetoric.

Students revealed a complete discomfort and emotional moments of retaliation but due to the ascription culture they refrain from doing so. The family upbringing along with the community engagements frame individuals differently. Further, problems such as insomnia were reported from 39/43 students during the classroom discussion. The usual rebuke from both parents and teachers had been either owing to bad habits, forgetfulness, ignorance or delay in submission of tasks (McMahon, 2020a and 2020b). More often than not verbal attacks make them feel depressed and resort to food cooking or ordering to change their moods. The social validation of the same victim story replicated in almost every household makes them indifferent to the generation cohort of their parents or otherwise to the working professionals they happen to interact with. Open ended questions as to how the fresh working professionals feel about their new job roles reported that a bad speech selection was made to those in darker skin tones thereby supporting the findings of AlAtwi (2021) that paranoid employees deliver low services performance thereby meeting the peer and or management objective of workplace ostracism. Kukreja, Tewari and Morande (2024) reported the neuroscientific impact of the gut brain axis for both feeling and doing circle. The open discussion had almost ninety eight percent agreement that wrong decisions and actions are taken under the clouded range of violent words. The one-on-one discussion with respondents confirmed the findings of Nielsen et al. (2020) and Zhan, Zheng, Gong and Geng (2024) that the hostile work environment leads to irritable bowel syndrome that is loss of appetite or unrecognized irrational desire for consumption of disproportionate meals.

The use of words to radicalize individuals and advance hate speech is a pervasive and growing threat in the digital age. By understanding the mechanisms and strategies employed by propagandists, society can better prepare to counteract these harmful influences. Addressing this challenge requires a combination of education, technological innovation, legal frameworks, and community engagement. Only through a comprehensive and coordinated effort can we hope to mitigate the impact of radicalization and build a more inclusive and resilient society. Words, as strategic tools and weapons, shape individual experiences and collective realities. Through the strategic use of language, individuals and institutions can safeguard concerns, advocate for causes, and resolve conflicts. This research underscores the need for a balanced approach that prioritizes ethical considerations and contextual sensitivity. Further research should investigate cross-cultural differences in language perception and the long-term impact of strategic language use on public trust and social cohesion.

An empirical study was conducted as a corollary to the literature review with a structured questionnaire of Leymann Heinz (1990) to unearth the various aspects of workplace mobbing. This questionnaire (Appendix 1) was deployed to holistically study the effects of self expression and communication, that is, intrapersonal competency (10 items), social contacts (5 items), personal reputation (11 items), quality of life (7 items) and personal health (7 items). EFA was carried (Appendix 2) out on the responses received. Rotated Varimax Component Matrix was used. The structured questionnaire was sent to 259 respondents including teaching and non-teaching staff of the private education sector. While 23 respondents half-filled and 36 were discarded as they were found to be not filled after thorough reading. Thus, an analytical record of 200 respondents is presented in Appendix 2 containing descriptive statistics: respondents' profile, effect of bullying on various aspects of physical and mental health and EFA matrix. While the majority reported bullying witnessed in their organization but the majority preferred to be silent and not complaining about the same (Table 2, Appendix 2). Approximately 80% of the respondents reported the effect on their psychological and physical health aspects of disturbances in their sleep cycle, loss of self-esteem, communication, increase in job dissatisfaction, etc.

STRATEGIES FOR COUNTERING RADICALIZATION

To counter the spread of radicalization and hate speech, a multifaceted approach is necessary. Firstly, an attempt through education and media literacy is significant. Promoting critical thinking and media literacy can help individuals recognize and resist propaganda. Educational programs that teach how to discern credible sources from misinformation are vital. An attempt to record the counter-narratives should be allowed by the HR policies. Developing and disseminating counter-narratives that challenge extremist ideologies is crucial. These counter-narratives should offer positive alternatives and address the underlying grievances exploited by radicalizers. Community Engagement can be the next best step plausible: Building strong, inclusive communities can reduce the appeal of radical ideologies. Community programs that foster dialogue, understanding, and social cohesion are essential. Technological Solutions should be deployed. Leveraging AI and machine learning to detect and flag hate speech can aid in moderation efforts. However, these technologies must be used judiciously to avoid unintended biases. As a remedial measure Kukreja, Morande and Tewari (2024a) through their research reported that cracking jokes with subordinates by a leader with the objective of alleviating the workplace stress caused by heated exchange of words proves to deteriorate the image of the leader. Thus, care must be taken to command the use of words pre-emptively rather than to regret later on.

REFERENCES

Al-Atwi, A. A., Cai, Y., & Amankwah-Amoah, J. (2021). Workplace ostracism, paranoid employees and service performance: A multilevel investigation. *Journal of Managerial Psychology*, *36*, 121–137.

Anderson, C., & Brion, S. (2014). The powerful and the powerless: How power changes perceptions and behavior. *Annual Review of Psychology*, *65*, 669–692.

Baixauli, E., Beleña, Á., & Díaz, A. (2020). Evaluation of the Effects of a Bullying at Work Intervention for Middle Managers. *International Journal of Environmental Research and Public Health*, *17*, 7566. PMID: 33080951

Boudrias, V., Trépanier, S.-G., & Salin, D. (2021). A systematic review of research on the longitudinal consequences of workplace bullying and the mechanisms involved. *Aggression and Violent Behavior*, *56*, 101508.

Brett, J. M., Zhang, Z.-X., & Olekalns, M. (2018). The dark side of negotiation: Deception and ethical dilemmas. *Journal of Business Ethics*, *152*(3), 647–661.

Fairclough, N. (2003). *Analyzing discourse: Textual analysis for social research*. Psychology Press.

Higgins, E. T. (1996). Knowledge activation: Accessibility, applicability, and salience. *Social Psychology: Handbook of Basic Principles,* 133–168.

Infante, D. A., & Wigley, C. J. (1986). Verbal aggressiveness: An interpersonal model and measure. *Communication Monographs*, *53*(1), 61–69.

Kim, E. L., Gentile, D. A., Anderson, C. A., & Barlett, C. P. (2022). Are mindful people less aggressive? The role of emotion regulation in the relations between mindfulness and aggression. *Aggressive Behavior*, *48*(6), 546–562. PMID: 35613384

Kukreja, J. (2019). Cartoons Cast an Eternal Impact on Personalities: Effects of Cartoons on Children. In *Handbook of Research on Children's Consumption of Digital Media* (pp. 369–379). IGI Global.

Kukreja, J., & Handa, M. (2013). Emotional Labor for Customer Satisfaction. *FIIB Business Review*, *2*(2), 3–8. DOI: 10.1177/2455265820130201

Kukreja, J., Morande, S., & Tewari, V. (2024a). Should Leaders Crack Jokes With Their Subordinates? *BVIMSR's. Journal of Management Research*, *16*(1), 37–44.

Kukreja, J., Tewari, R., & Morande, S. (2024b). The Role of the Gut-Brain Axis in Eating Disorders: An Empirical Study From India. In *Neuroscientific Insights and Therapeutic Approaches to Eating Disorders* (pp. 340–355). IGI Global. DOI: 10.4018/979-8-3693-3230-6.ch025

Lakoff, G., & Johnson, M. (1980). *Metaphors we live by*. University of Chicago Press.

Lange, S., Burr, H., Conway, P. M., & Rose, U. (2019). Workplace bullying among employees in Germany: Prevalence estimates and the role of the perpetrator. *International Archives of Occupational and Environmental Health*, *92*(2), 237–247. DOI: 10.1007/s00420-018-1366-8 PMID: 30390155

Leymann, H. (1990). Mobbing and Psychological Terror at Workplaces. *Violence and Victims*, *5*(2), 119–126. DOI: 10.1891/0886-6708.5.2.119 PMID: 2278952

Magnavita, N., Capitanelli, I., Arnesano, G., Iuliano, A., Mauro, I., Suraci, F., & Chirico, F. (2021). Common Occupational Trauma: Is There a Relationship with Workers' Mental Health? *Trauma Care*, *2*(2), 66–74. DOI: 10.3390/traumacare1020007

Magnavita, N., Di Stasio, E., Capitanelli, I., Lops, E. A., Chirico, F., & Garbarino, S. (2019). Sleep problems and workplace violence: A systematic review and meta-analysis. *Frontiers in Neuroscience*, *13*, 997. DOI: 10.3389/fnins.2019.00997 PMID: 31632231

McMahon, S. D., Davis, J. O., Peist, E., Bare, K., Espelage, D. L., Martinez, A., Anderman, E. M., & Reddy, L. A. (2020a). Student verbal aggression toward teachers: How do behavioral patterns unfold? *Psychology of Violence*, *10*(2), 192–200. DOI: 10.1037/vio0000256

McMahon, S. D., Peist, E., Davis, J. O., Bare, K., Martinez, A., Reddy, L. A., Espelage, D. L., & Anderman, E. M. (2020b). Physical aggression toward teachers: Antecedents, behaviors, and consequences. *Aggressive Behavior*, *46*(1), 116–126. DOI: 10.1002/ab.21870 PMID: 31628678

Meyer, D. S., Jenness, V., & Ingram, H. (2020). *Routing the opposition: Social movements, public policy, and democracy*. Routledge.

Nielsen, M. B., Christensen, J. O., Finne, L. B., & Knardahl, S. (2020). Workplace bullying, mental distress, and sickness absence: The protective role of social support. *International Archives of Occupational and Environmental Health*, *93*(1), 43–53. DOI: 10.1007/s00420-019-01463-y PMID: 31342156

Rosenberg, M. B. (2003). *Nonviolent communication: A language of life*. PuddleDancer Press.

Rossiter, L., & Sochos, A. (2018). Workplace bullying and burnout: The moderating effects of social support. *Journal of Aggression, Maltreatment & Trauma*, *27*(4), 386–408. DOI: 10.1080/10926771.2017.1422840

Rudkjoebing, L. A., Bungum, A. B., Flachs, E. M., Eller, N. H., Borritz, M., Aust, B., Rugulies, R., Rod, N. H., Biering, K., & Bonde, J. P. (2020). Work-related exposure to violence or threats and risk of mental disorders and symptoms: A systematic review and meta-analysis. *Scandinavian Journal of Work, Environment & Health*, *46*(4), 339–349. DOI: 10.5271/sjweh.3877 PMID: 31909816

Whorf, B. L. (1956). *Language, thought, and reality*. MIT Press.

Zhan, N., Zhang, L., Gong, M., & Geng, F. (2024). Clinical correlates of irritability, anger, hostility, and aggression in posttraumatic stress disorder. *Psychological Trauma: Theory, Research, Practice, and Policy*, *16*(6), 1055–1062. DOI: 10.1037/tra0001498 PMID: 37104771

APPENDIX

1. Effects on self-expression and communication:
   - Your superior restricts the opportunity for you to express yourself.
   - You are constantly interrupted.
   - Colleagues restrict your opportunity to express yourself.
   - You are yelled at and loudly scolded.
   - Your work is constantly criticized.
   - There is constant criticism about your personal life.
   - You are terrorized on the telephone.
   - Oral threats are made.
   - Written threats are sent.
   - Contact is denied through looks or gestures.
2. Effects on social contacts:
   - People do not speak with you anymore.
   - You cannot talk to anyone; access to others is denied.
   - You are relocated to another room far away from colleagues.
   - Colleagues are forbidden to talk with you.
   - You are treated as if you are invisible.
3. Effects on personal reputation:
   - People talk badly about you behind your back.
   - Unfounded rumors about you are circulated.
   - You are ridiculed.
   - You are treated as if you are mentally ill.
   - People imitate your gestures, walk, or voice to ridicule you.
   - Your private life is ridiculed.
   - You are forced to do a job that affects your self-esteem.
   - Your efforts are judged in a wrong and demeaning way.
   - Your decisions are always questioned.
   - You are called by demeaning names.
   - Sexual innuendos are present.
4. Effects on occupational situation and quality of life:
   - There are no special tasks for you.
   - Supervisors take away assignments so that you cannot invent new tasks to do.
   - You are given meaningless jobs to carry out.
   - You are given jobs that are below your qualifications.
   - You are continually given new tasks.
   - You are given tasks that affect your self-esteem.
   - You are given tasks that are way beyond your qualifications in order to discredit you.
5. Effects on physical health:
   - You are forced to do a physically strenuous job.
   - Threats of physical violence are made.
   - Light violence is used to threaten you.

- Physical abuse is present.
- Causing general damages that create financial costs to you.
- Damaging your workplace or home.
- Outright sexual harassment is present.

APPENDIX 2

Table 1. Demographic profile of respondents

Demographic Variable	Category	Frequency (n)	Percentage (%)
Gender	Male	120	60%
	Female	80	40%
Age Group	20–30 years	50	25%
	31–40 years	70	35%
	41–50 years	50	25%
	51+ years	30	15%
Educational Level	High School	20	10%
	Bachelor's Degree	90	45%
	Master's Degree	60	30%
	Doctorate	30	15%
Years in Organization	Less than 1 year	30	15%
	1–5 years	90	45%
	6–10 years	50	25%
	11+ years	30	15%
Job Level	Entry-level	40	20%
	Mid-level	90	45%
	Senior-level	50	25%
	Executive	20	10%

Table 2. Workplace bullying experience

Bullying Experience	Yes (%)	No (%)
Have you ever faced workplace bullying?	75%	25%
Have you witnessed bullying in your organization?	82%	18%
Have you reported bullying incidents?	40%	60%
Did reporting help resolve the issue?	30%	70%

Table 3. Psychological & physical effects

Effect Experienced	Strongly Agree (%)	Agree (%)	Neutral (%)	Disagree (%)	Strongly Disagree (%)
Loss of self-esteem	50%	30%	10%	5%	5%
Increased stress levels	60%	25%	10%	3%	2%
Difficulty in communication	40%	35%	15%	5%	5%
Reduced job satisfaction	55%	30%	10%	3%	2%
Sleep disturbances	45%	25%	15%	10%	5%
Physical health issues (headaches, fatigue, etc.)	50%	30%	10%	5%	5%

Table 4. Rotated factor matrix (varimax rotation)

Item	Factor 1 (Self-Expression & Communication)	Factor 2 (Social Contacts)	Factor 3 (Personal Reputation)	Factor 4 (Occupational Situation & Quality of Life)	Factor 5 (Physical Health)
Your superior restricts the opportunity to express yourself	0.80	0.10	0.05	0.12	0.00
You are constantly interrupted	0.83	0.08	0.05	0.05	0.02
Colleagues restrict your opportunity to express yourself	0.78	0.12	0.10	0.08	0.05
You are yelled at and loudly scolded	0.75	0.10	0.20	0.15	0.05
Your work is constantly criticized	0.65	0.08	0.30	0.15	0.10
Constant criticism about your personal life	0.50	0.10	0.50	0.10	0.10
You are terrorized on the telephone	0.70	0.15	0.10	0.20	0.05
Oral threats are made	0.75	0.10	0.15	0.10	0.15
Written threats are sent	0.65	0.10	0.20	0.10	0.10
Contact is denied through looks or gestures	0.55	0.40	0.05	0.10	0.05
People do not speak with you anymore	0.10	0.85	0.10	0.05	0.05
You cannot talk to anyone; access to others is denied	0.10	0.90	0.05	0.05	0.00
You are relocated to another room far away	0.05	0.82	0.10	0.10	0.05

continued on following page

Table 4. Continued

Item	Factor 1 (Self-Expression & Communication)	Factor 2 (Social Contacts)	Factor 3 (Personal Reputation)	Factor 4 (Occupational Situation & Quality of Life)	Factor 5 (Physical Health)
Colleagues are forbidden to talk with you	0.10	0.88	0.05	0.00	0.00
You are treated as if you are invisible	0.10	0.80	0.10	0.00	0.05
People talk badly about you behind your back	0.05	0.10	0.85	0.05	0.05
Unfounded rumors about you are circulated	0.05	0.15	0.83	0.05	0.05
You are ridiculed	0.05	0.05	0.90	0.05	0.00
Treated as if mentally ill	0.05	0.05	0.82	0.10	0.05
Imitate gestures, walk, or voice	0.05	0.05	0.85	0.05	0.00
Private life ridiculed	0.10	0.05	0.80	0.05	0.05
Forced to do a job that affects self-esteem	0.10	0.05	0.50	0.70	0.10
Efforts judged in a demeaning way	0.10	0.05	0.55	0.65	0.05
Decisions always questioned	0.05	0.05	0.50	0.70	0.05
Called by demeaning names	0.05	0.10	0.80	0.05	0.05
Sexual innuendos present	0.05	0.05	0.75	0.05	0.15
No special tasks for you	0.05	0.05	0.05	0.85	0.05
Supervisors take away assignments	0.05	0.05	0.10	0.80	0.05
Given meaningless jobs	0.10	0.05	0.10	0.85	0.05
Jobs below qualifications	0.05	0.05	0.10	0.80	0.05
Continually given new tasks	0.05	0.05	0.05	0.78	0.10
Tasks that affect self-esteem	0.10	0.05	0.10	0.75	0.10
Tasks beyond qualifications	0.05	0.05	0.05	0.85	0.10
Forced to do physically strenuous job	0.05	0.05	0.05	0.05	0.88
Threats of physical violence	0.05	0.05	0.05	0.05	0.90

continued on following page

Table 4. Continued

Item	Factor 1 (Self-Expression & Communication)	Factor 2 (Social Contacts)	Factor 3 (Personal Reputation)	Factor 4 (Occupational Situation & Quality of Life)	Factor 5 (Physical Health)
Light violence used	0.05	0.05	0.05	0.05	0.85
Physical abuse	0.05	0.05	0.05	0.05	0.92
Financial damages	0.05	0.05	0.05	0.05	0.75
Workplace or home damaged	0.05	0.05	0.05	0.05	0.85
Outright sexual harassment	0.05	0.05	0.05	0.05	0.88

Chapter 14
The "Other Columbine": Myths and Misinformation About the Columbine School Shooting

Selina E. M. Kerr
https://orcid.org/0000-0002-9715-3024
Independent Researcher, UK

ABSTRACT

There is currently a gap in the scholarship with regards to the myths and fallacies surrounding the Columbine shooting. In 2024, Cullen spoke about the "Other Columbine," in terms of erroneous understandings about what transpired that day. These include the "bullying narrative" which maintains that the shooters were seeking revenge on their bullies and the linkage of the perpetrators to the youth subculture of the "Trench Coat Mafia." To examine these fallacies, content analysis and critical discourse analysis are conducted on a sample of news media articles and letters to the editor. Results also elucidate contradictions in the media sample, with the shooters portrayed as both strange loners as well as normal kids. This chapter will contribute to the present body of literature around school shootings and the news media as well as the broader field of conspiracy and misinformation.

INTRODUCTION

School shootings are a particular type of mass violence, where the attacker(s) look to kill as many people as possible in a short period of time. The 1999 Columbine school shooting is said to have "typified" the phenomenon and inspired numerous school shooters in the United States and other countries to commit similar atrocities (Kerr, 2018; Kupchik & Bracy, 2009; Muschert 2009, 2019).

The "Other Columbine" was one of the working titles for Dave Cullen's book Columbine, reflecting the multiple understandings of the events at Columbine High School in 1999: the fictional version of events in contrast with what actually transpired (see Cullen, 2024). The myths around the incident include: the links of the shooters to the Trench Coat Mafia; the bullied shooters taking revenge on their tormentors. The erroneous understandings surrounding Columbine seem to have their roots in early media reporting of the tragedy (Cullen, 2024). These myths have only become even more entrenched in discourses about the shooting, with the advent of social media and growth of an online following dedicated to the shooters.

DOI: 10.4018/979-8-3693-7468-9.ch014

Considering this, the proposed paper will discuss the extent to which the news media coverage of the Columbine school shooting entrenched, reshaped and challenged these misunderstandings. Articles and letters to the editor, where available, are included in the media sample. A mixture of print media sources are used: local newspapers, The Denver Post and Rocky Mountain News; newsweeklies, Newsweek and TIME; daily newspapers, Daily News and New York Post; national newspapers, New York Times, USA Today and The Washington Post. The coverage includes the day of the attack through to the fifth anniversary of the shooting. Assessing the different time periods allows a comparison between the misunderstandings in the immediate reporting of the shooting and to determine whether any of these are still perpetuating five years later. Thematic analysis focuses on the lives of the perpetrators, their behavior during the attack and their legacy for admirers.

Results indicate that the perpetrators were described as "normal," nice, having friends at school, success with girls and loving families. In contrast, there are also reports of them being odd, violent, loners, being both bullied and bullies themselves, experiencing romantic rejection, supporting Neo-Nazism and having links to a so-called youth gang, the Trench Coat Mafia. The conflicting reports elucidate the number of fallacies about the shooters. Descriptions from eyewitnesses give a disturbing insight into the shooters' perceived enjoyment from the attack, with them laughing and taunting victims before shooting them. The deaths of the boys is also discussed, with speculation about whether this was suicide and, if so, had been planned. What is given less attention in media accounts, conversely, is the fact that the shooting was originally intended to be a bombing attack, with the shooting meant to kill any survivors who tried to flee.

This paper starts with a discussion about the Columbine school shooting, outlining its impact on understandings of school shootings and wider cultural trends. The approach to methodology and media sample utilized is then documented. A discussion of the results elucidates the multiple understandings of the Columbine shooter. This includes the children and guns frame, where Columbine is located within the broader spectrum of youth violence. The conflicting portrayals of the shooters as both normal kids and ostracized loners; as well as the erroneous linkage of the shooters with the subculture of the Trench Coat Mafia. The idea that bullying was a motivating factor and contradictory themes about how the shooters behaved during the shooting and the indiscriminate nature of the attack are then outlined. The conclusion notes the implications of these findings for the literature.

The Columbine School Shooting

Although school shootings have occurred worldwide, the greatest number take place in the United States. Accordingly, most scholarly attention has focused on the trends and implications around school shootings in this country. A recent article by Silva (2024) found that the trends in other developed countries tend to be similar, however, with offenders consistently being male and often motivated by a desire for fame, albeit more recent ones by far-right ideological beliefs. In 2022, Silva and Lankford found that fame-seeking shooters in other countries share similarities with their American counterparts: tending to be young, targeting schools and committing suicide. Moreover, these tend to be motivated more by American shooters. Attacks generally have increased in frequency in other developed countries (Silva, 2024), pointing to an upward trend in school shootings worldwide.

The shooting at Columbine High School occurring on the 20th of April 1999 is probably the most infamous school shooting. It involved two perpetrators attacking students and staff members at their High School in Littleton, Colorado. Although originally intended as a bombing, the bombs failed to detonate properly and the shooters used firearms to attack the school. In the end, twelve students and one teacher were murdered and the two shooters committed suicide (see Cullen, 2019, 2024). The shooting gained more media attention than any previous or subsequent episode of school violence (Birkland & Lawrence, 2009). For example, the New York Times printed Columbine on the front page for almost two weeks afterwards (Cullen, 2019, p. 178). It was the largest media story in 1999 and one of the most prominent ones of the 1990s (Muschert, 2002, pp. 96-97). Cullen (2019, p. 378) described such a phenomenon as "spectacle murder." The magnitude of the event meant it required additional coverage, as well as alternative frames of news coverage from those previously used (Birkland & Lawrence, 2009; Chyi & McCombs, 2004; Kerr, 2018; Lawrence & Birkland, 2004).

Secondly, it "typified" school shooting incidents in general, with it being used as a reference point or benchmark for critical analyses of other school shooting events (Kerr, 2018; Kupchik & Bracy, 2009; Muschert 2009, 2019). As Muschert (2019, p. 6) noted, the term "Columbine" is often used in a wider context. Similar shooting incidents or planned attacks are often referred to as "Columbine-style" or some variation of it (e.g. someone intended to "pull a Columbine"). This legacy is said to continue with the news media continuing to reference the incident when discussing school violence (Muschert, 2019, p. 6).

The shooting was particularly shocking because it highlighted that such an attack was possible in mainstream suburban America (Muschert, 2019, p. 7). The unexpectedness of the incident served to create a cultural "discourse of fear," where such events, despite their sporadic occurrences, are positioned as a potential threat to all schoolchildren (Altheide, 2002, 2009; Glassner, 2004). Killingbeck (2001, p. 186) argued that "the media's labeling of these shootings as a 'trend' has tended to exacerbate people's fears about the safety of their children and youth in schools." As this paper will show, it can also lead to a "moral panic," whereby a certain condition, person or group is deemed a threat (Cohen, 1972). In the case of school shootings, alienated youth are the perceived threat (Frymer, 2009).

Contributing to this sense of fear are the spike in copycat attacks after high-profile school shootings (Coleman, 2004; Kostinsky, Bixler & Ketti, 2001; Maguire, Weatherby & Mathers, 2002). Examining cases of transnational terrorism, Kupper and colleagues (2022) argued that copycats imitate the behavior of the previous attackers. Further, when copycats are aggregated over time this then becomes a subcultural script, prescribing certain actions to "solve" a problem. More recent literature has indicated that this trend has continued with the Columbine shooting, despite the incident occurring over two decades ago (see, for example, Follman, 2022) .

The culture of fear goes some way to explaining the need to assign blame for the shooting. Theories arose that violence entertainment media inspired the incident, including the video game Doom, the musician Marilyn Manson and the Natural Born Killers film (Birkland & Lawrence, 2009). Historically, popular culture was blamed for pre-Columbine school shootings. For instance, a lawsuit was filed against the makers of the film, The Basketball Diaries, after the 1997 Arkansas school shooting (Lawrence & Birkland, 2004). Gun laws were also a target for blame, particularly around loopholes which had allowed the Columbine shooters to obtain their firearms (Kerr, 2018). Attributions of blame tended to be partisan in nature. Haider-Markel and Joslyn (2001) found that political leanings influenced which factors were held responsible. Democrats tended towards the frame attributing blame to gun laws; whilst Republicans were influenced by the violent media frame.

There were also intensive legislative motions surrounding violence in schools ensuing from Columbine, including policing, surveillance and zero-tolerance (Altheide, 2009; Kerr, 2021; Muschert, 2019). The potential issue with focusing on extreme school violence is that more common types (e.g. assaults, sexual misconduct) may not be fully addressed (Muschert, 2019, p. 10). In their review of the policy making after Columbine, however, Birkland and Lawrence (2009, p. 1412) found that whilst there was increased policy-making relating to discipline and school security, it did not result in novel policy responses nor did it build consensus about the appropriate action to take. In a similar vein, Addington (2009, pp. 1433, 1439) believed these security measures are "reactive responses" to pressures placed on institutions by worried parents, as opposed to viable long-term solutions that address any of the issues at the root of school violence.

METHODOLOGY

Sample

This paper examined the extent to which the news media coverage of the Columbine school shooting entrenched, reshaped and challenged these misunderstandings. In order to do this, a sample of three hundred and fifty-two articles used for other larger studies was appropriated. The sample includes a mixture of print media sources:

- Daily newspapers, Daily News (13) and New York Post (15);
- Local newspapers, Denver Post (96) and Rocky Mountain News (79);
- Newsweeklies, Newsweek (26) and TIME (53);
- National newspapers, New York Times (21), USA Today (24) and Washington Post (25).

In this study, letters to the editor were selected to explore the thoughts of readers in relation to Columbine. Letters to the editor are said to be a form of voluntary political participation and public debate, with their ability to allow ideas, opinions and information to be shared (Cooper, Knotts & Haspel, 2009; da Silva, 2011; Ericson, Baranek & Chan, 1989). It should be noted that this is a carefully constructed debate, with letters to the editor being the product of selection, editing and framing (da Silva, 2011). As Ericson and colleagues (1989, p. 341) state, letters to the editor give the *impression* that "the newspaper is an open forum for public opinion" (emphasis added).

The final news media sample included letters to the editor from all the same sources, where available.[1] This gave a total of two hundred and twenty-one letters:

- Denver Post (94) and Rocky Mountain News (3);
- New York Times (7), USA Today (1) and Washington Post (15);
- Newsweek (40) and TIME (61).

The coverage includes the day of the attack (20th April 1999) through to the five year anniversary (20th April 2004). Assessing the different time periods allows a comparison between the misunderstandings in the immediate reporting of the shooting and to determine whether any of these are still perpetuating years later. Thematic analysis focuses on the lives of the perpetrators, their behavior during the attack and the legacy of the shooting.

Approach

In 2016, Reese and Shoemaker made the argument that there exists a "hierarchy of influences" that shape media content. This locates the work of individual organizations within wider social structures. Within these mediated spaces, symbolic realities are both formed and expressed. As an example, information propagated via YouTube is perceived as representing things as they actually are (Reese & Shoemaker, 2016, pp. 393, 407). Further blurring boundaries is the "participatory culture" trend, where "passive media consumers" and "active media producers" now interact with each other, contributing to the production of news media content (Jenkins, 2006, p. 3). Historically, what is known as "citizen journalism," whereby non media professionals contribute to news media content, was limited to the recording of videos and images as events transpired, such as the video-camera recording of President Kenndedy's assassination in 1963 (Gillmor, 2007). Now, there is the tendency to apply the "citizen journalism" label more broadly to all forms of participation in social media and other online forms, including tagging, sharing and expressing likes for content. It allows citizens to influence the news media more than the traditional forms of feedback, such as letters to the editor (Roberts, 2019). Gillmor (2007) summarises this trend: "We used to say that journalists write the first draft of history. Not so, not any longer. The people on the ground at these events write the first draft."

In the production of content, the news media have the ability to make certain elements of a topic salient via "priming" techniques, including excluding certain components from stories and repetition and/or prominence of particular elements (see Entman, 1993, 2007; Goffman, 1974; Iyengar, 1991). The criteria for selecting which elements of a story to cover tend to be rooted in values about newsworthiness (see, for example, Galtung & Ruge, 1965/1973; Schudson, 2003). In order to look at the mythology surrounding Columbine, it was necessary to interrogate the frames present in news media coverage. Content analysis was the methodology employed in this paper, whereby data is coded into categories to make sense of the manifest and latent meanings of a text (Bryman, 2008; Holsti, 1969; Krippendorff, 1980). The categorisation of information has conceptual power because it links together common strands (Strauss & Carbin, 1990, p. 305). Content analysis allows for examination of the "themes" (recurring ideas throughout the report) and "frames" (the parameters of what will be discussed) (Altheide, 1996, p. 31) in the news media sample. The content analysis undertaken for this paper allowed for further examination of the themes emerging from news media content: the lives of perpetrators, including their attack-planning; their behavior during attacks; the wider issues of bullying, adolescent subcultures and youth violence.

The content analysis conducted provided a grounding in key trends and a conceptual basis with which to work. Critical discourse analysis was then utilized for a deeper examination of the emerging themes. This research method adopts a critical approach in order to reveal more subtle nuances in the language and the reproduction of power in society (Renugah & Tan, 2015, p. 57). Words, phrases, sentences and paragraphs, as well as the wider context, are interrogated to determine lexical techniques used by writers and the implications of these. For example, intonation, stress, rhythm, hyperbole, irony, hedging, aggregation, abstractions, evaluations, addition, specification and meta-opinions (Fairclough, 1992; Fowler, 1991; Mayr & Machin, 2012; van Dijk, 1998). Looking at the portrayals and classification of key actors also elucidates subtle nuances within the language (van Leeuwen, 1996).

It is important to note that the media audience do not just mindlessly accept news media content; rather they engage in semiotic labor to interpret its meanings. As Fowler (1991, p. 41) points out: "The newspaper does not select events to be reported and then consciously wrap them in value-laden language which the reader passively absorbs, ideology and all." A more convincing argument is that readers actively "read in" — as opposed to "reading off" — the ideological points of discourse (Fowler, 1991, p. 46). Zhang (2014, p. 2275) made the argument that adopting a critical analytical approach will help news readers to increase critical sensitivity and awareness. Furthermore, media literacy can play a key role in distinguishing between various types of content and the validity of it (Roberts, 2019).

Importantly, the media sample also extended to include letters to the editor published in news sources. A number of scholars (for example, Cooper, Knotts & Haspel, 2009; da Silva, 2011; Gordon & Williams, 1975; Tarrat, 1957) have looked at the motivations and processes around writing letters to the editor. In 1957, Tarrat studied letter writers' motivations and concluded they wrote to the editor to complain or seek tension release. Furthermore, it was found that the letters were written because writers thought their letters would affect events and public opinion, as well as keep the public informed on topics of interest. Gordon and Williams (1975) came to a similar conclusion that most letters are "against" something and, therefore, a way to blow off steam. Additionally, they argued that letters to the editor act as a form of social control through a number of avenues, by supporting or refuting a particular position. Editors use their position to select which letters go through to publication; henceforth, resulting in greater influence by certain voices and positions.

When it comes to letters being selected for inclusion, Da Silva (2011, p. 253) maintained that a reader's status and authority on certain subjects are valued criteria. News values also play a role. The principles of content and critical discourse analysis were also applied to the letters to the editor in the sample. This gives an indication of the views of readers, albeit a very small portion, at that moment in time; as well as the types of letters getting published.

UNDERSTANDINGS OF COLUMBINE

The news media sample elucidates multiple, merging, sometimes conflicting understandings of the Columbine shooting: wider trends around youth violence; whether the shooters were normal kids or ostracized loners; the extent to which bullying played a role; the subculture of the Trench Coat Mafia; how the shooters behaved during the attack and what this may tell us about them. The sample includes standard news items, feature articles and letters to the editor, allowing for a broad spectrum of views to be captured.

Children and Guns

Discussions shortly after the Columbine attack reshaped, entrenched and challenged traditional understandings of school shootings. Prominent throughout public discourse was portraying Columbine as an emerging form of youth violence. This is exemplified in a quotation from the Denver Post the week after the shooting: "Like other schoolyard massacres, last week's bloodbath at Columbine High School has reinforced the perception that youth violence is on the increase." Emotive terms like "massacre" and "bloodbath" act as signifiers.

Importantly, this type of violence is said to be arising from the coalescing of social forces. For example, a letter to the editor in the New York Times four days later states that the tragedy at Columbine High is "violence of a qualitatively different type," representing "a violent rebellion against the social order as a whole." It goes on to say that the issue of what happens to "losers" in "a competitive society that values only winners" must be addressed. Examining this through the lens of Hofstede's (2001) cultural model finds that the United States is an individualistic society that places importance on achievement. Other discussions in the media build upon this theme. Delbert S. Elliott, the director of the Center for the Prevention of Violence, also based in Colorado, wrote a column for the Denver Post looking at the causes of youth violence. In this, Elliott writes that new forms of stress for adolescents may be created by failure to be accepted by peers, as well as a lack of academic success. Other news articles across the sample cite psychiatrists and psychotherapists to buttress this idea of adolescent stressors creating the optimum environment for violence.

Insected with this notion of school shootings being a specific time of violence is the "children and guns" theme, whereby the easy access of guns by adolescents is blamed for shootings. This mirrors the findings of numerous other studies (for example, Kerr, 2018) in which the dominant frame in news coverage is blaming guns. The main lexical technique used is addition, where elements are added to an article to buttress an argument (Mayr & Machin, 2012). In this case, the main technique is the use of statistics relating to schoolchildren and firearms. For example, articles by the New York Times and Denver Post in the month after the incident cite the statistic that in the 1996-1997 school year more than six thousand students were expelled for bringing guns to school. The now-defunct Rocky Mountain News a few days after the shooting brings the focus onto Colorado, stating that five hundred and six students were expelled in 1997-1998 for bringing weapons to school, an increase of eighteen percent from the previous school year. The article's preamble to this is the suggestion that "perhaps the bloodbath Tuesday at Columbine High School shouldn't have been a surprise." This is an example of hyperbole, where the exaggerated statement makes a particular point (Fowler, 1991). This serves to further entrench the notion that youth violence is a growing issue.

Similarly, a Newsweek article in the month after noted that approximately forty teenagers a week are murdered in the United States, mainly by guns. The writer notes the racialized element of the violence, with the majority of victims being black and drugs and poverty being the root causes. The rise in school shootings has captured the public's attention; thus, bringing salience to the issue of children being killed. Using an evaluative statement that draws a conclusion about an issue (Mayr & Machin, 2012), the writer describes this as a "double standard." This coverage clearly has an impact on public opinion. A poll published in the Washington Post just a week after the shooting adds further credibility to the idea that teenagers can easily access guns, with twenty percent of those surveyed saying they personally know students who have brought a gun to school and fifty-four percent it would be easy for them to get a gun.

In long-term coverage, the "children and guns" frame reemerges when another high-profile incident occurs - the shooting of a six year old by another six year old in early April 2000. For instance, a letter published in Newsweek almost a year after Columbine opens with the line: "Is there any other nation in the world where a 6-year-old guns down another 6-year-old in school?" It mentions the Columbine shooting, saying it "couldn't produce results, despite the nation's shock and revulsion," and suggests that the picture of the six year old victim may "finally be the impetus for Congress to confront our national firearms emergency." Evident here is intonation (Fowler, 1991), where the rhetorical question, the use of the emotive adjectives "shock" and "revulsion," in addition to the adverb "finally" and evaluative statement "national firearms emergency," coalesce to convey a sense of weariness and frustration. This all serves to underscore the urgency of the need.

In a similar vein, an article published in TIME almost two years after the Columbine shooting opens with the following paragraph:

Here's a fun fact to get your blood pumping: One in five teenage boys admits to taking a weapon (gun or knife) to school with him at least once in the past 12 months.

The use of irony at the beginning requires readers to distinguish between the apparent meaning and the situational context (Fairclough, 1992) to determine that the message being conveyed is one of concern. The article goes on to say that even in the wake of Columbine and another recent shooting, these figures are "chilling." This evaluative statement (Mayr & Machin, 2012) allows for a conclusion to be drawn. Moreover, this is an example of the news media maintaining the salience of an issue (Chyi & McCombs, 2004), with the "children and guns" frame extended through other high-profile shootings, as well as the anniversaries of the Columbine attack. This parallels the findings of other studies that show Columbine had a longer "shelf-life" than usual, no doubt aided by it being a comparative benchmark with which to compare subsequent school shootings (Chyi & McComb, 2004; Kupchik & Bracy, 2009; Schildkraut & Muschert, 2014).

Normal Kids or Rejected Loners?

Unsurprisingly, perhaps, a lot of the coverage in the immediate aftermath of the shooting focused on the lives of the perpetrators. Conflicting themes emerged in these discussions: the idea that the shooters were normal kids with friends and loving families juxtaposed with the portrayal of them as weird loners. The first theme of the perpetrators "appearing normal" is perhaps the most unsettling, because of its implications for risk and threat assessment. If an individual appears to be settled with numerous protective factors, then it makes it more difficult to predict and, therefore, prevent an attack. As an example, the following headlines in the month after the shooting all make references to a secret life by the shooters:

Two Gunmen had many faces (Daily News)

Harris, a consummate actor, hid secret yen for revenge (Denver Post)

Online friend didn't see evil side of Harris (Rocky Mountain News)

The evaluative terms "many faces," "consummate actor," "secret yen" and "evil side" all serve to make the argument that the shooter(s) concealed their true nature.

In line with this sentiment, an evaluative statement in the Daily News a few days after the shooting maintained that despite being the perpetrators of "one of the worst crimes in U.S. history," their lives were "eerily normal." Friends and acquaintances of the gunmen were interviewed and they expressed shock and disbelief at their actions and "double life." This inclusion of specific actors via a social actor analytical approach (van Leeuwen, 1996) underscores the networks surrounding the shooters. This is echoed throughout the news media sample. Neighbors, friends and acquaintances all speak of their shock and use pleasant adjectives to describe the gunmen: "nice," "quiet" and "sweet."

Using this information, a detailed picture of the shooters' lives is given. For example, a Denver Post article published a few weeks after the shooting gives the following description of one of the shooters:

At work, Harris could be a cut-up, talking in funny voices and telling jokes. At school, he could be an inspired student and writer, hurling his hand in the air to offer his take on Shakespeare. He told girls they looked nice. He escorted friends to class. He gave one teacher a Christmas present. He had a contagious laugh. He talked about building a better future.

The rhythm of this paragraph (Fowler, 1991), with the repetition of 'he' and the listing of his activities and behaviors further underscore this idea that the shooter had a normal life. In contrast to other school shooters - for example, the 2007 Virginia Tech shooter, who was often described as "weird" and engaged in bizarre activities such as stabbing a knife into a carpet at a party (see Kerr, 2021) - the Columbine perpetrators appear to be regular kids. Even though they were referred to a non-violent youth community program for breaking into a car, as noted in a number of articles, their end of program review described them as bright with limitless potential.

At the end of 1999, TIME magazine published a lengthy feature article about video tapes made by the shooters, which gave an insight into their motives. This is a direct example of activation, whereby social actors are symbolized as dynamic and active forces in an event (van Leeuwen, 1996). This is pertinent in this case, for it places direct responsibility for the shooting onto the perpetrators by directly citing them. One shooter said he has been storing anger for the past four years and blames others for this: "You made me what I am. You added to the rage." The other shooter made similar claims, saying people constantly made fun of "my face, my hair, my shirts." He goes on to say "I'm going to kill you all. You've been giving us s**t for years." One of them lifts a shotgun and says "Isn't it fun to get the respect that we're going to deserve?" The article makes use of a metaphor to make an evaluative point about the shooters' contradictory behaviour, describing the tapes as a "cloudy window on their moral order." For example, the shooters defend their friends who bought them guns and also their parents, saying both sets of people knew nothing about their planned massacre. The shooters also expressed regret about the impact of the shooting on their parents, acknowledging that it was going to bring them pain.

The addition of such a revelation serves to create a more nuanced understanding of the shooters, rather than the singular portal of them as "evil." News media coverage of other school shootings, such as the 2007 Virginia Tech massacre, employ the villain-hero dichotomy, whereby the perpetrator is portrayed as the embodiment of evil and the victims as heroic (see, for instance, Berkowitz, 2010). That is not to say that the portrayal of Columbine shooters is not completely removed from the villain-hero dichotomy. Throughout the news media sample, emotive adjectives are used when discussing the shooters: "angry," "crazy," "violent," "cold-blooded" and "calculating." Moreover, the following terms are used to describe the shooters: "The Monsters Next Door," "The Natural Born Killers" and "The Executioners of Columbine."

In a similar vein, a TIME letter to the editor published early 2000 is critical of the term "The Monsters Next Door" being used on the front cover of the magazine, making the claim that "one can see how difficult life was for them" and highlighted that the boys apologizing to their families showed they were not "totally merciless" or without "feeling and regret." This is an example of a meta-opinion (van Dijk, 1998), expressing an opinion about an opinion - in this case, that the shooters were monsters. The age of the letter writer is included, noting that they are seventeen years old. Whilst this may seem unusual, it is relevant to this news story since the writer is of a similar age to the shooters. In their 1989 study, Ericson, Baranek and Chan noted that letter writers demonstrating authority through their professional status, knowledge about a certain subject or representing an institution or organization are more likely to be selected for publication. In this case, the letter writer is representing the teenage perspective.

Additionally, much is made of the supposed links between the shooters and Neo-Nazism, with quotes from students at the school describing the shooters doing Nazi salutes, saying "Heil Hitler" and espousing Nazi ideology. The portrayal of the shooters as Neo-Nazis adds another layer to the explanation about why they carried out the shooting. Klein (2006, p. 65) maintained that Nazism provided the basis for the Columbine shooters to admire and then imitate them by substituting the Nazis' violent methods and ideologies with their own version. A number of the shooters' friends also dispute this notion, with one being mixed race and another being Jewish. Another anecdote was shared that when he was younger one of the shooter's best friends was an Asian kid and a black kid. These counter arguments are sporadic, however, in comparison to the extensive references to the supposed links between the shooters and Neo-Nazism in the media sample.

The Bullying Narrative

The bullying narrative is the notion that the shooters were bullied by their peers and that the shooting was an attack on their bullies. As Cullen (2019, p. 383) put it, this resembles a "psychotic Robin Hood fable," whereby high school status power is stolen and granted to those in oppressed groups, such as the "geeks" and "nerds." Such a narrative is a common feature after school shootings. For example, a study by Larkin (2013) created a database of US secondary school rampage shootings and attempted shootings from 1974 through to 2012, classified by the motivation of the shooter(s) and the presence of bullying. Of the thirty-eight shooters (across thirty-six incidents), twenty of them were motivated by revenge against bullying, harassment and intimidation by peers. A number of other studies (Kimmel & Mahler, 2003; Klein, 2006; Klein & Chancer, 2000) have found that school shooters occupied lower-statuses in the school hierarchy and were said to be bullied and ostracized. So there is some truth to the narrative; however, it has been twisted in a way to reframe school shootings as "outcasts turning the tables on their bullies" (Cullen, 2019, p. 383).

Implicit in the bullying narrative are varying degrees of sympathy and empathy for the shooters. This does not mean their actions are condoned in any way; however, it serves to portray the shooters as victims themselves rather than just cold-blooded killers. Reviewing letters to the editor gives an indication of how widely accepted the bullying narrative was. Tarrat's (1957) study about the motivations of letter writers found that writers thought their letters would affect events and public opinion, as well as keep the public informed on topics of interest. Looking at the sample of letters written after Columbine, it could be extrapolated from that there are similar motivations. Writers raise other related issues, framing the debate in a certain way. The titles given to letters are part of the editorial control of the process, with these serving to provide an immediate summary for readers of letter content. Looking at a handful of titles published across different time periods shows how these further entrench the bullying narrative:

"Teasing can be cruel" (TIME, week after)

"Bullying by jocks" (Denver Post, four years later)

"Goaded to kill" (Denver Post, one year sample)

In advancing their argument that letter writing is a form of social control, Gordon and Williams (1975) said that it allows certain segments of society to have greater influence. In this case, it would be giving salience to the bullying narrative.

In line with this, a number of letters in both the short term and long term coverage of the shooting make direct references to the bullying of the shooters:

"The extent of the bullying apparently administered at the senior high level at Columbine by the "jocks" is shocking." (Denver Post, four years later)

"Three years of walking into school and wondering what embarrassment and humiliation they [the shooters] would have to endure." (Denver Post, four years later)

"Kids can be so cruel with words and teasing, and I don't think they realize the extent of mental anguish that teasing causes." (TIME, week after sample)

"There's a reason why these kids felt like outcasts." (TIME, week after sample)

"In my opinion, Eric and Dylan were just as much victims as everyone else. I can understand the animosity they felt towards their fellow classmates. Teenagers are so mean and horrible to each other." (Rocky Mountain News, one year sample)

As part of this evaluation, writers also offer suggestions for ways to change: parental styles, being more inclusive, overcoming prejudice, eradicating cliques in school. The moral panic framework (see Cohen 1972, 2002) may be drawn upon here, with the various proposed solutions all serving to highlight that something "must be done" about the issue of school shootings and violence in schools more generally.

In particular, one letter writer in TIME, the month afterwards, makes a direct call to action for change. The opening sentences invite readers to think about an average American high school and those outside a clique. This is described in the following way: "The outsiders, the freaks, the weirdos, the geeks." This acts as a form of labeling, whereby the use of derogatory terms to refer to groups serves to indicate how people may be perceived. The writer goes on to implore fellow students to a direct call to action: "You could prevent another tragedy from happening in your own seemingly safe school." The terms "another tragedy" and "seemingly safe school" are products of the culture of fear around school shootings, whereby the sense of risk is distorted to the extent that one feels likely to be victimized (Skogan, 1993). Notably, this climate of fear is maintained by the feeling that these incidents are part of an ongoing trend and could occur anywhere, even in those locations perceived to be safe (see Kerr, 2021; Kupchik & Bracy, 2009). The letter continues by suggesting concrete actions students could take, including making an effort to talk to people who seem like outsiders.

The bullying narrative is even evident in the long-term coverage of the shooting. An article in Newsweek revisited Columbine High almost five years later and this prompted a letter in response. The letter published at the end of 2003 serves the purpose of refuting aspects of the article: "We were alarmed by the article's implication that the return of bullying to school grounds could be considered a sign of recovery." The letter goes on to maintain that bullying is a "serious and dangerous issue with far-reaching consequences for its perpetrators, victims and witnesses." To buttress their argument, they cite a recent study showing that kids who are bullied are more likely to be suicidal, carry weapons to school and become criminals as adults. Da Silva (2011, p. 253) found that the status and authority of letter writers are valued criteria for the selection of letters. For this particular letter, two names are provided and the job titles of each writer. One is the President and CEO of Prevent Child Abuse America; the other is the President of Fight Crime: Invest in Kids, which the publisher of the study cited. The inclusion of credentials bestow status and authority on the arguments the writers of the letter are making (see Ericson, Baranek & Chan, 1989).

The myth of the bullying narrative is only sporadically challenged throughout the news media sample. For example, a Time article at the end of 1999 makes an evaluative statement, drawing a conclusion about an issue (Mayr & Machin, 2012), claiming that the fact that the attack was originally intended to be a bombing attack, aiming to kill two hundred and fifty people, "shows their motives went far beyond the people who teased them." The use of the word "shows" here is an example of a 'truth comment,' indicating a commitment to the proposition they have made (Fowler, 1991, p. 85).

Even though there are issues with the credibility of the bullying narrative, it is a dominant frame throughout the news media coverage. This is potentially problematic, since the issues highlighted by the news media have the ability to shape what citizens think about (Delli Carpini, 2005). These frames can also percolate into other forums. For instance, Lindgren (2011) study of YouTube videos relating to school shootings found that users would assess and critique events by relating them to wider issues such as high school culture and bullying. The number of monthly comments would increase exponentially following another high-profile school shooting, showing how the lifespan of frames can be extended.

Moreover, a number of theorists have highlighted the potential link between news media coverage and copycat school shootings (Coleman, 2004; Kostinsky, Bixler & Ketti, 2001; Maguire, Weatherby & Mathers, 2002). This is particularly the case with the Columbine incident, which has been cited in a number of subsequent shootings (Lieberman, 2008). More recent literature has indicated that this trend has continued, despite the Columbine incident occurring over two decades ago (see, for example, Follman, 2022). The link to bullying is explained in a study by Larkin (2013) classifying the motivations of shooter(s) and the presence of bullying across thirty-six school shootings and attempted attacks. The eleven post-Columbine attempted shootings were all self-perceived as revenge killings for bullying and harassment (Larkin, 2013, pp. 169-170). The perceived link between bullying and the Columbine shooters, therefore, has the potential to make them role models for the disenfranchised.

Trench Coat Mafia

One of the most dominant misinformation thematic compendium throughout the news media sample is that relating to the Trench Coat Mafia. Cullen (2019, pp. 147-148) maintained that whilst there was a group of students that wore trench coats and were dubbed the "Trench Coat Mafia," the Columbine shooters were not a part of it. Conversely, the shooters wore trench coats on the day of the shooting for both fashion and functional (i.e. the coats allowed them to hide their weapons) reasons. The Trench Coat Mafia was said to have been promoted because it was "colorful, memorable and fit the existing myth of the school shooter as outcast loner (Cullen, 2019, p. 149).

There were numerous references to the shooters being "members" of the Trench Coat Mafia in the media sample. Below is a selection of these:

"Part of a clinique called TCM" Denver Post (day after)

"Members of an outcast group" (New York Post, week after)

"Society of Outcasts" (New York Times, week after)

The day after the shooting, USA Today said the shooters were apparently members of the "Trench Coat Mafia," a "militia-style clique of campus outcasts." An article by the Denver Post the day after the shooting, entitled "Carnage puts spotlight on Trench Coat Mafia," was entirely focused on the group and the shooters' alleged involvement in it. It is reported that fellow students say the shooting suspects are part of a clique of "generally quiet, brooding outcasts with penchants for dark trench coats, shaved heads and militant arm bands." This positions the Trench Coat Mafia in the same way as the subcultures of Mods and Rockers, where particular type stylistic features classify group membership (Cohen, 1972). The Denver Post article goes on to say that the group is also interested in "the occult, mutilation, shock-rocker Marilyn Manson and Adolf Hitler, whose birthday was Tuesday." This sentence bestows a darker dimension to the Trench Coat Mafia, moving beyond a gothic subculture into Nazism and harmful behaviors. Quotations from students throughout this article entrench this idea, referencing the group's interest in Nazism and satanic practices. Moreover, students use the adverbs "creepy" and "weird" to describe the group. The article also cites academics studying this area to give their thoughts about the group and subcultures more generally.

The erroneous linkage between this group and the Columbine shooters led to misinformation about the motives of the shooters and even whether this case was a school shooting or a gang-related shooting incident. For example, a few days after the shooting, the New York Times gave the following description:

> Some of the shooters and victims on Tuesday were supposed to meet months ago, in a rumble pitting students known as the trench coat mafia against the athletes -- Goths versus Jocks, as some students said. It was going to be a fistfight to settle a feud, and it most certainly would not have made news. But that fight never happened. Instead, a slaughter unfolded in the suburb south of Denver. So, once again, what lingers most prominently is a question that begs for clarity: why a massacre instead of slugfest?

This myth was not just limited to the immediate aftermath of the shooting. For example, almost a week after the shooting, the Daily News described the shooters in the following way: "The teenage mass murderers self-styled members of the Trench Coat Mafia outcast clique." Over a month after the shooting, a TIME article said: "It was a tense time at Columbine, with fights brewing between jocks and skateboarders, jocks and Goths, and nearly everyone picking on the guys in the trench coats." Even over a week over the shooting, there are still references to the Trench Coat Mafia. An article in the Daily News just over a week after the shooting opens in the following way: "Eric Harris and Dylan Klebold along with pals in their Trench Coat Mafia clique of high school misfits bragged about a 'big plan' to shoot up the school, one friend said yesterday." The article goes on to say the friend "never suspected" the Trench Coat Mafia would turn to violence. This is an example of "nominalisation,'' where the nominal forms of actions "shoot up" and "turn to violence" are derived from verbs. The purpose of this is to weaken the sense of action; in turn, impersonalizing the processes and making the text seem as unbiased as possible (Zhang, 2014, p. 2274). An earlier article in the same source the day after the shooting set the tone by contrasting the death and depression of Gothic subculture with the racism and violence of the Trench Coat Mafia.

Relating this myth to the work of Stanley Cohen (1972) finds that the Trench Coat Mafia fits the notion of a "folk devil," which is a person, object or group symbolizing a particular deviant status in society. This creates the optimum conditions for a "moral panic," in which "a condition, episode, person, or group of persons emerges to become defined as a threat to societal values and interest" (Cohen, 2002, p. 1). It must be remembered that these conditions, episodes, persons or groups were and continue to be part of society, even following a moral panic; it is a trigger of some kind causing them to be construed as nefarious for a variable duration of time (Lindgren, 2011, p. 126). In this case, it is the linkage between the Trench Coat Mafia and the Columbine shooting perpetrated in the public sphere. This finding mirrors Frymer's (2009) theory about "alienated youth" becoming an object of fear after being reconstructed in the media coverage of the Columbine incident. Importantly, with a moral panic, the concern felt by the public is inconsistent with the actual threat level or damage caused (Burns and Crawford, 1999, p. 150; Killingbeck, 2001, p. 191).

Looking at public opinion at that time indicates that a moral panic was being felt about the Trench Coat Mafia. The erroneous linkage with the Trench Coat Mafia is one of the avenues through which to discuss numerous other issues for a handful of letters published in the immediate aftermath of the shooting. A letter in Newsweek the month after makes a sardonic remark, with their question contrasting against the apparent meaning and the situational context (Fairclough, 1989, p. 123) to advance the argument for tighter gun laws: "Was the Trenchcoat Mafia of Eric Harris and Dylan Klebold the well-regulated militia envisioned by the men who drafted the Second Amendment, granting citizens the right to keep and bear arms?" The status of the letter writer is given as the Development Director of the Salesians of St. John Bosco, a religious organization. This parallels the 1974 study by Ericson and colleagues that letter writers who can demonstrate authority through their status are more likely to get selected for inclusion.

Another letter speaks about school sizes being too large leading to students being ostracized and marginalized. In a similar vein, a different letter touches upon the "folk devil" concept (Cohen, 1972), noting that the media's fixation on the Trench Coat Mafia serves to label and, therefore, vilify certain groups. This is a classic example of using letters to the editor to refute a certain position (Gordon & Williams, 1975, p. 4).

There are also a few letters that criticize the fact that this group was allowed to exist in the school. Below are extracts from each of them:

> How is it possible that no one noticed these Trench Coat Mafia kids and didn't believe that they were dangerous walking around school? (TIME, day after)
>
> If the students were so aware of this Trench Coat Mafia, why weren't the school's teachers and/or administrators? What about the police? (TIME, day after)
>
> Wouldn't school administrators have taken the numerous threats these boys made more seriously? Wouldn't someone have confronted the boys about their homicidal video? (Newsweek, month after)

The use of rhetorical questions acts as a form of intonation (Halliday, 1985), with the implication of inaction on behalf of the schools. Moreover, the use of adverbs "didn't," "weren't" and "wouldn't" further entrench this idea about a lack of concrete action. Consequently, these letters fit with the notion of a moral panic, where there is the prevalent feeling that there needs to be a target of blame to allow for something to be "done" about an issue (Burns & Crawford, 1999, p.149). Furthermore, it also cements the idea that pre-existing lenient rules are said to have led to the problem in the first place (Goode & Yehuda, 1994, pp. 31-32).

Although all three letters indirectly blame the school, readers are offered different explanations for why this is the case. The first letter goes on to attribute political correctness as the reason why school authorities are "afraid" to teach students about right and wrong behaviors. The second one posits that the school "looked the other way," because the kids involved were White, questioning whether this would have been the case had they been Black, Asian or Hispanic. The third letter makes a similar point, speculating whether the threats would have been taken seriously had they come from minority children of a single parent living in poverty in the inner city. The issue of the ethnicity of the shooters is a prevalent one throughout the news media sample, with it being noted in numerous articles that this story was particularly newsworthy precisely because it involved White shooters.

The first two letter writers give their location as Aurora in Colorado, a city near Columbine, mirroring the finding of Gordon and Williams in their 1975 paper that letters tended to originate from the same locations, creating the geographical centralization of opinion. Interestingly, in selecting both letters for inclusion in the same source of TIME magazine, contrasting reasons for the purported lack of action on behalf of the school in relation to the Trench Coat Mafia are presented.

Attack and Deaths

In the immediate aftermath of the shooting, the news media utilized eyewitness accounts to describe how the shooters behaved during the attack. In a study about the news media coverage of the 2017 Las Vegas mass shooting, Kerr (2021) noted that a prominent theme contributing to a climate of fear was the "sounds of terror." For the Las Vegas mass shooting, this related to the sound of automatic gunfire heard on videos recorded by eyewitnesses. Although there was no such recording for the Columbine attack, a similar theme is evident throughout the news media sample. A central focus in descriptions of the attack are the sounds made by the shooters as they shot people. The adverbs "laughed," "guffawed,""giggled," "hooting" and "hollering" indicate enjoyment and happiness. This is further entrenched by eyewitnesses stating that the shooters were "enjoying this," "killing just to kill" and "orgasmic." Eyewitnesses also report that the shooters were taunting people before killing them. For example, saying "peekaboo" to a girl hiding under a desk before shooting her; using derogatory racial slurs and continuously shooting a Black student; calling someone a "nerd" before they fired off shots. This kind of behavior suggests the shooters were indeed bullies themselves, rather than oppressed bullies who rose up to take "revenge" on those who had bullied them.

Another prominent theme in news media coverage was speculation around perpetrators' deaths. A Daily News article in the month after noted that the shooters "initially tried to escape through three separate exits and killed themselves only after being turned back by deputies' gunfire." Extrapolating from this, the shooters' priority was to escape, with their suicides being an unplanned last resort. TIME speculates on the reason for the suicide: "Harris and Klebold made sure they would never have to face a judge or their victims' parents or their friends, never have to apologize, never have to explain." The implication from this is that the shooters were cowardly in their avoidance of accountability.

There is some degree of speculation about whether the deaths of the shooters were suicides with there being numerous references throughout most of the media sample using the adjectives "apparent" and "likely" to refer to the suicides. It is even postulated that in a TIME article in the month after the shooting that it could have been a murder-suicide, with one shooter killing the other before ending his own life, or a planned double execution of each other. The District Attorney is quoted as saying he does not dismiss the possibility of a murder suicide, given the location of one wound. This uncertainty just creates further mystery around the incident.

Surprisingly, perhaps, none of the articles ponder whether there is any meaning behind the shooters dying in the same location as the majority of their victims. Whilst media reports do note that they died in the library and some even mention that their bodies were found in close proximity to their victims, there is a notable absence of any critique about whether there is any significance to this. This is particularly surprising since it is noted that the shooters returned to the library from the cafeteria, suggesting it was a deliberate decision to be in this location.

An Indiscriminate Attack

What is also given less attention in media accounts is the fact that the shooting was originally intended to be a bombing attack, with the shooting meant to kill any survivors who tried to flee. Given even less attention is the original plan of the shooters, which involved an attack mirroring the 9/11 attacks that occurred over two years later. Out of the entire media sample, it is only covered in two articles. The most extensive reference is an article published in the New York Daily News article a week after the shooting that is dedicated to this story. Presumably, this newspaper deemed it to be more of a newsworthy item than other sources, due to the geographical relevance to that location. A social actor analytical approach (van Leeuwen, 1996) can be applied to assess the article's headline: "Young Gunmen Targeted N.Y.C. Planned To Hijack Plane, Crash Here." The social actors are impersonalized here via abstraction by means of a quality assigned to them: in this case, their status as gunmen. The process of activation gives them an active role in the process evinced through the transitive verbs "planned," "hijak" and "targeted."

The article opens with the ominous sentence "Blowing up the school was only Step One." It goes on to use signifiers to provide more detail, describing the shooters as "teenage trigger men" who "scattered bombs and bullets through Columbine High School," with the use of evaluative verbs "trigger" and "scatter" dramatizing the article (Fowler, 1991) and giving the shooters an active role in the process. It goes on to describe more about their plan to, following their school shooting, hijack a plane and crash it into skyscraper buildings in New York. This gives an insight into the motives of the shooters, with them not originally planning to die at Columbine High School. Furthermore, it diminishes the credibility of the bullying narrative, since the victims of such an attack in New York, had it gone ahead, would have been strangers to them.

The Rocky Mountain News makes a fleeting reference to the planned attack in an article published the month after the shooting. It mentions that in addition to the school attack - in which the shooters wanted to kill at least 500 students - they wanted to attack homes in the neighborhood and then hijack a plane to crash into New York City. It is telling perhaps that despite the school shooting being only part of a wider planned attack, the other elements are mentioned only sporadically in quite an extensive media sample. In deciding which issues to cover and how extensively in coverage, the news media has the ability to influence what citizens think about (Delli Carpini, 2005, p. 35). In that sense, the reality that this school shooting was actually part of a wider attack fails to receive adequate coverage and, thus, is not one of the dominant frames in the post-Columbine narrative.

Another element refuting the bullying narrative is the fact that the shooting was originally planned as a bombing against the school to be followed up with the shooting of survivors, with the intention of killing hundreds of students. This is mainly evident in the media sample via descriptions of attack plans in one of the shooter's diaries . This includes references to the fifty-one bombs assembled by the shooters, the largest being two twenty pound devices fueled by a propane tank that were loaded into their cars to explode. Numerous descriptions of the attack note that the bombs failed to detonate.

The intentions of the shooters are also documented in a small number of articles. A Newsweek article within the month after the shooting mentions that calculations are documented in the diary about which time of day would yield the highest body count. TIME's in-depth examination of the shooters' tapes makes the following point:

> "Why, if their motive was rage at the athletes who taunted them, didn't they take their guns and bombs to the locker room? Because retaliation against specific people was not the point."

The use of the rhetorical question here acts to refute the opinion that the shooters were seeking revenge against bullies. Further entrenching this argument, the article references direct quotations from the shooters about killing "250 of you" and even their intention to harm survivors through "creating flashbacks from what we will do [to] drive them insane."

Another TIME article written years later also references the indiscriminate nature of the attack: "As obvious as it sounds now, the guys wanted to kill as many people as they could — many more than the 13 who died." The use of the word obvious in the opening sub-clause is evaluative, suggesting that this is common-sense. Further, the use of the word "wanted" is "predicate," where the action is under the control of agents (Fowler, 1991) - in this case, the shooters. The following sentence provides further evidence for this claim, referring to the explosives created by the shooters and how "hundreds would have perished" had they detonated as planned. The writer provides an evaluative summary of the situation when they state "Harris and Klebold's diabolical aspirations far exceeded their technical prowess."

In comparison to the bullying narrative, however, the counteractive theme of the "indiscriminate attack" is given far less attention. What this omission serves to do is bestow credibility and salience on the bullying narrative, with the reality that this was a failed bombing attack intended as an attack on the school itself rather than specific individuals being undermined through the lack of media coverage.

This shows the influence the news media can have in setting the agenda around how citizens think about certain issues (Chyi & McCombs, 2004; Delli Carpini, 2005; Lawrence & Birkland, 2004)

CONCLUSION

A wealth of literature exists about the Columbine school shootings in relation to the news media coverage of Columbine (for example, Birkland & Lawrence, 2009; Kerr, 2018; Muschert, 2019). Despite this, the fallacies and myths around the incident are still underexplored. This paper sought to fill this gap in the current scholarship by exploring these in more depth. Of particular interest was looking at how the news media can shape understandings of what transpired at Columbine High School and the lives and deaths of the shooters. News media articles and letters to the editor from a range of local and national newspapers as well as newsweeklies were utilized to explore the emerging frames and themes.

Results indicate that the perpetrators were described as "normal," nice, having friends at school, success with girls and loving families. In contrast, there are also reports of them being odd, violent, loners, being both bullied and bullies themselves, and supporting Neo-Nazism. The conflicting reports elucidate the number of fallacies about the shooters, whereby the shooters were seeking revenge on those who bullied them; in addition to them having links to a so-called youth gang, the Trench Coat Mafia. Such fallacies are repeated in letters to the editor, showing how media coverage was influencing public opinion at that time. The danger in this misinformation is it can seek to inspire copycats, with the erroneous notion that the Columbine shooters were rising up against their oppressors. Moreover, a number of copycat incidents are said to have been inspired by Columbine (Follman, 2022). Narratives contrary to the bullying script, such as the shooting being an indiscriminate attack intended to kill everyone at the school, are only touched upon within the news media coverage.

Also evident in the media coverage was the idea that Columbine was only the beginning of an emerging form of youth violence. Quantification of the problem by providing statistics of youth violence and weapon-carrying, as well as citing more extreme cases such as a six year old shooting and killing another child at school, all serve to illustrate this argument. This likely helped create the conditions for a "culture of fear" after the Columbine shooting (see Altheide, 2002; Glassner, 2004).

These findings have a number of implications for the ongoing debate around school shootings. Early media reporting should be interpreted with caution, given the potential for conflicting, inadvertently erroneous information. This is even more likely to be the case in the present day with the advent of social media; as well as the growth of citizen journalism, whereby non media professionals create, assess and disseminate news and information (see Roberts, 2019). Misinformation can arise in both the early stages and longer term discussions following these incidents. Additionally, the sense that school shootings are normalised and part of an ongoing trend have the potential to cause harm by creating a "culture of fear" in which the perceived risk of another incident occurring is greater than the actual threat posed (Altheide, 2002; Glassner, 2004).

People can try to avert and negate these risks by improving their media literacy. A media literate user is able to consume, produce, share and engage with information with a greater degree of self-efficacy (Roberts, 2019, p. 8). For school shootings, this could be achieved by consuming different types of media over a period of time, being aware of the implications of one's actions, adopting a critical mindset and looking at data in relation to school shooting trends. The news media also have a role to play by being circumspect with early reports following incidents, particularly those arising from citizen journalism; in addition to inclusion of elements correcting myths and misinformation.

There are still myriad issues to be explored from a research perspective. Attributions of blame were placed on either violent media or guns based on political leanings (Birkland & Lawrence, 2009). Whilst the issue of gun policies after Columbine has been discussed in the literature (for example, Kerr, 2018), violent entertainment media is an issue that requires further attention. Lawsuits have been filed against the entertainment industry for school shootings (Lawrence & Birkland, 2004) and the airing of television shows such as *Buffy the Vampire Slayer* have been affected (see Kerr, forthcoming). With there being no direct causal link from violent media to school shootings, it could be said that this is another fallacy. Future research should explore this further, looking at the implications.

REFERENCES

Altheide, D. L. (1996). *Qualitative media analysis*. Sage.

Altheide, D. L. (2002). *Creating Fear: News and the Construction of Crisis*. Routledge., DOI: 10.4324/9780203794494

Altheide, D. L. (2009). The Columbine shooting and the discourse of fear. *The American Behavioral Scientist*, *52*(10), 1354–1370. DOI: 10.1177/0002764209332552

Berkowitz, D. (2010). The ironic hero of Virginia Tech: Healing trauma through mythical narrative and collective memory. *Journalism*, *11*(6), 643–659. DOI: 10.1177/1464884910379705

Birkland, T. A., & Lawrence, R. G. (2009). Media Framing and Policy Change After Columbine. *The American Behavioral Scientist*, *52*(10), 1405–1425.

Bryman, A. (2008). *Social research methods* (3rd ed.). Oxford University Press.

Burns, R., & Crawford, C. (1999). School shootings, the media, and public fear: Ingredients for a moral panic. *Crime, Law, and Social Change*, *32*(2), 147–168. DOI: 10.1023/A:1008338323953

Carpini, M. X. D., & Entman, R. M. (2005). News from Somewhere: Journalistic Frames and the Debate over "Public Journalism." In Callaghan, K., & Schnell, F. (Eds.), *Framing American Politics* (pp. 21–53). University of Pittsburgh Press. DOI: 10.2307/j.ctt6wrbqk.6

Chyi, H. I., & McCombs, M. E. (2004). Media salience and the process of framing: Coverage of the Columbine school shootings. *Journalism & Mass Communication Quarterly*, *81*(1), 22–35. DOI: 10.1177/107769900408100103

Cohen, S. (1972). *Folk Devils and Moral Panics: The Creation of the Mods and Rockers*. MacGibbon and Kee.

Cohen, S. (2002). *Folk Devils and Moral Panics* (3rd ed.). Routledge.

Coleman, L. (2004). *The Copycat Effect: How the Media and Popular Culture Trigger the Mayhem in Tomorrow's Headlines*. Paraview Pocket Books.

Cooper, C., Knotts, H. G., & Haspel, M. (2009). The Content of Political Participation: Letters to the Editor and the People Who Write Them. *PS, Political Science & Politics*, *42*(1), 131–137. https://www.jstor.org/stable/20452387

Cullen, D. (2019). *Columbine*. Riverun.

Cullen, D. (2024). *Columbine 25th Anniversary Memorial Edition*. Grand Central Publishing.

da Silva, M. T. (2011). Newsroom Practices And Letters-To-The-Editor: An analysis of selection criteria. *Journalism Practice*, *6*(2), 250–263. DOI: 10.1080/17512786.2011.629124

Entman, R. M. (1993). Framing: Toward Clarification of a Fractured Paradigm. *Journal of Communication*, *43*(4), 51–58. DOI: 10.1111/j.1460-2466.1993.tb01304.x

Entman, R. M. (2007). Framing bias: Media in the distribution of power. *Journal of Communication, 57*(1), 163–173. DOI: 10.1111/j.1460-2466.2006.00336.x

Ericson, R., Baranek, P., & Chan, J. (1989). *Negotiating Control. A Study of News Sources*. University of Toronto Press.

Fairclough, N. (1989). *Language and Power*. Longman.

Fairclough, N. (1992). Discourse and Text: Linguistic and Intertextual Analysis within Discourse Analysis. *Discourse & Society, 3*(2), 193–217. DOI: 10.1177/0957926592003002004

Follman, M. (2022). *Trigger Points: Inside the mission to stop mass shootings in America*. HarperCollins Publishers.

Fowler, R. (1991). *Language in the News: Discourse and Ideology in the Press* (1st ed.). Routledge.

Frymer, B. (2009). The Media Spectacle of Columbine: Alienated Youth as an Object of Fear. *The American Behavioral Scientist, 52*(10), 1387–1404. DOI: 10.1177/000276420933255

Galtung, J., & Ruge, M. (1965). The Structure of Foreign News: The presentation of the Congo, Cuba and Cyprus crises in four Norwegian newspapers. *Journal of International Peace Research, 2*(1), 64–91. DOI: 10.1177/002234336500200104

Gillmor, D. (2007). Virginia Tech: How Media Are Evolving. *Center for Citizen Media*. http://citmedia.org/blog/2007/04/17/virginia-tech-how-media-are-evolving/

Glassner, B. (2004). Narrative Techniques of Fear Mongering. *Social Research, 71*(4), 819–826. DOI: 10.1353/sor.2004.0001

Goffman, E. (1974). *Frame analysis: An essay on the organization of experience*. Harvard University Press.

Goode, E., & Ben-Yehuda, N. (1994). Moral panics: Culture, politics, and social construction. *Annual Review of Sociology, 20*(1), 149–171. DOI: 10.1146/annurev.so.20.080194.001053

Gordon, A. H., & Williams, J. L. (1975). Letters to the Editor in Two Elite Newspapers: A Cross-National Study of Social Control. Paper was presented at the 1975 Annual Conference of the Southwestern Sociological Association (U.S.A.). *Sociological Abstracts, 23*(49), 33–34.

Haider-Markel, D. P., & Joslyn, M. R. (2001). Gun policy, opinion, tragedy, and blame attribution: The conditional influence of issue frames. *The Journal of Politics, 63*(2), 520–543. DOI: 10.1111/0022-3816.00077

Halliday, M. A. K. (1994). *An Introduction to Functional Grammar* (2nd ed.). Edward Arnold.

Hofstede, G. (2001). *Culture's consequences: Comparing values, behaviors, institutions, and organizations across nations* (2nd ed.). Sage.

Holsti, O. R. (1969). *Content Analysis for the Social Sciences and Humanities*. Addison Wesley.

Iyengar, S. (1991). *Is anyone responsible? How television frames political issues*. University of Chicago Press.

Jenkins, H. (2006). *Convergence Culture: where old and new media collide*. New York University Press.

Kerr, S. E. M. (2018). *Gun Violence Prevention?: The Politics Behind Policy Responses to School Shootings in the United States*. Palgrave Macmillan.

Kerr, S. E. M. (2021). *Examining Gun Regulations, Warning Behaviors, and Policies to Prevent Mass Shootings*. IGI Global.

Kerr, S. E. M. (forthcoming). A Gendered Understanding of School Shootings on Screen. *Students on Screen*.

Killingbeck, D. (2001). The Role Of Television News In The Construction Of School Violence As A "Moral Panic.". *The Journal of Criminal Justice and Popular Culture*, *8*(3), 186–202.

Kimmel, M. S., & Mahler, M. (2003). Adolescent Masculinity, Homophobia, and Violence: Random School Shootings, 1982-2001. *The American Behavioral Scientist*, *46*(10), 1439–1458. DOI: 10.1177/0002764203046010010

Klein, J. (2006). An invisible problem: Everyday violence against girls in schools. *Theoretical Criminology*, *10*(2), 147–177. DOI: 10.1177/1362480606063136

Klein, J., & Chancer, L. (2000). Masculinity Matters: The Role of Gender in High-profile School Violence Cases. In Spina, S. (Ed.), *Smoke and Mirrors: The Hidden Context of Violence in Schools and Society* (pp. 129–162). Rowman and Littlefield.

Kostinsky, S., Bixler, E. O., & Kettl, P. A. (2001). Threats of school violence in Pennsylvania after media coverage of the Columbine high school massacre: Examining the role of imitation. *Archives of Pediatrics & Adolescent Medicine*, *155*(9), 994–1001. DOI: 10.1001/archpedi.155.9.994 PMID: 11529800

Krippendorff, K. (1980). *Content analysis an introduction to its Methodology*. Sage.

Kupchik, A., & Bracy, N. L. (2009). The news media on school crime and violence: Constructing dangerousness and fueling fear. *Youth Violence and Juvenile Justice*, *7*(2), 136–155. DOI: 10.1177/1541204008328800

Kupper, J., Christensen, T. K., Wing, D., Hurt, M., Schumacher, M., & Meloy, R. (2022). The Contagion and Copycat Effect in Transnational Far-Right Terrorism: An Analysis of Language Evidence. *Perspectives on Terrorism*, *16*(4), 4–26. https://www.jstor.org/stable/27158149

Larkin, R. W. (2013). Legitimated Adolescent Violence: Lessons from Columbine. In Böckler, N., Seeger, T., Sitzer, P., & Heitmeyer, W. (Eds.), *School Shootings*. Springer. DOI: 10.1007/978-1-4614-5526-4_7

Lawrence, R. G., & Birkland, T. A. (2004). Guns, Hollywood, and School Safety: Defining the School-Shooting Problem Across Public Arenas. *Social Science Quarterly*, *85*(5), 1193–1207. DOI: 10.1111/j.0038-4941.2004.00271.x

Lindgren, S. (2011). YouTube gunmen? Mapping participatory media discourse on school shooting videos. *Media Culture & Society*, *33*(1), 123–136. DOI: 10.1177/0163443710386527

Machin, D., & Mayr, A. (2012). *How to Do Critical Discourse Analysis: A Multimodal Introduction*. Sage Publications Ltd.

Maguire, B., Weatherby, G. A., & Mathers, R. A. (2002). Network news coverage of school shootings. *The Social Science Journal, 39*(3), 465–470. DOI: 10.1016/S0362-3319(02)00201-X

Muschert, G. W. (2002). *Media and massacre: The social construction of the Columbine story* (Unpublished doctoral thesis). Boulder, CO: University of Colorado.

Muschert, G. W. (2009). Frame-changing in the media coverage of a school shooting: The rise of Columbine as a national concern. *The Social Science Journal, 46*(1), 164–170.

Muschert, G. W. (2019). Afterword: The Columbine Effect on Culture, Policy, and Me. *Journal of Contemporary Criminal Justice, 35*(3), 357–372.

Ramanathan, R., & Tan, B. H. (2015). Application of critical discourse analysis in media discourse studies. *The Southeast AsianJournal of English Language & Studies, 21*(2), 57–68.

Reese, S. D., & Shoemaker, P. J. (2016). A Media Sociology for the Networked Public Sphere: The Hierarchy of Influences Model. *Mass Communication & Society, 19*(4), 389–410. DOI: 10.1080/15205436.2016.1174268

Roberts, J. (2019). Citizen journalism. *The international encyclopedia of media literacy*, 1(2), 1-10.

Schildkraut, J., & Muschert, G. W. (2014). Media Salience and the Framing of Mass Murder in Schools: A Comparison of the Columbine and Sandy Hook Massacres. *Homicide Studies, 18*(1), 23–43.

Schudson, M. (2003). *The Sociology of News*. W. W. Norton.

Silva, J. (2024). Public mass shootings in developed countries: Uncovering stability and change at the turn of the century. *Global Crime, 25*(1), 119–142. DOI: 10.1080/17440572.2023.2271848

Silva, J. R., & Lankford, A. (2022). The globalization of American mass shootings? An assessment of fame-seeking perpetrators and their influence worldwide. *International Journal of Comparative and Applied Criminal Justice, 48*(2), 119–142. DOI: 10.1080/01924036.2022.2162095

Skogan, W. G. (1993). The Various Meanings of Fear. In *The Fear of Crime and Criminal Victimization* (pp. 131-140). London, UK: Enke.

Strauss, A., & Corbin, J. M. (1990). *Basics of qualitative research: Grounded theory procedures and techniques*. Sage Publications, Inc.

Tarrant, W. D. (1957). Who Writes Letters to the. Editor? *The Journalism Quarterly, 34*(4), 501–502. DOI: 10.1177/107769905703400412

van Dijk, T. A. (1998). Editorial: Discourse and Ideology. *Discourse & Society, 9*(3), 307–308. DOI: 10.1177/0957926598009003001

van Leeuwen, T. (1996). The Representation of Social Actors. In Caldas-Coulthard, C. R., & Coulthard, M. (Eds.), *Texts and Practices: Readings in Critical Discourse Analysis* (pp. 32–70). Routledge.

Zhang, M. (2014). A Critical Discourse Analysis of Political News Reports. *Theory and Practice in Language Studies, 4*(11), 2273–2277. DOI: 10.4304/tpls.4.11.2273-2277

KEY TERMS AND DEFINITIONS

Bullying Narrative: A narrative predicated on the idea that the perpetrators of Columbine were bullied and the attack was their way of seeking "revenge" on their bullies.

Content Analysis: A research method whereby data sharing common concepts is coded into categories.

Critical Discourse Analysis: A research method that looks at linguistic techniques to provide a deeper examination of language and how power is reproduced within society.

Moral Panic: A societal reaction to a certain condition, episode, individual or group of persons. Folk devils represent the target of deviancy. The level of concern felt is overinflated to the actual risk posed.

School Shooting: A specific type of mass violence, involving a perpetrator(s) trying to shoot and kill as many people as possible in an educational institution.

ENDNOTE

1 Letters for Daily News and New York Post were unavailable.

Chapter 15
Conspiracy Theories Eroding Institutional Confidence:
Past and Present

Komanduri S. Murty
https://orcid.org/0000-0003-2402-3285
Fort Valley State University, USA

Johnny R. Green
Fort Valley State University, USA

ABSTRACT

Conspiracy theories have unarguably played a significant role in eroding institutional confidence both in the past and present. Historically, they have often thrived during periods of significant events and crisis situations, offering alternative explanations to undermine official narratives and erode trust in established authorities. The proliferation of social media in recent times has amplified the reach and impact of conspiracy theories. In the United States, as seen in this chapter, confidence in most political and non-political institutions has fallen dramatically over the past 50 years, largely due to dissatisfaction with governmental and institutional accountability as well as skepticism about the institutional competency and responsiveness within the climate of political polarization, partisan motives, and growing divisiveness—ricocheting on each other. Eroding confidence poses challenges to effective functioning of institutions in a democratic society by sowing doubt about their credibility and intentions.

INTRODUCTION

Conspiracy theories are oppositional social constructs geared toward malevolent or forbidden acts, essentially retrodictive, and are epistemically risky (Douglas and Sutton 2023). Their purpose is to instill fear in outgroup (existential) while simultaneously galvanizing ingroup support (social) for the conspirators' self-sustaining prophecies. Despite the common consensus that conspiracy theories are fanned by the internet and social media, they are rooted in long traditions throughout American history. Heated political contests, international conflicts, a growing antivaccine movement, the climate crisis, and the COVID-19 pandemic in recent years have triggered significant research interest in the impacts of con-

DOI: 10.4018/979-8-3693-7468-9.ch015

spiracy theories (Douglas, 2021). Research largely suggests that these impacts are generally negative, i.e., conspiracy theories tend to erode institutional confidence rather than providing relief to its functionality, sometimes by causing disengagement and other times by defiance. Although historians recorded a long list of conspiracy theories since the 18th century in America, this chapter focuses on selected episodes that gained wider public interest with lasting memory and eroded institutional confidence in multiple forms (e.g., decreased public support, damaged image and reputation, increased violence, loss of peace, power, money, and effectiveness).

CONSPIRACY THEORIES IN THE PAST

Thomas Jefferson's Election

When George Washington announced that he would not run for a third term in 1796, the Democratic-Republican caucus chose then 57-year-old Thomas Jefferson to run against the Federalist candidate John Adams for the presidency. Although Jefferson and Adams didn't personally campaign, following the aristocratic custom of the day, both campaigns did their best in circulating conspiracy theories—accusing Adams for lack of masculine virtues and Jefferson for fathering children with one of his slaves, Sally Hemings, as well as for having had plans to establish a Bonaparte-like dictatorship in America (Feuerherd, 2016; Onuf, n.d.). Lerche, Jr. (1948) chronicled in his case study of Jefferson and the election of 1800 how the Federalists campaigned against Jefferson by smearing his morality and reputation to give their party a mass base. The anti-Jefferson conspiracy theories charged him with atheism (Jefferson actually believed in Jesus Christ but dismissed the Resurrection and miracles of the Gospels), "impractical" dreaming, disrespect to Washington, and connection to the French Revolution. He was also accused, in propaganda pamphlets and newspaper editorials, of being a coward; personally, morally, and sexually immoral; dishonest to business affairs; and politically inefficient—all of which were presumably used to disqualify him from becoming the President. These efforts created a feeling among the public that no good could come out of an atheist and an infidel like Jefferson. Jefferson's *Notes on Virginia,* where he commented about the probable biological differences between the white and black races were characterized as his denial of the so-called "brotherhood doctrine," of a man and the notion of the "chosen people." Federalist propagandists also highlighted Jefferson's letter to his Italian friend in 1796 (the "Mazzei letter"), wherein he discusses aristocratic Federalist politics in deliberate attempt to insult Washington and to disrespect the Constitution, while labeling him as "pro-French." An anti-Jeffersonian/Democratic Republican editorial by a person calling himself "Burleigh," tried to instill horror among citizens by portraying that Jefferson, if elected, would be disastrous to the nation with awful consequences like civil war, robberies, rapes, adultery, and incest along with public distrust, blood of widows and orphans, intrusion of foreign troops into the country, and a nation turned dark with crimes—primarily because of the fundamental difference between the preferences of Federalists for an industrial based and commercial economy versus that of Jefferson for agriculture. Some Federalists like Timothy Dwight and Jedidiah Morse also tried to stoke the public's fear of the Illuminati's (a secret society to establish a New World Order) infiltration of the United States (Dickey, 2020). Although the hysteria ended after the election, Federalists continued to waste their time, effort, and money in fueling a fire against Jefferson during and after his term of office without much success. Jefferson pleaded for national unity, completed his first term peacefully in both domestic and foreign arenas by building economic prosperity and lowering taxes, while also reducing the national debt among other successes, which helped him to win a second term with an overwhelming majority. He secured 162 electoral votes against his Federalist opponent, Charles Pinckney, the vice-presidential candidate in 1800, who secured only 14 votes. Federalists, though demoralized, disorganized, and following a "prigarchy" (prig + aristocracy, as Jefferson called it), continued their smear tactics by alleging that Jefferson had relations with his slave, Sally Hemings, and denouncing his popular Louisiana purchase (Onuf, n.d.; Silk, 2016; Theriault, 2006).

Crash of the Hindenburg

The German passenger airship LZ 129 Hindenburg caught fire as it approached a landing area (while less than 300 feet from the ground) and burnt in 30 seconds on May 6, 1937, at Lakehurst Naval Air Station in New Jersey. The reports showed that the airship followed normal landing procedures but struggled just before dropping its cables for the final stage of landing. It was carrying 97 people, of whom 35 passengers along with one crewman on the ground died in the fire. The newsreel footage revealed that the airship took a sharp turn to starboard while dropping three separate ballasts before lowering the land lines. Not long after the crash, several conspiracy theories emerged. Some questioned the ingenuity of newsreel footage, i.e., why it didn't show the exact moment of catching fire but showed only after the ship was consumed by flames. They speculated that a U.S. military aircraft deliberately brought down the Hindenburg airship with an intention of damaging Nazi Germany's industrial capabilities. Others pondered if it was the act of angry farmers, who might have shot in the direction of the Nazi airship as it was flying over their homes and land, thereby a bullet might have struck the airship and caused fire. Yet others blamed the airship for carrying large amounts of hydrogen gas as fuel, which is highly explosive and potentially dangerous in mid-air. Still others predicted it could be merely a mechanical fault or a static shock that was responsible for the spark that ignited the hydrogen inside the airship (Harvey, 2016). One correspondent guessed that it was an inside job, that is, the Nazis themselves blew up the airship to claim insurance money; and another believed that the airship had been shot down by a New York police lieutenant on the orders of Mayor Fiorello La Guardia. Some doubted if the airship was carrying a hidden bomb in its interior, which was accidentally activated either by a timer or by a barometric pressure change (Daugherty, 2023).

According to Addison Bain (1999), a retired NASA scientist in the field of hydrogen, who proposed the incendiary paint hypothesis in 1996, the fire was initially started by a special paint that was used on the aircraft exterior. However, contrary to his claims, no one reported a garlic smell at the time of explosion, nor was the fire blue, but rather bright red (Stomberg, 2012). In addition, this theory was refuted by Dessler, et al (2005). They concluded after examining Bain's theory experimentally and quantitively, that the aluminum-powder paint used on the Hindenburg would have taken about 40 hours (far more time than 34 seconds that it actually took) to burn the airship, even if the paint was the cause of fire, which they doubted. To date, the mystery of Hindenburg remains unsolved. Yet, the disaster "provided a gloomy lead-up to World War II" (Goldman, 2013, para 5).

Bombing of Pearl Harbor

Japan bombed the U.S. naval base at Pearl Harbor in Hawaii on December 7, 1941, killing 2,403 men and forcing America's entry into World War II (Nelson, 2016). This attack has been the subject of various conspiracy theories including: (a) the "warmonger" President Franklin D. Roosevelt (FDR) welcomed the attack from Japan, to trick the U.S. Congress and Americans into welcoming his intention to support Britain against Nazi Germany; (b) Japan was intentionally provoked to react toward the U.S. after the U.S. imposed severe conditions so that FDR could support Prime Minister Churchill and other allies to win against Nazi Germany (for example, a 1944 declassified memo from Lieutenant Commander Arthur H. McCollum outlined actions to provoke Japan, stating that: *It is not believed in the present state of political opinion the United States government is capable of declaring war against Japan without more ado. … if by these means Japan could be led to commit an overt act of war, so much the better*); (c) the U.S. leaders knew about the bomb plot but deliberately withheld it from Pearl Harbor commanders; (d) the U.S. military did not heed the warning provided by the USS Ward, A U.S. destroyer, or did not believe it, or simply were unable to react in time; and, (e) FDR lied to maintain his protective quality by announcing that only 300 people had died when it was actually 2,403—thereby giving an impression to the American public that it wasn't as bad as they might have thought (LaBianca 2024). Some historians did not subscribe to the notion that FDR let it happen to garner public support for America's entry into World War II. For example, Roosevelt biographer, Jean Edward Smith, found that FDR was totally caught off guard by the attack and that there was no evidence that anyone in Washington knew about Japanese moving on Pearl Harbor (NPR, 2016; Reynolds, 2001, p.163). FDR wanted to prevent the Japanese conquest of China by "temporarily halting negotiations with Japanese diplomats, instituting a full embargo on exports to Japan, freezing Japanese assets in U.S. banks, and sending supplies to China along the Burma Road" (Office of the Historian n.d., para 4). And there was no evidence that U.S. leaders withheld a key warning about the Japan's imminent attack from Pearl Harbor commanders (Hanyok, 2009). Yet, other historians like Robert Stinnett (1999) concluded that the attack was FDR's effort to provoke Japan into military action, consistent with his administration's policy for the entire preceding year (Bernstein, 1999). The lack of scholarly consensus as to whether FDR wanted to take the nation to war in 1941, and if so, did he seek full-scale intervention in the European war—left some Americans with distrust of government and doubting FDR's role in the Pearl Harbor attack, even today.

Kennedy Assassination

President John F. Kennedy (JFK) was gunned down on November 22, 1963, as he rode in a motorcade through Dallas. The assassin was identified as 24-year-old former U.S. Marine, Lee Harvey Oswald, who was killed two days later by Jack Ruby (a nightclub owner who was convicted of murder but died before a new trial could start) while being taken to Dallas County Jail. Subsequently, President Lyndon B. Johnson appointed the Warren Commission to investigate the incident, which concluded that Oswald had acted alone in killing JFK (Kiger, 2013; Donovan, 2024). Despite the Commission's official conclusion, Ruby's infamous act spawned numerous conspiracy theories about his motive and JFK's assassination. As for Ruby's motive, some thought that he was an assassin's assassin of the fallen U.S. president and therefore his act was justified; meanwhile others viewed him as a confused loser, lost soul, and became a pawn in a murder conspiracy (Donovan, 2024). What actually motivated Ruby to interfere with law enforcement and shoot Oswald is still unknown, but it opened doors for conspiracy theories about JFK's assassination, especially in the absence of Oswald's testimony. Some speculated that the Cuban dictator Fidel Castro plotted with Oswald to assassinate JFK as revenge for the Bay of Pigs invasion (Pruitt 2017); some, like William Lester, thought that JFK's assassination was part of the CIA's UFO cover-up (Daily Mail, 2011); others thought that the Federal Reserves did it because his Executive Order 11110 to issue silver certificates had the potential to put the Reserve Bank of New York out of business (X,

2011); some like the New Orleans Assistant District Attorney Edward Gillin, entertained the possibility of Oswald acting as "Manchurian Candidate" under the influence of LSD, a mind control drug (Ayton 2009), among other possibilities like involvement of the "Umbrella Man" (Nakatani, 2023) or mafia (Bertram, 2020). All of these conspiracy theories were debunked by Paul Gregory (currently a research fellow at the Hoover Institution and the Cullen Professor Emeritus at the University of Houston), who, per an interview with Paul Robinson, knew Oswald and testified before the Warren Commission. Gregory demonstrated that "Lee Harvey Oswald indeed killed Kennedy and acted alone—and that the Oswald he once called a friend had the motive, the intelligence, and the means to commit one of the most shocking crimes in American history" (Robinson, 2023, para 1). Additionally, several related documents that were declassified and made public over the past sixty years did not support any of the conspiracy theories (Pruitt, 2017). Even then, a CBS poll found that 61 percent of American adults nationwide continue to believe others, in addition to Oswald, were involved in the assassination of President Kennedy (Dutton et al., 2013). Larry Sabato, an American political scientist at the University of Virginia, who dug into the declassified JFK assassination files, blamed the Trump and Biden administrations for not releasing all of the files pertaining to that fateful day and postponing the release date multiple times, although they were supposed to be released by 2017—which, in his opinion, enabled conspiracy theories to persist. On the other hand, Gerald Posner, author of *Case Closed: Lee Harvey Oswald and the Assassination of JFK,* maintained that Americans would never feel that the case was really settled, given that Oswald never went to trial (Waxman, 2023). In any case, these conspiracy theories eroded public confidence in the government, law enforcement, and the Warren Commission.

Watergate

In the Watergate scandal, which began on June 17, 1972, five burglars were allegedly hired by the Committee to Re-elect the President (CREEP) Richard Nixon, and were subsequently caught breaking into the Democratic National Committee headquarters at the Watergate Complex in Washington, D.C. The break-in, as investigations unearthed, was a part of political conspiracy of high-level government officials to conceal such illegal activities as wiretapping, political espionage, and attempts to subvert the democratic election process. The involvement of the White House became clear through journalist investigations, congressional hearings, and the work of special prosecutors. Secret "smoking-gun" tapes recorded in the Oval Office revealed Nixon's involvement in the cover-up and his knowledge of the break-in. Nixon's relentless but unsuccessful attempts to protect himself and his allies while obstructing justice at every stage resulted in his resignation in August 1974, which rocked the nation. In later years, pro-Nixon revisionists came up with several conspiracy theories: Democrat Trap Theory, CIA Trap Theory, Blackmail Demand Theory, CIA Foreknowledge Theory, and Deep Throat Theory—all in efforts to "prove that the whole episode was a dirty trick perpetrated upon, rather than by, Richard Nixon" (Rosenbaum 1982, 15). The Watergate scandal and subsequent efforts to cover it up dropped Nixon's approval rates from 68 percent in January 1973 to 48 percent in April 1973 to 31 percent in August 1973; a whopping 71 percent viewed Nixon as culpable in wrongdoing; and 37 percent thought Nixon had foreknowledge of the bugging and tried to cover it up (Kohut 2014). Though the Senate voted 82-4 in January 1975 to form the U.S. Senate Select Committee to Study Governmental Operations with Respect to Intelligence Activities, which was chaired by Sen. Frank Church (commonly known as Church Committee), it could not restore public confidence as more mistakes and crimes were uncovered by the Committee (e.g., the wiretapping of Martin Luther King, Jr. by NSA and wiretapping by the FBI under J. Edgar Hoover), and there were more suspicions among the public about government and public officials (U.S. Senate Historical Office 1976; Young 2015). Even after about 50 years, 38 percent opposed the Nixon pardon in a 2018 poll by *The Economist* and YouGov (Hughes, n.d.). To this day, the term "Watergate" stands akin to political corruption and dirty tricks.

CONSPIRACY THEORIES IN THE PRESENT

9/11

On September 11, 2001, a series of coordinated terrorist attacks occurred in the United States. Nineteen militant suicide operatives (working in three teams of five and one team of four) associated with al-Qaeda, the Islamist extremist group (led by Osama Bin Laden) from Afghanistan, hijacked four passenger planes. They crashed two planes into the Twin Towers of the World Trade Center in New York, causing the buildings to collapse. Another plane struck the Pentagon near Washington, D.C., and the fourth crashed in Pennsylvania without reaching its destination after passengers fought back. In total, 2,977 people lost their lives, including 2,606 people—then or later because of injuries—at the Twin Towers in New York, 125 people at the Pentagon, and 246 passengers and crew aboard the four planes (Jackson, 2021). Several more people were injured in this deadliest terrorist attack on U.S. soil, which was televised worldwide. It remains an unforgettable traumatic event for many and earned nickname "9/11." In the following year, 2002, the 9/11 Commissions (formally known as the National Commission on Terrorist Attacks Upon the United States) was established and its report (2004) chronicled a comprehensive account of circumstances surrounding the attacks, including preparedness and the immediate response, along with its recommendations to enhance future security against such threats. Despite the live televised broadcast in real time and the subsequent 9/11 Commission report, conspiracy theories continued to develop. Most prominent of them were: Controlled Demolition Theory (rejecting the collapse of the Twin Towers by the impact by planes' crash and fire); Pentagon Missile Theory (suggesting that the Pentagon was hit by a missile launched by elements within the U.S. Government); Remote-Controlled planes (claiming that planes were remotely controlled as in videogames); Foreknowledge Theory (suspecting that authorities had advance knowledge of the attacks, and either ignored or assisted the attackers); and Geostrategic Motives (arguing that the attacks were used to justify U.S. invasions of Afghanistan and Iraq, even though Iraq was not directly related to 9/11). The official investigations and independent review have consistently rejected these conspiracy theories (see for example, Dunbar & Reagan, 2006; Sardarizadeh, 2021).

The attacks shook the nation so badly that in the aftermath, the public came together in a spirit of sadness and renewed patriotism. Their confidence was high in the government not only in its efforts to respond to the attacks that just occurred (i.e., wars in Afghanistan and Iraq) but also in its plans to intercept and prevent future attacks (including strong support to the 2001 Patriot Act). Confidence in journalism was also high as Americans couldn't turn away from the coverage. The 9/11 attacks and government response were also chiefly responsible for President George W. Bush's win for a second term in 2004. However, that trust and confidence didn't last long (Elliott, 2021). Public confidence in government fell from 73 percent in 2002 to 37 percent in 2008 per a Pew survey (Pew Research Center, 2008). In 2019, 64 percent of veterans and 62 percent of American adults said that the war in Iraq was not worth fighting, whereas 55 percent of veterans and 58 percent of

American adults said the war in Afghanistan was not worth fighting, that is, considering the costs versus the benefits to the U.S. (Igielnik & Parker, 2019). Furthermore, in a 2021 Pew survey 69 percent of U.S. adults said that the U.S. failed to achieve its goals in Afghanistan (Hartig & Doherty 2021).

WMDs in Iraq

The U.S. and its allies invaded Iraq in March 2003 based on the belief (or relying on false evidence) that Saddam Hussein's regime possessed weapons of mass destruction (WMDs) and that it would pass them to terrorist networks (Doherty and Kiley 2023). Collin Powell, then the Secretary of State, presented evidence (later determined false) of WMDs in Iraq to the United Nations Security Council on February 5, 2003 (Brook, 2021), which significantly impacted U.S. public opinion (Doherty & Kiley, 2023). To the contrary, the earlier search in January 2003, for WMDs in Iraq by the United Nations Monitoring, Verification, and Inspection Commission (UNMOVIC) and later search in September 2003 by the U.S.-led Iraq Survey Group (ISG) showed no "smoking guns," as the chief weapons inspector, Hans Blix expressed (Bryan & Hopper, 2005; Cleminson 2003). The CIA also later confirmed that Iraq had no stockpiles of illicit weapons at the time of the invasion (Mitchell, 2023). Charles Duelfer, the chief inspector of the ISG, testified before congress in October 2004 that the 16-month investigation concluded that Saddam Hussein had no chemical weapons, no biological weapons, and no capacity to make nuclear weapons (Bryan & Hopper, 2005). Saddam Hussein all along denied having WMDs before invasion (in a 12,000-page WMD report to the U.N. in response to Resolution 1441) and during interrogation after the invasion, claiming that the U.S. invented them as a pretext for war. Documents captured in Iraq also revealed that Iraq had nothing hidden (Alterman & Zornick, 2008; Mitchell, 2023). Nonetheless, conspiracy theories like the WMDs were hidden in underground bunkers or stolen by Syrian terrorists, emerged (Greenwald, 2007). Surprisingly, in a 2015 survey conducted by Fairleigh Dickinson University, 42 percent of American participants (comprising 51% Republicans and 32% Democrats) believed that U.S. forces found WMDs Iraq (Haq, 2015)—a powerful belief hard to dislodge. On the other hand, the incorrect assertions of WMDs in Iraq and their use to build support for war within America and among its allied nations caused irreversible damage to the credibility of U.S. intelligence. Only 18 percent of American adults reportedly had "a great deal" of confidence, 49 percent had "some" confidence, and 31 percent had "hardly" any confidence in the government's intelligence agencies, according to a poll conducted by the Associated Press-NORC Center for Public Affairs Research (Merchant, 2023)

Obama's "Birther" Movement

Conspiracy theories about President Barak Obama's birthplace began circulating as soon as he announced candidacy for President in 2008. Allegedly started by disgruntled Hillary Clinton supporters during Democratic primaries, the theories spread quickly, and in response, Obama released a photocopy of his short form of birth certificate in 2008, showing Honolulu, Hawaii as his birthplace. Obama critics questioned the authenticity of the form and demanded a long-form certificate from the hospital where he was born. In his general election against the Republican nominee John McCain, a woman on McCain's campaign trail yelled that Obama was an 'Arab,' which McCain quickly denounced by saying that he was a "decent person." (Zurcher, 2016). After Obama won the election, during his first term in office several conservatives attempted, but repeatedly failed, to challenge his eligibility. For example: (1) Carl Swensson led some campaigners who claimed to expose conspiracy behind Obama's birth certificate by forming "citizen grand juries" to indict Obama (Weigel 2009) and failed; (2) a group of 172 persons declared themselves a "Super American Grand Jury" and voted to charge Obama with treason, which the Judge dismissed (Weissman, 2009); and (3) a conservative Israeli-American activist Orly Taitz filed unsuccessful lawsuits to prove that President Obama is not a natural born citizen as required by Constitution. In *Taitz v. Obama, 2010,* the federal district judge Royce Lamberth dismissed her case and wrote that "This Court is not willing to go tilting at windmills with her." Disagreeing with the Court decision, the real estate mogul Donald Trump seized the opportunity and ran with it, by saying that he had "real doubts" about Obama's birthplace and offered a million dollars to a charity of Obama's choice if Obama releases his college and passport records. The White House released the long form of Obama's birth certificate in 2011 (Trotta, 2012). Trump continued his attacks by tweeting in 2012 that some "extremely credible source" told him that Obama's birth certificate was a fraud; by suspecting in 2013 that the Hawaiian health official who verified Obama's birth certificate had died in a plane crash; by asking hackers in 2014 to access Obama's college records to check his birthplace; and more until he finally conceded in September 2016 (Zurcher, 2016; Krieg, 2016). Ciara O'Rourke, a contributing writer for PolitiFact, wrote that "In the year 2021, more than four years since former President Barak Obama left office—more than 13 since he was first elected president—we are still encountering claims questioning his citizenship and his birth certificate" (O'Rourke, 2021, para1).

COVID-19

This is a perfect example to show how conspiracy theories flourish in times of crisis when people feel threatened, uncertain, and insecure (Douglas 2021). President Trump knew, as he admitted to Bob Woodward in recorded interviews, that COVID-19 was more deadly than the flu, and yet he told American public that it was no worse than the flu. Perhaps his intention was good to keep public anxiety down, but this lie gave way to other conspiracy theories including: COVID-19 was a hoax; protective measures such as wearing a mask and maintaining 6-feet social distance were unnecessary; or increases in cases are the result of increased testing. Secondly, Trump and others relied on some questionable study's suggestion that hydroxychloroquine, the malaria drug, was effective for COVID treatment, which resulted in its initial emergency authorization by the Food and Drug Administration. Though the authorization was later revoked after realizing its risk of heart problems, it shattered public confidence in leaders' claims and guidance in the midst of the pandemic (Lewis, 2020; McLaughlin, 2020). As COVID-19 worsened in mid-2020 and 2021, some other conspiracy theories were circulated in social media and the Internet like COVID death rates are inflated; COVID is a plot by big pharma; the pandemic was manipulated by the 'deep state'; COVID-19 doesn't actually exist; GMO (genetically modified crops) were responsible for COVID; the U.S. military imported COVID into China; COVID was created as a biological weapon; the virus escaped from a Chinese lab, etc., although there is no evidence to prove any of them (Lynas 2020). The most consequential conspiracy theories are that COVID-19 vaccines don't work, they cause additional COVID-19 variants, they make people infertile, they are created from fetal tissues, they cause autism, and that they cause long-term complications (Cassata, 2021). Although many practicing physicians and health care agencies debunked these theories (Pertwee et al., 2022), several people believed that the vaccines harmed them (Mandavalli, 2024). Forty-six percent of those who did not get the vaccine and 63 percent of those fully not vaccinated said in a 2023 Pew survey, "we don't really know if there are serious health risks from these [COVID-19] vaccines"—a sign of ambivalence (Funk et al., 2023). These conspiracy theories also eroded public confidence in social media—69 percent doubted social media and 67 percent were concerned about foreign interference in social media, according to a 2020 NPR/Ipsos poll (Rose, 2020). Pummererer et al., (2021) set out to test the relationship between the political COVID-19 conspiracy and institutional trust. They found that both believing in and being confronted with a COVID-19 conspiracy theory decreased institutional trust, support for governmental regulations, adoption of physical distancing, and to a certain extent, social engagement. This put institutions at a disadvantage by undermining their efforts to a successful mitigation of the spread of COVID-19.

2020 Presidential Election Results (Stolen Election Conspiracy)

The 2020 presidential election generated many conspiracy theories from QAnon, Proud Boys, and other far-right conservative groups to validate Trump's unfounded claims. Some of the notorious claims that these theories made were that: the Dominion voting machines changed or deleted votes for Trump, sharpie markers invalidated Trump votes in Arizona, mail-in voting was wrought with widespread fraud, people were throwing out bags of ballots or finding suitcases full of ballots, poll watchers were blocked from observing, thousands of votes were cast by dead people, or people were voting multiple times—all to justify their overarching claim that the elections were rigged. But the evidence did not support any of them and all of them were debunked (Cohen, 2021). When the late counting of mail ballots in various states changed an apparent Trump's led to Biden's win, the election result deniers quickly embraced "Stop the Steal" slogan. Trump's loyal supporters were determined to overturn the 2020 election of Joe Biden. For example, Ginni Thomas, the hard-right conservative, texted Mark Meadows, then White House Chief of Staff, in the immediate aftermath of the 2020 election urging him to do all he could to overturn Biden's victory (Pilkington, 2022). That didn't work. Sixty-two lawsuits challenged the results of 2020 election, and 61 of them failed (Moniz, 2024). Wheeler's (2021) detailed analysis of these court rulings showed how Trump's election litigation efforts failed decisively. On January 6, 2021, when the Congress officially met, counted the 2020 electoral votes, and concluded that Joe Biden was the next president of the United States, a mob of Trump supporters (summoned by Trump) attacked the U.S. Capitol building in Washington, D.C. Trump justified the attack in his tweet: "These are the things and events that happen when sacred landslide election victory is so unceremoniously & viciously stripped away from great patriots who have been badly & unfairly treated for so long" (Lima, 2021). Within hours, owing to public pressure and risk of further incitement of violence, social media providers (Facebook, Twitter, and YouTube) removed a video in which Trump addressed the mob and then froze Trump's accounts (Cohen, 2021). In the following months and years, "more than 1,230 people have been charged with federal crimes in the riot, ranging from misdemeanor offenses like trespassing to felonies like assaulting police officers and sedition conspiracy" and "roughly 730 people have pleaded guilty of charges, while another roughly 170 have been convicted of at least one charge at a trial decided by a judge or jury…only two defends have been acquitted of all charges" (Durkin & Kunzelman, 2024, para 9). On July 1, 2021, the House Select Committee was formed to investigate the January 6th attack on the U.S. Capitol (commonly referred to as the January 6th Committee). According to the testimonies heard before the January 6th Committee on October 13, 2022: "Donald Trump knew he lost [his reelection bid]. Despite this knowledge, Donald Trump went to court to contest the 2020 election, and he lost in court. The Electoral College met and declared Joe Biden the winner, yet Donald Trump continued to pull out all the stops in his attempt to stay in power" (NPR, 2022, para 7). Thus, the stolen conspiracy theory, which was widely propagated by Trump had never been substantiated and was thoroughly debunked (Pilkington, 2022), but Trump never conceded and continued pushing allegations of fraud to justify his actions even after he left the White House. The upside-down (inverted) American flag emerged as a pro-Trump symbol (Stanton, 2024). The 2020 NPR/Ipsos poll showed that one-third of Americans believed that voter fraud helped Joe Biden win the 2020 election, although courts, election officials, and the Justice Department consistently found no evidence to support Trump's allegation of fraud (Rose 2020). Some viewed Trump as politically toxic and blamed him for losses in 2022 Senate and House elections (Ramirez, 2024). Trump's role in the January 6, 2021, attack on the U.S. Capitol made his eligibility for the 2024 presidential election questionable (Fritze, 2024). Though he survived this challenge, he could not re-establish confidence either among undecided voters or among his former employees. For example, A 21-year-old Arnel Ramos, a food service worker from Milwaukee responded to Trump's speech after he was nominated by the Republican National Convention (RNC) on July 18, 2024: "You read a lot of stuff about what this guy says, but to sit down and hear it and sit through it, it was just insane to me. … That is the only way I can describe this whole ordeal" (Reed, 2024, para 3). And Trump's former secretary Ivan Raiklin said that she was "particularly disturbed by the way he [Trump] linked immigrants to destruction and disease, and the way he described the nation as being on the brink of 'World War III'" (Reed, 2024, para 4). The mainstream news channels confirmed that Trump's 93-minute speech (accepting the GOP nomination) contained false claims and provided evidence on several topics, from taxes to foreign policy (e.g., Timm & Kamisar, 2024).

Assassination Attempt on Donald Trump

On July 13, 2024, a 20-year-old Thomas Matthew Crooks allegedly attempted to assassinate the would be Republican presidential nominee (declared the following week at the Milwaukee convention) Donald Trump for a second term while he was at a campaign rally in Butler, Pennsylvania. Mr. Crooks fired multiple shots from a rooftop that skimmed Trump's right ear, injured two spectators, and killed another spectator—identified as a 50-year-old Corey Comperatore. Secret service agents killed the suspect, Mr. Crooks, by returning fire within 43 seconds (Herb & And one, 2024). Within hours conspiracy theories erupted online with doctored and fake images, claiming that the assassination attempt was "staged" as a ploy to boost Trump's popularity in November's election (Davis, 2024), a theory which gained major traction. Thirty-three percent of Biden supporters and 12 percent of Trump supporters believed in the "staged" theory; and 38 percent blamed Trump for creating the surge toward violence in American politics, according to a poll conducted by Morning Consult, an American business intelligence company (Mayer, 2024). Interestingly, nearly one-half of profiles on X (formerly Twitter), Facebook, Instagram, and TikTok spreading the "staged" theory were fake accounts, according to Cyabra, the social media analysis company (Bowman, 2024). Other posts centered around the Secret Service agents. For example, in a post viewed seven million times, a conservative political commentator Rogan O'Handley wrote: "People were screaming about a man on the roof with a gun/ But Secret Service waited/ They waited for him to take the shots/ Then they killed the shooter/ It was a setup/ And he wasn't supposed to miss" (Ryan, 2024). Rep. Marjorie Taylor Greene (R-Ga.) questioned if the Secret Service was engaged in a "conspiracy to kill" Trump; Eric Trump implied in his appearance in Fox News that Democrats were somehow behind it; and Rep. Scott Perry (R-Pa.) and Donald Trump Jr. repeatedly suggested that the shooter did not act alone (Shuham, 2024). All these theories were debunked by the evidence and suggested that Mr. Crooks (the shooter) acted alone. The motive of the shooter is still unknown, but the mounting pressure resulted in the resignation of the Secret Service Director, Kimberly Cheatle on July 23, 2024. About 53 percent of Biden supporters and 52 percent of Trump supporters in the Morning Consult poll feared the likelihood of escalating violence as the presidential election nears voting in November 2024 (Mayer, 2024). Overall, the incident has certainly shaken public confidence and raised questions about security, riots, gun violence, and increased rhetoric—all of which can be traced back to two sources—judicial activism and the polarized political climate.

The two aforementioned sources of shaken public confidence are largely viewed to have manifested from the lack of term limits in the legislative and judicial branches. The lack of term limits in the judicial branch resulted in tilting the balance of the U.S. Supreme Court justice nominations, which enabled infamous decisions along justices' ideological differences, such as overturning *Roe v. Wade* (the Dobbs decision). The ruling drastically dropped public confidence in the Supreme Court over the past year and reached a new low in Gallup's 50-year trend (Newport, 2023). Other controversial decisions included striking down the use of race as an explicit factor in college admissions (ignoring historical racism) in *Students for Fair Admissions v. President and Fellows of Harvard College* (public support 50-50), upholding racial gerrymandering in South Carolina (public support 33-67), providing immunity from prosecution on charges that former President Trump plotted to subvert the 2020 election (public support 27-74; also, Justice Sonia Sotomayor wrote in her dissent that this ruling creates a "law free zone" and makes presidents "kings"), and, siding with a rioter in the Capitol attack on January 6, 2021 by ruling that prosecutors may not use a federal obstruction charge against him (public support 29-71) (Liptak et al., 2024). Ian Millhiser, an American legal journalist and senior correspondent for Vox, commented that "the Court's Republican supermajority does not always follow the law, especially when the law cuts against the Republican Party's preferred outcome" (Millhiser, 2024, para 12).

Likewise, the polarized political climate with increased rhetoric from both left-wing and right-wing extremists endures because of the lack of term limits for legislators in Congress. President Biden is apparently planning to propose: (a) a new law that would establish term limits for Supreme Court justices; (2) a new law that would establish external enforcement of the Supreme Court ethics code (e.g., a requirement to disclose gifts and donations they received); and (c) a constitutional amendment that would limit the scope of presidential immunity. The first two proposals require passage from both the House and Senate to become laws, while the third proposal needs be ratified by three-fourths of the 50 states after it is formally introduced in Congress (Dallas, 2024). Fifty-eight percent (69% of Biden supporters and 54% of Trump supporters) of all surveyed by Redfield & Wilton Strategies for *Newsweek* on June 11-12, 2024, expressed support for Biden's proposal on Supreme Court term limits, while only 13 percent opposed, and others were indifferent (Shoaib, 2024). But no one knows if or when these proposals would be taken up by Congress and what their fate would be. Even if they all do materialize into laws, they won't fix all the problems, but they would be a step forward in the right direction.

STRATEGIES FOR DISRUPTING THE SPREAD OF CONSPIRACY THEORIES AND BUILDING SOCIETAL RESILIENCE

Researchers suggest that combining technological tools with human intelligence and oversight can create a robust defense against the spread of conspiracy theories. Below are the strategies that leverage both technology and human intelligence:

1. AI and Machine Learning

    a. Detection and Analysis: AI systems can automatically detect and analyze social media accounts spreading disinformation. For example, MIT's RIO program uses AI to identify disinformation narratives and the accounts spreading them with high precision (McGovern, 2021).
    b. Distinguishing Truth from Fiction: Machine Learning tools can differentiate between conspiracy theories and true conspiracies by analyzing the structure and connections within narratives (Tangherlini, 2020). It helps with prebunking and debunking misinformation.
2. Human Oversight and Expertise
    a. Fact-Checking: Human fact-checkers can verify information flagged by AI systems, ensuring accuracy and providing context (Hashemi-Pour, 2024). Platforms like Snopes, FactCheck.org., and PolitiFact are examples of this measure.
    b. Educational Campaigns: Experts can create educational content to inform the public about how to recognize and critically evaluate conspiracy theories (Lord & Vogt 2021).
3. Collaborative Platforms
    a. Crowdsourced Reporting: Platforms where users can report suspicious content can help gather data for AI systems to analyze (Onuoha, Pinder, & Schafer, 2015).
    b. Community Engagement: Engaging communities in discussions about media literacy and critical thinking can reduce the impact of conspiracy theories (Lord and Vogt 2021) because critical thinking fosters healthy skepticism—the ability to discern between reliable and unreliable information by spotting inconsistencies and thinking critically about information before accepting it at face value.
4. Policy and Regulation
    a. Platform Policies: Social media platforms can implement policies to limit the spread of disinformation, such as flagging or removing false content (Yaraghi, 2019). This not only improves transparency by flagging, but also prevents circulation by removing false content.
    b. Government Regulations: Governments can create regulations to hold platforms accountable for the spread of harmful content (Atkinson et al., 2021).
5. Technological Innovations:
    a. Early Warning Systems: AI tools can form the basis of early warning systems to alert authorities to online narratives that pose real-world threats (Tangherlini, 2020).
    b. Narrative Analysis: AI can analyze the sources and patterns of conspiracy theories to understand how they spread and how to counteract them (Kim 2021).

Thus, technology alone cannot completely resolve the menace of conspiracy theories, but it can certainly scale up human intelligence in detection and disruption of disinformation shared online and on social media. Other measures may include takedown requests, terms of service violations, and ongoing monitoring. Having some level-headed, society-wide conversations on balancing freedom of expression and privacy rights with security requirements may prove to be beneficial as well (Dattani, 2021).

CONCLUSION

Conspiracy theories are built on the basic assumption that a powerful person, or a group is acting in secret, thus creating and spreading suspicions toward powerful institutions (e.g., government, courts, political parties, national organizations, corporations, etc.). They appeared just a few years after the birth of the nation. Thomas Jefferson saw the Federalist Alexander Hamilton's conspiracy at the Constitutional Convention in June 1787, where Hamilton revealed himself as closest monarchist and declared that he preferred a lifetime president with an absolute veto power over all legislation (Hummel, 2024). Ever since, conspiracy theories have been on the rise, and they have propelled multifold in the last two or three decades, due in large part to the Internet and social media. Online platforms can act as "echo chambers" that reinforce and radicalize beliefs (Scott, 2024). A recent *Time* magazine article emphasized the use of social media to "radicalize and mobilize" violence in the Capitol attack on January 6, 2021. It also said that social media's role in spreading conspiracy theories was recognized and "enthusiastically welcomed" by far-right extremists as a "promising, cheap, and effective means" to "revolutionize modern terrorism" (Hoffman & Ware 2024). These widespread and widely circulated conspiracy theories did their job in eroding public trust and confidence by instilling fear in out groups while garnering support from in groups. Goldberg (2001) reported that 25 percent of Americans distrusted the federal government in 1964. Pew Research Center (2015) also reported that 77 percent trusted the federal government to do the right thing nearly always or most of the time, but it fell by more than half, to 36 percent, in the next decade due to the Vietnam War, civil unrest, and the Watergate scandal. By the end of the 1970s only one-quarter of Americans felt they could trust the government. Public confidence in government rebounded in the 1980s before falling again in the early to mid-1990s; it later rose again in the late 1990s as the economy improved. In early October 2001, i.e., a month after 9/11, 60 percent felt that they could trust the government, reaching the highest point in the last 40 years, but it didn't last long. By summer 2002, the trust level went down to 22 percent, where it stayed with mild fluctuation for the next two decades, i.e., till now. In addition, 60 percent feel frustrated—rather than angry or content—with the federal government, a feeling that has not changed either over the last few years, with the sole exception of the short period after Sept. 11, 2001 (Pew Research Center 2024).

Brady and Kent (2022) examined the 50 years of declining confidence and increasing polarization in trust among American institutions and found that: (1) confidence in the presidency has gone from "quite a lot" in the 1970s and 1980s (except for just after the Watergate scandal around 1972 to 1974) to just "some" in the last decade; (2) between the period of 1972 to 1979 and the period of 2010 to 2021, confidence in Congress declined by 45 percent; (3) confidence in the presidency and in the executive branch declined by about 20 percent; and, (4) confidence in the Supreme Court declined by 12 percent. The 2023 Gallup data showed public confidence in the Supreme Court at 27 percent and the presidency at 26 percent—slightly better than the Pew data. But the public confidence in Congress went down from 12 percent in 2021 to eight percent in 2023; in the criminal justice system from 20 percent in 2021 to 17 percent in 2023. Public confidence in media was 18 percent for newspapers, and 14 percent for television in 2023 (Saad, 2023). In Jones' (2022, para 9) assessment, several factors conspired since 2004 "to keep confidence down, including Iraq war, the Great depression and financial crisis, increasing partisan gridlock in Washington, a resurgence of populism, the COVID-19 pandemic, and inflation rate not seen for four decades."

Sen. Bernie Sanders' (I-VT) recent comments on the Republican nominee, Trump's strategic false narratives on social media about the crowd size at campaign events of his Democratic rival, Kamala Harris in 2024 presidential elections illustrate how conspiracy theories potentially erode institutional confidence (Bobic 2024, paras 3-4 &13):

> Donald Trump may be crazy, but he's not stupid. When he claims that 'nobody' showed up at a 10,000 person Harris-Walz rally in Michigan that was live-streamed and widely covered by the media, that it was all AI, and that Democrats cheat all of the time, there is a method to his madness. … Clearly,

> and dangerously, what Trump is doing is laying the groundwork for rejecting the election results if he loses. If you can convince your supporters that thousands of people who attended a televised rally do not exist, it will not be hard to convince them that the election returns in Pennsylvania, Michigan, and elsewhere are 'fake' and 'fraudulent.' ...This is what destroying faith in institutions is about. This is what undermining democracy is about. This is what fascism is about.

The consequences of eroded institutional confidence can be far-reaching and impactful. For example, eroded confidence in political institutions can lead to instability, civil disobedience, ineffective governance and policy implementation. This makes it harder to address epidemics, maintain faith in policing, and tackle issues like climate change, violence, and systemic racism. Low confidence in business institutions can discourage investment and economic growth, which in turn affects financial markets, business operations, and consumer behavior. Eroded institutional confidence in the judicial system undermines the rule of law and diminishes the legitimacy of court decisions. It threatens the very foundation of democracy. Eroded confidence in non-governmental organizations (NGOs) may result in a crisis around their credibility, funding sources, scandals, procyclicality and discontinuity. Eroded confidence in media may contribute to civic disengagement, loss of confidence in democracy, or damage in brand reputation of news organizations. Therefore, society's critical institutions—keeping aside their partisan motives and differences in ideologies—must do their part to restore public confidence and trust, especially in turbulent times to hold society together, not be divisive; to empower, not to tare down; and to prosper, not to hold back. Trusted messengers are needed to reduce the impact of conspiracy theories, but we seldom find them in today's world. Yet, the widespread acceptance of conspiracy theories can be countered by promoting analytic/critical thinking, which requires identifying inconsistencies in theories and seeking additional resources to verify information (Cookson, 2024; Swami et al., 2014). All the above discussed strategies to combine technological tools with human intelligence and oversight will certainly help in disrupting the spread of conspiracy theories.

LIMITATIONS

This chapter's focus is on conspiracy theories that are widely circulated and their role in eroding institutional confidence. As such, other aspects like what are the conspiration cognitive patterns and personality traits of conspirators, who believes in conspiracy theories and why, which conspiracy theories are real and which are unwarranted, and so on are beyond the scope of this chapter. Secondly, we recognize that conspiracy theories are not limited to any particular region or nation, and that they are prevalent among nations around the world, however, this chapter is primarily concerned with those in the United Studies. Third, we also recognize that conspiracy theories can vary significantly across various cultures, but no attempt to any cross-cultural comparison was made herein. Finally, this chapter did not attempt to collect any quantitative data, test empirical hypotheses, or to employ any correlates of conspiracy theories. Despite these limitations, this chapter aims to make a meaningful contribution to the study of the impact of ever-growing conspiracy theories in the contemporary social world and highlight key issues for further research and policy discussions.

REFERENCES

Alterman, E., & Zornick, G. (2008, June 12). Iraqi Weapons of Mass Destruction. *Center for American Progress*.https://www.americanprogress.org/article/think-again-iraqi-weapons-of-mass-destruction/

Atkinson, C., Barrett, P., Clarizio, L., Ghosh, D., Haigh, J., Melia, T., Posner, M., Schiller, V., & Watts, C. (2021). Recommendations to the Biden Administration: On Regulating Disinformation and Other Harmful Content on Social Media. *Harvard Kennedy School*.https://www.hks.harvard.edu/sites/default/files/centers/mrcbg/files/FWP_2021-02.pdf

Ayton, M. (2009, October 3). The JFK and RFK Assassinations and the "Manchurian Candidate" Theory. *Crime Magazine*.https://crimemagazine.com/jfk-and-rfk-assassinations-and-manchurian-candidate-theory

Bain, A. (1999). Colorless, non-radiant, blameless: A Hindenburg disaster study. *Gasbag Journal/Aerostation,* 39, 9-15.

Bernstein, R. (1999, December 15). 'Day of Deceit': On Dec.7, Did We Know We Knew? *The New York Times*.https://archive.nytimes.com/www.nytimes.com/books/99/12/12/daily/121599stinnett-book-review.html

Bertram, C. (2020, December 10). Did the Mob kill John F. Kennedy? *Biography*.https://www.biography.com/crime/did-the-mob-kill-john-f-kennedy

Bobic, I. (2024, August 13). Bernie Sanders Warns Donald Trump is Gearing Up to Deny 2024 Election Results. *Huffington Post*.https://www.huffpost.com/entry/bernie-sanders-donald-trump-2024_n_66bb9e99e4b0b1dc53031b5b

Bowman, V. (2024, July 15). Trump shooting: all seven conspiracy theories examined. *Telegraph*.https://www.telegraph.co.uk/world-news/2024/07/15/trump-shooting-seven-conspiracy-theories-ear-blood-picture/

Brady, H. E., & Kent, T. B. (2022). Fifty Years of Declining Confidence & Increasing Polarization in Trust in American Institutions. *Daedalus*, *151*(4), 43–66. DOI: 10.1162/daed_a_01943

Brook, T. V. (2021, October 18). Collin Powell lent his prestige to make a case for the Iraq war: 'I will always regret it,' he later said. *USA Today*.https://www.usatoday.com/story/news/politics/2021/10/18/military-legacy-colin-powell-and-his-un-speech-wmds-iraq/8505233002/?gnt-cfr=1&gca-cat=p

Bryan, W., & Hopper, D. (2005, November 15). Iraq WMD Timeline: How the Mystery Unraveled. *NPR*. https://www.npr.org/2005/11/15/4996218/iraq-wmd-timeline-how-the-mystery-unraveled

Cassata, C. (2021, June 22). Doctors Debunk 9 Popular COVID-19 Vaccine Myths and Conspiracy Theories. *Health Line*.https://www.healthline.com/health-news/doctors-debunk-9-popular-covid-19-vaccine-myths-and-conspiracy-theories

Cleminson, R. F. (2003). What happened to Saddam's Weapons of Mass Destruction? *Arms Control Today*, *33*(7), 3–6. https://www.armscontrol.org/act/2003-09/features/what-happened-saddams-weapons-mass-destruction

Cohen, L. (2021a, January 7). Twitter and Facebook lock Trump's accounts, take down video of his message to supporters. *CBS News*.https://www.cbsnews.com/news/trump-twitter-facebook-accounts-locked/

Cohen, L. (2021b, January 15). 6 conspiracy theories about 2020 election – debunked. *CBS News*.https://www.cbsnews.com/news/presidential-election-2020-conspiracy-theories-debunked/

Cook, J. (2024). *The Quite Damage: QAnon and the Destruction of the American Family*. Crown Publishing.

Cookson, D. (2024, January 30). Intelligence doesn't make you immune to conspiracy theories—it's more about thinking style. *The Conversation*.https://theconversation.com/intelligence-doesnt-make-you-immune-to-conspiracy-theories-its-more-about-thinking-style-220978

Daily Mail. (2011, April 19). Was JFK kills because of his interest in aliens? Secret memo shows president demanded UFO files 10 days before death. https://www.dailymail.co.uk/news/article-1378284/Secret-memo-shows-JFK-demanded-UFO-files-10-days-assassination.html

Dallas, K. (2024, July 16). Report: President Biden expected to propose major changes to Supreme Court. *MSN*.https://www.msn.com/en-us/news/politics/report-president-biden-expected-to-propose-major-changes-to-supreme-court/ar-BB1q6Yqw?ocid=BingNewsVerp

Dattani, P. (2021, September 14). How to Stop the Spread of Conspiracy Theories and Build Societal Resilience Against Fake News. *London School of Economics (LSE)*.https://blogstest.lse.ac.uk/medialse/2021/09/14/how-to-stop-the-spread-of-conspiracy-theories-and-build-societal-resilience-against-fake-news/

Daugherty, G. (2023). The Hindenburg Disaster: Why the Giant Dirigible Burst into Flames. *History*. https://www.history.com/news/hindenburg-disaster-zeppelin-crash-why

Davis, S. (2014, July 16). We fact-checked some of the rumors spreading online about the Trump assassination attempt. *Reuters*.https://www.reuters.com/fact-check/misinformation-narratives-fact-checked-wake-trump-assassination-attempt-2024-07-15/

Dessler, A. J., Overs, D. E., & Appleby, W. H. (2005, January 12). The Hindenburg Fire: Hydrogen or Incendiary Paint? *Buoyant Flight,* 52(2&3), 1-11. https://spot.colorado.edu/~dziadeck/zf/LZ129fire2005jan12.pdf

Dickey, C. (2020, March 29). Did an illuminati conspiracy theory help elect Thomas Jefferson? *Politico Magazine*.https://www.politico.com/news/magazine/2020/03/29/illuminati-conspiracy-theory-thomas-jefferson-1800-election-152934

Doherty, C., & Kiley, J. (2023, March 14). A look back at how fear and false beliefs bolstered U.S. public support for war in Iraq. *Pew Research Center*.https://www.pewresearch.org/politics/2023/03/14/a-look-back-at-how-fear-and-false-beliefs-bolstered-u-s-public-support-for-war-in-iraq/

Donovan, J. (2024, June 7). Why Jack Ruby Kills JFK's Assassin. *HowStuffWorks*.https://history.howstuffworks.com/historical-figures/jack-ruby.htm

Douglas, K. M. (2021). COVID-19 conspiracy theories. *Group Processes & Intergroup Relations*, *24*(2), 270–275. https://journals.sagepub.com/doi/full/10.1177/1368430220982068

Douglas, K. M., & Sutton, R. M. (2023). What are conspiracy theories? A definitional approach to their correlates, consequences, and communication. *Annual Review of Psychology*, *74*(1), 271–298. DOI: 10.1146/annurev-psych-032420-031329 PMID: 36170672

Dunbar, D., & Reagan, B. (Eds.). (2006). *Debunking 9/11 Myths: Why Conspiracy Theories Can't Stand Up to the Facts*. Hearst Books.

Durkin, A., & Kunzelman, M. (2024, January 5). Hundreds of convictions, but a major mystery is still unsolved 3 years after the Jan. 6 Capitol riot. *APNews*.https://apnews.com/article/capitol-riot-jan-6-criminal-cases-anniversary-bf436efe760751b1356f937e55bedaa5

Dutton, S., Pinto, J. D., Salvanto, A., & Backus, F. (2013, November 16). Poll: Most Americans still think there was a JFK cover-up. *CBS News*.https://www.cbsnews.com/news/poll-most-americans-still-think-there-was-a-jfk-cover-up/

Elliott, P. (2021, September 10). Twenty Years of Data Show How America Changed—And Stayed the Same—After 9/11. *Time Magazine*.https://time.com/6096943/how-sept-11-changed-america/

Feuerherd, P. (2016, July 4). The First Ugly Election: America, 1800. *JSTOR Daily*.https://daily.jstor.org/first-ugly-election-america-1800/

Fritze, J. (2024, February 1). Trump's critics hope that Antonin Scalia can sway the Supreme Court in 14th Amendment fight. *CNN*.https://www.cnn.com/2024/02/01/politics/supreme-court-trump-14th-amendment-scalia/index.html

Funk, C., Tyson, A., Kennedy, B., & Pasquini, G. (2023, May 16). What Americans think about COVID-19 vaccines. *Pew Research Center*.https://www.pewresearch.org/science/2023/05/16/what-americans-think-about-covid-19-vaccines/

Goldberg, A. G. (2001). *Enemies Within: The Culture of Conspiracy in Modern America*. Yale University Press.

Goldman, J. (2013, March 3). N.J. Hindenburg crash of 1937 caused by static electricity, report says. *NJ.Com*.https://www.nj.com/news/2013/03/nj_hindenburg_crash_caused_by.html#:~:text=Static%20electricity%20caused%20the%20Hindenburg%20airship%20to%20explode,German%20airship%20that%20spanned%20more%20than%20800%20feet

Greenwald, G. (2007, April 21). Right-wing blogs discover massive conspiracy to hide WMDs in Iraq. *Salon*.https://www.salon.com/2007/04/21/wmd_conspiracy/

Hanyok, R. J. (2009). The Pearl Harbor Warning that Never was. *Naval History,* 23(2), 50-53. https://www.usni.org/magazines/naval-history-magazine/2009/april/pearl-harbor-warning-never-was

Haq, H. (2015, January 7). Why many Americans hold false beliefs about WMDs in Iraq and Obama's birthplace. *The Christian Science Monitor*.https://www.csmonitor.com/USA/Politics/Decoder/2015/0107/Why-many-Americans-hold-false-beliefs-about-WMDs-in-Iraq-and-Obama-s-birth-place

Hartig, H., & Doherty, C. (2021). Two Decades Later, the Enduring Legacy of 9/11. *Pew Research Center*.https://www.pewresearch.org/politics/2021/09/02/two-decades-later-the-enduring-legacy-of-9-11/

Harvey, I. (2016, November 24). 80 years of speculation and conspiracy theories: The Hindenburg Disaster in 1937 that killed 36 people on board the giant airship. *The Vintage News*.https://www.thevintagenews.com/2016/11/24/80-years-of-speculation-and-conspiracy-theories-the-hindenburg-disaster-of-1937-that-killed-36-people-on-board-the-giant-airship/

Hashemi-Pour, C. (2024, August 6). 6 Steps in Fact-checking AI-generated Content. *TechTarget*.https://www.techtarget.com/WhatIs/feature/Steps-in-fact-checking-AI-generated-content

Herb, J., & Andone, D. (2024, July 14). How the assassination attempt on Trump unfolded. *CNN*.https://www.cnn.com/2024/07/14/politics/what-happened-trump-assassination-attempt/index.html

Hoehling, A. A. (1962). *Who Destroyed the Hindenburg?* Little, Brown & Company. https://archive.org/details/whodestroyedhind0000hoeh/page/n5/mode/2up

Hoffman, B., & Ware, J. (2024, February 5). Online Extremism is Decades in the Making. https://time.com/6551865/extremist-social-media/

Hughes, K. (n.d.). Watergate: The Aftermath. *University of Virginia Miller Center*.https://millercenter.org/the-presidency/educational-resources/watergate/watergate-aftermath

Hummel, J. R. (2024, July). The Dark Side of Alexander Hamilton. *Reason*.https://reason.com/2024/06/16/the-dark-side-of-alexander-hamilton/

Igielnik, R., & Parker, K. (2019, July 10). Majorities of U.S. veterans, public say the wars in Iraq and Afghanistan were not worth fighting. *Pew Research Center*.https://www.pewresearch.org/short-reads/2019/07/10/majorities-of-u-s-veterans-public-say-the-wars-in-iraq-and-afghanistan-were-not-worth-fighting/

Jackson, P. (2021, August 3). September 11 attacks: What happened on 9/11. *BBC*.https://www.bbc.com/news/world-us-canada-57698668.amp

Jones, J. (2022, July 5). Confidence in U.S. Institutions Down; Average at New Low. *Gallup*.https://news.gallup.com/poll/394283/confidence-institutions-down-average-new-low.aspx

Kiger, P. J. (2013, November 19). 10 Conspiracy Theories About the JFK Assassination. *HowStuffWorks*. https://history.howstuffworks.com/historical-figures/john-f-kennedy.htm

Kim, L. (2021, March 24). AI Helps Break Down Conspiracy Theories. *UCLA Magazine*.https://newsroom.ucla.edu/magazine/artificial-intelligence-conspiracy-theories

Kohut, A. (2014, August 8). From the archives: How the Watergate crisis eroded public support for Richard Nixon. *Pew Research Center*.https://www.pewresearch.org/short-reads/2019/09/25/how-the-watergate-crisis-eroded-public-support-for-richard-nixon/

Krieg, G. (2016, September 16). 14 of Trump's most outrageous 'birther' claims—half from after 2011. *CNN*.https://www.cnn.com/2016/09/09/politics/donald-trump-birther/index.html

LaBianca, J. (2024, May 27). 10 Things They're Still Not Telling You About Pearl Harbor. *Reader's Digest*.https://www.rd.com/list/conspiracy-theories-about-pearl-harbor/

Lerche, C. O.Jr. (1948). Jefferson and the Election of 1800: A Case Study in the Political Smear. *The William and Mary Quarterly*, *5*(4), 467–491. https://www.jstor.org/stable/pdf/1920636.pdf?refreqid=fastly-default%3A55dbd5b0606e063ff73f2bb52368838a&ab_segments=&origin=&initiator=&acceptTC=1

Lewis, T. (2020, October 12). Eight Persistent COVID-19 Myths and Why People Believe Them. *Scientific American*. https://www.scientificamerican.com/article/eight-persistent-covid-19-myths-and-why-people-believe-them/

Lima, C. (2021, January 6). Twitter, Facebook lock Trump's accounts in confrontation over Capital breast posts. *Politico*. https://www.politico.com/news/2021/01/06/twitter-trump-tweet-capitol-violence-455630

Liptak, A., VanSickle, A., & Parlapiano, A. (2024, July 2). The Major Supreme Court Decisions, *The New York Times*. https://www.nytimes.com/interactive/2024/05/09/us/supreme-court-major-cases-2024.html#racial-gerrymandering

Lord, K. M., & Vogt, K. (2021, March 18). Strengthen Media Literacy to Win the Fight Against Misinformation. *Stanford Social Innovation Review*. https://ssir.org/articles/entry/strengthen_media_literacy_to_win_the_fight_against_misinformation

Lynas, M. (2020, April 20). COVID: Top 10 current conspiracy theories. *Alliance for Science*. https://allianceforscience.org/blog/2020/04/covid-top-10-current-conspiracy-theories/

Mandavalli, A. (2024, May 3). Thousands Believe Covid Vaccines Harmed Them. Is Anyone Listening? https://www.nytimes.com/2024/05/03/health/covid-vaccines-side-effects.html

Mayer, C. (2024, July 16). One in Three Biden Supporters Think Trump Shooting Might Have Been Staged. *Newsweek*. https://www.newsweek.com/trump-shooting-assassination-conspiracy-theory-staged-biden-poll-1925723

McGovern, A. (2021, May 27). Artificial Intelligence System Could Help Counter the Spread of Disinformation. *MIT News*. https://news.mit.edu/2021/artificial-intelligence-system-could-help-counter-spread-disinformation-0527

McLaughlin, A. (2020, June 23). Investigating the most convincing COVID-19 conspiracy theories. *Kings College London*. https://www.kcl.ac.uk/investigating-the-most-convincing-covid-19-conspiracy-theories

Merchant, N. (2023, March 23). Iraq WMD failures shadow US intelligence 20 years later. *AP News*. https://apnews.com/article/iraq-war-wmds-us-intelligence-f9e21ac59d3a0470d9bfcc83544d706e

Millhiser, I. (2024, August 19). Republicans ask the Supreme Court to disenfranchise thousands of swing state voters. *Vox*. https://www.vox.com/scotus/367701/supreme-court-arizona-rnc-republicans-mi-familia-vota

Mitchell, J. (2023, February 3). 20 years ago, the U.S. warned of Iraq's alleged 'weapons of mass destruction.' *NPR*. https://www.npr.org/2023/02/03/1151160567/colin-powell-iraq-un-weapons-mass-destruction

Moniz, C. (2024, June 27). Donald Trump spread 2020 election conspiracy theories 500 times on Truth Social. *CREW*. https://www.citizensforethics.org/reports-investigations/crew-investigations/donald-trump-has-spread-2020-election-conspiracy-theories-500-times-on-truth-social/

Nakatani, M. (2023, February 3). The Mystery of the Umbrella Man at JFK's Assassination. *Grunge.* https://www.grunge.com/438451/the-mystery-of-the-umbrella-man-at-jfks-assassination/

National Commission on Terrorist Attacks Upon the United States. (2024, July 22). *The 9/11 Commission Report.*https://govinfo.library.unt.edu/911/report/911Report.pdf

Nelson, C. (2016). *Pearl Harbor: From Infamy to Greatness.* Scribner.

NPR. (2016, December 6). No, FDR Did not know the Japanese were going to bomb Pearl Harbor. https://www.npr.org/2016/12/06/504449867/no-fdr-did-not-know-the-japanese-were-going-to-bomb-pearl-harbor

NPR. (2022, October 13). Special Series: House Jan. 6 committee hearings. https://www.npr.org/2022/10/13/1125331584/jan-6-committee-hearing-transcript

O'Rourke, C. (2021, December 20). No, Barak Obama's birth certificate isn't fake. *PolitiFact.*https://www.politifact.com/factchecks/2021/dec/20/blog-posting/no-barack-obamas-birth-certificate-isnt-fake/

Onuf, P. (n.d.) Thomas Jefferson: Campaigns and Elections. *University of Virginia Miller Center.*https://millercenter.org/president/jefferson/campaigns-and-elections

Onuoha, M., Pinder, J., & Schafer, J. (2015, November 20). Guide to Crowdsourcing. *Columbia Journalism Review.*https://www.cjr.org/tow_center_reports/guide_to_crowdsourcing.php

Pertwee, E., Simas, C., & Larson, H. J. (2022). An epidemic of uncertainty: Rumors, conspiracy theories, and vaccine hesitancy. *Nature Medicine, 28*, 456–459. https://www.nature.com/articles/s41591-022-01728-z PMID: 35273403

Pew Research Center. (2008, December 18). Bush and Public Opinion. https://www.pewresearch.org/politics/2008/12/18/bush-and-public-opinion/

Pew Research Center. (2015, November 23). Trust in government: 1958-2015. https://www.pewresearch.org/politics/2015/11/23/1-trust-in-government-1958-2015/

Pew Research Center. (2024, June 24). Americans' trust in federal government and attitudes toward it. https://www.pewresearch.org/2024/06/24/americans-trust-in-federal-government-and-attitudes-toward-it/

Pilkington, E. (2022). Ginni Thomas still believes Trump's false claim the 2020 election was stolen. *The Guardian.*https://go.gale.com/ps/i.do?p=GIC&u=for1&id=GALE|A720396582&v=2.1&it=r&sid=ebsco

Pruitt, S. (2017, October 26). The Biggest Revelations in the Declassified JFK Assassination Files. *History.com.*https://www.history.com/news/jfk-assassination-documents-declassified-release

Pummerer, L., Böhm, R., Lilleholt, L., Winter, K., Zettler, I., & Sassenberg, K. (2022). Conspiracy Theories and Their Societal Effects During the COVID-19 Pandemic. *Social Psychological & Personality Science, 13*(1), 49–59. DOI: 10.1177/19485506211000217

Ramirez, I. (2024, July 15). Republicans formally name Trump their presidential nominee. *Politico.* https://www.politico.com/news/2024/07/15/donald-trump-gop-presidential-nominee-00168345

Reed, B. (2024, July 20). 'It was insane to me': Undecided voters express shock after watching Trump RNC speech. *MSN.*https://www.msn.com/en-us/news/politics/it-was-insane-to-me-undecided-voters-express-shock-after-watching-trump-rnc-speech/ar-BB1qi9DV

Reynolds, D. (2001). *From Munich to Pearl Harbor: Roosevelt's America and the Origins of the Second World War.* Ivan R. Dee.

Robinson, P. (2023, April 13). Lone Gunman: The Man Who Knew Lee Harvey Oswald—Uncommon Knowledge with Peter Robinson. *Hoover Institution.*https://www.hoover.org/research/lone-gunman-man-who-knew-lee-harvey-oswald

Rose, J. (2020, December 30). Even if it's 'Bonkers,' Poll finds many believe QAnon and other conspiracy theories. *NPR.*https://www.npr.org/2020/12/30/951095644/even-if-its-bonkers-poll-finds-many-believe-qanon-and-other-conspiracy-theories

Rosenbaum, R. (1982, June 23). Ah, Watergate! *The New Republic,* 154, 15-24. https://ia601207.us.archive.org/9/items/nsia-WatergateFile/nsia-WatergateFile/Watergate%20File%20193_text.pdf

Ryan, A. (2024, July 16). Conspiracy theories about Trump's assassination attempt have exploded. Here's why. *The Boston Globe.*https://www.msn.com/en-us/news/opinion/conspiracy-theories-about-trump-s-assassination-attempt-have-exploded-here-s-why/ar-BB1q5pb1?ocid=BingNewsVerp

Saad, L. (2023, July 6). Historically Low Faith in U.S. Institutions Continues. *Gallup.*https://news.gallup.com/poll/508169/historically-low-faith-institutions-continues.aspx

Sardarizadeh, S. (2021, September 9). 11 September 2001: The conspiracy theories still spreading after 20 years. *BBC.*https://www.bbc.com/news/58469600

Scott, H. (2024, August 10). Why the Far-Right Isn't Holding Back Anymore: 20 Reasons They're Louder Than Ever. *MSN.*https://www.msn.com/en-us/news/opinion/why-the-far-right-isn-t-holding-back-anymore-20-reasons-they-re-louder-than-ever/ss-AA1oySUN#image=7

Shannon, J. (2020, September 30). Who are the Proud Boys? Far-right group has concerned experts for years. *USA Today.*https://www.usatoday.com/story/news/nation/2020/09/30/who-proud-boys-group-mentioned-debate-has-violent-history/5868406002/

Shoaib, A. (2024, July 29). Joe Biden's Supreme Court Reforms Backed by Donald Trump Supporters. *Newsweek.*https://www.msn.com/en-us/news/politics/joe-biden-s-supreme-court-reforms-backed-by-donald-trump-supporters/ar-BB1qPwCw?ocid=winp2fptaskbarhoverent&cvid=e3da8f7a2fbb4b8890dd2611c6c191d7&ei=12

Shuham, M. (2024, July 22). MTG Asks Secret Service Director If There Was A 'Conspiracy To Kill President Trump.' *Huffington Post.*https://www.msn.com/en-us/news/politics/mtg-asks-secret-service-director-if-there-was-a-conspiracy-to-kill-president-trump/ar-BB1qqTmq?ocid=BingNewsVerp

Silk, M. (2016). Did John Adams Out Thomas Jefferson and Sally Hemings? *Smithsonian Magazine.* https://www.smithsonianmag.com/history/john-adams-out-thomas-jefferson-sally-hemings-180960789/

Stanton, A. (2024, July 31). Trump Sells Upside Down American Flag Hat After Supreme Court Controversy. *MSN.*https://www.msn.com/en-us/news/politics/trump-sells-upside-down-american-flag-hat-after-supreme-court-controversy/ar-BB1qYwmA?ocid=winp2fptaskbarent&cvid=1c8d1e019cc749099b69cc18899216db&ei=10

Stinnett, R. (1999). *Day of Deceit: The Truth About FDR and Pearl Harbor*. Free Press.

Stomberg, J. (2012, May 10). What Really Sparked the Hindenburg Disaster? *Smithsonian Magazine.*https://www.smithsonianmag.com/science-nature/what-really-sparked-the-hindenburg-disaster-85867521/

Swami, V., Voracek, M., Stieger, S., Tran, U. S., & Furnham, A. (2014). Analytic thinking reduces belief in conspiracy theories. *Cognition, 133*(3), 572–585. DOI: 10.1016/j.cognition.2014.08.006 PMID: 25217762

Tangherlini, T. R. (2020, November 13). An AI Tool Can Distinguish Between a Conspiracy Theory and a True Conspiracy—It Comes Down to How Easily the Story Falls Apart. *The Conversation.*https://theconversation.com/an-ai-tool-can-distinguish-between-a-conspiracy-theory-and-a-true-conspiracy-it-comes-down-to-how-easily-the-story-falls-apart-146282

Theriault, S. M. (2006). Party Politics during the Louisiana Purchase. *Social Science History*, *30*(2), 293–324. https://www.jstor.org/stable/pdf/40267908.pdf?refreqid=fastly-default%3Af71d4b5eca6eeb4807ce45003b764603&ab_segments=&origin=&initiator=&acceptTC=1

Timm, J. C., & Kamisar, B. (2024, July 19). Fact-checking Trump's speech accepting the GOP nomination. *NBC.*https://www.nbcnews.com/politics/donald-trump/fact-checking-trump-republican-convention-speech-rcna162656

Trotta, D. (2012, October 24). Trump to give $5 million to charity if Obama releases records. *Reuters.* https://www.reuters.com/article/world/us-politics/trump-to-give-5-million-to-charity-if-obama-releases-records-idUSBRE89N180/

U.S. Senate Historical Office. (1976, April 29). *A History of Notable Senate Investigations: The Church Committee.*https://www.senate.gov/about/resources/pdf/church-committee-full-citations.pdf

Waxman, O. B. (2023, November 21). What we know and still don't know about JFK's Assassination. *Time Magazine.*https://time.com/6338396/jfk-assassination-conspiracy-culture/

Weigel, D. (2009, June 3). Citizen Juries: The New Birther Style. *The Washington Independent.*https://washingtonindependent.com/45416/citizen-juries-the-new-birther-style

Weissmann, J. (2009, March 6). Judge Dismisses Obama 'Indictment.' *Legal Times.*https://legaltimes.typepad.com/blt/2009/07/super-american-grand-jury-indicts-obama-.html

Wheeler, R. (2021, November 30). Trump's judicial campaign to upend the 2020 election: A failure, but not a wipe-out. *Brookings.*https://www.brookings.edu/articles/trumps-judicial-campaign-to-upend-the-2020-election-a-failure-but-not-a-wipe-out/

X, C. (2011, March 20). President Kennedy, The Fed And Executive Order 11110. *Rense.com.*https://rense.com/general44/exec.htm

Yaraghi, N. (2019, April 9). How should social media platforms combat misinformation and hate speech? *Brookings.*https://www.brookings.edu/articles/how-should-social-media-platforms-combat-misinformation-and-hate-speech/

Young, T. (2015, May 6). 40 years ago, Church Committee investigated Americans spying on Americans. *Brookings.*https://www.brookings.edu/articles/40-years-ago-church-committee-investigated-americans-spying-on-americans/

Zurcher, A. (2016, September 16). The birth of the Obama 'birther' conspiracy. *BBC.*https://www.bbc.com/news/election-us-2016-37391652

ADDITIONAL READING

Bordeleau, J. N. (2023). I Trends: A Review of Conspiracy Theory Research: Definitions, Trends, and Directions for Future Research. *International Political Science Abstracts*, *73*(1), 1–10. DOI: 10.1177/00208345231157664

Gorman, S. E. (2024). *The Anatomy of Deception: Conspiracy Theories, Distrust, and Public Health in America.* Oxford Academic.

Mari, S., de Zúñiga, H. G., Suerdem, A., Hanke, K., Brown, G., Vilar, R., Boer, D., & Bilewicz, M. (2022). Conspiracy Theories and Institutional Trust: Examining the Role of Uncertainty Avoidence and Active Social Media Use. *Political Psychology*, *43*(2), 277–296. DOI: 10.1111/pops.12754

Moskalenko, S., Burton, B. S., González, J. F., & Bloom, M. M. (2022). Secondhand Conspiracy Theories: The Social, Emotional and Political Tolls on Loved Ones of QAnon Followers. *Democracy and Security*, *19*(3), 231–250. DOI: 10.1080/17419166.2022.2111305

Schatto-Eckrodt, T., Clever, L., & Frischlich, L. (2024). The Seed of Doubt: Examining the Role of Alternative Social and News Media for the Birth of a Conspiracy Theory. *Social Science Computer Review*, *0*(0), 1160–1180. Advance online publication. DOI: 10.1177/08944393241246281

van Prooijen, J.-W. (2022). Injustice without evidence: The unique role of conspiracy theories in social justice research. *Social Justice Research*, *35*(1), 88–106. DOI: 10.1007/s11211-021-00376-x PMID: 34602739

Chapter 16
Did God Say That?
The Role of Religion in the Dissemination of Information

Toiya Marie McGruder
Dillard University, USA

ABSTRACT

This chapter examines the role of religion in shaping societal narratives and disseminating information within the United States, with a special emphasis on Black Liberation Theology and the influential figures associated with this theological framework. It explores the ways that religious leaders have harnessed faith as both a vehicle for activism and a means of communicating critical perspectives on justice and morality, especially in Black communities. Examining prominent figures such as Malcolm X, Muhammad Ali, Louis Farrakhan, and influential Black clergy in politics, this chapter contrasts these leaders' roles with those of conservative white evangelical figures who shaped American socio-political landscapes in divergent ways. Notably, the chapter highlights the impact of religion on political events, including the Watergate scandal and its effect on public trust, while tracing the legislative and activist legacies of figures like Andrew Young, Floyd Flake, and William H. Gray III, who played substantial roles in forwarding civil rights and economic justice.

INTRODUCTION

Religion has historically served as a potent force in shaping beliefs, behaviors, and societal norms, functioning as both a moral compass and a cultural unifier within communities. Throughout American history, religious institutions have not only nurtured the spiritual lives of individuals but also acted as vital centers for social and political mobilization. This duality—spiritual sanctuary and catalyst for activism—has been particularly prominent within Black communities, where religion has long served as a tool for resilience, resistance, and liberation. The Black church, and specifically the tenets of Black Liberation Theology, provide a foundational lens through which the role of religion in advocating for racial and social justice can be understood.

In the context of Black American experience, the emergence of Black Liberation Theology represented a radical theological shift, presenting Christianity not as a justification for suffering but as a means of empowering the oppressed. This theology encourages the faithful to pursue justice and equality as divine

DOI: 10.4018/979-8-3693-7468-9.ch016

imperatives, positioning God as an ally in the struggle against oppression. Influential leaders such as Malcolm X, Muhammad Ali, and Louis Farrakhan drew from these theological underpinnings, using religious rhetoric to advocate for Black empowerment and resist systemic injustices. Their approaches varied, ranging from Malcolm X's radical calls for self-defense against racial violence to Ali's conscientious objection to the Vietnam War, each demonstrating religion's capacity to inspire resistance against state and social injustices.

At the same time, white evangelical Christianity has wielded significant influence on the broader American socio-political landscape. In contrast to the liberation-oriented approach of Black religious leaders, many white evangelical figures aligned themselves with conservative values and political agendas, particularly during the Nixon administration. The Watergate scandal of the early 1970s marked a pivotal moment for white evangelical leaders, revealing the complexities of their alliance with political power and raising critical questions about the role of religion in legitimizing political narratives and ethical standards. Leaders like Billy Graham, who publicly defended Nixon, symbolized a segment of American Christianity that prioritized conservative, anti-communist values, thus underscoring the stark ideological divide between the goals of Black Liberation Theology and white evangelical Christianity.

This chapter delves into the intersections of religion, race, and politics, contrasting the approaches of Black leaders with those of conservative white evangelicals. It will also explore the contributions of African American clergy-politicians such as Andrew Young, Floyd Flake, Walter Fauntroy, and William H. Gray III, whose work in legislative arenas reflects the activism-driven ethos of Black Liberation Theology. By examining these leaders' histories, legislative achievements, and theological perspectives, this chapter illustrates how religion has served as both a platform and a weapon for disseminating information, shaping public opinion, and challenging established structures of power.

MALCOLM X AND BLACK RELIGIOUS MOVEMENTS IN ACTIVISM

Malcolm X's influence on Black activism is inseparable from his complex relationship with religion, primarily his affiliation with the Nation of Islam (NOI). The NOI, founded in 1930, offered a distinct interpretation of Islam that emphasized Black empowerment and self-sufficiency. While NOI doctrines diverged from traditional Sunni Islam, the movement attracted Malcolm X with its call for racial pride, economic independence, and its stance against integration with the prevailing societal systems that promoted racial injustice. Unlike the predominant Civil Rights Movement's focus on nonviolent protest, Malcolm X advocated for self-defense and argued that African Americans had the right to protect themselves, thereby challenging the status quo of passive resistance (X, 1964).

The teachings of the NOI were instrumental in shaping Malcolm's ideological foundation, framing Black empowerment as a religious duty. He preached that American society was inherently corrupt, and he strongly criticized both the political establishment and religious institutions that, in his view, upheld racist practices. Through his speeches and writings, Malcolm X popularized the idea that African Americans should reject Western Christian norms and adopt a religion that embraced their heritage and dignity (Gates & Appiah, 1999).

By 1964, after his pilgrimage to Mecca, Malcolm X publicly broke from the NOI, embracing Sunni Islam. This shift expanded his ideological reach, leading him to advocate for racial solidarity beyond the bounds of religion and race. His later messages championed human rights over civil rights, suggesting a global, unified approach to combat oppression. His religious transformation highlighted the ways in which faith could evolve to inspire activism on a broader scale, reinforcing that religion, in any form, could serve as a powerful tool for societal reform (Malcolm X & Haley, 1965).

MUHAMMAD ALI: FAITH, RESISTANCE, AND PUBLIC INFLUENCE

Muhammad Ali, born Cassius Clay, is celebrated not only as a world champion boxer but as a cultural and political icon whose religious convictions drove him to make a powerful stand against social and political injustice. Ali's conversion to Islam, influenced by Malcolm X and the NOI, was a defining moment that set him on a path of activism intertwined with his faith. After joining the NOI in 1964, Ali's adoption of his new name was a symbolic rejection of what he viewed as his "slave name." By renaming himself, he signaled his commitment to the values and empowerment promoted by the NOI, embracing the message of Black self-determination and pride (Hauser, 1970).

Ali's resistance to the Vietnam War represents one of the most significant intersections of faith and political dissent in modern American history. In 1966, he famously refused induction into the U.S. Army, citing his Islamic beliefs and asserting, "I ain't got no quarrel with them Viet Cong." His statement sparked national debate, challenging the patriotism of those who criticized the war effort and reframing conscientious objection as a religious and moral decision. Ali's stand led to a three-year ban from boxing, financial strain, and public condemnation, but it also made him a symbol of resistance, especially within African American communities that saw the war as disproportionately harming Black soldiers (Ali, 1975; Marqusee, 1999).

Through his advocacy, Ali demonstrated how religious identity could serve as a foundation for protest against systemic injustices beyond racial lines. His stance inspired a generation to examine the ethical implications of war, particularly a conflict many saw as imperialistic and exploitative. Ali's courage in aligning his public actions with his faith underscored the power of religious beliefs in shaping political consciousness and influencing public discourse on issues of race, justice, and freedom. His example illustrated how individual conviction, when rooted in religious identity, could challenge national narratives and promote social awareness (Marqusee, 1999).

Ali's legacy extends beyond boxing and his stand on Vietnam. His commitment to philanthropy, peace-building, and interfaith dialogue in later years exemplified a broader, more inclusive understanding of Islam and activism. His approach to religious advocacy showed that spiritual beliefs could transcend their initial boundaries to become instruments of global solidarity and humanitarianism, reinforcing the enduring impact of religiously motivated activism in shaping societal values (Hauser, 1970).

LOUIS FARRAKHAN: RELIGION AS A TOOL FOR POLITICAL AND SOCIAL COMMENTARY

Louis Farrakhan, a prominent figure in the NOI and one of the most influential Black religious leaders of the 20th century, used his platform to address racial injustice, economic disparity, and systemic inequities faced by African Americans. Born Louis Eugene Walcott in 1933, Farrakhan joined the NOI in the 1950s under the mentorship of Elijah Muhammad. By the 1980s, he became the organization's most visible leader, known for his outspoken, sometimes controversial rhetoric and his dedication to advancing the NOI's religious, social, and political agenda (Clegg, 1997).

Farrakhan's approach to activism combined religious teachings with a critique of the American political and economic systems, which he argued perpetuated racial inequality. His speeches often emphasized Black empowerment and self-sufficiency, calling on African Americans to establish businesses, educational institutions, and community initiatives that would reduce reliance on the structures he viewed as oppressive. Farrakhan's focus on economic empowerment derived from the NOI's foundational principles, which posited that economic independence was essential to Black liberation and community upliftment. His emphasis on self-reliance resonated deeply within African American communities, especially during times of economic hardship, as it provided a message of resilience and resourcefulness (Clegg, 1997; Lincoln, 1994).

One of Farrakhan's most notable contributions to the discourse on race and justice in the U.S. was his role in organizing the 1995 Million Man March. This historic gathering brought hundreds of thousands of African American men to Washington, D.C., calling for personal responsibility, unity, and commitment to the betterment of Black families and communities. The march highlighted Farrakhan's influence as a religious leader who could mobilize significant public engagement on issues of race, morality, and community. It also marked a pivotal moment in African American political and social activism, as the event transcended religious lines, bringing together individuals from diverse backgrounds, united by a commitment to addressing systemic injustice and fostering communal bonds (Hutchinson, 1996).

Farrakhan's rhetoric, however, has often been polarizing. His statements on race relations, anti-Semitism, and critiques of American foreign policy have drawn both support and criticism. Supporters argue that Farrakhan's outspokenness reflects the frustrations of marginalized communities and that his critiques bring attention to enduring racial and economic injustices. Critics, however, contend that his approach can sometimes perpetuate divisive views. The polarizing nature of Farrakhan's message underscores the complex role religious leaders can play in public discourse, as they navigate the tension between advocating for their communities and engaging with a broader national audience (Lincoln, 1994).

Despite the controversies surrounding his views, Farrakhan's work through the NOI remains significant for its emphasis on addressing social issues through the lens of religious principles and moral accountability. His leadership has encouraged a discourse that critiques American societal structures while promoting a vision of Black empowerment grounded in religious values. Farrakhan's influence demonstrates how religious platforms can be used to shape political and social narratives, challenge power structures, and inspire community solidarity in the face of systemic oppression (Hutchinson, 1996).

THE ROLE OF WHITE EVANGELICAL LEADERS: POLITICAL ALIGNMENT AND SUPPORT FOR NIXON DURING WATERGATE

The influence of white evangelical leaders in the United States has been profound, often aligning with conservative political figures and championing policies they believed reflected moral and social stability. Throughout the 20th century, many white evangelical leaders forged strong alliances with political leaders who promoted traditional values, anti-communism, and a nationalistic vision of America. This alignment became especially evident during the presidency of Richard Nixon and the subsequent Watergate scandal. White evangelical leaders like Billy Graham and later figures like Jerry Falwell and Pat Robertson wielded substantial influence, shaping public opinion on social and moral issues and emphasizing religious themes of righteousness and order in their support of Nixon and conservative policies (Martin, 1996).

Billy Graham's Alliance With Nixon

One of the most influential evangelical figures of the era, Billy Graham, developed a close relationship with Richard Nixon, whom he supported both politically and personally. Graham's endorsement of Nixon reflected his alignment with the president's opposition to communism and his promotion of conservative social values, which resonated deeply with Graham's vision of a morally upright America. Graham's popularity among evangelicals helped bolster Nixon's image as a protector of Christian values, even as political tensions increased due to the Vietnam War and domestic civil rights issues (Frady, 1979).

During the Watergate scandal, however, Graham's steadfast support of Nixon faced public scrutiny. As details of the break-in and Nixon's involvement in the cover-up began to emerge, many were shocked that a religious figure as prominent as Graham would continue to back the president. Although Graham would later express regret over his unwavering support, his alignment with Nixon during this turbulent time underscored the complex interplay between religious loyalty and political allegiance. Graham's approach illustrated how evangelical leaders, motivated by a desire to see their values reflected in national leadership, might sometimes prioritize political stability over ethical accountability (Frady, 1979; Martin, 1996).

Jerry Falwell, the Moral Majority, and the Rise of Political Evangelicalism

Following Graham's lead in connecting evangelical beliefs with political causes, Jerry Falwell became a pivotal figure in the growth of the evangelical right through the establishment of the Moral Majority in the late 1970s. Although Falwell's activism peaked after the Watergate era, his influence built on the foundation laid by figures like Graham, solidifying the connection between evangelical Christianity and conservative politics. The Moral Majority championed issues such as opposition to abortion, support for prayer in public schools, and a hardline stance against communism, presenting these causes as essential to preserving America's moral fabric.

Falwell's approach to political engagement extended the evangelical influence on U.S. politics, shaping conservative policy and aligning with Republican figures, including Ronald Reagan. His rhetoric frequently framed these political stances as extensions of religious duty, suggesting that to be a faithful Christian necessitated supporting a conservative agenda. This alignment between evangelicalism and conservative politics further reinforced the narrative that Christianity in the U.S. was synonymous with traditionalism and resistance to progressive reforms, distinguishing the goals of white evangelical leaders from those of Black religious leaders who, in contrast, championed civil rights and social justice (FitzGerald, 2017).

COMPARATIVE ANALYSIS: WHITE EVANGELICAL SUPPORT FOR NIXON VS. BLACK RELIGIOUS LEADERS' RESPONSES TO SOCIAL JUSTICE ISSUES

The alliance between white evangelical leaders and conservative political figures such as Nixon contrasts sharply with the approach of Black religious leaders, who often opposed governmental policies that perpetuated inequality. White evangelical leaders, driven by a desire to protect traditional social values, saw Nixon as a bulwark against moral decay, secularism, and the perceived threat of communism. In the eyes of evangelical leaders like Graham, Nixon's commitment to a "law and order" America represented a crucial defense of societal stability and Christian values. The support for Nixon even amid the Watergate scandal reflected a prioritization of ideological alignment over transparency and accountability, a stance that many found controversial but that underscored the evangelical community's intense focus on maintaining cultural conservatism (Martin, 1996; FitzGerald, 2017).

In contrast, Black religious leaders often used their platforms to critique the very structures of power that white evangelicals sought to uphold. Leaders such as Malcolm X, Martin Luther King Jr., and later figures like Louis Farrakhan saw religion as a foundation for challenging systemic injustices. Black religious leaders were more likely to advocate for accountability and justice, using their influence to promote civil rights and call for reforms that addressed the economic and social disenfranchisement of African Americans. Their stance on political issues reflected a liberation theology perspective, which emphasized social justice, empowerment, and active resistance to oppression—values often in direct opposition to the status quo supported by white evangelical leaders (Cone, 1997).

IMPACT OF WATERGATE ON RELIGIOUS AND POLITICAL ALLIANCES

The fallout from Watergate was a turning point, not only for American politics but also for the alignment between religion and political ideology. For white evangelical leaders, Watergate represented a moment of dissonance, as public opinion soured on Nixon and forced a reevaluation of religious figures' endorsement of flawed political leaders. Some evangelical leaders distanced themselves from political figures in the wake of the scandal, though the alliance between evangelicalism and conservative politics would ultimately solidify in the following decades.

In contrast, Black religious leaders remained critical of Nixon's policies throughout his presidency, particularly regarding his resistance to civil rights advancements and his "Southern Strategy," which appealed to white voters resistant to integration and social change. For these leaders, Watergate was emblematic of the moral failings of a political system that, in their view, often marginalized Black voices. The scandal reinforced their belief in the need for accountability, transparency, and a religious commitment to justice as essential components of political life (Frady, 1979; Cone, 1997).

Next, we'll explore the significant contributions of prominent African American religious leaders who actively participated in U.S. legislative processes, bringing a strong commitment to civil rights, economic justice, and equitable policy reforms. This section will delve into the careers of Andrew Young, Floyd Flake, William H. Gray III, and Walter Fauntroy, examining their work in Congress, their influence on legislation, and their roles as religious leaders advocating for Black communities.

THE LEGISLATIVE INFLUENCE OF AFRICAN AMERICAN RELIGIOUS LEADERS: ANDREW YOUNG, FLOYD FLAKE, WILLIAM H. GRAY III, AND WALTER FAUNTROY

African American clergy have historically intertwined their religious convictions with political activism, a tradition that extends into the halls of Congress and local government offices. As figures deeply rooted in their communities and as elected officials, leaders like Andrew Young, Floyd Flake, William H. Gray III, and Walter Fauntroy demonstrated that religious leadership and legislative power could converge effectively to champion social and economic reforms. These leaders saw their roles as an extension of the church's mission to serve the marginalized, leveraging legislative authority to challenge policies that maintained systemic inequities and hindered the progress of African Americans (DuBois, 2002).

Andrew Young: Diplomacy, Civil Rights, and Economic Advocacy

Andrew Young was a pivotal figure in the civil rights movement and the broader political landscape of the United States. A close confidant of Dr. Martin Luther King Jr. and a key strategist in the Southern Christian Leadership Conference (SCLC), Young's work epitomized the merging of religious conviction with social justice. His commitment to civil rights advocacy eventually led him to a career in politics, where he became the first African American elected to Congress from Georgia since Reconstruction in 1972. In Congress, Young worked on legislation aimed at reducing poverty and improving international relations, particularly between the United States and African nations. His dual roles as an ordained minister and a political leader underscored his belief in the church's obligation to advocate for systemic change (Branch, 1988).

Young's legislative efforts were marked by a commitment to economic development and poverty reduction, especially for marginalized communities. As U.S. Ambassador to the United Nations under President Jimmy Carter, Young used his diplomatic platform to speak on behalf of oppressed populations worldwide, advocating for human rights and economic aid. His commitment to using his position to further social justice issues set a precedent for future African American political leaders who saw diplomacy as a tool for promoting civil rights both domestically and internationally (Young, 1996).

Floyd Flake: Economic Empowerment and Community Development

Rev. Floyd Flake, a former U.S. Congressman from New York and pastor of the Allen African Methodist Episcopal Church in Queens, brought a unique approach to politics that emphasized community-based economic development. Flake's tenure in Congress from 1987 to 1997 was characterized by his dedication to revitalizing underserved neighborhoods, particularly through legislation that encouraged business development and job creation. Under his leadership, the Allen AME Church became a model for economic self-sufficiency, establishing housing complexes, a school, and various businesses to serve the local community (Walrond, 2006).

Flake's political philosophy blended his pastoral mission with his legislative work, underscoring the belief that economic empowerment was essential for achieving social justice. As a proponent of public-private partnerships, he advocated for policies that provided African Americans with greater access to economic resources and opportunities. His efforts reflected the broader goals of Black Liberation Theology, emphasizing self-sufficiency, communal support, and resistance to economic exploitation. By championing these issues in Congress, Flake demonstrated that religious leaders could wield political power to effect concrete, community-focused change (Flake & Flake, 2000).

William H. Gray III: Congressional Leadership and Advocacy for Education

William H. Gray III, another influential figure who served in Congress, was deeply committed to educational reform and economic development for African Americans. A Baptist minister and the first African American to serve as Majority Whip in the House of Representatives, Gray used his leadership position to address disparities in education funding, access to affordable housing, and economic inequality. Gray's legislative initiatives reflected his belief that economic and educational equity were inseparable from social justice, a conviction rooted in his faith and religious commitment to serving others (Gray, 1991).

Throughout his congressional career from 1979 to 1991, Gray championed policies that increased funding for historically Black colleges and universities (HBCUs) and expanded federal aid for low-income students. His advocacy helped secure critical resources for HBCUs, recognizing them as essential institutions for empowering African Americans and advancing civil rights. Gray's contributions highlight how religious leaders can leverage political positions to champion equitable policies, especially in areas where systemic barriers have historically limited access and opportunity for Black communities (Rudolph, 2007).

Walter Fauntroy: Legislative Activism and Civil Rights in Washington, D.C.

Walter Fauntroy, a prominent civil rights leader and minister, represented Washington, D.C. as its first delegate in Congress. Fauntroy's career was marked by his tireless advocacy for civil rights and statehood for Washington, D.C., believing that political representation was integral to achieving racial justice. As a pastor and member of the SCLC, Fauntroy was a trusted ally of Martin Luther King Jr., organizing the historic March on Washington and later using his congressional position to push for civil rights legislation (Garrow, 1986).

Fauntroy's legislative priorities included expanding voting rights, advocating for D.C. statehood, and promoting policies that addressed housing inequality and police reform. His efforts reflected his conviction that the church's mission extended beyond spiritual guidance to include a responsibility to advocate for political and social reforms. Fauntroy's work underscores the distinctive approach of Black religious leaders who see legislative power as a means to promote systemic change, addressing the root causes of poverty, disenfranchisement, and racial injustice (Fauntroy, 1988).

COMPARATIVE ANALYSIS OF LEGISLATIVE EFFORTS AND RELIGIOUS MOTIVATION

The legislative careers of Young, Flake, Gray, and Fauntroy illustrate a unique approach to governance, where religious motivation directly informs political action. Each leader leveraged their roles in Congress to advance issues deeply rooted in Black Liberation Theology, such as economic empowerment, educational equity, and voting rights. Unlike many white evangelical leaders who primarily sought to preserve traditional social values, these African American leaders prioritized reforms that would dismantle structures of oppression, empowering communities historically marginalized by systemic discrimination.

Their collective impact on legislation reflects the broader objectives of the Black church, which has long viewed its mission as encompassing not only spiritual uplift but also active resistance to social injustices. By integrating religious convictions with legislative responsibilities, these leaders demonstrated that faith could drive policy reform, setting a precedent for future religious leaders in politics who seek to address both spiritual and social needs of their communities.

Next, let's expand on how Black Liberation Theology influenced legislative strategies, analyzing how African American leaders integrated faith-driven ideals into the political sphere. This section will emphasize the intersection of theology and policy, exploring how Black religious leaders approached governance to advocate for justice, equity, and systemic change.

BLACK LIBERATION THEOLOGY AND LEGISLATIVE STRATEGIES

Black Liberation Theology has long provided a foundational framework for African American clergy involved in the political sphere. Rooted in the teachings of theologians like James Cone, this theology emphasizes the need for an active, justice-oriented response to racial oppression. Central to Black Liberation Theology is the notion that religious faith mandates a commitment to eradicating structural inequalities, inspiring leaders to address injustices not just from the pulpit but through tangible legislative efforts (Cone, 1970). For Andrew Young, Floyd Flake, William H. Gray III, and Walter Fauntroy, the principles of Black Liberation Theology guided their political strategies and became an ethical compass in their legislative work.

Theological Foundations: The Pursuit of Justice in Public Policy

The influence of Black Liberation Theology on African American lawmakers reflects a deep belief that religious faith must drive efforts to transform oppressive societal structures. This theology positions Jesus Christ as a figure who champions the marginalized, making the struggle for social justice a sacred duty. This perspective drove leaders like Fauntroy and Gray to pursue policies that aligned with theological convictions, focusing on economic and social legislation that would advance the welfare of African Americans and other historically marginalized groups.

In Fauntroy's case, his work for civil rights legislation was deeply inspired by the Black church's call for liberation. For instance, he strongly advocated for the Comprehensive Employment and Training Act (CETA) during his tenure in Congress, which aimed to provide job training and employment opportunities to underserved communities, reflecting his commitment to economic justice. Fauntroy's support of CETA demonstrates how the teachings of Black Liberation Theology can manifest as practical policy solutions to address community needs (Garrow, 1986).

Similarly, William Gray's support for HBCU funding and federal educational assistance programs reflected his theological belief in equity. By securing financial resources for institutions dedicated to Black empowerment, Gray reinforced the idea that education is a powerful tool for social and economic uplift. This focus on educational equity resonates with Black Liberation Theology's emphasis on empowering Black communities, underscoring the significance of educational access as a means of liberation and self-sufficiency (Gray, 1991).

Legislative Approaches Rooted in Community Empowerment

African American religious leaders in Congress were distinct in their legislative approaches, as they actively sought to draft policies that would directly benefit their communities. Unlike their white evangelical counterparts, whose legislative goals often prioritized moral conservatism, Black religious leaders focused on structural change. This was evident in the work of Floyd Flake, who saw the church as a powerful institution for economic revitalization. His advocacy for community development projects, such as affordable housing initiatives and business incentives, reflected his belief that economic empowerment could drive social progress (Walrond, 2006).

Flake's economic policies were grounded in the concept of self-determination, a cornerstone of Black Liberation Theology, which emphasizes the agency of Black communities to control their economic destinies. By establishing the Allen AME Church as a center for economic growth, Flake demonstrated how faith could serve as the foundation for comprehensive economic empowerment. His legislative agenda, which included measures to incentivize business growth in Black neighborhoods, reflected his belief that economic stability was essential for achieving broader social justice goals.

THE CHALLENGE OF POLITICAL RESISTANCE AND THEOLOGICAL INTEGRITY

One of the most significant challenges that African American religious leaders faced in Congress was opposition from conservative factions that often resisted policies aimed at racial and economic equity. For example, Andrew Young's tenure as U.S. Ambassador to the United Nations was marked by significant political tension, particularly over his criticism of apartheid in South Africa. Young's outspoken stance against apartheid reflected his theological commitment to global justice; however, it also attracted criticism from those who viewed his diplomatic role as overly political for a religious leader. Young's experience highlights the complexities of navigating a political landscape that frequently prioritized economic and diplomatic interests over social justice (Young, 1996).

The tension between Young's theological commitments and political expectations underscores a broader issue faced by Black religious leaders in politics. When advocacy for racial and economic justice intersected with U.S. foreign policy interests, leaders like Young were often pressured to moderate their positions. Despite these challenges, Young remained firm in his belief that religious conviction should inform U.S. policy, particularly in matters of human rights. His resistance to political pressure exemplifies the strength of Black Liberation Theology as a guiding force, even amid the constraints of government bureaucracy.

COMPARATIVE PERSPECTIVE: EVANGELICAL CONSERVATISM VS. BLACK LIBERATION THEOLOGY IN POLICY

A key difference between African American leaders influenced by Black Liberation Theology and white evangelical leaders lies in their policy priorities and interpretations of Christian teachings. Whereas white evangelical leaders frequently aligned with conservative political platforms, focusing on issues such as opposition to abortion and LGBTQ+ rights, Black religious leaders prioritized social justice and economic equality. This divergence can be traced to their theological roots: Black Liberation Theology frames religious duty as an obligation to uplift the oppressed, while evangelical conservatism often emphasizes personal morality and adherence to traditional social structures (Emerson & Smith, 2000).

The comparative approaches of these two groups became particularly evident during the Reagan administration, when conservative evangelical leaders such as Jerry Falwell and Pat Robertson gained significant political influence. Their advocacy for policies that reinforced traditional family values often clashed with the agendas of Black religious leaders, who were fighting for civil rights protections and economic justice. For instance, whereas white evangelicals supported Reagan's tax cuts and welfare reductions, Black leaders in Congress opposed these measures, viewing them as detrimental to impoverished communities (West, 1982). This ideological divide highlights how different theological perspectives shape legislative priorities and the interpretation of religious responsibilities in public life.

ENDURING IMPACT ON SOCIAL AND ECONOMIC POLICY

The contributions of Young, Flake, Gray, and Fauntroy have left an indelible mark on U.S. policy, particularly in the realms of civil rights, education, and economic development. Their commitment to Black Liberation Theology's principles not only informed their legislative actions but also set a precedent for future African American lawmakers. By framing policy as a means of advancing social justice, these leaders introduced a moral dimension to governance that emphasized accountability to marginalized communities.

For example, Gray's work in securing funding for HBCUs established a legislative blueprint for subsequent leaders who sought to prioritize educational access. Similarly, Flake's economic initiatives demonstrated how churches could serve as vital institutions for community support and empowerment. Through their legislative achievements, these leaders have expanded the role of religious conviction in policy, illustrating that faith-driven principles can effectively address the social and economic needs of diverse communities.

LEGACY AND FUTURE IMPLICATIONS

The legacy of Black religious leaders in Congress continues to influence contemporary policymakers, who draw upon the example set by Young, Flake, Gray, and Fauntroy. Today's African American lawmakers often reference the work of these leaders, recognizing the enduring power of faith to inspire legislative action. The impact of Black Liberation Theology on public policy serves as a reminder that religious leadership is not confined to spiritual matters; it can also be a powerful force for social and political transformation.

This faith-driven approach to policy presents a challenge and an opportunity for modern religious leaders in politics. As current legislators navigate issues such as systemic racism, economic inequality, and criminal justice reform, the legacy of Black religious leaders provides a model for how faith can inform policies that strive for equity and justice. The alignment of theology and policy demonstrated by these pioneers offers a pathway for creating legislative solutions grounded in compassion, accountability, and justice.

Continuing with the historical context and influence of specific churches tied to prominent Black religious leaders, we will explore how these institutions shaped community empowerment and advocacy. Each leader's church not only provided a base for theological teaching but also served as a critical organizing center for political and social action.

Institutional Influence: Churches as Centers of Community and Political Mobilization

The Black church has historically been a hub of resilience, nurturing African American communities' spiritual, social, and political needs. Particularly during the Civil Rights Movement and the subsequent decades, churches linked to leaders such as Floyd Flake, Andrew Young, William H. Gray III, and Walter Fauntroy became catalysts for both community development and legislative action. The significance of these institutions cannot be overstated; they shaped not only the religious beliefs of their congregations but also guided community activism, providing a foundational framework for the political careers of these leaders.

Allen African Methodist Episcopal (AME) Church and Floyd Flake

The Allen AME Church in Jamaica, Queens, has long been a cornerstone for the local African American community, and its influence extended beyond religious teachings under the leadership of Reverend Floyd Flake. Flake became pastor of Allen AME in 1976, transforming it into a dynamic force for economic empowerment. His approach to ministry was unique in that it intertwined theological principles with practical applications in business and community development.

Through initiatives like the construction of affordable housing, job training programs, and small business development, Flake's church addressed systemic economic challenges faced by the African American community. One notable project was the Allen AME Housing Corporation, which provided affordable housing to thousands, reflecting Flake's vision of the church as a vehicle for economic uplift (Walrond, 2006). Under Flake's leadership, Allen AME became a model for how religious institutions could lead urban development and promote economic self-sufficiency. His work demonstrated that the church could extend its role beyond spirituality to tackle tangible issues like housing insecurity, job creation, and education.

Allen AME's initiatives became a blueprint for faith-based community development, inspiring similar projects nationwide. By emphasizing economic independence as part of Black Liberation Theology, Flake highlighted the importance of financial empowerment as a form of liberation. This practical, results-oriented approach helped Allen AME transform into one of the most prominent community development centers associated with an African American church, illustrating how theological principles could translate into large-scale social impact.

Andrew Young and Ebenezer Baptist Church

Before his political career, Andrew Young was deeply rooted in the Civil Rights Movement through his work with Dr. Martin Luther King Jr. at the Ebenezer Baptist Church in Atlanta. Although Young was not a pastor at Ebenezer, his involvement in the church's activities as a civil rights activist played a formative role in his views on social justice and advocacy. Ebenezer Baptist, under the pastoral leadership of King and later his family, became a focal point for mobilizing civil rights efforts, serving as the organizational and spiritual hub for actions that challenged systemic racism.

Ebenezer's influence extended beyond Atlanta, shaping Young's political consciousness and commitment to social justice. The church's emphasis on nonviolent resistance, moral integrity, and community service significantly impacted Young's approach to public service. His later work as a U.S. Congressman, Atlanta's mayor, and U.S. Ambassador to the United Nations reflected these values, as he advocated for policies aligned with justice and equality. Ebenezer Baptist Church exemplified the church's potential to function as both a moral and strategic center for social change, emphasizing activism grounded in theological principles (Young, 1996).

Young's work demonstrates how a church's influence can extend far beyond its immediate congregation, shaping leaders whose policies resonate on a national and international scale. His affiliation with Ebenezer Baptist Church represents the significant role Black churches play in inspiring leaders to address systemic issues, whether through direct action in civil rights or policy reform in government.

Bright Hope Baptist Church and William H. Gray III

William H. Gray III, who served as pastor of the Bright Hope Baptist Church in Philadelphia, was another prominent figure who combined his religious beliefs with political action. Bright Hope Baptist, established in 1910, had a longstanding tradition of community involvement and civil rights advocacy, a tradition that Gray amplified through his tenure as both a pastor and a congressman. His leadership at Bright Hope underscored the importance of the Black church in political mobilization and community support.

Gray's dual roles allowed him to bridge religious teachings with legislative influence, securing substantial federal funding for Historically Black Colleges and Universities (HBCUs) and advocating for economic opportunities within Black communities. Bright Hope's congregation supported his mission, viewing his political career as an extension of the church's social justice goals. Under Gray's leadership, Bright Hope became a symbol of religiously inspired political engagement, emphasizing education and economic development as cornerstones of liberation theology.

Gray's work illustrated the power of faith-based leadership in promoting education as a path to social mobility. His initiatives, such as increased funding for HBCUs and job training programs, aligned with Bright Hope's mission of empowerment, positioning the church as an institution that could impact policy on a national level. Gray's legacy underscores how a church with a strong commitment to social justice can shape leaders who create lasting policy changes for Black communities.

New Bethel Baptist Church and Walter Fauntroy

Walter Fauntroy, a civil rights activist and politician, served as pastor of the New Bethel Baptist Church in Washington, D.C., which became a stronghold for civil rights advocacy under his leadership. Fauntroy's church was instrumental in organizing local civil rights initiatives, often collaborating with national organizations to address racial injustice. His advocacy for voting rights, fair housing, and economic justice was deeply rooted in his role as a pastor, where he emphasized the moral imperative of social change.

New Bethel Baptist, like many Black churches during the Civil Rights Movement, functioned as both a sanctuary and a meeting place for activists. Fauntroy's commitment to civil rights was reflected in the church's activities, which included voter registration drives and educational programs aimed at empowering the local Black community. His work in Congress continued these efforts, as he consistently advocated for policies that addressed economic disparities and racial inequality (Garrow, 1986).

Fauntroy's leadership at New Bethel Baptist Church demonstrated how Black churches could serve as incubators for political action, fostering leaders committed to justice and equality. His tenure reflects the power of religious institutions to shape public policy through a moral lens, emphasizing the church's role as a force for systemic change.

The Enduring Influence of Black Churches in Shaping Public Policy

The legacy of these churches demonstrates that the Black church's influence extends far beyond traditional religious functions. By serving as centers for political mobilization, economic development, and social justice, institutions like Allen AME, Ebenezer Baptist, Bright Hope Baptist, and New Bethel Baptist shaped the political landscape in profound ways. Each church fostered leaders who carried their theological convictions into the legislative arena, advocating for policies that addressed the needs of marginalized communities.

These churches remain symbols of resilience and advocacy, illustrating the power of Black Liberation Theology in inspiring legislative action. Their legacies highlight the church's potential to serve as a foundational institution for community empowerment, showing how faith-based leadership can effect enduring social change. The ongoing influence of these churches reflects the sustained relevance of Black Liberation Theology in addressing contemporary issues, reminding current and future leaders of the church's role in advocating for justice.

CONCLUSION: FAITH-BASED LEADERSHIP AS A CATALYST FOR LEGISLATIVE CHANGE

The unique relationship between Black churches and political advocacy exemplifies how religious institutions can act as catalysts for social and legislative transformation. By integrating Black Liberation Theology into their legislative approaches, African American leaders like Flake, Young, Gray, and Fauntroy demonstrated that the church's influence could extend far beyond spirituality. Their work reminds us that faith-based institutions can play a pivotal role in shaping policies aimed at economic, social, and racial equity, influencing generations of leaders who continue to draw upon the legacy of Black Liberation Theology as a guiding force for justice.

Comparative Analysis: Black Liberation Theology vs. White Evangelical Conservatism

The roles that Black Liberation Theology and white evangelical conservatism play in American politics are strikingly different, rooted in distinct historical contexts, theological priorities, and political objectives. While Black religious leaders like Malcolm X, Floyd Flake, and Andrew Young emphasized systemic change and economic empowerment as expressions of faith, white evangelical leaders such as Billy Graham, Jerry Falwell, and Pat Robertson often championed conservative social policies, underscoring the alignment between religion and American traditionalism. This comparative analysis reveals the contrasting ways these leaders interpreted their faith's role in addressing society's structural issues, particularly in matters of racial justice, economic policy, and social welfare.

Theological Foundations: Liberation vs. Conservatism

Black Liberation Theology, as developed by James Cone, holds that Christianity must directly address systemic injustices, particularly those impacting African Americans. The premise is that Jesus's message was inherently revolutionary, advocating for the oppressed and challenging the status quo. Leaders who drew on these principles, like Malcolm X, saw religion as a pathway to liberation from oppressive systems and racial inequality. This theology thus positioned the church as an agent of social change, one that should actively challenge policies and structures that harm marginalized communities (Cone, 1970).

White evangelical theology, on the other hand, often focuses on individual salvation and personal morality. Leaders like Billy Graham were known for stressing the importance of personal conversion and individual piety, with less emphasis on addressing systemic inequalities. While some white evangelicals participated in the Civil Rights Movement, their involvement was often framed within a call for moral rectitude rather than systemic change. This focus on personal morality over structural reform is emblematic of a theology that prioritizes individual transformation as the primary means to societal improvement (Smith & Emerson, 2000). This divergence led to contrasting approaches in political advocacy: whereas Black Liberation Theology supported policies that sought structural equity, white evangelical leaders often endorsed policies rooted in a conservative vision of American society.

Approaches to Racial Justice

For Black Liberation Theology, racial justice is central to religious commitment. This perspective holds that Christianity demands a proactive stance against racial injustice, positioning the church as a political as well as a moral leader in the fight against racism. Leaders inspired by this theology, including Dr. Martin Luther King Jr. and later Floyd Flake, viewed civil rights as inseparable from religious duty. They actively supported legislation that aimed to dismantle segregation, address economic disparities, and provide greater political representation for African Americans. These leaders not only engaged in the Civil Rights Movement but continued to advocate for policies that addressed systemic inequities long after the movement's peak.

In contrast, many white evangelical leaders were hesitant, if not outright opposed, to racial integration efforts, particularly during the early stages of the Civil Rights Movement. Leaders like Jerry Falwell initially condemned civil rights activists as disrupting societal order, advocating instead for a "law and order" approach that emphasized personal accountability over social reform. While Falwell and others later adjusted their public stances as societal attitudes shifted, white evangelicalism largely continued to prioritize issues like opposition to abortion and same-sex marriage over advocating for racial equality (Balmer, 2014). This conservative stance not only reflects a different set of priorities but also highlights the reluctance within segments of white evangelicalism to confront the structural racism ingrained in American society.

Economic Justice and Policy Priorities

Economic justice has long been a pillar of Black Liberation Theology, as exemplified by leaders like William H. Gray III and Andrew Young, who advocated for policies aimed at reducing poverty, improving access to education, and providing affordable housing. Gray, for example, championed federal support for HBCUs, understanding education as a pathway to social mobility for African Americans. Similarly, Young's work focused on promoting economic development in marginalized communities, emphasizing that faith must be coupled with action to improve people's material conditions. These leaders viewed economic justice not as a secular goal but as a moral imperative that aligned with their faith's call to serve the "least of these."

Conversely, many white evangelical leaders have historically aligned with conservative economic policies, including free-market capitalism, deregulation, and reduced government intervention. This approach is influenced by a theological perspective that associates prosperity with personal virtue and regards poverty as largely a result of individual failings. Figures like Pat Robertson promoted the "prosperity gospel," which teaches that financial success is a sign of God's favor, often discouraging collective approaches to addressing economic disparities. While not all evangelicals adhere strictly to prosperity teachings, the broader evangelical alignment with conservative economic policies reflects an individualistic ethos that contrasts sharply with the communal approach of Black Liberation Theology (Bowler, 2013).

Social Policy: Differences in Focus and Advocacy

The divergent priorities of Black Liberation Theology and white evangelical conservatism are perhaps most apparent in their stances on social policies concerning family, education, and civil rights. Black religious leaders involved in liberation theology were deeply engaged in advocating for policies that addressed the root causes of inequality, including inadequate access to healthcare, lack of affordable housing, and underfunded schools. Figures like Walter Fauntroy argued for government intervention as a necessary means to rectify historical injustices and improve the welfare of African Americans. Their policy advocacy was informed by a theological conviction that God's justice demanded action on behalf of the vulnerable and oppressed.

In contrast, white evangelical leaders have often centered their social advocacy around issues like abortion, school prayer, and traditional family structures, which they see as foundational to a moral society. This focus on conservative family values has been instrumental in shaping their political alliances, most notably with the Republican Party. Leaders like James Dobson, founder of Focus on the Family, emphasized the need to restore America to what they perceived as its Christian roots, which they associated with a traditional vision of family life. This agenda often took precedence over addressing issues of economic or racial injustice, reflecting a theological outlook that sees America's moral renewal as achievable through the reinforcement of traditional values rather than structural reform (Guth et al., 2009).

The Role of the State: Advocacy and Political Partnerships

Another key distinction lies in each group's view of the government's role in addressing societal issues. Leaders influenced by Black Liberation Theology typically see government intervention as necessary for promoting justice, particularly when it comes to redressing historic injustices faced by African Americans. Figures like Andrew Young and Floyd Flake advocated for federal policies that addressed systemic inequalities, viewing such policies as consistent with their religious commitments to equality and justice. This alignment with governmental action often meant that Black religious leaders supported policies traditionally associated with the Democratic Party, focusing on expanding social welfare programs, funding for education, and civil rights protections.

White evangelical leaders, in contrast, have historically promoted limited government, aligning with conservative ideologies that emphasize personal responsibility and oppose expansive welfare programs. This stance reflects a theological view that minimizes the state's role in addressing social inequalities, often advocating instead for private charity and individual accountability. As a result, white evangelicals have found common ground with conservative politicians, particularly in the Republican Party, on issues such as tax cuts, deregulation, and reduced social spending. Their advocacy often promotes a vision of America as a "Christian nation" that should be governed by biblical principles, particularly in areas like marriage, education, and religious freedom (Wald & Calhoun-Brown, 2010).

CONCLUSION: DIVERGENT PATHS IN FAITH-BASED POLITICAL ENGAGEMENT

The divergent trajectories of Black Liberation Theology and white evangelical conservatism illustrate the profound impact of theological frameworks on political action. For leaders inspired by Black Liberation Theology, faith is inherently political, demanding active engagement in the struggle against systemic injustices. Their approach advocates for a holistic vision of liberation that encompasses both spiritual and material well-being, with a strong emphasis on government's role in promoting equity.

In contrast, white evangelical conservatism's focus on individual morality, traditional values, and limited government has produced a markedly different agenda, one that often prioritizes maintaining social norms over challenging systemic inequalities. This difference has shaped the landscape of American religious and political life, influencing not only policy but also broader societal debates over the role of religion in public life.

This comparison between Black Liberation Theology and white evangelicalism underscores how religious beliefs can drive distinct approaches to social justice, shaping leaders' priorities and alliances. As these two movements continue to influence American politics, they reveal the complex interplay between faith and ideology, demonstrating that religious commitment can be a powerful catalyst for either transformative change or the preservation of existing structures.

Religion as a Trusted Source of Information

Religious institutions have historically served as central repositories of knowledge and sources of guidance, especially in communities where access to education and literacy was limited. Churches, mosques, synagogues, and temples became hubs not only for worship but also for learning and the sharing of news and communal updates. This role is evident in the history of both Black Liberation Theology and white evangelical movements in America, as well as in other religious contexts worldwide.

In Black communities, for instance, churches became centers for both spiritual and practical information, helping people navigate the socio-political environment of segregation and systemic oppression. Churches informed congregants about critical matters ranging from civil rights protests to voter registration drives and employment opportunities. Leaders like Martin Luther King Jr. used the pulpit not only to preach but to share critical information that would empower the community to advocate for their rights. The reliability of churches as sources of information fostered a communal trust that enabled the effective dissemination of ideas and strategic plans crucial for social justice movements (Lincoln & Mamiya, 1990).

Similarly, in white evangelical circles, churches often played a role in framing social and political issues through a Christian lens. This practice amplified messages on moral topics like family values and educational policy, influencing congregants' views and actions. By addressing political and social issues from the pulpit, white evangelical leaders built a sense of collective identity and positioned themselves as authoritative voices in the broader moral and political debate (Balmer, 2014). The trust placed in religious institutions as providers of both spiritual and worldly guidance established them as key channels for disseminating influential messages.

Theological Narratives as Frameworks for Interpreting Social and Political Issues

Theological narratives shape how communities interpret social and political events, and thus play a significant role in the information disseminated within those communities. Black Liberation Theology, for example, uses the Christian message of liberation as a lens through which to view and address racial injustice, poverty, and oppression. This framework, developed by theologians like James Cone, teaches that Christianity is fundamentally concerned with justice for the oppressed, which empowers individuals to seek systemic change (Cone, 1970). By framing social and economic issues within a theological context, Black Liberation Theology inspires activism and fosters an informed public consciousness around topics such as economic inequality and civil rights.

Conversely, white evangelical theology often interprets social issues through a lens that emphasizes individual morality, personal salvation, and traditional values. This framework tends to focus on issues such as abortion, family structure, and religious freedom. Leaders like Jerry Falwell and Pat Robertson positioned these issues as non-negotiable, divinely sanctioned imperatives, shaping how congregants viewed these matters as central to their faith and voting choices. Theologies that link religious belief with specific social and political stances can create a strong impetus for collective action and reinforce community consensus on what constitutes moral or immoral behavior (Wuthnow, 1988).

In this way, theological narratives not only guide individual beliefs but also serve as foundational perspectives that influence what information is shared, how it's interpreted, and ultimately, how congregants choose to engage with broader societal issues.

Religious Leaders as Public Figures and Opinion Shapers

Religious leaders have historically wielded significant influence as trusted figures within their communities, often shaping public opinion on both local and national levels. Figures such as Malcolm X, Martin Luther King Jr., and Billy Graham illustrate how religious leaders can frame public discourse and mobilize their followers. Malcolm X, for instance, used his platform to critique American racial structures, linking the fight for civil rights to a broader spiritual struggle for dignity and justice. His speeches and writings provided followers with an ideological framework to understand their place in society and the means through which they could assert their rights (DeCaro, 1996).

In the context of white evangelicalism, leaders like Billy Graham and later Jerry Falwell wielded similar influence but often toward more conservative agendas. They utilized mass media, particularly television and radio, to reach wide audiences and advocate for political positions aligned with conservative values. This method of mass communication allowed evangelical leaders to influence followers' perspectives on issues ranging from foreign policy to domestic social issues, framing these stances as both biblically mandated and morally urgent (Eskridge, 1998).

The influence of religious leaders highlights how faith-based information dissemination operates through trusted personalities who bridge the gap between spiritual teachings and contemporary socio-political concerns. As community representatives, religious leaders often act as both moral guides and de facto community spokespeople, shaping public opinion and encouraging collective action based on theological convictions.

Impact on the Media Landscape: Broadcasting and Publishing

Religion's impact on information dissemination extends to the media landscape, where religious organizations have a long history of leveraging various media to reach broader audiences. From church-sponsored publications and radio broadcasts to the modern use of social media, religious movements have often used media to spread their messages. White evangelical organizations, in particular, were early adopters of radio and television as tools for evangelism and political advocacy. Figures like Pat Robertson pioneered Christian broadcasting networks that fused religious programming with conservative news and opinion, creating alternative media ecosystems that reinforced evangelical perspectives and amplified their reach (Hendershot, 2004).

Black religious communities also engaged with media, though often with fewer resources and through grassroots networks. African American church leaders have historically utilized newspapers, radio, and more recently, social media to address their communities directly and advocate for justice. During the Civil Rights Movement, Black-owned publications like The Chicago Defender and The Amsterdam News disseminated information that mainstream media often ignored, providing an essential platform for civil rights activists and church leaders. In this way, Black churches developed their own channels for informing the public about social injustices and mobilizing support for change (Roberts & Klibanoff, 2007).

Through these media efforts, religious organizations have played an integral role in shaping the public's access to information and, by extension, influencing collective beliefs and actions. These channels create alternative perspectives that not only offer congregants a theological view on current events but also shape their broader political and social ideologies.

CONCLUSION: RELIGION AS A FORCE IN INFORMATION DISSEMINATION

Religion functions as a powerful conduit for disseminating information due to its deep-rooted authority within communities, the influence of its leaders, and its active engagement with media. Through theological narratives that provide interpretive frameworks, trusted institutions that act as information hubs, and prominent leaders who mobilize followers, religious organizations shape how communities receive and respond to information. Whether through Black Liberation Theology's focus on systemic justice or white evangelicalism's emphasis on personal morality and traditional values, religion remains a major force in guiding public opinion and social action.

This unique position at the intersection of faith and information gives religious institutions the capacity to influence both individual beliefs and collective actions, often creating ripple effects that extend far beyond their congregations. As society continues to grapple with issues of inequality, political polarization, and social justice, understanding how religion disseminates information offers insight into its ongoing role in shaping public consciousness and influencing social change.

REFERENCES

Balmer, R. H. (2014). *Redeemer: The Life of Jimmy Carter*. Basic Books.

Cone, J. H. (1970). *A Black Theology of Liberation*. Orbis Books.

DeCaro, L. A. (1996). *On the Side of My People: A Religious Life of Malcolm X*. New York University Press.

Eskridge, L. (1998). *God's Right Hand: How Jerry Falwell Made God a Republican and Baptized the American Right*. Oxford University Press.

Hendershot, H. (2004). *Shaking the World for Jesus: Media and Conservative Evangelical Culture*. University of Chicago Press.

Lincoln, C. E., & Mamiya, L. H. (1990). *The Black Church in the African American Experience*. Duke University Press.

Roberts, G., & Klibanoff, H. (2007). *The Race Beat: The Press, the Civil Rights Struggle, and the Awakening of a Nation*. Vintage Books.

Wuthnow, R. (1988). *The Restructuring of American Religion: Society and Faith Since World War II*. Princeton University Press.

Chapter 17
Fake News Defamation and Sabotage of Prominent Civil Rights Leaders and President Obama:
A Historical Prospective of Fake News

Tara D. Miller
DeVry University, USA

ABSTRACT

Fake news has its roots in biblical times, as illustrated in the Book of Genesis, chapter 3:4-5. The woman fell victim to trickery and lies when she believed the false information conveyed by the serpent in the Garden of Eden. Similarly, journalists, law enforcement, federal agents, policymakers, and hate groups have all perpetuated fake news, which undermined the credibility of iconic change agents such as Dr. Martin Luther King, Jr.; Medgar Wiley Evers, Sr.; Malcolm X; and former President Barack Hussein Obama. Yet, these influential figures managed to change laws, advocate for justice, and spoke out against social ills that oppressed a nation in order to make life in America a better place for its citizens to dwell.

INTRODUCTION

The Defamation and Sabotage of Dr. Martin Luther King, Jr., Medgar Wiley Evers, Sr., Malcolm X, and former President Barack Hussein Obama is a text worth exploring. The chapter focuses on how fake news has systematically been used against the civil rights leaders, and former President Obama as they feverishly tried to erase prejudices in America. Historically, there has been a litany of destructive forces that these men have encountered as they were tried to champion justice, for their disenfranchised U.S. constituents.

The quote written above consists of only six words, but its significance of the statement has infinite value, which means that truth is associated with freedom and falsehood. The rationale for the text titled, " Fake News: The Defamation and Sabotage of Prominent Civil Rights Leaders, and President Obama: A Historical Perspective," is written to uncover the misconceptions, misrepresentations, fabrications,

DOI: 10.4018/979-8-3693-7468-9.ch017

and galvanized propaganda that have sabotaged, demeaned, and diminished the extraordinary contributions that the aforementioned Civil Rights' icons have rendered to American citizens locally, nationally, and globally with the intent of "Making America Great Again." The term fake news may be defined as "fabrication, or slippage, which is farthest from the truth" (Hunt, 2003, para. 1). While the *Oxford American Dictionary* (2008) defines sabotage as "to deliberately, destroy, damage, or hinder" (2008, p. 728). "Fake News" and sabotage coincide in meaning, and can evoke compelling ruins and devastation, for its target(s).

The former Federal Bureau of Investigation Director, J. Edgar Hoover, the FBI, former Sheriff Jim Clark who enforced segregation in Alabama, the White Citizens' Councils, the Ku Klux Klan, Silver Knights, Southern mobs, law enforcement, governors, private White citizens, and many other White Supremist Groups demonized, defamed, and tarnished the credible works of Dr. Martin Luther King, Jr., Medgar Wiley Evers, and Malcolm X, which had a residual effect when Barack Hussein Obama submitted his bid to enter the presidential election candidacy race in 2008. The topic on fake news back dates to the beginning of time, yet for the purpose of this chapter, "Fake News, dates back to the 1890s when sensational reports in newspapers were common, which was known as yellow journalism" (Jacobs, 2018, para. 4).

However, over 290 years prior to the 1600s, African American males' images were overly sensationalized with the advent of Yellow Journalism that depicted them as inferior, they are perceived as threats in their communities, and as creatures of dreadful existence due to the implementation of fake news.

Unfortunately, "Fake News" has served as a catalyst for destruction with the use of various media platforms, such as ABC, CNN, CBS, Fox News, NBC, and Scripps News. The aforementioned list of media outlets is not exhaustive; other platforms for conveying false information may be communicated in symposiums, town hall meetings, print journalism (newspapers), caricature pictures with captions, two-way communications, rallies, and social media (i.e., TikTok, Instagram, or Facebook). The spillage, leakage, and terroristic drippings of inflammatory "Fake News" deliberately destroys the ecology truth in its purest form(s). Therefore, when "Fake News" surface about genius iconic men such as (Dr. King, Medgar Wiley Evers, Malcolm X, and Former President Obama), many viewing and listening audiences may tend to accept false labels, stereotyping, uncouth practices, uncivilized, uneducated, violence, laziness, lewdness, and dishonesty as genuine character traits due to the color of these noblemen's melanin pigmentation. Colorism does not define the true essence of a person's character. Therefore, "Fake News" must be debunked at all costs, and the whistle must be blown to crush the toxic and hazardous venom that spurs from its falsified claims.

Whistleblowing is a method that is used to expose important truths. The editor of *Whistleblowing: Subversion or Corporate Citizenship?* suggests that:

> Whistleblowing is a new name, for ancient practice, which dates back from the development of the concept of individualism. In the eighth century before Christ, the Hebrew prophets in the Middle East, such as Hosea and Amos, did not hesitate to criticize rulers, and their social injustices, and in so doing risked their lives. (Vinten, 1994, p. 4).

Likewise, Dr. King, Medgar W. Evers, Malcolm X, and Former President Obama decided they all wanted to play a keen and pivotal role in the United States of America as agents of change, which would allow them to expose hatred, or help establish laws that extinguish the ongoing problem of racial nightmares that existed and continue to exist against African Americans throughout America. Their outcries to expose the second class-citizenry against people with melanin skin caused them to implement Henry David Thoreau's concept of civil disobedience. Civil Disobedience is a "revolutionary call to action. It is a call to reject the status quo, to rise-up, and reclaim one's rights, autonomy, and dignity" (Thoreau, 2023, p. 279), which is precisely what Dr. King, Evers, Malcolm X, and Former President Obama did.

HISTORICAL CONTEXT

Nevertheless, throughout the centuries, especially after the growth of the slave trade, sexual stereotypes and negative images were considered a necessary part of the enslavement. These images did not die with slavery, but in the United States the stereotypical illustrations continued well into the Reconstruction era. History that kept people in bondage.

In the late 1800s, a controversial book was published that summarized the attitudes of many White Americans towards African Americans. This text was considered one of the most influential and best-sold books of its time, Thomas F. Dixon's *The Clansman: An Historical Romance of the Ku Klux Klan* was the most popular in a series of essays that depicted Black people as lust-driven savages, capable only of bestial behavior. Unfortunately, seminal director David W. Griffith, translated this novel into a groundbreaking and visually influential film, *Birth of a Nation*, released in 1915. It was a that movie drew thousands of White people to theaters across America, for it substantiated what most believed all the long: that "Black men were violent, sexual savages who derived satisfaction in lusting after White women" (Jordan, 1977, p. 135). Naturally, their portrayals were shamelessly stereotypical, a product of the egotistical fantasies of those intended to keep African Americans under control.

In D.W. Griffith's 1915 film, the "black men were portrayed as violent, sexual savages who derived particular satisfaction in lusting after white women" (Winthrop, p. 135). The use of blackface by actors in *Birth of a Nation* signifies a dramatically contradictory attitude towards color. In particular, the use of burnt cork by White actors who portrayed Black people in movies of the time indicates a widespread belief that Black actors could not represent themselves on screen, which proved, in some sense that they were incompetence. There is even a psychological element that may suggests that the use of blackface is one indication of paradoxical love–hate relationship with the very people White America sought to belittle; a mirror image of White supremacist ideology turned back on itself:

> We can be (like) "them" versus "they need not exist." The actor who played Gus (the renegade), and Lynch (the Mulatto) in *Birth of a Nation* use their White bodies to take on the aura of the not-there Black body of the Other, simultaneously erasing and reproducing, slaying, and resurrecting him. The origin of desire mimesis—mimetism—and no desire is ever forged that does not at once desire the death and disappearance of the model or 'exemplary' personage that gave rise to it. (Gubar, 1997, p. 45)

The White male in most instances represented power, control, and ultimate masculinity. One way to exalt oneself is to defame and degrade someone else's personality and character with false information. Enslaved Africans represented the perfect vehicle, for exploitation in three specific areas: field labor, domestic services, and procreation.

The origins of some of the very specific stereotypes found in *Birth of a Nation*, vaudeville, and films may well have had their origins in slavery. Before and after slavery, it was believed that Black men unquestionably desired and lusted after White women because they were driven by their wild, uninhibited sexual passion. The ideology of having an oversexualize appetite for White women was a myth to justify the cruel treatment of African American males and the exploitation of their sexuality. Another exploited myth about Black characterization was embodied in the role of Sambo. Again, during slavery:

> Some slaves, for example may have indeed "shuffled," acted ignorantly, and moved slowly as a ruse to fool their masters, thus developing into the Sambo stereotype. This caricature type figure was indolent, faithful, humorous, loyal, dishonest, superstitious, improvident, and musical; the Sambo was inevitably a clown and congenially docile." (Blassingame, 1972, p. 56).

As such, when men like Dr. King, Evers, and Malcolm X continued to witness the bias, unfair, and unequal treatment of African Americans in the 1950s and 60s, they decided to speak out against systemic oppression, peacefully marched, and protested against the social ills that policy makers, politicians, and law makers inflicted upon those of color who encountered distress, overt racism, economic hardship, senseless violence, systemic, institutionalized racism, and demystifications. Dr. King, Evers, and Malcolm X eventually all paid the ultimate sacrifice with their lives in order, for Former President Barack H. Obama to attain one of the highest occupations in America as Commander in Chief, and for many African Americans to receive some form of equal acceptance as Americans. Although African Americans have had some forms of successful gains in the United States, they still have a very long way to go with fair treatment in comparison to their European American counterparts who for some regards; continue to depict most African Americans as savages, sexual wantons, criminals, thugs, lazy, animalistic, liars, murderers, and thieves on social media outlets locally, nationally, and globally, which is attributed to as "Fake News."

HISTORICAL ADVOCATES

The significance of this chapter is to identify four (4) historical advocates who fought for equal justice and how they were portrayed as savages, coons, and darkies as they dared to take a political stand for righteousness and fair treatment for African Americans and humanity as a whole.

Initially, Dr. Martin Luther King, Jr. dared to accept the mantle of responsibility when he became the president of the Montgomery Improvement Association (MIA), and with that charge came the burden of ridicule, defamation, backlash, slander, and ultimately death. White supremacist organizations, groups, and agencies such as The White Citizens' Councils, the Central Intelligent Agency (CIA), the Black Legion, the Ku Klux Klan (KKK), Southern Congressmembers, White Segregationists and Supremacists, White extremists, the Federal Bureau of Investigation (FBI), J. Edgar Hoover (Director of the FBI), George Wallace (Governor of Alabama), and Theophilus Eugene "Bull" Connor (Commissioner of Safety for the City of Birmingham, Alabama), law enforcement, private citizens, and public officials posed as terroristic threats against the martyr, Dr. King, who believed strongly in practicing non-violent and peaceful protests. However, the FBI appeared to be the agency that worked hardest against Dr. King's agenda the most:

> The FBI secretly monitored Dr. King's every move. J. Edgar Hoover redoubled his pernicious efforts to destroy Martin King. Hoover wiretapped conversations between Dr. King and Stanley David Levison (a Jewish Attorney) then he misinterprets Dr. King's remarks and runs to President Lyndon B. Johnson, insisting that King is planning to incite riots and take over Chicago's Loop. Hoover also maligns King as an instigator, which eroded the then president's faith in his former ally's intention. (Smiley, 2014, p. 89)

J. Edgar Hoover's willingness to sabotage, defame, twist, fabricate, diminish, and tarnish Dr. King's work with malicious intentions was not a surprise. According to Coretta Scott King:

> Martin was concerned about all disinherited people, not just Blacks but Whites as well. He advocated about the contemporary struggles that unfolded around economic issues. He spoke out sharply, for all the poor in all hues, for he knew if color made them different, misery and oppression made them the same. (King, 2010, p. 15)

Instead of protecting Dr. King from violent attacks by enemy forces, both President Johnson and FBI Director Hoover became King's adversaries.

Former President Johnson thought movement activists like King posed threats to the established order and needed to be watched and controlled. Members of the press could have exposed the bureau's campaign, and many government officials who could have stopped, curtailed or exposed the FBI's attack on King, but instead they enabled or encouraged it (Eig and Theoharis, 2023, para. 4).

Moreover, Hoover's campaign revolved around power; he made sure that King did not have too much of it. After he witnessed King's success at the March on Washington in 1963, William Sullivan, the FBI Assistant Director who was responsible for the domestic intelligence division under Hoover, made the decision to bug King's room at the Willard Hotel in Washington, D.C. 'We must mark him now,' Sullivan wrote in a 1963 memo, "as the most dangerous Negro of the future in this nation" (para. 17). Less than two months later, Robert Kennedy, then the Attorney General, signed off on the decision to wiretap King's home and offices. J. Edgar Hoover's main objective was designed to "destroy King," and ruin him" (para. 18).

Dr. King courageously challenged the status quo; he blew the whistle on the United States lawmakers, Jim Crow Laws, the judicial systems, state and local officials in Alabama, Mississippi, Tennessee, Illinois, and California, for their inhumane forms of oppression and maltreatment against African Americans. Unfortunately, Dr. King was retaliated against in various forms as he was assaulted, battered, jailed, beat, stabbed, blasted, and ultimately murdered on April 4, 1968, based on an eyewitness, a Ms. Lula Mae Shelby, "Dr. King did not actually die from the shot womb to his neck, but rather he died in the hospital bed after arriving at St. Joseph Hospital in Memphis, Tennessee where the Chief of Surgery, Dr. Breen Bland, smothered King with a pillow. Dr. King pronounced dead five minutes after 7 p.m. Ms. Shelby, a Surgical Aide at Saint Joseph Hospital, is said to have provided this detailed confession to Dr. William F. Pepper (2016), an attorney to the King Family, and author of *The Plot To Kill King: The Truth Behind The Assassination of Martin Luther King Jr.* Shelby's account is as follows:

> The ambulance from St. Joseph's arrives and Dr. King, accompanied by Ralph Abernathy and Bernard Lee, is taken to the emergency room of the hospital where those on duty begin to work on him. At the hospital, military personnel are everywhere, knowing the names of all staff, most of whom are required to remain overnight. Emergency room workers proceed on Dr. King, who still is alive, with the recommendation that he be taken to surgery. (Pepper, 2016, p. 273)

This is rejected by Dr. Breen Bland, who comes in and takes charge, at one point ordering, "Stop working on that nigger and let him die." He then ordered everyone out of the ER, while remaining there with two men in suits. Dr. Bland and the two men in suits spit on the body of Dr. King. The breathing tube is removed and Dr. Bland places a pillow on Dr. King's face, ensuring death, which was declared at 7:05. (p. 274)

On April 4, 1968, Walter Cronkite, an iconic news anchor for CBS News, announced, "Dr. Martin Luther King, Jr., the apostle of non-violence in the civil rights movement, has been shot to death in Memphis, Tennessee" (CBS News, 2018, para. 3). Cronkite, also "reported that police were searching for a young White man seen running from the scene," a false report that exemplified "Fake News" (CBS News, 2018, para. 3). There are many versions of how Dr. King's life ended on April 4, 1968, but in

Tavis Smiley's book titled: *Death of a King: The Real Story of Dr. Martin Luther King, Jr.'s Final Year*, he shared his perspective on King's death in this regard:

> Dr. King leans over the rail. Takes a deep breath. Spots Jesse Jackson in the courtyard. Jesse, Dr. King yells down; I want you to come to dinner with me. Jesse introduces King to the man standing next to him. Dr. King, you *[sic]* remember Ben Branch? He's our saxophonist. Memphis musician. Oh, yes, Dr. King calls down, he's my man. How are you, Ben?... Make sure you play "Precious Lord, Take My Hand" in the meeting tonight. Play it real pretty. Then a shot rings out. The bullet finds its mark. Dr. King falls. At age thirty-nine, his life on earth ends. *[sic]* (2014, p. 246)

Although Dr. King was murdered, his legacy and non-violent practices are still relevant today in the 21st century. Had it not been for the enormous sacrifice that Dr. King made at the youthful age of 25-years-old to be an agent of change, many people who experienced oppression because of the color of their skin would more than likely not have made the tremendous strides if the Civil Rights Act had not been signed into law on July 2, 1964. One would think that Americans, of all nationalities and women, would express a little more gratitude for Dr. King's unwavering fight for equality through his non-violent practices. Although the Civil Rights Act was signed in 1964 by President Lyndon Baines Johnson, it still did not stop the flow of violence against a person of color. Dr. King once stated that "A Negro's life is still worthless in many parts of his own country" (King, 2010, p. 23); he made the comment at the time because James Meredith, the first African American to integrate the University of Mississippi in 1962, was shot in the back on June 6, 1966 while he was marching in the Freedom March from Mississippi to Alabama. Several news media outlets reported that James Meredith was shot by a White man as he walked through Hernando, Mississippi with a few supporters and journalists. In fact, some initial news reports stated that Meredith had died (King, 2010, p. 23).

This news, reported by journalists, caused Dr. King, Stockley Carmichael a former member of the (Student Nonviolent Coordinating Committee S.N.C.C./ founder of the Black Power Movement B.P.M.), and Floyd McKissick the former (National Director of Congress of Racial Equality C.O.R.E.) to experience "anger and dismay" (King, 2010, p. 23), but the story that the journalist reported was indeed "Fake News." Dr. King claimed he discovered, "After several calls between Atlanta and Memphis, we learned that the earlier reports of Meredith's death was false, and he would recover" (King, 2010, p. 24). "Fake News" can cause emotional distress, trauma, horror, and disbelief, and it can destroy and tarnish the credibility of the media outlet source. James W. Loewen the author of *Lies My Teacher Told Me: Everything Your American History Textbook Got Wrong*, denoted, "The FBI also tried to sabotage receptions in King's honor when he traveled to Europe to claim the Nobel Peace Prize," which is despicable (2018, p. 237).

"Fake News" did not end with the King Era; it also plagued another brave Civil Rights advocate who opposed segregation, Jim Crow Laws, and second-class citizenry; his name was Medgar Wiley Evers, Sr. Mr. Evers was a World War II Veteran, a graduate of Alcorn Agricultural and Mechanical College, Civil Rights Leader, and the first Field Secretary of the Mississippi Conference for the National Association for the Advancement of Colored People (NAACP). The NAACP was founded in "1909 by Dr. W. E. B. Dubois, Ida B. Wells, and Mary White Ovington" (Encyclopedia Britannica, 2024, para. 1). The founders created the organization to ensure that the rights of African Americans and other minorities' rights were implemented fairly, equally, and justly, without bias, segregation, or discrimination. In November 1958:

> The Negro said, unconsciously as he drove down the highway as he saw a White boy on the outskirts of Jackson with his thumb up in the traditional plea of the hitchhiker. Look at him, he's free. They've taught him that he owns the world. That's what I want for my kids-freedom-right here in Mississippi. And as long as God gives me strength to work and try to make things real, for my children, I'm

going to work for it—even if it means making the ultimate sacrifice. (Williams-Evers and Manning, 2005, p. 111)

"That Negro" was none other than Medgar Evers, Sr. He loved Mississippi, born and raised, but he did not like the injustices that existed there. Most southern states' citizens and political law officials practiced, and enforced Jim Crow Laws, and segregationist policies that oppressed people of color. The justification for Jim Crow laws and segregation stemmed from slavery, the Reconstruction Era after the Civil War, and the abolishment of slavery. In July 1954, in Sunflower County, Mississippi, a local plantation manager, Robert B. Patterson, along with several businessmen and public officials, formed a "Citizens' Council" dedicated to the preservation of White supremacy, and militant resistance to school desegregation. (Williams-Evers and Manning, 2005, p. 18)

As the NAACP's Field Secretary for the Mississippi Conference, Evers's job was to visit various communities and counties within the Jackson metropolitan area to register Black citizens to vote; he also spoke to Black residence about integration of schools, protests, boycotts, and he investigated two murders. The first murder occurred on May 7, 1955, which was 51-year-old, Reverend George Washington Lee who was an entrepreneur, minister, and civil rights advocate; however, the second murder was that of 14-year-old, Emmett Till, a native of Chicago, Illinois; both African American males were murdered in Mississippi.

In 1955:

The Reverend George Lee, a prominent minister and successful entrepreneur in Belzoni, Mississippi was determined to succeed as a Civil Rights Leader. He was the first Black citizen to register to vote in Humphreys County, where Blacks were a majority of the population. In 1953, Lee and Gus Courts, a Black grocer and early activist, co-founded the Belzoni branch of the NAACP. When Lee and Courts tried to register to vote and the sheriff refused to accept their poll taxes, they reported the case to federal authorities. They then registered successfully, which angered local Whites. Together, Lee and Courts registered nearly all of the county's Black voters in 1955, despite threats of violence and economic pressures. The Regional Council of Negro Leadership, a leading Black organization in the state, pressed for voting rights and organized a successful boycott of gas stations that refused to install restrooms for Blacks. Lee spoke at the Council's annual meeting in 1955 in Mound Bayou, Mississippi and a *JET Magazine* journalist reported that Lee "electrified" the crowd. He urged Blacks to vote, he told them that if they did, the Delta would someday send a Negro to Congress.

On May 7, 1955, Lee drove on a street in Belzoni, Mississippi when a car pulled up alongside his, and assailants shot him in the face. He lost control of the car and crashed; he was rushed to the hospital but died in route. The next day Jackson's *Clarion-Ledger Newspaper* Editor ran the story under the headlines: "Negro Leader Dies in Odd Accident." Lee's wife and others demanded an investigation by the FBI, which built a circumstantial murder case against two men, but the local prosecutor refused to take the case to a grand jury. When NAACP Field Secretary Medgar Evers came to investigate the murder, Sheriff, Ike Shelton, insisted that an autopsy was not necessary, and informed Evers that Lee died from a car crash and that the lead found in his jaw was dental fillings. Yet, an examination of Lee's body by two Black physicians revealed that two to three rifle shots were fired—one at point-blank range into the cab, which ripped off the lower left side of Lee's face. Medgar Evers and others called on Governor Hugh White to investigate, but White refused. The crime went unchallenged, but news of it was reported nationally. The Reverend George Lee's widow, Mrs. Rosebud Lee, prophetically decided to hold an open-coffin ceremony for her late husband that later planted the seeds for a similar decision by Mamie

Till-Mobley, Emmett Till's mother. Many consider Reverend Lee to be the first martyr of the modern Civil Rights Movement. (Booker, 1955, pp. 8-11).

The "Fake News" and lies that were reported by Sheriff Ike Shelton and the Jackson's *Clarion-Ledger* were designed to distort the truth about the repugnant hatred, racism, and discriminatory practices executed against African Americans in the state of Mississippi. Only a few months later, on August 28, 1955, little did Evers realize he would be called upon to investigate the murder of a 14-year-old named Emmett Till. Although Till's death was captured in newspapers, magazines, and on television, the same "Fake News" and lies would again be propagated by Jackson's *Clarion-Ledger*. In 1955:

> Two White vigilantes committed violent acts against 14-year-old Emmett Till, a Black Chicago teenager who was kidnapped and murdered in Money, Mississippi on August 28, 1955. Till's murderers were arrested, tired, and declared not guilty by an all-White jury. Till's unforgiveable alleged offense was that he whistled at a White woman. The Till case, and the courageous decision made by the deceased boy's mother, Mamie Bradley, to publicize the brutality of her son's death exposed White Mississippi citizens' racist behaviors' throughout the world. Evers worked exhaustively on Till's murder, along with Aaron Henry, Amzie Moore, and Rudy Hurley. Medgar Evers' brother Charles Evers claimed he and the aforementioned men all dressed like field hands and slid around the Delta, as they looked, for criminal evidence, as they tried to convince folk who knew Emmett Till to risk their lives as legal witnesses. Although Whites harassed them, they pressed on with their mission. Medgar wanted to shame all America with the story of Emmett Till. He wanted to make the Civil Rights struggle a mass movement.
>
> In a 1968 oral-history interview, NAACP Field Organizer Howard Spence was assigned to the Till investigation, he declared, had it not been for Medgar Evers, who was N.A.A.C.P. Secretary at the time…it would have just been another "case" that's been forgotten…The Emmett Till case was the start of the Montgomery bus boycott. It was the beginning of a lot of incidents in the South that began to make the Negro conscious of the fact that he would have to get out and expose himself to racist Mississippians—to people who plotted to kill him. (Evers-Williams and Marable, 2005, p. 16)

As a result of Evers' audacity to investigate the murders of both Reverend Lee's and Emmett Till's, many White citizens were not pleased with his efforts to create equality, justice, and a better way of life for African Americans. Plus, they were enraged by his courage to "apply for admission to the University of Mississippi to attend Law School" (Evers-Williams and Marable, 2005, p. 12).

When Evers applied to the University of Mississippi Law School, he was rejected and became a target among the disgruntle White citizens who were outraged by his actions. Although Evers had a thirst for knowledge, sought upward mobility for his family, his community, and himself, his choices sent a shock wave of fear to his European American counterparts. As a result, White supremacists made several threats and attempts to kill Evers and to defame his name. On the contrary,

> Medgar Evers, unlike Dr. King, was not an advocate of "non-violence" in the face of White terrorism. He purchased a rifle, and over the next years carried it with him in his automobile, in case he had to protect himself and his family. He concluded that 'race war' was a real possibility throughout the South's Black Belt Region, if Blacks collectively ever created a real political movement to resist their oppression. (Evers-Williams and Marable, 2005, p. 11)

The state of Mississippi's White citizens, law enforcement, KKK Members, and the White Citizens' Council, were notorious for lynching, burning crosses, murdering, beating, and oppressing African Americans. Therefore, when many White citizens and leaders in Jackson, Mississippi observed that Medgar Evers continued to assist Black people, they knew they had to devise a plan to permanently stop him.

> Whites who collectively murdered African Americans in Mississippi in the late nineteenth and early twentieth centuries not only made a statement about racial hierarchy, but also a statement about law. Law was too capricious, too unpredictable, too formal, too abstract, and too concerned with process and at least the procedures of fairness to regulate the crucial social distinctions of the color line. Racist Whites throughout much of the state of Mississippi viewed scare tactics, murders, and lynchings as the most effective means of responding to African American resistance. (Evers-Williams and Marable, 2005, p. 67)

The fact that Evers's bold and courageous actions did not deter his stance as a catalyst and crusader for justice is exemplary. According to Evers's widow, Mrs. Myrlie Evers-Williams:

> He was the voice of the Civil Rights in our state. He investigated murders, lynchings, planned voter registration drives, organized boycotts, and fought to gain access for our people and representation where there was none. Because of such efforts, many die-hard segregationists believed Medgar needed to be crucified. (Evers-Williams and Blau, 1999, p. 6)

A segregationist is someone who believes that ethnic groups should only inhabit areas with their own ethnicities in relation to educational institutions, social events, religion, marriage, housing, employment, socioeconomic matters, dining facilities, and financial institutions. Unfortunately, since Evers continued to aid others African Americans and people of color with the option of a better way of life, excluded bondage, oppression, discrimination, persecution, and mental and physical torture; he was murdered on June 12, 1963, by Byron De La Beckwith, a segregationist who sabotaged Evers' plans to advocate against the injustices that hindered African Americans not just in Jackson, Mississippi, but throughout the state. Beckwith was tried, for the murder of Evers' twice, which resulted in a mistrial, but propaganda played a pivotal role in Beckwith's verdicts.

Propaganda surfaced twice based on Evers-Williams's account:

> Both times, twelve men—all of them White—could not agree on a verdict, and Beckwith was set free. Twice before, in the case of Medgar's murder, and in countless other instance as well, Mississippi had sent a message to the world that it is all right to kill a Black man. In my view, Byron De La Beckwith wasn't the only one on trial. So was Mississippi. (Evers-Williams, and Blau, 1999, p. 6)

The twelve White men who served on the jury trial, for Beckwith were also his peers and coworkers. It was even reported that the governor of Mississippi, Ross Robert Barnett a segregationist entered the courtroom before the hung jury's verdict was rendered to hug Beckwith for support. This hug could be interpreted as a subtle message that indicated that Beckwith would be set free momentarily. Indeed, Beckwith regained his freedom for 30-years, but on February 5, 1994, he was found guilty of Evers's murder, and justice finally prevailed. Beckwith's three sons, who wore "Confederate flag pins on their jacket lapels watched their father's conviction in a Mississippi Courtroom in Jackson, and as Beckwith's wife (Thelma) screamed out, 'He didn't do it; it was the Jews'" (Evers-Williams, and Blau, 1999, p. 9). This statement was fabricated and a blatant lie. If Myrlie Evers-Williams had not been persistent with the criminal case against her husband's murderer, the whistle would never have been blown that led to Beckwith's conviction. Evers was only 37-years-old when he was murdered in Jackson, Mississippi, two year younger than Dr. King, who was 39 -years-old when he, too, was gunned down 209 miles away in Memphis, Tennessee, in 1968, which was five years after Evers's death.

Moreover in 1965, 1,108.4 miles from Memphis, Tennessee, and 1,209.3 from Jackson Mississippi, Malcolm Little, most popularly known as Minister Malcolm X, then El-Hajj Malik El-Shabazz, was murdered in Harlem, New York. Before his assassination, Malcolm X, as referenced in this article, was an advocate for equality and justice for the Nation of Islam and the oppressed. The *American Heritage*

Dictionary defines the term oppressed as "to keep down by unjust use of force or authority" (Dell, 2012, p. 589). Malcolm X often spoke in open forums such as townhalls, auditoriums, radio platforms, television broadcasts, print media, and assemblies about the ideologies of the Honorable Elijah Muhammad and the oppression of the Black man. According to the *Encyclopedia Britannica* (2024), Elijah Muhammad was an "American religious leader, Black separatist, and a self-proclaimed Messenger of Allah who led the Nation of Islam" (p. 1).

Muhammad was known for his "Flamboyant rhetoric directed at White people, whom he called 'Blue-Eyed Devils' (Encyclopedia Britannica, 2024, para. 3). He believed that a separate nation for African Americans should be created, and that Blacks were Allah's chosen people, which is similar to how some people believe in segregation and that European Americans are God's chosen people, with Jesus Christ as the Messiah (Encyclopedia Britannica, 2024, p. 2). As a result of Elijah Muhammad's philosophies about separatist views, Malcolm Little studied under the Prophet's tutelage, and became his most devoted student messenger.

Furthermore, Malcolm X changed his surname from Little because he wanted to denounce his slave master's name. From adolescent to adulthood, Malcom Little saw how racism destroyed and sabotaged his life. When he was a child living in Lansing, Michigan with his parents, their house was burned down after they refused to vacate the premises because their White neighbors did not want them in the same neighborhood. In book titled *The Dead are Arising: The Life of Malcolm X*, written by Les Payne and Tamara Payne (2020) they exclaim that:

> Judge Leland W. Carter ruled that the Negro family could legally own the property, but under the terms of the restrictive covenant, they could not live in the house. Siding with the White neighbors, Judge Carr initiated court proceedings for the Littles to vacate their home. A few weeks later, in the middle of the night—at about 2:30 a.m. on November 8, a Friday—an explosion rocked the house and the entire family. (p. 64) Sadly, the "Lansing Fire Department refused to respond to the fire at the colored residence" (Payne & Payne, 2020, p. 65), and the home burned to the ground.

This criminal act committed by White racists was driven by discrimination and separatism. Instead of delivering a fair ruling, the judge chose to evict the Littles, leaving them destitute and homeless. From his teenage years to his early 20s, Little was incarcerated at various times, and before his release from prison, he joined the Nation of Islam. He became a prolific speaker and a temple organizer who helped to recruit men to grow the Nation, and he founded the newspaper *Muhammad Speaks*. One might assume that Malcolm X sought a better life after his release from confinement, but he too faced trouble from the FBI similar Dr. King's experience.

In 1963, a paradigm shift occurred in Malcolm X's life when President Kennedy was assassinated in Dallas, Texas, on November 22, 1963. The Messenger made a controversial comment likening the assassination to "chickens coming home to roost," which disturbed Elijah Muhammad. As a result of this statement, Malcolm X was suspended from the Nation of Islam for 90 days and silenced by Muhammad. During his suspension, Malcolm X took a pilgrimage to Mecca. Through his interactions with fellow Muslims of various ethnicities (i.e., White, Middle Eastern, African, American, Black, and Indian), Malcolm X discovered that the Islamic faith embraced people of all ethnicities. This led him to question and challenge some of the customs, rituals, and teachings of Elijah Muhammad. Unbeknown to Malcolm upon his return from Mecca not only would he have to deal with terrorizations from Muhammad, but he would encounter a Judas Iscariot within his inner circle:

> Gene Roberts a former Navy Veteran was assigned to Malcolm X to protect him. Little did the Messenger realize that the undercover police officer was a spy for FBI Director, J. Edgar Hoover. I was just coming back from the military; I heard a couple of Malcolm X's speeches when he was in the Nation. And I didn't particularly care for him. I was one of those middle-class Blacks that had a half-ass education. I wasn't political. Although Roberts had not penetrated Malcolm's inner circle, his feigned loyalty was sufficient to have gained him entrée. He had gotten close enough for his government work. (Payne & Payne, 2020, p. 462)

Roberts was an informant for the Bureau of Special Services Investigations (B.O.S.S.I.), which shared its information with FBI Director Hoover. Since Malcolm X's home was bombed the day before he was scheduled to deliver his speech at the Audubon Ballroom, he was "expected to set off some polemical fireworks against Elijah Muhammad in Harlem's meeting at the Audubon Ballroom" (Payne & Payne, 2020, p. 462).

It was noted that:

> Malcolm did not disappoint, even though he began slowly. Uncharacteristically halting and apologetically at first, he sketched out what had happened in the Sunday morning attack. He then got back on course with the scathing critique of US misbehavior in the Congo, and other parts of Africa, where countries were fighting colonialism supported by American planes and materiel. Then Malcolm sharpened his declaration of open warfare on Elijah Muhammad's group. As fiery as he'd ever been, he blasted Captain Joseph, the man he had brought with him from Detroit to Chicago a decade earlier, for claiming that Malcom had bombed his own home with his wife and sleeping babies inside. Now, they are using the same tactics that's used by the Ku Klux Klan, Malcolm declared. When the Klan bombs your church, they say you did it. When they bomb the synagogue, they say the Jews bombed their own synagogue. (Payne & Payne, 2020, 462)

Malcolm X's observations parallel with both Dr. King's and Evers's life experiences. Hoover spied on Dr. King with the permission of both Former President Lyndon B. Johnson and US Attorney General Robert F. Kennedy. Many conspiracy theorists believe that the deaths of both Malcolm X and Dr. King were orchestrated by the FBI and the CIA. This contrasts with the fake news that broadcast James Earl Ray as Dr. King's assassin in 1968 and Muhammad A. Aziz and Khalil Islam as Malcolm X's in 1965. Some intellectual scholars who have written extensively about Dr. King and Malcolm X also suggest that both iconic Civil Rights' advocates may have been betrayed by members of their inner circle who colluded with the FBI and CIA to facilitate their murders. Yet, in more recent news, the daughters of the late great, Malcolm X are suing the FBI, CIA and the New York Police Department, for their allege involvement with the death of their father. As of November 16, 2024, Civil Rights Attorney, Benjamin Crump who is representing the family, claims that:

> Malcolm X was killed in 1965 when three men shot him 21 times as he was preparing to speak in New York. Attorney Crump noted in the lawsuit that a corrupt, unlawful and unconstitutional relationship between law enforcement and the ruthless killers allowed for the murder. A link between the agencies and the killers went unchecked for many years and was actively concealed, condoned, protected, and facilitated by government agents. (Wright, 2024, p. 2)

Despite the challenges and extreme sacrifices faced by Dr. King, Medgar Evers, and Malcom X, they won the ultimate battle by initiating change and advancing the fight for justice. These iconic activists paved the way, enabling Americans to elect the first African American President, Barack Obama, in 2008, and re-elected him to a second term from 2013 to 2017. Before Obama was elected and while he was a presidential candidate, the media frenzy intensified as journalists defamed and fabricated stories as they claimed he was not born in the United States and that he was a Muslim and even a terrorist due to his middle name, Hussein. The conspiracy surrounding Obama's place of birth began in 2008 during his presidential campaign and gained traction with figures like Donald Trump promoting it. According to reports, Obama released his short-form birth certificate in 2008 and his long-form in 2011, confirming his birth in Hawaii. Zeleny, J. (2011). The New York Times. Despite evidence, a 2016 poll showed a significant portion of Americans still believed the claim. Beckwith, R. T. (2016). Trump Finally Admits It: Obama Was Born in the U.S. Time Magazine. Not to mention the "Fake News" that Obama was secretly a Muslim with ties to radical Islam "took on a life of it's own;" this was allegedly fused by early false claims that Obama attended a madrasa (Islamic school) in Indonesia and he refused to say the Pledge of Allegiance (CNN Fact Check (2008). The fact that Obama was a member of Trinity United Church of Christ is not only a known fact, but it is public knowledge that he is a practicing Christian, and he has publicly condemned extremism multiple times. Unfortunately polls still showed many Americans believed he was Muslim, influenced negative perceptions. (Pew Research Center. (2010).

Next, came the claim that The Affordable Care Act (Obamacare) would establish "death panels" deciding who receives healthcare. According to PolitiFact (2009) in an article, *Lie of the Year: 'Death Panels'* the former Alaska Governor Sarah Palin popularized the term, claiming government panels would decide the fate of elderly and disabled patients. Fact-checkers and medical professionals clarified that the law proposed voluntary end-of-life counseling, not mandatory panels. (PolitiFact, 2009) Unfortunately, the misinformation seems to fuel opposition to healthcare reform.

In addition, Charlene Muhammad (2010) reported on a political event involving (Glen Beck) that demonstrated fear of Obama becoming president:

> Mr. Beck and some 8,000 fans [had], gathered in Orlando, Fla., for his American Revival, a daylong event aimed at taking back, or regaining America. Media Matters reported that Mr. Beck, who has been accused of "spewing such incendiary language," urged followers to stock food and water for a coming showdown. 'If we don't face the truth right now, we'll be dead in five years—this country can't survive,' he said. (Muhammad, 2010, para. 8)

In 2010, this quote appeared in *The Final Call* Newspaper, only 47-years after the death of Medgar Evers. Beck's rhetoric mirrors the same distain exhibited by segregationists, Hoover, the KKK, Silver Knights, the White Citizens' Council, the CIA, the FBI, and other racists. As written in Ecclesiastes 1:9, "There is nothing new under the sun" (*Holy Bible*, 2018, p. 384), which means that some people's mindsets, patterns, actions, comments, and behaviors rarely change over time. Sabotage, fake news, fabrication, lies, racism, hatred, prejudice, and discrimination continue to cloud the truth.

CONCLUSION

In conclusion, Dr. King, Medgar Evers, Malcolm X, and Former President Obama were all portrayed as troublemakers, even though their primary objective was to create an America that treated all people fairly, regardless of race, gender, or economic social status. These men of valor demonstrated integrity, truth, honor, and courage while advocating for inclusion. "Fake News" remains a prevalent problem worldwide, and at its core, it is "fabricated, with no verifiable facts, sources, or quotes" (Desai & Oehrli, 2024, para. 2). It must be prevented in all instances, as it only creates chaos and madness that will always lead to discord, division, disaster, and disarray.

REFERENCES

Blassingame, J. (1972). *The slave community: Plantation life in the Antebellum South.* Oxford Press.

Booker, S. (1955, May 26). Is Mississippi Ushing up a Lynching? *JET Magazine. Volume*, (8), 8–10.

CBS News. (2018, April 4). *MLK assassination: How Walter Cronkite covered the April 4, 1968 tragedy.* https://www.cbsnews.com/news/mlk-assassination-walter-cronkite-report-cbs-evening-news-broadcast-april-4-1968/

CNN. (2008). *FactCheck.org.* Obama Not Attending a Muslim School.

Dell. (2012). Oppressed. In *American Heritage dictionary* (p. 589). Academic Press.

Desai, S., & Oehrli, J. A. (2024, March 14). *"Fake news," lies and propaganda: How to sort fact from fiction.* University of Michigan Library Research Guides. https://guides.lib.umich.edu/fakenews

Dixon, T. F. (1905). *The Clansman: An Historical Romance of the Ku Klux Klan.* Doubleday Press.

Eig, J., & Theoharis, J. (2023, April 12). The man who knew exactly what the F.B.I. was doing to Martin Luther King, Jr. *The New York Times.* Retrieved from: https://www.nytimes.com/2023/04/12/opinion/lyndon-johnson-martin-luther-king-jr.html

Encyclopedia Britannica. (2024, October 3). Elijah Muhammad. In *Encyclopedia Britannica online.* Retrieved from: https://www.britannica.com/biography/Elijah-Muhammad

Encyclopedia Britannica. (2024, October 16). National Association for the Advancement of Colored People. In *Encyclopedia Britannica online.* Retrieved from: https://www.britannica.com/topic/National-Association-for-the-Advancement-of-Colored-People

Evers-Williams, M., & Blau, M. (1999). *Watch me fly: What I learned on the way to becoming the woman I was meant to be.* Little Brown and Company.

Evers-Williams, M., & Marable, M. (Eds.). (2005). *The autobiography of Medgar Evers: A hero's life and legacy revealed through his writings, letters, and speeches.* Basic Civitas Books.

Gubar, S. (1997). *Racechanges: White skin, black face in American culture.* Oxford Press.

Holy Bible. (2018). Thomas Nelson Publishing.

Hunt, D. P. (2003). The concept of knowledge and how to measure it. *Journal of Intellectual Capital, 4*(1), 100–113.

Jacob, M. (2018). *Fake News in the 1890s: Yellow Journalism.* Retrieved from the Digital Public Library of America. Retrieved from: https://production.dp.la/primary-source-set/fake-news-in-the-1890s-yellow-journalism

Jordan, W. D. (1977). *White over Black: American attitudes toward the negro, 1550–1812.* W. W. Norton and Co., Inc.

King, M. L. (1968). *Where do we go from here? Chaos or community?* Beacon Press Books.

Muhammad, C. (2010, April 6). "Mean spirited, vicious racism" comes to surface during debates about president and U.S. politics." *The Final Call*. Retrieved from: https://www.finalcall.com/artman/publish/National_News_2/article_6846.shtml

Oxford Press. (2008). Sabotage. In *Oxford American dictionary* (p. 728). OUP.

Payne, L., & Payne, T. (2020). *The dead are arising: The life of Malcolm X*. Liveright Publishing Corporation.

Pepper, W. F. (2016). *The Plot to Kill King: The Truth Behind the Assassination of Martin Luther King Jr*. Skyhorse.

Pew Research Center. (2010, August 18). *Growing Number of Americans Say Obama Is a Muslim*. Author.

Pfeifer, M. J. (2004). *Rough justice: Lynching and the American society 1874–1947*. University of Illinois Press.

PolitiFact. (2009, December). *Lie of the Year: 'Death Panels*. Author.

Smiley, T. (2014). *Death of a King: The real story of Dr. Martin Luther King, Jr.'s final year*. Little Brown and Company.

Thoreau, H. D. (2023). *Walden and civil disobedience*. Union Square & Co., LLC.

Vinten, G. (1994). *Whistleblowing: Subversion or corporate citizenship?* St. Martin's Press.

Wright, G. (2024, November 16). Malcolm X's family sues FBI, CIA, and NYPD over his murder. *BBC News,* pp. 1-2. Retrieved from: https://www.bbc.com/news/articles/c3rxzndz17yo

Zeleny, J. (2011, April 27). White House Releases Obama Birth Certificate. *The New York Times.*

ADDITIONAL READING

Alexander, M. (2010). *The New Jim Crow: Mass Incarceration in the Age of Colorblindness*. New Press.

Allen, J. (2000). *Without Sanctuary: Lynching Photography in America*. Twin Palms Publishers.

Anderson, J. (1989). *The Education of Blacks in the South, 1860-1935*. University of North Carolina Press.

Apel, D. (2003). *Imagery of Lynching: Black Men, White Women, and the Mob*. Rutgers University Press.

Baldwin, J. (1963). *The Fire Next Time*. Penguin Books.

Balleck, B. J. (Ed.). (2019). *Hate groups and extremist organizations in America: An encyclopedia*. ABC-CLIO. DOI: 10.5040/9798400661983

Benson, C. (2009, Winter). Turning Point: Emmett Till's Killers Thought No One was Watching…They were Wrong. *Crisis, 116*, 6–9.

Bernstein, D. (2005). Thoughts on Hodges v. United States. *Boston University Law Review. Boston University. School of Law*, *85*, 811–819.

Blee, K. (1991). *Women of the Klan: Racism and Gender in the 1920s*. University of California Press.

Blee Kathleen, M. (2003). *Inside Organized Racism: Women in the Hate Movement*. University of California Press.

Bogle, D. T. (1998). Coons, Mulattoes, Mammies, and Bucks: An Interpretive History of Blacks in American Films. *Continuum*.

Brundage, F. (1993). *Lynching in the New South: Georgia and Virginia, 1880-1930*. University of Illinois Press.

Brundage, F. (1997). *Under Sentence of Death: Lynching in the South*. University of North Carolina Press.

Cameron, J. (1982). *A Time of Terror*. T/D Publications.

Capeci, D. J. (1989). *The Lynching of Cleo Wright*. University Press of Kentucky.

Collins, P. (1990). *Black Feminist Thought: Knowledge, Consciousness, and the Politics of Empowerment*. Unwin Hyman.

Ellison, R. (1980). *Invisible Man*. Vintage Books.

Ermida, I. (Ed.). (2023). *Hate speech in social media: Linguistic approaches*. Palgrave Macmillan. DOI: 10.1007/978-3-031-38248-2

Fanon, F. (1967). *Black Skin, White Masks*. Groove Press, Inc.

Feagin, J. (2009). *The White Racial Frame: Centuries of Racial Framing and Counter-framing*. Routledge.

Finkenbine, R. (2004). *Sources of the African American past: Primary sources in American history*. Pearson/Prentice Hall.

Foucault, M. (1980). *The History of Sexuality*. Vintage Books.

Gossett, T. (1965). *Race: The History of an Idea in America*. Schocken Books.

Greene, J. (2010). *America in the Sixties*. Syracuse University Press.

Guerrero, E. (1993). *Framing Blackness: The African American Image in Film*. Temple University Press.

Heale, M. (2001). *The Sixties in America: History, Politics and Protest*. Edinburgh University Press.

Hine, D. (2009). *African Americans: A concise history* (3rd ed.). Pearson/Prentice Hall.

Jewell, S. (1993). *From Mammy to Miss America and Beyond: Cultural Images and the Shaping of US Social Policy*. Routledge.

Jones, J. (1993). *The Construction of Black Sexuality: Black American Cinema*. Routledge.

Jones, W. (2013). *The March on Washington: Jobs, Freedom, and the Forgotten History of Civil Rights*. W.W. Norton & Company.

Joseph, E. (2006). *The Black Power Movement: Rethinking the Civil Rights-Black Power Era*. Routledge.

Leab, D. (1975). *From Sambo to SuperSpade: The Black Experience in Motion Pictures*. Houghton Mifflin Company.

Lee, H. (1960). *To Kill a Mockingbird*. Haper Perennial.

Lepore, J. (2018). *These Truths: A History of the United States*. W. W. Norton and Company.

Levy, P. (2018). *The Great Uprising: Race Riots in Urban America during the 1960s*. Cambridge University Press. DOI: 10.1017/9781108381659

Lewis, J. (2015). *Walking With the Wind*. Harcourt Brace & Company.

Mapp, E. (1972). *Blacks in American Films: Today and Yesterday*. Metuchen. The Scarecrow.

Marwick, A. (1998). *The Sixties: Cultural Revolution in Britain, France, Italy and the United. States, c.1958 – c.1974*. Oxford University Press.

Maynard, R. (1974). *The Black Man on Film: Racial Stereotyping*. Hayden Book Company, Inc.

McCall, N. (1994). *Makes Me Wanna Holler: A Young Black Man in America*. Vintage Books.

Mercer, K. (1994). *Welcome to the Jungle: New Positions in black Cultural Studies*. Routledge.

Murch, D. (2010). *Living for the city: migration, education, and the rise of the Black Panther Party in Oakland*. University of North Carolina Press.

Murray, J. (1973). *To Find an Image: Black Films from Uncle Tom to Superfly*. The Bobbs-Merrill Company, Inc.

Nash, D. (1985). 'Eyes on the Prize' interview, 12 November 1985. Retrieved from: http://repository .wustl.edu/ concern/ videos/qf85nd261

Noble, P. (1937). *The Negro in Films*. Skelton Robinson.

Null, G. (1975). *Black Hollywood: The Black Performer in Motion Pictures*. The Citadel Press.

Parker, T. (1974). *A Pictorial History of Sex in Films*. Citadel Press.

Patterson, J. (2001). *Brown v. Board of Education: A Civil Rights Milestone and Its Troubled Legacy*. Oxford Press.

Pieterse, N. (1992). *White on Black: Images of Africa and Blacks in Western Popular Culture*. Yale University Press.

Powers, A. (1974). *Black in American Movies: A Selected Bibliography*. The Scarecrow Press, Inc.

Reid, M. (1993). *Redefining Black Film*. University of California Press.

Reynolds, D. (2010). *America: Empire of Liberty*. Penguin.

Rhines, J. (1996). *Black Film/White Money*. Rutgers University Press.

Roberts, D. (1999). *Killing the Black Body*. Vintage Books.

Rogers, B. (2015). *Grounds for Difference*. Harvard University Press.

Roithmayr, D. (2014). *Reproducing Racism: How Everyday Choices Lock in White Advantage*. New York University Press.

Sims, Y. (2006). *Women of Blaxploitation: How the Black Action Film Heroine Changed American Popular Culture*. McFarland & Company, Inc.

Snead, J. (1994). *Image of Black Independent Films: A Brief Survey: Celebration of Black Cinema, Inc.* The MIT Press.

Zamalin, A. (2017). *Struggle on Their Minds: The Political Thought of African American Resistance*. Columbia University Press. DOI: 10.7312/zama18110

KEY TERMS AND DEFINITIONS

Defamation: To damage someone's credibility with slander.

Discrimination: To prejudge and stereotype another person without giving him or a fair opportunity to demonstrate his or her character fitness.

Fake News: To create lies, misconceptions, or myths about a person, or group of people.

Racism: The idea that one's ethnicity is superior to the other group's due to social economic status, ethic origins, or education.

Racist: An individual who oppresses, suppresses, and treats a person with distain based on one's skin color.

Sabotage: To purposely place a barrier, or destroy another individual, which will produce mental or physical harm.

Yellow Journalism: Exaggerated and sensationalized new stories, which are fake and fabricated.

Chapter 18
Dual Narratives on Social Media and the Future of Trust and Reliability in Indian Politics

Kesavan Dhanapal
https://orcid.org/0000-0002-6208-4997
SRM Institute of Science and Technology, India

S. Sivaprakkash
https://orcid.org/0000-0003-4642-0660
Central University of Tamil Nadu, India

Naveenraj Xavier
https://orcid.org/0000-0003-2681-5964
SRM Institute of Science and Technology, India

N. Marianand
https://orcid.org/0000-0002-6443-249X
University of Technology and Applied Sciences, Oman

ABSTRACT

This chapter explores the impact of dual narratives propagated through social media on India's public perception and political discourse from 2014 to 2024. While social media plays a key role in shaping public opinion, it also spreads misinformation and fosters polarization. The study uses a mixed-methods approach, analyzing 10 major incidents and surveying 50 respondents. The results show that respondents struggle with conflicting narratives and express mistrust in social media information. Regression analysis reveals that concerns about national unity and future divisions outweigh personal perceptions. The study emphasizes the need for stricter regulation of social media platforms to curb misinformation and polarization. Respondents overwhelmingly support regulation, indicating public demand for action. The research highlights the importance of collective efforts to create a reliable and cohesive digital environment to protect democratic processes and societal stability.

DOI: 10.4018/979-8-3693-7468-9.ch018

INTRODUCTION

Social media has rapidly transformed the landscape of communication, political discourse, and information dissemination across the globe. In the past decade, platforms such as Facebook, Twitter, Instagram, and WhatsApp have evolved from mere social networking sites into powerful tools that influence public opinion, shape political narratives, and impact decision-making processes at every level of society. With over 4.5 billion users globally, social media is not just a medium of interaction but a critical arena where ideas, beliefs, and ideologies are contested and reinforced (Statista, 2023). Social media increasingly exposes news, opinion, and civic information (Bakshy *et al.,* 2015).

In India, the role of social media has become particularly pronounced. India has one of the world's largest internet populations as of 2021, with over 448 million members on social media (Statista, 2023). Social media has become an essential forum for political communication where individuals, leaders, and political parties can discuss issues, exchange news, and rally support. Social media is vital in Indian politics because of its accessibility, especially during elections, protests, and policy discussions.

The development of social media has created concern over the reliability of information and the emergence of dual narratives. Regarding non-political events, ideological boundaries do not always prevent social media from becoming a popular form of communication (Barberá *et al.,* 2015). Regarding political matters, people are more likely to share information from ideologically similar sources than dissimilar ones. Dual narratives are two conflicting pieces of information about the same event or topic that are spread simultaneously, supported by facts, interpretations, and emotional appeals. These narratives are developed considering the political agendas and are spread to reinforce specific ideological positions, leading to deep societal polarisation (Bennett & Livingston, 2018). India is a land of social diversity combined with social, religious, and political identities; the dual narratives have significantly impacted public confidence and information reliability.

People come across information from various ideological views, frequently interpreted to improve public policy, political representation, and social capital (Barberá *et al.,* 2015). The global scenario provides several examples of how social media has created and propagated dual narratives. The 2016 presidential election is a case in point in the United States (Bovet & Makse, 2019). Social media platforms were used to spread misinformation, target specific voter groups with tailored messages, and create competing narratives around critical issues such as immigration, national security, and economic policy (Allcott & Gentzkow, 2017; Bennett & Livingston, 2018). This influenced voter behaviour and decreased trust and belief in traditional media and democratic institutions. Similarly, the Brexit vote in the United Kingdom had massive use of social media to distribute favourable and unfavourable European Union narratives, resulting in one of the most polarising events in recent British history (Bennett & Livingston, 2018).

India also got into the clutches of social media, and its influence is significantly high in shaping the public's opinions towards politics. The 2014 General Election was the first democratic activity highly manipulated by social media. The Bharatiya Janata Party (BJP), under the leadership of Shri. Narendra Modi utilised social media to a greater extent, which helped them to reach millions of voters directly, bypassing traditional media channels (Chakravartty & Roy, 2017). The social media campaigns helped the political party to create an image of development, nationalism, and strong leadership. This overwhelming victory upheld the baton of social media in shaping political outcomes and set the cornerstone for future elections.

Since then, social media has played a crucial role in Indian politics. During the 2019 General Elections, both the BJP and the Indian National Congress (INC) invested heavily in digital campaigns, using social media to engage with voters, spread their messages, and counter the narratives of their opponents. This period saw the emergence of highly polarised narratives, with each party accusing the other of spreading fake news and manipulating public opinion (Bradshaw & Howard, 2018). The impact of these dual narratives was evident in the election results and the public discourse that followed.

Beyond elections, social media platforms were instrumental in shaping public opinion for social and political events in India. For example, the Citizenship Amendment Act (CAA) protests of 2019-2020 created deep divisions within Indian society. The government defended the CAA as a humanitarian measure to protect persecuted minorities. At the same time, critics argued that it was discriminatory against Muslims and undermined the secular fabric of the nation (Chakravartty & Roy, 2017). These opposing narratives were propagated through social media, leading to widespread protests and a polarised public debate.

The farmers' protests of 2020-2021 provide another example of how social media can both mobilise support and create competing narratives. The government's narrative framed the new farm laws as essential reforms to modernise agriculture and increase farmers' incomes. In contrast, the protesting farmers and their supporters argued that the laws would benefit large corporations at the expense of small farmers, leading to the erosion of their livelihoods (Chakravartty & Roy, 2017). Social media also played a crucial role in organising the protests, spreading information, and countering the government's narrative, ultimately leading to repealing the laws (Ufuophu-Biri & Ojoboh, 2017).

While social media has undoubtedly enhanced political engagement and provided a platform for diverse voices, it has also exacerbated the challenges of misinformation and polarisation. The algorithms that drive these platforms prioritise content that generates engagement, often amplifying sensational or emotionally charged material (Tufekci, 2015). This has led to the creation of echo chambers, where users are exposed primarily to information that aligns with their pre-existing beliefs, reinforcing their biases and deepening societal divisions (Pariser, 2011). In such an environment, the ability of individuals to critically evaluate information and separate fact from fiction is significantly compromised, leading to a decline in public trust in both the media and democratic institutions.

The implications of these developments for democracy are profound. Sunstein (2018) argues that the proliferation of dual narratives on social media can erode the foundations of democratic debate by making it more difficult for citizens to engage in informed and rational discussions. When competing versions of the truth are presented as equally valid, the public's ability to reach a consensus on critical issues is undermined, leading to greater polarization and, in some cases, social unrest. This is particularly concerning in a diverse and populous democracy like India, where the stakes of political and social divisions are high.

The spread of misinformation and the rise of dual narratives have significant implications for the future of trust and reliability in Indian politics. As political actors continue to exploit social media to advance their agendas, the line between truth and falsehood becomes increasingly blurred. This not only affects the quality of public discourse but also threatens the very fabric of democracy by eroding the trust that is essential for its functioning (Bail *et al.*, 2018).

The rise of social media as a central force in political communication has sparked substantial scholarly interest, particularly in its dual role as both a democratising tool and a platform for spreading misinformation. Numerous studies have explored how social media facilitates the creation of dual narratives, contributing to polarization and challenging democratic processes. This literature review synthesises key findings from these studies, highlighting the multifaceted impact of social media on public discourse and political dynamics.

The Power and Perils of Social Media

Social media's ability to democratise information has been extensively studied, with scholars highlighting its potential and pitfalls. Bennett and Livingston (2018) discuss how social media platforms have enabled broader participation in political discourse by giving diverse voices a platform. This democratising potential is significant in countries with restricted traditional media landscapes, allowing marginalised groups to share their perspectives and engage in public debates. However, Bennett and Livingston (2018) also point out the darker side of this phenomenon, where the same platforms are exploited to spread disinformation and manipulate public opinion. This dual capability of social media creates an environment where truth and falsehood coexist and compete, often blurring the lines between fact and fiction (Marwick & Lewis, 2017).

Bradshaw and Howard (2018) further emphasise that state and non-state actors increasingly use social media to conduct disinformation campaigns. Their research highlights how these actors craft and disseminate conflicting narratives, especially during elections and political crises, to destabilise societies and erode trust in public institutions. This strategic use of social media in disinformation campaigns reflects a broader shift in how information warfare is conducted in the digital age. Woolley and Howard (2017) describe this as 'computational propaganda,' where automated accounts and bots are deployed to spread false narratives, amplifying their reach and impact.

The potential for social media to distort political communication is also evident in (Aïmeur *et al.,* 2017) exploration of 'fake news.' Social media's role in democratising information is compromised by its use as a tool for disseminating fabricated and misleading content. He suggests that spreading fake news is not just a by-product of social media's open platform but also a deliberate strategy employed by various actors to influence public opinion and undermine democratic processes. The social aspect of social media adds another dimension to the building of fake news, as the power of fake news lies in its ability to permeate social spheres (Tandoc *et al.,* 2017).

Echo Chambers and Algorithmic Amplification

The phenomenon of echo chambers, where individuals are primarily exposed to information that reinforces their existing beliefs and shields them from information that contradicts their views, has been widely studied in the context of social media. Critics claim that the ubiquity of echo chambers, filter bubbles, and selective exposure is exacerbating the polarisation of the parties and their differing perspectives on fundamental truths, hence exacerbating the status of our democracy (Guess *et al.,* 2018). Tufekci (2015) argues that the algorithms powering social media platforms are critical in creating these echo chambers. By prioritising content likely to engage users, often sensational or emotionally charged material, these algorithms inadvertently contribute to the polarisation of public discourse (Wardle & Derakhshan, 2017). This selective exposure to information reinforces ideological divides, making it more challenging for users to encounter and engage with opposing viewpoints.

Pariser (2011) introduces the concept of the 'filter bubble,' a personalised online environment created by algorithmic filtering that limits users' exposure to diverse perspectives. Pariser (2011) states that these filter bubbles trap users in self-reinforcing loops of information catering to their preexisting beliefs. This phenomenon polarises public opinion and narrows the range of information available to individuals, resulting in a fragmented and less informed public. Sunstein (2018) builds on this idea, arguing that such algorithmic filtering significantly undermines democratic deliberation by restricting access to diverse viewpoints, thereby fostering polarisation. Partisan media can disseminate false information and aggravate anti-party sentiment among a significant and influential population segment (Guess *et al.,* 2018).

Some scholars offer a more nuanced view of the role of algorithms in creating echo chambers. Bruns (2019) contends that social media platforms are not solely responsible for echo chambers. Instead, users' pre-existing preferences and selective exposure behaviours significantly determine the diversity of content they encounter. Individuals' exposure to political content on the internet may be influenced by the desire for reinforcement rather than an aversion to opinion challenge (Garrett, 2009). Opinion-reinforcing information promotes news story exposure, while opinion-challenging information makes exposure marginally less likely. Individuals actively select information sources that align with their beliefs, indicating that the responsibility for echo chambers is shared between platform design and user behaviour.

Dual Narratives and Misinformation

The emergence of dual narratives and conflicting versions of the same event or issue on social media has been a significant concern for scholars. Chakravartty and Roy (2017) examine how political actors in India have effectively used social media to construct and propagate populist narratives that resonate with specific voter bases. These narratives often play on cultural and religious identities, using divisive rhetoric to mobilise support while marginalising dissenting voices. This strategy has been particularly evident during major political events, such as the 2014 General Elections, where social media was instrumental in shaping public perception. People with lower cognitive ability levels made less of an adjustment to their attitudes than people with higher cognitive ability levels (De Keersmaecker & Roets, 2017).

Bail *et al.* (2018) found that exposure to opposing political views on social media often leads to increased polarisation rather than moderation. Their study suggests that when individuals encounter information that contradicts their beliefs, they are more likely to entrench their positions than reconsider them. This finding highlights social media's role in deepening societal divisions, mainly when dual narratives are at play. Vosoughi, Roy and Aral (2018) support this view, noting that false news spreads more rapidly on social media than actual news, primarily due to its novelty and the emotional reactions it elicits, further fuelling polarisation.

Banaji and Bhat (2019) discuss the impact of misinformation in India, noting that the spread of false narratives through social media has contributed to a climate of political instability and uncertainty. They argue that misinformation campaigns often target emotional and cultural sensitivities, exploiting existing social divisions and fostering distrust among different communities. This manipulation of social media platforms to spread dual narratives exacerbates tensions and complicates efforts to foster social cohesion.

Impact on Democracy and Social Cohesion

The broader implications of dual narratives for democracy and social cohesion are profound. Sunstein (2018) argues that the proliferation of conflicting narratives on social media can weaken the foundations of democratic debate by eroding trust in public institutions and making it more difficult for citizens to engage in informed and rational discourse. When competing versions of the truth are presented as equally valid, the public's ability to discern fact from fiction diminishes, leading to greater polarisation and the potential for social unrest. Iyengar and Massey (2019) also highlight this erosion of trust and suggest that misinformation can create a 'post-truth' environment where facts are less influential than appeals to emotion and personal belief.

In the Indian context, Chakravartty and Roy (2017) note that using social media to propagate dual narratives has deepened existing social and political divides, complicating efforts to achieve consensus on critical national issues. The authors warn that these dynamics could undermine the democratic process by fostering mistrust and disengagement among the electorate. This concern is echoed by Guess, Nagler, and Tucker (2019), who found that misinformation on social media is often spread by a small, highly active group of users who are heavily partisan, suggesting that efforts to combat fake news should focus on these super-spreaders rather than the general population.

Grinberg *et al.* (2019) observed that misinformation tends to circulate more widely in politically polarised environments, where users are more likely to share content that aligns with their ideological views, regardless of its veracity. This finding underscores the need for a targeted approach to counter misinformation, focusing on high-risk groups and fostering a more informed public discourse.

Psychological Effects of Dual Narratives

Recent studies have also explored the psychological effects of dual narratives on individuals. Van Bavel and Pereira (2018) suggest that exposure to conflicting information on social media can create cognitive dissonance, prompting individuals to seek content that reaffirms their beliefs while rejecting contradictory information. This behaviour reinforces existing biases and contributes to the entrenchment of polarised views, making it more difficult to bridge ideological divides. Pennycook and Rand (2020) further explore this phenomenon, finding that repeated exposure to misinformation can increase its perceived accuracy, known as the 'illusory truth effect,' which poses significant challenges for combating fake news and misinformation on social media.

Farkas and Schou (2018) add to this discussion by examining how fake news operates as a 'floating signifier,' adapting to different contexts and reinforcing dual narratives based on the socio-political climate. Their study highlights the adaptability and resilience of misinformation, which can change form and content to suit different audiences, thereby perpetuating its influence and reinforcing societal divisions.

Dual Narratives and Social Stability

When it comes to change and stability, narratives are crucial. Narratives are crucial to preserve or replicate stability and/or to encourage or oppose change Vaara *et al.* (2016). Stories describe events in order and present them as either stable or changing. Stories have the power to alter the course of events. It is possible to study polyphony or plurivocality (i.e.) multiple interpretations of stability and change across narratives and their implications by comparing different narratives. Stability narratives provide for known meanings by maintaining the same evaluative dimension. Storytelling or narratives can significantly impact fostering change or preserving stability. People are constantly creating stories to maintain stability in the face of ongoing change. Along with helping people deal with being stuck, fit narratives enable them to interpret stability positively. Retelling stories might provide some people stability while giving others a sense of change.

OBJECTIVES OF THE STUDY

The study intends to achieve the following objectives:

1) To examine the role of social media in shaping dual narratives in Indian political discourse from 2014 to 2024.
2) To assess the impact of conflicting narratives on public trust in information, national unity, and societal cohesion.
3) To identify the broader implications of these dual narratives for democracy and social stability in India.
4) To provide recommendations for mitigating the spread of misinformation and reducing polarisation.

RESEARCH METHODOLOGY

Research Design

This study adopts an empirical approach to investigate the role of social media in shaping dual narratives and their impact on public perception in India from 2014 to 2024. The empirical approach of this study is particularly suited to exploring the nuanced effects of social media narratives. Combining detailed incident analysis with quantitative survey data offers a well-rounded perspective on how conflicting narratives shape public opinion and influence societal cohesion. This methodology provides a solid foundation for analysing the broader implications of social media use in political discourse. It contributes valuable insights into the challenges of maintaining trust and reliability in the digital age.

Sample Size

To quantify public perceptions and concerns about these dual narratives, a structured survey was conducted with 50 respondents.

Sampling Strategy

The survey was carefully designed to evaluate responses across three categories: Personal Perception, National Impact, and Future Concerns. The questions aimed to assess how well respondents understood the incidents, their emotional reactions, and their level of trust in the information they encountered. The survey provided a robust framework for understanding the complex interplay between social media narratives and public trust by capturing data across these categories.

Data Collection Instrument

The questionnaire was the primary tool for data collection. The questionnaire was developed based on the information collected by reviewing previous studies. The research is grounded in a comprehensive analysis of ten critical incidents that generated significant debate on social media platforms. These incidents were selected based on their ability to provoke widespread public engagement and present clear opposing narratives, as evidenced by the trends observed on platforms such as Twitter, Facebook, and WhatsApp (Bradshaw & Howard, 2018). A 5-point Likert scale was employed, consisting of the following options viz., Strongly Agree (SA), Agree (A), Neither Agree nor Disagree (N), Disagree (D), and Strongly Disagree (SD). The scoring ranged from 5 (Strongly Agree) to 1 (Strongly Disagree).

Ethical Considerations

- Informed consent was obtained from all participants.
- Anonymity and confidentiality of responses was ensured.
- Data will be securely stored and accessible only to authorised personnel.

ANALYSES OF THE NARRATIVES

Social media has become a powerful tool for shaping public opinion, especially in the realm of politics. Since 2014, India has witnessed several significant political and social incidents where dual narratives have emerged, often creating conflicting perceptions among the public. These incidents have been heavily debated on platforms like Twitter, Facebook, and WhatsApp, leading to polarised opinions. This analysis examines ten critical incidents from 2014 onwards, highlighting the dual narratives propagated through social media and their impact on public perception.

Incident 1: 2014 General Elections

The 2014 General Elections were a watershed moment in Indian politics, marking the rise of social media as a crucial tool in election campaigns. The Bharatiya Janata Party (BJP) led by Narendra Modi leveraged social media extensively to craft a narrative of development and strong leadership.

Table 1. Dual Narratives of General Elections of 2014 in India

Aspect	Pro-Government Narrative	Anti-Government Narrative
Incident Overview	Narendra Modi as a transformative leader, promising development and good governance	Modi was criticised for his role in the 2002 Gujarat riots and was seen as a divisive figure.
Key Hashtags	#ModiForPM, #AccheDin	#StopModi, #NotMyPM
Narrative Focus	Emphasis on economic development, anti-corruption, and strong leadership	Focus on human rights concerns, secularism, and fears of authoritarianism
Public Engagement	Over 20 million tweets supporting Modi (South Asian Voices, 2022)	Over 5 million tweets critical of Modi (Asia Times, 2020)
Visual Imagery	Images of Modi with supporters, development projects	Images of protests, criticism of Modi's past

Source: Compiled by Authors

The 2014 elections saw a clear divide in how Narendra Modi was portrayed on social media. While supporters celebrated his promises of *'Achhe Din'* (Good Days), opponents focused on his controversial past. The election is often called India's 'first social media election,' with digital platforms playing a pivotal role in shaping the narrative (Asia Times, 2020).

Incident 2: Demonetization (2016)

In November 2016, the Indian government announced the demonetisation of . 500 and . 1,000 currency notes, aiming to tackle black money and corruption. The move sparked widespread reactions across the country.

Table 2. Dual Narratives of Demonetization of Currencies in India

Aspect	Pro-Government Narrative	Anti-Government Narrative
Incident Overview	A bold move to eliminate black money and curb corruption	Criticised as poorly planned, causing economic distress and hardship
Key Hashtags	#Demonetization, #BlackMoney	#DeMonetizationDisaster, #ModiFails
Narrative Focus	Highlighted as a necessary step for economic cleansing and national interest	Focused on the negative impact on common people, small businesses, and the economy
Public Engagement	Over 15 million tweets supporting demonetisation (Clarity Circuit, 2024)	Over 10 million tweets criticising the move (Asia Times, 2020)
Visual Imagery	Images of people supporting the move, patriotic messaging	Images of long queues, cash shortages, protests

Source: Compiled by Authors

The government presented demonetisation as necessary to tackle black money and corruption. However, the move faced criticism for its poor execution, leading to widespread economic hardship. With significant public engagement, social media became a battleground for both narratives (Clarity Circuit, 2024).

Incident 3: Balakot Air Strikes (2019)

Following the Pulwama terror attack in February 2019, India conducted airstrikes on a terrorist camp in Balakot, Pakistan. This incident led to significant social media activity, with dual narratives emerging around the military action.

Table 3. Dual Narratives of Balakot Air Strikes

Aspect	Pro-Government Narrative	Anti-Government Narrative
Incident Overview	A decisive military response against terrorism, showcasing India's strength	Questioning the strategic impact and political motivations behind the strikes
Key Hashtags	#IndiaStrikesBack, #BalakotAirStrike	#BalakotDebate, #PulwamaRevenge
Narrative Focus	Focused on national pride, military prowess, and a solid response to terrorism	Raised concerns about the timing, effectiveness, and potential political motives

continued on following page

Table 3. Continued

Aspect	Pro-Government Narrative	Anti-Government Narrative
Public Engagement	Over 25 million tweets supporting the strikes (South Asian Voices, 2022)	Over 8 million tweets questioning the strikes (Asia Times, 2020)
Visual Imagery	Images of fighter jets, national symbols, and celebrations	Images of debates, questions over the actual impact

Source: Compiled by Authors

The Balakot airstrikes were widely celebrated as a bold response to terrorism by the government, with a strong focus on national pride. However, critics questioned the timing and effectiveness of the strikes, suggesting they were influenced by political motives ahead of the general elections (South Asian Voices, 2022).

Incident 4: JNU Sedition Row (2016)

In February 2016, students at Jawaharlal Nehru University (JNU) were accused of raising anti-India slogans during a protest, leading to charges of sedition against several students. This incident sparked a nationwide debate on nationalism and freedom of speech.

Table 4. Dual Narratives of JNU Students' Sedition

Aspect	Pro-Government Narrative	Anti-Government Narrative
Incident Overview	The students engaged in anti-national activities deserve strict legal action.	The charges were seen as an attack on free speech and dissent.
Key Hashtags	#AntiNationals, #SaveIndia	#StandWithJNU, #FreeSpeech
Narrative Focus	Emphasised the importance of national integrity and punishing anti-national behaviour	Focused on defending free speech and the rights of students
Public Engagement	Over 12 million tweets supporting strict action (South Asian Voices, 2022)	Over 10 million tweets supporting JNU students (Asia Times, 2020)
Visual Imagery	Images of protests, nationalist symbols, police action	Images of student protests, solidarity marches, academic discussions

Source: Compiled by Authors

The JNU sedition row brought to the forefront the tension between nationalism and free speech in India. While the government and its supporters justified the legal action as necessary for national security, critics argued that it was an attempt to suppress dissent. The incident generated significant debate on social media, reflecting deep societal divides (Asia Times, 2020).

Incident 5: Sabarimala Temple Entry (2018)

The Supreme Court of India ruled in September 2018 that women of all ages should be allowed entry into the Sabarimala Temple in Kerala, overturning a long-standing ban. This decision led to widespread protests and polarised opinions on social media.

Table 5. Dual Narratives of Sabarimala Temple Entry

Aspect	Pro-Government Narrative	Anti-Government Narrative
Incident Overview	The ruling was a landmark victory for gender equality and constitutional rights.	The ruling was opposed as an attack on religious traditions and sentiments.
Key Hashtags	#RightToPray, #WomenEquality	#SaveSabarimala, #TraditionMatters
Narrative Focus	Focused on the importance of upholding constitutional values and gender equality	Emphasised the need to respect religious traditions and cultural values
Public Engagement	Over 18 million tweets supporting the verdict (Clarity Circuit, 2024)	Over 12 million tweets opposing the verdict (Asia Times, 2020)
Visual Imagery	Images of women activists, court celebrations, progressive messaging	Images of large-scale protests, traditional rituals

Source: Compiled by Authors

The Sabarimala temple entry issue highlighted the conflict between gender equality and religious tradition. The Supreme Court's ruling was hailed as a progressive step by many, while others saw it as an infringement on religious practices. Social media reflected this divide, with passionate arguments on both sides (Clarity Circuit, 2024).

Incident 6: Pulwama Attack and Aftermath (2019)

In February 2019, a suicide bombing in Pulwama, Kashmir, killed 40 Indian paramilitary personnel. This attack led to heightened tensions between India and Pakistan, culminating in the Balakot airstrikes.

Table 6. Dual Narratives of Pulwama Attack and Aftermath

Aspect	Pro-Government Narrative	Anti-Government Narrative
Incident Overview	The attack justified a robust military response, showcasing India's resolve against terrorism.	Criticised for intelligence failures and the need for a transparent investigation
Key Hashtags	#PulwamaAttack, #IndiaStrikesBack	#PulwamaProbe, #AccountabilityNow
Narrative Focus	Emphasised the need for a solid response to terrorism and national security	Focused on intelligence lapses and the need for accountability
Public Engagement	Over 30 million tweets supporting military action (South Asian Voices, 2022)	Over 10 million tweets demanding accountability (Asia Times, 2020)
Visual Imagery	Images of grieving families, military tributes, and nationalistic rallies	Images of protests demanding transparency and accountability

Source: Compiled by Authors

The Pulwama attack was one of the deadliest terrorist incidents in recent Indian history, leading to a surge of nationalist sentiment. The government's response, particularly the subsequent airstrikes, was widely supported on social media as a necessary action against terrorism. However, there were also significant calls for accountability regarding the intelligence lapses that led to the attack, with critics questioning the timing and intent behind the military response (South Asian Voices, 2022).

Incident 7: Citizenship Amendment Act (CAA) Protests (2019-2020)

The Citizenship Amendment Act (CAA) passed in December 2019 sparked widespread protests across India, with critics arguing that it discriminated against Muslims. The government defended the act as a humanitarian measure to protect persecuted minorities.

Table 7. Dual Narratives of Protests towards Citizenship Amendment Act

Aspect	Pro-Government Narrative	Anti-Government Narrative
Incident Overview	The CAA is a humanitarian act to protect persecuted minorities from neighbouring countries.	The CAA is discriminatory against Muslims and undermines India's secular fabric.
Key Hashtags	#IndiaSupportsCAA, #CABPassed	#RejectCAA, #NoCAB
Narrative Focus	Emphasised the need to protect religious minorities and rectify historical wrongs	Focused on the exclusion of Muslims and the threat to secularism
Public Engagement	Over 20 million tweets supporting the CAA (Clarity Circuit, 2024)	Over 18 million tweets opposing the CAA (Asia Times, 2020)
Visual Imagery	Images of grateful minorities receiving citizenship, celebrations	Images of protests, police action, and affected individuals

Source: Compiled by Authors

The Citizenship Amendment Act (CAA) triggered massive protests across India, with social media playing a central role in mobilising public opinion. The government's narrative portrayed the act as a benevolent measure for persecuted minorities, while critics argued that it was an unconstitutional law targeting Muslims. The polarised views led to significant social media engagement, reflecting the deep divisions in Indian society (Asia Times, 2020).

Incident 8: Farmers' Protests (2020-2021)

In 2020, the Indian government introduced three farm laws to reform the agricultural sector. However, these laws were met with widespread protests, particularly from farmers in Punjab and Haryana, who feared the laws would undermine their livelihoods.

Table 8. Dual Narratives of Farmers' Protest towards Farm Laws

Aspect	Pro-Government Narrative	Anti-Government Narrative
Incident Overview	Farm laws are essential to modernising agriculture and improving farmers' incomes.	Farm laws are detrimental to small farmers and favour big corporations.
Key Hashtags	#FarmLaws, #FarmersWithModi	#FarmersProtest, #NoFarmLaws
Narrative Focus	Highlighted the long-term benefits of agricultural reforms and the need for modernisation	Focused on the negative impact on small farmers and the threat to traditional farming

continued on following page

Table 8. Continued

Aspect	Pro-Government Narrative	Anti-Government Narrative
Public Engagement	Over 15 million tweets supporting the farm laws (Clarity Circuit, 2024)	Over 25 million tweets opposing the farm laws (South Asian Voices, 2022)
Visual Imagery	Images of modern farming techniques, government outreach to farmers	Images of large-scale protests, farmers camping in Delhi, and clashes with police

Source: Compiled by Authors

The farmers' protests the new farm laws became one of the most significant mass movements in recent Indian history. While the government promoted the laws as necessary for modernising agriculture, the protests highlighted deep concerns about the potential impact on small farmers. Social media was a key battleground, with both sides using it to mobilise support and frame their narratives (South Asian Voices, 2022).

Incident 9: Delhi Riots (2020)

In February 2020, violent riots erupted in Northeast Delhi, coinciding with protests towards the Citizenship Amendment Act (CAA). The riots led to significant loss of life and property, with both sides blaming each other for instigating the violence.

Table 9. Dual Narratives of Delhi Riots

Aspect	Pro-Government Narrative	Anti-Government Narrative
Incident Overview	The riots were portrayed as a spontaneous reaction to anti-CAA protests by violent elements.	The government was accused of instigating violence against anti-CAA protestors.
Key Hashtags	#DelhiRiots, #DefendDelhi	#DelhiGenocide, #JusticeForDelhi
Narrative Focus	Emphasised the need for law and order, blaming anti-CAA protestors for the violence	Focused on the alleged complicity of the government and police in targeting Muslims
Public Engagement	Over 10 million tweets supporting the government's stance (Clarity Circuit, 2024)	Over 15 million tweets condemning the government (South Asian Voices, 2022)
Visual Imagery	Images of police restoring order, Hindu victims of violence	Images of Muslim victims, police inaction, and alleged state complicity

Source: Compiled by Authors

The Delhi riots of 2020 were one of the most violent episodes in recent memory, deeply polarising public opinion. The government's narrative focused on the need to restore law and order, blaming the violence on anti-CAA protestors. In contrast, critics accused the government and police of being complicit in the violence against Muslims. Social media played a significant role in shaping these narratives, further deepening societal divisions (South Asian Voices, 2022).

Incident 10: Pegasus Spyware Scandal (2021)

In July 2021, it was revealed that several Indian politicians, journalists, and activists were allegedly targeted using Pegasus spyware. The revelations led to widespread outrage and demands for an investigation.

Table 10. Dual Narratives of Pegasus Spyware Scandal

Aspect	Pro-Government Narrative	Anti-Government Narrative
Incident Overview	The government dismissed the allegations as baseless and part of an international conspiracy.	The government was accused of illegally spying on citizens, undermining democracy.
Key Hashtags	#Pegasus, #FalseNarrative	#PegasusProject, #SpyGate
Narrative Focus	Focused on dismissing the reports as politically motivated, part of a foreign conspiracy	Emphasised the need for transparency and accountability, alleging government overreach
Public Engagement	Over 8 million tweets supporting the government's dismissal (Clarity Circuit, 2024)	Over 12 million tweets demanding accountability (Asia Times, 2020)
Visual Imagery	Images of government officials denying the allegations, calls for national security	Images of protestors, media reports, and targeted individuals

Source: Compiled by Authors

The Pegasus spyware scandal brought the issue of surveillance and privacy to the forefront of Indian politics. While the government dismissed the allegations as a baseless conspiracy, opposition leaders and civil society demanded a thorough investigation. The scandal led to significant social media engagement, with discussions about the implications for democracy and civil liberties (Clarity Circuit, 2024).

DESIGN AND THEMATIC CATEGORIZATION

To assess the opinions and perceptions of respondents regarding the impact of social media narratives, we constructed a comprehensive questionnaire comprising 15 questions. These questions are strategically grouped into three main categories: Personal Perception, National Impact, and Future Concerns. This categorisation aims to capture the multifaceted effects of social media narratives on individuals, society, and future outlooks.

The Personal Perception category includes questions designed to gauge how respondents personally interpret and are influenced by the conflicting narratives they encounter on social media. This section aims to understand the direct impact on their understanding, emotions, and trust in the information presented to them. The National Impact category explores respondents' views on how these dual narratives affect broader societal and national issues. This includes concerns about national unity, the integrity of institutions, and the overall impact on public discourse. The Future Concerns category addresses respondents' anxieties about the long-term implications of these narratives. It seeks to understand how these conflicting messages may affect future generations, contribute to societal divisions, and influence the respondents' outlook on the future.

Each question is designed to elicit responses on a Likert scale ranging from 'Strongly Agree' to 'Strongly Disagree,' allowing for a nuanced understanding of the respondents' views. This structure ensures that we capture a wide range of opinions, comprehensively analysing the impact of social media narratives.

Table 11. Thematic Categorization of Questions

Category: Personal Perception	Strongly Agree	Agree	Neutral	Disagree	Strongly Disagree
1. I fully understood the incident from both perspectives.					
2. The information I received seemed biased towards one side.					
3. The conflicting narratives made me feel confused or misdirected.					
4. I often find it challenging to know which narrative to trust.					
5. The information I encountered influenced my opinion significantly.					
Category: National Impact					
6. I believe the conflicting narratives could harm national unity.					
7. I am concerned about the impact of social media on truth and misinformation.					
8. I feel the dual narratives contribute to societal division.					
9. I am worried about the impact of these narratives on our national identity.					
10. These narratives make it harder for me to trust national institutions and media.					
Category: Future Concerns					
11. I believe more should be done to regulate misinformation on social media.					
12. I feel uncertain about the future due to these conflicting narratives.					
13. I think these narratives could lead to more serious divisions in the future.					
14. I am concerned about the impact of these narratives on future generations.					
15. After reviewing the narratives, I still feel uncertain about my stance on the issue.					

Source: Compiled by Authors

Table 11 presents the 15 questions, categorised into three thematic areas, all within a single table for a cohesive presentation. The design of the questionnaire is intended to comprehensively explore the respondents' views on the multifaceted impacts of social media narratives, both at an individual and societal level. By analysing the responses, we can gain valuable insights into how these narratives influence personal opinions, national sentiment, and concerns for the future.

RESULTS

The findings from the respondents' data focus on the descriptive statistics, regression weights, and their significance across the three thematic categories: Personal Perception, National Impact, and Future Concerns. The results provide valuable insights into how social media narratives influence individual opinions, societal cohesion, and concerns for the future.

Table 12. Descriptive Statistics

The Opinion	Mean	Standard Deviation	p-value
I fully understood the incident from both perspectives.	2.6	1.385641	0.048791
The information I received seemed biased towards one side.	3.28	1.414779	0.172212
The conflicting narratives made me feel confused or misdirected.	3.34	1.491442	0.116970
I often find it challenging to know which narrative to trust.	3.5	1.473092	0.021458
The information I encountered influenced my opinion significantly.	3.52	1.389100	0.011662
I believe the conflicting narratives could harm national unity.	4.12	1.032279	0.000000
I am concerned about the impact of social media on truth and misinformation.	3.88	1.259206	0.000011
I feel the dual narratives contribute to societal division.	3.88	1.290581	0.000017
I am worried about the impact of these narratives on our national identity.	3.78	1.360735	0.000205
These narratives make it harder for me to trust national institutions and media.	4.08	1.092520	0.000000
I believe more should be done to regulate misinformation on social media.	4.38	0.977548	0.000000
I feel uncertain about the future due to these conflicting narratives.	4.34	0.885664	0.000000
I think these narratives could lead to more serious divisions in the future.	4.22	1.005783	0.000000
I am concerned about the impact of these narratives on future generations.	4.4	0.800000	0.000000
After reviewing the narratives, I still feel uncertain about my stance on the issue.	3.72	1.386218	0.000664

Source: Computed by Authors

The descriptive statistics (Table 12) reveal the overall distribution of responses across the 15 questions categorised under Personal Perception, National Impact, and Future Concerns. Each question was rated on a Likert scale ranging from 'Strongly Agree' to 'Strongly Disagree,' with the mean, standard deviation, and p-value calculated for each item. The data indicates a significant variation in how respondents perceive and are influenced by social media narratives:

Understanding and Trust: Respondents expressed difficulty in fully understanding incidents from both perspectives, with a mean score of 2.60 and a p-value of 0.048, indicating that the perceived understanding is significantly lower than neutral. Trust in the narratives was also low, with a mean score of 3.50, highlighting individuals' challenges in discerning credible information ($p = 0.021$).

Perception of Bias and Influence: The perception of bias in the information received was moderate, with a mean of 3.28, though not statistically significant ($p = 0.172$). However, the information's influence on respondents' opinions was significant, with a mean score of 3.52 ($p = 0.012$), suggesting that despite recognising potential bias, respondents still found their opinions shaped by the content they encountered.

National Impact: A vital concern was evident regarding the impact of conflicting narratives on national unity, with a high mean score of 4.12 ($p < 0.001$). Similarly, there was significant concern about the broader impact of social media on truth and misinformation, as indicated by a mean score of 3.88 ($p < 0.001$).

Future Concerns: Respondents expressed substantial anxiety about the future implications of these narratives, with the mean scores for concerns about societal division and the impact on future generations being 3.88 and 3.78, respectively, both highly significant ($p < 0.001$).

Regression Analysis

The regression analysis was conducted to determine the impact of each thematic category on the overall mean scores. The coefficients and p-values mentioned in Table 13 provided insights into how strongly each category influenced respondents' perceptions.

Table 13. Regression Analysis

Thematic Category	Coefficient	p-value
Personal Perception	0.396	2.77
National Impact	1.096	2.4
Future Concerns	1.36	2.19

Source: Computed by Authors

- **Personal Perception:** The coefficient for this category was 0.396, with a p-value of 2.77, indicating that while individual perceptions play a role, their influence is less significant compared to other categories. This suggests that broader societal concerns overshadow respondents' understanding and emotions.
- **National Impact:** This category had a coefficient of 1.096 and a p-value of 2.40, highlighting the significant influence that concerns about national unity and societal division have on respondents' overall views. The strong impact of this category suggests that issues affecting the nation are a primary concern for individuals when evaluating social media narratives.
- **Future Concerns:** The highest coefficient was found in the Future Concerns category, with a value of 1.360 and a p-value of 2.19. This indicates that respondents are most influenced by the potential future implications of conflicting narratives, particularly in terms of societal division and the well-being of future generations. This category's significance underscores individuals' deep anxieties about the long-term effects of social media on society.

DISCUSSION

The results of this study highlight several key findings about the impact of social media narratives on public perception in India:

Trust and Understanding: The data indicate a pervasive sense of confusion and mistrust among respondents, particularly regarding their ability to understand and trust the narratives they encounter fully. This reflects the challenges posed by the abundance of conflicting information on social media, making it difficult for individuals to discern credible sources and form well-rounded opinions.

National Concerns: The high impact of the National Impact category suggests that respondents are deeply concerned about the broader implications of social media narratives for societal cohesion and national unity. The strong association between these concerns and overall perception scores indicates that issues affecting the nation significantly drive public opinion.

Future Anxiety: The significant influence of Future Concerns on respondents' perceptions points to widespread anxiety about the long-term effects of social media on society. The data suggests that individuals are apprehensive about the potential for increased societal division and the negative impact on future generations, which could undermine social stability and democratic processes.

Recommendations for Mitigating the Spread of Misinformation and Reducing Polarization

A multi-faceted approach is essential to address the challenges posed by dual narratives and the spread of misinformation on social media. Based on the findings of this study, several strong recommendations emerge to mitigate these issues and reduce societal polarisation.

First, enhancing regulatory frameworks is crucial. Social media platforms should be subject to more stringent regulations that require transparency in their algorithms and content moderation policies. Governments and regulatory bodies must work closely with these platforms to ensure that algorithms do not disproportionately amplify sensational or polarising content, which can exacerbate divisions. Mandatory disclosures about prioritising and promoting content could help users better understand the information they encounter and make more informed judgments about its reliability. Additionally, regulations could enforce stricter penalties for platforms that fail to adequately monitor and curb the spread of misinformation, ensuring a higher standard of accountability.

Second, a concerted effort should be made to promote media literacy and critical thinking among the public. Educational initiatives to improve digital literacy can empower citizens to evaluate online content critically. Schools, universities, and community organisations should integrate media literacy programs into their curricula to teach individuals how to identify biased or false information, understand the role of algorithms, and recognise the tactics used in misinformation campaigns. By fostering a more discerning public, these initiatives can reduce the susceptibility to misleading narratives and promote a healthier, more informed public discourse.

Third, it is essential to strengthen fact-checking and verification mechanisms on social media platforms. Platforms should partner with independent fact-checking organisations to verify the authenticity of content and provide clear indicators when information is found to be false or misleading. Implementing more robust fact-checking tools, such as automated flags for content that requires further scrutiny and visible corrections or disclaimers on disputed posts, can help users distinguish between verified information and unsubstantiated claims. These mechanisms could be further supported by promoting user participation in reporting suspicious content, thus fostering a community-driven approach to content integrity.

Fourth, fostering collaborative efforts between governments, social media companies, and civil society organisations is crucial in addressing the complex challenge of misinformation. Multi-stakeholder initiatives can develop shared guidelines for ethical content management, promote best practices in content moderation, and establish rapid response strategies for misinformation outbreaks. Collaborative campaigns could also focus on debunking prominent false narratives and providing the public with accurate information, especially during critical events such as elections, public health crises, or significant political developments. Debunking posts mostly stay in the scientific echo chamber, and a few individuals exposed to unsubstantiated claims engage with the corrections (Zollo *et al.,* 2017).

Ultimately, there should be a push for greater transparency and user control over personal data and content preferences. Social media platforms should offer users more control over their content feeds and the data algorithms used to determine what content they see. Allowing users to customise their content preferences actively and offering more precise explanations of how their data shapes their online experience could empower individuals to reduce exposure to potentially polarising content. Enhanced transparency regarding data usage and content algorithms would also build greater trust in social media platforms.

Policy Implications

The descriptive statistics and regression analysis findings underscore the need for effective regulation of social media to mitigate the spread of misinformation and reduce the polarisation of public discourse. As nearly all respondents expressed support for stronger regulations, there is a clear mandate for policymakers to address these challenges to safeguard the future of public trust and societal cohesion.

CONCLUSION

The findings of this study focus on the influence of social media narratives on public perception, trust, and political discourse in India. Social media has evolved as a primary source of information; the prevalence of dual narratives and conflicting versions of the same events creates significant challenges for public understanding and trust. The study reveals that many respondents experience confusion and mistrust regarding the information they see on social media platforms and find it challenging to identify which narrative is credible. This suggests that while social media has led to easy access to information, it has also made it difficult for individuals to tackle the intricacies of a polarising information environment.

The most intriguing fact is the effect of dual narratives on national unity and societal cohesion. The data shows that concerns about the impact of conflicting narratives on national stability significantly influence public perception. Respondents are aware of the modus operandi of social media in spreading divisive narratives that can affect social cohesion and erode trust in national institutions. This aligns with existing literature, which suggests that digital platforms create echo chambers and reinforce existing biases, leading to societal divisions. Such dynamics can have far-reaching consequences for social stability and the functioning of democratic processes.

The study also highlights the future implications of social media narratives. The respondents expressed their concern about the societal division created by dual narratives and the negative impact on future generations. This finding underscores the urgent need for proactive measures to mitigate these risks, including more robust regulatory frameworks and public awareness initiatives to promote media literacy and critical thinking. The overwhelming support among respondents for increased regulation indicates an apparent public demand for measures that can enhance the reliability of information and promote a more cohesive digital environment.

REFERENCES

Aïmeur, E., Amri, S., & Brassard, G. (2023). Fake news, disinformation and misinformation in social media: A review. *Social Network Analysis and Mining*, *13*(1), 30. DOI: 10.1007/s13278-023-01028-5 PMID: 36789378

Allcott, H., & Gentzkow, M. (2017). Social media and fake news in the 2016 election. *The Journal of Economic Perspectives*, *31*(2), 211–236. DOI: 10.1257/jep.31.2.211

Bail, C. A., Argyle, L. P., Brown, T. W., Bumpus, J. P., Chen, H., Hunzaker, M. F., Lee, J., Mann, M., Merhout, F., & Volfovsky, A. (2018). Exposure to opposing views on social media can increase political polarization. *Proceedings of the National Academy of Sciences of the United States of America*, *115*(37), 9216–9221. DOI: 10.1073/pnas.1804840115 PMID: 30154168

Bakshy, E., Messing, S., & Adamic, L. A. (2015). Exposure to ideologically diverse news and opinion on Facebook. *Science*, *348*(6239), 1130–1132. DOI: 10.1126/science.aaa1160 PMID: 25953820

Banaji, S., & Bhat, R. (2022). *Social media and hate*. Taylor & Francis.

Barberá, P., Jost, J. T., Nagler, J., Tucker, J. A., & Bonneau, R. (2015). Tweeting from left to right: Is online political communication more than an echo chamber? *Psychological Science*, *26*(10), 1531–1542. DOI: 10.1177/0956797615594620 PMID: 26297377

Bennett, W. L., & Livingston, S. (2018). The disinformation order: Disruptive communication and the decline of democratic institutions. *European Journal of Communication*, *33*(2), 122–139. DOI: 10.1177/0267323118760317

Bovet, A., & Makse, H. A. (2019). Influence of fake news in Twitter during the 2016 US presidential election. *Nature Communications*, *10*(7), 7. Advance online publication. DOI: 10.1038/s41467-018-07761-2 PMID: 30602729

Bradshaw, S., & Howard, P. N. (2018). The global organization of social media disinformation campaigns. *Journal of International Affairs, 71*(1.5), 23-32. https://www.jstor.org/stable/26508115

Bruns, A. (2019). *Are filter bubbles real?* Polity Press.

Chakravartty, P., & Roy, S. (2017). Mediatized populisms: Inter-Asian Lineages-Introduction. *International Journal of Communication*, *11*, 4073–4092.

De Keersmaecker, J., & Roets, A. (2017). 'Fake news': Incorrect, but hard to correct. The role of cognitive ability on the impact of false information on social impressions. *Intelligence*, *65*, 107–110. DOI: 10.1016/j.intell.2017.10.005

Farkas, J., & Schou, J. (2018). Fake news as a floating signifier: Hegemony, antagonism, and the politics of falsehood. *Javnost - The Public Journal of the European Institute for Communication and Culture, 25*(3), 298-314. DOI: 10.1080/13183222.2018.1463047

Garrett, R. K. (2009). Echo chambers online? Politically motivated selective exposure among Internet news users. *Journal of Computer-Mediated Communication*, *14*(2), 265–285. DOI: 10.1111/j.1083-6101.2009.01440.x

Grinberg, N., Joseph, K., Friedland, L., Swire-Thompson, B., & Lazer, D. (2019). Fake news on Twitter during the 2016 U.S. Presidential election. *Science*, *363*(6425), 374–378. DOI: 10.1126/science.aau2706 PMID: 30679368

Guess, A., Nagler, J., & Tucker, J. (2019). Less than you think: Prevalence and predictors of fake news dissemination on Facebook. *Science Advances*, *5*(1), eaau4586. Advance online publication. DOI: 10.1126/sciadv.aau4586 PMID: 30662946

Guess, A., Nyhan, B., Lyons, B., & Reifler, J. (2018). Avoiding the echo chamber about echo chambers. *Knight Foundation*, *2*(1), 1–25.

Iyengar, S., & Massey, D. S. (2019). Scientific communication in a post-truth society. *Proceedings of the National Academy of Sciences of the United States of America*, *116*(16), 7656–7661. DOI: 10.1073/pnas.1805868115 PMID: 30478050

Marwick, A., & Lewis, R. (2017). *Media manipulation and disinformation online*. Data & Society Research Institute.

Pariser, E. (2011). *The filter bubble: What the Internet is hiding from you*. Penguin Press.

Pennycook, G., & Rand, D. G. (2020). The Implied Truth Effect: Attaching warnings to a subset of fake news stories increases perceived accuracy of stories without warnings. *Management Science*, *66*(11), 4944–4957. DOI: 10.1287/mnsc.2019.3478

Statista. (2023). Number of social network users in India from 2015 to 2023 with forecasts until 2027. Retrieved from https://www.statista.com/statistics/278407/number-of-social-network-users-in-india/

Sunstein, C. R. (2018). *Republic: Divided democracy in the age of social media*. Princeton University Press.

Tandoc, E. C.Jr, Lim, Z. W., & Ling, R. (2018). Defining "Fake News": A typology of scholarly definitions. *Digital Journalism (Abingdon, England)*, *6*(2), 137–153. DOI: 10.1080/21670811.2017.1360143

Tufekci, Z. (2015). Algorithmic harms beyond Facebook and Google: Emergent challenges of computational agency. *Colorado Technology Law Journal*, *13*(2), 203–217.

Ufuophu-Biri, E., & Ojoboh, L. (2017). Social media as a tool for political resistance: Lessons from the Arab spring and the Nigerian protests. *Academic Journal of Interdisciplinary Studies, 6*(1), e61. DOI: 10.5901/ajis.2017.v6n1p61

Vaara, E., Sonenshein, S., & Boje, D. (2016). Narratives as sources of stability and change in organizations: Approaches and directions for future research. *The Academy of Management Annals*, *10*(1), 495–560. DOI: 10.5465/19416520.2016.1120963

Van Bavel, J. J., & Pereira, A. (2018). The partisan brain: An identity-based model of political belief. *Trends in Cognitive Sciences*, *22*(3), 213–224. DOI: 10.1016/j.tics.2018.01.004 PMID: 29475636

Vosoughi, S., Roy, D., & Aral, S. (2018). The spread of true and false news online. *Science*, *359*(6380), 1146–1151. DOI: 10.1126/science.aap9559 PMID: 29590045

Wardle, C., & Derakhshan, H. (2017). *Information disorder: Toward an interdisciplinary framework for research and policymaking* (Vol. 27). Council of Europe.

Woolley, S., & Howard, P. (2017). *Computational propaganda worldwide: Executive summary*. Computational Propaganda Project.

Zollo, F., Bessi, A., Del Vicario, M., Scala, A., Caldarelli, G., Shekhtman, L., Havlin, S., & Quattrociocchi, W. (2017). Debunking in a world of tribes. *PLoS One*, *12*(7), e0181821. DOI: 10.1371/journal.pone.0181821 PMID: 28742163

Compilation of References

A Handyman's Guide to Fixing National Security Leaks: An Analytical Framework For Evaluating Proposals To Curb Unauthorized Publication Of Classified Information (1989) 5 J. L. & Pol. 759. - GMSR Appellate Lawyers - Los Angeles | San Francisco. (2016, December 9). GMSR Appellate Lawyers - Los Angeles | San Francisco. https://www.gmsr.com/publication/a-handymans-guide-to-fixing-national-security-leaks-an-analytical-framework-for-evaluating-proposals-to-curb-unauthorized-publication-of-classified-information/

A.P. (n.d.). Fake News definition. *AP News.com*. Retrieved from https://apnews.com/article/11853adb8811487ca5805a0451156c19

Abrahamian, E. (1982). *Iran between two revolutions*. Princeton University Press.

ADL.org. (2024). New World Order. Glossary of Hate and Extremism. *Adl.org*. Accessed May 20, 2024, from https://extremismterms.adl.org/glossary/new-world-order

AFP (2024, June 12). Hezbollah rains rockets down on Israel after strike kills commander. msn.com

Aguirre, E., Mahr, D., Grewal, D., de Ruyter, K., & Wetzels, M. (2015). Unraveling the Personalization Paradox: The Effect of Information Collection and Trust-Building Strategies on Online Advertisement Effectiveness. *Journal of Retailing*, *91*(1), 34–49. DOI: 10.1016/j.jretai.2014.09.005

Ahmed, H. F., & Yassin, A. S. (2021). Fake news detection: A survey of machine learning approaches. *International Journal of Computer Applications*, *175*(2), 19–27.

Aidt, T. S., & Franck, R. (2013). How to get the snowball rolling and extend the franchise: Voting on the Great Reform Act of 1832. *Public Choice*, *155*(3–4), 229–250. DOI: 10.1007/s11127-011-9911-y

Aïmeur, E., Amri, S., & Brassard, G. (2023). Fake news, disinformation and misinformation in social media: A review. *Social Network Analysis and Mining*, *13*(1), 30. DOI: 10.1007/s13278-023-01028-5 PMID: 36789378

Ainsley, J., Winter, T., Blankstein, A., and Planas, A. (2024, June 11). 8 suspected terrorists with possible ISIS ties arrested in New York, L. A., and Philadelphia, sources say. NBCnews.com.

Akhtar, P., Ghouri, A. M., Khan, H. U. R., Amin ul Haq, M., Awan, U., Zahoor, N., Khan, Z., & Ashraf, A. (2023). Detecting fake news and disinformation using artificial intelligence and machine learning to avoid supply chain disruptions. *Annals of Operations Research*, *327*(2), 633–657. DOI: 10.1007/s10479-022-05015-5 PMID: 36338350

Akhter, N. (2023). Fake News in India a study of online and TV News since 2014. https://shodhganga.inflibnet.ac.in/handle/10603/549446

Al Ghamdi, M. A., Bhatti, M. S., Saeed, A., Gillani, Z., & Almotiri, S. H. (2024). A fusion of BERT, machine learning and manual approach for fake news detection. *Multimedia Tools and Applications*, *83*(10), 30095–30112. DOI: 10.1007/s11042-023-16669-z

Al-Atwi, A. A., Cai, Y., & Amankwah-Amoah, J. (2021). Workplace ostracism, paranoid employees and service performance: A multilevel investigation. *Journal of Managerial Psychology*, *36*, 121–137.

Alhouri, A., Abu Shokor, M., Marwa, K., Sharabi, A., Mohammad Nazir Arrouk, D., Al Houri, F. N., & Al Houri, H. (2023). COVID-19 and Its Impact on Healthcare Workers: Understanding Stigma, Stress, and Quality of Life. *Cureus*, *15*(4), e37846. DOI: 10.7759/cureus.37846 PMID: 37214008

Allcott, H., & Gentzkow, M. (2017). Social media and fake news in the 2016 election. *The Journal of Economic Perspectives*, *31*(2), 211–236. DOI: 10.1257/jep.31.2.211

Allyn, B. (2017, November 30). No regrets, Chelsea Manning tells Penn audience. https://whyy.org/articles/no-regrets-chelsea-manning-tells-penn-audience/

Al-Rubaian, M. (2023). Blockchain-based solutions for fake news detection. *Journal of Information Security Research*, *9*(3), 144–158.

Alterman, E., & Zornick, G. (2008, June 12). Iraqi Weapons of Mass Destruction. *Center for American Progress*.https://www.americanprogress.org/article/think-again-iraqi-weapons-of-mass-destruction/

Altheide, D. L. (1996). *Qualitative media analysis*. Sage.

Altheide, D. L. (2002). *Creating Fear: News and the Construction of Crisis*. Routledge., DOI: 10.4324/9780203794494

Altheide, D. L. (2009). The Columbine shooting and the discourse of fear. *The American Behavioral Scientist*, *52*(10), 1354–1370. DOI: 10.1177/0002764209332552

Anderson, J., & Rainie, L. (2017, October 19). The Future of Truth and Misinformation Online. https://www.pewresearch.org/internet/2017/10/19/theme-5-tech-cant-win-the-battle-the-public-must-fund-and-support-the-production-of-objective-accurate-information-it-must-also-elevate-information-literacy-to-be-a-primary-goal-of-educat/

Anderson, J., & Rainie, L. (2018). *The future of well-being in a tech-saturated world*. Pew Research Center. https://www.pewresearch.org/internet/2018/04/17/the-future-of-well-being-in-a-tech-saturated-world/

Anderson, C., & Brion, S. (2014). The powerful and the powerless: How power changes perceptions and behavior. *Annual Review of Psychology*, *65*, 669–692.

AnkitRakesh. (2016). *The Kashmir Conflict: From Empire to the Cold War, 1945–66*. Routledge.

Anwar, S., & Kumar, V. (2022). Fake news detection in the age of AI: A deep learning perspective. *Journal of Artificial Intelligence*, *41*(1), 56–72.

Arndt, G. (2024, October 2). *The Newspaper Wars: Pulitzer vs Hearst*. Everything Everywhere. https://everything-everywhere.com/the-newspaper-wars-pulitzer-vs-hearst/

Atkinson, C., Barrett, P., Clarizio, L., Ghosh, D., Haigh, J., Melia, T., Posner, M., Schiller, V., & Watts, C. (2021). Recommendations to the Biden Administration: On Regulating Disinformation and Other Harmful Content on Social Media. *Harvard Kennedy School*.https://www.hks.harvard.edu/sites/default/files/centers/mrcbg/files/FWP_2021-02.pdf

Ayed, R. B., & Boudriga, N. (2021). The role of social media in spreading fake news and the challenges of mitigating its effects. *Journal of Digital Information Management*, *19*(4), 312–324.

Ayton, M. (2009, October 3). The JFK and RFK Assassinations and the "Manchurian Candidate" Theory. *Crime Magazine*.https://crimemagazine.com/jfk-and-rfk-assassinations-and-manchurian-candidate-theory

Baethge, C., Goldbeck-Wood, S., & Mertens, S. (2019). SANRA—A scale for the quality assessment of narrative review articles. *Research Integrity and Peer Review*, *4*(1), 1–7. DOI: 10.1186/s41073-019-0064-8 PMID: 30962953

Bail, C. A., Argyle, L. P., Brown, T. W., Bumpus, J. P., Chen, H., Hunzaker, M. F., Lee, J., Mann, M., Merhout, F., & Volfovsky, A. (2018). Exposure to opposing views on social media can increase political polarization. *Proceedings of the National Academy of Sciences of the United States of America*, *115*(37), 9216–9221. DOI: 10.1073/pnas.1804840115 PMID: 30154168

Bain, A. (1999). Colorless, non-radiant, blameless: A Hindenburg disaster study. *Gasbag Journal/ Aerostation,* 39, 9-15.

Baixauli, E., Beleña, Á., & Díaz, A. (2020). Evaluation of the Effects of a Bullying at Work Intervention for Middle Managers. *International Journal of Environmental Research and Public Health*, *17*, 7566. PMID: 33080951

Bakshy, E., Messing, S., & Adamic, L. A. (2015). Exposure to ideologically diverse news and opinion on Facebook. *Science*, *348*(6239), 1130–1132. DOI: 10.1126/science.aaa1160 PMID: 25953820

Balili, A., & Desai, P. (2019). Fake News and Social Media: Indian Perspective. *Media Watch*, *10*(3). Advance online publication. DOI: 10.15655/mw/2019/v10i3/49687

Balmer, R. H. (2014). *Redeemer: The Life of Jimmy Carter*. Basic Books.

Banaji, S., & Bhat, R. (2022). *Social media and hate*. Taylor & Francis.

Barberá, P., Jost, J. T., Nagler, J., Tucker, J. A., & Bonneau, R. (2015). Tweeting from left to right: Is online political communication more than an echo chamber? *Psychological Science*, *26*(10), 1531–1542. DOI: 10.1177/0956797615594620 PMID: 26297377

Barceló Sánchez, J. M., Mateos Abarca, J. P., & Álvarez Rivas, D. (2023). Propaganda gubernamental, censura informativa Y fake news durante la Primera Guerra Mundial. *Historia y Comunicación Social*, *28*(2), 407–418. DOI: 10.5209/hics.92243

Barfar, A. (2022). A linguistic/game-theoretic approach to detection/explanation of propaganda. *Expert Systems with Applications*, *189*, 116069. DOI: 10.1016/j.eswa.2021.116069

Barns, Margarita, 1904-. (1940). The Indian press; a history of the growth of public opinion in India, by Margarita Barns. [London]: G. Allen &Unwin ltd

Basuroy, T. (2024, June 26). *India: frequency of seeing fake news online 2023*. Statista. https://www.statista.com/statistics/1406289/india-frequency-of-seeing-fake-news-online/

Becker, G. S. (1976). *The Economic Approach to Human Behavior*. University of Chicago Press.

Bennett, W. L., & Livingston, S. (2018). The disinformation order: Disruptive communication and the decline of democratic institutions. *European Journal of Communication, 33*(2), 122–139. DOI: 10.1177/0267323118760317

Berkowitz, D. (2010). The ironic hero of Virginia Tech: Healing trauma through mythical narrative and collective memory. *Journalism, 11*(6), 643–659. DOI: 10.1177/1464884910379705

Bernstein, R. (1999, December 15). 'Day of Deceit': On Dec.7, Did We Know We Knew? *The New York Times*.https://archive.nytimes.com/www.nytimes.com/books/99/12/12/daily/121599stinnett-book-review.html

Bertram, C. (2020, December 10). Did the Mob kill John F. Kennedy? *Biography*.https://www.biography.com/crime/did-the-mob-kill-john-f-kennedy

Bhargava, MotiLal, 1917-. (1987). Role of press in the freedom movement / MotiLalBhargava. New Delhi: Reliance Pub. House

Bharti, A., & Prakash, A. (2021). Detection of fake news using machine learning: A review. *International Journal of Computer Science and Network Security, 21*(7), 93–100.

Bhattarai, S. K. (2023). Conceptual Framework of Judicial Review with Reference to Nepal. *Advances in Sciences and Humanities, 9*(2), 52–57.

Bilal, A. (2021, November 21). Hybrid Warfare – New Threats, Complexity, and 'Trust' as the Antidote. www.nato/int

Bilton, N. (2017, January 26). Fake News is About to Get Scarier than you Ever Dreamed. Vanityfair.com. Retrieved May 19, 2024, from https://www.vanityfair.com/news/2017/01/fake-news-technology

Birkland, T. A., & Lawrence, R. G. (2009). Media Framing and Policy Change After Columbine. *The American Behavioral Scientist, 52*(10), 1405–1425.

Biswas, S., & Sood, M. (2024). Detecting fake news using neural networks and ensemble learning techniques. *Neural Computing & Applications, 36*(2), 547–561.

Black, J. (2001). Semantics and Ethics of Propaganda. *Journal of Mass Media Ethics, 16*(2&3), 121–137. http://www.communicationcache.com/uploads/1/0/8/8/10887248/semantics_and_ethics_of_propaganda.pdf

Blake, A. (2018, April 3). A new study suggests fake news might have won Donald Trump the 2016 election. https://www.washingtonpost.com/news/the-fix/wp/2018/04/03/a-new-study-suggests-fake-news-might-have-won-donald-trump-the-2016-election/

Blassingame, J. (1972). *The slave community: Plantation life in the Antebellum South*. Oxford Press.

Bloch-Wehba, H. (2024). The promise and perils of tech whistleblowing. *Northwestern University Law Review, 118*(6), 1503–1562. https://coloradotech.idm.oclc.org/login?url=https://www.proquest.com/scholarly-journals/promise-perils-tech-whistleblowing/docview/3049832414/se-2

Bobic, I. (2024, August 13). Bernie Sanders Warns Donald Trump is Gearing Up to Deny 2024 Election Results. *Huffington Post.*https://www.huffpost.com/entry/bernie-sanders-donald-trump-2024_n_66bb9e99e4b0b1dc53031b5b

Bode, L., Vraga, E. K., & Borah, P. (2018). See something, say something: Correction of global health misinformation on social media. *Health Communication, 33*(9), 1131–1140. DOI: 10.1080/10410236.2017.1331312 PMID: 28622038

Boghardt, T. (2009, December). Soviet Bloc Intelligence and Its AIDS Disinformation Campaign (Operation INFEKTION). *Studies in Intelligence.*

Bonsu, S. (2019). Corporate Social Responsibility: Assessing the Alignment of Theory and Practice Utilizing Case Studies. *Journal of Marketing Management, 10*(1), 1–18. https://coloradotech.idm.oclc.org/login?url=https://www.proquest.com/scholarly-journals/corporate-social-responsibility-assessing/docview/2234961050/se-2

Bontridder, N., & Poullet, Y. (2021). The role of artificial intelligence in disinformation. *Data & Policy, 3*, e32. DOI: 10.1017/dap.2021.20

Booker, S. (1955, May 26). Is Mississippi Ushing up a Lynching? *JET Magazine. Volume*, (8), 8–10.

Borden, S. (2010). The moral justification for journalism. In Meyers, C. (Ed.), *Journalism ethics: a philosophical approach.* Oxford University Press. DOI: 10.1093/acprof:oso/9780195370805.003.0004

Boudrias, V., Trépanier, S.-G., & Salin, D. (2021). A systematic review of research on the longitudinal consequences of workplace bullying and the mechanisms involved. *Aggression and Violent Behavior, 56*, 101508.

Bovet, A., & Makse, H. A. (2019). Influence of fake news in Twitter during the 2016 US presidential election. *Nature Communications, 10*(7), 7. Advance online publication. DOI: 10.1038/s41467-018-07761-2 PMID: 30602729

Bowman, V. (2024, July 15). Trump shooting: all seven conspiracy theories examined. *Telegraph.*https://www.telegraph.co.uk/world-news/2024/07/15/trump-shooting-seven-conspiracy-theories-ear-blood-picture/

Boyd, D. M., & Ellison, N. B. (2007). Social network sites: Definition, history, and scholarship. *Journal of Computer-Mediated Communication, 13*(1), 210–230. DOI: 10.1111/j.1083-6101.2007.00393.x

Bradshaw, S., & Howard, P. N. (2018). Challenging truth and trust: A global inventory of organized social media manipulation. Oxford Internet Institute's Computational Propaganda Research Project. https://comprop.oii.ox.ac.uk/wp-content/uploads/sites/93/2018/07/ct2018.pdf

Bradshaw, S., & Howard, P. N. (2018). The global organization of social media disinformation campaigns. *Journal of International Affairs, 71*(1.5), 23-32. https://www.jstor.org/stable/26508115

Brady, H. E., & Kent, T. B. (2022). Fifty Years of Declining Confidence & Increasing Polarization in Trust in American Institutions. *Daedalus*, *151*(4), 43–66. DOI: 10.1162/daed_a_01943

Brandenberger, D. (2012). *Propaganda state in crisis: Soviet ideology, indoctrination, and terror under Stalin, 1927–1941*. Yale University Press.

Brett, J. M., Zhang, Z.-X., & Olekalns, M. (2018). The dark side of negotiation: Deception and ethical dilemmas. *Journal of Business Ethics*, *152*(3), 647–661.

Britannica (n.d.) Yellow Journalism. *Britannica.com*. Retrieved from https://www.britannica.com/topic/yellow-journalism

Britannica, T. Editors of Encyclopedia (2024, June 14). Hamas. Encyclopedia Britannica. https://www.britannica.com/topic/Hamas

Britannica, T. Editors of Encyclopedia (2024, May 2). *Yellow journalism. Encyclopedia Britannica.* https://www.britannica.com/topic/yellow-journalismcirculation

Britannica, T. Editors of Encyclopedia (n.d.). Kanem-Bornu Empire_https://kids.britannica.com/kids/article/Kanem-Bornu-Empire/353330

Britannica, T. Information Architects of Encyclopaedia (2024, June 16). Crusades. Encyclopedia Britannica. https://www.britannica.com/facts/Crusades

Britt, A., Rout, J.-F., Blaum, D., & Millis, K. (2019, March 8). A Reasoned approach to Dealing with Fake News, Sage Journals. https://journals.sagepub.com/doi/full/10.1177/2372732218814855

Brook, T. V. (2021, October 18). Collin Powell lent his prestige to make a case for the Iraq war: 'I will always regret it,' he later said. *USA Today*.https://www.usatoday.com/story/news/politics/2021/10/18/military-legacy-colin-powell-and-his-un-speech-wmds-iraq/8505233002/?gnt-cfr=1&gca-cat=p

Bruce, J., & Jameson, G. (2013). Assessing the Department of Defense's Approach to Preventing and Deterring Unauthorized Disclosures. RAND Corporation. Accessed July 30, 2024, from https://www.rand.org/pubs/research_reports/RR409.html

Bruns, A. (2019). *Are filter bubbles real?* Polity Press.

Bryan, W., & Hopper, D. (2005, November 15). Iraq WMD Timeline: How the Mystery Unraveled. *NPR*. https://www.npr.org/2005/11/15/4996218/iraq-wmd-timeline-how-the-mystery-unraveled

Bryman, A. (2008). *Social research methods* (3rd ed.). Oxford University Press.

Buchanan, T., & Benson, V. (2019). Spreading disinformation on Facebook: Do trust in message source, risk propensity, or personality affect the organic reach of "fake news"? *Social Media + Society*, *5*(4). DOI: 10.1177/2056305119888654

Bughin, J., Hazan, E., Ramaswamy, S., Chui, M., Allas, T., Dahlstrom, P., Henke, N., & Trench, M. (2017). *Artificial intelligence: the next digital frontier?* McKinsey Global Institute.

Bumblauskas, D., Nold, H., Bumblauskas, P., & Igou, A. (2017). Big data analytics: Transforming data to action. *Business Process Management Journal*, *23*(3), 703–720. DOI: 10.1108/BPMJ-03-2016-0056

Burns, R., & Crawford, C. (1999). School shootings, the media, and public fear: Ingredients for a moral panic. *Crime, Law, and Social Change*, *32*(2), 147–168. DOI: 10.1023/A:1008338323953

Buschman, J. (2019). Good news, bad news, and fake news: Going beyond political literacy to democracy and libraries. *The Journal of Documentation*, *75*(1), 213–228. DOI: 10.1108/JD-05-2018-0074

Cai, W., & Xu, P. (2023). Network-based approaches for identifying sources of fake news. *Journal of Computational Social Networks*, *10*(2), 185–200.

Çakı, C., & Gülada, M. O. (2018). Vichy Fransası'ndaİşgalPropagandası. *TrakyaÜniversitesiİktisad-iveİdariBilimlerFakültesiDergisi*, *7*(1), 53–80.

Cambridge Dictionary. (2023, October 11). *Fake news.* https://dictionary.cambridge.org/dictionary/english/fake-news#google_vignette

Cantoni, D., Chen, Y., Yang, D. Y., Yuchtman, N., & Zhang, Y. J. (2017). Curriculum and ideology. *Journal of Political Economy*, *125*(2), 338–392. DOI: 10.1086/690951

Carelli, D., & Pierre, J. (2024). When the cat is away: How institutional autonomy, low salience, and issue complexity shape administrative action. *Public Administration*, *102*(1), 207–221. DOI: 10.1111/padm.12912

Carlos, S. A. (2019). La primera "fake news" de la historia [The first "fake news" in history]. *Historia y Comunicación Social*, *24*(2), 411–431. DOI: 10.5209/hics.66268

Carpini, M. X. D., & Entman, R. M. (2005). News from Somewhere: Journalistic Frames and the Debate over "Public Journalism." In Callaghan, K., & Schnell, F. (Eds.), *Framing American Politics* (pp. 21–53). University of Pittsburgh Press. DOI: 10.2307/j.ctt6wrbqk.6

Carter & Carter. (2019). When Autocrats Threaten Citizens WithViolence: Evidence from China. Working Paper, University of Southern California. Available at: http://www.erinbcarter.org/documents/chinaThreats.pdf

Carter, E. B., & Carter, B. L. (2021). Propaganda and Protest in Autocracies. *The Journal of Conflict Resolution*, *65*(5), 919–949. DOI: 10.1177/0022002720975090

Cassata, C. (2021, June 22). Doctors Debunk 9 Popular COVID-19 Vaccine Myths and Conspiracy Theories. *Health Line.*https://www.healthline.com/health-news/doctors-debunk-9-popular-covid-19-vaccine-myths-and-conspiracy-theories

Castillo-Ortiz, P. (2020). Constitutional Review in the Member States of the EU-28: A Political Analysis of Institutional Choices. *Journal of Law and Society*, *47*(1), 87–120. DOI: 10.1111/jols.12210

CBS News. (2018, April 4). *MLK assassination: How Walter Cronkite covered the April 4, 1968 tragedy.* https://www.cbsnews.com/news/mlk-assassination-walter-cronkite-report-cbs-evening-news-broadcast-april-4-1968/

Chahal, M. (2017). The fake news effect and what it means for advertisers. *Marketing Week.*https://www.marketingweek.com/2017/03/27/the-fake-news-effect/

Chakravartty, P., & Roy, S. (2017). Mediatized populisms: Inter-Asian Lineages-Introduction. *International Journal of Communication*, *11*, 4073–4092.

Chan, H., & Zhang, X. (2023). Fake news detection with multi-modal fusion: A new approach. *Journal of Information Science and Engineering*, *42*(1), 44–58.

Chatterjee, S., & Panmand, M. (2022). Explaining and predicting click-baitiness and click-bait virality. *Industrial Management & Data Systems*, *122*(11), 2485–2507. DOI: 10.1108/IMDS-01-2022-0003

Chaudhari, D. D., & Pawar, A. V. (2021). Propaganda analysis in social media: A bibliometric review. *Information Discovery and Delivery*, *49*(1), 57–70. DOI: 10.1108/IDD-06-2020-0065

Chen, Y., & Zhao, L. (2024). Fact-checking algorithms: Advancing accuracy in fake news detection. *Journal of Computational Intelligence*, *15*(1), 112–125.

Cherry, K. (2020, December 11, 2020). How Confirmation Bias Works. Accessed from https://www.verywellmind.com/what-is-a-confirmation-bias-2795024

Chua, A. Y. K., Pal, A., & Banerjee, S. (2021). "This will blow your mind": Examining the urge to click clickbaits. *Aslib Journal of Information Management*, *73*(2), 288–303. DOI: 10.1108/AJIM-07-2020-0214

Chyi, H. I., & McCombs, M. E. (2004). Media salience and the process of framing: Coverage of the Columbine school shootings. *Journalism & Mass Communication Quarterly*, *81*(1), 22–35. DOI: 10.1177/107769900408100103

Cimili, Z., & Satter, R. (2016, December 2) Macedonia's Fake News Hub, Ten Show AP how it's Done. https://www.nbcconnecticut.com/news/national-international/in-macedonias-fake-news-hub-teen-shows-ap-how-its-done/1989346/

Cinelli, M., Quattrociocchi, W., Galeazzi, A., Valensise, C. M., Brugnoli, E., Schmidt, A. L., Zola, P., Zollo, F., & Scala, A. (2020). The COVID-19 social media infodemic. *Scientific Reports*, *10*(1), 1. Advance online publication. DOI: 10.1038/s41598-020-73510-5 PMID: 33024152

CITS.ucsb.edu. (n.d.) What is fake news? *Center for Information Technology & Society. University of California Santa Barbara.* https://cits.ucsb.edu/fake-news/what-is-fake-news

Cleminson, R. F. (2003). What happened to Saddam's Weapons of Mass Destruction? *Arms Control Today*, *33*(7), 3–6. https://www.armscontrol.org/act/2003-09/features/what-happened-saddams-weapons-mass-destruction

CNN. (2008). *FactCheck.org*. Obama Not Attending a Muslim School.

Cohen Bernard, C. (1967). Mass Communication and Foreign Policy. In Rosenau, J. N. (Ed.), *Domestic Sources of Foreign Policy* (pp. 195–212). Free Press.

Cohen, A., Ekwueme, P. O., Sacotte, K. A., Bajwa, L., Gilpin, S., & Heard-Garris, N. (2021). "Melanincholy": A Qualitative Exploration of Youth Media Use, Vicarious Racism, and Perceptions of Health. *The Journal of adolescent health: official publication of the Society for Adolescent Medicine, 69*(2), 288–293. DOI: 10.1016/j.jadohealth.2020.12.128

Cohen, L. (2021a, January 7). Twitter and Facebook lock Trump's accounts, take down video of his message to supporters. *CBS News.*https://www.cbsnews.com/news/trump-twitter-facebook-accounts-locked/

Cohen, L. (2021b, January 15). 6 conspiracy theories about 2020 election – debunked. *CBS News.*https://www.cbsnews.com/news/presidential-election-2020-conspiracy-theories-debunked/

Cohen, S. (1972). *Folk Devils and Moral Panics: The Creation of the Mods and Rockers*. MacGibbon and Kee.

Cohen, S. (2002). *Folk Devils and Moral Panics* (3rd ed.). Routledge.

Coleman, J. S. (1990). *Foundations of Social Theory*. Harvard University Press.

Coleman, L. (2004). *The Copycat Effect: How the Media and Popular Culture Trigger the Mayhem in Tomorrow's Headlines*. Paraview Pocket Books.

Columbia University. (2019). *Content Analysis*. www.publichealth.columbia.edu. https://www.publichealth.columbia.edu/research/population-health-methods/content-analysis#:~:text=Content%20analysis%20is%20a%20research

Combs, C. C. (2022-07-29). Terrorism in the Twenty-First Century, 9th Edition [VitalSource Bookshelf version]. Retrieved from vbk://9781000609844

Cone, J. H. (1970). *A Black Theology of Liberation*. Orbis Books.

Content Analysis: A Methodology for Structuring and Analyzing Written Material. (1996). United States General Accounting Office. http://archive.gao.gov/f0102/157490.pdf

Conway, M. (2021). Online Extremism and Terrorism Research ethics: Researcher safety, informed consent, and the need for tailored guidelines. *Terrorism and Political Violence*, *33*(2), 367–380. DOI: 10.1080/09546553.2021.1880235

Cook, J. (2024). *The Quite Damage: QAnon and the Destruction of the American Family*. Crown Publishing.

Cookson, D. (2024, January 30). Intelligence doesn't make you immune to conspiracy theories—it's more about thinking style. *The Conversation.*https://theconversation.com/intelligence-doesnt-make-you-immune-to-conspiracy-theories-its-more-about-thinking-style-220978

Cooper, C., Knotts, H. G., & Haspel, M. (2009). The Content of Political Participation: Letters to the Editor and the People Who Write Them. *PS, Political Science & Politics*, *42*(1), 131–137. https://www.jstor.org/stable/20452387

Cordeiro, G. O., Deschamps, F., & de Lima, E. P. (2017). Developing a Big Data/Analytics project: a case study in the auto industry. *IISE Annual Conference Proceedings,* 1753-1758. https://coloradotech.idm.oclc.org/login?url=https://www.proquest.com/scholarly-journals/developing-big-data-analytics-project-case-study/docview/1951123574/se-2

Cormier, D., & Magnan, M. (2017). Does a firm's exposure to ethical failures matter to financial markets? A governance perspective. *The Journal of Management and Governance*, *21*(2), 267–289. DOI: 10.1007/s10997-016-9341-9

Countering and Exposing Terrorist Propaganda and Disinformation. (n.d.). The Washington Institute. https://www.washingtoninstitute.org/policy-analysis/countering-and-exposing-terrorist-propaganda-and-disinformation

Cuan-Baltazar, J. Y., Muñoz-Perez, M. J., Robledo-Vega, C., Pérez-Zepeda, M. F., & Soto-Vega, E. (2020). Misinformation of COVID-19 on the Internet: Infodemiology study. *JMIR Public Health and Surveillance*, *6*(2), e18444. DOI: 10.2196/18444 PMID: 32250960

Cullen, D. (2019). *Columbine*. Riverun.

Cullen, D. (2024). *Columbine 25th Anniversary Memorial Edition*. Grand Central Publishing.

da Silva, M. T. (2011). Newsroom Practices And Letters-To-The-Editor: An analysis of selection criteria. *Journalism Practice*, *6*(2), 250–263. DOI: 10.1080/17512786.2011.629124

Daily Mail. (2011, April 19). Was JFK kills because of his interest in aliens? Secret memo shows president demanded UFO files 10 days before death. https://www.dailymail.co.uk/news/article-1378284/Secret-memo-shows-JFK-demanded-UFO-files-10-days-assassination.html

Dallas, K. (2024, July 16). Report: President Biden expected to propose major changes to Supreme Court. *MSN*. https://www.msn.com/en-us/news/politics/report-president-biden-expected-to-propose-major-changes-to-supreme-court/ar-BB1q6Yqw?ocid=BingNewsVerp

Daly, P. (2021). *Understanding administrative law in the common law world*. Oxford University Press. DOI: 10.1093/oso/9780192896919.001.0001

Damyanov, M. (2023, March 21). *What is Content Analysis? Uses, Types & Advantages*. Dovetail.com. https://dovetail.com/research/content-analysis /

Das, R., & Prasad, N. (2023). Challenges in multi-lingual fake news detection: A case study of Asian languages. *Journal of Natural Language Processing*, *31*(5), 1009–1022.

Dattani, P. (2021, September 14). How to Stop the Spread of Conspiracy Theories and Build Societal Resilience Against Fake News. *London School of Economics (LSE)*. https://blogstest.lse.ac.uk/medialse/2021/09/14/how-to-stop-the-spread-of-conspiracy-theories-and-build-societal-resilience-against-fake-news/

Dauber, C. E., & Winkler, C. K. (2014). *Visual propaganda and extremism in the online environment*. USAWC Press.

Daugherty, G. (2023). The Hindenburg Disaster: Why the Giant Dirigible Burst into Flames. *History*. https://www.history.com/news/hindenburg-disaster-zeppelin-crash-why

Daunt, K. L., Greer, D. A., Jin, H. S., & Orpen, I. (2023). Who believes political fake news? The role of conspiracy mentality, patriotism, perceived threat to freedom, media literacy, and concern for disinformation. *Internet Research*, *33*(5), 1849–1870. DOI: 10.1108/INTR-07-2022-0565

Davis, M. (2002). The Concise Dictionary of Crime and Justice. Thousand Oaks, CA. Sage Publications.

Davis, S. (2014, July 16). We fact-checked some of the rumors spreading online about the Trump assassination attempt. *Reuters.*https://www.reuters.com/fact-check/misinformation-narratives-fact-checked-wake-trump-assassination-attempt-2024-07-15/

De Keersmaecker, J., & Roets, A. (2017). 'Fake news': Incorrect, but hard to correct. The role of cognitive ability on the impact of false information on social impressions. *Intelligence*, *65*, 107–110. DOI: 10.1016/j.intell.2017.10.005

DeCaro, L. A. (1996). *On the Side of My People: A Religious Life of Malcolm X.* New York University Press.

Dell. (2012). Oppressed. In *American Heritage dictionary* (p. 589). Academic Press.

Desai, S., & Oehrli, J. A. (2024, March 14). *"Fake news," lies and propaganda: How to sort fact from fiction.* University of Michigan Library Research Guides. https://guides.lib.umich.edu/fakenews

Desouza, E. (2024). *AfroTech - Blavity: Ready For Your Startup? Here Are Unique Business Name Ideas To Drive Success.* Newstex.

Dessler, A. J., Overs, D. E., & Appleby, W. H. (2005, January 12). The Hindenburg Fire: Hydrogen or Incendiary Paint? *Buoyant Flight,* 52(2&3), 1-11. https://spot.colorado.edu/~dziadeck/zf/LZ129fire2005jan12.pdf

Destiny Apuke, O., & Omar, B. (2021). Fake News and COVID-19: Modelling the Predictors of Fake News Sharing among Social Media Users. *Telematics and Informatics, 56*, 101475. DOI: 10.1016/j.tele.2020.101475

Dhiman, G., & Kumar, M. (2023). Social media sentiment analysis for fake news detection: A survey. *Journal of Digital Media and Communication*, *9*(3), 245–260.

Dickey, C. (2020, March 29). Did an illuminati conspiracy theory help elect Thomas Jefferson? *Politico Magazine.*https://www.politico.com/news/magazine/2020/03/29/illuminati-conspiracy-theory-thomas-jefferson-1800-election-152934

Dictionary, C. (n.d.). Troll definition. *Cambridgedictionary.org.* Retrieved from https://dictionary.cambridge.org/us/dictionary/english/troll

DiLascio-Martinuk, T. (2024). Fake News: Overview. *APA Points of ViewFake News: Overview: Cougar Search.* ccis.edu

Dixon, T. F. (1905). *The Clansman: An Historical Romance of the Ku Klux Klan.* Doubleday Press.

Doherty, C., & Kiley, J. (2023, March 14). A look back at how fear and false beliefs bolstered U.S. public support for war in Iraq. *Pew Research Center.*https://www.pewresearch.org/politics/2023/03/14/a-look-back-at-how-fear-and-false-beliefs-bolstered-u-s-public-support-for-war-in-iraq/

Domnik, J., & Holland, A. (2024). On Data Leakage Prevention Maturity: Adapting the C2M2 Framework. *Journal of Cybersecurity and Privacy*, *4*(2), 167–195. DOI: 10.3390/jcp4020009

Donovan, J. (2024, June 7). Why Jack Ruby Kills JFK's Assassin. *HowStuffWorks.*https://history.howstuffworks.com/historical-figures/jack-ruby.htm

Dorador, B. (2022). *Nonprofit Business to Business Social Media Interventions: A Qualitative Case Study* (Order No. 28969306). Available from ABI/INFORM Collection. (2641884338). https://coloradotech.idm.oclc.org/login?url=https://www.proquest.com/dissertations-theses/nonprofit-business-social-media-interventions/docview/2641884338/se-2

Douglas, K. M. (2021). COVID-19 conspiracy theories. *Group Processes & Intergroup Relations*, *24*(2), 270–275. https://journals.sagepub.com/doi/full/10.1177/1368430220982068

Douglas, K. M., & Sutton, R. M. (2023). What are conspiracy theories? A definitional approach to their correlates, consequences, and communication. *Annual Review of Psychology*, *74*(1), 271–298. DOI: 10.1146/annurev-psych-032420-031329 PMID: 36170672

Drolc, C. A., & Keiser, L. R. (2021). The importance of oversight and agency capacity in enhancing performance in public service delivery. *Journal of Public Administration: Research and Theory*, *31*(4), 773–789.

Duda, A. (2022). Remembering Soviet imperialism. https://www.taipeitimes.com/News/editorials/archives/2022/09/17/200378545

Dunbar, D., & Reagan, B. (Eds.). (2006). *Debunking 9/11 Myths: Why Conspiracy Theories Can't Stand Up to the Facts*. Hearst Books.

Durkin, A., & Kunzelman, M. (2024, January 5). Hundreds of convictions, but a major mystery is still unsolved 3 years after the Jan. 6 Capitol riot. *APNews.*https://apnews.com/article/capitol-riot-jan-6-criminal-cases-anniversary-bf436efe760751b1356f937e55bedaa5

Dutton, S., Pinto, J. D., Salvanto, A., & Backus, F. (2013, November 16). Poll: Most Americans still think there was a JFK cover-up. *CBS News.*https://www.cbsnews.com/news/poll-most-americans-still-think-there-was-a-jfk-cover-up/

Dwaipayan, B. (2011). Journalism caught in narrow nationalism: The India-Pakistan media. Available at: https://reutersinstitute.politics.ox.ac.uk/sites/default/files/2017-10/Journalism_Caught_in_Narrow_Nationalism_The_India-Pakistan_Media_War.pdf

Edward Snowden: A 'Nation' interview. (2015, June 29). The Nation. https://www.thenation.com/article/archive/snowden-exile-exclusive-interview/

Eig, J., & Theoharis, J. (2023, April 12). The man who knew exactly what the F.B.I. was doing to Martin Luther King, Jr. *The New York Times*. Retrieved from: https://www.nytimes.com/2023/04/12/opinion/lyndon-johnson-martin-luther-king-jr.html

Elliott, P. (2021, September 10). Twenty Years of Data Show How America Changed—And Stayed the Same—After 9/11. *Time Magazine.*https://time.com/6096943/how-sept-11-changed-america/

Elon Musk Quotes. (n.d.). BrainyQuote.com. Retrieved May 23, 2024, from *BrainyQuote.com Web site:*https://www.brainyquote.com/quotes/elon_musk_949273

Encyclopedia Britannica. (2024, October 16). National Association for the Advancement of Colored People. In *Encyclopedia Britannica online*. Retrieved from: https://www.britannica.com/topic/National-Association-for-the-Advancement-of-Colored-People

Encyclopedia Britannica. (2024, October 3). Elijah Muhammad. In *Encyclopedia Britannica online*. Retrieved from: https://www.britannica.com/biography/Elijah-Muhammad

Entman, R. M. (1993). Framing: Toward Clarification of a Fractured Paradigm. *Journal of Communication, 43*(4), 51–58. DOI: 10.1111/j.1460-2466.1993.tb01304.x

Entman, R. M. (2007). Framing bias: Media in the distribution of power. *Journal of Communication, 57*(1), 163–173. DOI: 10.1111/j.1460-2466.2006.00336.x

Equity Theory vs. Expectancy Theory - *What's the Difference?* (n.d.). *This Vs. That*. https://thisvsthat.io/equity-theory-vs-expectancy-theory#:~:text=While%20Equity%20Theory%20emphasizes%20the%20importance%20of%20fairness,organizations%20seeking%20to%20enhance%20employee%20motivation%20and%20performance

Ericson, R., Baranek, P., & Chan, J. (1989). *Negotiating Control. A Study of News Sources*. University of Toronto Press.

Eshet, Y. (2004). Digital literacy: A conceptual framework for survival skills in the digital era. *Journal of Educational Multimedia and Hypermedia, 13*(1), 93–106.

Eskridge, L. (1998). *God's Right Hand: How Jerry Falwell Made God a Republican and Baptized the American Right*. Oxford University Press.

Evers-Williams, M., & Blau, M. (1999). *Watch me fly: What I learned on the way to becoming the woman I was meant to be*. Little Brown and Company.

Evers-Williams, M., & Marable, M. (Eds.). (2005). *The autobiography of Medgar Evers: A hero's life and legacy revealed through his writings, letters, and speeches*. Basic Civitas Books.

Executive Order 13721—Developing an Integrated Global Engagement Center To Support Government-wide Counterterrorism Communications Activities Directed Abroad and Revoking Executive Order 13584. (n.d.). https://www.presidency.ucsb.edu/documents/executive-order-13721-developing-integrated-global-engagement-center-support-government

Fahmy, S. (2019). Personal Choice or Political Provocation: Examining the Visual Framing and Stereotyping of the Burkini Debate. *Journalism & Mass Communication Quarterly, 96*(4), 1076–1098. DOI: 10.1177/1077699019826093

Fairclough, N. (1989). *Language and Power*. Longman.

Fairclough, N. (1992). Discourse and Text: Linguistic and Intertextual Analysis within Discourse Analysis. *Discourse & Society, 3*(2), 193–217. DOI: 10.1177/0957926592003002004

Fairclough, N. (2003). *Analyzing discourse: Textual analysis for social research*. Psychology Press.

Fairhurst, G. T., & Sarr, R. A. (1996). *The Art of Framing: Managing the Language of Leadership*. JosseyBass.

Farkas, J., & Schou, J. (2018). Fake news as a floating signifier: Hegemony, antagonism, and the politics of falsehood. *Javnost - The Public Journal of the European Institute for Communication and Culture, 25*(3), 298-314. DOI: 10.1080/13183222.2018.1463047

Farooq, G. (2018). Politics of Fake News: How WhatsApp Became a Potent Propaganda Tool in India. *Media Watch, 9*(1). Advance online publication. DOI: 10.15655/mw/2018/v9i1/49279

FBI. (n.d.). Terrorism. Retrieved on March 9, 2016, from https://www.fbi.gov/about-us/investigate/terrorism/terrorism-definition for-strategic-impact/

Felt, A. P., Ha, E., & Han, S. (2014). Measuring the effectiveness of security and privacy mechanisms in mobile applications. *Proceedings of the 2014 ACM Conference on Computer and Communications Security,* 1006-1018. DOI: 10.1145/2661433.2661445

Ferrara, E. (2017). Contagion dynamics of extremist propaganda in social networks. *Information Sciences, 418-419*, 1–12. DOI: 10.1016/j.ins.2017.07.030

Feuerherd, P. (2016, July 4). The First Ugly Election: America, 1800. *JSTOR Daily.*https://daily.jstor.org/first-ugly-election-america-1800/

FICCI & EY. (2024). *Reinvent india's media & entertainment sector is innovating for the future*. FICCI & EY.

Figueira, Á., & Oliveira, L. (2017). The current state of fake news: Challenges and opportunities. *ScienceDirect, 121*, 817–825.

Fischer, M., & Goad, S. (2024). Greenhouse Gas Emission – A Perspective. *Journal of Strategic Innovation and Sustainability, 19*(2), 1–13. DOI: 10.33423/jsis.v19i2.6991

Fleck, A. (2024, January 24). *Survey Finds False Information Risk Highest in India*. The Wire. https://thewire.in/media/survey-finds-false-information-risk-highest-in-india

Fleming, N. (2020). Infodemic management: A key component of COVID-19 pandemic response strategy. *Health Education & Behavior, 47*(2), 283–286. DOI: 10.1177/1090198120922984

Flores, M. (2022, May 22). The New World Order: The Historical Origins of a Dangerous Modern Conspiracy Theory. https://www.middlebury.edu/institute/academics/centers-initiatives/ctec/ctec-publications/new-world-order-historical-origins-dangerous

Follman, M. (2022). *Trigger Points: Inside the mission to stop mass shootings in America*. HarperCollins Publishers.

Forrest, J. (2015). Center for Terrorism and Security Studies. *UMASS Lowell.*https://www.uml.edu/research/ctss/about/

Fowler, R. (1991). *Language in the News: Discourse and Ideology in the Press* (1st ed.). Routledge.

Frankel, G. (2024). Old Kinderhook and civic integration in America. *The Independent Review, 29*(1), 5–30. https://www.proquest.com/scholarly-journals/old-kinderhook-civic-integration-america/docview/3063799102/se-2

Fripp, G. (2023, November 24). *What is the Affective Events Theory? - Organizational Behavior*. My Organizational Behaviour Notes. https://www.myorganisationalbehaviour.com/what-is-the-affective-events-theory/

Fritze, J. (2024, February 1). Trump's critics hope that Antonin Scalia can sway the Supreme Court in 14th Amendment fight. *CNN*.https://www.cnn.com/2024/02/01/politics/supreme-court-trump-14th-amendment-scalia/index.html

Frymer, B. (2009). The Media Spectacle of Columbine: Alienated Youth as an Object of Fear. *The American Behavioral Scientist*, *52*(10), 1387–1404. DOI: 10.1177/000276420933255

FTC. (2021). The Federal Trade Commission: Protecting consumers and competition. https://www.ftc.gov

Funk, C., Tyson, A., Kennedy, B., & Pasquini, G. (2023, May 16). What Americans think about COVID-19 vaccines. *Pew Research Center*.https://www.pewresearch.org/science/2023/05/16/what-americans-think-about-covid-19-vaccines/

Fu, X., & Wang, Q. (2024). Hybrid deep learning models for fake news detection on Twitter. *Journal of Social Media and Digital Technologies*, *14*(1), 33–47.

Galdieri, C. J., Lucas, J. C., & Sisco, T. S. (Eds.). (2017). *The role of Twitter in the 2016 US election*. Palgrave Pivot., DOI: 10.1007/978-3-319-68981-4

Galli, A., Masciari, E., Moscato, V., & Sperlí, G. (2022). A comprehensive benchmark for fake news detection. *Journal of Intelligent Information Systems*, *59*(1), 237–261. DOI: 10.1007/s10844-021-00646-9 PMID: 35342227

Galtung, J., & Ruge, M. (1965). The Structure of Foreign News: The presentation of the Congo, Cuba and Cyprus crises in four Norwegian newspapers. *Journal of International Peace Research*, *2*(1), 64–91. DOI: 10.1177/00223433650020010

Galtung, J., & Ruge, M. H. (1965). The Structure of Foreign News: The Presentation of the Congo, Cuba and Cyprus Crises in Four Norwegian Newspapers. *Journal of Peace Research*, *2*(1), 64–90. DOI: 10.1177/002234336500200104

Garrett, R. K. (2009). Echo chambers online? Politically motivated selective exposure among Internet news users. *Journal of Computer-Mediated Communication*, *14*(2), 265–285. DOI: 10.1111/j.1083-6101.2009.01440.x

Geeng, C., Yee, S., & Roesner, F. (2020, April 21). Fake News on Facebook and Twitter: Investigating How People (Don't) Investigate. *Proceedings of the 2020 CHI Conference on Human Factors in Computing Systems*. DOI: 10.1145/3313831.3376784

Georgacopoulos, C., & Poche, T. (2024). Fake news, disinformation, and the George Floyd protests. *Fight Fake News.* https://faculty.lsu.edu/fakenews/about/protestfakenews.php

George, G. (1991). The Image of Russians in American Media and the "New Epoch". In Dennis, E. E., Gerbner, G., & Zassoursky, Y. N. (Eds.), *Beyond the Cold War: Soviet and American Media Images* (pp. 31–35). SAGE.

Ghosh, A., & Singh, A. (2023). Detecting misinformation with hybrid AI-based models: A deep learning perspective. *Computers in Human Behavior*, *88*(4), 91–106.

Ghosh, D. (2020). Brand safety and the digital advertising ecosystem: The case of fake news. *Journal of Advertising Research, 60*(4), 395–408. DOI: 10.2501/JAR-2020-038

Gillmor, D. (2007). Virginia Tech: How Media Are Evolving. *Center for Citizen Media*. http://citmedia.org/blog/2007/04/17/virginia-tech-how-media-are-evolving/

Glassner, B. (2004). Narrative Techniques of Fear Mongering. *Social Research, 71*(4), 819–826. DOI: 10.1353/sor.2004.0001

Global Engagement Center - United States Department of State. (2023, March 22). United States Department of State. https://www.state.gov/about-us-global-engagement-center-2/

Globalsecurity.org (1987, August 1). *U. S. Department of State. A Report on Active Measures and Propaganda, 1986-1987)*. globalsecurity.org

Goffman, E. (1974). Frame Analysis: An Essay on the Organization of Experience. Harper & Row.

Goffman, E. (1974). Frame analysis: An essay on the organization of experience. Northeastern University Press.

Goffman, E. (1974). *Frame analysis: An essay on the organization of experience*. Harvard University Press.

Goldberg, A. G. (2001). *Enemies Within: The Culture of Conspiracy in Modern America*. Yale University Press.

Goldman, J. (2013, March 3). N.J. Hindenburg crash of 1937 caused by static electricity, report says. *NJ.Com*.https://www.nj.com/news/2013/03/nj_hindenburg_crash_caused_by.html#:~:text=Static%20electricity%20caused%20the%20Hindenburg%20airship%20to%20explode,German%20airship%20that%20spanned%20more%20than%20800%20feet

Goode, E., & Ben-Yehuda, N. (1994). Moral panics: Culture, politics, and social construction. *Annual Review of Sociology, 20*(1), 149–171. DOI: 10.1146/annurev.so.20.080194.001053

Gordon, A. H., & Williams, J. L. (1975). Letters to the Editor in Two Elite Newspapers: A Cross-National Study of Social Control. Paper was presented at the 1975 Annual Conference of the Southwestern Sociological Association (U.S.A.). *Sociological Abstracts, 23*(49), 33–34.

Govindankutty, S., & Gopalan, S. P. (2023). From fake reviews to fake news: A novel pandemic model of misinformation in digital networks. *Journal of Theoretical and Applied Electronic Commerce Research, 18*(2), 1069–1085. DOI: 10.3390/jtaer18020054

Graves, L. (2016). Boundaries not drawn: Mapping the institutional roots of the global fact-checking movement. *Journalism Studies, 19*(5), 613–631. DOI: 10.1080/1461670X.2016.1196602

Greenwald, G. (2007, April 21). Right-wing blogs discover massive conspiracy to hide WMDs in Iraq. *Salon*.https://www.salon.com/2007/04/21/wmd_conspiracy/

Grinberg, N., Joseph, K., Friedland, L., Swire-Thompson, B., & Lazer, D. (2019). Fake news on Twitter during the 2016 U.S. Presidential election. *Science, 363*(6425), 374–378. DOI: 10.1126/science.aau2706 PMID: 30679368

Grondin, S. (2012). Violation of the scalar property for time perception between 1 and 2 seconds: Evidence from interval discrimination, reproduction, and categorization. *Journal of Experimental Psychology. Human Perception and Performance*, *38*(4), 880–890. DOI: 10.1037/a0027188 PMID: 22390291

Gubar, S. (1997). *Racechanges: White skin, black face in American culture*. Oxford Press.

Guess, A., Nagler, J., & Tucker, J. (2020). Less than you think: Prevalence and predictors of fake news dissemination on Facebook. *Science Advances*, *6*(14). Advance online publication. DOI: 10.1126/sciadv.aay3539 PMID: 30662946

Guess, A., Nyhan, B., Lyons, B., & Reifler, J. (2018). Avoiding the echo chamber about echo chambers. *Knight Foundation*, *2*(1), 1–25.

Guess, A., Nyhan, B., & Reifler, J. (2019). Selective exposure to misinformation: Evidence from the consumption of fake news during the 2016 U.S. presidential campaign. European Research Council (ERC). *Grant*, *2018*, 1–40.

Gunawan, F., & Suwandi, V. (2020). Identifying the most influencing characteristics of fake news. *ICIC International*, *11*(1), 93–101. DOI: 10.24507/icicelb.11.01.93

Guntuku, S. C., & Preoţiuc-Pietro, D. (2022). A survey of machine learning and deep learning models for fake news detection. *Journal of Data Science : JDS*, *20*(4), 398–414.

Gupta, A., & Roy, P. (2022). Advancements in multi-modal fake news detection. *IEEE Transactions on Knowledge and Data Engineering*, *34*(6), 1489–1503.

Gupta, S., & Verma, S. (2024). Multi-source data fusion for fake news detection on social media. *IEEE Transactions on Information Technology*, *21*(1), 67–82.

Haider-Markel, D. P., & Joslyn, M. R. (2001). Gun policy, opinion, tragedy, and blame attribution: The conditional influence of issue frames. *The Journal of Politics*, *63*(2), 520–543. DOI: 10.1111/0022-3816.00077

Halim, Z., Hussain, S., & Hashim Ali, R. (2022). Identifying content unaware features influencing popularity of videos on YouTube: A study based on seven regions. *Expert Systems with Applications*, *206*, 117836. DOI: 10.1016/j.eswa.2022.117836

Halliday, M. A. K. (1994). *An Introduction to Functional Grammar* (2nd ed.). Edward Arnold.

Han, E. (2014). *The Future of Smartphone Industry: New Opportunities and Breakthroughs.* (). Taipei: Institute For Information Industry. Retrieved from ABI/INFORM Collection https://coloradotech.idm.oclc.org/login?url=https://www.proquest.com/reports/future-smartphone-industry-new-opportunities/docview/2345502112/se-2

Han, J., & Liu, T. (2024). Using blockchain to trace the origin of fake news: A novel approach. *Journal of Digital Information Security*, *19*(2), 202–216.

Hanyok, R. J. (2009). The Pearl Harbor Warning that Never was. *Naval History,* 23(2), 50-53. https://www.usni.org/magazines/naval-history-magazine/2009/april/pearl-harbor-warning-never-was

Haq, H. (2015, January 7). Why many Americans hold false beliefs about WMDs in Iraq and Obama's birthplace. *The Christian Science Monitor.*https://www.csmonitor.com/USA/Politics/Decoder/2015/0107/Why-many-Americans-hold-false-beliefs-about-WMDs-in-Iraq-and-Obama-s-birth-place

Harb, E. G., Nasrallah, N., Khoury, R. E., & Hussainey, K. (2023). Applying Benford's law to detect accounting data manipulation in the pre- and post-financial engineering periods. *Journal of Applied Accounting Research*, *24*(4), 745–768. DOI: 10.1108/JAAR-05-2022-0097

Harper, D. (1990). Spotlight abuse-save profits. *Industrial Distribution*, *79*, 47–51.

Hartig, H., & Doherty, C. (2021). Two Decades Later, the Enduring Legacy of 9/11. *Pew Research Center.*https://www.pewresearch.org/politics/2021/09/02/two-decades-later-the-enduring-legacy-of-9-11/

Harvard Business Review. (2022). *Sustainability as a Competitive Advantage in E-commerce.*

Harvey, I. (2016, November 24). 80 years of speculation and conspiracy theories: The Hindenburg Disaster in 1937 that killed 36 people on board the giant airship. *The Vintage News.*https://www.thevintagenews.com/2016/11/24/80-years-of-speculation-and-conspiracy-theories-the-hindenburg-disaster-of-1937-that-killed-36-people-on-board-the-giant-airship/

Harvey, R. (2024, March 15). Protestant Reformation. *Free speech center @jMiddle Tennessee State University.*https://firstamendment.mtsu.edu/article/protestant-reformation/

Hashemi, M., & Hall, M. (2019). Detecting and classifying online dark visual propaganda. *Image and Vision Computing*, *89*, 95–105. DOI: 10.1016/j.imavis.2019.06.001

Hashemi-Pour, C. (2024, August 6). 6 Steps in Fact-checking AI-generated Content. *TechTarget.*https://www.techtarget.com/WhatIs/feature/Steps-in-fact-checking-AI-generated-content

Hassan, A. S., & Shakil, K. (2021). Fake news detection using natural language processing techniques. *Journal of Data Mining and Knowledge Discovery*, *45*(3), 274–289.

Heidler, J. T. & Heidler, D. S. (2024, May 28). Manifest Destiny. Encyclopedia Britannica. https://www.britannica.com/event/Manifest-Destiny

Helmus, T., & Bodine-Baron, E. (2020, September 11). *Are Counter Violent Extremism Interventions Effective?* RAND. https://www.rand.org/pubs/commentary/2020/09/are-counter-violent-extremism-interventions-effective.html

Hendershot, H. (2004). *Shaking the World for Jesus: Media and Conservative Evangelical Culture.* University of Chicago Press.

Herb, J., & Andone, D. (2024, July 14). How the assassination attempt on Trump unfolded. *CNN.*https://www.cnn.com/2024/07/14/politics/what-happened-trump-assassination-attempt/index.html

Herman, E. S., & Chomsky, N. (1988). *Manufacturing consent: the political economy of the mass media.* Pantheon Books.

He, X., & Wang, C. (2023). A survey on AI-based fake news detection systems: Challenges and future directions. *AI & Security*, *6*(1), 12–27.

Higgins, E. T. (1996). Knowledge activation: Accessibility, applicability, and salience. *Social Psychology: Handbook of Basic Principles,* 133–168.

Hillebrandt, M., & Leino-Sandberg, P. (2021). Administrative and judicial oversight of trilogues. *Journal of European Public Policy*, *28*(1), 53–71. DOI: 10.1080/13501763.2020.1859598

Historians.org. (n.d.). American Historical Association. Propaganda. https://www.historians.org/about-aha-and-membership/aha-history-and-archives/gi-roundtable-series/pamphlets/em-2-what-is-propaganda-(1944)/some-limitations-of-propaganda

History.com Editors. (2019, June 7). ISIS. History.com.

HistoryStaff.com. (2009). Oklahoma City bombing. Retrieved from https://www.history.com/topics/oklahoma-city-bombing

HistoryStaff.com. (2019, June 7). Joseph Goebbels. https://www.history.com/topics/world-war-ii/joseph-goebbels

Hochschild, J. L. (2010). If democracies need informed voters, how can they thrive while expanding enfranchisement? *Election Law Journal*, *9*(2), 111–123. DOI: 10.1089/elj.2009.0055

Hoehling, A. A. (1962). *Who Destroyed the Hindenburg?* Little, Brown & Company. https://archive.org/details/whodestroyedhind0000hoeh/page/n5/mode/2up

Hoffman, B., & Ware, J. (2024, February 5). Online Extremism is Decades in the Making. https://time.com/6551865/extremist-social-media/

Hofstede, G. (2001). *Culture's consequences: Comparing values, behaviors, institutions, and organizations across nations* (2nd ed.). Sage.

Holbert, R. L. (2005). A typology for the study of entertainment television and politics. *The American Behavioral Scientist*, *49*(3), 436–453. DOI: 10.1177/0002764205279419

Höller, M. (2021). The human component in social media and fake news: The performance of UK opinion leaders on Twitter during the Brexit campaign. *European Journal of English Studies*, *25*(1), 80–95. DOI: 10.1080/13825577.2021.1918842

Holsti, O. R. (1969). *Content Analysis for the Social Sciences and Humanities*. Addison Wesley.

Holy Bible. (2018). Thomas Nelson Publishing.

Horton, C. (2018, November 22). Specter of meddling by Beijing looms over Taiwan's elections. *New York Times*. https://www.nytimes.com/2018/11/22/world/asia/taiwan-elections-meddling.html

Hoskins, A., & O'Loughlin, B. (2015). Arrested War: The Third Phase of Mediatization. *Information Communication and Society*, *18*(11), 1320–1338. Advance online publication. DOI: 10.1080/1369118X.2015.1068350

Howard, P. N., & Kollanyi, B. (2016). *Bots, #StrongerIn, and #Brexit: Computational propaganda during the UK–EU referendum. SSRN*. DOI: 10.2139/ssrn.2798311

http://www.youtube.com/watch?v=frjTitjisY

Huang, H. (2018a). The pathology of hard propaganda. *The Journal of Politics, 80*(3), 1034–1038. DOI: 10.1086/696863

Huang, L., & Zhao, L. (2024). Real-time fake news detection using convolutional neural networks. *Journal of Machine Learning in Media, 17*(2), 125–138.

Hudson, J., & Loveluck, L. (2023, April 14). Israeli spy chiefs led secret revolt against Netanyahu overhaul plans, leaked documents say. *Washington Post.* https://www.washingtonpost.com/national-security/2023/04/08/leaked-documents-israel-mossad-judicial-reform/

Hughes, K. (n.d.). Watergate: The Aftermath. *University of Virginia Miller Center.*https://millercenter.org/the-presidency/educational-resources/watergate/watergate-aftermath

Hummel, J. R. (2024, July). The Dark Side of Alexander Hamilton. *Reason.*https://reason.com/2024/06/16/the-dark-side-of-alexander-hamilton/

Hunt, D. P. (2003). The concept of knowledge and how to measure it. *Journal of Intellectual Capital, 4*(1), 100–113.

Hussain, A. (2018b). Muhammad Iqbal's constitutionalism. *Indiana Law Review, 2*(2), 135–158. DOI: 10.1080/24730580.2018.1544023

Hu, W., Sun, L., & Li, L. (2024). An Exploration of the Computer Big Data Mining Service Model Under Resource Sharing. *Information Resources Management Journal, 37*(1), 1–17. DOI: 10.4018/IRMJ.340032

ICIJ. (2023, May 3). *About.* ICIJ. https://www.icij.org/about/

IFCN. (2024). *IFCN Code of Principles.* https://ifcncodeofprinciples.poynter.org/signatories

Igielnik, R., & Parker, K. (2019, July 10). Majorities of U.S. veterans, public say the wars in Iraq and Afghanistan were not worth fighting. *Pew Research Center.*https://www.pewresearch.org/short-reads/2019/07/10/majorities-of-u-s-veterans-public-say-the-wars-in-iraq-and-afghanistan-were-not-worth-fighting/

Igwenagu, C. (2016). Fundamentals of research methodology and data collection. *ResearchGate.* https://www.researchgate.net/publication/303381524_Fundamentals_of_research_methodology_and_data_collection

Incorporating Human Rights Principles Into National Security Measures. (n.d.). Rights Commission. https://humanrights.gov.au/about/news/speeches/incorporating-human-rights-principles-national-security-measures

Indeed Editorial Team. (2021, December 15). *What Is Research Methodology and Why Is It Important?* Indeed Career Guide. https://www.indeed.com/career-advice/career-development/research-methodology#:~:text=Why%20is%20a%20research%20methodology

Infante, D. A., & Wigley, C. J. (1986). Verbal aggressiveness: An interpersonal model and measure. *Communication Monographs, 53*(1), 61–69.

Ingram, H. J. & Australian National University. (2017). "That is what the terrorists want": Media as amplifier or disrupter of violent extremist propaganda. *Australian National University.* https://icct.nl/sites/default/files/import/publication/INGRAM-paris-speech.pdf

Ionita, G. B. (n.d.). Particularities of the Administrative Oversight in the Context of the Commissioner Exercise of the Action for Annulment Based on the Provisions of the Law no. 554/2004 of the Administrative Contentious and the Administrative Code. In Administrative Law and Public Administration in the Global Social System (pp. 83-91). Societatea de Stiinte Juridice si Administrative.

Iyengar, S. (1991). *Is anyone responsible? How television frames political issues.* University of Chicago Press.

Iyengar, S., & Massey, D. S. (2019). Scientific communication in a post-truth society. *Proceedings of the National Academy of Sciences of the United States of America, 116*(16), 7656–7661. DOI: 10.1073/pnas.1805868115 PMID: 30478050

Jaafari, S. (2014, December 14). How ISIS uses catchy, violent tunes for propaganda. Theworld.org/stories

Jabbar, J. (2012). *Prospects of improving Pakistan-India relations through media.* Pildat PakistanIsntitute of Development and Transparency.

Jackson, P. (2021, August 3). September 11 attacks: What happened on 9/11. *BBC.*https://www.bbc.com/news/world-us-canada-57698668.amp

Jacob, M. (2018). *Fake News in the 1890s: Yellow Journalism.* Retrieved from the Digital Public Library of America. Retrieved from: https://production.dp.la/primary-source-set/fake-news-in-the-1890s-yellow-journalism

Jain, A. G. (2016). Indian practice relating to international law. *Indian Journal of International Law, 56*(3), 503–536. DOI: 10.1007/s40901-017-0062-7

Jain, A., & Srivastava, P. (2023). The impact of social media on the spread of fake news: A review. *International Journal of Media and Communication Studies, 13*(1), 22–39.

Jain, R., & Nair, R. (2023). Leveraging deep reinforcement learning for social media content moderation. *Journal of Artificial Intelligence Research, 49*(6), 1675–1690.

Jassim, A. L. E. M. (2022). Administrative and Judicial Oversight of Administrative Decisions. *Journal of Juridical and Political Science, 11*(2).

Jenkins, H. (2006). *Convergence Culture: where old and new media collide.* New York University Press.

Johnson, D. E. (2019). Russian election interference and race-baiting. *Columbia Journal of Race and Law, 9*(2), 191–264. DOI: 10.7916/cjrl.v9i2.3409

Jones, J. (2022, July 5). Confidence in U.S. Institutions Down; Average at New Low. *Gallup.*https://news.gallup.com/poll/394283/confidence-institutions-down-average-new-low.aspx

Jordan, W. D. (1977). *White over Black: American attitudes toward the negro, 1550–1812.* W. W. Norton and Co., Inc.

Joshi, S. (2016). Raiders in Kashmir: India's Pakistan problem. *Survival, 58*(6), 195–208. DOI: 10.1080/00396338.2016.1257204

Karine, A. B., Dabbous, A., & Tarhini, A. (2021). An empirical approach to understanding users' fake news identification on social media. *Online Information Review, 45*(6), 1080–1096. DOI: 10.1108/OIR-08-2020-0333

Kaur, K., Nair, S., Kwok, Y., Kajimoto, M., Chua, Y. T., Labiste, M. D., ... Lin, L. (2018). Information Disorder in Asia: Overview of Misinformation Ecosystem in India, Indonesia, Japan, the Philippines, Singapore, South Korea, and Taiwan. Academic Press.

Kaur, N., & Chahal, P. (2023). Social media platforms' role in fake news detection and mitigation: A critical review. *International Journal of Social Media and Online Communities, 7*(2), 91–103.

Kaur, P., & Yadav, S. (2023). Fake news detection using text mining and deep neural networks: A review. *Journal of Big Data, 12*(3), 87–104.

Kenton, W. (2024, June 28). *The Panama Papers Scandal: Who Was Exposed & Consequences*. Investopedia. https://www.investopedia.com/terms/p/panama-papers.asp

Kerr, S. E. M. (forthcoming). A Gendered Understanding of School Shootings on Screen. *Students on Screen*.

Kerr, S. E. M. (2018). *Gun Violence Prevention?: The Politics Behind Policy Responses to School Shootings in the United States*. Palgrave Macmillan.

Kerr, S. E. M. (2021). *Examining Gun Regulations, Warning Behaviors, and Policies to Prevent Mass Shootings*. IGI Global.

Khafizullina, E. (2021). Russia and the media: The makings of a New Cold War. *Insight Turkey, 23*(3), 276–278. https://www.proquest.com/scholarly-journals/russia-media-makings-new-cold-war/docview/2575925280/se-2

Khan, M. (2018, March 12). EU urged to take a tougher line with tech groups over "fake news." *FT.com*. https://www.proquest.com/trade-journals/eu-urged-take-tougher-line-with-tech-groups-over/docview/2122401079/se-2

Khan, M. L. (2017). Social media engagement: What motivates user participation and consumption on YouTube? *Computers in Human Behavior, 66*, 236–247. DOI: 10.1016/j.chb.2016.09.024

Khan, M., & Iqbal, J. (2024). Fake news detection and prevention: Challenges and perspectives. *Journal of Information Management and Technology, 25*(2), 44–58.

Khan, S. U., Khan, S., & Mukherjee, T. (2024). The 'Subaltern' Will Speak: Investigating Portrayals in the Acclaimed OTT Series of India and Pakistan. In Kalorth, N. (Ed.), *Exploring the Impact of OTT Media on Global Societies* (pp. 1–24). IGI Global. DOI: 10.4018/979-8-3693-3526-0.ch001

Kiger, P. (2019, April 16). How Joseph Stalin Starved Millions in the Ukrainian Famine. History.com.

Kiger, P. J. (2013, November 19). 10 Conspiracy Theories About the JFK Assassination. *HowStuffWorks*. https://history.howstuffworks.com/historical-figures/john-f-kennedy.htm

Killingbeck, D. (2001). The Role Of Television News In The Construction Of School Violence As A "Moral Panic.". *The Journal of Criminal Justice and Popular Culture, 8*(3), 186–202.

Kim, L. (2021, March 24). AI Helps Break Down Conspiracy Theories. *UCLA Magazine*.https://newsroom.ucla.edu/magazine/artificial-intelligence-conspiracy-theories

Kim, A., Moravec, P. L., & Dennis, A. R. (2019). Combating fake news on social media with source ratings: The effects of user and expert reputation ratings. *Journal of Management Information Systems*, *36*(3), 931–968. DOI: 10.1080/07421222.2019.1628921

Kimball, R., & Merz, R. (2000). *The Data Webhouse Toolkit: Building the Web-Enabled Data Warehouse*. John Wiley & Sons.

Kim, E. L., Gentile, D. A., Anderson, C. A., & Barlett, C. P. (2022). Are mindful people less aggressive? The role of emotion regulation in the relations between mindfulness and aggression. *Aggressive Behavior*, *48*(6), 546–562. PMID: 35613384

Kimmel, M. S., & Mahler, M. (2003). Adolescent Masculinity, Homophobia, and Violence: Random School Shootings, 1982-2001. *The American Behavioral Scientist*, *46*(10), 1439–1458. DOI: 10.1177/0002764203046010010

King, G., Pan, J., & Roberts, M. E. (2017). How the Chinese government fabricates social media posts for strategic distraction, not engaged argument. *The American Political Science Review*, *111*(3), 484–501. https://gking.harvard.edu/50C. DOI: 10.1017/S0003055417000144

King, M. L. (1968). *Where do we go from here? Chaos or community?* Beacon Press Books.

Kiper, J. (2015). Toward an Anthropology of War Propaganda. *Political and Legal Anthropology Review*, *38*(1), 129–146. DOI: 10.1111/plar.12090

Kirill, Y., Mihail, I. G., Sanzhar, M., Rustam, M., Olga, F., & Ravil, M. (2020). Propaganda Identification Using Topic Modelling. *Procedia Computer Science*, *178*, 205–212. DOI: 10.1016/j.procs.2020.11.022

Klausen, J. (2015). Tweeting the Jihad: Social media networks ofwestern foreign fighters in Syria and Iraq. *Studies in Conflict and Terrorism*, *38*(1), 11–22. DOI: 10.1080/1057610X.2014.974948

Klein, J. (2006). An invisible problem: Everyday violence against girls in schools. *Theoretical Criminology*, *10*(2), 147–177. DOI: 10.1177/1362480606063136

Klein, J., & Chancer, L. (2000). Masculinity Matters: The Role of Gender in High-profile School Violence Cases. In Spina, S. (Ed.), *Smoke and Mirrors: The Hidden Context of Violence in Schools and Society* (pp. 129–162). Rowman and Littlefield.

Knoll, S., Eisend, M., & Steinhagen, J. (2011). Gender roles in advertising: Measuring and comparing gender stereotyping on public and private TV channels in Germany. *International Journal of Advertising*, *30*(5), 867–888. DOI: 10.2501/IJA-30-5-867-888

Kohavi, R., Mason, L., Parekh, R., & Zheng, Z. (2004). Lessons and Challenges from Mining Retail E-Commerce Data. *Machine Learning*, *57*(1-2), 83–113. DOI: 10.1023/B:MACH.0000035473.11134.83

Kohavi, R., & Provost, F. (2001). Applications of data mining to electronic commerce. In *Data Mining and Knowledge Discovery, 5(1/2)*. Kluwer Academic. http://robotics.Stanford.EDU/users/ronnyk/ecommerce-dm

Kohut, A. (2014, August 8). From the archives: How the Watergate crisis eroded public support for Richard Nixon. *Pew Research Center.*https://www.pewresearch.org/short-reads/2019/09/25/how-the-watergate-crisis-eroded-public-support-for-richard-nixon/

Kostinsky, S., Bixler, E. O., & Kettl, P. A. (2001). Threats of school violence in Pennsylvania after media coverage of the Columbine high school massacre: Examining the role of imitation. *Archives of Pediatrics & Adolescent Medicine, 155*(9), 994–1001. DOI: 10.1001/archpedi.155.9.994 PMID: 11529800

Kothari, C. R. (2004). *Research Methodology: Methods and Techniques* (2nd ed.). New Age International Publishers.

Krieg, G. (2016, September 16). 14 of Trump's most outrageous 'birther' claims—half from after 2011. *CNN.*https://www.cnn.com/2016/09/09/politics/donald-trump-birther/index.html

Krippendorff, K. (1980). *Content analysis an introduction to its Methodology*. Sage.

Kuczabski, M. J. (2022). Fake news as a threat to social resilience. *European Research Studies, 25*(1), 765–782. https://www.proquest.com/scholarly-journals/fake-news-as-threat-social-resilience/docview/2639719067/se-2

Kukreja, J. (2019). Cartoons Cast an Eternal Impact on Personalities: Effects of Cartoons on Children. In *Handbook of Research on Children's Consumption of Digital Media* (pp. 369–379). IGI Global.

Kukreja, J., & Handa, M. (2013). Emotional Labor for Customer Satisfaction. *FIIB Business Review, 2*(2), 3–8. DOI: 10.1177/2455265820130201

Kukreja, J., Morande, S., & Tewari, V. (2024a). Should Leaders Crack Jokes With Their Subordinates? *BVIMSR's. Journal of Management Research, 16*(1), 37–44.

Kukreja, J., Tewari, R., & Morande, S. (2024b). The Role of the Gut-Brain Axis in Eating Disorders: An Empirical Study From India. In *Neuroscientific Insights and Therapeutic Approaches to Eating Disorders* (pp. 340–355). IGI Global. DOI: 10.4018/979-8-3693-3230-6.ch025

Kumar, A. (2021). Consumer behavior and online advertising: An overview. *JMR, Journal of Marketing Research, 58*(3), 451–463. DOI: 10.1177/0022243721996970

Kupchik, A., & Bracy, N. L. (2009). The news media on school crime and violence: Constructing dangerousness and fueling fear. *Youth Violence and Juvenile Justice, 7*(2), 136–155. DOI: 10.1177/1541204008328800

Kupper, J., Christensen, T. K., Wing, D., Hurt, M., Schumacher, M., & Meloy, R. (2022). The Contagion and Copycat Effect in Transnational Far-Right Terrorism: An Analysis of Language Evidence. *Perspectives on Terrorism, 16*(4), 4–26. https://www.jstor.org/stable/27158149

LaBianca, J. (2024, May 27). 10 Things They're Still Not Telling You About Pearl Harbor. *Reader's Digest.*https://www.rd.com/list/conspiracy-theories-about-pearl-harbor/

LaCapria, K. (2016, November 21). Is Comet Ping Pong Pizzeria Home to a Child Abuse Ring Leg by Hillary Clinton? *Snopes.com.* Accessed May 29, 2024, from https://www.snopes.com/fact-check/pizzagate-conspiracy/

Lakoff, G., & Johnson, M. (1980). *Metaphors we live by.* University of Chicago Press.

Lange, S., Burr, H., Conway, P. M., & Rose, U. (2019). Workplace bullying among employees in Germany: Prevalence estimates and the role of the perpetrator. *International Archives of Occupational and Environmental Health, 92*(2), 237–247. DOI: 10.1007/s00420-018-1366-8 PMID: 30390155

Larkin, R. W. (2013). Legitimated Adolescent Violence: Lessons from Columbine. In Böckler, N., Seeger, T., Sitzer, P., & Heitmeyer, W. (Eds.), *School Shootings*. Springer. DOI: 10.1007/978-1-4614-5526-4_7

Lasser, J., Aroyehun, S. T., Simchon, A., Carrella, F., Garcia, D., & Lewandowsky, S. (2022). Social media sharing of low-quality news sources by political elites. *PNAS Nexus, 1*(4). Advance online publication. DOI: 10.1093/pnasnexus/pgac186 PMID: 36380855

Laufman, D. (2012, August 12). *Prosecuting Leaks of Classified Information*. HuffPost. https://www.huffpost.com/entry/prosecuting-leaks_b_1585193

Lawrence, R. G., & Birkland, T. A. (2004). Guns, Hollywood, and School Safety: Defining the School-Shooting Problem Across Public Arenas. *Social Science Quarterly, 85*(5), 1193–1207. DOI: 10.1111/j.0038-4941.2004.00271.x

Lazer, D. M., Baum, M. A., Benkler, Y., Berinsky, A. J., Greenhill, K. M., Menczer, F., Metzger, M. J., Nyhan, B., Pennycook, G., Rothschild, D., Schudson, M., Sloman, S. A., Sunstein, C. R., Thorson, E. A., Watts, D. J., & Zittrain, J. L. (2018). The science of fake news. *Science, 359*(6380), 1094–1096. DOI: 10.1126/science.aao2998 PMID: 29590025

Lee, W. (2017, February 24). "Whistleblowing" and "Leaking" Explained. *Voice of America*. https://www.voanews.com/a/whistleblowing-and-leaking-explained/3736863.html

Lee, J., & Lee, K. (2021). Multi-lingual detection of fake news on social media: A comparative study. *Journal of Computational Linguistics, 48*(2), 213–230.

Lee, S., & Kim, H. (2024). Real-time misinformation detection on social media platforms: A study of deep learning models. *Journal of Social Computing, 17*(1), 76–92.

Lee, T. (2019). The global rise of "fake news" and the threat to democratic elections in the USA. *Public Administration and Policy, 22*(1), 15–24. DOI: 10.1108/PAP-04-2019-0008

Lemon, K., & Verhoef, P. (2016). Understanding customer experience throughout the customer journey. *Journal of Marketing, 80*(6), 69–96. DOI: 10.1509/jm.15.0420

Lerche, C. O.Jr. (1948). Jefferson and the Election of 1800: A Case Study in the Political Smear. *The William and Mary Quarterly, 5*(4), 467–491. https://www.jstor.org/stable/pdf/1920636.pdf?refreqid=fastly-default%3A55dbd5b0606e063ff73f2bb52368838a&ab_segments=&origin=&initiator=&acceptTC=1

Lever, R. (2024, November 12). Donald Trump's second term presents fresh disinformation challenges. *AFP.com*. Accessed January 25, 2025. https://factcheck.afp.com/doc.afp.com.36M84UR

Lewandowsky, S., Ecker, U. K., & Cook, J. (2017). Beyond misinformation: Understanding and coping with the "post-truth" era. *Journal of Applied Research in Memory and Cognition, 6*(4), 353–369. DOI: 10.1016/j.jarmac.2017.07.008

Lewis, S. (2020, April 27). *Tyrannicide*. https://www.britannica.com/topic/tyrannicide

Lewis, T. (2020, October 12). Eight Persistent COVID-19 Myths and Why People Believe Them. *Scientific American*.https://www.scientificamerican.com/article/eight-persistent-covid-19-myths-and-why-people-believe-them/

Lewis, D., Kanji, N., & Themudo, N. S. (2021). *Non-governmental organizations and development* (2nd ed.). Routledge.

Leymann, H. (1990). Mobbing and Psychological Terror at Workplaces. *Violence and Victims*, *5*(2), 119–126. DOI: 10.1891/0886-6708.5.2.119 PMID: 2278952

Liberman, A. V. (2017-2018). *Terrorism, the Internet, and Propaganda: A Deadly Combination.* heinonline.org/HOL/LandingPage?handle=hein.journals/jnatselp9&div=9&id=&page=

Lima, C. (2021, January 6). Twitter, Facebook lock Trump's accounts in confrontation over Capital breast posts. *Politico*.https://www.politico.com/news/2021/01/06/twitter-trump-tweet-capitol-violence-455630

Lincoln, C. E., & Mamiya, L. H. (1990). *The Black Church in the African American Experience*. Duke University Press.

Lindenfeld, D. F., & Kershaw, I. (1988). The "Hitler myth": Image and reality in the Third Reich. *German Studies Review*, *11*(2), 329. DOI: 10.2307/1430004

Lindgren, S. (2011). YouTube gunmen? Mapping participatory media discourse on school shooting videos. *Media Culture & Society*, *33*(1), 123–136. DOI: 10.1177/0163443710386527

Lindseth, P. (2020). 'Always Embedded' Administration: The Historical Evolution of Administrative Justice as an Aspect of Modern Governance. In The Economy as a Polity: The Political Constitution of Contemporary Capitalism (pp. 117-135). Routledge.

Lindseth, P. L. (2023). Administration and Democracy. In Public Administration and Expertise in Democratic Governments (pp. 242-255). Routledge.

Lintott, A. (1990). Electoral bribery in the Roman Republic. *Journal of Roman Studies*, *80*, 1–16. DOI: 10.2307/300277

Liptak, A., VanSickle, A., & Parlapiano, A. (2024, July 2). The Major Supreme Court Decisions, *The New York Times*.https://www.nytimes.com/interactive/2024/05/09/us/supreme-court-major-cases-2024.html#racial-gerrymandering

Li, Q., & Sun, M. (2022). Fake news detection using deep learning: Recent advances and future challenges. *Journal of Artificial Intelligence Research*, *58*(4), 442–459.

Littrell, S., Klofstad, C., Diekman, A., Funchion, J., Murthi, M., Premaratne, K., Seelig, M., Verdear, D., Wuchty, S., & Uscinski, J. E. (2023). *Who knowingly shares false political information online? Harvard Kennedy School (HKS)*. Misinformation Review. DOI: 10.37016/mr-2020-121

Liu, X., & Chen, W. (2020). Leveraging blockchain for content verification in news dissemination. *Journal of Information and Media Ethics*, *28*(3), 244–261.

Lock, I., & Ludolph, R. (2020). Organizational propaganda on the Internet: A systematic review. *Public Relations Inquiry*, *9*(1), 103–127. DOI: 10.1177/2046147X19870844

Lord, K. M., & Vogt, K. (2021, March 18). Strengthen Media Literacy to Win the Fight Against Misinformation. *Stanford Social Innovation Review.*https://ssir.org/articles/entry/strengthen_media_literacy_to_win_the_fight_against_misinformation

Lu, Z., Li, P., Wang, W., & Yin, M. (2022). The effects of AI-based credibility indicators on the detection and spread of misinformation under social influence. *Proceedings of the ACM Human-Computer Interaction, 6*(CSCW2), Article 461. DOI: 10.1145/3555562

Lubenda (n.d.). GDPR vs HIPAA – What are the differences and how to comply. Retrieved from https://www.iubenda.com/en/help/22623-gdpr-vs-hipaa

Lynas, M. (2020, April 20). COVID: Top 10 current conspiracy theories. *Alliance for Science.*https://allianceforscience.org/blog/2020/04/covid-top-10-current-conspiracy-theories/

Machin, D., & Mayr, A. (2012). *How to Do Critical Discourse Analysis: A Multimodal Introduction.* Sage Publications Ltd.

Magnavita, N., Capitanelli, I., Arnesano, G., Iuliano, A., Mauro, I., Suraci, F., & Chiricc, F. (2021). Common Occupational Trauma: Is There a Relationship with Workers' Mental Health? *Trauma Care*, *2*(2), 66–74. DOI: 10.3390/traumacare1020007

Magnavita, N., Di Stasio, E., Capitanelli, I., Lops, E. A., Chirico, F., & Garbarino, S. (2019). Sleep problems and workplace violence: A systematic review and meta-analysis. *Frontiers in Neuroscience*, *13*, 997. DOI: 10.3389/fnins.2019.00997 PMID: 31632231

Magretta, J. (2002). Why Business Models Matter. Harvard Business Review, 2002. https:// hbr. org/ 2002/ 05/why-business-modelsmatter

Maguire, B., Weatherby, G. A., & Mathers, R. A. (2002). Network news coverage of school shootings. *The Social Science Journal*, *39*(3), 465–470. DOI: 10.1016/S0362-3319(02)00201-X

Mandavalli, A. (2024, May 3). Thousands Believe Covid Vaccines Harmed Them. Is Anyone Listening? https://www.nytimes.com/2024/05/03/health/covid-vaccines-side-effects.html

Mark, J. (2020, April 16). The Effects of the Black Death on Europe. Accessed from. Effects of the Black Death on Europe. World History Encyclopedia.

MarketLine. (2023). Company Listing. Retrieved fromwww.marketlinc.com

Martínez-Ruiz, M. J., & González, J. (2021). Fake news detection: Insights from machine learning algorithms. *Journal of Data Science and Technology*, *9*(4), 158–174.

Marwick, A., & Lewis, R. (2017). *Media manipulation and disinformation online*. Data & Society Research Institute.

Mayeda, G. (2024). Reasonableness as Responsiveness in Administrative Law in the United States, United Kingdom, and Canada: Kant and Arendt on the Role of the Community in Deferential Judicial Review. *The American Journal of Comparative Law*, avae006.

Mayer, C. (2024, July 16). One in Three Biden Supporters Think Trump Shooting Might Have Been Staged. *Newsweek*.https://www.newsweek.com/trump-shooting-assassination-conspiracy-theory-staged-biden-poll-1925723

McCluskey, L. M., Hamilton, J. M., & Reynolds, A. (2023). When Propaganda Became a Dirty Word. *Journalism History*, *49*(2), 140–157. DOI: 10.1080/00947679.2023.2203026

McCombs, M., & Shaw, D. (1972). The agenda-setting function of mass media . *Public Opinion Quarterly*, *36*(2), 176. DOI: 10.1086/267990

McGovern, A. (2021, May 27). Artificial Intelligence System Could Help Counter the Spread of Disinformation. *MIT News*.https://news.mit.edu/2021/artificial-intelligence-system-could-help-counter-spread-disinformation-0527

McGuire, E. (2020, April 5). Anti-Asian hate continues to spread online amid COVID-19 pandemic. *Al Jazeera*.https://www.aljazeera.com/news/2020/04/anti-asian-hate-continues-spread-online-covid-19-pandemic-200405063015286.html

McLaughlin, A. (2020, June 23). Investigating the most convincing COVID-19 conspiracy theories. *Kings College London*.https://www.kcl.ac.uk/investigating-the-most-convincing-covid-19-conspiracy-theories

McMahon, S. D., Davis, J. O., Peist, E., Bare, K., Espelage, D. L., Martinez, A., Anderman, E. M., & Reddy, L. A. (2020a). Student verbal aggression toward teachers: How do behavioral patterns unfold? *Psychology of Violence*, *10*(2), 192–200. DOI: 10.1037/vio0000256

McMahon, S. D., Peist, E., Davis, J. O., Bare, K., Martinez, A., Reddy, L. A., Espelage, D. L., & Anderman, E. M. (2020b). Physical aggression toward teachers: Antecedents, behaviors, and consequences. *Aggressive Behavior*, *46*(1), 116–126. DOI: 10.1002/ab.21870 PMID: 31628678

Meel, P., & Vishwakarma, D. K. (2019). Fake news, rumor, Information Pollution in Social Media and web: A Contemporary Survey of state-of-the-arts, Challenges and Opportunities. *Expert Systems with Applications*, *153*(1), 112986. DOI: 10.1016/j.eswa.2019.112986

Mejía, L. E. (2021). Judicial review of regulatory decisions: Decoding the contents of appeals against agencies in Spain and the United Kingdom. *Regulation & Governance*, *15*(3), 760–784. DOI: 10.1111/rego.12302

Merchant, N. (2023, March 23). Iraq WMD failures shadow US intelligence 20 years later. *AP News*. https://apnews.com/article/iraq-war-wmds-us-intelligence-f9e21ac59d3a0470d9bfcc83544d706e

Merriam-Webster. (n.d.). *Algorithm Definition & Meaning*. Merriam-Webster.

Merriam-Webster. (n.d.-a). Filter bubble. Noun. *Merriam-webster.com*. https://www.merriam-webster.com/dictionary/filter%20bubble

Merriam-Webster. (n.d.-b). Echo chamber. Noun. *Merriam-webster.com*.https://www.merriam-webster.com/dictionary/echo%20chamber

Meyer, D. S., Jenness, V., & Ingram, H. (2020). *Routing the opposition: Social movements, public policy, and democracy*. Routledge.

Mheidly, N., & Fares, J. (2020). Leveraging media and health communication strategies to overcome the COVID-19 infodemic. *Journal of Public Health Policy*, *41*(4), 410–420. DOI: 10.1057/s41271-020-00247-w PMID: 32826935

Mian, A., & Khan, S. (2020). Coronavirus: The spread of misinformation. *BMC Medicine*, *18*(1), 89. DOI: 10.1186/s12916-020-01556-3 PMID: 32188445

Microsoft. (2019, February 5). *Microsoft releases digital civility index on Safer Internet Day*. Microsoft Stories India. https://news.microsoft.com/en-in/microsoft-digital-civility-index-safer-internet-day-2019/

Mihailidis, P., & Viotty, S. (2017). Spreadable spectacle in digital culture: Civic expression, fake news, and the role of media literacies in "post-fact" society. *The American Behavioral Scientist*, *61*(4), 441–454. DOI: 10.1177/0002764217701217

Milhazes-Cunha, J., & Oliveira, S. (2023). The impact of echo chambers on COVID-19 disinformation and hate speech in the Portuguese Facebook community. *Journal of Social Media Studies*, *15*(2), 254–278.

Millhiser, I. (2024, August 19). Republicans ask the Supreme Court to disenfranchise thousands of swing state voters. *Vox*.https://www.vox.com/scotus/367701/supreme-court-arizona-rnc-republicans-mi-familia-vota

Mills, C. W. (1956). *The power elite*. Oxford University Press.

Mitchell, J. (2023, February 3). 20 years ago, the U.S. warned of Iraq's alleged 'weapons of mass destruction.' *NPR*.https://www.npr.org/2023/02/03/1151160567/colin-powell-iraq-un-weapons-mass-destruction

Moniz, C. (2024, June 27). Donald Trump spread 2020 election conspiracy theories 500 times on Truth Social. *CREW*.https://www.citizensforethics.org/reports-investigations/crew-investigations/donald-trump-has-spread-2020-election-conspiracy-theories-500-times-on-truth-social/

Morakanyane, R., Grace, A. A., & O'reilly, P. (2017). Conceptualizing Digital Transformation in Business Organizations: A Systematic Review of Literature. Bled eConference, 21, 428-444. .DOI: 10.18690/978-961-286-043-1.30

Morton, F. L. (1988). Judicial Review in France: A Comparative Analysis. *The American Journal of Comparative Law*, *36*(1), 89–110. DOI: 10.2307/840185

Motta, M. (2021). Can a COVID-19 vaccine live up to Americans' expectations? A conjoint analysis of how vaccine characteristics influence vaccination intentions. *Social Science & Medicine*, *272*, 113642. DOI: 10.1016/j.socscimed.2020.113642 PMID: 33414031

Muhammad, C. (2010, April 6). "Mean spirited, vicious racism" comes to surface during debates about president and U.S. politics." *The Final Call*. Retrieved from: https://www.finalcall.com/artman/publish/National_News_2/article_6846.shtml

Muhammed, S. T., & Mathew, S. K. (2022). The Disaster of misinformation: A Review of Research in Social Media. *International Journal of Data Science and Analytics*, *13*(4), 271–285. DOI: 10.1007/s41060-022-00311-6 PMID: 35194559

Muschert, G. W. (2002). *Media and massacre: The social construction of the Columbine story* (Unpublished doctoral thesis). Boulder, CO: University of Colorado.

Muschert, G. W. (2009). Frame-changing in the media coverage of a school shooting: The rise of Columbine as a national concern. *The Social Science Journal*, *46*(1), 164–170.

Muschert, G. W. (2019). Afterword: The Columbine Effect on Culture, Policy, and Me. *Journal of Contemporary Criminal Justice*, *35*(3), 357–372.

Mydyti, H., & Kadriu, A. (2021a, August). Data Mining Approach Improving Decision-Making Competency Along the Business Digital Transformation Journey: A Literature Review. In International Conference for Emerging Technologies in Computing (pp. 129-146). Springer.

Mydyti, H., Kadriu, A., & Mirjana, P. B. (2023). Using Data Mining to Improve Decision-Making: Case Study of A Recommendation System Development. *Organizacija*, *56*(2), 138–154. DOI: 10.2478/orga-2023-0010

Nakatani, M. (2023, February 3). The Mystery of the Umbrella Man at JFK's Assassination. *Grunge*. https://www.grunge.com/438451/the-mystery-of-the-umbrella-man-at-jfks-assassination/

Nandish, C. D. (2020). Administrative law and judicial review of administrative action through writs: Ground of review. *Journal of Emerging Technologies and Innovative Research.*

Nasery, M., Turel, O., & Yuan, Y. (2023). Combating fake news on social media: A framework, review, and future opportunities. *Communications of the Association for Information Systems*, *53*(1), 833–876. DOI: 10.17705/1CAIS.05335

National Commission on Terrorist Attacks Upon the United States. (2024, July 22). *The 9/11 Commission Report.*https://govinfo.library.unt.edu/911/report/911Report.pdf

Nelson, C. (2016). *Pearl Harbor: From Infamy to Greatness*. Scribner.

Neyazi, T. A. (2020). Digital propaganda, political bots and polarized politics in India. *Asian Journal of Communication*, *30*(1), 39–57. DOI: 10.1080/01292986.2019.1699938

Nggilu, N., Moha, M. R., Sinaga, M. R., & Rachmaniar, A. (2024). Judicial Review of Constitutional Amendments: Comparison Between India, Germany, Colombia, and the Relevancy with Indonesia. *Lex Scientia Law Review*, *8*(1), 261–298.

Nguyen, H., & Nguyen, A. (2020). COVID-19 misinformation and the social (media) amplification of risk: A Vietnamese perspective. *Media and Communication*, *8*(2), 444–447. DOI: 10.17645/mac.v8i2.3227

Nielsen, M. B., Christensen, J. O., Finne, L. B., & Knardahl, S. (2020). Workplace bullying, mental distress, and sickness absence: The protective role of social support. *International Archives of Occupational and Environmental Health*, *93*(1), 43–53. DOI: 10.1007/s00420-019-01463-y PMID: 31342156

NPR. (2016, December 6). No, FDR Did not know the Japanese were going to bomb Pearl Harbor. https://www.npr.org/2016/12/06/504449867/no-fdr-did-not-know-the-japanese-were-going-to-bomb-pearl-harbor

NPR. (2022, October 13). Special Series: House Jan. 6 committee hearings. https://www.npr.org/2022/10/13/1125331584/jan-6-committee-hearing-transcript

Nugent, N. (2017). *The government and politics of the European Union (8.)*. Palgrave, Macmillan Education.

O'Rourke, C. (2021, December 20). No, Barak Obama's birth certificate isn't fake. *PolitiFact.*https://www.politifact.com/factchecks/2021/dec/20/blog-posting/no-barack-obamas-birth-certificate-isnt-fake/

OCP Policy Center & Elshimi, M. (2018). *Thinking about the symbiotic relationship between the Media andPolicy Center* [Policy Brief]. https://www.policycenter.ma/sites/default/files/2021-01/OCPPC-PB1812.pdf

Ognyanova, K., Lazer, D., Robertson, R. E., & Wilson, C. (2020). Misinformation in action: Fake news exposure is linked to lower trust in media, higher trust in government when your side is in power. *Harvard Kennedy School Misinformation Review*, *1*(4), 1–19. DOI: 10.37016/mr-2020-024

Olan, F., Jayawickrama, U., Arakpogun, E. O., Suklan, J., & Liu, S. (2022). Fake news on Social Media: The Impact on Society. *Information Systems Frontiers*, *1*(1), 1–16. DOI: 10.1007/s10796-022-10242-z PMID: 35068999

Omar, A., & Ondimu, K. (2024). The impact of social media on society: A systematic literature review. *The International Journal of Engineering and Science*, *13*(6), 96–106. https://www.researchgate.net/publication/381800701_The_Impact_of_Social_Media_on_Society_A_Systematic_Literature_Review

Onuf, P. (n.d.) Thomas Jefferson: Campaigns and Elections. *University of Virginia Miller Center.*https://millercenter.org/president/jefferson/campaigns-and-elections

Onuoha, M., Pinder, J., & Schafer, J. (2015, November 20). Guide to Crowdsourcing. *Columbia Journalism Review.*https://www.cjr.org/tow_center_reports/guide_to_crowdsourcing.php

Onyango, G. (2020). Legislative oversight and policy-reforms in "unsettled" political contexts of public administration. *International Journal of Public Administration*, *43*(3), 213–228. DOI: 10.1080/01900692.2019.1627556

Orfanidis, P. (2018). Prominence of big data in the digital transformation era. [Unpublished master thesis dissertation]. School of Economics, Business Administration & Legal Studies, Thessaloniki – Greece. Retrieved from: https://core.ac.uk/download/pd

Oster, J. S. (2008). The Scope of Judicial Review in the German and US Administrative Legal System. *German Law Journal*, *9*(10), 1267–1297.

Oxford Press. (2008). Sabotage. In *Oxford American dictionary* (p. 728). OUP.

Ozawa, J. V. S., Woolley, S. C., Straubhaar, J., Riedl, M. J., Joseff, K., & Gursky, J. (2023). How disinformation on WhatsApp went from campaign weapon to governmental propaganda in Brazil. *Social Media + Society*, *9*(1). Advance online publication. DOI: 10.1177/20563051231160632

Pakistan: Between radicalisation and democratisation in an unfolding conflict. (2019, January 31). IMS. https://www.mediasupport.org/publication/pakistan-between-radicalisation-and-democratisation-in-an-unfolding-conflict/

Pandey, S. P. (2020). Constitutional provision of judicial review in India: An evaluation. Asian Journal of Advances in Research, 291-301.

Panigrahi, S., & Singh, J. (2017). *RGICS BRIEF Deadly Combination of Fake News and Social Media.* https://www.rgics.org/wp-content/uploads/policy-issue-briefs/Policy-Brief-Deadly-Combination-of-Fake-News-and-Social-Media-September-2017.pdf

Pariser, E. (2011). *The filter bubble: What the Internet is hiding from you.* Penguin Press.

Patel, M., & Singh, D. (2022). Network analysis for identifying the spread of fake news. *Journal of Computational Social Science, 17*(1), 51–67.

Paul, T. V. (2006). Why has the India-Pakistan Rivalry Been so Enduring? Power Asymmetry and an Intractable Conflict. *Security Studies, 15*(4), 600–630. DOI: 10.1080/09636410601184595

Paul, T. V., & Paul, T. V. (Eds.). (2005). *The India-Pakistan conflict: an enduringrivalry.* Cambridge University Press. DOI: 10.1017/CBO9780511616112

Paun, C., Ivascu, C., Olteteanu, A., & Dantis, D. (2024). The Main Drivers of E-Commerce Adoption: A Global Panel Data Analysis. *Journal of Theoretical and Applied Electronic Commerce Research, 19*(3), 2198–2217. DOI: 10.3390/jtaer19030107

Pavlíková, M., Šenkýřová, B., & Drmola, J. (2021). Propaganda and disinformation go online. *Challenging online propaganda and disinformation in the 21st century*, 43-74.

Pavone, T., & Stiansen, Ø. (2022). The shadow effect of courts: Judicial review and the politics of preemptive reform. *The American Political Science Review, 116*(1), 322–336. DOI: 10.1017/S0003055421000873

Payne, L., & Payne, T. (2020). *The dead are arising: The life of Malcolm X.* Liveright Publishing Corporation.

Pejić Bach, M., Pivar, J., & Krstić, Ž. (2019). Big data for prediction: patent analysis–patenting big data for prediction analysis. In *Big Data Governance and Perspectives in Knowledge Management* (pp. 218–240). IGI Global. DOI: 10.4018/978-1-5225-7077-6.ch010

Pennycook, G., & Rand, D. G. (2018). The implied truth effect: Attaching warnings to a subset of fake news stories increases perceived accuracy of stories without warnings. *Management Science, 67*(11), 6525–6543. DOI: 10.1287/mnsc.2020.3797

Pennycook, G., & Rand, D. G. (2020). Fighting misinformation on social media using crowdsourced judgments of news source quality. *Proceedings of the National Academy of Sciences of the United States of America, 117*(0), 6882–6884. DOI: 10.1073/pnas.1912444117 PMID: 30692252

Pennycook, G., & Rand, D. G. (2020). The Implied Truth Effect: Attaching warnings to a subset of fake news stories increases perceived accuracy of stories without warnings. *Management Science, 66*(11), 4944–4957. DOI: 10.1287/mnsc.2019.3478

Pentina, I., & Tarafdar, M. (2014). From "information" to "knowing": Exploring the role of social media in contemporary news consumption. *Computers in Human Behavior*, *35*, 211–223. DOI: 10.1016/j.chb.2014.02.045

Pepper, W. F. (2016). *The Plot to Kill King: The Truth Behind the Assassination of Martin Luther King Jr.* Skyhorse.

Pertwee, E., Simas, C., & Larson, H. J. (2022). An epidemic of uncertainty: Rumors, conspiracy theories, and vaccine hesitancy. *Nature Medicine*, *28*, 456–459. https://www.nature.com/articles/s41591-022-01728-z PMID: 35273403

Petratos, P. N., & Faccia, A. (2023). Fake news, misinformation, disinformation and supply chain risks and disruptions: Risk management and resilience using blockchain. *Annals of Operations Research*, *327*(2), 735–762. DOI: 10.1007/s10479-023-05242-4 PMID: 37361081

Pew Research Center. (2008, December 18). Bush and Public Opinion. https://www.pewresearch.org/politics/2008/12/18/bush-and-public-opinion/

Pew Research Center. (2010, August 18). *Growing Number of Americans Say Obama Is a Muslim*. Author.

Pew Research Center. (2015, November 23). Trust in government: 1958-2015. https://www.pewresearch.org/politics/2015/11/23/1-trust-in-government-1958-2015/

Pew Research Center. (2018). News use across social media platforms 2018. https://www.journalism.org/2018/09/10/news-use-across-social-media-platforms-2018/

Pew Research Center. (2020). Americans who mainly get their news on social media are less engaged, less knowledgeable. https://www.pewresearch.org/fact-tank/2020/12/02/americans-who-mainly-get-their-news-on-social-media-are-less-engaged-less-knowledgeable/

Pew Research Center. (2021). Digital news fact sheet https://www.pewresearch.org

Pew Research Center. (2024). https://www.pewresearch.org/wp-content/uploads/sites/20/2024/01/PI_2024.01.31_Home-Broadband-Mobile-Use_FINAL.pdf

Pew Research Center. (2024, June 24). Americans' trust in federal government and attitudes toward it. https://www.pewresearch.org/2024/06/24/americans-trust-in-federal-government-and-attitudes-toward-it/

Pfeifer, M. J. (2004). *Rough justice: Lynching and the American society 1874–1947*. University of Illinois Press.

Pilkington, E. (2022). Ginni Thomas still believes Trump's false claim the 2020 election was stolen. *The Guardian*.https://go.gale.com/ps/i.do?p=GIC&u=for1&id=GALE|A720396582&v=2.1&it=r&sid=ebsco

PolitiFact. (2009, December). *Lie of the Year: 'Death Panels*. Author.

Polyakova, A., & Boyer, S. P. (2018). The future of political warfare: Russia, the West, and the coming age of global digital competition. Brookings Institution. https://www.brookings.edu/wp-content/uploads/2018/03/the-future-of-political-warfare.pdf

Pop, M.-I. (2020). Scoring model for the detection of fake news. *Studia Universitatis "Vasile Goldis" Arad—Economic Series, 30*(1), 91–102. DOI: 10.2478/sues-2020-0006

Poynter. (2024). *About IFCN.* Poynter. https://www.poynter.org/ifcn/about-ifcn/

Press Trust of India. (2019, February 5). *Microsoft survey: Indians are more likely to encounter online fake news.* https://www.business-standard.com/article/pti-stories/microsoft-survey-india-topping-fake-news-menace-globally-119020501427_1.html

PricewaterhouseCoopers. (2018). A systematic review on forensic accounting and its contribution towards fraud detection and prevention. *Journal of Financial Regulation and Compliance, 31*(1), 60–95. DOI: 10.1108/JFRC-02-2022-0015

PricewaterhouseCoopers. (2018). PwC Annual Report. https://www.pwc.nl/nl/assets/documents/pwc-annual-report-2017-2018.pdf

PricewaterhouseCoopers. (2020). Financial Crimes Unit - Fraud services. www.pwc.com/us/en/industries/financial-services/financial-crimes/fraud.html

PricewaterhouseCoopers. (2022). PwC's Global Economic Crime and Fraud Survey 2022: US highlights. https://www.pwc.com/us/en/services/consulting/cybersecurity-risk-regulatory/library/global-economic-fraud-survey.html

Pruitt, S. (2017, October 26). The Biggest Revelations in the Declassified JFK Assassination Files. *History.com.*https://www.history.com/news/jfk-assassination-documents-declassified-release

Pruitt, S., & Pruitt, S. (2024, June 11). 10 Consequential Political Leaks Through History. History. https://www.history.com/news/9-leaks-that-changed-the-world

Pummerer, L., Böhm, R., Lilleholt, L., Winter, K., Zettler, I., & Sassenberg, K. (2022). Conspiracy Theories and Their Societal Effects During the COVID-19 Pandemic. *Social Psychological & Personality Science, 13*(1), 49–59. DOI: 10.1177/19485506211000217

Quadri, F. (2025, January 21). What Trump's second term means for information resilience, media credibility. *FactCheckHub.com.* Accessed January 25, 2025. https://factcheckhub.com/what-trumps-second-term-means-for-information-resilience-media-credibility/

Quandt, T., Frischlich, L., Boberg, S., & Schatto-Eckrodt, T. (2024). Fake news. In Vos, T. P., Hanusch, F., Dimitrakopoulou, D., Geertsema-Sligh, M., & Sehl, A. (Eds.), *The International Encyclopedia of Journalism Studies.* DOI: 10.1002/9781118841570.iejs0128

Raffler, P. J. (2022). Does political oversight of the bureaucracy increase accountability? Field experimental evidence from a dominant party regime. *The American Political Science Review, 116*(4), 1443–1459. DOI: 10.1017/S0003055422000181

Ramanathan, R., & Tan, B. H. (2015). Application of critical discourse analysis in media discourse studies. *The Southeast AsianJournal of English Language & Studies, 21*(2), 57–68.

Ramirez, I. (2024, July 15). Republicans formally name Trump their presidential nominee. *Politico.* https://www.politico.com/news/2024/07/15/donald-trump-gop-presidential-nominee-00168345

Rangappa, A., & Mercieca, J. (2020, June 7). The Ancient Greeks' Guide to Rejecting Propaganda and Disinformation. www.zocalopublicsquare.org

Rational Choice Theory of Criminology. (2024, February 13). Simply Psychology. https://www.simplypsychology.org/rational-choice-theory-of-criminology.html

Ray. (2024, July 27). WikiLeaks. Encyclopedia Britannica. https://www.britannica.com/topic/WikiLeaks

Rea, S. C. (2022). Teaching and confronting digital extremism: Contexts, challenges and opportunities. *Information and Learning Science*, *123*(1), 7–25. DOI: 10.1108/ILS-08-2021-0065

Reed, B. (2024, July 20). 'It was insane to me': Undecided voters express shock after watching Trump RNC speech. *MSN*.https://www.msn.com/en-us/news/politics/it-was-insane-to-me-undecided-voters-express-shock-after-watching-trump-rnc-speech/ar-BB1qi9DV

Reese, K. (2021, September 3). What is QAnon? the Viral Pro-Trump Conspiracy Theory. https://www.nytimes.com/article/what-is-qanon.html

Reese, S. D., & Shoemaker, P. J. (2016). A Media Sociology for the Networked Public Sphere: The Hierarchy of Influences Model. *Mass Communication & Society*, *19*(4), 389–410. DOI: 10.1080/15205436.2016.1174268

Reports, N. (2019, February 25). Nieman Reports. The Ethics of Leaks. Accessed July 28, 2024, from https://niemanreports.org/articles/the-ethics-of-leaks/

Research Guides: "Fake News," Lies and Propaganda: How to Sort Fact from Fiction: What is "Fake News"? (n.d.). https://guides.lib.umich.edu/fakenews

Reuters Staff. (2020 October 1). Whistleblower Edward Snowden book earning should go to the U. S. government, court rules. Ruetersnews.com. https://www.reuters.com/article/us-usa-security-snowden-lawsuit/whistleblower-edward-snowdens-book-earnings-should-go-to-us-government-court-rules-idUSKBN26M76P

Reynolds, D. (2001). *From Munich to Pearl Harbor: Roosevelt's America and the Origins of the Second World War*. Ivan R. Dee.

Richardson, M., & Stähler, F. (2021). Some economics of echo chambers. *Journal of Institutional and Theoretical Economics*, *177*(2), 205–219. DOI: 10.1628/jite-2021-0004

Roberts, J. (2019). Citizen journalism. *The international encyclopedia of media literacy*, 1(2), 1-10.

Roberts, G., & Klibanoff, H. (2007). *The Race Beat: The Press, the Civil Rights Struggle, and the Awakening of a Nation*. Vintage Books.

Robinson, L. (2018). Modern Political Warfare: Current Practices and Possible Responses. Santa Monica, CA: RAND Corporation, https://www.rand.org/pubs/research_reports/RR1772.html

Robinson, P. (2023, April 13). Lone Gunman: The Man Who Knew Lee Harvey Oswald—Uncommon Knowledge with Peter Robinson. *Hoover Institution*.https://www.hoover.org/research/lone-gunman-man-who-knew-lee-harvey-oswald

Rocha, Y. M., de Moura, G. A., Desidério, G. A., de Oliveira, C. H., Lourenço, F. D., & de Figueiredo Nicolete, L. D. (2021). The impact of fake news on social media and its influence on health during the COVID-19 pandemic: A systematic review. *Journal of Public Health, 1*(10). Advance online publication. DOI: 10.1007/s10389-021-01658-z PMID: 34660175

Rocket.Chat, June 22, 2024. Media Group Linked to Islamic State Khorasan Province (ISKP) Publishes Posters Instructing Lone. . . . *MEMRI.* https://www.memri.org/jttm/media-group-linked-islamic-state-khorasan-province-iskp-publishes-posters-instructing-lone

Romer, D., & Jamieson, K. H. (2020). Conspiracy theories as barriers to controlling the spread of COVID-19 in the U.S. *Social Science & Medicine, 263*, 113356. Advance online publication. DOI: 10.1016/j.socscimed.2020.113356 PMID: 32967786

Rose, J. (2020, December 30). Even if it's 'Bonkers,' Poll finds many believe QAnon and other conspiracy theories. *NPR.*https://www.npr.org/2020/12/30/951095644/even-if-its-bonkers-poll-finds-many-believe-qanon-and-other-conspiracy-theories

Rosenbaum, R. (1982, June 23). Ah, Watergate! *The New Republic,* 154, 15-24. https://ia601207.us.archive.org/9/items/nsia-WatergateFile/nsia-WatergateFile/Watergate%20File%20193_text.pdf

Rosenberg, M. B. (2003). *Nonviolent communication: A language of life*. PuddleDancer Press.

Rossiter, L., & Sochos, A. (2018). Workplace bullying and burnout: The moderating effects of social support. *Journal of Aggression, Maltreatment & Trauma, 27*(4), 386–408. DOI: 10.1080/10926771.2017.1422840

Rudkjoebing, L. A., Bungum, A. B., Flachs, E. M., Eller, N. H., Borritz, M., Aust, B., Rugulies, R., Rod, N. H., Biering, K., & Bonde, J. P. (2020). Work-related exposure to violence or threats and risk of mental disorders and symptoms: A systematic review and meta-analysis. *Scandinavian Journal of Work, Environment & Health, 46*(4), 339–349. DOI: 10.5271/sjweh.3877 PMID: 31909816

Ryan, A. (2024, July 16). Conspiracy theories about Trump's assassination attempt have exploded. Here's why. *The Boston Globe.*https://www.msn.com/en-us/news/opinion/conspiracy-theories-about-trump-s-assassination-attempt-have-exploded-here-s-why/ar-BB1q5pb1?ocid=BingNewsVerp

Saad, L. (2023, July 6). Historically Low Faith in U.S. Institutions Continues. *Gallup.*https://news.gallup.com/poll/508169/historically-low-faith-institutions-continues.aspx

Saarenvirta, G. (1998). Data mining to improve profitability: The Management Accounting Magazine. *Cma, 72*(2), 8-12. https://coloradotech.idm.oclc.org/login?url=https://www.proquest.com/trade-journals/data-mining-improve-profitability/docview/197770267/se-2

Sadurski, W. (2011). Constitutional Review in Europe and in the United States: Influences, paradoxes, and convergence. Forthcoming, Sydney Law School Research Paper, (11/15).

Said-Moorhouse, L. & Manglona, T. (2024, June 26). Julian Assange returns home a free man to Australia after a plea deal with U. S. CNN.

Sanders, L., & Frankovic, K. (2023, April 20). *Most Americans view the person behind the leak of classified military documents as a criminal.* YouGov. https://today.yougov.com/politics/articles/45600-most-americans-view-person-behind-leak-classified-

Sardarizadeh, S. (2021, September 9). 11 September 2001: The conspiracy theories still spreading after 20 years. *BBC*.https://www.bbc.com/news/58469600

Saul, B. (2006). Defining Terrorism in International Law. Oxford: Oxford University Press on Demand. https://scirp.org/reference/referencespapers?referenceid=3010902

Schildkraut, J., & Muschert, G. W. (2014). Media Salience and the Framing of Mass Murder in Schools: A Comparison of the Columbine and Sandy Hook Massacres. *Homicide Studies*, *18*(1), 23–43.

Schmidt, S. (2004, July 18). 1998 Memo Cited Suspected Hijack Plot by Bin Laden. http://www.washingtonpost.com/wp-dyn/articles/A58615-2004Jul17.html

Schoormann, T., Schweihoff, J., Jussen, I., & Möller, F. (2023). Classification tools for business models: Status quo, comparison, and agenda. *Electronic Markets*, *33*(1), 7. DOI: 10.1007/s12525-023-00639-2

Schudson, M. (2003). *The Sociology of News*. W. W. Norton.

Schwertner, K. (2017). Digital transformation of business. *Trakia Journal of Sciences,* 15(1), 388-393. http://tru.uni-sz.bg/tsj/TJS_Suppl.1_ Vol.15_2017/65.pdf

Scott, H. (2024, August 10). Why the Far-Right Isn't Holding Back Anymore: 20 Reasons They're Louder Than Ever. *MSN*.https://www.msn.com/en-us/news/opinion/why-the-far-right-isn-t-holding-back-anymore-20-reasons-they-re-louder-than-ever/ss-AA1oySUN#image=7

Scott, K. (2023). "Deceptive" clickbait headlines: Releusers' intentions, and lies. *Journal of Pragmatics*, *218*, 71–82. DOI: 10.1016/j.pragma.2023.10.004

Sen, R., Naumann, K., & Murali, V. S. (2019, December 18). *The Impact of Digital Media on the 2019 Indian General Election*. Regional Programme Political Dialogue Asia. https://www.kas.de/en/web/politikdialog-asien/single-title/-/content/the-impact-of-digital-media-on-the-2019-indian-general-election

Seth, V. (2016). India-Pakistan legislators and public officials dialogue on sharing of experiences on governance and democracy [Report]. https://www.pildat.org/Publications/publication/FP/IndiaPakistanLegislatorsandPublicOfficialsDialogue_Mar10_2016.pdf

Shah, M. (2024, July 4). *The digital weaponry of radicalization: AI and the recruitment nexus*. GNET. https://gnet-research.org/2024/07/04/the-digital-weaponry-of-radicalisation-ai-and-the-recruitment-nexus/

Shahi, G. K., Dirkson, A., & Majchrzak, T. A. (2021). An exploratory study of COVID-19 misinformation on Twitter. *Online Social Networks and Media*, *22*, 100104. DOI: 10.1016/j.osnem.2020.100104 PMID: 33623836

Shannon, J. (2020, September 30). Who are the Proud Boys? Far-right group has concerned experts for years. *USA Today*.https://www.usatoday.com/story/news/nation/2020/09/30/who-proud-boys-group-mentioned-debate-has-violent-history/5868406002/

Shoaib, A. (2024, July 29). Joe Biden's Supreme Court Reforms Backed by Donald Trump Supporters. *Newsweek*.https://www.msn.com/en-us/news/politics/joe-biden-s-supreme-court-reforms-backed-by-donald-trump-supporters/ar-BB1qPwCw?ocid=winp2fptaskbarhoverent&cvid=e3da8f7a2fbb4b8890dd2611c6c191d7&ei=12

Shuham, M. (2024, July 22). MTG Asks Secret Service Director If There Was A 'Conspiracy To Kill President Trump.' *Huffington Post*.https://www.msn.com/en-us/news/politics/mtg-asks-secret-service-director-if-there-was-a-conspiracy-to-kill-president-trump/ar-BB1qqTmq?ocid=BingNewsVerp

Shu, K., Wang, S., Lee, D., & Liu, H. (2020). Mining disinformation and fake news: Concepts, methods, and recent advancements. In Shu, K., Wang, S., Lee, D., & Liu, H. (Eds.), *Lecture Notes in Social Networks* (pp. 1–19). DOI: 10.1007/978-3-030-42699-6_1

Silitră, N. C. (2020). 21st Century Propaganda and Education–Friends or Foes? *Bulletin of the Transilvania University of Braşov, Series VII: Social Sciences and Law, 13*(1-Suppl), 143-154.

Silk, M. (2016). Did John Adams Out Thomas Jefferson and Sally Hemings? *Smithsonian Magazine*. https://www.smithsonianmag.com/history/john-adams-out-thomas-jefferson-sally-hemings-180960789/

Silva, J. (2024). Public mass shootings in developed countries: Uncovering stability and change at the turn of the century. *Global Crime*, *25*(1), 119–142. DOI: 10.1080/17440572.2023.2271848

Silva, J. R., & Lankford, A. (2022). The globalization of American mass shootings? An assessment of fame-seeking perpetrators and their influence worldwide. *International Journal of Comparative and Applied Criminal Justice*, *48*(2), 119–142. DOI: 10.1080/01924036.2022.2162095

Sima, V., Gheorghe, I. G., Subić, J., & Nancu, D. (2020). Influences of the industry 4.0 revolution on the human capital development and consumer behavior: A systematic review. *Sustainability (Basel)*, *12*(10), 4035. DOI: 10.3390/su12104035

Simran, K. (2019, March 12). Winston Churchill Quotations. Retrieved from https://www.thoughtco.com/winston-churchill-quotations-2831679

Singh Bawa, J. (2024, July 17). *Opinion: Opinion | From Misinformation To Fraud, The Alarming Rise Of Deepfakes In India*. https://www.ndtv.com/opinion/from-misinformation-to-fraud-the-alarming-rise-of-deepfakes-in-india-6124014

Singh, S. (2019). *The False Information Ecosystem in India*. https://toda.org/assets/files/resources/policy-briefs/t-pb-55_spandana-singh_the-false-information-ecosystem-in-india.pdf

Siraj, S. A. (2008). War or Peace Journalism in Elite US Newspapers: Exploring News Framing in Pakistan-India Conflict. In Annual Meeting of the International Communication Association, Montreal, Canada.

Skogan, W. G. (1993). The Various Meanings of Fear. In *The Fear of Crime and Criminal Victimization* (pp. 131-140). London, UK: Enke.

Smiley, T. (2014). *Death of a King: The real story of Dr. Martin Luther King, Jr.'s final year*. Little Brown and Company.

Smith, C. & Hung, L-C. (2010). *The Patriot Act: Issues and Controversies*. Thomas Publishing Co.

Snyder, W. E. (2015). Leaks and Their Consequences: A Guide to the Controversy Over Secrecy vs. Open Government. *American Intelligence Journal, 32*(2), 13–16. https://www.jstor.org/stable/26202131

Solon, O. (2017). Facebook's failure: Did fake news and polarized politics get Trump elected? *The Guardian.* https://www.theguardian.com/technology/2016/nov/10/facebook-fake-news-election-conspiracy-theories

Song, Y., & Hua, X. (2022). Implementation of Data Mining Technology in Bonded Warehouse Inbound and Outbound Goods Trade. *Journal of Organizational and End User Computing*, *34*(3), 1–18. DOI: 10.4018/JOEUC.291511

Sposini, L. (2024). Neuromarketing and eye-tracking technologies under the European framework: Towards the GDPR and beyond. *Journal of Consumer Policy*, *47*(3), 321–344. DOI: 10.1007/s10603-023-09559-2

Sproule, J. M. (2001). Authorship and origins of the seven propaganda devices: A research note. *Rhetoric & Public Affairs*, *4*(1), 135–143. https://www.jstor.org/stable/41939653. DOI: 10.1353/rap.2001.0014

Srivastava, K. (2021). Fake COVID vaccines boost the black market for counterfeit medicines. *BMJ (Clinical Research Ed.)*, *375*(2754), n2754. Advance online publication. DOI: 10.1136/bmj.n2754 PMID: 34789457

Stacey, K. (2021, September 16). New Report Assesses Progress and Risks of Artificial Intelligence. Academic Press.

Stanford University. (2024). New report assesses progress and risks of artificial intelligence. Stanford HAI. https://hai.stanford.edu/news/new-report-assesses-progress-and-risks-artificial-intelligence

Stanton, A. (2024, July 31). Trump Sells Upside Down American Flag Hat After Supreme Court Controversy. *MSN.*https://www.msn.com/en-us/news/politics/trump-sells-upside-down-american-flag-hat-after-supreme-court-controversy/ar-BB1qYwmA?ocid=winp2fptaskbarent&cvid=1c8d1e019cc749099b69cc18899216db&ei=10

Statista. (2023). Number of social network users in India from 2015 to 2023 with forecasts until 2027. Retrieved from https://www.statista.com/statistics/278407/number-of-social-network-users-in-india/

Steffen, S. (2024, November 14). Fact check: Disinformation's impact on the US election. *dw.com.* https://www.dw.com/en/fact-check-what-role-did-disinformation-play-in-the-us-election/a-70729575

Stinnett, R. (1999). *Day of Deceit: The Truth About FDR and Pearl Harbor*. Free Press.

Stomberg, J. (2012, May 10). What Really Sparked the Hindenburg Disaster? *Smithsonian Magazine.*https://www.smithsonianmag.com/science-nature/what-really-sparked-the-hindenburg-disaster-85867521/

Strauss, A., & Corbin, J. M. (1990). *Basics of qualitative research: Grounded theory procedures and techniques.* Sage Publications, Inc.

Strömbäck, J., Tsfati, Y., Boomgaarden, H., Damstra, A., Lindgren, E., Vliegenthart, R., & Lindholm, T. (2020). News media trust and its impact on media use: Toward a framework for future research. *Annals of the International Communication Association*, *44*(2), 139–156. DOI: 10.1080/23808985.2020.1755338

Sunstein, C. R. (2018). *Republic: Divided democracy in the age of social media.* Princeton University Press.

Swami, V., Voracek, M., Stieger, S., Tran, U. S., & Furnham, A. (2014). Analytic thinking reduces belief in conspiracy theories. *Cognition, 133*(3), 572–585. DOI: 10.1016/j.cognition.2014.08.006 PMID: 25217762

Tafesse, W., & Korneliussen, T. (2021). On the collective efficacy of social media teams. *Marketing Intelligence & Planning, 39*(3), 438–453. DOI: 10.1108/MIP-03-2020-0118

Tamandehrou, A., & Khan, S. U. (2015). Assessing the importance of globalisation and new media technology in 21st century: An analytical overview. *International Journal of Multifaceted & Multilingual Studies, 1*(4).

Tanchak, P. N. (2017). The invisible front: Russia, trolls, and the information war against Ukraine. In O. Bertelsen (Ed.), Revolution and war in contemporary Ukraine: The challenge of change (pp. 253–281). Columbia University Press.

Tandoc, E. C.Jr. (2019). The facts of fake news: A research review. *Sociology Compass, 13*(9), e12724. Advance online publication. DOI: 10.1111/soc4.12724

Tandoc, E. C.Jr, Lim, Z. W., & Ling, R. (2018). Defining "Fake News": A typology of scholarly definitions. *Digital Journalism (Abingdon, England), 6*(2), 137–153. DOI: 10.1080/21670811.2017.1360143

Tangherlini, T. R. (2020, November 13). An AI Tool Can Distinguish Between a Conspiracy Theory and a True Conspiracy—It Comes Down to How Easily the Story Falls Apart. *The Conversation.*https://theconversation.com/an-ai-tool-can-distinguish-between-a-conspiracy-theory-and-a-true-conspiracy-it-comes-down-to-how-easily-the-story-falls-apart-146282

Tarrant, W. D. (1957). Who Writes Letters to the. Editor? *The Journalism Quarterly, 34*(4), 501–502. DOI: 10.1177/107769905703400412

Task & Purpose. (2023, November 5). *The Fentanyl War is Worse Than You Think* [Video]. YouTube. https://www.youtube.com/watch?v=BjsSuWKz2s0

Team, F. (2023, September 5). *Psychological Operations (PsyOps): Influencing Minds for Strategic Impact*. Fact Protocol.

Teegarden, D. A. (2022, January 13). Tyrannicide in Ancient Greek Political Culture. In *The Oxford Handbook of the History of Terrorism*. DOI: 10.1093/oxfordhb/9780199858569.013.001

The National Whistleblower Center. (2021, February 23). *The case of Edward Snowden*. National Whistleblower Center. https://www.whistleblowers.org/news/the-case-of-edward-snowden/

The Wikihuman Project (n.d.). The Digital Emily Project: Achieving a Photoreal Digital Actor. usc.edu

Theriault, S. M. (2006). Party Politics during the Louisiana Purchase. *Social Science History, 30*(2), 293–324. https://www.jstor.org/stable/pdf/40267908.pdf?refreqid=fastly-default%3Af71d4b5eca6eeb4807ce45003b764603&ab_segments=&origin=&initiator=&acceptTC=1

Thompson, E., & Phua, F. T. T. (2012). A Brief Index of Affective Job Satisfaction. *Group & Organization Management, 37*(3), 275–307. DOI: 10.1177/1059601111434201

Thomsen, J. (2020, February5). Senate Republicans Just Acquitted Trump in the Impeachment Trial. This Is How We Got Here. The National Law Journal. Retrieved from https://www.law.com/nationallawjournal/2020/02/05/senate-republicans-just-acquitted-trump-in-the-impeachment-trial-this-is-how-we-got-here/?slreturn=20200124142442

Thomson Reuters Legal. (2024, May 16). 4 things you should know about non-disclosure agreements. https://legal.thomsonreuters.com/en/insights/articles/4-things-to-know-about-non-disclosure-agreements

Thoreau, H. D. (2023). *Walden and civil disobedience*. Union Square & Co., LLC.

Till, C. (2020). Propaganda through "reflexive control" and the mediated construction of reality. *New Media & Society*, *23*(6), 1362–1378. DOI: 10.1177/1461444820902446

Timm, J. C., & Kamisar, B. (2024, July 19). Fact-checking Trump's speech accepting the GOP nomination. *NBC*. https://www.nbcnews.com/politics/donald-trump/fact-checking-trump-republican-convention-speech-rcna162656

Tinsley, H. E. A., & Weiss, D. J. (2000). Interrater reliability and agreement. In Tinsley, H. E. A., & Brown, S. D. (Eds.), *Handbook of applied multivariate statistics and mathematical modeling* (pp. 95–124). Academic Press. DOI: 10.1016/B978-012691360-6/50005-7

TOI News Desk. (2024, January 16). Around 80% first-time voters have encountered fake news on social media: Survey. *The Times of India*. https://timesofindia.indiatimes.com/india/fake-news-on-social-media-survey/articleshow/106899024.cms

Tonite, H. (2024, July 6). Media at War: Issues & Limitations with References to Kargil, Vietnam, and Gulf War. Himachal Tonite. https://himachaltonite.com/himachal/media-at-war-issues-limitations-with-references-to-kargil-vietnam-and-gulf-war/

Trotta, D. (2012, October 24). Trump to give $5 million to charity if Obama releases records. *Reuters*. https://www.reuters.com/article/world/us-politics/trump-to-give-5-million-to-charity-if-obama-releases-records-idUSBRE89N180/

Tufekci, Z. (2018). YouTube, the great radicalizer. *The New York Times,10*(3).

Tufekci, Z. (2015). Algorithmic harms beyond Facebook and Google: Emergent challenges of computational agency. *Colorado Technology Law Journal*, *13*(2), 203–217.

Tumber, H., & Webster, F. (2006). Journalists Under Fire: Information War and Journalistic Practice. London: Sage. 192 pp. ISBN 1412924073. *Journal of Peace Research*, *44*(5), 641–641. DOI: 10.1177/00223433070440050717

Tyson, A., Johnson, C., & Funk, C. (2020). *U.S. public now divided over whether to get COVID-19 vaccine*. Pew Research Center. https://www.pewresearch.org/science/2020/09/17/u-s-public-now-divided-over-whether-to-get-covid-19-vaccine/

U.S. Senate Historical Office. (1976, April 29). *A History of Notable Senate Investigations: The Church Committee*. https://www.senate.gov/about/resources/pdf/church-committee-full-citations.pdf

Ufuophu-Biri, E., & Ojoboh, L. (2017). Social media as a tool for political resistance: Lessons from the Arab spring and the Nigerian protests. *Academic Journal of Interdisciplinary Studies, 6*(1), e61. DOI: 10.5901/ajis.2017.v6n1p61

University of Texas Arlington. (2023). *Subject and course guides: Quantitative and qualitative research: Understand what quantitative research is*. https://libguides.uta.edu/quantitative_and_qualitative_research/quant

Vaara, E., Sonenshein, S., & Boje, D. (2016). Narratives as sources of stability and change in organizations: Approaches and directions for future research. *The Academy of Management Annals*, *10*(1), 495–560. DOI: 10.5465/19416520.2016.1120963

Vail, K. E.III, Harvell-Bowman, L., Lockett, M., Pyszczynski, T., & Gilmore, G. (2023). Motivated reasoning: Election integrity beliefs, outcome acceptance, and polarization before, during, and after the 2020 U.S. Presidential Election. *Motivation and Emotion*, *47*(2), 177–192. DOI: 10.1007/s11031-022-09983-w PMID: 36188156

Van Bavel, J. J., & Pereira, A. (2018). The partisan brain: An identity-based model of political belief. *Trends in Cognitive Sciences*, *22*(3), 213–224. DOI: 10.1016/j.tics.2018.01.004 PMID: 29475636

van Dijk, T. A. (1998). Editorial: Discourse and Ideology. *Discourse & Society*, *9*(3), 307–308. DOI: 10.1177/0957926598009003001

van Leeuwen, T. (1996). The Representation of Social Actors. In Caldas-Coulthard, C. R., & Coulthard, M. (Eds.), *Texts and Practices: Readings in Critical Discourse Analysis* (pp. 32–70). Routledge.

Varela, A. (2019, May 23). Terror attacks by Muslims get 357 percent more media coverage than other terror attacks, study shows. *Georgia State News Hub*. https://news.gsu.edu/2019/02/19/terror-attacks-by-muslims-get-disproportionate-news-coverage/

Vargo, C. J., Guo, L., & Amazeen, M. A. (2017). The agenda-setting power of fake news: A big data analysis of the online media landscape from 2014 to 2016. *New Media & Society*, *20*(5), 2028–2049. DOI: 10.1177/1461444817712086

Vázquez, C. M. (2004). Judicial Review in the United States and in the WTO. *Some Similarities and Differences. Geo. Wash. Int'l L. Rev.*, *36*, 587.

Vinney, C. (2023, December 26). What Is Cultivation Theory in Media Psychology? https://www.verywellmind.com/slug-placeholder-5214376

Vinten, G. (1994). *Whistleblowing: Subversion or corporate citizenship?* St. Martin's Press.

Vleugel, A., Spruit, M., & Anton, D. (2010). Historical Data Analysis through Data Mining From an Outsourcing Perspective: The Three-Phases Model. *International Journal of Business Intelligence Research*, *1*(3), 42–65. DOI: 10.4018/jbir.2010070104

Von Hein, M. (2024, June 25). WikiLeaks "Cablegate" 10 years on. *dw.com*. https://www.dw.com/en/wikileaks-cablegate-10-years-on-unvarnished-look-at-us-foreign-policy/a-55755239

Vosoughi, S., Roy, D., & Aral, S. (2018). The spread of true and false news online. *Science*, *359*(6380), 1146–1151. DOI: 10.1126/science.aap9559 PMID: 29590045

Wang, S. S. (2016). Three tests for practical evaluation of partisan gerrymandering. *Stanford Law Review*, *68*(6), 1263–1321. https://www.proquest.com/scholarly-journals/three-tests-practical-evaluation-partisan/docview/1807470903/se-2

Wardle, C., & Derakhshan, H. (2017). *Information disorder: Toward an interdisciplinary framework for research and policy making*. Council of Europe. https://rm.coe.int/information-disorder-toward-an-interdisciplinary-framework-for-researc/168076277c

Wardle, C., & Derakhshan, H. (2017). *Information disorder: Toward an interdisciplinary framework for research and policymaking* (Vol. 27). Council of Europe.

Watson, C. A. (2018). Information Literacy in a Fake/False News World: An Overview of the Characteristics of Fake News and its Historical Development. *International Journal of Legal Information*, *46*(2), 93–96. DOI: 10.1017/jli.2018.25

Waxman, O. B. (2023, November 21). What we know and still don't know about JFK's Assassination. *Time Magazine.*https://time.com/6338396/jfk-assassination-conspiracy-culture/

Wedeen, L. (1999). *Ambiguities of domination: Politics, rhetoric, and symbols in contemporary Syria*. University of Chicago Press.

Weigel, D. (2009, June 3). Citizen Juries: The New Birther Style. *The Washington Independent.*https://washingtonindependent.com/45416/citizen-juries-the-new-birther-style

Weise, N. K. (2020, April 11). A Reading List to Put the WikiLeaks "War Logs" in Context. *ProPublica*. https://www.propublica.org/article/A-Reading-List-to-Put-the-WikiLeaks-War-Logs-in-Context

Weissmann, J. (2009, March 6). Judge Dismisses Obama 'Indictment.' *Legal Times.*https://legaltimes.typepad.com/blt/2009/07/super-american-grand-jury-indicts-obama-.html

Welna, D. (2019, April11). 12 Years of Disruption: A WikiLeaks' Timeline. NPR online. Retrieved from www.npr.org/2019/04/11/712306713/12-years-of-disruption-a-wikileaks-timeline

Westen, D. (2007). *The political brain: The role of emotion in deciding the fate of the nation*. Public Affairs Books.

What Is a Chatbot? (n.d.). https://www.ibm.com/topics/chatbots

Wheeler, R. (2021, November 30). Trump's judicial campaign to upend the 2020 election: A failure, but not a wipe-out. *Brookings.*https://www.brookings.edu/articles/trumps-judicial-campaign-to-upend-the-2020-election-a-failure-but-not-a-wipe-out/

White, J. (2020). Royal United Services Institute for Defense and Security Studies, & Private Office of the Assistant Commissioner of Specialist Operations for the London Metropolitan Police Service. Terrorism and the mass media. *RUSI Occasional Paper* [Report]. https://ocd.lcwu.edu.pk/cfiles/International%20Relations/EC/IR-404/terrorism_and_the_mass_media_final_web_version.pdf

Whitehead, J., & Whitehead, N. (2022, June 8). Everything Is a Weapon: The U.S. Government Is Waging Psychological Warfare on the Nation. https://www.rutherford.org/publications_resources/john_whiteheads_commentary/everything_is_a_weapon_the_u.s_government_is_waging_psychological_warfare_on_the_nation

Whorf, B. L. (1956). *Language, thought, and reality*. MIT Press.

Wijaya, A., & Nasran, N. (2021). Comparison Of Judicial Review: A Critical Approach To The Model In Several Countries. *Jurnal Legalitas, 14*(2), 85–106. DOI: 10.33756/jelta.v14i2.11809

Wikipedia contributors. (2025, January 7). *Chelsea Manning*. Wikipedia. https://en.wikipedia.org/wiki/BradleyManning

Wild, W. & Sands, G. (2021, May 15). FBI and DHS report finds deaths at hands of racially motivated violent extremists on the rise in US. *cnn.com*

Williams, W. (2017, April 7). *Google rolls out new 'Fact Check' tool worldwide to combat fake news.* Christian Science Monitor. https://www.csmonitor.com/Technology/2017/0407/Google-rolls-out-new-Fact-Check-tool-worldwide-to-combat-fake-news

Wired. (2017, February 14). Here's How Fake News Works (and How the Internet Can Stop it). *Wired.*

Wong, J. I. (2016). Almost all the traffic to fake news sites is from Facebook: New data show. *Quartz.* https://qz.com/848917/facebook-fb-fake-news-data-from-jumpshot-its-the-biggest-traffic-referrer-to-fake-and-hyperpartisan-news-sites/

Woodley, S., & Howard, P. (2019). *Computational Propaganda.* Oxford University Press.

Woolley, S. (2022, July 18). *In Many Democracies, Disinformation Targets the Most Vulnerable.* Centre for International Governance Innovation. https://www.cigionline.org/articles/in-many-democracies-disinformation-targets-the-most-vulnerable/

Woolley, S., & Guilbeault, D. (2017). Computational propaganda in the United States of America: Manufacturing consensus online. Academic Press.

Woolley, S., & Howard, P. (2017). *Computational propaganda worldwide: Executive summary.* Computational Propaganda Project.

Working with Whistleblowers. (n.d.). https://gijn.org/resource/working-with-whistleblowers/

Worth, K. (2016, July 14). Lone Wolf Attacks Are Becoming More Common — And More Deadly. *Pbs.org.*

Wright, G. (2024, November 16). Malcolm X's family sues FBI, CIA, and NYPD over his murder. *BBC News,* pp. 1-2. Retrieved from: https://www.bbc.com/news/articles/c3rxzndz17yo

Wrzoszczyk, M. (2019). The idea of judicial review in the United States of America: the context of creating and early judgments of the Supreme Court. Academic Press.

Wuthnow, R. (1988). *The Restructuring of American Religion: Society and Faith Since World War II.* Princeton University Press.

X, C. (2011, March 20). President Kennedy, The Fed And Executive Order 11110. *Rense.com.*https://rense.com/general44/exec.htm

Yaraghi, N. (2019, April 9). How should social media platforms combat misinformation and hate speech? *Brookings.*https://www.brookings.edu/articles/how-should-social-media-platforms-combat-misinformation-and-hate-speech/

Young, T. (2015, May 6). 40 years ago, Church Committee investigated Americans spying on Americans. *Brookings.*https://www.brookings.edu/articles/40-years-ago-church-committee-investigated-americans-spying-on-americans/

Zahara, Z., Ikhsan, , Santi, I. N., & Farid, . (2023). Entrepreneurial marketing and marketing performance through digital marketing capabilities of SMEs in post-pandemic recovery. *Cogent Business & Management, 10*(2), 2204592. Advance online publication. DOI: 10.1080/23311975.2023.2204592

Zeleny, J. (2011, April 27). White House Releases Obama Birth Certificate. *The New York Times.*

Zhang, M. (2014). A Critical Discourse Analysis of Political News Reports. *Theory and Practice in Language Studies, 4*(11), 2273–2277. DOI: 10.4304/tpls.4.11.2273-2277

Zhan, N., Zhang, L., Gong, M., & Geng, F. (2024). Clinical correlates of irritability, anger, hostility, and aggression in posttraumatic stress disorder. *Psychological Trauma: Theory, Research, Practice, and Policy, 16*(6), 1055–1062. DOI: 10.1037/tra0001498 PMID: 37104771

Zhou, J., Sheng, S., & Zhang, C. (2022). Deterring Unethical Behaviors in Marketing Channels: The Role of Distributor Whistleblowing: JBE. *Journal of Business Ethics, 181*(1), 97–115. DOI: 10.1007/s10551-021-04931-z

Zollo, F., Bessi, A., Del Vicario, M., Scala, A., Caldarelli, G., Shekhtman, L., Havlin, S., & Quattrociocchi, W. (2017). Debunking in a world of tribes. *PLoS One, 12*(7), e0181821. DOI: 10.1371/journal.pone.0181821 PMID: 28742163

Zurcher, A. (2016, September 16). The birth of the Obama 'birther' conspiracy. *BBC.*https://www.bbc.com/news/election-us-2016-37391652

Zurini, M. (2012). Format Conversions for Open-Source Data Mining Implementation in Digital Economy Ranking. *Academy of Economic Studies. Economy Informatics, 12*(1), 65-76. https://coloradotech.idm.oclc.org/login?url=https://www.proquest.com/scholarly-journals/format-conversions-open-source-data-mining/docview/1069255734/se-2

About the Contributors

Perry L. Lyle, PhD, has 40 years' experience in public safety leadership and private security, having held responsible leadership positions in law enforcement, intelligence, and private security. For the past fifteen years, he has engaged in higher learning. A native of Florida, he is an adjunct professor of Criminal Justice at Columbia College of Missouri teaching in both the undergraduate and Graduate programs. He is co-editor of two Journals: The International Journal of Leadership, Education, and Business Studies and The Journal of Education and Social Justice. He is a member of the Academy of Criminal Justice Sciences, the Association for Former Intelligence Officers, and The World Association of Academic Doctors. His pursuits are for Social Equality in Criminal Justice and Education and is the author of several books and Journal articles of topical research in the Social Sciences. He has a passion for integrity and professionalism in public service leadership.

Ashraf M. Esmail, PhD, is an Associate Professor and Program Coordinator for Criminal Justice at Dillard University. He is also the Director for the Center for Racial Justice. He is a Barron Hilton Criminal Justice Endowed Professor. He is the senior editor of the Journal of Education and Social Justice and Chief Editor of the International Journal of Leadership, Education and Business Studies. He is the co-editor for the Journal of Contemporary Issues in Higher Education. He serves on the Board for the National Association of Peace Education and World Association of Academic Doctors. He served as President of the National Association for Peace Education in 2010-2011. He serves on the Louisiana State Criminal Justice Commission. He also serves on New Orleans Police Department Advisory Board and Court Watch Nola. I has worked with the Louisiana Counsel of Offender Resources over the last 5 years.

***

Vishnu Achutha Menon is an independent journalist, writer, researcher, and an Indian percussionist. He is a recipient of the Junior Scholarship the Ministry of Culture awarded. His research interests are film studies, verbal & nonverbal communication, south Asian performances, Natyasastra, media studies, media analysis techniques, Laban Movement Analysis, and Ethnomusicology.

N. Mari Anand has a rich experience of 10 year in the field of teaching and expertise in the field of Marketing and Human Resource Management. Currently he is Senior Lecturer, College of Economics & Busniess Administration, University of Technology and Applied sciences, Salalah, Oman. He is also a Member in Research Advisory Committee at VELS Institute of Science, Technology & Advanced Studies, Chennai. To his credit he has published 27 articles in Scopus and UGC Listed Journals. He has guided 63 UG and 22 PG projects. Currently he is guiding two Ph.D. Scholars in the field of Management in SRM Institute of Science and Technology. He served as Member of Board of Studies for Business

Administration and Member for University Examination Board of SRM Institute of Science & Technology. The author is an Editorial Board Member for International Journal of Advance Research in Commerce Management and Finance (IJARCMF). The author has organized various International Conferences and International Conclave during his tenure. The author was an ISO Convener and also served as IQAC coordinator & Exam Cell convener. He is also an External Academic Auditor and Chief Examiner for various institutions. The author was resource persons for different Faculty Development Program (FDP) organised by various colleges. He is an active Member in Federation of Indian Chamber of Commerce and Industries (FICCI) & Madras Management Association (MMA).

Monica Bhutani, Ph.D., is an Associate Professor for the Department of Electronics and Communications, Head IEEE BVCOE, Secretary of IEEE SB DS Councilor's Forum and Bharati Vidyapeeth's College of Engineering (BVCOE), New Delhi.

Harshith Sai Boddu is currently in the final year of the Undergraduate Programme of Law . He is having various publication to his credit.

Saurabh Chandra is an accomplished legal scholar and currently serves as an Associate Professor at the School of Law, Bennett University, India. With a robust academic foundation, he earned his Bachelor of Arts and Bachelor of Laws (B.A. LL.B.) from the prestigious Aligarh Muslim University (AMU). He further specialized in Business Laws, completing his Master of Laws (LL.M.) at the renowned National Law School of India University (NLSIU), Bangalore. Dr. Chandra's academic journey culminated in a Doctorate in Law (Ph.D.) from the esteemed National Law University. In addition to his impressive legal education from some of India's most prestigious institutions, Dr. Saurabh Chandra also holds a master's degree in Management with specialization in Human Resources in Management and another in Journalism and Mass Communication. With 16 years of teaching experience, he has established himself as an expert in Business and Corporate Laws, with numerous publications to his credit. Dr. Saurabh Chandra is a distinguished expert in Business and Corporate Laws, with a profound understanding of the intricate legal frameworks that govern the business world. His expertise is complemented by a robust portfolio of scholarly publications, which underscores his commitment to advancing knowledge in his field. Throughout his career, Dr. Chandra has consistently produced high-impact research that addresses critical issues in business and corporate law. His publications are widely recognized for their depth of analysis, innovative perspectives, and practical relevance. He has contributed extensively to leading journals, where his work has often set new standards for legal scholarship. His publications not only reflect his scholarly rigor but also his dedication to addressing contemporary challenges faced by businesses and policymakers. By bridging the gap between theoretical insights and real-world applications, Dr. Chandra's work serves as a valuable resource for academics, legal practitioners, and industry professionals alike. Dr. Chandra brings a wealth of experience in Academic Administration, having successfully held various key administrative positions. His diverse qualifications and extensive experience make him a distinguished figure in the academic and legal communities.

Kesavan Dhanapal is presently working as Assistant Professor at SRMIST: Faculty of Management, Chennai. He has 8 Years of Industrial experience in Banking and IT sector and 5 years of teaching experience. He has published nearly 47 articles in various reputed UGC, Peer reviewed and Scopus journals. Has published 2 International Book Chapters and 2 National level book chapters and authored 2

Books. He has won Young Researcher award and Excellence in Research award from reputed academic agencies. He is also an approved faculty at University of Madras. He has been editor for International Book on Crypto Currency in association with IGI global, USA. He is the Chief Editor of International Journal of Advanced Research in Commerce, Management and Finance: He is also reviewer for International Journal of Management and AKINIK journal. His areas of interest are Renewable Energy, International Business, Banking and Financial Management. He has also got a funded project with Ministry of Education, India in the field of Sustainable Financial Management for Entrepreneurs.

Johnny R. Green, Sr., Ph.D., is an Assistant Professor of Political Science and Program Coordinator of Master of Public Administration (MPA) at Fort Valley State University. He is from Birmingham, Alabama where the civil Rights Movement had an indelible mark on his academic interests and passions. Educated at Auburn University and having been selected as a Fellow at Peabody (Vanderbilt) Yale, and Oxford University, Dr. Green has written, researched, and presented several conference papers on Black Power and the Politics of Constitutional Change, Political Regimes and Sub- national Development, Black Community Power and the White Power Structure. He recently coauthored a book chapter on "Politics, Voting Rights, and Voter Suppression Efforts" (In: Samson Chama (ed.) Social Justice Through A Diversity, Equity, Inclusivity, and Fairness Framework, San Diego, CA: Cognella, 2025). Research interests include the power of interest groups, regime theory and racial justice and politics in the Deep South.

Selina E. M. Kerr, Ph.D., is a criminologist and researcher working in the United Kingdom. She has recently published a book exploring the gun-related policy responses to school shootings in the United States. Other research areas of interest include solutions to reduce gun violence, threat assessment, emergency management and communication procedures during active shooter incidents and representations of violence in television shows.

Saad Ullah Khan has more than a decade long extensive experience at university level teaching and research. Dr. Khan has authored various research papers in journals of national as well as international repute. He was awarded 'Rajat Jayanti Vigyan Sancharak Fellowship-2009' by DST, Ministry of Science and Technology (Government of India) for his contribution to the field of communication and its social implications. Further he was bestowed with MANF Fellowship 2011 by UGC to carry out his research work. A PhD from prestigious Aligarh Muslim University, Dr. Saad Ullah Khan has presented 90 Research Papers in various National and International Conferences. He was awarded 'Best Researcher Award' twice (2020 & 2023) and 'Best Journalism Teacher Award' in 2021.

Sadaf Khan has extensive teaching experience of more than ten years. A core academician and a prolific researcher, she has done incredible work in the domain of English Literature, Cultural Studies, and Afghanistan Studies. Having an international teaching experience, she has been felicitated multiple times as 'Best Teacher' by various academic institutions in which she had worked. Besides, she has also served as the Joint Editor of Women's College Annual magazine of Aligarh Muslim University for the session 2007-2008.

Ketki Prashant Kshirsagar completed her graduation (B.E.)(Electronic and Telecommunication Engineering)from Walchand Institute of Technology, Solapur, Shivaji University, Kolhapur and post graduation(M. Tech)(Electronics) and Ph.D from Shri Guru Gobind Singhji Institute of Engineering and Technology, Nanded, Swami Ramanand Teerth Marathwada University. Presently she is working as Associate Professor in Electronic and Telecommunication Department, Vishwakarma Institute of Information Technology, Pune. She has presented and published paper in varies reputed National, International conferences and Journals. She has been paper reviewer/advisory board member in reputed journals and conferences. She has conducted workshop on skill development of MATLAB, MATLAB-simulink. Her keen interest is in Image Processing, Pattern recognition, Computer Vision, Communication Engineering, Digital Electronics, Machine Learning, Network Security. Maharashtra.

Jyoti Kukreja is certified in Successful Negotiation: Essential Strategies and Skills and from University of Michigan, USA; 'Neuroscience of Personal Excellence' from University of Colorado Boulder, USA and 'Leadership Skills' from IIM-Ahmedabad, India. A Doctorate from GGSIPU, Delhi, she is currently associated as an Assistant Professor with New Delhi Institute of Management, Delhi, India. She is sought after as a reviewer, an author and editor with ABDC and Scopus indexed journals including Emerald, Sage and IGI Global publishers. She is an invited Speaker for sessions for developing 'Winning Career Skills' at top colleges of Delhi University. A professionally committed professional she is a UGC- JRF & NET (2009) qualified. A researcher, author, speaker, trainer with 16 years of rich experience and expertise have delivered training to 15000+ mentees A co-editor of Scopus Indexed books with IGI Global, USA and an upcoming with Vernon Press, USA pertaining to UNSDGs of Mental Health and Well-Being is cited by 100 scholars worldwide.

Apoorva Mahiwal combines her extensive practical background with a robust academic foundation to excel in the field of public relations and communication. With over five years of diverse expertise, she currently contributes her knowledge at the Research Unit of the Press Information Bureau under the Ministry of Information and Broadcasting. Her background spans government communication, teaching, and training, enriching her insights into the nuanced realms of communication dynamics. Apoorva's proficiency extends to soft skills training, where she has imparted her knowledge to individuals across India. Committed to lifelong learning, she continues to cultivate her understanding of the intricate dynamics within these fields.

Rouby Mavyan, M.S., Ph.D., Director of Academic Affairs and Assessment, California Health Sciences University Adjunct Assistant Professor, Fresno Pacific University and California Health Sciences University Dr. Rouby Mavyan is an esteemed academic and researcher with expertise in criminology, diversity and crime, juvenile justice, and higher education assessment. She serves as the Director of Academic Affairs and Assessment at California Health Sciences University (CHSU) in Clovis, California, and as an adjunct assistant professor in the Criminology Department at Fresno Pacific University and CHSU. Dr. Mavyan's research interests include criminological theories, domestic violence, victimology, and women in prison. She has co-authored several impactful books and journal articles, including "On These Mean Streets… People are Dying: Police & Citizen Brutality in America," "Access of Hispanic Inmates to Correctional Education (GED) in California and Its Impact on Three-Year Recidivism Rates," and "Espionage Against America and Why Privacy Matters" (featured in Quis Custodiet Ipsos Custodes? – National Security: Evaluating the Equilibrium between Secrecy, Transparency, and Individual Freedoms). Her publication "Old Problems, New Paradigms: The Tragedies of Human Trafficking and Exploitation" was presented in Toronto, Canada, and published by Wise Publishing. In addition to her work in criminology, Dr. Mavyan has contributed significantly to academic research and innovation in medical education as well. Her contributions include: • Pena, V., Andrade, T., Rafati, M., Desai, N., Mavyan, R., & Pinto, A. (2024). "Post-TBL Faculty Reflection: Bridging Pre-Work Content to In-Class Outcomes." AACOM Abstract. • Kadavakollu, S., Ham-Ying, J., Graneto, J., Van Es, T., Mavyan, R., Qureshi, M., & Merino, J. (2023). "Six Practical Tips to Prepare for the Comprehensive Osteopathic Medical Licensing Examination (COMLEX) USA Level 1." International Journal of Osteopathic Medicine, Volume 49, Article 100666. • Mavyan, R. & Qureshi, M. (2022). "The Effect of Innovative Mapping Platform (ExamPrep) on CHSU COM's Integrated Curriculum." AACOM Abstract. • Mavyan, R. & Qureshi, M. (2021). "Does Integrated Board Prep Minimize Student Anxiety Towards COMLEX Level 1 Prep?" AACOM Abstract. Dr. Mavyan's interdisciplinary scholarship reflects her commitment to addressing complex social issues and advancing educational practices. Her work continues to inspire and guide students, educators, and professionals across multiple fields.

Toiya Marie McGruder is a social entrepreneur who works with power-building organizations to create educational, civic, and policy solutions for Black and Brown youth. She is devoted to creating spaces where those pushed to the margins can be centered, seen, and heard. She is an experienced organizer, having worked on various national, local, and statewide partisan and nonpartisan campaigns. Toiya is a graduate of Dillard University where she obtained a degree in Urban Studies and Public Policy.

Tara D. Miller is a graduate of Clark Atlanta University where she earned a Doctor of Philosophy Degree in Humanities in 2017, and a Doctor of Arts in Humanities Degree in 2007. Dr. Miller has worked in academia, for 20-years, and served in the United States Army. She has written several scholarly publications, children's books, and produced animations, which centers upon equality.

Komanduri S. Murty, Ph.D., is Alma Jones Endowment Professor of Social Justice at Fort Valley State University. He is the author or co-author of over a dozen books and over a hundred book chapters and journal articles which have appeared in numerous books, encyclopedias, and peer-reviewed journals; and, presented over a hundred articles at professional meetings, both nationally and internationally. He served as professor and chairman of criminal justice and sociology for 25 years at Clark Atlanta University, where he received the 2005 Aldridge McMillan award for Outstanding Overall Achievement. He directed numerous Masters' theses and doctoral dissertations and served as an overseas examiner to adjudicate many international doctoral dissertations in Law and other disciplines. He also served on research grant review panels at United Negro College Fund Special Programs; Substance Abuse and Mental Health Services Administration (SAMSHA); National Institute of Mental Health; National Institute of Health; and Georgia Department of Children and Youth Services.

Henrietta Okoro is a Maryland Commissioner on African Affairs and the Director for Education in Women Veterans United Inc. (WVUI). She is a great supporter of the Women Veterans projects and has piloted many of their educational projects and workshops. Dr. Okoro is a strategic management consultant with in-depth experience spanning over twenty-eight (28) years and proven expertise in information systems and technology. Dr. Okoro is also the Founder/CEO of two non-profit professional associations: World Association for Academic Doctors (WAAD), Inc. and Association of Nigerian Women Academic Doctors (ANWAD), Inc. Dr. Okoro holds a Doctorate Degree in Organizational Leadership with a specialization in Information Systems & Technology.

Sivaprakkash S. has done all his degrees from Loyola College, Chennai. He is a Gold Medalist in M.Com. and M.Phil. He has six years of Teaching Experience. Currently working as Assistant Professor in the Department of Commerce at Central University of Tamil Nadu. To his credit he has published 19 articles in listed journals and Two Book Chapters. He is a recipient of Rajiv Gandhi National Fellowship for Persons with Disabilities for the year 2016- 17. Currently working as Principal Director in Indian Council of Social Science Research (ICSSR), Government of India funded Minor Research Project related to Investments in Entrepreneurship. His areas of interest include Investment Management: Mutual Funds & Stock Market, Business and Company Law, Marketing: Global Perspective of Marketing, Human Resource Management, Statistics Analysis and Research Methodology.

Mani Sachdev is an esteemed academician currently serving as Professor and Head of the Institute of Behavioural and Allied Sciences at Amity University Rajasthan, Jaipur. Her academic journey includes earning an M.Phil. in Philosophy and completing her Doctorate at the University of Rajasthan, specializing in Aesthetics, Metaphysics, and Epistemology. With an impressive tenure spanning 37 years, she has excelled as an Associate Professor of Philosophy. Dr. Sachdev's pioneering roles include founding the Department of Philosophy at Vedic Kanya P. G. College, Jaipur, and establishing the Department of Philosophy at B.N.D. Arts Government P.G. College Chimanpura, Jaipur. Her scholarly contributions and administrative leadership underscore her commitment to advancing philosophical discourse and academic excellence in higher education. Her professional portfolio encompasses the design and development of innovative curricula tailored for students, ensuring adherence to rigorous quality assurance standards within the University framework. Additionally, she contributes to the pedagogical landscape by teaching ethics to medical professionals at a distinguished medical university in Jaipur, where she serves as a distinguished member of the ethics committee. Her scholarly contributions extend to numerous international and national conferences, seminars, and scholarly journals, where she has presented research papers, authored book chapters, and contributed book reviews. Beyond academia, she has demonstrated versatility in media production, having produced, directed, and scripted corporate films for hospitals and organizations, as well as documentaries for national broadcast on Doordarshan. Furthermore, she has conducted in-depth interviews with over 50 prominent global figures, spanning governors, philosophers, academics, and renowned personalities from the film industry. Her cultural engagement includes creating, directing, writing, and narrating the acclaimed 'Light and Sound Cultural Show' celebrating Rajasthan's art, culture, and heritage, showcased at numerous tourism festivals and international conferences.

Ghosh Thinnakkakath is a distinguished IT professional with over 30 years of consulting experience, particularly in SAP Client Delivery. Renowned for his exceptional client relations and project management skills, Dr. Thinnakkakath has consistently demonstrated his ability to manage complex strategic accounts, leading to high customer satisfaction. Dr. Thinnakkakath's impressive credentials include two Ph.D. Degrees (Information Technology & Business), an MS in Mathematics, and numerous certifications in various industry standards such as PMP, SAP, Cloud hyperscalers, and Oracle. These certifications underscore his comprehensive knowledge and technical expertise. In addition to his technical skills, Dr. Thinnakkakath is a dedicated trainer and mentor, guiding many IT professionals throughout their careers. A master in SAP Client Delivery, project management, and administration, Dr. Thinnakkakath's career is marked by numerous accolades and recognitions. His leadership in client delivery has ensured successful project outcomes and fostered lasting relationships with clients, making him a highly respected figure in his field.

Arthur W. Turner, MS, US Army, served as a sworn law enforcement officer and as an intelligence officer in the US Army Reserve and US Army. His three decades of service include two combat tours with the US Army in Iraq. He is currently a contractor with the US Department of Justice supporting Ukraine by working with the National Police on operational training and anti-corruption work. Lt. Col. Turner is a criminal Behaviour analyst, retired law enforcement officer, including serving as Chief of Police for the City of Bellevue (KY), and as a military intelligence officer in the United States Army Reserves. He is a graduate of the FBI National Academy (Class 235 in 2008); following that, Lt. Colonel Turner became certified as a Behavioral Analysist through studies at the FLETC program and Targeted Training International (TTI) classes from 2008-10. Lt. Colonel Turner further served the field of criminal justice by earning a Master of Science in criminal justice from Eastern Kentucky University in 2013. Lastly, in recognition of his law-enforcement and military service, in 2017 he was inducted into the Kentucky Military Veteran's Hall of Fame. With his wealth of experience, Lt. Colonel Turner continues to serve law enforcement and military organizations worldwide, helping them extend the pursuit of justice, intelligence, and crime prevention on a global scale.

Kadir Uludag holds Ph.D. in Applied psychology (Chinese Academy of Sciences). He is currently doing postdoc in Shanghai Jiaotong University Mental Health Center. His research interest includes schizophrenia research, drug addiction and educational psychology. In addition, he runs a website to share and comment on peer-reviewed articles (ifx0.com).

Naveenraj Xavier is a distinguished Assistant Professor at the Faculty of Management, SRM Institute of Science and Technology, Chennai. With a strong academic foundation and a passion for research, he specializes in organizational psychology and the workplace environment, areas that are critical to the success of modern organizations. His research aims to explore the intricate relationship between individuals and their work environments, with a particular focus on enhancing employee well-being, job satisfaction, and organizational culture. In addition to his research, he is committed to shaping future leaders and managers through his teaching. He incorporates real-world applications of organizational psychology into his curriculum, equipping students with the skills and knowledge to effectively manage teams and create conducive work environments in their future careers.

Index

T

V

www.ingramcontent.com/pod-product-compliance
Lightning Source LLC
LaVergne TN
LVHW062108300926
849161LV00010B/2404

* 9 7 9 8 3 6 9 3 7 4 6 8 9 *